the social web

the social web

an introduction to sociology

john and erna perry
cuyahoga community college

Canfield Press · San Francisco
A Department of Harper & Row, Publishers, Inc.
New York · Evanston · London

Photo Credits

Ilka Hartmann, *Jeroboam*, p. 20, 69, 189, 212
Victor Friedman, *Rapho Guillumette*, p. 22, 354, 495
Alan Becker, *Photofind*, p. 23, 28, 104
Ken Graves, *Jeroboam*, p. 30, 36, 37, 72, 82, 106, 145, 246, 248, 354, 371, 409, 465, 548
Susan Ylvisaker, *Jeroboam*, p. 34, 312, 427
Howard Harrison, *Jeroboam*, p. 79, 261, 429, 502, 514
Leonard Freed, *Magnum*, p. 110
Joanne Leonard, *Photofind*, p. 115, 205, 310
Mitchell Payne, *Photofind*, p. 118
Sam Coombs, *Photofind*, p. 120
Ernst Haas, *Magnum*, p. 122
Gerhard E. Gscheidle, *Jeroboam*, p. 150, 233, 375, 451, 472
Burt Glinn, *Magnum*, p. 151
Ernest Lowe, *Photofind*, p. 157, 209, 500
Roger Lubin, *Jeroboam*, p. 192, 245, 257, 323, 423, 552
Elliott Erwitt, *Magnum*, p. 201
Larry Keenan, *Photofind*, p. 302
Hank Lebo, *Jeroboam*, p. 318, 422
Morton Beebe, *Photofind*, p. 353
Phiz Mezey, *Jeroboam*, p. 373, 489
Roger Birt, *Photofind*, p. 460
David Powers, *Jeroboam*, p. 461
Jim Goldberg, p. 551

International Standard Book Number: 0-06-386760-3

Library of Congress Catalog Card Number: 72-10902

73 74 75 5 4 3 2 1

*To our parents and our children, who
represent yesterday and tomorrow, with love.*

Students are often attracted to sociology because they expect to hear and read about themselves, about what makes them as they are, how they can change, or what they can demand of the future. But they become bored when they are confronted, instead, with turgid recitations of terms like socialization, stratification, interaction, urbanization, and countless other concepts of the discipline.

Of course, if sociology is to have any meaning for them, students must confront these terms out of their own frame of reference. But this is where most textbooks run afoul: They present the concepts and define them, and many even offer examples. They leave the concepts, however, at an abstract level so the student does not see why he should care about them. They do not engage the student's attention by saying, "Look, you better know what a stratification system is, and whether you live in a stratified society. Stratification will affect your life in these ways: It will determine the extent of your education; it will influence your choice of a career; it will shape your life style, your choice of a marriage partner, the public officials you vote for, and so on."

We have tried to avoid this problem in several ways. First, we have presented only those concepts that are most vital to the discipline, and in each case, we have tried to offer the simplest and clearest definition. Second, we have chosen several practical examples to clarify the concepts. Most important, we have included articles that show how some of the concepts, which sound abstract and irrelevant when merely defined, are central to everyday life.

The articles have several characteristics that make them different from those in other texts. First, they are not intended to be sociological research. Because they were not written by sociologists for other sociologists, they do not use the jargon of the discipline. Yet the articles are concerned with the issues that sociologists analyze. In most instances, they are lively and contemporary and should generate much student interest. Taken from the educated layman's press, the articles have been chosen to illustrate such concepts as role and status, group formation, culture, modal personality, social change, and so on.

For example, in discussing social roles and statuses, we present an article written by a black woman who expresses the black woman's ideas about her own status and roles in our society and about the status and roles of white women. When we discuss various kinds of groups, their formation, and the processes within them, we include an article about a number of groups existing in San Francisco's Chinatown today. The article points out which needs prompted the formation of specific groups and what processes occurred within and among the groups. Furthermore, it discusses which groups survived, which were dissolved, and why.

In stressing the basic similarity of the human experience regardless of its particular societal setting, as well as in pointing out cultural differences among societies, we have attempted to choose articles with a cross-cultural point of view. Unfortunately, we were limited by the availability of articles written in this vein. We do portray the effects on personality of specific cultural values and norms with an article on members of a society in the Asiatic part of the Soviet Union. And we do show that the problems of race and minority relations exist in other societies, even in such strongly unified ones as Israel.

Following the articles are a series of discussion questions, which point out to students which items in the text are illustrated by the articles. In addition, each chapter is followed by a glossary of terms, in order of their appearance, to highlight points of importance in the chapter and to help students review the material. Each chapter is followed by an annotated bibliography, consisting chiefly of contemporary paperbacks, with which the instructor can round out the course, if he deems it necessary.

Another problem to which we have addressed ourselves is clarity of expression and general intelligibility. There is no denying that many of the texts now on the market are sadly lacking in these areas. Some are complex in vocabulary; others demand the kind of background that few students possess. We have attempted to attain simplicity without oversimplification and readability without meaninglessness.

Our text is flexible and lends itself to use on both a semester and a quarter basis. Of the eleven chapters and Introduction, the first six chapters present the fundamental concepts of sociology, and the last five discuss pivotal institutions. The Conclusion is a survey of contemporary society, including speculations about its future direction.

The completion of the text was considerably hastened and its quality improved by the cooperation of many persons to whom we are profoundly grateful. Canfield Press Sociology Editor, Howard Boyer, provided many helpful hints and offered much needed moral support at crucial times. Production editor Wendy Cunkle did her usual competent job in her area of specialization. Jacqueline Wiseman of San Francisco State College, Chaim I. Waxman of Central Connecticut State College, and Irving Witt of the College of San Mateo, all read our manuscript, pinpointing its weaknesses as well as its strengths. We were also guided by the critical comments of a number of students who read the manuscript. Among them, the most diligent and helpful were Carol Goldberg and Dolores Leventhal. In addition to her role of critic, Dolores also assumed much responsibility for handling permissions and other secretarial chores which she performed with utmost excellence. Librarians Pamela Hess and Ruth Lederer considerably lightened many of the time-consuming endeavors involved in writing. Finally, we would like to thank our children and our parents for the patience and understanding they showed us during the sometimes harrowing months of writing.

John and Erna Perry, 1973

CONTENTS

xi

CHAPTER TWO: SOCIETY AND CULTURE   65

Society □ Society and Culture □ Cultural Content □ Culture as Structure □ Cultural Differences and Uniformities □ Subcultures and Countercultures □ Summary

CHAPTER THREE: THE INDIVIDUAL AND SOCIETY   103

What Is Personality? □ Humans: Biological Animals □ Biological Determinism □ Psychodynamic Theories of Personality □ Theories of Personality Based on Individual Inheritance □ Cultural Determinism □ Behaviorism, or Environmental Determinism □ Personality: A Social Product □ Maturation and Socialization □ The Chief Agent of Socialization: The Family □ The Acquisition of Self □ Normal Versus Abnormal Personality □ Summary

CHAPTER FOUR: SOCIAL RANKING   143

Social Stratification, or Social Ranking □ Social Class □ Status □ Power □ Systems of Stratification □ Social Mobility □ Life Chances □ Summary

CHAPTER FIVE: MAJORITY AND MINORITY   186

Minorities □ Race □ Racism □ Ethnicity □ Prejudice □ Discrimination □ Conceptual Models of Minority Assimilation □ Black Americans □ Jews □ Spanish-Speaking Minorities □ American Indians □ Summary

CHAPTER SIX: SOCIETY AND CULTURE IN FLUX   232

Some Explanations of Social and Cultural Change □ Processes of Cultural

Change □ Processes of Social Change and Sociocultural Drift □ Population □ Industrialization and Urbanization □ Causes and Mechanisms of Collective Behavior □ Crowds □ Rumors □ Fashions, Fads and Crazes □ Public Opinion □ Social Movements □ Summary

PART TWO: SOCIAL INSTITUTIONS   297

CHAPTER SEVEN: THE SOURCE OF LIFE—THE FAMILY   301

Life Without the Family □ Basic Patterns of Family Organization □ Universal Family Functions □ The American Family □ The Russian Family □ Summary

CHAPTER EIGHT: ASSURING SURVIVAL: THE ECONOMY   351

What Is the Economy? □ A Glance at the Past □ The Philosophy of Capitalism □Karl Marx's View of the Origin of Capitalism □ Max Weber's View of the Origin of Capitalism □ American Capitalism □ Corporate Power □ The Industrial Hierarchy: Management □ The Industrial Hierarchy: Middle-Management □ The Industrial Hierarchy: Blue-Collar Workers □ Organized Labor □ The Rise of Bureaucracy □ The American Economy Today □ Summary

CHAPTER NINE: THE POLITICAL INSTITUTION   405

Government □ The State □ The Nation □ Political Ideology □ Democracy □ Autocracy □ Ideology in Action: Democracy in the United States □ Extremist Political Ideologies: Right and Left □ The Political Behavior of the American Voter □ Summary

A sk the mythical "man in the street" to describe sociology, and you will receive wrong or, at best, incomplete answers. Recognizing the prefix "social," he might tell you that sociology has something to do with social work, or public relations, or, heaven forbid, socialism. Most people, unless they happen to be specialists of some kind or students who are studying for an exam, do not have exact definitions on the tips of their tongues. But people probably have even a hazier idea of sociology than they have of other fields of knowledge.

Part of this vagueness is understandable because sociology is a young discipline, although it has a long tradition behind it. Not until the latter part of the nineteenth century did the discipline even acquire a name, and it is only in the last two decades that many universities established separate sociology departments. Possibly, another reason why people fail to understand the nature of the discipline is that sociology has not received a unanimously favorable reaction from either intellectuals or the public. Many people maintain that what sociology attempts to do—scientifically study humans in interaction—is impossible. And outspoken critics have even said that sociology does nothing more than take common sense knowledge and turn it into words no one understands.

Most likely, criticisms of this kind occur because the content of sociology is not exotic, or distant, or abstract. It is not necessary to place social phenomena under a microscope to see them, or dissect them to understand them, or observe them through a telescope to learn their functions. The content of sociology has not only existed for a long time, but everyone feels he is an expert on it. Sociological content is so common and so much concerned with everyday phenomena that it did not occur to people to examine it scientifically until well after most other phenomena of the human environment had been logically organized by the physical sciences.

WHAT IS SOCIOLOGY?

What, then, is this ordinary content that is the subject of sociology? In a nutshell, *sociology* is the scientific study of the human being as he relates with other human beings. Recognizing that humans are social beings who never naturally live in isolation, sociologists analyze them not as individuals but in their natural habitat—groups of various kinds. Thus, sociology is the study of humans in groups. Other definitions, shorter and at a higher level of abstraction, are often quoted to beginning students of the subject. For instance, sociology is often defined as the science of human interaction, the study of human relationships, or the science of social action systems. But all definitions revolve around the goals of sociology: the discovery of facts, their explanation, and their role in predicting human behavior as it occurs among humans in association with other humans.

What Sociology Is Not

What makes sociology special? Other disciplines are also concerned with human beings. But the sciences, art, and the humanities view the human being from different perspectives than does sociology. Biology looks at the physical organism. Medicine tries to cure ills. Psychology looks at individual mental processes. Religion attempts to satisfy spiritual longings. The other social sciences attempt to explain and order particular facets of human experience. Only sociology studies the individual in the totality of his experience as a social being—one who interrelates with others.

Sociology is not the first discipline to look at humans in this way. The curiosity of humans about their natural surroundings, about themselves, their origins, the motives for their behavior, and their ultimate purpose in life did not develop in modern times. It is likely that even precivilized humans, as soon as they were able to communicate with their fellows, engaged in speculations about their being. Comments about humans, their nature, and their societies, have come down to us from the Greek philosophers, from the pages of the Old Testament, and from the learned men of the Renaissance.

In the prescientific era, when facts were few and had to be gathered with the aid of only the imperfect human senses, all knowledge, factual and speculative, came under the heading of philosophy. As Western civilization grew in complexity, the knowledge gradually began to separate into different disciplines. The accumulated facts about the stars became the science of astronomy. The accumulated facts about earthly phenomena became the sciences of physics, chemistry, biology, and geology. But other areas of knowledge remained for a much longer period in the domain of philosophy, sometimes called the mother of sciences. Among these was the branch of knowledge called social philosophy, which eventually developed into sociology.

As the shapeless knowledge of what had once been philosophy began to take the form of the various scientific disciplines, the first division made was that between the natural and the social sciences. The natural sciences deal with the physical universe and include principally astronomy, physics, chemistry, geology, and biology. The social sciences are concerned with the man-made universe and thus include history, economics, political science, law, and sociology. There are some scientific disciplines—psychology, anthropology, geography, for instance—that straddle this division, studying both natural and man-made phenomena.

Sociology and the Social Sciences

Although sociology's place is among the social sciences, its distinction from them may not seem clear. Someone may justly say, for instance, that history also deals with humans as they interact with others. Without interaction, there would be no history. History, however, focuses on the narration and explanation of a chain of past events to form a complete record of a society or a number of societies—American history or the history of Western civilization, for example. Sociology, on the other hand, uncovers in the same events certain processes that occur when people relate with one another under certain circumstances. Specifically, sociologists want to know whether historical events show a definite pattern that repeats itself every time people find themselves in the same circumstances. They look for generalities in the events, not for specifics; they look for regularities, not for the exceptional; they look for the universal, not for the particular.

Sociology and History: A Difference in Focus

To further illustrate the differences in the way a historian and a sociologist look at the same phenomenon, let's consider the subject of war. A historian studying war would list the names and dates of all the important wars that ever occurred. He would uncover who and what circumstances brought about each war. He would speculate about how each war could have been prevented. And he would distinguish one war from another according to cause, duration, extent of cruelty, and so on. The sociologist, when confronted with such a list, would be interested in the phenomenon of war itself. He would not ask, "Why did World War II break out?" or "Why did it break out in Europe and not in Africa?" Instead, he would ask, "Why do people ever engage in war? Under what conditions do wars in general break out? Do such conditions always bring on war?"

Similarly, whereas the historian would be concerned with the differences between the French and the American revolutions, the sociologist would be interested in the phenomenon of revolution per se. The historian would be acquainted with the biographies of the great personalities of history, but the sociologist would wonder what made these persons, rather than others, leaders. In short, history focuses on descriptions of particulars, of specifics, of the unique. Sociologists generalize, analyze, and find recurring variables. As sociologist Robert Bierstedt comments, "If the past is to be thought of as a continually unrolling cloth, then the historian would be interested in picking out the individual threads; the sociologist, in the overall pattern."[1]

A similar distinction may be made regarding the other social sciences and sociology. The emphases of the social sciences differ, each dealing with a distinct facet of man's experience. Very often, their borders overlap. In fact, many social scientists feel that such borders are artificial and that the social sciences should be approached as a whole. But although sociologists are interested in all facets of man's experience, they are interested in them in a particular way. Specifically, their goals are to uncover the structure—or regular pattern—of social relationships, which the individual creates and recreates to give order to his life. As another well-known sociologist Peter Berger says, "The fascination of sociology lies in the fact that its perspective makes us see in a new light the very world in which we have lived all our lives."[2] Also, "The sociologist does not look at phenomena that nobody is aware of. But he looks at the same phenomena in a different way."[3]

SOCIOLOGY: A SCIENCE

Many of sociology's insights into the nature of people and society are identical with those of poets, playwrights, essayists, novelists, and philosophers. Throughout the centuries, however, philosophers and others have obtained insights by using four main tools. One tool is *intuition*, a sudden insight, the source of which cannot be explained. Another tool is *authority*, or acceptance of statements by people who are specialists in a subject or who are thought to be divinely inspired. A third tool used in the search for truth is *tradition*. That is based on the belief that what has been considered right and true in the past should be considered so in the present. The last tool is *common sense*. Knowledge gained through common sense is based on superficial observation, incomplete data, and the imperfect perception of the human senses.

A New Tool: The Scientific Method

These tools of inquiry are not disregarded today. Many people still rely on them for most of their everyday knowledge. And knowledge gained through the use of such tools tends to persist. That is why people refused for so long

[1]Robert Bierstedt, "Toynbee and Sociology," *The British Journal of Sociology* (June, 1959), pp. 95-104. Also, Pitirim A. Sorokin, "On Sociology Among the Social Sciences," in Marcello Truzzi, ed., *Sociology: The Classic Statements* (New York: Random House, 1971), pp. 3-13.

[2]Peter L. Berger. *Invitation to Sociology* (Garden City, N. Y.,: Doubleday Anchor Books, 1963), p. 21.

[3]Ibid., p. 28.

to acknowledge the evidence that the earth was not flat and that it was not the center of the universe. And that is why many superstititious beliefs and old wives' tales are still accepted today.

The search for truth and knowledge can, however, be carried much further through the use of a new tool of inquiry: the scientific method. It is the scientific method, and not any particular body of content, that gives science a unique way of looking at things. The objective of the scientific method is to obtain verifiable evidence to the basic question, How does it work? And its basis is to make no judgment about even the most obvious facts until original suppositions are overwhelmingly supported by proof.

The Scientific Spirit

Underlying the scientific method is an attitude called the *scientific spirit*. The first principle of this spirit is that the scientist approaches everything with great *doubt* and skepticism, taking nothing for granted. This attitude is displayed even in regard to his own findings, which are always subject to change after further analysis. The second principle is *objectivity*. This means that the scientist tries to rid himself completely of personal attitudes, desires, beliefs, values, and tendencies when confronting data. He must try to be completely dispassionate, not permitting his individual biases to affect his judgment. Naturally, objectivity is an ideal to which the scientist can only aspire. No one is totally objective all the time. Furthermore, some scientists no longer believe that total objectivity is desirable. An increasing number maintain that the scientist as a human being has a moral obligation toward his fellow human beings. Therefore, he should not permit the products of his research to be used in immoral ways. We shall see later how this issue affects sociology.

Closely related to objectivity is *ethical neutrality*. According to this principle, the scientist must not make value judgments about his findings. In his function as a scientific researcher, he cannot maintain that his conclusions are good or bad, right or wrong. He must be concerned only with whether they are true or false. Finally, the scientist's conclusions must never be considered final, absolute, or universal truths. His conclusions are always relative to the time and place in which they are made and always subject to change.

Techniques of the Scientific Method

The basic technique of the scientific method is observation. But it must be observation of a special kind. Above all, observation must be accurate and precise. In collecting data, the scientist must subject it to careful checking, rechecking, and cross-checking. He must also subject it to careful measurement. For instance, he cannot permit himself to say, "The big universities are full of radicals." He would have to say, instead, "In universities with enrollments of 15,000 and over, 60.5 percent of the students were found to be members of political action groups."

Scientific observation must also proceed systematically. In other words, the scientist must select and define a problem and then make an organized plan for collecting data. A haphazard collection of facts, taken from memory or from a small sample, obviously proves nothing. In defining his problem, the scientist forms an hypothesis. This is a statement, in general terms, of the problem and its probable solution. An hypothesis may be simply a hunch or a guess by the researcher, which research may prove valid, may reform, or may contradict altogether.

After data have been systematically collected, the scientist must classify, organize, and record the data. Because human memory is imperfect and subject to personal prejudices, research that has not been so recorded is considered invalid. Furthermore, the data must be made public, so others may have access to both the findings and the procedures through which they were obtained. The scientist's obligation is to make public his findings even if they displease him or endanger him.

Scientific observation should take place under controlled conditions. In other words, the researcher should be able to make particular features of the environment remain constant. Then, when other features change, he can be sure of which specific cause is determining which effect. This is difficult in the area of the social sciences because research cannot always be performed in a laboratory setting. Finally, scientific observation must be made by a trained observer. Only such a person knows which data are relevant and which are unimportant.

Clearly, scientific observation is not the same as looking at things. Those of us who have the use of our vision look at things all the time. But seldom do we arrive at scientific observations. Sometimes the evidence of our senses can be confirmed through the method of science. Sometimes that same method proves us wrong.

THE SCIENTIFIC METHOD IN SOCIOLOGY

We have seen that sociology is a science because it uses the scientific method as its system of inquiry. But because it is a social science, it cannot use exactly the same methodology as the physical sciences do. The scientific method of sociology is based on the use of concepts, theory, and research.

Concepts

People think in terms of concepts about things that they observe and experience, and then they express these concepts through language. *Concepts* are generalized ideas about people, objects, and processes that are related to one another. Concepts are abstractions, ways of classifying things that are similar. For instance, the concept of *chair* includes all those objects that people sit in. Although this concept embraces all variations of the object, each of us interprets it in his own way. Those who have been brought up in mansions may think of a gilded Louis XIV chair. Others are likely to think of plain chrome kitchen chairs. However, we all know and understand the generalized idea of chair.

Sociological concepts are generalizations made about human interaction. For example, conflict is a concept that we all understand; it refers to a particular kind of behavior among a number of people. It may refer to a fistfight between two men who both want to dance with the same woman; it may refer to the "silent treatment" one marriage partner gives the other when a large portion of the paycheck has been spent in one way; or it may refer to guerilla warfare practiced by a group against another group that has control of a nation's government. We know about conflict because we have experienced it ourselves, we have observed it among others, we have thought about it on occasion, and are therefore able to generalize about it.

Concepts are learned and are continually altered in our minds as we obtain additional information. The child who believes that all chairs are made of wood adds another dimension to his concept of chair when he discovers that some chairs are upholstered and covered with fabric.

Sociologists use concepts as their technical vocabulary. But sociological concepts often have precise meanings that differ considerably from the layman's meaning. It is therefore essential for a student of sociology to become acquainted with sociological concepts. Such concepts as group, culture, society, and association, to mention but a few, mean one thing to the man and woman in the street and another to sociologists. When dealing with sociological concepts, however, the student should be aware that they are generalized abstractions, instead of being concrete and real. Thus, when they define the concept of group, sociologists do not mean to imply that each and every group has characteristics identical to those in their definition. In other words, they have no particular group in mind but a generalized abstraction of a group. Concepts, then, are merely guidelines that direct sociologists as they try to interpret and analyze reality.

Theory

Concepts form the basis of theories. *Theories* are attempts at predicting possible and probable relationships among data. They are also formulations of principles of behavior through which we try to increase our knowledge of human interaction. Theories are generalizations too, but they are founded on observation and analysis. Their intent is to explain the connection between and among occurrences in human interaction. Without theories, the accumulation of sociological knowledge would be impossible, just as the formulation of theories would be impossible without concepts.

In sociology, theories are helpful not only in the explanation of current situations but also in the prediction of future ones. Suppose, for instance, we use available data to theorize that under conditions of large-scale unemployment minority groups will vote the Democratic ticket. If election results proved our theory right, it would be reasonable to expect that these groups will vote similarly whenever they are faced with unemployment. This does not mean that every member of a minority group will always vote Democratic. It simply suggests that most will, under the same circumstances, vote Democratic most of the time.

A theory, then, does not have the force of a law. The latter is an unchanging explanation of relationships among events, According to the law of gravity, for example, an object always falls in the same direction under given conditions. Sociology has no laws. It has many theories, some of which, because of the poor availability of data, are really little more than hypotheses. Working with concepts as his tools and using the techniques of the scientific method, the sociologist arrives at a theory. A theory, however, is never considered the final word on a subject. It is always open to change and even to total rejection if new evidence is brought forth to challenge it.

Research

Research tests and bolsters theories. The two aspects of the sociological method complement each other: Theory without the proper research remains in the realm of speculation, whereas research without theory is meaningless. However, most sociologists specialize in either one or the other. They either refine the concepts from which theories are constructed, fitting concepts into a theoretical framework, or they engage in empirical research. Empirical research has already been described in general terms when we discussed the techniques of the scientific method. But sociological research makes heavy use of three fundamental formats: the sample survey—and its variation, observation of social interaction—the case study, and the experiment. In all of these formats, mathematical statistics have become a frequently used and valued research tool.

The case study.   The case study is a detailed investigation of a specific social unit. The unit may be the black family, the patients of mental hospitals, or the middle-class suburban family. The focus of the case study approach is on the total behavior of the selected unit rather than on one aspect of it, as in the sample survey. Its advantage is that it permits the researcher—through depth interviewing—to explore quite thoroughly the factors that may cause specific behavior. Its disadvantage is that because the social units analyzed are generally rather small, generalizations cannot always be made about similar units. However, if enough case studies yield similar results, such generalizations are possible.

The experiment.   In the experimental method, the researcher controls one variable and then observes and records the results. For example, suppose a sociologist wants to test his hypothesis that marijuana has a negative effect on motor coordination. Using the experimental method, the researcher selects about one hundred people of approximately the same age and physical build. He then puts them through a test, measuring their motor coordination when they have not smoked marijuana for twenty-four hours. He carefully records their performance under this condition. Then, he permits them to smoke progressively larger quantities of marijuana, recording their performance after each increase in dosage. If, after a maximum amount of marijuana smoking, the performance of the participants does not differ markedly from their performance when not under the stimulant's influence, the sociologist rejects his hypothesis. If, on the other hand, the opposite is true, he has proved that his hypothesis is correct. The result of this experiment would permit the sociologist to make definite predictions. He would know that under specific circumstances, the smoking of marijuana affects smokers in specific ways and to a specific degree.

This method has limitations in sociology, because it cannot be used to test many hypotheses. People are not objects or white mice that can be manipulated at will so a researcher may test their reactions. However, the method has possibilities and has been used to advantage by a number of researchers. The most obvious recent example is furnished by Masters and Johnson, who seem to have been quite successful in obtaining evidence about human sexual behavior.

The sample survey and observation of social interaction. The sample survey is an attempt at determining the occurrence of a given act or option within a given sample of people. The sociologist, having decided to analyze a specific group—called a population—selects a statistically valid sample of it. For example, if he wants to study the political behavior of thirty-five-year-old, college-educated housewives residing in the Midwest, he must choose a reasonably large group of women with these characteristics. Data are collected through questionnaires and personal interviews. It is then assumed that the findings represent the political behavior of *all* thirty-five-year-old, college-educated housewives residing in the Midwest. This method is quite effective as a research technique, but it is not equally effective for all topics, because its accuracy depends on the frankness with which questions are answered.

Observation of actual interaction among people is sometimes substituted for, or used in addition to, the survey approach although that method is not entirely satisfactory either. When people know they are being observed, they often don't act naturally.

We must stress again that in spite of the use of the scientific method social scientists have more difficulty obtaining verifiable data than do physical scientists. Examining a piece of moon rock in the laboratory is very different from examining a human being as he relates to others. Not only does the human being not lend himself to many of the experiments that the inert moon rock does but the human being also evokes a reaction from the researcher. The researcher can remain objective and perfectly impassive as he uncovers all the elements of the moon rock. But the researcher cannot help reacting positively or negatively to the human being he is analyzing: He may find the person ugly or beautiful, intelligent or dumb, interesting or boring. And as objective as he tries to be, the researcher's conclusions may be tinged by his bias. Thus, in sociology, there are no absolute conclusions and no absolutely objective interpretations.

CHARACTERISTICS OF SOCIOLOGY

We have been mentioning characteristics of sociology throughout this discussion, but it may be helpful to list them together, under one heading. In addition to being a social science, sociology is categorical rather than normative. In other words, it is concerned with what is and never with what ought to be. Science, in general, does not attempt to probe into matters that are not perceived by the human senses but is concerned strictly with empirical phenomena. Sociology is also limited to the description of events as they are, as they were, or as they probably will be. Sociologists cannot, however, make statements about whether these events are good or bad, right or wrong, or whether they should be pursued or changed.

In addition, sociology is a pure, not an applied, science. In other words, its goal is the acquisition of knowledge about the behavior of human beings in society, not the use of that knowledge. That task is left to such fields as social work, diplomacy, administration, teaching, and so on.

Another characteristic of sociology is that it is an abstract science, rather than a concrete one. This means that it is more concerned with the forms and patterns that human behavior takes than it is with the specific consequences of behavior. Thus, sociologists are not interested in the U.S. Steel Corporation as such but in the human tendency to organize into various associations to get things done. They are not interested in the nations of the globe per se but in the universality of human societies, which display structural similarities.

Related to the abstract nature of sociology is its involvement with general, rather than particular, principles governing human interaction. Sociologists are not interested in a particular society that waged war on another society and was strengthened as a result. They study that event only because it provides further evidence of the principle that external aggression tends to solidify the internal unity of a group.

Finally, sociology is a general and not a special social science. By this, we mean that sociologists seek out the principles that govern *all* interaction and social relationships, regardless of the area of human life in which they occur. In this, it differs from the rest of the social sciences, which do make this distinction and thus treat only specific areas of human life.

THE RELEVANCE OF SOCIOLOGY

Max Weber, one of the great sociological thinkers, perceived a threefold function in the social sciences: the ability to control the forces of society, the training of future social scientists, and the attainment of intellectual clarity. It appears that the first two functions have been generally accepted by academicians, the second function having, in addition, been actively pursued. But the last function, which Weber considered the most important, has been neglected. Yet intellectual clarity would enable the individual citizen of a society to judge alternative courses of action because he would be aware of their present basis and their future consequences.

It is to this last function, intellectual clarity, that this text addresses itself. It is only by attaining intellectual clarity that the first of Weber's functions—the ability to control the forces of society—can be considered a reasonable goal. For much of human history, people have been buffeted by forces beyond their control. Today, through technology, people can control many of these forces. But their control has been most successful in the physical world. In the social realm, people have remained slaves to tradition and to provincialism, which limit their ability to perceive things as they are. As a consequence, a substantial portion of the people in most societies live in conditions beneath the dignity of a human being.

Sociology has no specific answers that will cure the ills of humanity or that will help to bring about utopia. But by relentlessly asking Why? and How? and by continually probing into causes, sociology can tear off some of the veils that have covered social reality for so long. It matters little how these veils were imposed—whether through ignorance, greed, or the thirst for power. What matters is that they be seen for what they are, not for what they appear to be. In bringing this about, sociology and its followers are, and no doubt will be, faced with much antagonism. No one likes to see his idols shattered. No one likes to be told that the group he belongs to is not actually superior—that only his ethnocentrism, or belief in the superiority of his group makes it seem so. No one likes to be told that the family he is trying to prevent from moving into his neighborhood is not inferior—that only his prejudice makes it seem so. No one likes to be told that his hate of communism is not patriotism but is only a compensatory mechanism he has developed because he feels frustrated by changes beyond his control.

People must, however, understand social reality if they are to become the true masters of their destiny and if they are to make rational, constructive choices and to experience a complete life. Unfortunately, even though we live in society and it is our immediate reality, we understand very little about it. (After all, we are living organisms but this does not mean that we automatically understand biology!)

Sociology does not claim to be the only discipline that helps people understand and know society and the individuals within it. Sociology only claims to provide one means of achieving such understanding, but the means are uniquely appropriate to exploration of a changed and changing world. The novelist James Joyce expressed his horror at some of the morbid aspects of human experience by saying that history was a nightmare from which he was trying to awake. Sociology may help us all to awake from the nightmares not only of history but of the present.

SOCIOLOGY: THE RAGE WITHIN

Sociology is not only the target of cynical attacks and criticisms from the outside but it is also the victim of a controversy within its own ranks. This controversy has several themes. Whereas the majority of sociologists are convinced that sociology is rightly, and should continue to be, a scientific study, a minority challenges this contention. They accuse sociologists of having betrayed their discipline, which arose, to a great extent, in response to a movement for social reform, but has become strictly objective and ethically neutral. Others accuse sociologists of having "sold out to the Establishment," by which they mean that sociologists have helped to maintain the status quo by accepting grants and subsidies from government and corporate agencies.

Still others maintain that the sociologist's attempt at maintaining strict neutrality is at best an impossibility—some personal bias always creeps in—and at worst a way to deliberately avoid seeking solutions to the pressing problems confronting humanity. The responsibility of a sociologist, these critics maintain, should be not only to survey, research, and analyze at a distance but to participate in and try to solve critical issues.

Finally, many sociologists differ among themselves about the fundamental question of whether sociology should, or whether it even can, be both a humanistic and a scientific discipline. Critics have observed that the increasingly statistical and empirical methods of research have linked sociology to exact science, while the humanistic methods of inquiry—observation, depth interviewing, and so on—are being neglected.

The controversy is not likely to be resolved in the near future partly because all the participants are right from their own point of view. An exclusive stress on methodology and research may obscure the larger issue, which is the study of humans. Also, much of sociology has become bureaucratized and some of it has gone for sale to the highest bidder. Furthermore, some sociologists may have closed their eyes to the inequalities and injustices of society with the excuse that they must remain objective. At the same time, use of the scientific method does not preclude concern with the human element. Nor does ethical neutrality preclude involvement in today's issues.

In a healthy discipline, there is room for many people with many points of view: sociologists who man the barricades and those who remain in their ivory towers; sociologists who use mathematical formulas and those who feel more comfortable with the lessons of philosophy or history; sociologists enamored with information processed by a computer and those who prefer to rely on information processed through their own brains. After all, human life is such that it is filled with dichotomies. Humans experience cooperation and conflict, love and hate, attraction and repulsion. The human individual is a product of society; yet in many respects he is in conflict with it. If sociology studies humans in their habitat, then nothing human—no individual reaction, no mass movement—should be alien to it.

TERMS TO REMEMBER

Sociology. The study of the human being as he relates with other human beings, or the study of humans in groups.

Intuition. A method of gaining knowledge through a sudden insight, the source of which cannot be explained.

Authority. A method of gaining knowledge through acceptance of statements by people who are experts.

Tradition. A method of gaining knowledge based on the belief that what has been considered right and true in the past should be considered so in the present.

Common sense. A method of gaining knowledge based on superficial observation, incomplete data, and the imperfect perception of the human senses.

Scientific spirit. A principle of the scientific method, requiring the scientist to approach everything with doubt and skepticism.

Objectivity. A principle of the scientific method, requiring the scientist to divest himself of personal attitudes, desires, beliefs, values, and tendencies.

Ethical neutrality. A principle of the scientific method, requiring that the scientist not pass judgment on his findings.

Concept. A generalized idea about people, objects, and processes that are related to one another; abstractions; ways of classifying things that are similar.

Theory. A series of concepts that attempts to predict possible and probable relationships among data.

Sample survey. A method of research consisting in an attempt to determine the occurrence of a given act or opinion within a given sample of people.

Case study. A method of research consisting in a detailed investigation of a specific social unit.

Experiment. A method of research in which the researcher controls one variable and observes and records the results.

PART ONE ◈

THE social web

The German sociologist Max Weber, whose numerous works make him an end-less source of inspiration for modern sociological writers, considered the proper sub-ject matter of sociology to be the understanding of all social action for the purpose of determining its cause and its effects. By social action, Weber meant human behavior of which the individual is aware and which is directed toward others. In other words, the reflex action of blinking at an object approaching the eye is not a social action. But blinking at someone in order to attract his attention is a social action. Sociology is concerned with all social action, so we can see how broad the field becomes.

Because the subject matter is vast and difficult to analyze, sociologists abstract it into concepts. They then place the concepts within a specific frame of reference. The social action of Weber may be analyzed from many points of view—in other words, from within many conceptual frameworks. For instance, human behavior may be studied from the point of view of the individual human being. Then, the focus is on the individual's motives, emotions, feelings of identity, and so on. This is usually the psychologist's frame of reference, and much of social psychology involves this particular conceptual framework.

Another conceptual framework with which the sociologist deals is the group. Although the group is made up of individuals, it is usually dealt with as a unit. Then, human beings are viewed primarily as group members rather than individuals.

Other conceptual frameworks may be built around the interaction that goes on among the individuals making up a group and the interaction between and among groups. These conceptual frameworks give rise to even more possibilities. Social behavior may be analyzed from the point of view of interaction between individuals in terms of their roles: husband and wife, manufacturer and consumer, candidate and voter. Or it may be analyzed from the point of view of social structure, the patterns of roles that cluster around a definite social function: the educational struc-ture, the religious structure, the economic structure. Social behavior may even be analyzed within the conceptual framework of a social system, which is the patterned relationship of the several social structures.

Regardless of how sociologists choose to conceptualize human behavior, they must reckon with another factor: Human behavior is subject to social regulation. The regulation of social behavior is the function of sanctions, norms, and values.

These conceptual abstractions of human behavior, and the constraints placed on behavior by social regulation, make up the principle analytical tools of sociology and its chief ingredients. The sociologist has abstracted human behavior because he wants to analyze it and explain it. He wants to know how it originated, why it originated in one form rather than another, why it persists, and why it changes. He wants to know both the regularities of human behavior and the variations.

The task of the first six chapters will be to familiarize the student with the conceptual framework within which sociologists analyze the bulk of human behavior. The first chapter clarifies the sociological meaning of the concept of group, suggests the kinds of processes that take place in interaction, and illustrates how interaction can be analyzed from the point of view of roles and statuses. The second chapter considers the sociological meanings of society and culture and their interrelationships, universality, and variation. Chapter 3 shows how the individual human becomes a social being. Chapters 4 and 5 deal with the organizational aspects of society, specifically with how societies organize in hierarchical fashion and how they deal with minority groups within them. Chapter 6 presents several theories of social change in an attempt to explain the origin of sociocultural change and some of its results: industrialization, urbanization, and population growth. The chapter also deals with a type of behavior often provoked by sudden social change: collective behavior.

Part II of the text examines the pivotal institutions of society—family, economy, government, education, and religion—using the sociological tools and the conceptual framework with which the student became acquainted in the first part. In this process, we hope that students will learn to look with new eyes at old territory.

CHAPTER ONE

GROUPS: FROM TWO TO MILLIONS

A glance at the daily newspaper is sufficient to convince us that groups are much more newsworthy than are single individuals. We read that members of a union affiliated with the UAW-CIO are threatening to strike. We read that spokesmen for the automotive industry are bargaining for more time to comply with new safety and antipollution specifications. On the late news we hear that teachers in a neighboring school system are protesting their lack of autonomy and academic freedom. A local citizens committee is formed to fight proposed public housing in a community. A California family is moving to Alaska where it hopes to find some of the old-fashioned virtues absent from our large cities. The United Nations has issued yet another warning to a member nation to stay out of the internal affairs of its neighbor.

Organizations, families, communities, and nations are the subject of news far more often than are the individuals who make up these groups. This comes as no surprise to us, because we know, through observation and experience, that we live in groups, and not in isolation. When the news media do concern themselves with individuals, it is because the individuals have been singled out for some honor, because they represent a powerful or prestigious group, or because they have committed an act for which society must punish them.

Occasionally, we hear and read about other individuals—persons who have lost their sense of community and their membership in their groups. Many old men and women are forced to live in antiseptic convalescent homes or alone in the misery of their own homes. Frequently unable to face such aloneness, they simply die. Prison inmates who are kept in solitary confinement too long often take their own lives or renounce life by going mad. Boys and girls abandon their blood families in search of communal, though primitive, life in rural areas of America. Children reared in isolation, without access to nurturing adults, grow into subhuman beings, incapable of performing the simplest tasks, unable even to walk or feed themselves. When brought out of isolation, such children acquire human characteristics only through intense interaction with others.

A LIFE LIVED IN GROUPS

What do all the preceding examples of the importance of groups tell us about ourselves and the human species? Essentially, they suggest the extent to which we need one another. In no part of the world do people live absolutely alone by choice. Isolation is considered an extreme punishment, and it is a brutalizing experience. When people do seek isolation voluntarily, they are usually pursuing an ideological principle or symbolizing their rejection of society. But isolation has never been considered a natural way to live.

We are well aware that we live in groups. In fact, we know all too well how crowded the earth is becoming and what price we must pay for privacy. Yet it is doubtful whether many of us realize the extraordinarily pervasive nature of group life.

The individual human being is created by a group, and he remains under the influence of innumerable groups from the time he is born until he dies. From the moment of conception, the biological being about to become an individual is hardly ever alone. In the womb, he forms a strong, physical bond with the mother; his life depends on her body. Even after he is born, his survival depends on a group, usually his immediate family.

The child's maturation into a human being, as well as his survival, depends on continued interaction with other people. A constant relationship with those around him teaches him the foremost characteristic of humanness: language. All other social characteristics, from the most elementary group habits of our society to the most complex attitudes, are learned through observation of and association with others. As a young child, the individual belongs to a peer group of playmates. Later, he forms friendship groups at school and then at work. Finally, he is a member of a family group of his own creation, and his children repeat the cycle of maturation through interaction in groups.

Throughout his life, the individual belongs to temporary and permanent groups, organized for specific or general goals. What kind of person he becomes depends greatly on the groups to which he belongs and on the quality of relationships that exist in them.

SOCIOLOGICAL TERMINOLOGY

In the Introduction, we pointed out that the fundamental aim of sociology is to study humans in their natural setting—society. In practice, this means that the sociologist attempts to categorize, classify, order, describe, and discover the principles governing the behavior of individuals in groups and the behavior of groups with one another. Intragroup and intergroup interaction provide the basic framework of sociology; whether the sociologist explores personality and the self, institutions, culture and society, or any one of a thousand topics, he proceeds from the standpoint of interaction within and among groups.

We also said that the sociologist's principal tool of inquiry is the concept. Some sociological concepts are familiar to us because they are part of everyday usage. But because the sociologist approaches the study of phenomena with a scientific methodology, he usually defines and uses concepts in a different and more precise way than we do. Thus, it is necessary to devote much of the content of the following chapters to definitions of sociological concepts.

Definitions do not make for exciting reading, but they are essential if all of us are to have a common understanding of the subject under discussion. Lastly, we must warn students that definitions of concepts should not be accepted as the gospel of the god Sociology. Definitions are simply tools to aid analysis: they provide a language of specific meanings which we can use to make certain we are all speaking about the same thing.

THE NATURE OF GROUPS

In view of what we have said about terminology, it is not surprising that the sociological definition of the word *group* is different from the common definition of "a number of people congregated at the same time and at the same place." In the context of sociology, fifteen students cramming for an exam in a student lounge are not necessarily a group. Twenty commuters on the morning train into town are not necessarily a group. Nor are eight salesmen eating lunch at the counter of Moe's Delicatessen. If we know nothing else about these people except that they are in the same place at the same time, we call them *aggregates*, not groups.

There are many individuals, across the nation and across the world, who share specific characteristics. There are, for example, millions of people who were born on the Fourth of July of a particular year, who have flaming red hair, who are lefthanded, and who part their hair in the middle. We cannot say that these people make up a group, either. Instead, we say that they form a *category*.

Suppose, however, that three of the fifteen students cramming in the student lounge have been studying there since the beginning of the school year. What's more, they have an English class together, and they eat lunch at the same time. Because they are human and, therefore, social beings, the students exchange only greetings at first. Later they sit together in English class and in the cafeteria, complaining about the difficulty of the courses, the boredom of life, and the ugliness of the local scenery. Out of an aggregate of fifteen, then, three have formed a group. By the same token, suppose that all the redheads who were born on the Fourth of July in 1945 organized a club. The members of the club corresponded regularly and met periodically for the purpose of setting up a scholarship fund for redheads born on the Fourth of July, 1945. The redheads, then, would have ceased to be a category and would have become a social group.

The Sociological Definition of a Group

In sociological terms, an aggregate or a category is not a group, regardless of its size, goals, or origin, unless it meets the following conditions: (1). There is physical and, more important, symbolic interaction among the members: (*Symbolic interaction* is communication through speech, gestures, writing or even music. In this kind of communication, members are aware of one another; mutual awareness causes them to respond, or behave, in particular ways and, thus, to influence one another.) (2) Each member recognizes that he is part of the group. Conversely, the group recognizes him as a member. (3) Members accept the roles, duties, and obligations, as well as the privileges, resulting from group membership.

In short, physical interaction alone is not sufficient to generate a group; when you bump into ten people in a crowded elevator, you are part of an aggregate. For sociologists, symbolic interaction is the vital prerequisite for determining whether a collection of people is a group.

Symbolic interaction need not involve face-to-face communication. If relatives and friends who live at opposite points of the earth are still able to affect

one another through correspondence, they remain a group. Moreover, members of a group need not be personal friends. As long as there is some kind of communication among people that results in mutual adjustment of behavior, the people make up a group. In this sense, citizens of a nation, who are united by common political processes and who share a number of similar loyalties, a common history, and the sense of a common future, are considered a group.

Classifications of Groups

There are an extraordinarily large number of groups and great diversity among them. Groups vary in size from two members to many more than two million, as the chapter title suggests (from a pair of individuals to a whole society, or in some contexts, even to the entire population of the earth). The number of groups in every society is countless; it surpasses the number of individuals, because each individual belongs to more than one group. Small wonder, then, that researchers find classification of groups to be problematic. A researcher must decide whether to categorize groups according to size, interests, duration, type of organization, quality of interaction, and so on, in an infinite variety of ways. None of these classifications is either right or wrong; classification depends on the researcher's purpose in examining the group.

Primary and secondary groups and relationships.   Sociologists invariably classify groups into primary and secondary groups. The term *primary group* was coined by Charles Horton Cooley (1864-1929), a pioneer American sociologist. Cooley designated primary groups as groups in which members engage in intimate interaction and cooperation, the influence of which is basic to the development of an individual's personality.

Later sociologists decided that additional characteristics distinguished primary from other groups. Among these characteristics are relatively small group size, physical nearness of members, intense interaction among members, group stability, and relatively long duration of group existence. In addition, interaction in primary groups occurs informally and spontaneously, as individuals begin to know and deal with one another on an individual, personal, and total basis. Clearly, the family provides the foremost example of a primary group. However, a clique of friends, a circle of playmates or fellow students, and even one's neighborhood or community may also be considered primary groups.

If we imagine a long, straight, horizontal line called an ideal continuum and if we place primary groups on one end of this continuum, the other end will be occupied by *secondary groups*. Secondary groups tend to be large and to exist for a short period of time. Most important, the interaction among members is formal, utilitarian, specialized, and, most likely, temporary. In a secondary group, the members are not interested primarily in one another as persons but in one another in terms of the roles and functions they perform in society. If you have to ask yourself "What's in it for me?" you are probably involved in a secondary relationship.

To illustrate the difference between primary and secondary groups, let's assume that you and Tony, the owner of a pizza parlor, have known each other since kindergarten. Suppose that you and he have some of the same friends, bowl on the same team, and confide in each other and frequently visit each other's homes. You and Tony, then, form a primary group, and the two of you interact in a primary relationship. On the other hand, suppose

TABLE 1-1   PRIMARY AND SECONDARY RELATIONSHIPS

	Primary	**Secondary**
Typically found in Such groups as:	family playmates clique village	nation religious denomination trade union professional association
Such dyadic relationships as:	husband-wife parent-child teacher-pupil friend-friend	officer-subordinate clerk-customer performer-spectator congressman-constituent
Social characteristics	informal feeling of freedom and spontaneity inclusive knowledge of other person identity of ends other-oriented personal	formal feeling of external constraint specialized and limited knowledge of other person disparity of ends self-oriented impersonal
Physical conditions	small number long duration physical proximity	large number short duration physical distance

SOURCE: Adapted, with modifications, from Kingsley David, *Human Society*, 1949, p. 306, by permission of The Macmillian Company, New York. Copyright 1948, 1949 by the Macmillian Company.

that you remember Tony only when the craving for pizza overtakes you, and the only dealings you have with him are to order and pick up pizzas. Regardless of how friendly you are during the transaction, you and he form a secondary group and interrelate in a secondary relationship.

Although some relationships may be recognized as purely primary and others as purely secondary, most relationships fall somewhere between the two extremes. Moreover, some primary relationships may in the course of time slide into secondary relationships, and very often secondary relationships become primary ones.

Another way of looking at primary and secondary groups is in terms of what they *do* for us. The secondary group satisfies a particular goal, whether it is the taste for pizza or the necessity of providing a livelihood. But we judge the primary group by the emotional satisfaction it affords us and not by useful functions that it performs for us.

Primary groups are universal and have probably existed since the beginning of mankind. When an individual is totally removed from primary relationships, his spirit is soon broken, and his mental health may be severely affected. Even so, not all primary relationships are of a harmonious nature, nor are they always satisfying to the individual. Primary relationships may involve a large amount of conflict or the enforcement of conformity, which stifles individuality.

The importance of primary relationships, as well as several interesting points about group formation, is discussed in Stanford M. Lyman's article, "Red Guard on Grant Avenue," included at the end of this chapter.[1] The author talks about the kinds of groups formed by the original Chinese settlers in America. Because there were twenty-seven men for every Chinese woman in the United States, the men developed groups that served as substitutes for the primary group of the family. These groups provided lonely men with some sense of solidarity and familiarity, and some emotional support. Clan associations and secret societies helped fulfill the men's emotional needs, and prostitution houses, opium smoking, and gambling provided other forms of support. Later immigrants, as well as a generation of Chinese-Americans, created additional groups. Both the early and the later immigrants exhibited the social processes that we will describe later in the chapter as making up social interaction.

Other Classifications of Groups.   In examining groups, we find the concepts of in-group and out-group useful. These concepts describe the "we" as opposed to "they" feelings of which every group member is at least somewhat conscious. These feelings are a universal feature of group formation. Their advantage is that they produce a feeling of unity within in-groups. But they are sometimes harmful to interaction in a society, especially when out-groups are perceived as enemies by in-groups.

Groups can also be classified into reference groups and membership groups. *Membership groups* are the formal (the YMCA) or informal (clique of friends) organizations to which an individual belongs. *Reference groups* are groups to which an individual aspires to belong and on which he patterns his present behavior. A reference group need not be a particular kind of group or have special characteristics; it may be a political, economic, religious, ethnic, kinship, or social organization. Again, an individual may already be a member of it, and participate in its activities, or he may not. The important point is that he refers to and accepts its values so strongly that its influence on him is *apparent* to a greater extent than the influence of any other group.[2] (It is important to remember, however, that the family group has more *actual* influence in the long run.)

In examining groups, we may also notice that some are of a voluntary and others of an involuntary nature. We cannot choose the kind of family into which we are born. This primary group, then, is an *involuntary group.* Secondary groups may also be of an involuntary nature. Young men who are drafted into the Armed Forces are usually not able to select their favorite branch of service or the location of their tour of duty. Conversely, there are hundreds

---

[1]Stanford M. Lyman, "Red Guard on Grant Avenue," *Transaction* (April, 1970).

[2]Robert A. Nisbet, *The Social Bond* (New York: Alfred A. Knopf, 1970), pp. 107–108.

of thousands of organizations, ranging from fraternities to political parties and from fan clubs to bridge clubs, that an individual may join entirely of his free will—or sometimes for reasons of social and economic expediency. Such groups are called *voluntary groups*.

The Size of Groups

Sociologists also consider groups from the standpoint of their size. Small groups such as the family, a circle of close friends, a clique within a large organization, and a committee formed for specific problem solving share several common characteristics: (1) Relations among members are usually on a face-to-face basis; (2) in general, members share common values; (3) the group is usually durable; (4) members exhibit feelings of identification with the group and group loyalty; (5) in general, members accept one another; (6) members perceive the group as a separate entity; (7) members perceive the group as striving to fulfill definite goals.[3] In addition, small groups usually value stable membership; the difficulty of joining them enhances membership; they greatly influence the behavior of their members; and within them, democratic leadership is more effective than it is within large groups.

Large groups, of necessity, have characteristics that differ from those of small groups. Above all, they tend to be much more highly organized, often assuming the proportions, and titles, of formal organizations and bureaucracies. Formal organizations usually possess some kind of definite structure: Their goals, programs, and the roles of their personnel are fairly specific.

When formal organizations reach large-scale dimensions—as do giant corporations, state and federal governments, and huge university complexes—they are called bureaucracies. A *bureaucracy* is a hierarchical system in an organization. The hierarchy depends on job specialization—or division of labor—on a set of rules and standards designed to promote uniformity, and on an attitude of impersonal impartiality.[4]

We are all familiar with some facets of bureaucracy because in large, complex societies bureaucracy becomes, to a great extent, a way of life. Our bureaucratic way of life has been undergoing criticism for quite some time, especially by young people, who believe that overorganization stifles creativity, and is generally dehumanizing. This may be true. Yet bureaucratic organization is largely responsible for our high standard of living, including high productivity, rapid transportation, and the advancements in medical science. By organizing our lives so efficiently, then, bureaucracy can give us more time to pursue our creative impulses. In the end, it may actually be enhancing our personal freedom.

Finally, the largest group to which people belong is one with which we all are familiar—society. This group is considered in detail in the following chapter. For now, it is sufficient to know that, in general, societies are examined from the standpoint of their attributes—whether they are urban or rural, traditional or modern, Gemeinschaft or Gesellschaft.

[3]David Dressler, *Sociology: The Study of Human Interaction* (New York: Alfred A. Knopf, 1969), p. 288.

[4]Peter M. Blau, *Bureaucracy in Modern Society* (New York: Random House, 1956), pp. 28-31.

Gemeinschaft and Gesellschaft

The German sociologist Ferdinand Tönnies (1855-1936), in examining different kinds of societies, arrived at concepts similar to those of primary and secondary groups. He noted that in small, homogeneous societies members interacted with one another on an informal, personal, face-to-face basis and that tradition dictated behavior. Tönnies called this kind of society a *Gemeinschaft*, which is translated more or less as "a communal, or traditional, society."

Relationships are much different in societies that are large and heterogeneous, like modern industrial societies. In these societies, relationships among members are impersonal, formal, functional, and specialized. Furthermore, they are often contractual—dealings are spelled out in legal contracts rather than being governed by tradition. Tönnies called these societies *Gesellschaft*, or "associational societies."

In the modern world, there has been an easily observable shift from Gemeinschaft to Gesellschaft societies. The large size of the societal group and the complexities of a technological economy make secondary groups, dedicated to efficiency rather than sentiment, a necessity. Therefore, in Gesellschaft societies, many of the tasks of primary groups, such as education and economic transactions, have passed to secondary groups.

The great reliance in Gesellschaft societies on secondary groups has both disadvantages and advantages. Many behavioral problems—even the high incidence of suicide—have been blamed on the breaking of primary group ties. On the other hand, the large-scale impersonal organizations we call corporations have greatly enhanced our physical comfort because of their efficiency in handling economic matters. Furthermore, secondary groups, by taking into account a wide range of interests, counteract some of the narrow interests and viewpoints often found in small, tightly knit groups.

It is important to remember, too, that primary groups continue to be formed within the confines of secondary groups. As a matter of fact, successful primary interaction in large formal organizations and in bureaucracies is vital to the organizations' success. If the interests of a large organization are perceived as running counter to those of the primary groups in it, the large organization may fail. This is so because an organization's success is measured by its productivity. Productivity, in turn, depends, to a large degree, on employees. Successful primary group interaction in a large organization may lead to satisfied employees, who produce well. If, however, employees are dissatisfied with the goals of an organization, successful primary group interaction will strengthen and encourage them to sabotage the organization.

SOCIAL INTERACTION AND SOCIAL PROCESSES

The various kinds of groups that exist in societies—as well as societies themselves—are not static. They change and become modified. Interaction among members of a group and among groups is continually taking place. Remember that in a sociological sense, interaction refers to behavior, or action, that is symbolic—verbal or gestural. The behavior is directed toward others, and the individual is aware of how others will probably respond. Interaction

is reciprocal, then; each person is aware of and responsive to the actions and reactions of others. If, for example, you say "Hello" to an acquaintance, you expect a "Hello" in return. If you open the door for a woman carrying packages, you expect her to say "Thank you."

Thus, although interaction is not governed by rigid rules, it is not completely haphazard either. There are enough patterns and repetitions for us to study and predict human behavior in given situations. Many of these patterns were established long ago. We, and others in our society, follow these patterns to simplify our lives; it would be ridiculous for us to have to decide every moment of the day how to behave in a given situation. In small, non-technological, homogeneous societies, most interaction is structured in this way. In complex societies, however, we also face situations for which we do not have established patterns of behavior.

Whether established long ago or fairly recently, a number of key patterns of interaction are present in all societies. These key patterns constitute, in the words of sociologist Robert Nisbet, "the microelements of the social bond, or the molecular cement of society."[5] One or more of these patterns, also called *social processes*, are at work any time interaction takes place.

Cooperation

Cooperation is a basic social process involving two or more persons or groups working jointly in a common enterprise for a shared goal. Cooperation is considered basic because without it life would be difficult, if not impossible. Cooperation, however, is not equally strong in all groups. For instance, there will probably be more cooperation in a primary group than in a secondary group (although many examples to the contrary can be found).

Furthermore, some groups and societies stress cooperation to a much greater

[5]Robert A. Nisbet, *The Social Bond*, p. 50.

degree than do others. Our society, for instance, although it appears to value cooperation, in reality encourages individuals to compete with one another in achieving specific goals.

Conflict

The opposite of cooperation is conflict. *Conflict* is a struggle between two or more persons for an object or value that each prizes.[6] Conflict may also be considered the process in which opposing parties attempt to injure or destroy each other to achieve the ultimate goal in question.[7]

Although conflict, like cooperation, is present in every facet of human life, and is believed by many to be a permanent condition of humanity, it is characteristically intermittent—it cannot exist constantly. One of the opposing parties eventually emerges as a victor, and the other as a loser. Then conflict ceases, at least temporarily.

Conflict does not necessarily involve violence, although very often it does. Conflict is present in every group, from the most intimate to the most impersonal, and it may revolve around societal rewards that are in short supply, or around ideological disagreements.

The effects of conflict are not entirely disruptive and negative. In the face of a common antagonist, group cohesiveness is greatly enhanced.[8] In addition, a society entirely devoid of conflict would become lifeless, because conflict, like friction in the physical world, is a force that impels toward action.[9]

This argument leads us to conclude that societies should not attempt to eliminate conflict entirely; instead, they should provide channels through which conflict can be solved with as little violence and psychological harm as possible. This solution is more likely to be used in loosely structured societies, with many centers of power, than in rigid, closed societies. In the latter, the antagonists tend to be more intimately involved with one another, and their conflicts require them to become more emotionally involved.

Competition. Among the social processes that may be placed under the general category of conflict is competition. *Competition* is a form of oppositional interaction that is less obvious than conflict. Here, the antagonists focus on the reward rather than on each other. In other words, the antagonists have nothing against each other personally; both simply want the same scarce object or intangible value.

If competition is not to erupt into conflict, everyone involved must work out and agree upon some rules. These rules are peculiar to each society and culture, and they vary in importance from society to society. In some, competition is unimportant or nonexistent. In our own society, however, competition

---

[6]Ibid., p. 75.

[7]Kimball Young and Raymond W. Mack, *Systematic Sociology* (New York: American Book, 1962), p. 103.

[8]Georg Simmel, *Conflict and the Web of Group Affiliations*, trans. by Kurt H. Wolff and Reinhard Bendix (New York: Free Press, 1955). Also, Lewis Coser, *The Functions of Social Conflict* (New York: Free Press, 1956).

[9]Robert A. Nisbet, *The Social Bond*, p. 77.

is essential to the operation of the economic system, and plays an important part in other facets of life. Because of the importance of competition, we have developed rules, sometimes strengthened by laws or governmental intervention, that prevent competition from becoming ruthless conflict.

Ambition. Ambition is also a form of conflict. It differs from competition in that what individuals or groups desire is a value rather than an object. The student who wants the highest score on all his exams, the accountant who wants to be corporation executive, and all those whose desires include an increase in wealth, status, and privilege are said to be driven by ambition.

Rivalry. Rivalry is a form of conflict in which the antagonists are aware of and seek to defeat each other. If the student competing for the highest score on an exam is more concerned with not being outdone by anyone else—particularly by the girl in the third row who always knows all the answers—than with the actual grade he will receive, he is a rival of everyone who is competing for the high grade. The same is true of an athletic team whose desire to win is strongly colored by the desire to see the opposing team defeated. In short, in rivalry, both the scarce commodity for which one competes and one's competitor are important.

Coercion. Coercion is a form of conflict in which an individual or group imposes its will on another individual or group, often, but not always, through the threat of force. In fact, coercion can take the form of the deliberate avoidance of force. Mahatma Gandhi and Martin Luther King effectively used this mode of coercion.[10]

[10]Ibid., p. 73.

At first glance, coercion seems to lack reciprocity because the coercer acts on the coerced. On closer examination, however, we see that the response of the coerced—which may be anger, passivity, rebellion, or so on—reflects back on the coercer, demanding a further response from him.

For many people, coercion has negative connotations; slavery and imprisonment are examples of the process. Nevertheless, some forms of coercion are responsible for our learning not only the fundamentals of our culture but also basic survival. When, for example, a mother holds a small child's hand against his will while they cross a busy street, she is coercing him to act in a particular way. But she is also preventing him from being run over and is teaching him a safe method of crossing streets. Furthermore, because a human being is capable of thinking of himself as both subject and object (the "I" and the "Me"), coercion may also be directed by the individual upon himself. What we call morality, willpower, and conscience are developed by such self-coercion.

Coercion is a fundamental social process, present in varying degrees in all societies and cultures. Although it often becomes intermixed with other social processes, primarily conflict and cooperation, coercion is important because some element of it is present in almost all social relationships.

Accommodation and Assimilation

Two social processes that are by-products of conflict are accommodation and assimilation. We have already called attention to the temporary, or intermittent, nature of conflict. After one or the other of the antagonists in conflict emerges as victor, there is a peace-making, conflict-settling period called *accommodation*.

Accommodation does not permanently settle issues. It simply keeps things cool, in a state of temporary, peaceful coexistence. Conflict remains present under the surface and may eventually erupt again. But the stage is also set for cooperation and the ultimate solution of conflicts.

If two groups formerly in conflict cooperate and arrive at an ultimate solution of the conflict, the process is called assimilation. *Assimilation* is essentially a process of fusion, in which one individual or group becomes completely accepted as part of another group. This is usually a slow process, whereby the group that becomes assimilated adopts the culture of the other group, becomes a part of all social systems within the society, and has absolute freedom to intermarry with members of other groups.[11]

Exchange

Exchange can be described as interaction for the purpose of receiving something in return. At one time, exchange was considered a purely economic process. Although it has an essential function in several facets of the economy, sociologists now view exchange as a process that is present in almost every social relationship.

Exchange is basic to the intimate relationship between lovers and spouses. Not only does an individual work to receive a salary so he can buy food and shelter for his physical survival, but he also acts in a loving manner so he

[11]Alvin L. Bertrand, *Basic Sociology* (New York: Appleton-Century-Crofts, 1967), pp. 217–218.

receives love and, thus, ensures his psychological survival. This does not mean that love is totally selfish. The individual may not be aware that he wants love in return—and sometimes he does not get it. The expectation of requited love is, however, present at some level within the individual, and relationships based on totally one-sided love soon wither away.

Gratitude also plays a much more important role in human relationships than it is generally given credit for. In performing even the smallest act for another person, we expect that person's gratitude in return. If it is not forthcoming, the bond that temporarily united us to the other person is broken.

SOCIAL ORGANIZATION

A *social system* is an imaginary model, or sociologist's conceptualization, of social relationships. Every social group is a social system, within which each part is interdependent and interconnected to the other parts and to the whole. The elements of this system are individual group members relating to one another to attain a specific goal. (For analytical purposes, and not because it is so in reality, the social system is viewed as a unit that is distinct from the individuals who make it up.) In their effort to reach their goal, the members of the social system are guided both by actual behavior and shared, patterned, and recurrent expectations of behavior. These guides—in the form of patterns resulting from constant repetition of the social processes we have just examined—form the *social structure*.

The network of patterned behavior that both guides and is the product of interaction is called *social organization*. Some sociologists do not distinguish between social organization and social structure. Others interpret structure as the ideal pattern of behavior and social organization as the way people actually behave.[12] Still others view structure as one dimension of social organization, which also includes function (division of labor) and process (adaptation to change).

For our purposes, such distinctions are unnecessary. We may redefine social organization as the patterned and recurring manner in which individuals and groups interact. This does not mean that social organization is necessarily a fixed set of rules. It is instead a dynamic process in which stable and predictable patterns are continually redefined and changed to fit the changing conditions of the social and physical environment.

Levels of Social Organization

Social interaction occurs on three levels of social organization. The first is the *interpersonal*, or *social relationship*, level. Relationships at this level occur when two persons occupy definite positions in relation to each other: husband to wife, father to son, teacher to student, girlfriend to boyfriend, and so on. These relationships constitute the basic elements of social structure and underlie all other social relationships.

The second level is the *group, intergroup,* or *organizational,* level. Relation-

[12]Robin H. Williams, Jr., *American Society*, 2nd rev. ed. (New York: Alfred A. Knopf, 1960), pp. 22-38.

ships at this level occur within and between organized groups. Sociologists are particularly concerned with the process and structure of intergroup relationships.

Finally, at the *community*, or *social order*, level, sociologists examine the general patterns of group life that characterize entire communities or societies.[13]

Some sociologists include an additional level, an abstract "social reality" level which emerges as a result of the features that groups develop as they become organized. This social reality is external to the individual and is not merely a total of interpersonal relationships. In other words, even though the relationship at the interpersonal level is the basic unit of social structure, additional group laws, actions, and patterns of organization develop in relationships at the group and society levels. These laws, actions, and patterns are independent of those emerging at the interpersonal level.

Role and Status

Social organization can be examined from different standpoints: as it exists within groups or social systems and in its function as a link, joining separate social systems into a social organization network. The fundamental elements of social organization are norms, roles, and statuses. Here, we will discuss only roles and statuses, postponing the discussion of norms until the next chapter so they can be analyzed in the context of culture.

Role and status are different aspects of the same idea. In its simplest definition, a *status* is a position in a social group. It generally implies ranking (high or low), or value rating according to the prevailing values of the group or society. A *role* is the carrying out of the status—its dynamic aspect. Role guides the occupant of a status in behavior befitting that status.

Each society is faced with an immense number of functions that must be performed if the society is to operate effectively. Efficiency is improved when specific tasks, rather than being performed haphazardly by everyone, are allocated to particular individuals. The allocation of tasks leads to division of labor, which, in turn, creates statuses. As ways of behaving begin to cluster around allocated tasks and become crystallized, transmittable, and to a great extent predictable, roles are developed.

Statuses and the roles that grow up around them are not static. They are continually subject to change, modification, and replacement. In addition, social change and daily interaction cause constant redefinition of roles.

The role of female and of blacks in our society is a case in point. How black women view their own roles and those of their white counterparts and how the Women's Liberation movement is affecting this view are explored in the article "What the Black Woman Thinks About Women's Lib" by Toni Morrison, appearing at the end of this chapter.[14] This article is particularly revealing because it is written from the black perspective and shows how black women, as a social group, perceive their own role in an entirely different light

---

[13]Leonard Broom and Philip Selznick, *Sociology* (New York: Harper & Row, 1968), pp. 15-16.

[14]Toni Morrison, "What the Black Woman Thinks of Women's Lib," *The New York Times Magazine* (August 22, 1971), pp. 4-66.

from the way they perceive the role of white women. This different perception explains why a growing number of middle-class white women feel the need to be liberated, whereas most black women feel that they have been too liberated already (for liberated, read "self-sufficient," "self-supporting," "strong"). The article also makes clear how differences in the perception of role stem from differences in the quality of interaction within and between various social groups.

Ascribed and achieved status. Some statuses and their satellite roles are ours at birth; we cannot avoid occupying them. A newborn child is either a male or a female; it belongs to a given racial group; and its family already occupies the status of banker or farm laborer, or whatever. Such statuses are called *ascribed* because they are not attained through any individual effort or merit.

The family group makes sure that the child behaves in accordance with his status—in other words, that he fulfills his role. If the child is a male, the family provides him with toys and other objects that are associated with masculinity in our society—baseballs, bats, football helmets, and guns. Moreover, he is taught the values that are also associated with maleness: Big boys do not cry; they stand up for their rights and do not run home to mother; and so on. Parents also prepare the child to act according to his other statuses. If, for example, he is the son of a banker, he will be expected to attend a prep school and an Ivy League university and to engage in specific kinds of interaction with the "right" people.

If the child is a female, she will be presented with a different set of toys and values to prepare her for her role. Women's roles are, however, changing. In increasing numbers women are expressing dissatisfaction with the roles they are forced to assume and with the status society assigns them. The growing popularity of the Women's Lib movement, particularly among white, middle-class women, is evidence of this dissatisfaction. There are many causes for women's discontent; but perhaps none are as acute as the severe tensions created in the women of the preceding generation, who had to balance the roles of desirable sex object and "nice girl." The balancing of these roles was supposed to produce future wives and mothers.

In addition to ascribed statuses—which are involuntary and which depend on gender, age, race, ethnicity, and, to an extent, on the social position of one's family—there are statuses that are achieved through effort and choice. The statuses of husband and wife are *achieved statuses*, as are those of father and mother, and certainly those of teacher and plumber.

The multiplicity of statuses and roles. Each person occupies a large number of statuses in society and is expected to perform the roles associated with them. The president of a huge corporation occupies not only a status in the corporation but probably also occupies the status of son, brother, husband, and father. He also may be a trustee on the board of trustees of a university, a member of an exclusive country club, an elder in his church, and an official in the Republican party. On occasion, he is also a patient in a doctor's office and a client at his stockbroker's.

These statuses are not equally important, and in our society, the corporation president will probably be best known for his status of president of a corpora-

tion. His status may also vary according to the group that is ranking him. He may have a very high status in the corporation of which he is president, a very low one in his family, and a status equal to that of the other elders in his church.

Furthermore, no one performs all his roles equally well. The corporation president must be good at playing the role attached to his main status or he would not remain in his position very long. But if his wife is undergoing psychiatric treatment and his children are chronic runaways, we can assume that in his roles of husband and father, he leaves much to be desired.

A person performs one role better than another partly because of biologically determined facets of his personality and partly because of imperfect role learning. Role conflict also contributes to the problem.

Role conflict.   Frequently, our society prepares us for roles that in real life we do not have the opportunity to play. The young are often taught ideal, rather than real, patterns of behavior. This leads to role conflict and disillusionment. Sunday School teaches young people to love their neighbors, turn the other cheek, and to be honest, fair, and peace-loving. But these qualities are anything but descriptive of our society. Instead, our neighbors are confined to ghettos; injury is repaid with a worse injury; pacifism may lead to a jail sentence; and honesty and fairness, particularly in business, may very well lead to bankruptcy.

Such role conflicts are almost nonexistent in small, nontechnological, homogeneous societies. In such societies, the young live near to their elders and learn from them exactly what they are expected to do as they grow up. Our kind of society, however, has a complex economy in which most tasks are performed outside the home. Rapid social change makes it impossible to predict future life styles. For these reasons role expectation is, at best, fuzzy and, at worst, productive of serious personality disorders.

We are also often expected to play demanding roles simultaneously. To return to the corporation president, his role demands that he spend an unusually large proportion of his time on business connected with the corporation. To be an effective husband and father, however, he should also spend enough time in family activities so intimate interaction occurs. Which of these roles should take precedence?

Sometimes role conflict exists within the limits of a single role. Anyone in a position of leadership faces such a conflict. He can uphold discipline and thus increase the chance that the group will attain its goals. Or he can slacken discipline and be a well-liked leader, at the possible expense of an efficient attainment of goals.

Role confusion and role performance.   Role confusion often follows a change of status. A man who has spent most of his life behind a desk and is suddenly faced with retirement at age sixty-five may find that he cannot fill the leisure hours at his disposal. A young college-educated woman who had begun a promising career and is suddenly confronted with motherhood and the drudgery of housekeeping is ill prepared to cope with this new role.

Faulty role performance is another problem, which can result in mental illness, maladjustment, or general frustration. For many reasons—sometimes simply by chance— people fail in the roles for which they have been prepared. Sometimes they never even attain such roles. The old spinster with a trousseau hidden in her wardrobe has failed to attain her role. What is more, in our highly competitive economic system, people frequently fail in their professions and businesses. The high incidence of divorce demonstrates that large numbers of people fail in their marital roles.

Many people, especially today, are dissatisfied with the roles they are expected to perform. The current generation seems determined to break the bonds that hold us so rigidly to our roles. Surely, in our society, blacks are refusing to be limited to their inferior status, with its consequent role. Women are rebelling against their status as second-class citizens—sex objects who are expected to assume the role of housekeeper without pay. Young men have refused to fight in a war in which they do not believe and are not permitting themselves to be trained for occupations they consider demeaning and dehumanizing. The battle to break traditional roles and role stereotypes promises to be lengthy and uphill, but there is little doubt that it can be won.

SUMMARY

The essence of this chapter has been the fundamental nature of groups in human life. We have mentioned that people everywhere are members of some group at almost any time in their lives. We have distinguished groups from aggregages and categories. We have discussed some kinds of groups and have observed that groups can be classified in numerous ways. And we have established that any group, from two people to a society, may be viewed as a social system, containing interdependent parts, or elements.

The reciprocal relationships that take place within and among groups are called interaction. Interaction consists of several social processes, among which are cooperation, conflict (competition, ambition, rivalry, coercion), accommodation, assimilation, and exchange. Whatever the type of relationship—primary or secondary—one or more of these social processes are at work.

The structure, or social organization, of the social system is made up of shared and repeated patterns of behavior that have emerged, and continue to emerge, as a result of the interaction of group members. Social organization is a dynamic process rather than a rigid set of rules; it contains both stable and changing elements.

Interaction occurs on three levels of organization: on the interpersonal level (relationships between two persons who stand in a definite position to each other), on the group level (within and between groups), and on the community level (within a community or a society).

Interaction always occurs within a context. We relate to others from the standpoint of our own position (status) in our group, while we carry out behavior befitting that position (role). Status and role are basic elements of social organization, directing interaction within and between social systems.

We occupy some statuses involuntarily. Our ascribed statuses are those over which we have no control: our sex—male or female—our age, our racial and ethnic origin, and the economic standing of our families. Throughout our lives, we achieve other statuses as a result of our own effort or merit. Both these kinds of statuses have attendant roles that we are trained to fulfill.

In modern societies, many people face role conflict. Our society prepares us for some roles that we never have an opportunity to play. Frequently, we are expected to perform satisfactorily and at the same time in roles that make contradictory demands upon us. Then, too, we ourselves fail in the roles we have assumed.

Today, many groups are dissatisfied with their statuses and the roles they are expected to play. The changes that will probably occur in some stereotyped statuses and roles will have a definite effect on the social organization of our society.

In the next chapter, we will examine a social system in which we all participate—society. We will consider the normative structure of its social organization, as well as the product of the interaction within it—culture.

STANFORD M. LYMAN

Red Guard on Grant Avenue

To say that human beings live in groups is not to reveal a world-shattering secret. We all know it from experience. But, as often happens with familiar ideas, we seldom stop to consider why we live in groups, what moves us to form groups, what kind of groups we establish and for what purposes, and what takes place within these groups. Stanford Lyman's article is most illuminating from this point of view. He shows us how the original group of Chinese immigrants organized and what additional groups they formed, and why. He also shows how the kinds of groups and the interaction within and between groups changed with the changing times and the altered needs of members.

□□□

Visitors to San Francisco's historic Portsmouth Square on 7 May 1969 were startled to see the flag of the People's Republic of China flying over the plaza. The occasion had begun as a rally to commemorate the 50th anniversary of the May 4 movement in Peking, when Chinese students demonstrated to protest the ignominious treaties forced on a moribund Chinese Empire by Occidental imperialists. Now a half century later in San Francisco, a group of disaffected Chinatown youth took over the rally from its sponsors to protest against the community's poverty and neglect

and to criticize its anachronistic and conservative power elite.

Calling themselves the Red Guards, the youths asserted their right to armed self-defense against the city police and called for the release of all Asians in city, state and federal prisons on the ground that they had had unfair trials. On a more immediate and practical level, the Red Guards announced plans for a remarkably unradical petition campaign to prevent the Chinese Playground from being converted into a garage and for a breakfast program to aid needy children in the Chinatown ghetto. If the platform of the Red Guards sounded vaguely familiar, a spokesman for the group made it plain: "The Black Panthers are the most revolutionary group in the country and we are patterned after them."

To most San Franciscans the rise of youthful rebellion in the Chinese quarter of the city must come as a surprise. For the past three decades Chinese-Americans have been stereotyped in the mass media as quiet, docile and filial, a people who are as unlikely to espouse radicalism as they are to permit delinquency among their juveniles. In the last few years, however, evidence has mounted to suggest a discrepancy between this somewhat saccharine imagery and reality. Not only is there an unmistakable increase in delinquent activity among Chinese young people, there is a growing restlessness among them as well. Chinatown's younger generation feels a gnawing frustration over hidebound local institutions, the powerlessness of youth and their own bleak prospects for the future. The politics as well as the "crimes" of Chinatown are coming to resemble those of the larger society, with alienation, race consciousness and restive rebelliousness animating a new generation's social and organizational energies.

A basic cause for the emergence of youthful rebellion among the Chinese is the increase in the youthful population itself. There are simply more Chinese youth in the ghetto now than there ever have been before, a fact that can be attributed to an increasing birth rate among the indigenous population and a sudden rise in immigration from Hong Kong and other Asian centers of Chinese settlement.

By 1890, eight years after a wave of sinophobia had prompted Congress to block any further immigration of Chinese to this country, there were approximately 102,620 residents here. The vast majority were laborers or small merchants lured here by the promise of the "Gold Mountain" in California and work on the railroads. But a more significant fact is that the vast majority were also men. Before the turn of the century there were about 27 men for every woman among the Chinese in America. What this meant for white perceptions of these newcomers is probably familiar enough. Forced into ghettos, their women and children left behind to care for and honor their parents, these men joined together in clan associations and secret societies to provide them with some sense of familiarity and solidarity; and they turned as well to the typical pleasures of lonely men—prostitutes, stupefaction (through opium) and gambling. Just as typically, in a society known for its hostile racial stereotypes, the Chinese came to be identified with these "vices" in the minds of many white Americans and to be regarded as bestial, immoral and dangerous. But the alarming imbalance in the sex ratio also meant that the Chinese communities in America were almost incapable of producing a second generation of American-born Chinese. It wasn't until 1950 that the American-born made up more than half the total Chinese population, and even this growth only came about through the small trickle of illegal entries made by Chinese women prior to 1943 and the much larger number who entered since that date, thanks to gradual but important relaxations of the immigration laws.

The most radical of these relaxations came with the Immigration Act of 1965 which repealed the entire system of quotas based on national origins and substituted an entry procedure based on skills and the reuniting of families. Under this law, according to District Immigration Director C. W. Fullilove, there will be approximately 1,200 Chinese entering San Francisco every year with the intention of staying there. Although not all of them will do so, this new influx of Chinese makes up a significant proportion of San Francisco's burgeoning Chinese population, and many of them fall between what Fullilove calls "the problem ages" for Chinese youth 16 to 19.

THE GOLD MOUNTAIN

Of course, sheer numbers alone do not account for the rise of rebelliousness among young Chinese in San Francisco. A more significant factor is that conditions of life in Chinatown are by no means pleasant, productive or promising. We must distinguish, however, from among the Chinese those who have escaped the ghetto, those who are American-born but who still inhabit Chinatown and the foreign-born youth who reluctantly find themselves imprisoned within a ghetto even less of their own making than it is of the others'. Among those who have escaped there are, first, the scholars, scientists, intellectuals and professionals—many of whom hail from regions other than southeastern China, the original home of the bulk of America's Chinese immigrants—who have found work and residence within the larger society. Enclosed in university, corporation, professional or government communities, these Chinese do not for the most part feel themselves to be a part of Chinatown; they go there only occasionally for a banquet or for a brief sense of their ethnic origins. A second group much larger than the first, although actually quite small in relation to the total number of Chinese, consists of those American-born Chinese who have successfully completed high school and college and gone on to enter the professions—most frequently pharmacy and engineering—the American middle class and, when they can evade or circumvent the still prevalent discrimination in housing, the finer neighborhoods or the suburbs. This "gold bour-geoisie"—to paraphrase E. Franklin Frazier—is also estranged from Chinatown. Proud of his own achievements, wary of any attempt to thrust him back into a confining ghetto exis-tence and alternately angered, embarrassed or shamed by the presence of alienated, hostile and rebellious youth in Chinatown, the middle-class American Chinese holds tena-ciously to his newly achieved material and social success.

Nevertheless, middle-class native-born Chinese are discovering that the American dream is not an unmixed blessing. The "Gold Mountain" of American bourgeois promise seems somehow less glittering now that its actual pinnacle has been reached. Chinese, like other descendants of immigrants in America, are discovering that the gold is alloyed more heavily than they had supposed with brass; but, like their second and third generation peers among the Jews and Japa-nese, they are not quite sure what to do about it. The price of success has been very great—not the least payments being the aban-donment of language, culture and much of their ethnic identity. Among some there is a new search for cultural roots in Chinese his-tory, a strong desire to recover the ancient arts and a renewed interest in speaking Chi-nese—at least at home. Others emphasize, perhaps with too much protestation, their hap-piness within the American middle class and carry on a conspicuous consumption of leisure to prove it. Finally, a few recognize their Chinatown roots and return there with a desire to aid somehow in the advancement of the Chinese ghetto-dwellers. Sometimes their offers of help are rejected with curses by the objects of their solicitude, but in any event the growing number of restive Chinatowners con-stitutes another challenge to the comfort of bourgeois Chinese.

In its most primordial sense the visible con-trast between the style of life of the im-poverished ghetto-dweller and that of the middle-class professional promotes guilt and shame. Somehow it seems wrong that one's ethnic compatriots should suffer while one enjoys the benefits of success. Yet middle-class Chinese are quite ready to attribute their suc-cess to their own diligence, proverbial habits of thrift and hard work and to their conscious avoidance of delinquent or other kinds of unruly behavior. Naturally, then, some middle-class Chinese are equally quick to charge the angry Chinatown youth with indo-lence, impropriety and impiety. But even as they preach the old virtues as a sure cure for the young people's personal and social ail-ments, some perceive that there is more to these problems than can be solved by the care-ful nurturing of Confucian or Protestant ethics. They see more clearly than the Americanized and less alienated Chinese of the fifties that poverty, cultural deprivation and discrimina-tion are truly obdurate barriers to the advance-ment of the ghetto-dwellers of today. More-over, there is an even more profound problem. Like other alienated youthful minorities, the youth of Chinatown appear to reject just that dream which inspired and activated the now bourgeois Chinese. For the middle-class Chi-nese, then, the peak of the "Gold Mountain" seems to have been reached just when those still down below started to shout up that the arduous climb isn't worth the effort.

SOCIAL BANDITS AND PRIMITIVE REBELS

Among Chinatown's rebellious groups there are two distinguishable types of youth—those who are American-born but have dropped out of school and form part of the under- or unemployed proletariat of the Chi-nese community; and those recently arrived immigrant youth who, speaking little or no English and having little to offer in the way of salable skills, find themselves unable to enter the city's occupational and social main-stream. Both native and foreign-born Chinese are included among the ranks of the quasi-criminal and quasi-political gangs that are accused of contributing to the mounting inci-dence of delinquency in the Chinese quarter. Culture, language and background have divided the native from the foreign-born Chi-nese in the past, and it is only recently that there is any sign of a common recognition between the two groups.

It is traditional to focus on Chinatown gangs as an unfortunate form of juvenile delin-quency among a people otherwise noted for their social quiescence and honesty. A more fruitful approach however would adopt the perspective taken by E. J. Hobsbawm in his discussion of social bandits and primitive rebels. According to Hobsbawm, who has studied these phenomena in Europe, social banditry is a form of pre-ideological rebellion which arises among essentially agrarian, unskilled and unlettered peoples who are at great cultural distance from the official and oppressive power structure. It is led by those who enjoy a certain amount of local notoriety or awe. Often enough social banditry remains at a stage of petty criminality which is of concern, if at all, only to the local police. At a more refined stage, however, predatory gangs are formed which confine their criminal activities to attacks on strangers and officials and share any loot with local community members who, though not a party to the attacks, identify with and protect the robbers.

It is important to note that bandit gangs may adopt a populist or a conservative style. The former is symbolized by Robin Hood, who robbed the rich to feed the poor and attacked civic or state officialdom as intruders in the community's traditional way of life. In the conservative style, bandit gangs are co-opted as toughs and thugs to defend local satrapies and powerful petty interests. Social banditry may exist side by side with ideologically rebellious or revolutionary elements but is usually untouched by them except for particular reasons of strategy or tactics. Essentially, it is separated from ideological politics by its deep involvement with local ethnic rather than cosmopolitan class interests. However, it is not impossible for class and ethnic interests to merge and for the liberation of local groups to become enmeshed within the revolutionary aims of a radically politicized sector of a modern party state.

From the perspective of "primitive rebellion," Chinatown's gangs take on a greater significance for the understanding of loosely structured pluralistic societies like the United States. Gangs in Chinatown are by no means a new phenomenon, but their activities in the past describe mainly the early stages of social banditry. For the most part Chinatown's traditional social banditry has been of a particularly conservative type, identified with the recruitment of young toughs, thugs and bullies into the small criminal arm of Chinatown's secret

societies. They formed the "flying squads" of mercenaries who "protected" brothels, guarded gambling establishments and enforced secret society monopolies over other vice institutions of Chinatown. From their numbers came assassins and strong-arm men who fought in the so-called tong wars that characterized Chinatown's internecine struggles of a half century ago and which still occasionally threaten to erupt today. But this form of social banditry was an exclusive and private affair of Chinatown. Insofar as Chinatown's violent altercations were circumscribed not only by the invisible wall around the ghetto but also by the limited interests of the contending parties for women, wealth and power, the community was isolated by its internal conflicts. Whether manifested in fearful acquiescence or active participation, the ghetto's residents were bound together in a deadly kind of "antagonistic cooperation."

Since 1943 a progressive cycle of rebellion among Chinatown's youth has metamorphosed from crime to politics, from individual acts of agression to collective acts of rebellion and from nonideological modes of hostility to the beginnings of a movement of ideological proportions. From 1943 until 1949 juvenile crime in Chinatown was largely the activity of a small number of native-born boys about 15 years of age, hurt by unemployment, difficulties in home life or inadequate income. Their crimes were typical of the most individualized and inarticulate forms of primitive rebellion. Burglary, auto theft, robberies, larcenies, hold-ups and assault and battery constituted 103 of the 184 offenses for which Chinese male juveniles were referred to San Francisco's juvenile court in those years. There were also gangs of native-born youth, apparently sponsored by or under the protection of secret societies, who occasionally assaulted and robbed strangers in Chinatown, not a few of whom, incidentally, were Japanese-Americans recently returned from wartime internment camps and also organized into clubs, cliques and gangs.

Petty criminal gangs emerged more frequently among both the native and foreign-born youth in Chinatown from 1958 to 1964. In some cases these gangs were composed of young men sponsored in their criminal activities by secret societies. An example was the "cat" burglary ring broken up by police in 1958 and discovered to be a branch of the Hop Sing Tong. Three years later, two gangs, the "Lums" and the "Rabble Rousers," were reported to be engaged in auto thefts, extortion, street fights and petty larcenies. In January 1964 members of a San Francisco Chinatown gang were charged with the $10,000 burglary of a fish market in suburban Mountain View. A year later, the police broke up the "Bugs," a youthful criminal gang whose members dressed entirely in black, with bouffant hair style and raised-heel boots, and who, in committing 48 burglaries, made off with $7,500 in cash and $3,000 in merchandise in a period of six months. The "Bugs"—who capitalized on an otherwise stigmatizing aspect of their existence, their short stature—reemerged a year later despite an attempt by Chinatown's leaders to quell juvenile gangs by bringing in street workers from San Francisco's Youth for Service to channel the gang toward constructive activities. By the mid-1960s Chinatown's burglary gangs had begun to branch out and were working areas of the city outside the Chinese quarter.

The present stage of a more politicized rebellion may be dated from the emergence in May 1967 of Leway, Incorporated. In its history up to August 1969, the Leways experienced almost precisely the pattern of problems and response that typically give rise first to nonideological rebellion and then, under certain conditions, to the development of revolutionary ideology. Leway (standing for "legitimate way") began as a public-spirited self-help group among American-born Chinese teen-agers. Aged 17 to 22, these young men organized to unite Chinatown's youth, to combat juvenile delinquency and to improve conditions in the poverty-stricken Chinese ghetto through helping youths to help themselves. In its first months it gained the support of such Chinatown luminaries as Lim P. Lee, now San Francisco's postmaster and a former probation officer, and other prominent citizens. Through raffles, loans and gifts, these youths, many of whom could be classed as delinquents, raised $2,000 to rent a pool hall near the Chinatown-Filipino border area. And, with the help of the Chinese YMCA and Youth for Service, they outfitted it with five pool tables, seven pinball machines, some chairs

and a television set. "This is a hangout for hoods," said its president, Denny Lai, to reporter Ken Wong. "Most of us cats are misfits, outcasts with a rap sheet. What we're trying to do is to keep the hoods off the streets, give them something to do instead of raising hell."

Leway was a local indigenous group seeking to employ its own methods and style to solve its own members' problems. And it was precisely this that caused its downfall. Police refused to believe in methods that eschewed official surveillance, sporadic shakedowns and the not always occasional beating of a youth "resisting arrest." Leway tried a dialogue with the police, but it broke down over the rights of the latter to enter, search and seize members at Leway's headquarters, a tiny piece of "territory" which the young Chinese had hoped to preserve from alien and hostile intrusion. Leway claimed it wanted only to be left alone by this official arm of a society which they saw as already hostile. "We are not trying to bother them [the police] ... and we won't go out of our way to work with them either."

In addition to continuous harassment by white police, Leway failed to establish its legitimacy in Chinatown itself. The Chinese Chamber of Commerce refused it official recognition, and as a result Leway could not gain access to the local Economic Opportunity Council to obtain much-needed jobs for Chinatown youth. The Tsung Tsin Association, which owned the building where Leway had its headquarters, threatened to raise the rent or lease the premises to another renter. Finally, whether rightly or not, the members of Leway, together with other Chinatown youth groups, were blamed for the increasing violence in Chinatown. Throughout 1968-69 reports of violent assault on tourists and rival gangs were coming out of Chinatown. Police stepped up their intrusive surveillance and other heavy-handed tactics. Chinese youth charged them with brutality, but the police replied that they were only using proper procedures in the line of a now more hazardous duty. In late summer 1969 the combination of police harassment, rent hikes, Leway's failure to secure jobs for its chronically unemployed members and its general inability to establish itself as a legitimate way of getting Chinatown youth "straightened out" took its final toll.

Leway House closed its doors. Dreams of establishing on-the-job training for the unskilled, new business ventures for the unemployed, a pleasant soda fountain for Leway adolescents and an education and recreation program for Chinatown teen-agers—all this was smashed. The bitterness stung deep in the hearts of Chinatown young people. "Leway stood for legitimate ways," a 15-year-old youth told reporter Bill Moore. "Helluva lot of good it did them." The closing of Leway destroyed many Chinatown young people's faith in the official culture and its public representatives.

The stage was set for the next phase in the development of rebellion. Out of the shambles of Leway came the Red Guards, composed of the so-called radical elements of the former organization. But now Leway's search for legitimacy has been turned on its head. The Red Guards flout the little red book *Quotations from Chairman Mao Tse-tung* as their credo, make nonnegotiable demands on the power structure of Chinatown and the metropolis and openly espouse a program of disruption, rebellion and occasionally, it seems, revolution.

Leway had been modeled after other San Francisco youthful gang reform groups, but the Red Guards have adopted the organizational form, rhetorical style and political mood of the Black Panthers. A few years ago this would have seemed highly improbable. In the 1960s there were frequent bloody clashes between gangs of Chinese and Negroes, and interracial incidents at Samual Gompers School—a kind of incarceration unit for black and Oriental incorrigibles—had not encouraged friendly relations among the two groups. Nevertheless it was just these contacts, combined with a growing awareness of Panther tactics and successes, and some not too secret proselytization by Panther leaders among the disaffected Leway members, that brought the young Chinese to adopt the black militant style. Whatever prejudices Chinese might harbor against Negroes, Black Panther rhetoric seemed perfectly to describe their own situation. After all, Leway had tried to be good, to play the game according to the white man's rules, and all it had gotten for its pains were a heap of abuse and a few cracked skulls. Now it was time to be realistic—"to stop jiving" and "to tell it like it is." Police were "pigs"; white

men were "honkies"; officially developed reform programs were attempts to "shine" on credulous Chinese youth; and the goal to be attained was not integration, not material success, but power. "We're an organization made up mainly of street people and we're tired of asking the government for reforms," said Alex Hing, a 23-year-old Chinese who is the minister of information of the Red Guards. "We're going to attain power, so we don't have to beg any more."

URBAN POPULISM

The Red Guards are a populist group among Chinatown's "primitive" rebels. They stand against not one but two power structures in their opposition to oppression and poverty—that of old Chinatown and that of the larger metropolis. Ideologically they are located somewhere between the inarticulate rumblings of rustic rebels and the full-scale ideology of unregenerate revolutionaries. They cry out for vengeance against the vague but powerful complex of Chinese and white elites that oppress them. They dream of a world in which they will have sufficient power to curb their exploiters' excesses; meanwhile they do the best they can to right local wrongs and to ingratiate themselves with the mass of their Chinatown compatriots. The free breakfasts for indigent youngsters, a copy of the Panthers' program, attracts popular support among Chinatown's poor at the same time that it shames Chinatown's elites for allowing the community's children to go hungry. The demand for the release of all imprisoned Asians seems to place the Red Guards squarely on the side of all those "little people" of Chinatown who feel themselves victimized by an alien and oppressive police system. However, their ethnic consciousness usually supersedes and sometimes clashes with their alleged attachment to a class-oriented ideology, as it did when the Red Guards accepted an invitation to guard a meeting of the Chinese Garment Contractors' Association against a threatened assault by Teamsters seeking to organize Chinatown's heavily exploited dressmakers. But it is precisely their parochial dedication to a sense of Chinese ethnicity that endears them to the less hardy of young

Chinatowners who secretly share their dilemmas and dreams, as well as limits their political effectiveness.

Populist rebellion is not the only form of social politics in Chinatown. A conservative type of rebelliousness is illustrated in the evolution of the Hwa Ching and the Junior Hwa Ching. Hwa Ching emerged in 1967 as a loose association of mostly Hong Kong-born youth in Chinatown. Estimates of its size vary from 25 to 300, and this fact alone testifies to its low degree of cohesiveness and the sense of drift that characterizes its members. Until very recently Hwa Ching was represented in most public discussions by a "spokesman" (its looseness of organization prevented any greater clarification of title), George Woo, a former photographer who took on the task of bridging the communication gap between the largely Chinese-speaking youths and the officials of the metropolis. The aims of this association are difficult to ascertain exactly, partly because there was little agreement among its members and partly because spokesman Woo usually tended to a violently polemical speaking style in order to call attention to the situation of Chinatown's immigrants. Hwa Ching had less of a perfected program than a set of practical problems. Hong Kong youth were insufficiently educated and skilled to obtain any jobs other than Chinatown's dreary positions of waiter, busboy and sweated laborer; unequipped linguistically to enter the metropolis and, in the beginning, unwilling to accept confinement in a congested, poverty-stricken and despotically ruled ghetto.

Hwa Ching seemed to form itself around El Piccolo, an espresso coffeehouse opened in Chinatown in 1967 and operated by Dick and Alice Barkley. Alice Barkley, herself a Hong Kong-born Chinese, turned the coffeehouse into a haven for foreign-born Chinese youth. There they could meet in peace and with freedom to discuss, argue, complain and occasionally plan some joint activity. Reaction to their clubby fraternization at El Piccolo was mixed. Traditional Chinatowners accused the Barkleys of offering asylum to raffish criminal elements; a newly aroused college and university group of Chinese-Americans praised the establishment of a place for impoverished immigrants to congregate; and most San Franciscans didn't even know the Hwa Ching existed.

Early in 1968 Hwa Ching approached the Human Relations Commission, the Economic Development Council and the Chinese business elite to ask for their aid in establishing an educational program for alleviating the misery of Chinatown's immigrant youth. Their approach was unusually frank and plainly practical. They proposed the establishment of a comprehensive two-year educational program to provide Chinatown's young immigrants with a high school diploma and vocational training in auto repair, business machine operation, construction, sheet metal, electrical installation and plumbing. They closed with a statement that was unfortunately taken as a warning and a threat. "We've been hearing too many promises. The rise and fall of our hopes is tragic and ominous."

This first bid for help was unsuccessful. In late February, however, the Hwa Ching tried again and spoke to the Chinatown Advisory Board of the Human Relations Commission. This time Hwa Ching, represented by the fiery George Woo, was more modest in its request for a comprehensive program, but more militant in its presentation. Hwa Ching wanted $4,322 to build a clubhouse, but although Woo reiterated the same arguments as other Hwa Chings had presented in January, the tone was different. Describing his constituents, Woo said, "There is a hard core of delinquents in Chinatown who came from China. Their problems are the problems of all poor with the addition that they don't speak English." Then he added that "they're talking about getting guns and rioting. . . . I'm not threatening riots. The situation already exists, but if people in Chinatown don't feel threatened they won't do anything about it." The mention of guns and the warning of possible riots were too much for John Yehall Chin, a prominent Chinese businessman, principal of Saint Mary's Chinese Language School and member of the Human Relations Commission's Chinatown Advisory Board. In reply to the Hwa Ching's request he advised the commission, and indirectly the youths, "The have not shown that they are sorry or that they will change their ways. They have threatened the community. If you give in to this group, you are only going to have another hundred immigrants come in and have a whole new series of threats and demands." Although the commission expressed its interest, Hwa Ching's demand was rejected.

They tried again. In March the Hwa Ching's president, Stan Wong, presented the immigrant youths' case before the Chinese Six Companies, the oligarchy that controls Chinatown. Speaking in Cantonese, Wong repudiated the threat of riots made at the February meeting. "We made no threats," he said. "They were made by nonmembers. We need to help ourselves. We look to the future and are mindful of the immigrant youths who will be coming here later. We hope they do not have to go through what we've been through." Later he answered a question about possible Communist affiliation: "Hwa Ching is not involved with any political ideology." Although Commissioner Chin pointed out that the Hwa Ching had mended its ways, the Six Companies refused them help. Meanwhile the Human Relations Commission, under the direction of Chin, organized an Establishment-controlled Citizens for Youth in Chinatown. The Hwa Ching felt utterly rejected.

In their bitterness and anger, however, the Hwa Ching did not turn to populist revolt, as had the Leways. Instead they fragmented even more. Their loose coalition at El Piccolo ended when that establishment closed its doors in August 1968. The Hwa Ching had never in fact professed an ideology. What seemed to be one was more a product of the fervid imaginations of alarmed whites and of the fiery invective of George Woo than it was any coherent line of political or revolutionary thought. The Hwa Ching's practical needs were too immediate, their literacy in English too low and their limited but practical political experience in Hong Kong and Chinatown too real for them to accept an organization that used Mao's red book and which therefore ran for them the risks of political persecution and possible deportation. As Tom Tom, a 23-year-old immigrant who had been one of the earliest members of Hwa Ching, explained to a reporter, the immigrant youth were independent of the Leway and all other Chinatown groups, affected none of the hippie-Ché-Raoul-Panther styles and wanted little more than jobs, girls and to be left alone. The Hwa Ching found themselves oppressed by their supposed allies nearly as much as by their condition. Leway boys and other American-born Chinese called

them "Chinabugs" and attacked them in gang rumbles; Negroes picked on the diminutive Chinese until they learned to retaliate in numbers and with tactics; college students sought to tutor and to evangelize them with secular and sometimes political ideas but succeeded mostly in making them feel inferior and frightened by a kind of politics they abhorred.

By the middle of 1969 the Hwa Ching had split into three factions. One returned to the streets to fight, burglarize and assault all those available symbols and representatives of the seemingly monolithic power structure that had scorned them; two other factions apparently accepted cooptation into Chinatown's two most powerful though age-ridden secret societies—the Suey Sing and Hop Sing Tongs. There their anger could find outlet at the same time that their strength could be utilized for traditional aims. The secret societies could pay for the immigrant youths' basic needs and with the same expenditure buy the muscle to keep control of their own interests and institutions. And since the Tongs were part of the complex congeries of associations that make up Chinatown's power elite, it is not surprising that leaders of this same elite gave tacit approval to the Tongs' recruitment of what had appeared in early 1968 to be a serious threat to the old order. Unlike the Leway, which could not join the old order and may have been too Americanized to accept secret society patronage, the immigrant youth find in it a perhaps temporary expedient in their dilemma. Not being politicized, they can more readily join in the protection of old Chinatown. They have resumed a posture typical of earlier youthful generations' response to anger and poverty in Chinatown. They form the conservative wing of Chinatown's complex structure of conflict and rebellion.

In other areas and times of primitive rebellion, conservative and populist factions often fought each other as much as their professed enemies. Similarly, in Chinatown the young toughs who have become paid guards of the secret societies' and, occasionally, the Six Companies' meetings are not infrequently arrayed against the Leway-Red Guard gangs. And in this sense young Chinatown recapitulates a structure of conflict that characterized that of its earlier generations. Conservative-populist conflicts isolate the contending parties from outside groups and larger issues. The violent fights and smouldering feuds appear to noncomprehending outsiders to be exclusively Chinese in their nature and content. And this intramural conflict in turn circumscribes Chinatown and once again cuts it off from the metropolis.

OUTSIDE IDEOLOGIES

However, connections to the larger society of San Francisco in particular and the United States in general do exist. For the youth the most important one is the Intercollegiate Chinese for Social Action (ICSA). This group was formed at San Francisco State College from among the more socially concerned and politically aware Chinese-American students. For a while it managed the special program by which Chinese students from the ghetto were recruited to the college. But the long Third World strike at San Francisco State College in 1968-69 radicalized its members and propelled them into even greater contact with the Chinatown community. They became actively oriented toward conditions about which they had been only vaguely aware before. ICSA asserted aloud and with emphasis what had been but an open secret for decades—Chinatown was a racial ghetto—poverty-stricken, disease-ridden, overcrowded, underdeveloped and with a population growing in Malthusian proportions. To the remedy of all these defects they dedicated themselves and established offices not only in the college but in Chinatown itself. ICSA provides tutoring services to Chinatown's less educated youth and urges that San Francisco State College establish even more programs for community rehabilitation. The community-oriented Chinese college youth do not openly attack Leway or the Red Guards but remain in communication with them as well as with the erstwhile Hwa Ching. But, observes George Woo, now as an ICSA member, "We can also see the pitfalls in using too much of the blarney, as the Red Guards did. As a result, they alienated immigrant youths and the whole community in three months' time." By keeping open contacts among the native- and the foreign-born, among Hwa Ching and Leway-Red Guards, among status conscious diploma-bearers and

socially stigmatized delinquents and among the legitimated and the lowly, ICSA may yet be able to blunt the deadly edge of conflict and build a durable community for Chinatown.

What this means specifically is by no means clear even to the ICSA members themselves. "I'm still trying to figure out what I am supposed to be as a Chinese-American," complained a 21-year-old college student, echoing the inner nagging question of most of his compatriots. And George Woo replied, "I know how you feel, I don't identify with China either and I certainly don't identify with the petty American middle-class values of my aunts and uncles." ICSA emphasizes a two-way learning process between the lettered and the dropouts and calls for the formulation of a new ethic to replace the Confucian-Protestant ethos of Chinese America. As ICSA leader Mason Wong has said, "Our generation here will no longer accept the old and still prevalent Confucian doctrine of success coming only from hard work and humility." What that ethic will be is not yet known. However, the Chinese must still contend with the traditional social order that is Chinatown's Establishment.

THE OLD ORDER

Anyone at all conversant with San Francisco's Chinatown will have heard of the Chinese Six Companies. In a vague sense he might know about some of its activities, be able to point out its headquarters and note that it is a benevolent, protective and representational body of Chinese who enjoy unofficial but influential standing at City Hall. Beyond this he might know very little but the familiar litany that the Chinese take care of themselves, contribute little, if at all, to the welfare rolls or to the city's alarming rate of juvenile delinquency and, that while the Chinese were perhaps at one time a troublesome minority, they are now safely ensconced in their own quarter of the city where they enjoy a modicum of freedom to practice peculiar cultural expressions derived from a China that is no more. To him the Six Companies is one aspect of that cultural freedom.

Like many stereotypes that arise in racist societies, this one too contains some kernels of truth. The Chinese in San Francisco, like the Chinese in Calcutta, Singapore, Bangkok, Saigon, Manila and indeed in almost every large city to which Chinese have migrated, enjoy a measure of home rule that far exceeds that of any other minority group in the metropolis. During the colonial period in Southeast Asia, the British and Dutch formalized their practices of indirect rule into a specified system of titles. "Kapitan China" was the Dutch designation for the uniformed and bemedalled Chinese who represented his people in the colonial councils at Batavia, and the "Captain China" system prevailed in British Malaya and other colonies as well. For the colonial powers indirect rule was an expedient way of maintaining sufficient control over restless and hostile native peoples in a precariously pluralistic society in order to extract their labor and the colony's natural resources without having to contend with all their tribal and customary ways and woes. For the subject peoples it meant that they could freely organize their lives in accordance with traditional practices, so long as they didn't interfere with the rather limited interests of the imperial powers. Outside the colonial area, Chinese immigrant elites also managed to establish a kind of cultural extraterritoriality and to achieve an added legitimation to their traditional control over their fellow migrants by winning unofficial but practically useful recognition from white civic elites. In Vancouver, and in New York City the Chinese Benevolent Association has obtained such prerogatives; in San Francisco it is the Chinese Six Companies.

But to understand Chinatown's power structure fully, it is necessary to analyze the several kinds of traditional associations from which it is composed. First there are clan associations, or "family associations" as Occidental journalists and sociologists usually term them. Clan associations derive from the lineage communities so prevalent in Kwangtung and ideally unite all persons descended from a common male ancestor. Overseas, however, the more manageable lineage unit was replaced by a kinship network wider than that which originally enclosed only a compact village. The clan association includes all who bear the same surname. In the early days of Chinese immigration, the clan associations became a special kind of immigrant aid society providing the newcomer with food, shelter, employment, protection and advice. Furthermore, the clan leaders reminded the immigrant of his obligations to parents and family in the home village and, in the absence of the village elders, assumed a role in loco parentis, settling disputes, arbitrating disagreements and in general containing intraclan differences within the kinship fold. Some clan associations exercised a monopoly over a trade or profession in Chinatown and effectively resisted encroachments on these monopolies by ambitious Chinese upstarts from other clans. Until the recent arrival of large numbers of immigrants from Hong Kong, the clan associations had been declining in power and authority as a result of the aging of their members and the acculturation of the American-born Chinese. However, even this new lifeblood is less acquiescent than the former sojourner members. Chinatown clan associations are now challenged to provide something more than a paltry benevolence in exchange for their petty despotism.

In addition to clans, however, there developed among overseas Chinese a functionally similar but structurally different type of association. The *hui kuan* united all those who spoke a common dialect, hailed from the same district in China or belonged to the same tribal or ethnic group. (It is a mistake to suppose, as many Occidentals do, that the peoples of China are culturally homogeneous. In the tiny area around Canton from which most of America's immigrants have come, there are numerous dialects which, while they have a common script, are almost mutually unintelligible when spoken.) In many ways the hui kuan were similar to those immigrant aid and benevolent societies established by Germans, Irish, Jews and other Europeans in America. In San Francisco and other cities in which Chinese dwelt, the hui kuan, like the clan association, maintained a headquarters and served as caravansary, hostelry, credit association and employment agency. In all these matters it exercised authoritarian control, and since most of the Chinese in America were debtors, directly or indirectly, to their hui kuan, its officers were not infrequently suspected of taking an excessive interest or a corrupt profit from their charges. The hui kuan, again similar to the clan, conducted arbitration and mediation hearings between disputing members, managed and collected the debts of its members and in addition charged them various fees for its services. An aging membership and the flight of the American-born bourgeoisie tended to undermine hui kuan authority, but the old businesses in Chinatown still affiliate with them and accept their mediation and arbitration services. They are especially important in the ownership and control of Chinatown property which they administer in a traditional way quite different from real estate management in the Occidental parts of the city.

The third major type of association in Chinatown is the secret society. Like the clan and the hui kaun, the secret society originated in China where for centuries it served as a principal agency for popular protest, violent rebellion and social banditry. The overseas migrants from Kwangtung included not a few members of the Triad Society, the most famous of China's clandestine associations. In nearly every significant overseas community of Chinese they established chapters of, or models based on that order. In the United States secret societies among the Chinese were set up by the early immigrants in the cities and also in those outlying areas where clans and hui kuan could not form a solid base. Inside Chinatown the secret societies soon took over control of gambling and prostitution, and it is with these activities rather than with their political or charitable activities that they are most often associated in the minds of non-Chinese in America. Clans, hui kuan and the several chapters of secret societies often fell out with one another over their competition for women, wealth and power inside Chinatown, and these so-called tong wars raged intermittently until a Chinatown Peace Association established a still perilous peace between the warring factions in the 1920s. The charitable works of secret societies were confined for the most part to giving mutual aid to their own members, the establishment of headquarters and hostelries and in recent years the building of clubhouses where their aged bachelor members might find hospitable fraternity. The political activities of the secret societies have consisted in their intermittent interest in the fortunes of China's several regimes, but they

have not shown any particular interest in upsetting the national politics of the United States. Meanwhile the secret societies' most successful source of revenue in Chinatown —the control over gambling and prostitution—diminished as the Chinese bachelors aged and died and the American-born declined interest in these activities. The recruitment of the newly arrived and disaffected immigrant youth from Chinatown has undoubtedly done much to rejuvenate these societies, but it remains to be seen whether this will lengthen their life as institutions in America or change their function in accordance with new interests and current developments.

At the top of the community power structure of Chinatown is the Chinese Benevolent Association, commonly known as the Chinese Six Companies. It was formed in the late 1850s as a confederation of hui kuan—later it incorporated clans, guilds and, reluctantly, secret societies—in order to provide community-wide governance, to promote intracommunity harmony and to present at least the appearance of a common Chinese front to white society. Until the 1870s it functioned as an agency of international diplomacy and consular activity as well, since the Chinese Empire did not provide a specific overseas office for those duties. The Six Companies has been the principal spokesman for the Chinese to white America. It has protested against anti-Chinese legislation, helped fight discriminatory laws in the courts, petitioned federal, state and local governments in behalf of the Chinese and generally provided Chinatown with a modest respectability in the face of sinophobic stereotypy. One of its more recent efforts in defense of Chinese in America was a protest against Secretary of Transportation John Volpe's omission of the role that Chinese played in the building of the Transcontinental Railroad when he spoke at the centenary celebration of its completion.

Gradually the Six Companies established its legitimacy as rightful representatives of the Chinese in San Francisco. Composed of merchants and traders, the leaders of the Six Companies seemed to inspire assurance among civic leaders that the Chinese were not a threat to the city's economic base. Moreover, the anti-Chinese movement in America was largely a movement of small farmers and laborers against what they described as the unfair competition of Chinese laborers. Once labor agitation had succeeded in driving the Chinese workers out of the city's industries and into the confines of Chinatown—a mission largely accomplished by 1910—civic functionaries were quite prepared to negotiate with the Six Companies whatever agreements might have to be reached between the ghetto and the metropolis. For its part the Six Companies, although it protested against the excesses of ghettoization, must have realized the gain to be made in its own power by having the great majority of Chinese housed and employed in Chinatown. The final establishment of Chinatown as an unofficial but real quarter of the city consolidated and enhanced the power of the Six Companies over its denizens.

In effect the Six Companies' authority over Chinese in San Francisco was—until the advent of the American-born and the rise of intracommunity rebellion—an institutionalized version of the kind of control over Negroes in America exercised by Booker T. Washington and his "Tuskegee Machine" from 1890 until 1915. The slow growth of a second generation prevented an effective counteraction to its powers by an acculturated group demanding a new politics. To be sure, Chinatown's Six Companies had its W. E. B. DuBoises—men who opposed the despotic benevolence it exercised, the containment of Chinese in the ghetto that it tacitly espoused and the corruption in its offices. But they were too few in number to be effective, too readily co-opted into the controlled violence of Chinatown's secret societies or too easily frightened into silence by threats of financial loss, deportation or conviction of trumped-up crimes in the white man's courts, where Chinese interpreters could be bought and perjured witnesses were easily obtainable. When the American-born generation did reach maturity, many of its members went to college, entered the professions and departed from Chinatown. This caused the Six Companies some loss in its Chinese constituency, but since the Chinese-Americans *embourgeoisés* did not challenge the authority of the Six Companies, the loss did not undermine its control over Chinatown.

LEGITIMATE AND ILLEGITIMATE REBELLION

Today, in addition to the "illegitimate" rebellion of youth in Chinatown, there is a "legitimate" counteraction of adults against the communitywide authority of the Six Companies. This loyal opposition includes several intra-Chinatown associations composed of "respectable" members of the American-born and, occasionally, a foreign-born Chinese leader who opposes the associational oligarchy. Until 1956 the only significant organization among the American-born Chinese was the Chinese-American Citizens' Alliance, a group so small that in its early days, more than a half century ago, it was little more than a name promising assimilation. Since the mid-1950s, however, a new association has arisen—the Chinese-American Democratic Club (CADC). This organization of politically minded and socially conscious Chinese-Americans heralds a shift from communal-oriented traditionalism to civic-minded cosmopolitanism in Chinatown. Still another organization outside the domination of the Six Companies is the Concerned Chinese for Action and Change, a loose and informal association of middle-class Chinese-Americans who live outside the ghetto but who can be counted on to mass for support of more liberal social action in Chinatown. Third, the Chinatown-North Beach Area Youth Council, a product of the Economic Development Agency in Chinatown, seeks to link up the respectable middle-class Chinatowners with its less respectable youth groups. Finally, there is one aging Chinese, J. K. Choy, who almost alone has opposed the old order in Chinatown without effective reprisal. A Columbia-educated banker and a professed disciple of Fabianism, Choy has exposed the poverty and neglect hidden beneath the tinseled glitter of Chinatown's neon-lit ghetto. He organized a reading room and English classes for immigrants in the offices next to the branch bank which he oversees as general manager. When in October 1966 he advised the women employed in Chinatown's sweatshops to organize for better wages, shorter hours and improved conditions and offered a devastating criticism of the ghetto's poverty program, rumors were started in the community which resulted in a three-day run on the bank. Unlike the old Chinese boycotts, which were used so effectively in the early days of the economically isolated Chinatown, this attempt to destroy a Chinatown reformer failed because the bank was protected by its connections to the larger banking system of the state. The failure to silence Choy by traditional methods is a measure of the ghetto's growing interdependence with the nation and a testimony to the decreasing power of traditional sanctions available to intra-community elites.

In Chinatown the arena of battle between the new opposition and the old order has been for seats on the poverty board organized under the community action program of the Economic Opportunity Act of 1964. In April 1969, after three years of internecine in-fighting, the liberal opposition—largely composed of the members of the CADC—was finally able to depose the Six Companies' man on the board, Chairman Dapien Liang, and to replace him with a chairman more to its liking. The Six Companies charged that the poverty board was dominated by "left-wing militants"but was unable to secure its complete control over Chinatown's poverty program. However, the Chinatown program is budgeted so far only to the beginning of 1970. If the program is scrapped, the arena of conflict and opposition to Chinatown may shift on to some other plane.

Another challenge to the old order has been hurled recently by ICSA. In August 1969 a news reporter interviewed Foo Hum, tea merchant, mogul in the Chinese Six Companies and representative on the Chinatown antipoverty board, concerning Chinatown's social problems. In addition to denying that the community's problems were either exclusive or very grave, Hum refuted the assertion that they were attributable to newly arrived immigrants. Then he launched into an attack on the native-born youth, especially the Red Guards and the ICSA and was quoted in the press as saying, "The Red Guards and the Intercollegiate Chinese for Social Action—theirs are Communist activities. They should not be blamed on the new immigrants." ICSA promptly filed a slander suit against Hum for $100,000 general damages and $10,000 punitive damages. Hum, backed by a Six Companies legal defense fund of $10,000, refused to settle out of court to an

offer made by Mason Wong, ICSA president, that the suit be dropped in return for Hum's writing a letter of apology and publishing it in all local papers, paying all legal fees that have arisen thus far and donating a token gift of money to ICSA.

The crust of Chinatown's cake of customary control may be beginning to crumble. The old order must contend not only with the mounting opposition of the community's respectable, professional and American-born younger and middle-aged adults, but also with the militant organization of Chinatown's disaffected youth. In addition, one cannot count on the new immigrants to bow to Chinatown's traditional power elite in the future as they have in the past.

It is by no means clear, however, what the outcome of this continuing power struggle will be. Chinatown's more liberal-minded leaders may defeat themselves by their ambiguous support of both progressive policies and a new racial consciousness. The former may call for a need to push for the introduction of unionization and other characteristic features of white America into Chinatown's anachronistic institutions. But the new ethnic consciousness, a consciousness that in its extreme forms opposes both the old order of transplanted Cathay and the middle-class ways of white America, may forbid cooperation with those institutions—progressive or not—that are dominated by Caucasians. It is in this possible paralysis that Chinatown's old order coalesces with its new rebels. Both seem to oppose the imposition of the metropolis upon the ghetto, but for quite different reasons. For the old elites any greater intrusion might undermine their exclusive and "extraterritorial" power; for the new rebels any intrusion might wrest away their newly discovered desire for ethnic self-determination. It would not be impossible for Chinatown's garment workers, as well as the community's other unprotected and impoverished denizens, to be caught helplessly in the vice of this excruciating cultural conflict.

DISCRIMINATION AND NATIONAL OPPRESSION

Beyond the problems of the ghetto itself—some of which are typical of all poor ethnic enclaves in American cities, some of which are peculiarly Chinese—loom the attitude and action of the larger society. Chinatown's myth of social propriety, communal self-help, familial solidarity and a low crime rate was a carefully nurtured mystique, prepared to counteract the vicious stereotype of coolie laborers, immoral practices, murderous tong wars and inscrutable cunning that characterized the American white man's perspective. As a pervasive mystique coloring most reports of Chinatown for the past three decades, it has succeeded up to a point in its original purpose—to substitute a favorable stereotype for an unfavorable one. It had other latent functions as well, not the least of which was to protect the community's social and political structure from excessive scrutiny and destruction. So long as Chinatown could "contain" its problems, circumscribe its paragovernmental institutions with bourgeois or innocuously exotic descriptions and control its members, the community was safe, and the city adopted a relaxed attitude toward its own cosmopolitan character.

But Chinatown's safety rests also on American's foreign relations with China. The repeal of the exclusion laws in 1943 was a gesture of reconciliation toward the country's wartime ally in the war against Japan, just as the incarceration of the Japanese-Americans during that same war was a hostile move against those Americans who had the misfortune to be physically identifiable with America's enemy. Aware of the dangerously changeable character of America's friendliness toward her racially visible peoples, Chinatown has presented a picture of cultural identity with nineteenth-century Cathay and of moral sympathy for the Nationalist Regime in Taiwan. This is not a false picture, for the political identity of the aged aliens is of very low intensity, but if it must be linked to old China it is most probably to the Republic founded by Sun Yat Sen and continued under Chiang Kai-shek. The American-born Chinese are not "Zionists" to any degree and therefore feel themselves to be Americans politically and socially and do not identify with either China. Even the Red Guard's rhetorical usage of Mao's book is more a symbol of an American rebellion than the substance of Communist affiliation. And the new immigrants have shown a profound disinterest in associating even with the symbols of Maoism.

Nevertheless, the fires of fear and prejudice are still kindled in America. Not only are acts of prejudice and discrimination still visited upon Chinese-Americans in everyday life, at least one agency of the government itself is still not wholly satisfied with the loyalty of Chinese in America. On 17 April 1969 J. Edgar Hoover testified before a subcommittee of the House Committee on Appropriations that "the blatant, belligerent and illogical statements made by Red China's spokesmen during the past year leave no doubt that the United States is Communist China's No. 1 enemy." Hoover went on to warn the subcommittee of Communist Chinese intelligence activity "overt and covert, to obtain needed material, particularly in the scientific field." After hinting darkly that a Chinese-American who served a 60-day sentence in prison for making a false customs declaration about electronic parts being sent to Hong Kong might have been an agent of a Communist country, Hoover asserted, "We are being confronted with a growing amount of work in being alert for Chinese-Americans and others in this country who would assist Red China in supplying needed material or promoting Red Chinese propaganda." "For one thing," he continued, "Red China has been flooding the country with its propaganda and there are over 300,000 Chinese in the United States, some of whom could be susceptible to recruitment either through ethnic ties or hostage situations because of relatives in Communist China." Hoover went on to say that "up to 20,000 Chinese immigrants can come into the United States each year and this provides a means to send illegal agents into our Nation." Hoover concluded his testimony on this point by asserting that "there are active Chinese Communist sympathizers in the Western Hemisphere in a position to aid in operations against the United States." Thus the Chinese in America were reminded that perhaps all their efforts at convincing white America that they were a peaceable, law-abiding, family-minded and docile people who contributed much and asked little in return had gone for naught. In time of crisis they too might suffer the same fate that overtook the highly acculturated Japanese-Americans a quarter century before—wholesale incarceration. When Hoover's remarks are coupled with the widespread report in 1966 that China's atomic bomb was "fathered" by Dr. Tsien

Hwue-shen, an American-educated Chinese who was persecuted here for five years during the McCarthy era and then allowed to return to the country of his birth and citizenship, and with the fact that under Title II of the Emergency Detention Act of 1950 any person or group who is deemed to be a "threat to the internal security of the United States" may be incarcerated in the same detention camps in which the American Japanese were imprisoned, the safety of the Chinese in America from official persecution is by no means assured. The Chinese, of course, protested against Hoover's remarks, and one San Francisco paper labeled his testimony an irresponsible slur on "a large and substantial segment of American citizens." Meanwhile, Japanese-American, Chinese-American and several other kinds of organizations have joined together to attempt to get Congress to repeal the infamous Title II.

Race prejudice, as Herbert Blumer has reminded us, is a sense of group position. It arises out of the belief, supported and legitimated by various elites, that a racial group is both inferior and threatening. Such a belief may lie dormant beneath the facade of a long-term racial accommodation, made benign by a minority group's tacit agreement to live behind the invisible, but no less real for that, wall of a ghetto. Then when circumstances seem to call for new meanings and different explanations, the allegedly evil picture and supposedly threatening posture may be resuscitated to account for political difficulties or social problems that seem to defy explanation.

History, however, does not simply repeat itself. There is a new Chinatown and new sorts of Chinese in America. The old order holds its power precariously in the ghetto, and the new liberals and the now vocal radicals bid fair to supplant them and try new solutions to the old problems. Finally, the Japanese experience of 1942 may not be repeated either because the United States has learned that lesson too well or because too many Americans would not let it happen again.

TONI MORRISON

WHAT THE black WOMAN THINKS AbOUT WOMEN'S lib

The signs "White Ladies" and "Colored Women" used to mark separate facilities for black and white women in the American South. They are symbolic of the view the black woman has of herself, of her status and role, and of how she perceives the white woman and her status and role in our society. Novelist and Random House editor Toni Morrison explores these views in the following article. She explains that the sign "Colored Women" characterized the black woman, who developed strength, self-sufficiency, and independence. The white woman, trying to live up to her role of "lady," developed helplessness, softness, and modesty. The black woman, in fact, views her white counterpart as a spoiled child, instead of a complete adult, and views the white woman's search for "freedom" through Women's Lib as "responsibility"—something the black woman has always had.

□□□

They were always there. Whenever you wanted to do something simple, natural and inoffensive. Like drink some water, sit down, go to the bathroom or buy a bus ticket to Charlotte, N. C. Those classifying signs that told you who you were, what to do. More than those abrupt and discourteous signs one gets used to in this country—the door that says

From the NEW YORK TIMES MAGAZINE, August 22, 1972. Copyright © 1971 by The New York Times Company. Reprinted by permission.

"Push," the towel dispenser that says "Press," the traffic light that says "No"—these signs were not just arrogant, they were malevolent: "White Only," "Colored Only," or perhaps just "Colored," permanently carved into the granite over a drinking fountain. But there was one set of signs that was not malevolent; it was, in fact, rather reassuring in its accuracy and fine distinctions: the pair that said "White Ladies" and "Colored Women."

The difference between white and black females seemed to me an eminently satisfactory one. White females were *ladies*, said the sign maker, worthy of respect. And the quality that made ladyhood worthy? Softness, helplessness and modesty—which I interpreted as a willingness to let others do their labor and their thinking. Colored females, on the other hand, were *women*—unworthy of respect because they were tough, capable, independent and immodest. Now, it appears, there is a consensus that those anonymous sign makers were right all along, for there is no such thing as Ladies' Liberation. Even the word "lady" is anathema to feminists. They insist upon the "woman" label as a declaration of their rejection of all that softness, helplessness and modesty, for they see them as characteristics which served only to secure their bondage to men.

Significant as that shift in semantics is, obvious as its relationship to the black-woman concept is, it has not been followed by any immediate comradery between black and white women, nor has it precipitated any rush of black women into the various chapters of

NOW. It is the *Weltanschauung* of black women that is responsible for their apparent indifference to Women's Lib, and in order to discover the nature of this view of oneself in the world, one must look very closely at the black woman herself—a difficult, inevitably doomed proposition, for if anything is true of black women, it is how consistently they have (deliberately, I suspect) defied classification.

It may not even be possible to look at those militant young girls with lids lowered in dreams of guns, those middle-class socialites with 150 pairs of shoes, those wispy girl junkies who have always been older than water, those beautiful Muslim women with their bound hair and flawless skin, those television personalities who think chic is virtue and happiness a good coiffure, those sly old women in the country with their ancient love of Jesus—and still talk about The Black Woman. It is a dangerous misconception, for it encourages lump thinking. And we are so accustomed to that in our laboratories that it seems only natural to confront all human situations, direct all human discourse, in the same way. Those who adhere to the scientific method and draw general conclusions from "representative" sampling are chagrined by the suggestion that there is any other way to arrive at truth, for they like their truth in tidy sentences that begin with "all."

In the initial confrontation with a stranger, it is never "Who are you?" but "Take me to your leader." And it is this mode of thought which has made black-white relationships in this country so hopeless. There is a horror of dealing with people one by one, each as he appears. There is safety and manageability in dealing with the leader—no matter how large or diverse the leader's constituency may be. Such generalizing may be all right for plant analysis, superb for locating carcinogens in mice, and it used to be all right as a method for dealing with schools and politics. But no one would deny that it is rapidly losing effectiveness in both those areas—precisely because it involves classifying human beings and anticipating their behavior. So it is with some trepidation that anyone should undertake to generalize about still another group. Yet something in that order is legitimate, not only because unity among minorities is a political necessity, but because, at some point, one wants to get on with the differences.

What do black women feel about Women's Lib? Distrust. It is white, therefore suspect. In spite of the fact that liberating movements in the black world have been catalysts for white feminism, too many movements and organizations have made deliberate overtures to enroll blacks and have ended up by rolling them. They don't want to be used again to help somebody gain power—a power that is carefully kept out of their hands. They look at white women and see them as the enemy—for they know that racism is not confined to white men, and that there are more white women than men in this country, and that 53 per cent of the population sustained an eloquent silence during times of greatest stress. The faces of those white women hovering behind that black girl at the Little Rock school in 1957 do not soon leave the retina of the mind.

When she was interviewed by Nikki Giovanni last May in Essence magazine, Ida Lewis, the former editor-in-chief of Essence, was asked why black women were not more involved in Women's Lib, and she replied: "The Women's Liberation Movement is basically a family quarrel between white women and white men. And on general principles, it's not good to get involved in family disputes. Outsiders always get shafted when the dust settles. On the other hand, I must support some of the goals [equal pay, child-care centers, etc.].... But if we speak of a liberation movement, as a black woman I view my role from a black perspective—the role of black women is to continue the struggle in concert with black men for the liberation and self-determination of blacks. White power was not created to protect and preserve us as women. Nor can we view ourselves as simply American women. We are black women, and as such we must deal effectively in the black community."

To which Miss Giovanni sighed: "Well, I'm glad you didn't come out of that Women's Lib or black-man bag as if they were the alternatives...."

Miss Lewis: "Suppose the Lib movement succeeds. It will follow, since white power is the order of the day, that white women will be the first hired, which will still leave black men and women outside...."

It is an interesting exchange, Miss Lewis expressing suspicion and identifying closely with black men, Miss Giovanni suggesting that the two are not necessarily mutually exclusive.

But there is not only the question of color, there is the question of the color of experience. Black women are not convinced that Women's Lib serves their best interest or that it can cope with the uniqueness of their experience, which is itself an alienating factor. The early image of Women's Lib was of an élitist organization made up of upper-middle-class women with the concerns of that class (the percentage of women in professional fields, etc.) and not paying much attention to the problems of most black women, which are not in getting into the labor force but in being upgraded in it, not in getting into medical school but in getting adult education, not in how to exercise freedom from the "head of the house" but in how to *be* head of the household.

Black women are different from white women because they view themselves differently, are viewed differently and lead a different kind of life. Describing this difference is the objective of several black women writers and scholars. But even without this newly surfacing analysis, we can gain some understanding of the black women's world by examining archetypes. The archetypes created by women about themselves are rare, and even those few that do exist may be the result of a female mind completely controlled by male-type thinking. No matter. The most unflattering stereotypes that male minds have concocted about black women contain, under the stupidity and the hostility, the sweet smell of truth.

Look, for example, at Geraldine and Sapphire—Geraldine, that campy character in Flip Wilson's comic repertory, and Sapphire, the wife of Kingfish in the Amos and Andy radio and TV series. Unlike Nefertiti, an archetype that black women have appropriated for themselves, Geraldine and Sapphire are the comic creations of men. Nefertiti, the romantic black queen with the enviable neck, is particularly appealing to young black women, mainly because she existed (and there are few admirable heroines in our culture), was a great beauty and is remote enough to be worshiped. There is a lot of talk about Sojourner Truth, the freed slave who preached emancipation and women's rights, but there is a desperate love for Nefertiti, simply because she was so pretty.

I suppose at bottom we are all beautiful queens, but for the moment it is perhaps just as well to remain useful women. One wonders if Nefertiti could have lasted 10 minutes in a welfare office, in a Mississippi gas station, at a Parent Association meeting or on the church congregation's Stewardess Board No. 2. And since black women have to endure, that romanticism seems a needless *cul de sac*, an opiate that appears to make life livable if not serene but eventually must separate us from reality. I maintain that black women are already O.K. O.K. with our short necks. O.K. with our callused hands. O.K. with our tired feet and paper bags on the Long Island Rail Road. O.K. O.K. O.K.

As for Geraldine, her particular horror lies in her essential accuracy. Like any stereotype she is a gross distortion of reality and as such highly offensive to many black women and endearing to many whites. A single set of characteristics provokes both hatred and affection. Geraldine is defensive, cunning, sexy, egocentric and transvestite. But that's not all she is. A shift in semantics and we find the accuracy: for defensive read survivalist; for cunning read clever; for sexy read a natural unembarrassed acceptance of her sexuality; for egocentric read keen awareness of individuality; for transvestite (man in woman's dress) read a masculine strength beneath the accouterments of glamour.

Geraldine is offensive to many blacks precisely because the virtues of black women are construed in her portrait as vices. The strengths are portrayed as weaknesses—hilarious weaknesses. Yet one senses even in the laughter some awe and respect. Interestingly enough, Geraldine is absolutely faithful to one man, Killer, whom one day we may also see as caricature.

Sapphire, a name of opprobrium black men use for the nagging black wife, is also important, for in that marriage, disastrous as it was, Sapphire worked, fussed, worked and fussed, but (and this is crucial) Kingfish did whatever he pleased. Whatever. Whether he was free or irresponsible, anarchist or victim depends on your point of view. Contrary to the black-woman-as-emasculator theory, we see, even in these unflattering caricatures, the very opposite of a henpecked husband and emasculating wife—a wife who never did, and never could, manipulate her man. Which brings to the third reason for the suspicion black women have of Women's Lib: the serious one of the relationship between black women and black men.

There are strong similarities in the way black and white men treat women, and strong similarities in the way women of both races react. But the relationship is different in a very special way.

For years in this country there was no one for black men to vent their rage on except black women. And for years black women accepted that rage—even regarded that acceptance as their unpleasant duty. But in doing so, they frequently kicked back, and they seem never to have become the "true slave" that white women see in their own history. True, the black woman did the housework, the drudgery; true, she reared the children, often alone, but she did all of that while occupying a place on the job market, a place her mate could not get or which his pride would not let him accept. And she had nothing to fall back on: not maleness, not whiteness, not ladyhood, not anything. And out of the profound desolation of her reality she may very well have invented herself.

If she was a sexual object in the eyes of men, that was their doing. Sex was *one* of her dimensions. It had to be just one, for life required many other things of her, and it is difficult to be regarded solely as a sex object when the burden of field and fire is on your shoulders. She could cultivate her sexuality but dared not be obsessed by it. Other people may have been obsessed by it, but the circumstances of her life did not permit her to dwell on it or survive by means of its exploitation.

So she combined being a responsible person with being a female—and as a person she felt free to confront not only the world at large (the rent man, the doctor and the rest of the marketplace) but her man as well. She fought him and nagged him—but knew that you don't fight what you don't respect. (If you don't respect your man, you manipulate him, the way some parents treat children and the way white women treat their men—if they can get away with it or if they do not acquiesce entirely). And even so, the black man was calling most of the shots—in the home or out of it. The black woman's "bad" relationships with him were often the result of his inability to deal with a competent and complete personality and her refusal to be anything less than that. The saving of the relationship lay in her unwillingness to feel free when her man was not free.

In a way black women have known something of the freedom white women are now beginning to crave. But oddly, freedom is only sweet when it is won. When it is forced, it is called responsibility. The black Woman's needs shrank to the level of her responsibility; her man's expanded in proportion to the obstacles that prevented him from assuming his. White women, on the other hand, have had too little responsibility, white men too much. It's a wonder the sexes of either race even speak to each other.

As if that were not enough, there is also the growing rage of black women over unions of black men and white women. At one time, such unions were rare enough to be amusing or tolerated. The white woman moved with the black man into a black neighborhood, and everybody tried to deal with it. Chances are the white woman who married a black man liked it that way, for she had already made some statement about her relationship with her own race by marrying him. So there were no frictions. If a white woman had a child out of wedlock by a black man, the child was deposited with the black community, or grouped with the black orphans, which is certainly one of the reasons why lists of black foundling children are so long. (Another reason is the willingness of black women to have their children instead of aborting—and to keep them, whatever the inconvenience.)

But now, with all the declarations of independence, one of the black man's ways of defining it is to broaden his spectrum of female choices, and one consequence of his new pride is the increased attraction white women feel for him. Clearly there are more and more of these unions, for there is clearly more anger about it (talking black and sleeping white is a cliché) among black women. The explanations for this anger are frequently the easy ones: there are too few eligible men, for wars continue to shoot them up; the black woman who complains is one who would be eliminated from a contest with any good-looking woman—the complaint simply reveals her inadequacy to get a man; it is a simple case of tribal sour grapes with a dash of politics thrown in.

But no one seems to have examined this anger in the light of what black women understand about themselves. These easy explanations are obviously male. They overlook the fact that the hostility comes from both popular beauties and happily married black women. There is something else in this anger, and I think it lies in the fact that black women have always considered themselves superior to white women. Not racially superior, just superior in terms of their ability to function healthily in the world.

Black women have been able to envy white women (their looks, their easy life, the attention they seem to get from their men); they could fear them (for the economic control they have had over black women's lives) and even love them (as mammies and domestic workers can); but black women have found it impossible to respect white women. I mean they never had what black men have had for white men—a feeling of awe at their accomplishments. Black women have no abiding admiration of white women as competent, complete people. Whether vying with them for the few professional slots available to women in general, or moving their dirt from one place to another, they regarded them as willful children, pretty children, mean children, ugly children, but never as real adults capable of handling the real problems of the world.

White women were ignorant of the facts of life—perhaps by choice, perhaps with the assistance of men, but ignorant anyway. They were totally dependent on marriage or male support (emotionally or economically). They confronted their sexuality with furtiveness, complete abandon or repression. Those who could afford it, gave over the management of the house and the rearing of children to others. (It is a source of amusement even now to black women to listen to feminists talk of liberation while somebody's nice black grandmother shoulders the daily responsibility of child rearing and floor mopping and the liberated one comes home to examine the housekeeping, correct it, and be entertained by the children. If Women's Lib needs those grandmothers to thrive, it has a serious flaw.) The one great disservice black women are guilty of (albeit not by choice) is that they are the means by which white women can escape the responsibilities of womanhood and remain children all the way to the grave.

It is this view of themselves and of white women that makes the preference of a black man for a white woman quite a crawful. The black women regard his choice as an inferior one. Over and over again one hears one question from them: "But why, when they marry white women, do they pick the raggletail ones, the silly, the giddy, the stupid, the flat nobodies of the race? Why no real women?" The answer, of course, is obvious. What would such a man who preferred white women do with a real woman? And would a white woman who is looking for black exotica ever be a complete woman?

Obviously there are black and white couples who love each other as people, and marry each other that way. (I can think of two such.) But there is so often a note of apology (if the woman is black) or bravado (if the man is) in such unions, which would hardly be necessary if the union was something other than a political effort to integrate one's emotions and therefore, symbolically, the world. And if all the black partner has to be is black and exotic, why not?

This feeling of superiority contributes to the reluctance of black women to embrace Women's Lib. That and the very important fact that black men are formidably opposed to their involvement in it—and for the most part the women understand their fears. In The Amsterdam News, an editor, while deploring the conditions of black political organizations, warns his readers of the consequences: "White politicians have already organized. And their organizers are even attempting to co-opt Black women into their organizational structure, which may well place Black women against Black men, that is, if the struggle for women's liberation is viewed by Black women as being above the struggle for Black liberation."

The consensus among blacks is that their first liberation has not been realized; unspoken is the conviction of black men that any more aggressiveness and "freedom" for black women would be intolerable, not to say counterrevolutionary.

There is also a contention among some black women that Women's Lib is nothing more than an attempt on the part of whites to become black without the responsibilities of being black. Certainly some of the demands of liberationists seem to rack up as our thing: common-law marriage (shacking); children out of wedlock, which is even fashionable now if you are a member of the Jet Set (if you are poor and black it is still a crime); families without men; right to work; sexual freedom, and an assumption that a woman is equal to a man.

Now we have come full circle: the morality of the welfare mother has become the avant-garde morality of the land. There is a good deal of irony in all of this. About a year ago in The Village Voice there was a very interesting exchange of letters. Cecil Brown was explaining to a young black woman the "reasons" for the black man's interest in white girls: a good deal about image, psychic needs and what not. The young girl answered in a rather poignant way to this effect: Yes, she said, I suppose, again, we black women have to wait, wait for the brother to get himself together— be enduring, understanding, and, yes, she thought they could do it again ... but, in the meantime, what do we tell the children?

This woman who spoke so gently in those letters of the fate of the children may soon discover that the waiting period is over. The softness, the "she knows how to treat me" (meaning she knows how to be a cooperative slave) that black men may be looking for in white women is fading from view. If Women's Lib *is* about breaking the habit of genuflection, if it *is* about controlling one's own destiny, *is*

about female independence in economic, personal and political ways, if it is indeed about working hard to become a person, knowing that one has to work hard at becoming anything, *Man* or *Woman*—and if it succeeds, then we may have a nation of white Geraldines and white Sapphires, and what on earth is Kingfish gonna do then?

The winds are changing, and when they blow, new things move. The liberation movement has moved from shrieks to shape. It is focusing itself, becoming a hard-headed power base, as the National Women's Political Caucus in Washington attested last month. Representative Shirley Chisholm was radiant: "Collectively we've come together, not as a Women's Lib group, but as a women's political movement." Fannie Lou Hamer, the Mississippi civil-rights leader, was there. Beulah Sanders, chairman of New York's Citywide Coordinating Committee of Welfare Groups, was there. They see, perhaps, something real: women talking about human rights rather than sexual rights—something other than a family quarrel, and the air is shivery with possibilities.

DISCUSSING THE ARTICLES

1. What kinds of groups did Chinese males form before the turn of the century, when they were without wives and children in a foreign land? Would you have expected them to have formed such groups in view of the text's statements about the importance of groups to the individual? Was it more likely that the groups were of a primary or of a secondary nature? Were these men interested primarily in the functions the groups performed for them or in the emotional satisfactions provided by the groups?

2. Are the Chinese youths active in the Red Guards and other Chinatown organizations dissatisfied with their ascribed statuses or with their achieved statuses?

3. The Chinese of San Francisco appear to be divided into three groups according to class. Which social processes seem to be at work in each of these groups? Among the groups?

4. How do the American-born, middle-class Chinese feel about their achieved chief status? What has been the price of assimilation?

5. What does the author call the social process that had been at work in the Chinese ghetto before the 1940s? What social processes are at work now?

6. How did the reasons for forming youth groups in Chinatown change progressively from the 1940s to the 1970s?

7.   Was Leway a primary or a secondary group? Was it a formal or an informal organization? Was it a voluntary or an involuntary association?

8.   Which social processes were at work in Leway's interaction with the San Francisco police? With the local community?

9.   With which two groups are the Red Guards particularly in conflict? Is coercion likely to be playing a part in the conflict?

10. Which "we" against "they" feeling is stronger among the Red Guards, social class or ethnicity?

11. Have the Chinese become assimilated in the United States? Has accommodation between the Chinese minority group and society at large been successful? Does it threaten to erupt into conflict?

12. In the article "What the Black Woman Thinks of Women's Lib," what do the signs "White Ladies" and "Colored Women" imply about status? What roles did each of these statuses require?

13. What female role is the Women's Lib movement trying to change? Why aren't black women interested in this goal?

14. What characteristic of groups do black women display in their feelings toward white women? What social processes would you say have been involved in relations between white women and black women?

15. Do the fictional black male characters of Kingfish and Killer fit the stereotyped roles of the black male in our society?

16. According to the author of the article, how do black women perceive their own status and role compared with the status and role of white women?

17. What element of the white woman's role is particularly attractive to the black male? If Women's Lib is successful, will this element of her role continue to exist?

18. If Women's Lib is successful, will the white woman's role become more or less similar to the black woman's role than it is now? What would be some of the aims of a Black Women's Lib?

TERMS TO REMEMBER

Aggregate. A number of people who are in the same place at the same time but who do not interact with one another.

Category. A number of people who have some characteristics in common but who do not interact with one another.

Symbolic interaction. Communication through speech, gestures, writing, or even music. In this kind of communication, members are mutually aware of one another, and awareness causes them to behave in a particular way.

Group. A number of people who engage in symbolic interaction. The members of a group are mutually aware of and influence one another; they recognize their membership in the group, and are, in turn, recognized by the group as members; and they accept the roles, duties, obligations, and privileges that result from group membership.

Primary Group. A relatively small group of people who live physically near one another and who interact intensely. Primary groups tend to be stable and of relatively long duration. Interaction is informal and spontaneous; members deal with one another on an individual, personal, and total basis.

Secondary Group. A group that is, in general, larger and of shorter duration than is a primary group. Interaction among members is formal, utilitarian, specialized, and temporary. Members are interested in one another mainly in terms of the roles and functions they perform.

Membership Group. A formal (the YMCA) or informal (a clique of friends) organization to which an individual belongs.

Reference Group. A political, economic, religious, ethnic, kinship, or social organization to which an individual aspires to belong and on which he patterns his behavior.

Involuntary Group. A group to which a member cannot help belonging, such as a family, or if he is drafted, a branch of the military service.

Voluntary Group. A group that an individual joins of his own free will.

Bureaucracy. A hierarchical system in an organization. The hierarchy depends on job specialization—or division of labor—on a set of rules and standards designed to promote uniformity, and on an attitude of impersonal impartiality.

Society. The largest social group analyzed by sociologists.

Gemeinschaft. A small, homogeneous, communal, and traditional society. Relationships among members are personal, informal, and face-to-face, and behavior is dictated by tradition.

Gesellschaft. A large, heterogeneous society, such as modern industrial societies. Relationships among members tend to be impersonal, formal, contractual, functional, and specialized. Also called an associational society.

Interaction. In a sociological sense, the same as symbolic interaction.

Social Processes. Key patterns of interaction that seem to be present in all human societies.

Cooperation. A basic social process involving two or more individuals or groups working jointly in a common enterprise for a shared goal.

Conflict. A struggle engaged in by two or more persons for an object or value that each prizes.

Competition. A form of oppositional interaction that is less obvious than conflict; the antagonists focus on the reward rather than on each other.

Ambition. A form of interaction similar to competition, except that the scarce commodity that individuals or groups desire is a value rather than an object.

Rivalry. A form of competition in which antagonists are aware of and seek to defeat one another.

Coercion. A mode of interaction in which one individual or group compels or forces his will on another individual or group, often, but not necessarily, with the threat of force.

Accommodation. The peace-making, conflict-settling period following the victory of one antagonist in conflict.

Assimilation. A process of fusion in which one individual or group becomes completely accepted as part of another group.

Exchange. Interaction for the purpose of receiving something in return.

Social system. A conceptualized group in which each part is interdependent and interconnected to other parts and to the whole. The elements of this system are the individual group members relating to one another.

Social structure. The shared, patterned, and recurrent expectations of behavior that guide members of social systems in their relationships with one another.

Social organization. The network of patterned human behavior that both guides and is the product of interaction. Sometimes considered as the real, as opposed to the ideal, way people behave. It is not necessarily a stable set of rules but a dynamic process in which stable and predictable patterns are continually redefined and changed to fit the changing conditions of the environment.

Interpersonal, or social relationship, level. A level of social organization in which relationships occur between two persons standing in a definite position to each other: husband to wife, father to son, and so on. Such relationships are the basic elements of social structure.

Group, intergroup, or organizational, level. A level of social organization in which relationships occur within and among organized groups.

Community, or social order, level. A level of social organization in which relationships occur within entire communities or societies.

Status. A position, including ranking and rating, in a social group.

Role. The carrying out of a status. A way of behaving that befits a status and is transmittable and, to a great extent, predictable.

Ascribed status. An inherited position—one that is not attained through any individual effort or merit.

Achieved status. A position attained through individual effort or merit.

SUGGESTIONS FOR FURTHER READING

Blau, Peter M. *The Dynamics of Bureaucracy*. Chicago: University of Chicago Press, 1963. A distinguished sociologist illustrates the social processes that lead to change in a bureaucracy.

Cooley, Charles Horton. *Social Organization*. New York: Schocken Books, 1962. First edition, 1909. One of the classics of sociology, containing the original definition of a primary group, as well as other pertinent discussions of social structure and social organization.

Gans, Herbert J. *The Urban Villagers*. New York: The Free Press, 1962. An interesting analysis of primary groups and interpersonal relationships in an Italian, working-class community.

Gross, Edward. "Some Functional Consequences of Primary Groups in Formal Work

Organizations." *American Journal of Sociology* (August, 1953), pp. 368-373. Reprint S-106, The Bobbs-Merrill Company, Indianapolis. The effect of primary groups on formal organizations from the viewpoint of the positive support they engender.

Howton, William F. "Work Assignment and Interpersonal Relations in a Research Organization: Some Participant Observations." *Administrative Science Quarterly* (March, 1963), pp. 502-520. A more recent analysis of a phenomenon similar to that discussed in the article by Edward Gross.

Marine, Gene. *The Black Panthers.* New York: Signet Books, 1969. A vivid description of the formation and goals of this very contemporary social group.

Mills, Theodore. *The Sociology of Small Groups.* Englewood Cliffs, N. J.: Prentice-Hall, 1967. A brief compendium of small group theory, including the findings of numerous experiments in social psychology.

Olmstead, Michael S. *The Small Group.* New York: Random House, 1962. A readable paperback describing research on both primary and secondary groups and stressing that not all small groups are primary.

Presthus, Robert. *The Organizational Society.* New York: Random House, Vintage Books, 1962. This paperback emphasizes the conflicts between the aims of large-scale organizations and the needs for personal growth and creativity of the individuals who constitute them.

Redfield, Robert. *The Little Community and Peasant Society and Culture.* Chicago: University of Chicago Press, 1960. A classic description of the traditional, Gemeinschaft society.

Shils, Edward A., and Janowitz, Morris. "Cohesion and Disintegration in the Wehrmach in World War II." *Public Opinion Quarterly* (Summer, 1948). Reprint S-263, The Bobbs-Merrill Company, Indianapolis. A somewhat old but still valid study illustrating that morale remained high in the German army as long as primary groups remained operative.

Suttles, Gerald D. *The Social Order of the Slum.* Chicago: University of Chicago Press, 1968. A description of the differences in social organization among four ethnic groups in Chicago.

Much as we admire individuality, we are group animals who cannot survive without groups, who live organized into groups, who always identify with some group (even though we may not admit it), and who will not escape the impact of groups until death. Our understanding of the group nature of human beings might lead us to ask, "Do all humans on the earth form a group? Do people interact on a global level? And are they all alike?" Obviously, the answers are all negative. Humans may be considered a group under some circumstances—when they are differentiated from Martians, for instance—but only a small minority of people interact on a global level, and they are certainly not all alike.

If we continue to develop technologically and to find means of shortening distances, we may, in the distant future, become a global community. But for now, a global community remains in the realm of science fiction. Today, many groups have difficulty even existing in harmony with other groups within the largest group in which they function, the society.

As for differences among people, we hardly need examples. They are all around us. In our own society, we see that some of us are black, others white, and still others belong to additional racial groups. We recognize that we speak with different accents—a New England clip, a broad New York twang, a melodious Southern drawl, and an Appalachian singsong. We know that we attend different churches and celebrate different holidays. In cities, there are shops that specialize in pizza, kosher corned beef, Polish ham, Cantonese sub-gum, tacos, shishkebab, and bhkhlava. Some of us live in mansions, others in virtual hovels. Some of us vote Republican, others Democrat. Some of us think this is the best of all possible worlds; others think it is the worst. Some of us must diet because we are too well fed; others scrape up barely enough food for a meal. Some of us want more of the things we have—more cars, more houses, more material objects; others want an alternative, meaningful, life style.

If there are countless differences within our own society, imagine the number of differences on a world level! The rapidity and ease of travel now-adays and the effectiveness of the mass media have had an equalizing effect on groups of people, erasing many of their differences. Still, the differences that remain vastly outnumber those that have been erased.

To note differences, we need not go to exotic and remote places, where we can see natives adorned with plumes and grass skirts. We can remain on our own continent and visit our neighbors, the Canadians and the Mexicans. The Canadians speak English with an accent different from the American

accent, and in one area of their country, they speak French. In the French-speaking province, customs and food are as distinctive as is the language. In Mexican society, which is a complex mixture of Indian and Spanish traditions, values and beliefs are different from ours, as are language and customs.

Differences among societies can be obvious or subtle. In a recent article, the novelist Arthur Koestler described a recent trip to Marrakech, a city in Morocco, North Africa. Now, this is not a remote area of the world. It is easily reached by planes, which probably leave every day from our major airports. Yet some of the scenes the author witnessed are as foreign to us as if they had occurred on another planet.

Koestler tells, for instance, of the magnificent Berber women, who do all the physical work, it seems, while their men drink mint tea and gossip. For their daily labor in the fields, Berber women dress in gowns of gold lamé, a brocaded fabric into which metallic threads are woven. Even when they carry pitchers of water from the village well, the women wear silver necklaces and other jewelry.[1]

Much more subtle differences may be observed among people who live in societies very similar to our own and who share our common Western heritage. A native American male may be quite surprised (as one of the authors was) at the affectionate hug and kiss he may receive as a greeting from an Italian male. He may also be amazed at the trusting ways of the Scandinavians and perhaps pleased at the sexual customs which are more permissive than our own.

We could go on and on describing differences among people, for they are virtually without limit. At the same time, we must be aware that humans share significant similarities. Wherever we might travel in the world, we would find that, sooner or later, all people must eat (though what and how they eat differs), and all must sleep (though the accommodations are dissimilar). All people have some kind of dwelling for shelter, are grouped according to some kind of kinship ties, are organized according to some system of social organization, have some kind of economic system, and so on.

The fundamental question is, then, What makes people so different, although they are, in some respects, so similar? To answer the question with any degree of precision, it is necessary to understand two central concepts: society and culture. It is in the context of society and according to the dictates of culture that the drama of human life unfolds.

SOCIETY

A *society* may be defined as a fairly large group of individuals who interact with one another on a regular, continuous basis and according to patterns of behavior on which all more or less agree. Like all definitions of groups, the definition of society emphasizes social relationships, or interaction, rather than individuals. A basic distinction of a society is that "[It is a group] within which men can live a total common life, rather than an organization limited to some specific purpose or purposes."[2] In other words, of all groups, a society

[1]Arthur Koestler, "Reports and Comments: Marrakech," *Atlantic* (December, 1971), pp. 6-26.

[2]Ely Chinoy, *Sociological Perspective*, 2d ed. (New York: Random House, 1968), pp. 44–45.

has the highest degree of self-sufficiency, or the least degree of dependence on other groups. This self-sufficiency is based on the techniques set up by each society for obtaining and distributing resources and for otherwise fulfilling the needs of its members.

From a sociological standpoint, then, society is the interrelated network of social relationships that exists within the boundaries of the largest social system. In the past, the largest social system was often a clan, a tribe, or simply a family. Today, the largest social system is the national political state. In the national political state, individuals are grouped and interrelated as families, communities, racial and ethnic groups, political parties, social classes, and so on. When we speak of American society, then, we are referring to the approximately 200 million individuals (grouped in families, communities, and countless other classifications) who inhabit the territory of the United States and whose social relationships occur within its boundaries.

In addition, every society organizes representative groups and positions to which it gives the power of making decisions and settling conflicts. Finally, each society requires that its members feel greater loyalty to it than to any other group. Such loyalty is possible partly because the members share a language and a culture uniquely their own, even though a number of groups within the larger society have cultures and languages that are significantly different.[3]

Kinds of Societies

Throughout history, societies have assumed a number of different forms. As with other groups, societies can be classified in countless ways. For purposes of analysis, however, societies are generally classified according to either their chief mode of subsistence or their basic patterns of social organization.

The sociologist Gerhard Lenski distinguishes among eleven types of societies according to their mode of subsistence—the way they provide their members with food, shelter, and clothing:

The hunting and gathering society. The earliest and the least complex society is the hunting and gathering society, formed by people thousands of years ago. This kind of society is characterized by a small, nomadic population, an uncomplicated technology, almost no division of labor or any other kind of specialization, and particular stress on the importance of kinship ties. A few such societies still exist in the modern world: the Bushmen of southern Africa, some Eskimo tribes, and the Stone Age societies being discovered in Brazil and the Philippines. However, unavoidable contacts with modern societies doom all these comparatively simple societies to extinction or marked change.

The horticultural society. The second simplest society—the horticultural—appeared in history after people discovered how to cultivate grains. In the horticultural society, the cultivation and growing of wheat, rice, and other grains was the chief means of sustenance, whereas hunting and gathering performed

[3]Marvin E. Olsen, *The Process of Social Organization* (New York: Holt, Rinehart and Winston, 1968), p. 96.

a supplementary function. In this kind of society, domestic artifacts first appeared, and tools were more sophisticated than those of hunters and food-gatherers. For example, horticulturalists made stone cups, bowls, and, later, pottery. Buildings were also made of sun-dried clay blocks and were sturdy enough to last for at least two generations.

Moreover, the horticultural society contained reasonably large, settled communities; demonstrated development of the basics of trade; and produced, for the first time, a surplus which served to divide members of the society into social classes. The production of surpluses, or extra supplies of food, laid the foundation for social inequality, a condition that was to exist in all future societies. Eventually, surpluses led to a situation in which some people were rich and others poor, some led and others followed, and so on.

The agrarian society. The next milestone in the development of human societies was reached around 3000 B.C., following the invention of the plow. The plow led to the formation of the agrarian society. In this society, even greater surpluses were produced, and people no longer had to move about at all to search for fertile soils. Consequently, people become even more differentiated into landholders and landless peasants, and social stratification deepened. To maintain the system and to oversee the increasingly complex economy, members of the society developed a basic bureaucracy. Also found in the agrarian society were the initial stages of a money economy, gunpowder, iron smelting, and the use of windmills as a source of power.

Other preindustrial societies and industrial societies. Other preindustrial societies classified by Lenski are the fishing, maritime, and herding societies. All exhibit features that are, in general, similar to those of agrarian societies. The revolu-

tionary change in societal formation occurred with the emergence of the industrial society, characterized by urbanization, massive mechanization, complex bureaucratization, separation of institutional forms, and the substitution of kinship ties with impersonal ties.[4]

Classification According to Social Organization

Societies are more often classified according to their basic patterns of social organization rather than their mode of subsistence. To analyze organization, sociologists place societies on two extremes of an ideal continuum. These polar extremes are often called Gemeinschaft and Gesellschaft. As we said in Chapter 1, Gemeinschaft are communal traditional societies, whereas Gesellschaft are modern industrial, or associational, societies.

Much of the turmoil of our times is the result of a trend, begun in the late Middle Ages, away from the communal and toward the associational type of society. Today, even partially industrialized societies, particularly those of the Third World, are in the throes of this transition. But the transition has not yet been completed even in the industrial societies of the world.

Traditional, or communal, societies.   Gemeinschaft societies have the following characteristics: (1) They are usually small in size. (2) There is very little division of labor, or role specialization. (3) The family is the focal unit of society—on it, all social organization hinges. If larger groups than the family exist, they, too, are kinship groups—clans and tribes. (4) Social relationships are of a primary nature—durable, personal, and emotional. (5) Patterns of behavior are dictated by custom and tradition, and expectations of behavior are specific and well defined. (6) Lacking groups other than the family, clan, and tribe, the society is homogeneous and acts as an integrated social unit.

Modern industrial, or associational, societies.   Gesellschaft societies display characteristics that are almost the direct reverse of the characteristics of Gemeinschaft societies: (1) They are usually large in size. (2) There is a complex system of division of labor, or role differentiation. (3) The family's position as the essential social unit is eroded by social institutions and occupational, political, and social groups. Other kinship groups also lose importance. (4) Social relationships are of a secondary nature—transient, impersonal, and unemotional. (5) Formal and informal laws regulate patterns of behavior, whereas behavioral expectations are unclear and ill defined. (6) Because the society is heterogeneous and multigroup, unity diminishes.

SOCIETY AND CULTURE

The purpose of our discussion up to this point has been primarily to prepare you for a clear understanding of the principal and vital product of societies—their culture. Culture, like society, is a frequently misunderstood word. In everyday conversation, culture is used in general and sociologically

---

[4]Gerhard Lenski, *Human Societies* (New York: McGraw-Hill, 1970), pp. 118-142.

incorrect terms. For example, we tend to think of "cultured" people as individuals who have good manners, who attend concerts and symphonies, who go to art shows, and who have read the classics of world literature.

As a matter of fact, any individual who has been reared in a social group is cultured, even though he may lack the factual information that comes from years of study or the refined manners that come from associating with particular people. In short, an uneducated Indian peasant, an inhabitant of the Mongolian steppes, and an assembly line worker who finds modern art ridiculous are all equally cultured. Culture is the way of life of a people. Any part of that way of life, whether it concerns philosophy or theology, garbage collection or waste disposal, is part of culture.

We mentioned that culture is the product of a society. We should add that culture and society are two aspects of the same phenomenon, that they are interrelated and interdependent. Culture cannot exist without a society—or, at least, without a social group—and it would be impossible to conceive of society without a culture.

The interdependence of culture and society is understandable in terms of what was said in Chapter 1. No social group is immune to interaction, which takes place through a number of social processes. Furthermore, interaction is not entirely haphazard but is guided by recurring patterns of behavior. These patterns of behavior, in turn, are not simply set up but emerge as a result of the continued interaction of the members of a group. The outgrowth of interaction, then, is culture, which dictates further interaction.

For purposes of contrast, we can view culture and society in a theatrical context. Society can be considered a stage upon which individuals play roles befitting their statuses. The script that the actors use in playing their roles is culture. This script has been written for the actors by generations upon generations of their predecessors; each generation, including the present, has added, deleted, changed, or modified some parts of it.

A Definition of Culture

Culture is a central concept of sociology—and more importantly, of human life. It has many facets and includes many things. Therefore, it is not enough to define it simply as a way of life of a people, nor as the product of and guide for social interaction. On the other hand, it is equally senseless to pile definition on top of definition.

The difficulty of defining culture is apparent when we consider that anthropologists A. L. Kroeber and Clyde Kluckhohn, in their extensive investigation of culture, found no less than 164 definitions of the concept![5] Perhaps, however, we can obtain a composite view of culture by pointing out some of its fundamental characteristics: (1) Culture is that product of social interaction that is uniquely human. (2) Culture includes all the accumulated knowledge, ideas, values, goals, and material objects of a society that are shared by all the members of the society and that have been passed from generation to generation by individual members. (3) Culture is learned by each member

[5]A. L. Kroeber and Clyde Kluckhohn, "Culture: A Critical Review of Concepts and Definitions," Papers of the Peabody Museum of American Archaelogy and Ethnology, Vol. 47 (1952), Parts II and III, pp. 3-223.

of a society during his socialization—the process through which he learns to become human. Cultural learning takes place through symbolic interaction, a kind of communication in which language or gestures are used. (4) Culture provides each member of a society with ways of satisfying his biological and emotional needs in a manner approved by the society. Culture does this by supplying people with systems, or patterns, of organized behavior. (5) Each human society develops a culture that is distinct from other cultures. Yet all cultures share similarities, because they deal with biological and emotional needs that are universal. (6) Culture, as well as society—of which culture is a product and a guide—is in a constant state of flux. It changes either imperceptibly or rapidly, according to the circumstances.

In capsule form, we may define *culture* as the totality of what is learned and shared by the members of a society through interaction.

The Human Quality of Culture

We have noted that culture is the product of *human* social interaction. We emphasize the human aspect because animals also engage in social interaction. They live in groups, form more or less transient families, and even have basic forms of social organization and systems whereby members are divided into something akin to social classes. Yet they have no culture.

Animals lack culture mainly because they lack the ability to communicate *symbolically*. Animals communicate through a system of *signals* that are biologically determined and genetically transmitted responses to outside stimuli. An animal yelps in response to pain, runs in response to fear, and kills in response to hunger. These basic forms of communication are very limited in scope.

Biology and instinct determine how animals behave in particular situations. Genetically transmitted instinct tells salmon to return to fresh waters to spawn

and die. Instinct tells some birds—and not others—where and when to migrate. It tells bees and ants how to organize themselves for greatest efficiency, including what tasks each must perform.

Animals can be taught to act in ways that are not instinctual: You can teach a dog many tricks—how to lie down, sit up, and roll over. Unfortunately, the dog will never be able to tell his newborn pup how to perform these tricks. The owner will have to teach the young dog the same tricks over again.

Humans, on the other hand, communicate through *symbols*. Symbols are *not* biologically determined and genetically transmitted. They are learned and can be changed, modified, combined, and recombined in an infinite variety of ways. The most common example of a system of symbols is language, but music and art are also symbol systems.

The Effects of Biology on Culture

Biology is at the root of many human, as well as animal, limitations. In many respects, biology has limited our effectiveness in living on our planet. We cannot live in a vast part of the earth because we cannot breathe in water. Because we have a thin layer of skin, with very little hair on it, we need protection from the elements. We are comparatively small and defenseless, lacking the claws and fangs of many animals, as well as their sharp sense of smell and sight.

These shortcomings are more than made up for by the qualities we do possess: a grasping hand with a thumb that can be opposed to the other four fingers, which enables us to handle and make even the most delicate objects; an upright posture, which frees the forelimbs for handling objects; binocular vision, which enables us to focus far or near; complex vocal equipment, which enables us to speak; and an extremely well-developed brain, part of a complex nervous system, that makes it all possible.

The biological equipment of humans has enabled them to create culture, with which they adapt to their physical environment. Before people could create culture, however, they had to develop language. After the development of language, each member of a society was able to communicate his personal experiences, which then became shared by the whole society and eventually transmitted to the new generation. The members of the society could then respond to an experience they had not personally faced. They could learn from it, consider it good or bad, dismiss it as irrelevant or remember it as useful, or do whatever they chose with it. How much easier it is to acquire and accumulate knowledge in this manner than if each individual had to acquire it personally!

CULTURAL CONTENT

Culture is not visible or tangible in and of itself: You can't see it, you can't touch it, nor can you sell it over the counter. Nevertheless, culture is very much present among us. For this reason, we analyze its content, hoping to find clues that will bring us closer to solutions of the puzzle that is the human being.

Material Culture

What is both visible and tangible is the product of culture, or rather the products, for their numbers are astronomically high. All material objects, from a primitive stone ax to a complex guided missile, belong to the category of *material culture*. Material objects are created to fulfill a shared need and develop when one individual has an idea that is seized upon by other individuals, who add, modify, change, and put the idea to use.

The automobile, the foremost symbol of modern material culture, is an example of a product that is the result of the interaction of countless generations of people. The originator of the automobile, Henry Ford, owed much to those prehistoric cave dwellers who first honed stones into circular shapes (or found some ready-made by nature), saw how rapidly they rolled down inclines, stuck sticks through their middles, and attached to them heavy objects that they wanted moved. They, and the other members of their social group, must have been elated to realize that they had but to push or pull, rather than carry the weight.

Generations later, after people had domesticated several animals, other ingenious (or probably lazy) individuals carried the idea further. They attached wheeled equipment, such as a cart and, later, a plow, to animals. Now, humans did not need to use their own energy to push, pull, or carry but could use animal power.

Much later inventions, including the steam engine and the internal combustion engine, made it possible for people to sit safely in a train or a car, going wherever they wanted to go rapidly and in comfort. Henry Ford, at the beginning of the century, and General Motors, today, only applied the finishing touches to an idea born of the human brain and produced by human hands thousands of years ago.

Nonmaterial Culture

Another visible result of culture are the rules for human behavior, which are part of nonmaterial culture. *Nonmaterial culture* is made up not of the products of material culture but of behavioral expectations and ideas. These two categories of culture do not exist separately from each other, however. The sociologist Francis Merrill points out that material and nonmaterial are not different kinds of culture but merely different *levels*: "The basis of culture is found in the human mind, and the physical manifestations have meaning only in terms of these mental patterns. Ideas are the real foundation of culture. Material objects are useless without the knowledge of how to use them."[6]

Human behavior is shaped by the knowledge, beliefs, and values of a society and by a system of rules that regulates behavior. This system is called the *normative system*. The normative system did not develop in a day, a year, or even a generation; each society arrived at its normative system in a cumulative fashion.

The normative system.   A large part of a society's nonmaterial culture is dedicated to regulation of and prescriptions for behavior, called *norms*. Norms

[6]Francis E. Merrill, *Society and Culture* (Englewood Cliffs, N. J.: Prentice-Hall), 1969, p. 85.

cover a wide spectrum of behavioral standards, dictating conduct in informal and formal situations and in insignificant and serious ones. For example, norms dictate both the propriety of shaking hands with the left hand or with the right and the circumstances under which it is permissible to kill someone.

Norms emerge when a society, through experience, finds a particular act to be either harmful or beneficial to the society. If the act is found to be harmful, the society gives it negative value and forbids its performance. If the act is found to be beneficial, the society gives it positive value and encourages its performance. These ideas of right and wrong become the norms of the society. *Norms* are internalized; in other words, they become part of the individual's ideas of right and wrong. People, then, do not follow norms only because they fear punishment but also because they believe it is right to do so. People who act contrary to norms usually feel guilty.

There is disagreement over the origin of norms. Some social scientists believe that norms, or rules of behavior, emerge first and then values grow out of them. Other social scientists believe that a value, or distinction between that which is good and that which is bad, emerges first and norms develop around it. Such speculation is best left to social philosophers. What is important to remember is that cultural norms are essentially a set of behavioral expectations, a system that tells a member of a society how his society expects him to behave in specific circumstances.

Folkways. Because it is easier to examine a phenomenon if it can be viewed from different vantage points, sociologists have categorized cultural norms according to their importance and function. One such category is folkways, first used by the early American sociologist William Graham Sumner (1840-1910). *Folkways* are those norms that specify expected behavior in everyday situations. How many times a day members of a society are expected to eat, what types of food are eaten, how food is obtained, what types of clothes are worn to different social functions, and how people behave at a funeral—all these customary and habitual ways of acting are guided by folkways. Every culture develops a great number of folkways, but complex societies display an extraordinarily large number of them. Some folkways become permanent features of a society—celebration of holidays, for instance—but others are transitory, such as fashions in clothes, furniture, or automobiles.

People do not find it easy to ignore folkways. The violation of a folkway can cause great embarrassment to both the violator and those around him. Deliberate and repeated violation of folkways may cost a person his job or his reputation. Nevertheless, violation of folkways will not bring about severe punishment from the society, because folkways do not dictate behavior in the truly significant areas of human life.

Mores. Some behavior is considered either extremely harmful or extremely vital to society. The patterns that guide such behavior are called *mores*. Mores define the rightness or wrongness of an act, or its morality or immorality. People who consistently violate folkways may be excluded from some groups, but people who violate mores are punished by society itself. Violation of mores is considered a crime against the whole society.

Mores are perceived by members of society in terms of absolutes of right or wrong, but in reality, they are relative to time and place. As Sumner maintained, mores can make any act right or wrong because the society in which they exist *believes* the act to be right or wrong.

In many societies, at one time or another, mores permitted ritual murder, infanticide, cannibalism, incest, and other practices that we consider horrible today. But who are we to say that such actions are horrible? Who is to judge whether killing an infant at birth is crueler than exposing a whole society to starvation because of overpopulation? Often, we consider attitudes in India irrational and ridiculous because Indians refuse to kill their sacred cows even though people are starving. But a member of a society in which mores permit cannibalism as a means of survival would find our revulsion at the thought of eating human flesh equally irrational and ridiculous.

Even within a society, mores are not absolute. They have, for example, changed in our society. Child labor was considered perfectly justifiable in the United States only a century ago, but today we think of it as cruel. Mores concerned with the treatment of minority groups, capital punishment, and, especially, sex roles are in a state of change at the present time.

Mores that are couched in negative terms and that revolve around acts considered extremely repellent to the social group are called *taboos*. The biblical command "Thou shalt not kill" is an example of a taboo; other taboos have forbidden incest, cannibalism, and, at some times in history, adultery. Both mores and taboos are deeply etched on the members of society, some of whom actually become physically powerless to perform a forbidden act. Counterinfluences can, however, weaken the hold of mores and taboos on a substantial number of societal members, as the high crime rate in our society today indicates.

Laws. Mores may be somewhat ill defined, failing to draw a clear distinction between acts that are forbidden and those that are permitted. Furthermore, mores are frequently violated. To define and reinforce mores, then, most societies find it necessary to resort to laws. *Laws* are formal codes of behavior that are binding on a whole society. They specify both the behavior that deviates from norms and the punishment appropriate for each kind of norm-deviating behavior.

Laws are particularly necessary in a complex, heterogeneous society that is experiencing rapid social change, because many norms are not clear enough for all groups to understand or accept. In simpler societies, which have stronger kinship ties, a smaller number of norms are sufficient to prevent chaos and maintain order.

Whereas norms and mores are internalized by the members of a society, laws may not be. Thus, the more nearly laws reinforce mores that are universally accepted in a society, the more successful are the laws. In the United States, it is difficult to enforce the law against the smoking of marijuana. Enforcement is unsuccessful partly because a large number of people are not at all convinced of marijuana's dangers and don't accept the norm forbidding its use. Another law, Prohibition, was so unpopular and difficult to enforce in an unwilling population that it finally had to be repealed. Laws, then, can be repealed or modified when the values they reflect change sufficiently to warrant it. This gives laws an advantage over folkways and mores which tend to persist as habits.

Sometimes, people hope that by passing laws they can change mores and folkways that lead to injustice and cause conflict in a society. For example, the civil rights legislation enacted in this country has made specific forms of racism illegal. Although this legislation did not eliminate racism, the attitudes of which are functions of folkways and mores, it at least defined and reinforced certain values. Folkways and mores will probably eventually change to meet the conditions of the law.

Social Control

It is apparent that folkways, mores, taboos, and laws are a means of maintaining order within a society. In a sociological sense, their function is one of *social control*. The concept of social control will be discussed at some length in Chapter 9. For now, it is sufficient simply to be aware of this vital function of cultural norms.

Social control results from obedience to the norms of society. Obedience, in turn, is enforced by a system of *sanctions*. Positive sanctions consist of rewards, whereas negative sanctions consist of punishment. Official sanctions, whether positive or negative, are those given by representatives of a legal or formal organization. A judge who is appointed to the Supreme Court because he is outstanding in his profession receives a positive official sanction. A person who disobeys a law of the state and is sentenced to jail receives a negative official sanction.

More common than official sanctions are the unofficial sanctions, both positive and negative, that guide our behavior on an interpersonal, or intergroup, level of interaction. In other words, most of us conform to norms because of the rewarding or punishing words and actions of the people with whom we personally interact.

CULTURE AS STRUCTURE: AN ORGANIZED SYSTEM OF BEHAVIOR

We stated earlier that culture is an organized system of behavior, rather than a haphazard collection of folkways, mores, laws, and so on. (Remember, however, that culture is a conceptual system—an imaginary model.) To examine the various parts of this system—the structure of culture—sociologists find it helpful to divide culture into several components.

Traits

A *trait* is the smallest element, or unit, of culture. In material culture, every single object that society uses is a trait. In nonmaterial culture, every single idea, symbol, or belief existing in a society is a trait. Thus, a nail, a brick, and a house are all traits of material culture, whereas saluting the flag (patriotism), kissing (a symbol of affection), voting (a belief in democracy), or praying (a belief in God) are all traits of nonmaterial culture.

Culture Complexes

A number of related traits that accumulate around an activity form a *culture complex*. Football, for instance, is a culture complex. It consists of material traits—the football itself, uniforms, helmets, a field—and nonmaterial traits—the knowledge and ability of the players, a set of rules, a belief in winning, and team spirit. All areas of human life display numerous culture complexes.

Institutions

When a number of culture complexes cluster around a central human activity, an *institution* emerges. Institutions are formal systems of beliefs and behavior, composed of interrelated norms and culture complexes.

Institutions primarily center on and help to fulfill universal human needs. Sociologists usually consider that there are five basic institutions, which arose from five fundamental human needs. The need to regulate sexual interaction and care for the helpless newborn human being gave rise to the institution of the family. The need to provide food, shelter, and clothing resulted in the emergence of the economic institution. The need to maintain peace and order within a society led to the formation of the institution of government. The need to transmit culture and train the young gave rise to the institution of education. Finally, the dread and fear of the unknown created the institution of religion.

Although these basic institutions are common to all societies, the forms they assume vary from society to society. In following chapters, we will discuss, in detail, these and other institutions important to American society.

CULTURAL DIFFERENCES AND UNIFORMITIES

Anyone who has traveled abroad has personally observed that other societies do things differently from one's own. The degree to which societies differ depends on the distance between them—Canada will not greatly disorient an American, whereas China probably will—and on their cultural heritage and technological development.

Ethnocentrism Versus Cultural Relativity

Why societies differ has bothered thinkers and spawned theories throughout history. Unfortunately, judgments of particular societies have tended to be made from the viewpoint of *cultural ethnocentrism*, an attitude whereby one judges other societies by the standards of one's own. By indulging in this attitude, the ancient Greeks called barbarians all those foreigners who did not speak Greek but merely grunted (that is, who spoke their own language). Indulgence in the same attitude leads a tourist today to call immoral and lazy a people whose goals differ from those of his own culture.

Ethnocentrism is present, to some degree, in all social groups. It is reinforced by many of our institutions—the family and education, in particular—and, as we said in Chapter 1, of the "we" against "they" feeling that characterizes every group. In moderation, ethnocentrism has the positive value of promoting unity and loyalty within a group. On the social order level, cohesiveness and loyalty lead to patriotism. In excess, however, ethnocentrism acts like blinders on a horse, hiding from view all the good features of other cultures but permitting total acceptance of one's own culture. "America, right or

wrong," "America, love it or leave it," and the "God is with us" inscription that German soldiers wore in their belts are examples of extreme ethnocentrism.

Ethnocentrism can also be directed at groups within a culture. The damage it wreaks in such circumstances has been experienced by Americans, who are facing turmoil precisely because of racial ethnocentrism.

To counter the lack of objectivity of an ethnocentric approach, social scientists have suggested the alternative concept of *cultural relativity*. According to this concept, each culture is judged on its own terms, in the context of its own societal setting. No one is given the right to use the values and norms of his own culture to judge any trait of another culture. In other words, there are no universal norms, or moral absolutes. Under specific circumstances, any act can appear good or bad, and therefore any judgment we make of the act must be based on the context of the specific circumstance. In addition, cultural relativity requires that any act, even if it is completely contrary to one's own norms, should be regarded positively if it fulfills the needs or satisfies the goals of the society in which it is performed.

Unfortunately, some implications of cultural relativity are troublesome. For instance, if we accept this concept, are we to condone Nazi Germany's attempt to annihilate millions of people simply because the Nazis believed that the mass murder of people they considered inferior would benefit their society? Isn't the act of annihilating millions of people wrong under any circumstances?[7]

Questions like these have bothered many people, as well they should, for they appear to be unsolvable. All we can say, then, is that cultural relativity requires its followers to display tolerance and understanding of cultural features as they appear in societal settings. It does not require its followers to agree that a feature is good or to condone it in any way. Tolerance, respect, and understanding of cultural values, not their acceptance, is the objective of cultural relativity.

Theories of Cultural Differences

Adventurers, missionaries, and even some early anthropologists, unaware of the dangers of ethnocentrism, brought home tales of the fantastic and savage customs of the peoples they encountered in their travels. Not until social scientists used the scientific method in their research did they construct theories that attempted to solve the puzzle of cultural differences.

Some of these early theories were based on a racial explanation of cultural differences. But we now know that race is the result of biological differences and that we cannot explain a social product such as culture on the basis of biology.

Other theorists gave a geographic explanation of cultural differences, claiming that climate, elevation, topography, nearness to or isolation from other societies, and kinds of foods available were responsible for cultural variations. Much of the variation among cultures is, in fact, the result of geography. An Eskimo child will not be taught to build dwellings made out of palm fronds, nor will an inhabitant of the Amazonian region be taught how to build igloos.

Yet all cultural variation cannot be explained by geography. Societies located at great distances from each other have developed a number of cultural similarities, whereas societies located in the same area have often developed very dissimilar cultural patterns. A frequently used example of the latter circumstance is provided by two Indian tribes living in the American Southwest. Although the Hopi and the Navaho are neighboring tribes, the Hopi devote their time to peaceful pursuits, whereas the Navaho are warlike; the Hopi are sedentary and agricultural, the Navaho nomadic and pastoral; Hopi men have one wife, and Navaho men many wives. Allowing for the obvious influences of geography, then, cultural variations must, to a large extent, be the result of chance.

Culture, like an individual, is not changeless. Culture is an ongoing process, in which new elements are continually being added on to the elements already possessed. Thus, if a culture has adopted a given characteristic—peacefulness, violence, creativity, or whatever—that trend is not easily reversed, although, of course, it can be.

[7]Such issues are explored further in Robert Redfield, *The Primitive World and Its Transformations* (Ithaca, N.Y.: Cornell University Press, 1953), pp. 139-164 passim.

Cultural Universals

As striking as some cultural differences appear to us, a close examination of cultures shows us that there are also remarkable similarities. The similarities are particularly apparent in institutions, for institutions arise in response to biological and emotional needs shared by all humans. As an example, all social groups must regulate sexual relations to prevent haphazard reproduction and to provide for the welfare of offspring. Thus, the institution of the family exists in all known cultures.

Of course, the form that institutions assume varies greatly from society to society. In some societies, marriage takes a polygynous form (the male is permitted many wives); in others, a monogamous form (the male is permitted only one wife at a time); and in still others, it is polyandric (the woman is permitted more than one husband at a time). In like manner, kinship is traced through the father in some societies and through the mother in others. In some societies, the family institution performs almost all functions—including those of education, economics, and social control—whereas in others, separate institutions perform these functions.

Not only do institutional forms vary but all the other culture traits and complexes surrounding the institution also vary. The countless traditions and rituals that have developed around the family institution—puberty rites, marriageable age, the value placed on women and so on—differ greatly from society to society.

Cultural norms, values, and beliefs are also unexpectedly similar. All people enjoy adorning themselves, whether they wear a ring through their noses or on their little fingers; all people seem to have some taboo regarding a particular food, whether it is pork or dog; all people have some form of music and dancing and some form of art or handicraft; all people indulge in superstitious beliefs of one kind or another; and so on. The social anthropologist George P. Murdock compiled a long list of elements common to all known cultures. The list, prepared in alphabetical order, includes numerous and widely differing elements from age-grading to weather control.

Similarities common to all cultures are called *cultural universals*. They are general themes on which each culture develops its own variations. For example, Murdock included hospitality on his list of cultural universals. In the Eskimo culture, a hospitable host lends his wife out for the night; in the Chinese culture, a host feels obligated to give away any object admired by his guest; in the Arabic culture, no host is satisfied until his dinner guest approves the meal with a hearty belch. What is significant, however, is that the cultural universal of hospitality is present in all societies.

SUBCULTURES AND COUNTERCULTURES

Thus far, we have discussed culture on a societal level, noting uniformities and variations among whole societies. However, uniformities and variations also occur among the groups that make up a society. This is especially true of the heterogeneous, technologically developed societies that are beginning to predominate in the modern world.

Subcultures

In our society, which is extremely heterogeneous, groups are formed according to the members' race, ethnicity, religion, and numerous other distinguishing features. Even in homogeneous societies, in which members belong to the same ethnic and religious groups, people form additional groups based on the region in which they live, their occupation, their social class, their sex, and their age. Such groups are called subcultures. A *subculture* has distinctive features that set it apart from the wider culture of the society; yet it retains the principal features of the general culture.

The word "subculture" never implies any inferiority to the larger culture; it simply distinguishes a subdivision of it. As a matter of fact, membership in a subculture enriches an individual's life because it provides him with additional alternatives with which he can reach society's goals.

Because our society contains a number of subcultures, almost all of us have been brought up within one. For example, American teenagers form a subculture. They remain within the general framework of the overall culture and are guided by its patterns of behavior. At the same time, some of their interests and behavior are peculiar to their age group: teenagers have a special language, a distinctive manner of dress, a taste for particular kinds of music, and a fondness for particular foods.

In some instances, a single family may develop patterns of behavior that are sufficiently distinctive to qualify it as a subculture—for example, some of the families described in William Faulkner's novels and Tennessee Williams's plays. In other instances, a subculture may consist of people forgotten by time (or people who have forgotten time). The Amish and even the people of Appalachia speak, behave, and hold the values of their pioneer predecessors.

Often, subcultures arise around a particular occupation. The families of professional military men, astronauts, and even university professors (especially in small university towns) may, in some cases, be considered subcultures. Musicians, whether of the jazz, rock, or classical variety, form subcultures, too. Institutions—the school, the military, the government—develop behavior patterns and a language that may be considered subcultural.

The world of entertainment—show business—is another example of a subculture. Part of it is the sport/entertainment (some might argue that it is neither) world of wrestling. Wrestling, according to our article "Friday Night in the Coliseum," has many faithful supporters. The author, sociologist William C. Martin, explores this subculture, describing both the performers and the spectators, as well as the special world in which both operate. The article illustrates the richness of our culture, which includes elements many of us do not even know exist and certainly would not consider "cultural." It also points to the exotic quality of some of our subcultures—a quality that is sometimes difficult to detect under the equalizing mantle of the mass media.[8]

As exotic as a particular subculture may seem, however, it acts upon the general culture. The relationship between the overall culture of a society and its subcultures is not static. There is a continuous flow of influence from culture to subcultures, and vice versa. For example, the jargon of the jazz musician eventually found its way to the general public, as the jargon of the rock musician is doing today.

The United States is not the only society containing colorful subcultures. The Soviet Union, which is equally heterogeneous, contains many such groups. The article "Why They Live to Be 100, or Even Older, in Abkhasia," by anthropologist Sula Benet, is an interesting description of one Russian subculture. The Abkhasians have not only a language and behavior patterns peculiarly their own but they also seem to have found a formula for longevity.[9]

Countercultures

Some groups within a society possess a value system and goals that are in direct opposition to those of the larger culture. Such groups may or may not have other distinguishing features. In any case, these groups are not subcultures but contracultures, or *countercultures*. Some criminal groups may be considered countercultures, although not all, for many criminals accept the final goals of our society and reject only the means of attaining them.

In recent years, a countercultural movement has sprung from the ranks of young people, especially university students. The movement seems to have lost some of its initial momentum—witness the disappearance of the "flower children"—but it has created groups in our society that are definitely countercultures. These countercultures are made up of hippies, commune-dwellers, and others who find material goals and a complex technology that is designed to increase the standard of living completely irrelevant and of negative value. Members of today's countercultures express their views strongly and use parts of the mass media—primarily the press and music—to preach their gospel.

[8]William C. Martin, "Friday Night In The Coliseum," *Atlantic* (March, 1972), pp. 83-87.
[9]Sula Benet, "Why They Live to Be 100, or Even Older, in Abkhasia," *New York Times Magazine* (December 26, 1971), pp. 3 passim.

SUMMARY

The interacting human groups that were described in Chapter 1 as providing the basis of social structure are usually examined in the context of the largest social order, society. A society is a fairly large group of individuals who interact with one another on a regular, continuous basis and according to patterns of behavior on which all more or less agree. It is also an interrelated network of social relationships that exist within the largest social system. The members of a society lead a common, total life. In other words, of all groups, a society has the highest degree of self-sufficiency, or the least degree of dependence on other groups. Today, most societies correspond to the national political state.

Sociologists usually classify societies according to either their chief mode of subsistence, or their basic patterns of social organization. For several hundred years, societies have been moving from the traditional model toward the modern industrial model, which is characterized by great numbers of people, heavy reliance on secondary relationships, and emphasis on institutional forms.

The most important product of the interaction occurring in societies is culture. Culture is both the way of life of a people and the product of and guide for social interaction. Culture has both material content—tangible objects—and nonmaterial content—ideas, values, knowledge, and beliefs. Much of a society's nonmaterial culture is made up of norms, rules of behavior that are learned and shared by each member of the society through interaction. Norms include folkways, mores, and laws.

To examine culture as a structure, we may divide it into traits (the smallest units of culture), culture complexes (a number of related traits), and institutions. Institutions are formal systems of beliefs and behavior, composed of interrelated norms and culture complexes. Institutions primarily center on and help to fulfill universal human needs. Five basic institutions are common to all human societies: the family, the economy, education, government, and religion.

At a societal level, cultures display differences. Foreign cultures may appear irrational and silly if they are judged by the standards of one's own culture. This way of judging is called cultural ethnocentrism and is practiced, to some extent, by all social groups. The concept of cultural relativity counteracts ethnocentrism by requiring that each culture be judged in its societal context and on the basis of how well it fulfills its members' needs.

Cultural differences among societies are the result of geographic and other factors, of which little is known. The similar characteristics displayed by cultures arise because all cultures must help to fulfill universal human needs, both biological and emotional. Characteristics common to all cultures are called cultural universals.

Because societies are made up of varying groups, culture also varies within a single society. Groups within a society may be formed on the basis of geographic location, social class, occupation, race, ethnicity, religion, and so on. Individual groups, may have their own culture, including their own language or jargon, customs, traditions, and ritual. If the principal features of such a group are the same as those of the general culture, the group is called a subculture. If the principal values are in direct opposition to those of the larger culture, the group is called a counterculture.

WILLIAM C. MARTIN

friday night in the coliseum

The word "culture" suggests to many of us Leonard Bernstein directing the New York Philharmonic. But does it suggest wrestling, with contenders called Killers, Bruisers, Bulls and Mad Dogs? As a matter of fact, wrestling is as much a part of American culture as is classical music. What is more, this specialized activity, midway between a sport and entertainment, has given origin to a subculture embracing both performers and spectators. Rice University sociologist William C. Martin presents a masterful exploration of this subculture.

□□□

"When I die, I want to be cremated, and I want my ashes scattered in the Coliseum on Friday night. It's in my will." Thus spoke a little old lady who hasn't missed a Friday night wrestling match for—well, she's not exactly sure, but "it's been a long time, son, a long time." On Friday night, fifty times a year, more than 6500 fans stream into the Coliseum in downtown Houston for promoter Paul Boesch's weekly offering of Crushers, Killers, Bruisers, and Butchers, Commies, Nazis, Japs, and A-rabs, Dukes, Lords, and Barons, Professors and Doctors, Cowboys and Indians, Spoilers and Sissies, Farmers and Lumberjacks, Bulls and Mad Dogs, Masked Men and Midgets, Nice Girls and Bitches, and at least one Clean-cut, Finely Muscled Young Man who never fights dirty until provoked beyond

Reprinted from *The Atlantic Monthly*, March 1972. Copyright William C. Martin and Geoff Winningham. This material was prepared in collaboration with Geoff Winningham.

reason and who represents the Last, Best, Black, Brown, Red, or White Hope for Truth, Justice, and the American Way.

Though scoffed at by much of the public as a kind of gladiatorial theater in which showmanship counts for more than genuine athletic skill, professional wrestling enjoys steadily increasing success not only in Houston but in hundreds of tank towns and major cities all over America. This is not, of course, the first time around. Pro wrestling has been part of the American scene for more than a century and has enjoyed several periods of wide popularity. For most fans over thirty, however, it began sometime around 1949, with the arrival of television. Lou Thesz was world champion in those days, but the man who symbolized professional wrestling to most people was Gorgeous George, a consummate exhibitionist whose long golden curls, brocade and satin robes, and outrageously effeminate manner drew huge crowds wherever he went, all hoping to see a local he-man give him the beating he so obviously deserved.

The Gorgeous One's success at the box office ushered in a new era of wrestler-showmen, each trying to appear more outrageous than the others. For many, villainy has provided the surest route to fame and fortune. The overwhelming majority of professional wrestling matches pit the Good, the Pure, and the True against the Bad, the Mean, and the Ugly, and a man with a flair for provoking anger and hatred has an assured future in the sport. Since shortly after World War II, the most dependable source of high displeasure has been the Foreign Menace, usually an unreconstructed Nazi or a wily Japanese who insults the memory of our boys in uniform with actions so contemptuous one cannot fail to be proud that our side won the war.

Houston's most recent Nazi was Baron von Raschke, a snarling Hun with an Iron Cross on his cape and red swastikas on his shoes, who acknowledged his prefight introductions with a sharply executed goose step. Raschke, however, managed to make one think of George Lincoln Rockwell more often than Hitler or Goebbels, and so never really achieved first-class menacehood. It must be disappointing to be a Nazi and not have people take you seriously.

Now, Japs, especially Big Japs, are a different story. For one thing, they all know karate and can break railroad ties with their bare hands. For another, they are sneaky. So when Toru Tanaka climbs into the ring in that red silk outfit with the dragon on the back, and bows to the crowd and smiles that unspeakably wicked smile, and then caps it off by throwing salt all over everything in a ceremony designed to win the favor of god knows how many of those pagan deities Japanese people worship, you just know that nice young man up there in the ring with him is in serious trouble.

Another major Foreign Menace is, of course, the Russian. Russian wrestlers are named Ivan, Boris, or Nikita, and although they have defected from Russia in quest of a few capitalist dollars, they still retain a lot of typically Communist characteristics, like boasting that Russians invented certain well-known wrestling techniques and predicting flatly that the World Champion's belt will one day hang from the Kremlin wall. Furthermore, they value nothing unless it serves their own selfish aims. After a twenty-year partnership with Lord Charles Montague, Boris Malenko states flatly, "I owe his lordship nothing. Remember one thing about us Russians. When we have no more use for anybody or anything, we let them go. Friendship means nothing to a Russian. When we get through with the Arabs and Castro, you will see what I mean. When we want something we don't care who we step on."

Wrestling fans are generally an egalitarian lot, at least among themselves, and they do not appreciate those who put on airs. So they are easily angered by another strain of crowd displeaser one might call Titled Snobs and Pointy-Headed Intellectuals. These villains, who love to call themselves "Professor" or "Doctor" or "Lord" Somebody-or-other, use the standard bag of tricks—pulling a man down by his hair, rubbing his eyes with objects secreted in trunks or shoes, stomping his face while he lies wounded and helpless—but their real specialty is treating the fans like ignorant yahoos. They walk and speak with disdain for common folk, and never miss a chance to belittle the crowd in sesquipedalian put-downs or to declare that their raucous and uncouth behavior calls for nothing less than a letter to the *Times*, to inform proper Englishmen of the deplorable state of manners in the Colonies.

A third prominent villain is the Big Mean Sonofabitch, Dick the Bruiser, Cowboy Bill Watts, Butcher Vachone, Killer Kowalski—these men do not need swastikas and monocles and big words to make you hate them. They have the bile of human meanness by the quart in every vein. If a guileless child hands a Sonofabitch a program to autograph, he will often brush it aside or tear it into pieces and throw it on the floor. It isn't that he has forgotten what it was like to be a child. As a child, he kicked crutches from under crippled newsboys and cheated on tests and smoked in the rest room. Now, at 260 pounds, he goes into the ring not just to win, but to injure and maim. Even before the match begins, he attacks his trusting opponent from behind, pounding his head into the turn-buckle, kicking him in the kidneys, stomping him in the groin, and generally seeking to put him at a disadvantage. These are bad people. None of us is really safe as long as they go unpunished.

Fortunately, these hellish legions do not hold sway unchallenged by the forces of Right. For every villain there is a hero who seeks to hold his own against what seem to be incredible odds. Heroes also fall into identifiable categories. Most of them are trim and handsome young men in their twenties or early thirties, the sort that little boys want to grow up to be, and men want to have as friends, and women want to have, also. Personable Bobby Shane wins hearts when he wrestles in his red, white, and blue muscle suit with the "USA" monogram; and when Tim Woods, dressed all in white, is introduced as a graduate of Michigan State University, older folk nod approvingly. They want their sons and grandsons to go to college, even though they didn't have a chance to go themselves, and it is reassuring to see living proof that not everybody who goes to college is out burning draft cards and blowing up banks.

Though quick to capitalize on the jingoist appeal of matches involving Menacing Foreigners, few promoters will risk a match that might divide the house along racial lines. So black and brown wrestlers usually appear in the role of Hero, behind whom virtually the entire crowd can unite. Browns—Mexicans, Mexican-Americans, and Puerto Ricans—are almost invariably handsome, lithe, and acrobatic. They fight "scientifically" and seldom resort to roughhouse tactics until they have endured so much that the legendary Latin temper can no longer be contained. If a black chooses to play the villain, he will soften the racial element; when Buster Lloyd, the Harlem Hangman, came into town, he belittled the skills of his opponents not because they were white, but because they were Texans and therefore little challenge for a man who learned to fight at the corner of Lenox Avenue and 125th Street. Several white grapplers might have been able to handle Buster, but the hero selected to take his measure and send him packing back to Harlem was Tiger Conway, a black Texan.

The purest of pure Americans, of course, and a people well acquainted with villainy, are Red Indians. Most wrestling circuits feature a Red Indian from time to time; in Houston, ex-Jets linebacker Chief Wahoo McDaniel is the top attraction and has wrestled in the Coliseum more than a hundred times in the last three years. Like Chief White Owl, Chief Suni War Cloud, and Chief Billy Two Rivers, Wahoo enters the ring in moccasin-style boots, warbonnet, and other Indian authentica. He can endure great pain and injustice without flinching or retaliating in kind, but when enraged, or sometimes just to get the old adrenaline going, he will zip into a furious war dance and level his opponent with a series of karate-like Tomahawk Chops to the chest or scalp, then force him into submission with the dreaded Choctaw Death Lock.

Although no Nazi fights clean and few Red Indians fight dirty, not all wrestlers can be characterized so unambiguously. The Masked Man, for example, is sinister-looking, and usually evil, with a name indicative of his intentions: The Destroyer, The Assassin, The Hangman, and Spoilers One, Two, and Three. But some masked men, like Mr. Wrestling and Mil Mascaras (who stars in Mexican movies as a masked crime-fighting wrestler), are great favorites, and Clawman has tried to dignify mask-wearing by having Mrs. Clawman and the Clawchildren sit at ringside in matching masks.

The majority of Houston's wrestling fans appear to be working-class folk. The white and Mexican-American men still wear crew cuts and well-oiled pompadours, and many black men and boys cut their hair close to the scalp. Family men, often with several children in tow, wear Perma-Prest slacks and plaid sport shirts with the T-shirt showing at the neck. Others, who stand around before the matches drinking Lone Star Beer and looking for friendly ladies, favor cowboy boots, fancy Levis, and Western shirts with the top two or three pearl buttons already unsnapped. Occasionally, a black dude in a purple jump suit and gold ruffled shirt shows up, but the brothers in nondescript trousers and short-sleeve knits far outnumber him. The women cling stubbornly to bouffant hairstyles, frequently in shades blonder or redder or blacker than hair usually gets, and at least 80 percent wear pants of some sort.

One basic reason these people come to the Coliseum is reflected in the motto displayed in Boesch's office: "Professional Wrestling: the sport that gives you your money's worth." Approximately half the Houston cards feature at least one championship bout or a battle for the right to meet the men's, women's, midgets', tag-team, or Brass Knucks champion of Texas, the United States, or the World. If fans grow jaded with championships, Boesch adds extra wrestlers to produce two-, three-, and four-man team matches, heavyweight-midget teams, man-woman teams, and Battles Royale, in which ten men try to throw each other over the top rope, the grand prize going to the last man left in the ring.

Grudge matches, of course, are the backbone of professional wrestling, and Boesch's skillful exploitation of grudges allows him to draw large crowds and to use wrestlers like Johnny Valentine and Wahoo McDaniel over and over again without having the fans grow weary of them. Men fight grudge matches for many reasons, all of which are elaborately developed in the printed programs and on televised threat-and-insult sessions during intermissions.

They fight to uphold the honor of former associates, as when ex-gridders Ernie Ladd and Wahoo took on Valentine and Killer Karl Kox after the veteran wrestlers called them "big dumb football players" who did not have brains enough to engage in "the sport of the intelligentsia." They fight to avenge wrongs done to members of their family, as when Wild Bull Curry demanded to meet Valentine after the ruffian injured Wild Bull's popular son, Flying Freddy Curry, also known as Bull, Jr. And, in expression of a grudge more generic than personal, they fight to re-establish American supremacy over Foreign Menaces, as when Valentine turned hero-for-a-night by flying in from Asia to repay Toru Tanaka for the punishment the Dirty Jap had been handing out to the local heroes.

But not all grudge matches are fought for such lofty ideals. When Killer Karl Kox and Killer Kowalski wound up in Houston at the same time, they fought for the exclusive right to wear the nickname. In another long rivalry, marked by low but engaging comedy, Boris Malenko sought to humiliate Wahoo, who had kicked out several of the Russian's teeth a few weeks before, by challenging him to a match in which the loser's head would be shaved in the ring immediately afterward. Malenko lost, suffered the jeers of the fans for several weeks —"Hey, Baldy, why don't you go back to Russia?"—then challenged Wahoo to a rematch, the loser of which was to leave the state for a full year. The Russian, who had made himself doubly hateful by assuming the title of Professor, promised to punish Wahoo with his new steel dentures, and fans anguished over the possibility that their favorite Indian might bite the dust. Happily, Wahoo won the match, and Boris allegedly caught the first bus to Lake Charles, Louisiana.

To keep fans from tiring of a grudge series before it has yielded its full potential, promoters enhance the appeal of rematches by scheduling them under special rules and conditions that are something of a drawing card in themselves. The circumstances of previous matches often determine the conditions of the next. If one was decided by a questionable use of the ropes, the next might be fought with the ropes removed. If a cowardly villain frustrated a hero's attempt at vengeance by leaving the ring when the going got tough, he might find his way to safety blocked in the next match by a chain-link fence or a posse of eight or ten wrestlers stationed around the ring.

If Wahoo is involved, at least one match in the series will be an Indian Strap Match, in which the opponents are linked to each other by an eight-foot strap of rawhide. The strap can be used to beat, choke, and jerk, and the winner is the first man to drag his opponent around the ring twice. The Russian Chain Match is based on the same principle, but an eight-foot length of heavy chain is considerably more dangerous than a strip of leather.

For guaranteed action, however, none of these can equal a Texas Death Match. In this surefire crowd-pleaser, usually arranged after several battles have failed to establish which of the two rivals is tougher, there are no time limits, no specified number of falls, no grounds for disqualification. A victor is declared when one of the wrestlers can no longer continue, usually because he lies unconscious somewhere in or around the ring. Fans seldom leave a Texas Death Match without feeling they got their money's worth.

For many regulars, Friday night at the Coliseum is the major social event of the week. All over the arena blacks, browns, and whites visit easily across ethnic lines, in perverse defiance of stereotypes about blue-collar prejudices. A lot of people in the ringside section know each other, by sight if not by name. Mrs. Elizabeth Chappell, better known simply as "Mama," has been coming to the matches for more than twenty-five years. Between bouts, she walks around the ring, visiting with old friends and making new ones. When she beats on a fallen villain with a huge mallet she carries in a shopping bag, folks shout, "Attaway, Mama! Git him!" and agree that "things don't really start to pick up till Mama gets here." When a dapper young insurance salesman flies into a rage at a referee's decision, the fans nudge one another and grin about how "old Freddy really gets worked up, don't he?"

The importance of the opportunity to eat

and drink and laugh and scream in the company of one's peers should not be underestimated, but at least two other basic drives manifest themselves quite clearly on Friday night: Sex and Aggression.

For women in a culture that provides its men with a disproportionate share of visual aids to sexual fantasy, the wrestling matches offer some redress. With little effort, an accomplished voyeuress can find considerable stimulation in the spectacle of husky gladiators of varied hues hugging, holding, and hurting one another while clad in nothing but boots and colored trunks that sometimes get pulled daringly low.

Male fans in search of similar titillation have fewer opportunities for fulfillment, since there are simply not enough girl wrestlers to enable promoters to book even one ladies' bout each week. But when they are scheduled, they make every effort not to disappoint. Whatever else may happen in a girls' match, certain maneuvers are inevitable. Hair will be pulled, first by the tough, dark-haired grapplerette in the gaudy-sparkly black suit, then by the sweeter looking blond youngster in the white outfit. Each girl will treat the other to a form of punishment known as the Keester Bump, in which the bumpee is bounced sharply on her behind, producing a pain that requires extensive patting and rubbing. And finally, one or both girls will manage somehow to roll over the referee virtually every time he lies down beside them to check their shoulders or start the three-count.

Some women fans seem to enjoy these antics as much as the men; throughout one contest, a laughing middle-aged woman kept elbowing her husband and asking him, "How'd you like me to do that to you?" But others openly resent them, as did the young bride who said, "My husband is the only one I know that likes to watch the women. I really don't know why. This is a sport for men. Only thing I can figure is he's waiting for something to fall out."

Professional wrestling offers fans an almost unparalleled opportunity to indulge aggressive and violent impulses. A few appreciate the finer points of a takedown or a switch or a Fireman's Carry, but most would walk out on the NCAA wrestling finals or a collegiate match between Lehigh and Oklahoma. They want hitting and kicking and stomping and bleeding. Especially bleeding.

Virtually all bouts incite a high level of crowd noise, but the sight of fresh blood streaming from a wrestler's forehead immediately raises the decibel level well into the danger zone. This is what they came to see. If both men bleed, what follows is nothing less than orgiastic frenzy. Mere main events and world championships and tag-team matches eventually run together to form murky puddles in the back regions of the mind, but no one forgets the night he saw real blood. One woman recalled such a peak experience in tones that seemed almost religious: "One night, about six or seven years ago, Cowboy Ellis was hit against the post and got three gashes in his head. I grabbed him when he rolled out of the ring and got blood on my dress all the way from the neckline to the hem. I thought he would bleed to death in my arms. I never washed that dress. I've still got it at the house. I keep it in a drawer all by itself."

The lust for blood is not simply ghoulish, but a desire to witness the stigmata, the apparently irrefutable proof that what is seen is genuine. Wrestling fans freely acknowledge that much of the action is faked, that many punches are pulled, that the moisture that flies through the air after a blow is not sweat but spit, and that men blunt the full effect of stomping opponents by allowing the heel to hit the canvas before the ball of the foot slaps the conveniently outstretched arm. They not only acknowledge the illusion; they jeer when it is badly performed: "Aw my goodness! He can't even make it look good!" Still, they constantly try to convince themselves and each other that at least part of what they are seeing on a given night is real. When Thunderbolt Patterson throws Bobby Shane through the ropes onto the concrete, a woman shouts defiantly, "Was that real? Tell me that wasn't real!" And when Johnny Valentine and Ernie Ladd are both disqualified after a three-fall slugfest, a young man tells his buddy, "I think that was real. You know sometimes they do get mad. One time Killer Kowalski got so mad he tore old Yukon Eric's ear plumb off." But when blood flows, no one seeks or needs confirmation.

The effects on fans of viewing such violence are disputed. Some experiments with children and college students offer evidence that observing violent behavior either produces no change or raises the level of aggressive tendencies in the spectator. Other research, however, indicates that wrestling fans do experience a decrease in aggressive tendencies after viewing wrestling matches. Still, manipulating hatred and aggressive tendencies is not without its risks. Every wrestler has seen or heard about the time when some fan went berserk and clubbed or burned or cut or shot a villain who played his role too convincingly, and Tim Woods, it is said, has had only nine fingers since the night a challenger from the audience grabbed his hand, bit down extra hard, and spat the tenth out onto the mat. Then, too, the possibility always exists that in the highly charged atmosphere of the arena, a wrestler may lose control of himself and cause real damage to his opponent. If he were alive today, old Yukon Eric could tell you something about that.

At the Coliseum, as elsewhere, excitement, community, sex, and violence find their place in the context of a larger world view. One does not have to watch many matches or talk to many fans to sense that the action in the ring functions as a kind of quasi-religious ritual in which the hopes and fears of the gathered faithful are reflected in the symbolic struggle of Good and Evil. This ritual quality may help explain the indifference of fans to what happens at matches they do not see, either in person or on television. They may know that the same men they watch on Friday in Houston will wrestle on the other nights of the week, in some of the same combinations, in Fort Worth, Dallas, Austin, San Antonio, and Corpus Christi, but they do not care. It is not enough—it really isn't anything—that Wahoo defeat Tanaka in Fort Worth. For the event to have significance, for the ritual to work its power, it must occur on Friday Night in the Coliseum.

The Portrayal of Life that unfolds in the ring is no naïve melodrama in which virtue always triumphs and cheaters never win. Whatever else these folk know, they know that life is tough and filled with conflict, hostility, and frustration. For every man who presses toward the prize with pure heart and clean hands, a dozen Foreigners and so-called Intellectuals and Sonsofbitches seek to bring him down with treachery and brute force and outright meanness. And even if he overcomes these, there are other, basically decent men who seek to defeat him in open competition.

Nothing illustrates the frustrations of the climb to the top more clearly than the Saga of Wahoo McDaniel. For three years, Wahoo has been a top challenger for the National Wrestling Alliance world championship owned by Dory Funk, Jr. A quiet and rather colorless man, who still wears his letter jacket from West Texas State rather than the theatrical garb favored by his rivals, Funk is rough but seldom really dirty, and he knows what he is doing in the ring. Folks may not particularly like him, but they have to respect him. He is no fluke champion, and they know that neither Wahoo nor anyone else can be Number One until he has defeated Dory Funk, Jr., fair and square.

They believe Wahoo can do just that. Wahoo believes it himself and on a dozen occasions has come within seconds of proving it, only to have what seemed certain victory snatched from his hands. Two of their matches ended in a draw. Wahoo lost a third when the referee missed an obvious pin. Funk was disqualified in their next meeting, but titles do not change hands on disqualifications. The champion then won a Texas Death Match by knocking Wahoo out cold with a steel folding chair, a legal but grossly unsportsmanlike tactic.

Two years after they first met, Wahoo and Dory are still at it. In their latest match, the third fall apparently ended with Wahoo the winner and new champion, but as he danced around the ring in triumph, the timekeeper informed the referee that Dory's feet had been over the bottom rope, thus nullifying the decision. The referee ordered the match to continue, but Wahoo missed the signal and Funk grabbed him from behind to gain a quick pin. Fans fumed and screamed, then filed out in silent despair. Long after most of them were gone, Freddy the insurance salesman maintained a noisy vigil at ringside, beating on the mat and shouting to nobody in particular, "People paid good money to come see this, and the damn referee is so stupid he has to ask the timekeeper what happened. There's got to be a rematch."

There will be, Freddy, there will be. And some day, if he actually is the best man, Wahoo will win. Life has its temporary setbacks and disappointments, to be sure, but we can be confident that over the long haul men eventually get what they truly deserve, genuine ability is always rewarded, and the scales of justice ultimately balance. For life is like that, too, isn't it? Isn't it?

SULA BENET

why they live to be 100,
or even older, in abkhasia

We know that the United States contains many groups, particularly of a racial and ethnic kind, with behavioral patterns and other features that are sufficiently distinct from the "average" American culture to be called subcultures. But the societies in the rest of the world seem to us solidly homogeneous—they are made up of Frenchmen, Russians, or Germans. In reality, of course, subcultures exist in all societies. An unusual subculture is described by anthropologist Sula Benet, a professor at Hunter College, New York City. She has spent a great deal of time as a participant in and an observer of a long-living group of people in the Caucasus.

□□□

Not long ago, in the village of Tamish in the Soviet Republic of Abkhasia, I raised my glass of wine to toast a man who looked no more than 70. "May you live as long as Moses (120 years)," I said. He was not pleased. He was 119.

For centuries, the Abkhasians and other Caucasian peasants have been mentioned in the chronicles of travelers amazed at their longevity and good health. Even now, on occasion, newspaper reports in the United States and elsewhere (never quite concealing bemusement and skepticism) will tell of an Abkhasian who claims to be 120, sometimes 130. When I returned from Abkhasia to New York displaying photographs and statistics, insisting that the tales are true and preoc-

From the *New York Times Magazine*, December 26, 1971. © 1971 by The New York Times Company. Reprinted by permission.

cupied with the question of why, my American friends invariably responded with the mocking question that contained its own answer: "Yogurt?" As a matter of fact, no, not yogurt; but the Abkhasians *do* drink a lot of buttermilk.

Abkhasia is a hard land—the Abkhasians, expressing more pride than resentment, say it was one of God's afterthoughts—but it is a beautiful one; if the Abkhasians are right about its mythical origin, God had a good second thought. It is subtropical on its coast along the Black Sea, alpine if one travels straight back from the sea, through the populated lowlands and valleys, to the main range of the Caucasus Mountains.

The Abkhasians have been there for at least 1,000 years. For centuries they were herdsmen in the infertile land, but now the valleys and foothills are planted with tea and tobacco, and they draw their living largely from agriculture. There are 100,000 Abkhasians, not quite a fifth of the total population of the autonomous Abkhasian Republic, which is, administratively, part of Georgia, Joseph Stalin's birthplace; the rest are Russians, Greeks and Georgians. However, most of the people in government are Abkhasian, and both the official language and the style of life throughout the region are Abkhasian. The single city, Sukhumi, is the seat of government and a port of call for ships carrying foreign tourists. They are often visible in the streets of the city, whose population includes relatively few Abkhasians. Even those who live and work there tend to consider the villages of their families their own real homes. It is in the villages—575 of them between the mountains and the sea, ranging in population from a few hundred to a few thousand—that most Abkhasians live and work on collective farms.

I first went there in the summer of 1970 at the invitation of the Academy of Sciences of the USSR. The Abkhasians were fascinating; I returned last summer and will go again next year. It was while interviewing people who had participated in the early efforts at collectivization that I became aware of the unusually large number of people, ranging in age from 80 to 119, who are still very much a part of the collective life they helped organize.

After spending months with them, I still find it impossible to judge the age of older Abkhasians. Their general appearance does not provide a clue: You know they are old because of their gray hair and the lines on their faces, but are they 70 or 107? I would have guessed "70" for all of the old people that I encountered in Abkhasia, and most of the time I would have been wrong.

It is as if the physical and psychological changes which to us signify the aging process had, in the Abkhasians, simply stopped at a certain point. Most work regularly. They are still blessed with good eyesight, and most have their own teeth. Their posture is unusually erect, even into advanced age; many take walks of more than two miles a day and swim in the mountain streams. They look healthy, and they are a handsome people. Men show a fondness for enormous mustaches, and are slim but not frail. There is an old saying that when a man lies on his side, his waist should be so small that a dog can pass beneath it. The women are darkhaired and also slender, with fair complexions and shy smiles.

There are no current figures for the total number of aged in Abkhasia, though in the village of Dzhgerda, which I visited last summer, there were 71 men and 110 women between 81 and 90 and 19 people over 91—15 per cent of the village population of 1,200. And it is worth noting that this extraordinary percentage is not the result of a migration by the young: Abkhasians, young and old, understandably prefer to stay where they are, and rarely travel, let alone migrate. In 1954, the last year for which overall figures are available, 2.58 per cent of the Abkhasians were over 90. The roughly comparable figures for the entire Soviet Union and the United States were 0.1 per cent and 0.4 per cent, respectively.

Since 1932, the longevity of the Abkhasians has been systematically studied on several occasions by Soviet and Abkhasian investigators, and I was given full access to their findings by the Ethnographic Institute in Sukhumi. These studies have shown that, in general, signs of arteriosclerosis, when they occurred at all, were found only in extreme old age. One researcher who examined a group of Abkhasians over 90 found that close to 40 per cent of the men and 30 per cent of the women had vision good enough to read or thread a needle without glasses, and that over 40 per cent had reasonably good hearing. There were no reported cases of either mental illness or cancer in a nine-year study of 123 people over 100.

In that study, begun in 1960 by Dr. G. N. Sichinava of the Institute of Gerontology in Sukhumi, the aged showed extraordinary psychological and neurological stability. Most of them had clear recollection of the distant past, but partially bad recollection for more recent events. Some reversed this pattern, but quite a large number retained a good memory of both the recent and distant past. All correctly oriented themselves in time and place. All showed clear and logical thinking, and most correctly estimated their physical and mental capacities. They showed a lively interest in their families' affairs, in their collective and in social events. All were agile, neat and clean.

Abkhasians are hospitalized only rarely, except for stomach disorders and childbirth. According to doctors who have inspected their work, they are expert at setting broken arms and legs themselves—their centuries of horsemanship have given them both the need and the practice.

The Abkhasian view of the aging process is clear from their vocabulary. They do not have a phrase for "old people"; those over 100 are called "long living people." Death, in the Abkhasian view, is not the logical end of life but something irrational. The aged seem to lose strength gradually, wither in size and finally die; when that happens, Abkhasians show their grief fully, even violently.

For the rest of the world, disbelief is the response not to Abkhasians' deaths but to how long they have lived. There really should no longer be any question about their longevity. All of the Soviet medical investigators took great care to cross-check the information they received in interviews. Some of the men studied had served in the army, and military records invariably supported their own accounts. Extensive documentation is lacking only because the Abkhasians had no functioning written language until after the Russian Revolution.

But why *do* they live so long? The absence of a written history, and the relatively recent period in which medical and anthropological studies have taken place, preclude a clear answer. Genetic selectivity is an obvious possibility. Constant hand-to-hand combat during many centuries of Abkhasian existence may have eliminated those with poor eyesight, obesity and other physical shortcomings, producing healthier Abkhasians in each succeeding generation. But documentation for such an evolutionary process is lacking.

When I asked the Abkhasians themselves about their longevity, they told me they live as long as they do because of their practices in sex, work and diet.

The Abkhasians, because they expect to live long and healthy lives, feel it is necessary self-discipline to conserve their energies, including their sexual energy, instead of grasping what sweetness is available to them at the moment. They say it is the norm that regular sexual relations do not begin before the age of 30 for men, the traditional age of marriage; it was once even considered unmanly for a new husband to exercise his sexual rights on his wedding night. (If they are asked what is done to provide substitute gratification of normal sexual needs before marriage, Abkhasians smile and say, "Nothing," but it is not unreasonable to speculate that they, like everyone else, find substitutes for the satisfaction of healthy, heterosexual sex. Today, some young people marry in their mid-20's instead of waiting for the "proper" age of 30, to the consternation of their elders.)

Postponement of satisfaction may be smiled at, but so is the expectation of prolonged, future enjoyment, perhaps with more reason. One medical team investigating the sex life of the Abkhasians concluded that many men retain their sexual potency long after the age of 70, and 12.6 per cent of the women continue to menstruate after the age of 55.

Tarba Sit, 102, confided to me that he had waited until he was 60 to marry because while he was in the army "I had a good time right and left." At present, he said with some sadness, "I have a desire for my wife but no strength." One of his relatives had nine children, the youngest born when he was 100. Doctors obtained sperm from him when he was 119, in 1963, and he still retained his libido and potency. The only occasions on which medical investigators found discrepancies in the claimed ages of Abkhasians was when men insisted they were younger than they actually were. One said he was 95, but his daughter had a birth certificate proving she was 81, and other information indicated he was really 108. When he was confronted with the conflict he became angry and refused to discuss it, since he was about to get married. Makhti Tarkil, 104, with whom I spoke in the village of Duripsh, said the explanation was obvious in view of the impending marriage: "A man is a man until he is 100, you know what I mean. After that, well, he's getting old."

Abkhasian culture provides a dependent and secondary role for women; when they are young, their appearance is stressed, and when they are married, their service in the household is their major role. (As with other aspects of Abkhasian life, the period since the revolution has brought changes, and some women now work in the professions; but in the main, the traditions are still in force.) In the upbringing of a young woman, great care is taken to make her as beautiful as possible according to Abkhasian standards. In order to narrow her waist and keep her breasts small, she wears a leather corset around her chest and waist; the corset is permanently removed on her wedding night. Her complexion should be fair, her eyebrows thin; because a high forehead is also desirable, the hair over the brow is shaved and further growth is prevented through the application of bleaches and herbs. She should also be a good dancer.

Virginity is an absolute requirement for marriage. If a woman proves to have been previously deflowered, the groom has a perfect right to take her back to her family and have his marriage gifts returned. He always exercises that right, returning the bride and announcing to the family, "Take your dead one." And to him, as well as all other eligible men, she is dead: in Abkhasian society, she has been so dishonored by his rejection that it would be next to impossible to find a man to marry her. (Later on, however, she may be married off to an elderly widower or some other less desirable male from a distant village. When she is discovered, she is expected to name the guilty party. She usually picks the name of a man who has recently died, in order to prevent her family from taking revenge and beginning a blood feud.)

For both married and unmarried Abkhasians, extreme modesty is required at all times. There is an overwhelming feeling of uneasiness and shame over any public manifestation of sex, or even affection. A man may not touch his wife, sit down next to her or even talk to her in the presence of strangers. A woman's armpits are considered an erogenous zone and are never exposed, except to her husband.

A woman is a stranger, although a fully accepted one, in her husband's household. Her presence always carries the threat that her husband's loyalty to his family may be eroded by his passion for her. In the Abkhasian tradition, a woman may never change her dress nor bathe in the presence of her mother-in-law, and when an Abkhasian couple are alone in a room, they keep their voices low so that the husband's mother will not overhear them.

Despite the elaborate rules—perhaps, in part, because they are universally accepted —sex in Abkhasia is considered a good and pleasurable thing when it is strictly private. And, as difficult as it may be for the American mind to grasp, it is guiltless. It is not repressed or sublimated into work, art or religious-mystical passion. It is not an evil to be driven from one's thoughts. It is a pleasure to be regulated for the sake of one's health—like a good wine.

An Abkhasian is never "retired," a status unknown in Abkhasian thinking. From the beginning of life until its end, he does what he is capable of doing because both he and those around him consider work vital to life. He makes the demands on himself that he can meet, and as those demands diminish with age, his status in the community nevertheless increases.

In his nine-year study of aged Abkhasians, Dr. Sichinava made a detailed examination of their work habits. One group included 82 men,

most of whom had been working as peasants from the age of 11, and 45 women who, from the time of adolescence, had worked in the home and helped care for farm animals. Sichinava found that the work load had decreased considerably between the ages of 80 and 90 for 48 men, and between 90 and 100 for the rest. Among the women, 27 started doing less work between 80 and 90, and the others slowed down after 90. The few men who had been shepherds stopped following the herds up to the mountain meadows in spring, and instead began tending farm animals, after the age of 90. The farmers began to work less land; many stopped plowing and lifting heavy loads, but continued weeding (despite the bending involved) and doing other tasks. Most of the women stopped helping in the fields and some began to do less housework. Instead of serving the entire family—an Abkhasian family, extended through marriage, may include 50 or more people—they served only themselves and their children. But they also fed the chickens and knitted.

Dr. Sichinava also observed 21 men and 7 women over 100 years old and found that, on the average, they worked a four-hour day on the collective farm—the men weeding and helping with the corn crop, the women stringing tobacco leaves. Under the collective system, members of the community are free to work in their own gardens, but they get paid in what are, in effect, piecework rates for the work they do for the collective. Dr. Sichinava's group of villagers over 100, when they worked for the collective, maintained an hourly output that was not quite a fifth that of the norm for younger workers. But in maintaining their own pace, they worked more evenly and without waste motion, stopping on occasion to rest. By contrast, the younger men worked rapidly, but competitively and tensely. Competitiveness in work is not indigenous to Abkhasian culture but it is encouraged by the Soviet Government for the sake of increased production; pictures of the best workers are posted in the offices of the village collectives. It is too soon to predict whether this seemingly fundamental change in work habits will affect Abkhasian longevity.

The persistent Abkhasians have their own workers' heroes: Kelkiliana Khesa, a woman of 109 in the village of Otapi, was paid for 49 workdays (a collective's workday is eight hours) during one summer; Bozba Pash, a man of 94 on the same collective, worked 155 days one year; Minosyan Grigorii of Aragich, often held up as an example to the young, worked 230 days in a year at the age of 90. (Most Americans, with a two-week vacation and several holidays, work between 240 and 250 days, some of them less than eight hours, in a year.)

Both the Soviet medical profession and the Abkhasians agree that their work habits have a great deal to do with their longevity. The doctors say that the way Abkhasians work helps the vital organs function optimally. The Abkhasians say, "Without rest, a man cannot work; without work, the rest does not give you any benefit."

That attitude, though it is not susceptible to medical measurements, may be as important as the work itself. It is part of a consistent life pattern: When they are children, they do what they are capable of doing, progressing from the easiest to the most strenuous tasks, and when they age, the curve descends, but it is unbroken. The aged are never seen sitting in chairs for long periods, passive, like vegetables. They do what they can, and while some consider the piecework system of the collectives a form of exploitation, it does permit them to function at their own pace.

Overeating is considered dangerous in Abkhasia, and fat people are regarded as ill. When the aged see a younger Abkhasian who is even a little overweight, they inquire about his health. "An Abkhasian cannot get fat," they say. "Can you imagine the ridiculous figure one would cut on horseback?" But to the dismay of the elders, the young eat much more than their fathers and grandfathers do; light, muscular and agile horsemen are no longer needed as a first line of defense.

The Abkhasian diet, like the rest of life, is stable: investigators have found that people 100 years and older eat the same foods throughout their lives. They show few idiosyncratic preferences, and they do not significantly change their diet when their economic status improves. Their caloric intake is 23 per cent lower than that of the industrial workers in Abkhasia, though they consume twice as much vitamin C; the industrial workers have a much higher rate of coronary insufficiency and a higher level of cholesterol in the blood.

The Abkhasians eat without haste and with decorum. When guests are present, each person in turn is toasted with praise of his real or imaginary virtues. Such meals may last several hours, but nobody minds, since they prefer their food served lukewarm in any case. The food is cut into small pieces, served on platters, and eaten with the fingers. No matter what the occasion, Abkhasians take only small bites of food and chew those very slowly—a habit that stimulates the flow of ptyalin and maltase, insuring proper digestion of the carbohydrates which form the bulk of the diet. And, traditionally, there are no leftovers in Abkhasia; even the poor dispose of uneaten food by giving it to the animals, and no one would think of serving warmed over food to a guest—even if it had been cooked only two hours earlier. Though some young people, perhaps influenced by Western ideas, consider the practice wasteful, most Abkhasians shun day-old food as unhealthful.

The Abkhasians eat relatively little meat—perhaps once or twice a week—and prefer chicken, beef, young goat and, in the winter, pork. They do not like fish and, despite its availability, rarely eat it. The meat is always freshly slaughtered and either broiled or boiled to the absolute minimum—until the blood stops running freely or, in the case of chicken, until the meat turns white. It is, not surprisingly, tough in the mouth of a non-Abkhasian, but they have no trouble with it.

At all three meals, the Abkhasians eat *abista*, a corn meal mash cooked in water without salt, which takes the place of bread. *Abista* is eaten warm with pieces of homemade goat cheese tucked into it. They eat cheese daily, and also consume about two glasses of buttermilk a day. When eggs are eaten, which is not very often, they are boiled or fried with pieces of cheese.

The other staples in the Abkhasian diet— staple in Abkhasia means daily or almost so—include fresh fruits, especially grapes; fresh vegetables, including green onions, tomatoes, cucumbers and cabbage; a wide variety of pickled vegetables, and baby lima beans, cooked slowly for hours, mashed and served flavored with a sauce of onions, peppers, garlic, pomegranate juice and pepper. That hot sauce, or a variant of it, is set on the table in a separate dish for anyone who wants it. Large quantities of garlic are also always at hand.

Although they are the main suppliers of tobacco for the Soviet Union few Abkhasians smoke. (I did meet one, a woman over 100, who smoked constantly.) They drink neither coffee nor tea. But they do consume a locally produced, dry, red wine of low alcoholic content. Everyone drinks it almost always in small quantities, at lunch and supper, and the Abkhasians call it "life giving." Absent from their diet is sugar, though honey, a local product, is used. Toothaches are rare.

Soviet medical authorities who have examined the Abkhasians and their diet feel it may well add years to their lives; the buttermilk and pickled vegetables, and probably the wine, help destroy certain bacteria and, indirectly, prevent the development of arteriosclerosis, the doctors think. In 1970, a team of Soviet doctors and Dr. Samuel Rosen of New York, a prominent ear surgeon, compared the hearing of Muscovites and Abkhasians, and concluded that the Abkhasians' diet—very little saturated fat, a great deal of fruit and vegetables—also accounted for their markedly better hearing. The hot sauce is the only item most doctors would probably say "no" to, and apparently some Abkhasians feel the same way.

Although the Abkhasians themselves attribute their longevity to their work, sex and dietary habits, there is another, broader aspect of their culture that impresses an outsider in their midst: the high degree of integration in their lives, the sense of group identity that gives each individual an unshaken feeling of personal security and continuity, and permits the Abkhasians as a people to adapt themselves—yet preserve themselves—to the changing conditions imposed by the larger society in which they live. That sense of continuity in both their personal and national lives is what anthropologists would call their spatial and temporal integration.

Their spatial integration is in their kinship structure. It is, literally, the Abkhasians' all-encompassing design for living: it regulates relationships between families, determines where they live, defines the position of women and marriage rules. Through centuries of nonexistent or ineffective centralized authority, kinship was life's frame of reference, and it still is.

Kinship in Abkhasia is an elaborate, complex set of relationships based on patrilineage.

At its center is the family, extended through marriage by the sons; it also includes all those families which can be traced to a single progenitor; and, finally, to all persons with the same surname, whether the progenitor can be traced or not. As a result, an Abkhasian may be "kin" to several thousand people, many of whom he does not know. I first discovered the pervasiveness of kinship rules when my friend Omar, an Abkhasian who had accompanied me from Sukhumi to the village of Duripsh, introduced me to a number of people he called his brothers and sisters. When I had met more than 20 "siblings" I asked, "How many brothers and sisters do you have?"

"In this village, 30," he said. "Abkhasian reckoning is different from Russian. These people all carry my father's name."

I took his explanation less seriously than I should have. Later, when I expressed admiration for a recording of Abkhasian epic poetry I had heard in the home of one of Omar's "brothers," Omar, without a word, gave the record to me as a gift.

"Omar, it isn't yours," I said.

"Oh yes it is. This is the home of my brother," he said. When I appealed to the "brother," he said, "Of course he can give it to you. He is my brother."

The consanguineal and affinal relationships that make up the foundation of the kinship structure are supplemented by a variety of ritual relationships that involve lifetime obligations—and serve to broaden the human environment from which Abkhasians derive their extraordinary sense of security. Although there are no alternative life styles towards which the rebellious may flee, the Abkhasians are ready to absorb others into their own culture. During my visit, for instance, a Christian man was asked to be the godfather of a Moslem child; both prospective godfather and child were Abkhasians. When I expressed surprise, I was told, "It doesn't matter. We want to enlarge our circle of relatives."

The temporal integration of Abkhasian life is expressed in its general continuity, in the absence of limiting, defining conditions of existence like "unemployed," "adolescent," "alienated." Abkhasians are a life-loving, optimistic people, and unlike so many very old "dependent" people in the United States—who feel they are a burden to themselves and their families—they enjoy the prospect of continued life. One 99-year-old Abkhasian, Akhba Suleiman of the village of Achandara, told his doctor, "It isn't time to die yet. I am needed by my children and grandchildren, and it isn't bad in this world —except that I can't turn the earth over and it has become difficult to climb trees."

The old are always active. "It is better to move without purpose than to sit still," they say. Before breakfast, they walk through the homestead's courtyard and orchard, taking care of small tasks that come to their attention. They look for fences and equipment in need of repair and check on the family's animals. At breakfast, their early morning survey completed, they report what has to be done.

Until evening, the old spend their time alternating work and rest. A man may pick up wind-fallen apples, then sit down on a bench, telling stories or making toys for his grandchildren or great-grandchildren. Another chore which is largely attended to by the old is weeding the courtyard, a large green belonging to the homestead, which serves as a center of activity for the kin group. Keeping it in shape requires considerable labor, yet I never saw a courtyard that was not tidy and well-trimmed.

During the summer, many old men spend two or three months high in the mountains, living in shepherds' huts, helping to herd or hunting for themselves and the shepherds (with their arrested aging process, many are excellent marksmen despite their age). They obviously are not fearful of losing their authority during their absence; their time in the mountains is useful and pleasurable.

The extraordinary attitude of the Abkhasians—to feel needed at 99 or 110—is not an artificial, self-protective one; it is the natural expression, in old age, of a consistent outlook that begins in childhood. The stoic upbringing of an Abkhasian child, in which parents and senior relatives participate, instills respect, obedience and endurance. At an early age, children participate in household tasks; when they are not at school, they work in the fields or at home.

There are no separate "facts of life" for children and adults: The values given children are the ones adults live by and there is no hypocritical disparity (as in so many other societies) between adult words and deeds. Since what they are taught is considered important, and the work they are given is considered necessary, children are neither restless nor rebellious. As they mature, there are easy transitions from one status in life to another: a bride, for instance, will stay for a time with her husband's relatives, gradually becoming part of a new clan, before moving into his home.

From the beginning, there is no gap between expectation and experience. Abkhasians expect a long and useful life and look forward to old age with good reason: in a culture which so highly values continuity in its traditions, the old are indispensable in their transmission. The elders preside at important ceremonial occasions, they mediate disputes and their knowledge of farming is sought. They feel needed because, in their own minds and everyone else's, they are. They are the opposite of burdens; they are highly valued resources.

The Abkhasians themselves are obviously right in citing their diet and their work habits as contributing factors in their longevity; in my opinion, their postponed, and later prolonged, sex life probably has nothing to do with it. Their climate is exemplary, the air (especially to a New Yorker) refreshing, but it is not significantly different from many other areas of the world, where life spans are shorter. And while some kind of genetic selectivity may well have been at work, there simply is not enough information to evaluate the genetic factor in Abkhasian longevity.

My own view is that Abkhasians live as long as they do primarily because of the extraordinary cultural factors that structure their existence: the uniformity and certainty of both individual and group behavior, the unbroken continuum of life's activities—the same games, the same work, the same food, the same self-imposed and socially perceived needs. And the increasing prestige that comes with increasing age.

There is no better way to comprehend the importance of these cultural factors than to consider for a moment some of the prevalent characteristics of American society. Children are sometimes given chores to keep them occupied, but they and their parents know there is no *need* for the work they do; even as adults, only a small percentage of Americans have the privilege of feeling that their work is essential and important. The old, when they do not simply vegetate, out of view and out of mind, keep themselves "busy" with bingo and shuffleboard. Americans are mobile, sometimes frantically so, searching for signs of permanence that will indicate their lives are meaningful.

Can Americans learn something from the Abkhasian view of "long living" people? I think so.

DISCUSSING THE ARTICLES

1. In the article "Friday Night In the Coliseum," which value of the general American culture is represented by the different kinds of professional wrestlers? What value did the success of Gorgeous George represent?

2. Does the predominance of villains who call themselves Japs, Nazis, and Russians symbolize a subcultural prejudice or a general cultural prejudice? What other prejudices peculiar to our culture are evident from the names of some of the contenders?

3. Are black, brown, and red wrestlers cast in the role of heroes or villains? Does this follow our national stereotypes of these ethnic and racial groups?

4. What characteristics do the wrestling fans display? Are the "regulars" sufficiently distinct to merit the term subculture? What distinguishes them from the spectators of a NCAA wrestling match?

5. How would you assess the fans' desire to see blood? Are you sure your judgment is not ethnocentric? How would you explain this desire in the light of cultural relativity?

6. In the article "Why They Live to be 100, or Even Older, in Abkhasia," what makes the Abkhasians a subculture? To what kind of society did they once belong? In what kind of society do they live now?

7. Referring back to question 6, is the Abkhasians' culture representative of the first type of society or the second one?

8. What is the chief characteristic of the Abkhasian subculture? Would you say that this characteristic is easier to maintain in an urban industrial society or in an agrarian society?

9. The Abkhasians have no expression for old people. Is it because they all die young? How do you explain this absence? How do you suppose language is related to culture? Why don't Abkhasians have an expression for a condition that exists among all human groups? Is their reality different or do they perceive reality differently?

10. How do the sexual norms of the Abkhasians differ from our own? Are these norms changing, or have they remained the same? What enviable effect do these norms seem to have on members of the group?

11. What is the status of Abkhasian women? To what roles are they limited? What prerequisites must they fulfill for marriage? Is this a cultural universal or a cultural variable?

12. Do the modesty and secrecy surrounding sex in Abhkasia have the same origin as our Puritan Ethic? What is the ultimate value of sex to Abkhasians? How does this differ from the way we value sex in our culture?

13. Is competitiveness a trait of Abkhasian culture? How does this affect Abkhasian work habits?

14. Although the Abkhasians themselves attribute their longevity and good health to their moderation in sex, their work habits, and their diet, the author sensed another characteristic of their culture that she thought had greater bearing. What characteristic of Abkhasian culture did the author single out? Do you think our own culture has this characteristic? Do you think it will change as Abkhasian society becomes more urbanized and technological? In what direction do you think the change will occur?

15. Which structure is the vehicle of Abkhasian integration? Do we have a similar structure? Is it as important in our type of society as it is in theirs? Is it a cultural universal?

16. What are the extraordinary cultural factors that structure the existence of the Abkhasians? Is group and individual behavior uniform and certain or unpredictable and uncertain in Abkhasia? In our society? What about the Abkhasian attitude toward the old? How do the old—and the very young—think of themselves? How do these people think of themselves in our society?

TERMS TO REMEMBER

Society. A fairly large group of individuals who interact with one another on a regular, continuous basis and according to patterns of behavior on which all more or less agree. A society is also an interrelated network of social relationships that exists within the boundaries of the largest social system.

Culture. The way of life of a people. Culture is both the product of social interaction and a guide for further social interaction. It is the totality of all that is learned and shared by the members of a society through their interaction.

Signals. Biologically determined and genetically transmitted responses to outside stimuli.

Symbols. Genetically independent responses to stimuli. Symbols are learned and can be changed, modified, combined, and recombined in an infinite number of ways. Language, music, and art are common symbol systems.

Normative System. A system of rules regulating human behavior.

Norms. Behavioral standards that dictate conduct in both informal and formal situations; a set of behavioral expectations.

Folkways. Norms that direct behavior in everyday situations; customary and habitual ways of acting.

Mores. Norms that direct behavior that is considered either extremely harmful or extremely helpful to society. Mores define the rightness or wrongness of an act, or its morality or immorality. Violation of mores is punished by society as a whole.

Taboos. Mores stated in negative terms. Taboos center on acts deemed extremely repellent to the social group.

Laws. Formal codes of behavior. Laws, which are binding on the whole society, outline norm-deviating behavior and prescriptions for punishing it.

Social Control. The process by which order is maintained within society through obedience to norms—folkways, mores, taboos, and laws.

Sanctions. Rewards (positive) or punishment (negative), directed at individuals or groups by either legal and formal organizations (official sanctions) or the people with whom we interact (unofficial sanctions) to encourage or discourage some types of behavior.

Culture Trait. The smallest element, or unit, of culture. In material culture, it is any single object. In nonmaterial culture, it is every single idea, symbol, or belief.

Culture Complex. A number of related traits that accumulate around an activity.

Institution. A number of culture complexes clustering around a central human activity.

Cultural ethnocentrism. The attitude by which one assumes that one's own culture is right and that cultural patterns different from it are wrong.

Cultural relativity. An attitude by which each culture is judged on its own terms, in the context of its own societal setting.

Cultural universals. Similarities common to all cultures.

Subculture. A group that has distinctive features setting it apart from the wider culture of the society, but still retains the general features of the wider culture.

Counterculture, or contraculture. A group that possesses a value system and goals that are in direct opposition to those of the larger culture.

SUGGESTIONS FOR FURTHER READING

Benedict, Ruth. *Patterns of Culture* (Boston: Houghton Mifflin, 1961). A classic work in which a well-known anthropologist shows how different cultures function to produce useful members of their societies.

Hall, Edward T. *The Silent Language* (New York: Doubleday, 1959). Also, "Our Silent Language." *Americas*, Vol. 14 (February, 1962), pp. 5–8. A description of nonverbal actions and behavior, showing the differences between the cultural norms of North and South America.

Kluckhorn, Clyde. *Mirror for Man* (New York: Fawcett World Library, 1964). An illustrious anthropologist writes about the value of studying cultures and offers numerous examples of ethnocentrism and culture shock.

Linton, Ralph. *The Study of Man* (New York: Appleton-Century-Crofts, 1936). A classic of anthropology, in which the role of culture in human societies is analyzed.

Linton, Ralph. *The Tree of Culture* (New York: Alfred A. Knopf, 1955). A posthumous work delineating the development of culture in various parts of the world and presenting a theory of cultural development and cultural change.

Lipset, Seymour Martin. "The Value Patterns of a Democracy: A Case Study in Comparative Analysis," *American Sociological Review*, Vol. 28 (August, 1963), pp. 515–531. The value systems of four major contemporary societies are examined and compared by an eminent political sociologist.

Miner, Horace. "Body Ritual Among the Nacirema." *American Anthropologist*, Vol. 58 (June, 1956), pp. 503–507. Reprint S-185 by Bobbs-Merrill Company, Indianapolis. A humorous description of a familiar culture as though it were seen through the eyes of an anthropologist from another culture.

Roszak, Theodore. *The Making of a Counter Culture* (Garden City, N.Y.: Doubleday,

1969). An examination of the forces leading toward the establishment of a culture opposed to the dominant values of a technological society and with alternative cultural patterns.

Shapiro, Harry L., ed. *Man, Culture, and Society* (New York: Oxford University Press, 1956). A collection of essays providing examinations of various aspects of culture from the viewpoints of physical, cultural, and archaeological anthropology.

Sumner, William Graham. *Folkways* (New York: Mentor, 1960). A reprint of a classic and definitive work by one of the great men of sociology. Subjects include customs, folkways, and mores, and the emergence of the normative system.

Wolfe, Tom. *The Pump House Gang* (New York: Bantam Books, 1968) A view of the subcultures formed by surfers, teenagers, motorcyclists, and others who have chosen to drop out of the dominant culture.

Yinger, Milton J. "Contraculture and Subculture," *American Sociological Review*, Vol. 25 (October, 1960), pp. 625–635. An essay clarifying the two important concepts in the title.

CHAPTER THREE

THE individual and society

Imagine, for a moment, a situation that is probably familiar to you. It is a hot day in early fall. You, and a long line of other students, are waiting to register for the next academic term at your college or university. After forty-five minutes of standing in a small, airless room and of having been pushed from behind and shoved from in front, you are finally at the head of the line. You hand in fifteen different forms, and after a lengthy examination, the registration assistant tells you that Form XX is not in order. You will need another signature, for which you will have to track down the professor. He might be in his office two blocks away, in the cafeteria having lunch, in the library doing research, or even at home. After you have obtained the signature, you can return to the registration area, wait in line a second time, and find out whether all your classes are still available. Then maybe—but only maybe—you will be registered.

What is your reaction to this situation? Do you swallow hard, turn around, and leave muttering under your breath? Do you smile angelically, say thank you, and go to look for the professor whose signature you need? Do you slam the forms down on the table and scream that you don't have the time to go chasing after absentminded professors? Do you try to threaten or coax the assistant into registering you immediately?

All these reactions, and many more, are within the realm of possibility. People react differently to the same situation because personalities differ. But why are personalities different? What makes one person pleasant and optimistic, and another sullen and bleak? Why is one person generous to a fault, the other miserly; one person courageous, the other a coward; one person peaceful, the other belligerent? Are people born with temperaments that determine how they behave? Or are temperaments molded by the learning that takes place in society? Do personalities develop by chance or by design? Are they different because of genes or because of environment?

Thus far in our examination of man in his environment, we have emphasized the group aspect of human existence—the importance of group life and of social interaction. We discussed how social interaction leads to the organization of a social system in which members behave in a patterned, fairly predictable way, according to the statuses they occupy and the roles they fulfill. Furthermore, we saw that interaction within our largest social system—society—creates the peculiarly human phenomenon called culture. Culture is the basic factor differentiating humans from animals.

We must not lose sight, however, of the fundamental element of groups —the individual human being. After all, it is individuals who, in their interactions with one another, develop patterns of behavior for society. To understand how groups function, then, we must understand how the individual functions. In other words, we must examine human personality, including the forces —biological, psychological, and social—that create it and affect it.

WHAT IS PERSONALITY?

Personality is a familiar word. We all know what is meant by expressions like "What a nice personality she has!" and "He has no personality at all!" From a scientific point of view, however, such statements are nonsense. Every human being has a personality and whether he is "nice," "not nice," or "insignificant" is only part of his whole personality. Personality is a complex and dynamic system that includes all of an individual's behavioral and emotional traits—his attitudes, values, beliefs, habits, goals, and so on.

The study of personality involves examining the motivation for behavior. It involves investigating the reasons why one person behaves one way in a particular situation whereas another person behaves differently in the same situation. To understand why humans behave as they do, it is necessary to view them in their physical and social environments, their cultural structure, and from the point of view of how biological, psychological, and social factors affect them.

HUMANS: BIOLOGICAL ANIMALS

A study of personality must begin with an examination of the biological heritage of human beings, for biology affects personality. In Chapter 2, we mentioned the obvious limitations that biology sets on humans. We can live only in certain habitats, and to survive, we must satisfy our needs for air, water, food, warmth, and a degree of emotional security.

There are additional limitations that result from biological heritage. Such limitations are, however, often defined by society and its culture. For instance, society and culture determine whether it is better to be tall or short, thin or fat, strong or weak, blue-eyed or brown-eyed. Suppose that a particular society and culture determine that it is better to be tall, thin, blue-eyed, and strong. In the light of his society and culture then, an individual whose biological inheritance causes him to be short, fat, brown-eyed, and weak has been treated unfairly by biology. What is more, his personality will reflect his feelings of inadequacy. He may develop such traits as surliness, belligerence, and preference for solitude. Thus, although biology is responsible for some aspects of personality, society and culture are even more responsible, for they interpret biological characteristics in a way that affects personality.

BIOLOGICAL DETERMINISM

Biological determinism is the belief that human behavior is determined primarily by biology. This belief is an old one which gives few signs of disappearing. In the past, people thought that individuals behaved, or acted, in response to *instincts*—genetically transmitted, universal, and complex patterns of behavior. Instincts do, of course, exist and are the principal determinants of behavior in animals.

Although it is tempting to try to base explanations of human behavior on instincts, instinct theories have not stood the test of scientific research. One

problem arose when scientists tried to make lists of instincts to cover every aspect of human behavior. They soon realized not only that the number of instincts was ridiculously large but also that instincts frequently conflicted with one another. We can generalize, for instance, and say that humans have an instinct for adventure that makes them travel and wander. At the same time, their territorial instinct supposedly keeps them rooted to one place. It is also difficult to reconcile the supposed universal instinct for self-preservation with the number of suicides that occur in every society.

Most scientists now believe that, actually, it is the virtual absence of instincts in humans that makes it necessary for them to learn cultural patterns of behavior in order to survive. Still, the fascination with the animal ancestry of human beings continues. Witness the number of extremely popular books in which the authors contend that man is basically a "naked ape" or a "flesh-eating killer ape" who, because his personality is still molded by his drives, falls short of becoming fully human.

PSYCHODYNAMIC THEORIES OF PERSONALITY

Some of the theories that attempt to explain the structure of individual personality are based on the view that biological drives are of central importance to human behavior. Called psychodynamic theories, they use a sophisticated definition of the word "instinct" and give some importance to the effect culture and society have on behavior. The term "psychodynamic" may be interpreted as meaning that the behavior of an individual is motivated by mental and emotional factors present within him.

The Psychoanalytic Theory of Personality

The most significant of the psychodynamic theories is the psychoanalytic theory of Sigmund Freud. Freud's theory assumes the existence of unconscious, as well as conscious, processes. Unconscious processes are part of each individual, and develop partly as a result of his attempt to repress specific painful experiences. The unconscious reveals itself to us in dreams and as a result of psychoanalysis, a procedure developed by Freud in his treatment of personality disorders.

The id, the ego, and the superego.   Psychoanalytic theory also assumes the existence within all of us of an instinctual drive toward pleasure, called the *libido*. The libido, together with other unconscious processes, is the motivating energy for human behavior. In the personality, the representative of the libido is the *id*, which operates on an unconscious level and is the primitive, irrational part of personality. Because the unrestrained actions of the id might endanger the safety of the individual, another part of the personality, the ego, develops. The *ego* functions on a conscious level and attempts to force the id to satisfy its instinctual needs in a socially acceptable manner. Finally, as the individual absorbs the culture of his group, he develops a third element of personality, the superego. The *superego* exists mainly on an unconscious level, imposing inhibition and morality on the id. The commands of the superego conform to the cultural norms that the individual has absorbed through the teachings of parents and peers.

According to psychoanalytic theory, dysfunctions of personality—behavior that society labels abnormal or deviant—are caused by disharmony among the id, ego, and superego. This disharmony creates anxiety, and anxiety, in turn, leads to the development of defense mechanisms. *Defense mechanisms* are the frequently unconscious actions that an individual uses to ward off anxiety; such mechanisms hide from the individual his real motives and goals and thus protect him from a loss of self-esteem. Overreliance on defense mechanisms can cause individuals to show disturbed behavior of varying intensity.

Stages of psychosexual development.   An important characteristic of psychoanalytic theory is Freud's insistence that an individual's psychosexual development occurs in the period from infancy to adolescence. Personality structure is, then, to a large extent, determined in this period. Freud outlined five distinct stages in which psychosexual development occurs. Each stage represents the individual's attempts to gratify the libido at different periods of his physical maturation. The stages are (1) the oral stage, occurring during the first year of life, in which the child sucks, chews, swallows, and enjoys other activities restricted to the mouth and lips; (2) the anal stage, occurring during the second and third years, in which the child learns to control the muscles regulating elimination; (3) the phallic, or Oedipal, stage, occurring during the third through fifth years, in which male and female roles are introduced, and the child becomes attached to the parent of the opposite sex, rejecting the parent of the same sex; (4) the latency stage, occurring during the period from age five to the beginning of adolescence, in which the child explores his physical and intellectual environment, and not much personality change occurs; and (5) the genital stage, occurring during puberty, in which the id seeks gratification in the form of adult sexuality. In this last stage, especially, the ego and the superego must channel the energy unleashed by the id into socially approved activities. The success of the ego and superego depend mainly upon how well an individual has, in the previous stages, resolved the conflicts produced by the id.

Modern opinions of psychoanalytic theory.   Psychoanalytic theory, especially the concept of the unconscious, has been a source of fascination to those living in the twentieth-century. Freud's influence has extended far beyond the field of psychology, and his theory has given us valuable insights into the human personality.

Today, however, psychoanalytic theory is accepted by most behavioral scientists only with reservations. One reservation involves Freud's assumption that a conflict exists between the biological being and the external forces, represented by society and culture, that try to control him. This assumption is not universally shared.

A second reservation involves the importance assigned to the early years of an individual's life. Freud, you recall, believed that early experiences centering mainly on instinctual drives determine the main outlines of an individual's personality. Today, behavioral scientists are convinced that personality does not stop developing after puberty. Personality is viewed as a never-ending process, continually changing to respond to changing demands in an individual's environment.

Finally, many feel that psychoanalytic theory overemphasizes the instinctual aspects of personality and understates the effects of society and culture. Women's liberationists have a specific complaint against Freud for this very reason. His statement "Anatomy is fate" seems to mean that women are consigned to their inferior position in society because of what are considered their biological shortcomings.

Other Psychodynamic Theories of Personality

Psychoanalytic theory has been the source of additional theories that have enlarged and modified some of its basic assumptions. Numerous followers of Freud, called neo-Freudians, have been willing to give much more importance to society and culture in the molding of human personality than did their master. They have also recognized the ongoing quality of the process of personality formation. Among the neo-Freudians, the following have been the most influential: Carl Jung, who assumed that there exists a collective unconscious as well as Freud's individual one; Alfred Adler, who stressed the sense of inferiority as the motivating force in humans; Karen Horney, who believed that conflict between the individual and society results in neurotic needs; Erich Fromm, who thinks people have basic individual needs; and Erik Erikson, whose psychosocial stages of development parallel Freud's but span the entire life of the individual.[1]

---

[1]See the Suggestions for Further Reading at the end of this chapter for specific works of these behavioral scientists.

THEORIES OF PERSONALITY
BASED ON INDIVIDUAL INHERITANCE

Biology—in the form of the genetic inheritance that makes one individual different from another—is the basis of some other theories of personality. Two such theories are trait and body type theories. The foundation of *trait theory* is the speculation that personality results from a particular combination of inherited traits. *Body type theories* link the individual's physical build to his personality.

We are all familiar with the stereotypes of fat and thin people; fat people are supposedly jolly and easygoing, whereas thin people are supposedly tense and nervous.Because body type and personality have been associated in folklore throughout history, a number of scientists have tried to verify the relationship scientifically. The German scientist Ernest Kretschmer developed criteria according to which he classified people into pyknic types (short, fat, and jolly); asthenic types (tall, thin, and shy); and athletic types (combining the character traits of the other two).[2] The American psychologist William Sheldon developed a similar system, categorizing people into *endomorphs* (fleshy-bodied, calm, and outgoing); *mesomorphs* (athletically built, aggressive, and action seeking) and *ectomorphs* (tall, thin, hypersensitive, and intellectual).[3]

Doubtlessly, both traits and body build affect personality, but it seems likely that they do so mainly because of cultural patterns. For example, if a high school student who is six feet five inches tall and weighs 225 pounds decides to become a football player, he must act aggressively and seek action. Perhaps, however, he chooses to play football not so much because he has a natural bent toward the game—and toward that kind of behavior—but because of pressure from the coach and the expectations of his friends. (Not to mention the fact that it is easy to be aggressive when one is this size!)

At any rate, the theories that link traits and body structure to personality have been found inadequate by psychologists and other social scientists. Primarily they are incomplete, because they do not take social and cultural factors into account.

CULTURAL DETERMINISM

Theories involving *cultural determinism* are based on the view that human personality is a reflection of the individual's culture. The early sociologist Emile Durkheim (1858–1917) saw culture in terms of "collective representations," which result from the collective consciousness of a society. Each member of a society is coerced into conformity by these collective representations, which are unchangeable.

Later anthropologists reflect similar views. Leslie White conceives of culture as an irremovable force created for an individual by his ancestors. In White's view, culture manipulates the individual in the same way that a puppeteer controls a puppet. Humans must exist if a culture is to emerge, but they are

[2]Ernest Kretschmer, *Physique and Character* (New York: Harcourt, Brace & World, 1925).
[3]W. H. Sheldon, S. S. Stevens, and W. P. Tucker, *The Varieties of Human Physique* (New York: Harper & Row, 1940).

merely the instruments through which cultures express themselves. Culture, then, exists separately from humans, shaping them into what they are and, in the process, creating itself.[4]

Another anthropologist, Margaret Mead, does not place quite as much emphasis as White does on culture's function in molding human personality.

[4]Leslie White, *The Science of Culture* (New York: Grove Press, 1949), pp. 340–353.

Nevertheless, she maintains:

> We are forced to conclude that human nature is almost unbelievably malleable, responding accurately and contrastingly to contrasting cultural conditions. The differences between individuals who are members of different cultures, like the differences between individuals within a culture, are almost entirely to be laid to differences in conditioning, especially during early childhood; and the form of this conditioning is culturally determined.[5]

Mead is, in short, saying that the culture of a society and the culture of groups within a society are the forces most responsible for personality. The anthropologist was led to this conclusion by her study of three nontechnological societies; the different cultures of the societies apparently molded their members into entirely different human beings.

The National Character, or Modal Personality

Margaret Mead's study of three nontechnological societies also helped to support the theory of the modal personality, or national character. According to this theory, the cultural learning peculiar to a specific society produces a characteristic personality type. A culture that stresses competitiveness and one-upmanship—or success at the expense of others—and the importance of magic produces a personality characterized by traits such as hostility, suspicion, secretiveness, jealousy, and distrust.[6] In a society in which other cultural values are emphasized, entirely different personality types emerge.

There is no denying that common stereotypes such as "English humor," "Latin lover," and "Irish temper" are somewhat true. The basic personality type of Americans, at least in the mind of Europeans, is represented by an individual who is brash, loud, optimistic, and unconventional. The basic personality type of Englishmen, at least in the mind of Americans, is represented by a person who is reserved, unemotional, distant, traditionalist, and methodical. The encounter of two such personalities can have drastic results, as is illustrated by Calvin Trillin's short story "A Nation of Shopkeepers Loses Three of Them Through Contact with a Nation of Violence." Although this is not a scientific report but a work of fiction, we include it here because it deals masterfully with common stereotypes—along with their grains of truth.[7]

Objections to Cultural Determinism

Unquestionably, culture and personality are deeply intertwined. In fact, because the individual acquires his personality while he learns his culture, personality and culture are really not two different processes but two facets of the same process.[8] But culture alone cannot be responsible for the development of human personality. To say that it is is to ignore the differences among

---

[5]Margaret Mead, *Sex and Temperament in Three Primitive Societies* (New York: William Morrow, 1963), p. 280.

[6]Ruth Benedict, *Patterns of Culture* (Boston: Houghton Mifflin, 1934), Chapter 5.

[7]Calvin Trillin, "A Nation of Shopkeepers Loses Three of Them Through Contact with a Nation of Violence," *Atlantic* (January, 1971), pp. 71–74.

[8]Melford E. Spiro, "Culture and Personality: The Natural History of a False Dichotomy," *Psychiatry*, Vol. 14 (1951), pp. 19–46.

individuals. Furthermore, it is to discount the individual's ability to interpret events and choose alternative courses of action.

The theory of national character is also increasingly coming under attack because in heterogeneous societies like the United States there are a large number of subcultures, each of which has its own cultural traits. Generalizations about a national character, then, are impossible to make.

In addition, theories involving cultural determinism are based on the assumption that culture doesn't change. However, there is ample evidence that the favored cultural traits of societies are not deep-rooted and can change with time and circumstances. These changes explain the cyclical nature of history—periods in which mores are liberal, relaxed, and permissive seem to be followed by periods in which mores are conservative, rigid, and highly controlled. Following this line of reasoning, we can say that whereas the "typical" American is probably still materialistic, the emergence of a countercultural movement seems to indicate that a reversal of materialism is in progress.

BEHAVIORISM, OR ENVIRONMENTAL DETERMINISM

Behaviorism refers to another group of theories popular among numerous psychologists today. Behaviorists believe that scientific research can concern itself only with overt behavior, or behavior that can be objectively observed. Thus, they are not concerned with the way an individual perceives experience or with his unconscious processes. Scientific experiments on animals and humans have led them to conclude that the process governing behavior is essentially one of stimulus and response. A simple example of the operation of stimulus-response is that of a hungry person who responds to the stimulus of food by salivating.

The salivation of a hungry person is an instinctive response, one over which he has no control. Human beings, however, make many noninstinctive responses. Noninstinctive responses are the result of learning, which takes place through a method called *conditioning*. Conditioning is based on reinforcements—rewards and punishment. Responses that are rewarded are repeated and become a central part of an individual's behavior. Responses that are punished, or are not rewarded but ignored, are discontinued. Of the two kinds of reinforcement, the most effective is rewards. For humans, rewards can take many forms: money, candy, or a display of affection from another person.

To behaviorists, the newborn human being is a plastic organism, capable of being shaped in whatever ways people choose. Thus, behaviorism may also be called *environmental determinism*.

That behaviorism holds a great deal of fascination for people is shown by the mixture of criticism and acclaim that greeted publication of B. F. Skinner's book *Beyond Freedom and Dignity*. Skinner's basic argument is that society should, instead of concerning itself with people's freedom and individual dignity, use conditioning to cause them to behave in a morally ethical way. The problem with this argument is that what is morally ethical to one person may not be morally ethical to another. Whose interpretation of ethics are we to accept? And is it morally ethical to condition the members of a whole society to behave according to the standards of a small number of powerful people?

Many critics of behaviorism raise just such questions as these. They find the theory dangerous because it enables some people to control the behavior of others. A different group of critics, however, questions whether the theory is completely descriptive of behavior. Its view of human nature seems to them to be a greatly oversimplified one.

PERSONALITY: A SOCIAL PRODUCT

The theories of personality that we have presented—and they are only a small, if significant, sample of the many that exist—should give an idea of the complexity of the subject and the lack of definitive answers.

According to the psychoanalytic school, human personality emerges out of the conflict between the instinctual drive for pleasure, the libido, and the forces of society and culture that attempt to bring it under control. Early childhood experiences are considered important for the successful resolution of the conflict. It is in childhood that the outlines of the adult personality are formed.

Other theories of personality are based on the individual's biological heredity. According to these theories, a set of inherited traits determines personality, or an inherited body build matches a particular personality type.

Cultural determinists on the other hand, emphasize the effects of culture on the biological organism that is the human being. They view the human infant as an eminently malleable being molded by the culture into which he is born. The infant's personality, then, eventually reflects and is the product of his culture.

Behaviorists, substituting environment for culture, also claim that the biological organism can be taught any kind of behavior. Personality, in this view, is the result of conditioning. Conditioning is based on reinforcements—rewards and punishment.

The different conclusions reached in these theories are the result of emphasis on different aspects of the individual. Yet in each theory, the individual, rather than the group, is the central focus. This is understandable because the theories originated in fields other than sociology. A question that may arise here is, Why are we interested in theories that do not belong in the realm of sociology?

As we have insisted in the Introduction and in our first chapter, individuals do not live in isolation. They do not mature into human beings unless they interact with others. Thus, a personality develops only as a person relates to the people around him.

In looking at human personality, then, sociologists must take into account the findings of physical scientists who have done experiments on biological heredity. Sociologists must also take into account the theories constructed by all social scientists who have considered the effects of culture and society on the human being. Primarily, however, sociologists view personality as the product of heredity, culture, and society. Each individual inherits particular needs and potentials. These needs and potentials are shaped and developed by cultural and societal factors and by experiences unique to each individual. Sociologists refer to the overall process through which an individual develops personality as socialization.

MATURATION AND SOCIALIZATION

When we look into a hospital maternity ward, we note that the babies in the nursery are differentiated chiefly by the tone of their crying, by slight variations in size or head shape, and by the amount and color of hair. Twenty years later, however, those same babies will differ substantially both in their outward appearance and in their personalities. These differences will have been brought about by the twin processes of maturation and socialization.

Maturation is a physical process attained by all individuals, although at different rates of speed, in all societies, regardless of cultural or personal experiences. In short, every baby, unless there is some abnormality present, will learn to sit, stand, walk and run, in that order. In addition, all young people will attain sexual maturity at puberty, and all older people will eventually develop a wrinkled skin.

Socialization is broadly defined as the process by which a biological organism becomes a human being. In this process, the individual acquires a definite personality as well as those parts of his culture to which he is exposed. As such, then, socialization differs from society to society, and, to an extent, from group to group within the same society.

The central point of socialization is that it is a process in which the new member of society learns from the people around him. In other words, other people are necessary for the process to occur. The isolated individual cannot become human, develop a personality, or even become aware of the existence of a distinct self.

In the first chapter, we mentioned the studies of isolated individuals who were deprived of human interaction for the first several years of their lives. When they were found by other people, they were poorly functioning biological organisms, and little else. They could not speak and had no notion of any cultural norms, even the most simple folkways. Attempts at interaction caused them to respond with fear, withdrawal, and animal-like grunts.

Infants reared in total isolation are not the only people who fail to learn properly the characteristics of human beings. Infants may be raised in situations in which only their basic biological needs are tended to, and little or no interest and affection are shown them. Many such children simply die. Others may develop into stunted, retarded, or severely disturbed individuals.[9] Thus, inadequate interaction—the absence of communication, affection, and fondling—seems to affect the success of both maturation and socialization.

Socialization: A Two-Way Process

Socialization begins when the infant, tense from an imbalance in his organism—revealed by hunger, thirst, cold, discomfort, pain—discovers that someone helps him relieve his tensions. He soon comes to associate that someone—usually the mother and, later, other members of the household—with pleasure and the relief of tension. The presence of that person becomes a goal in itself, not simply a means of being fed and comforted.

In accepting the mother as pleasure giving, the infant has taken the first

[9]Rene A. Spitz, "Hospitalism," in Rose L. Coser, ed., *The Family: Its Structure and Functions* (New York: St. Martin's Press, 1964), pp. 399–425.

step toward accepting all others as necessary to his comfort. In tending to her newborn in culturally prescribed ways, the mother has, in turn, encouraged the child to solve his biological needs in socially approved ways. She has also introduced him, through gestures and language, to the pleasures of human communication, which the infant will attempt as soon as his vocal equipment becomes sufficiently matured. From this time on, the new individual will learn to take others into account and to define his self in terms of them.

Socialization, then, is a two-way process. It permits society to mold each new generation of biological beings into human beings who accept the culture of their elders. It permits the infant born into society to familiarize himself with and learn how to behave in an environment already prepared for him by the countless generations that preceded him. Furthermore, it permits the individual to develop his own unique personality in the process.

Social interaction, then, is a human necessity. Without it, society cannot pass culture from generation to generation, and the individual cannot develop a self and a personality. Social interaction, as we have said in previous chapters, is symbolic interaction. It takes place through the use of symbols, the chief of which is language.

To convince yourself of the truth of this statement, think of how significant your interaction would be if you were to find yourself stranded somewhere in Tibet and you did not know a word of the local language. Through gestures, you might be able to explain that you were hungry or were looking for a place to sleep. And through observation, you might receive a surface view of Tibetan culture, which you would interpret in the light of your previous experience. But you would be unable to engage in a relationship that would lead to understanding and participation in Tibetan culture. The importance of symbolic interaction prompted sociologist Robert Nisbet to state:

> *The whole experience of growing up is essentially the assimilation and internalization of values, ideas, techniques, and ways of behavior that are already in existence when each of us comes into the world. But we must think of symbolic interaction as forming the very stuff of human personality, character, self, and identity. Only through communication in terms of shared symbols is it possible for each of us to acquire his sense of self, character, and identity.*[10]

Resocialization

In addition to acquiring the culture of his society, the individual must sometimes undergo a drastic form of resocialization. Resocialization is necessary when an individual joins a "total institution." In such institutions, the individual lives with a number of people who, cut off from the rest of society for a period of time, reside and work in a controlled, rigidly structured environment. The armed services, convents or monasteries, mental institutions, prisons, and prisoner-of-war camps are examples of total institutions.

The resocialization that takes place in such situations involves a definite set of procedures. First, the institution's representatives try to destroy the individual's present identity, substituting for it feelings of inadequacy and dependence on the institution. They do this through isolating the individual from the outside world, by having him give up his personal possessions for a standardized uniform, by calling him by a number or a status rather than by his name, and by relieving him of his freedom. If these methods are insufficient for a speedy erasure of personality, other techniques are attempted. These techniques include degrading and humiliating the individual by forcing him to perform menial and meaningless tasks. The individual, no longer "what he used to be," is further made to feel inferior, insignificant, and inefficient. The individual's superiors claim absolute authority over him. The individual is more or less severely punished for the slightest disobedience to the rules. Finally, any independence left in the individual is quickly stamped out by his peers, who put pressure on him to conform so they can avoid punishment to themselves.

Through such procedures—and in extreme cases, through additional techniques of brainwashing—it is possible to cause the individual to deny his personality and to acquire a new one acceptable to the institution. There is, however, evidence that even under conditions of extreme stress (for example, brainwashing), some individuals cling stubbornly to their identities, literally refusing to accept the new identities being forced upon them.

From this, we must conclude that whereas some aspects of personality are

[10]Robert A. Nisbet, *The Social Bond* (New York: Alfred A. Knopf, 1970), p. 59.

susceptible to change, others resist it. Moreover, individuals react differently to attempts at resocialization. Logically, it seems as if individuals whose identities are the most firmly entrenched resist change most successfully, and individuals with less well-established identities more readily accept change.

Aims of Socialization

The specific aims of the process of socialization may be stated as follows: (1) Teaching the fundamentals of life in society. This includes teaching the infant and growing child the foods that he should eat and how and when he should eat them; customs centering on waste elimination; the times when it is permissible to show emotions and when they should be controlled; the customs of the society in regard to sex; the postponement of immediate pleasures for future goals; and all other knowledge necessary to get along in a group. (2) Instilling societal aspirations. The society must convince its new member that its values and goals are worth aspiring to and working toward. Thus, the individual learns the requirements for the attainment of high status in his society. (3) Transmitting skills important in the society. The transmission, or passing along, of skills is connected to the aim of instilling societal goals because it enables the individual to attain the goals of the society. The most important skill transmitted to the new member of society is language. Other skills differ from society to society and among the various classes and groups within a society. In our society, much of this training is done by institutions charged with the education of the young. (4) Teaching to fulfill social roles. The new member of society must be taught to interact with other members as an individual. But he must learn to interact in the statuses and roles he fulfills—as a child, a male, a son, a husband, a lawyer, and so on.[11]

Socialization occurs on both a conscious and an unconscious level. Adults may deliberately set out to teach children particular behavior, attitudes, and values, whether at home or at school. Often, other behavior, attitudes, and values—especially those of the society and of in-groups—are not deliberately taught. But a child may deduce what they are from the conversation and actions of the adults around him. Ethnocentric and racial feelings are often transmitted in such a manner.

THE CHIEF AGENT OF SOCIALIZATION: THE FAMILY

By now, it should be obvious that the attainment of human personality ordinarily takes place in the context of the family. The family plays a crucial role in the process of socialization for a variety of reasons. First, the family influences the child in his earliest stage of development. Second, the family attempts to meet all of the child's needs, both physical and emotional. Third, the family is the most constant influence in an individual's life, because he usually maintains a relationship with it from infancy into adulthood. Fourth, because the family is a primary group, socialization is aided. The individual learns most readily from persons with whom he has close personal and emo-

[11]Francis E. Merrill, *Society and Culture* (Englewood Cliffs, N. J.: Prentice-Hall, 1969), pp. 99–100.

tional ties. Finally, the child is born into the racial group and social class to which his family belongs. His class position greatly determines what he internalizes from the culture. Members of different social classes hav significantly different socialization experiences, as a discussion of life styles in Chapter 4 suggests.

The family, of course, is not the only influence on human social development. The school—beginning with nursery school or even with the sought after day-care centers—peer groups, specialized groups of which the individual becomes a member, and, to a great extent, the mass media also have a great impact on the socialization of the individual.

In his well-known work *The Lonely Crowd*, David Riesman and his coauthors suggest, in fact, that in modern societies the peer group is more important in socialization than are the parents. According to Riesman, the personality type that emerges from modern methods of socialization is "other directed." Unlike the individual who lived in less populated, nonindustrial societies, the other-directed person does not act primarily according to well-defined internal standards. Instead, he behaves in ways that make other people like and approve of him. The peer group is very important to the child, and parents, instead of instilling strict standards of behavior, accept the influence of the child's peer groups and instill values of popularity and approval.[12] Riesman, as do many other people, also points out the mass media's great influence on public opinion and, consequently, on behavior.

The peer group may indeed play a more important part in socialization than it did in the past. Generally, however, the peer group and the institutions and individuals who strongly influence socialization act upon foundations already instilled within the family.[13]

[12]David Riesman, Nathan Glazer, and Reuel Denney, *The Lonely Crowd* (New Haven, Conn.: Yale University Press, 1961).
[13]Kingsley Davis, *Human Society* (New York: Macmillan, 1949), pp. 405–406.

THE ACQUISITION OF SELF

As important as socialization is to society, it is still more important to the individual. In fact, not until the individual is sufficiently socialized does he assume a self, an identity, and an individuality of his own.

Following birth, the infant is totally unaware of self. He is even unable to distinguish between the parts of his body and other objects in his environment. Eventually, however, he notices that others act toward him in a specific manner, distinct from the manner in which they act toward objects and other people. From this, the new individual begins to realize that he is separate, distinct, and different. In short, the self—the awareness of one's distinctiveness —emerges as a result of interaction with others. Through interaction, the individual learns from others who and what he is in relation to them, and how he should feel toward himself as a result of this relationship. The individual's behavior also follows the clues given by those around him. In successful socialization, the individual generally behaves as he thinks those around him want him to behave.

Cooley and the Looking-Glass Self

Many theorists have attempted to describe the processes through which the self emerges. The most frequently accepted theories on the subject are those of Charles Horton Cooley and George Herbert Mead, two pioneer American sociologists. Modern research has tended to confirm many of Cooley's and Mead's insights into the individual and his social order.

Cooley believed that the development of human personality, and particularly the development of a socially defined self, must begin in the early stages of human life. In interaction with his immediate family and, later, with peer groups, the maturing individual learns that he is distinct from others and that his needs are satisfied because he is loved. He learns that he stands in a particular relationship to others and that they continually make judgments about his appearance and behavior according to standards, or norms, with which he soon becomes familiar.

The individual senses others' opinions of him from their reactions to him. On this basis, he determines whether his self is "good" or "bad," pleasant or unpleasant, and behaves accordingly. Cooley thought that this process, which he called the "looking-glass self," consists of three elements: (1) The individual imagines how his behavior appears to others; (2) the individual imagines how others judge his behavior; and (3) the individual feels pride or shame about others' judgments of him.[14]

In short, the individual looks into an imaginary mirror. The mirror reflects back to him his image as others see him. If the image is good, the individual is satisfied with himself. If the image is bad, he feels ashamed. We all know the feeling. When we dress for an important occasion, we wear our most becoming clothes because we anticipate other people's reaction to our attractive appearance. The imagined judgment of others is what, in reality, creates us. Throughout our lives, we continually "present" ourselves to others in the hope

---

[14]Charles Horton Cooley, *Human Nature and the Social Order* (New York: Schocken Books, 1964), p. 152. First edition, 1909.

of making a favorable impression that is reflected back to us. Then, we may feel good about ourselves.[15]

What we become, then, is in large measure determined by how we see ourselves reflected in others. To emerge and develop, the human self must have a mirror that reflects its image. In other words, it must have other people who react toward it. But others need not be physically present at all times. The individual soon generalizes others as "they," and perceives their reaction and judgment even in their absence. Moreover, the process does not end in childhood. The adult personality is equally in need of a social mirror to continually redefine itself.

Mead: Mind, Self, and Symbolic Interactionism

The theory that social interaction is the basis of the emergence of self and personality was moved further along by the work of George Herbert Mead (1863–1931). Mead was responsible for a social-psychological theory called *symbolic interactionism*. The ideas embodied in symbolic interactionism are many and complex, but they all center around the interrelationship of *mind* (the abstract whole of a person's ideas), *self* (the individual's self-conception, or self-awareness), and society. Symbolic interactionism clarifies the process

[15]Erving Goffman, *The Presentation of Self in Everyday Life* (New York: Doubleday Anchor Books, 1959), Introduction.

whereby the biological organism becomes an actual human being. It explains the procedure by which the agents of socialization accomplish their work.

In laying the foundation of his theory, Mead insisted that society cannot exist without humans, who have minds and selves. At the same time, rational minds and conscious selves can emerge only in society. Thus, society and the individual give rise to each other through interaction, especially symbolic interaction. Mead viewed interaction as a dynamic, rather than a static, process. Furthermore, he believed that the individual thinks and acts as a consequence of interpreting meanings, rather than because he responds and reacts to stimuli. Successful social interaction, which is the basis of the social order, is achieved when individuals, through socialization, acquire self-control over their behavior and are sensitive to the feelings and expectations of others.

The Self as Subject and Object

The human self is able to emerge only because the individual becomes capable of thinking about himself as he thinks about others. In other words, he becomes an object to himself. As soon as the child begins to realize the distinctions among "I," "me," and "you," he begins to treat himself as he does others. In Mead's words:

> The individual ... enters his own experience as a self or individual ... only in so far as he first becomes an object to himself just as other individuals are objects to him or in his experience; and he becomes an object to himself only by taking the attitudes of other individuals toward himself within a social environment ... in which both he and they are involved.[16]

In other words, according to Mead, an individual becomes John Smith or Jane White not simply because he is a living organism which, like other living organisms, reacts to stimuli, hunger, thirst, pain. Instead, he becomes the unique entity, himself, because he can think about himself, hate himself, love himself, communicate and interact with himself, and most important, because he can control his behavior and direct it into meaningful channels.

Taking the Role of Other

The uniquely human quality of being able to get outside ourselves and to see ourselves as others see us—and in so doing, to define our self—is possible because of role taking. At some time, all of us have observed children at play. We have noticed how they dress up as and pretend to be mothers, fathers, policemen, sales clerks, or whatever. During such games, each child speaks to himself and answers himself, both in his own role and in the role of the person he is playing. Pretending to be a policeman, a little boy may give himself a traffic ticket. Pretending to be the offender, he may try to talk himself out of it.

It is by *taking the role of other* that the child learns how others feel about him and how he must act in order to receive the desired response from them. Because he can put himself in the position of others, he learns how to anticipate

---

[16]George Herbert Mead, *Mind, Self, and Society* (Chicago: University of Chicago Press, 1934), p. 138.

their actions and reactions. This learning guides his behavior in his interaction with others.

Significant Others and the Generalized Other

At first, others whose role the individual takes are members of his family and of his peer group, or as Mead calls them, *significant others*. At a later stage in the development of the self, the individual learns to take the role of society as a whole. In Mead's terms, he takes into account the *generalized other*. This change occurs when the individual realizes that there are some situations in which he must take, at the same time, the role not only of one significant other but of several people. In short, he must react simultaneously to the expectations of a number of people. Mead uses the example of a baseball game to illustrate this process. In such a game, each player must know not only his role and that of each player, but he must also keep in mind the roles of groups of players and the role of the team as a unit. Furthermore, he must know the relationships among the various roles and, at any one time, the expectations and intentions of several other players. He does this by actually constructing an overall role out of the individual roles of specific people.

As in the ball game, the individual must take the role not simply of Bobby, Jimmy, or Billy, but of the whole team as a unit. Thus, in society, he must take into account not only mother, dad, and Aunt Patricia, but all his friends, his whole age group, his whole community, and eventually his whole society. The change from taking the role of significant others to taking the role of the generalized other is complete when the individual, in considering an action, no longer thinks, "Mommy says I must not do it," but rather, "It's not right to do it."

When we begin to act with the idea in mind that we ought or ought not do some things because "It is not right," we have internalized—made a part of ourselves—the folkways, mores, values, and other norms of society. We no longer refrain from some actions out of fear of punishment or the displeasure of others but because we want to avoid blaming ourselves or suffering in our own self-esteem. In short, we have acquired a conscience, which tells us what we ought or ought not do. We no longer need the physical presence of others to direct our behavior. Chapter 9, in which we discuss social control and the political institution, makes clear that it is this internalized understanding of the attitudes of the generalized other that controls the behavior of individuals sufficiently to permit the existence of a relatively free society.

In a small, fairly homogeneous society, taking on the attitudes of the generalized other is relatively easy, because most members of this kind of society are socialized to judge behavior in similar terms. In other words, everyone generally agrees on what is correct and what is incorrect behavior. In a large, heterogeneous society, however, it is almost impossible for an individual to achieve a perfect grasp of the attitudes of the generalized other. Because our society contains a number of subcultures, the child is exposed to and internalizes the attitudes of only several of many generalized others—most likely those of his own class, race, geographic region, and ethnic and religious groups. These attitudes are made real to him through his parents, his brothers and sisters, his peer groups, and his school. For instance, a child growing up in an urban ghetto receives a different version of the expectations of the generalized other than a child growing up in eastern Kentucky. A ghetto child is not shown the corn, the beets, and the best-laying chicken, as the child in our article is. He does not follow the song of a bird or the croak of a frog. And at three years old, the ghetto child has probably never even seen a stream, let alone waded and fished in one. To what degree socialization experiences differ among the various groups in our society is vividly illustrated in our article "A Domain of Sorts." The author, Robert Coles, portrays socialization in a section of Appalachia.[17]

Composition of the Self

Although the self that emerges as a result of the internalized attitudes of others is principally of a social nature, it has another, more creative and spontaneous element. This element, which Mead calls the "I", emerges before the social element, which he calls the "me". The "I" is the subjective, acting, natural, uninhibited part of the self. The "me," in contrast, is the objective representative of cultural and societal expectations which have been made part of his personality by the individual. The "I" is unique to each individual; the "me" is conventional in that it is shared with others.

In individuals in whom the "I" and the "me" are equally strong, behavior will, in general, be normal. Such individuals will attempt to solve any problem in a socially approved manner, according to their unique abilities and needs. However, behavior will be rigidly conventional if the individual is oversocialized—the "me" is stronger than the "I"—and may be destructively impul-

---

[17]Robert Coles, "A Domain of Sorts," *Harper's* (November, 1971), pp. 116–122.

sive if the individual is undersocialized—the "I" is stronger than the "me."[18]

The attainment of a definite identity and of self-respect are closely related to the development of the self. Neither condition will be reached unless the individual perceives that both the significant others and the generalized other react favorably to his personality.

NORMAL VERSUS ABNORMAL PERSONALITY

Our discussion of the human personality would be incomplete without reference to what is commonly called the "normal" personality and to what constitutes deviation from it. The concept of normality is extremely difficult to define, primarily because it varies not only from culture to culture but within cultures. If in our culture a man shows fear of a menstruating woman, we consider his behavior abnormal or neurotic. Yet in many nontechnological cultures, such fears are common and are considered perfectly normal.

Within cultures, the definition of normality varies according to time, class membership, and sex. Today, if a person tells us that sex is evil and the work of the devil, we are shocked and think that the person is greatly disturbed. Yet in Victorian times, that was the common view of sex. Furthermore, the conviction of the middle classes that hard work is a virtue is not completely shared by some members of the lower classes; nor is it shared by members of the counterculture, who may actually consider avoidance of hard work to be a virtue. Finally, worrying about wrinkles and impending old age is laughed off as normal for a woman, whereas it is viewed suspiciously when expressed by a man.

Perhaps we should note that the problem of definition is further complicated by the changes taking place in our society today. We live in an era of social and cultural turmoil. Aided by the mass media, social and cultural norms change more rapidly than ever before. Thus, a definition of normality based on standards acceptable to the community leads to the question, Standards acceptable in *which* community? Smoking marijuana, for instance, is both illegal and unacceptable in some communities but would definitely be common behavior in other communities. Homosexual behavior is frowned upon in the straight community, but gay communities, with their own churches and other institutions, are springing up in most large metropolitan centers. Finally, because of the much-talked-about sexual revolution, unmarried women who live with men are certainly not considered "fallen women," as they were a generation or two ago. With societal and cultural norms in such a flux, definitions of normality are almost nonsensical. Behavior must be judged on the basis of the effect it has on others.

Deviations from the Norm

Even though normality is extremely difficult to define, society must make some distinction between behavior that is acceptable and behavior that causes harm to both the individual and his society. Keeping in mind the problems we have discussed, then, we shall use the definitions commonly accepted by

---

[18]George Herbert Mead, *Mind, Self, and Society* (Chicago: University of Chicago Press, 1934).

psychologists and other behavioral scientists. *Normal* refers to behavior that is approved by our society and culture, and *abnormal* refers to behavior that is not. Deviations from the norm may consist of mild life adjustment problems or neuroses. Or they may be more severe, such as personality disorders and psychoses. Personality disorders include sexual deviation, alcoholism and drug addiction, lack of empathy, and lack of a conscience. Psychoses are sometimes accompanied by hallucinatory experiences and bizarre behavior or by chronic brain syndromes, in which normal functioning is prevented by a damaged brain.

Although abnormal conditions may require hospitalization, the borderline between abnormality and normality is frequently so fuzzy that an abnormal person may be able to function adequately, at least at intermittent intervals. The most frequent disorders dealt with by psychiatrists are neuroses and psychoses. The difference between the two is one of degree. In general terms, a *neurosis* is a feeling of profound anxiety that the affected individual tries to overcome by using defense mechanisms in exaggerated ways. Although the neurotic may at times be incapable of functioning in his environment, he at least tries to cope with his situation.

The psychotic, on the other hand, tries to adjust his enviroment to fit his peculiar scheme of things, and, in so doing, loses touch with reality. At most, we can state that *psychosis* is a more serious deviation from the norm than is neurosis. The psychotic cannot tell right from wrong and is more likely than the neurotic to be a threat to himself and to those around him.

Origins of Emotional Disorders

Some experts believe that mental illness results from psychological causes. Others think biological factors are the major cause. Those who accept the psychological viewpoint are convinced that emotional disorders are largely a product of damaging experiences in early childhood. On the other hand, the relief that some disturbed patients receive from drug therapy tends to support the biological viewpoint. And indeed many prominent scientists suggest that mental illness is a matter of body chemistry.

SUMMARY

We may make several general comments about human personality. First, we must agree with behavioral scientists who remark that each human being, to a certain extent, resembles all other human beings, resembles some other human beings, and resembles no other human being.[19] Each human resembles all other humans because we are all members of the same biological species, and, thus, are all born with the same basic drives and needs: the physical needs for oxygen, warmth, food, and the avoidance of pain and the emotional needs for affection and security. Each human resembles some other humans because as a member of a particular society, he shares in the culture of that society, having been socialized into its norms by a fairly standard process.

[19]Clyde Kluckhohn and Henry A. Murray, eds., *Personality in Nature, Society, and Culture* (New York: Alfred A. Knopf, 1949), p. 35.

And each human resembles no other human because experiences, unique to each individual and operating on an equally unique set of inherited potentials, create a personality that is like no other. Personality, then, develops on the basis of a unique genetic heredity; a unique physical environment; socialization into a shared culture; common, or group, experiences; and unique, or individual, experiences.

Behavioral scientists have approached human personality from different points of view. Some have attempted to explain it in terms of instincts. Others have maintained that personality is based on an inborn drive toward pleasure that is constantly in conflict with the forces of culture and society. Still others have thought that clusters of traits or body structure were the chief influences on personality.

Sociologists, who believe that the individual functions as a whole only within a group, almost universally agree that socialization is the determining factor in the development of personality. Socialization, unlike cultural determinism and behaviorism, does not lead to the conclusion that the individual can be molded into almost anything, provided the right environment or training is available. On the contrary, the individual is believed to come into the world equipped with a baggage of inherited traits and potentials—and perhaps with a specific temperament, as is being suggested in recent studies. He is also equipped with definite, powerful drives and a strong desire to have them fulfilled. Socialization, therefore, does not merely mold the individual; it simply teaches him how to satisfy his biological drives through social channels and how to fit his unique makeup into the fabric of his society.

In biology, researchers are trying to determine the extent of man's indebtedness to his physical nature. Perhaps we will ultimately discover that our roots are much deeper in our animal background than we care to admit. Maybe that is why neither our having created culture, nor our living in societies, nor our having attained a degree of civilization has saved us from much of the misery that we still experience periodically both as groups and as individuals. But all this remains in the realm of speculation. Only the future may be able to resolve such questions.

CALVIN TRILLIN

A NATiON of shopkEEpERS losEs thREE of thEM thROUGh CONTACT with A NATiON of violENCE

We have all heard that the Germans are punctual and exact, that the French and Italians are great lovers, and that the British are proper and have a special type of humor. Are these statements fact or folklore? Are cultural determinists correct in saying that each culture produces a personality type corresponding to the requirements of its society? And in a large, heterogeneous society, exactly which culture produces this personality? Whether fact or fancy, the idea of a national character persists in the minds of most people. How disastrous a clash of two different modal personalities can be is humorously reported in Calvin Trillin's fictional piece.

□□□

CYRIL CRENSHAW, STATIONER, 1905–1970

Crenshaw, a stationer of Knightsbridge, London SW2, perished in the attempt of Harvey R. ("Give-away") Gordon, a Pontiac dealer from Indianapolis, Indiana, to purchase a ballpoint pen. Gordon needed the pen in order to write his congressman that a country whose businessmen had no more initiative than British shopkeepers demonstrated should be cut off Marshall Plan aid immediately.

As the Metropolitan Police pieced the story

From *The Atlantic Monthly*, January 1971. Copyright © 1971 by Calvin Trillin.

together, Gordon's irritation at British business methods began on his first evening in London when, trying to relax from the flight over, he attempted to purchase a ticket at a Kensington cinema fourteen seconds after the final showing of the feature film had begun. The ticket seller informed Gordon that the box office was closing. When he tried to press his money upon her, she reminded him that he would not have received a fair return for it anyway, having already missed not only fourteen seconds of credits in the feature film but two trailers for coming attractions, a newsreel featuring a Manchester apprentice school's unique program for training Kenyan welders, and seven minutes of Horlicks advertisements. Gordon—who, on those occasions when he had to work on his books until three or four in the morning at Giveaway Gordon's Garden of Pontiacs, always kept all the showroom lights on just in case an insomniac station-wagon prospect wandered by—stormed into the theater, flinging a handful of coins at the ticket seller. Two police constables later agreed to remove Gordon physically from a seat in the front stalls, on the grounds not only that he entered when the box office was closing but also that he was improperly seated, having flung a total of ten shillings, the price for the loges (plus a house key), at the ticket seller and then taken a seven-shilling seat.

The following morning Gordon appeared to be less hostile. When the proprietor of a Saville

Row clothing store warned him that the two-hundred-dollar cashmere sport coat he was about to buy might not wear terribly well, Gordon, who had once persuaded a mildly alcoholic machine-tool heiress to buy a Pontiac with eighty-seven thousand four hundred dollars' worth of extras, merely suggested to the clothier that he seek medical attention. But that afternoon, Gordon himself has admitted, there was another throwing incident, this time involving a greengrocer near Victoria Station. Gordon told the greengrocer that he wanted four peaches, and then began to pick them out.

"I'll get them for you, sir, thanks very much," the greengrocer said.

"That's all right, I'll get them," Gordon replied.

"But you'll take all large ones," the greengrocer said.

"Well, of course I'll take all large ones," Gordon said.

"Well, that's hardly fair to the next chap, is it?" the greengrocer said.

"Fair!" Gordon said. "If you were interested in being fair you should have gone into refereeing."

"We can't all be picking out our own peaches, sir," the greengrocer said, whereupon Gordon picked out four of his own peaches, all large ones, and threw them at the greengrocer. The greengrocer and three of the peaches were bruised.

On the same day, Gordon apparently failed to arrange the mending of a shirt, having been told by one laundry that it didn't do small holes and by the laundry next door that it was not equipped for major mending unless Gordon wanted to book three weeks in advance. Two days later, Gordon threatened violence in a shop—the Minimum Delay Cleaners on Brompton Road. Gordon, noticing that the suit he had just had pressed was about to be taken off the hanger and folded up into a paper bag by the clerk, asked to take the suit on the hanger.

"But we would have to charge you tuppence for the hanger, sir," the clerk replied.

"Sold," said Gordon, who had, within a matter of seconds, calculated that paying tuppence for the hanger would be cheaper in the long run than paying to have the suit repressed after it became wrinkled in the paper bag.

"But you could buy hangers across the road for a penny each, sir," the clerk said.

Gordon stared at the clerk. "I'll give you four-pence for your hanger," he finally said. "But not a penny more."

"Oh, tuppence will be quite all right sir," the clerk said, not quite certain that he had understood Gordon correctly. The clerk then put the suit back on the hanger and started to fold it into the paper bag again. A Mrs. Jeffrey Jowell, who was in the store at the time, has confirmed the clerk's testimony that Gordon snatched the suit from the clerk's hand in a violent motion and, as he threw open the door to leave, threatened the destruction of the shop by arson.

Gordon went directly from the Minimum Delay Cleaners to Crenshaw's stationery shop for a pen, composing the letter in his mind as he walked.

"Terribly sorry, sir," Crenshaw said. "We don't do pens."

"You mean you don't sell them?" Gordon asked.

"I'm afraid not, sir," Crenshaw replied. "Odd—ten, fifteen people a day stop off here wanting to buy pens. I suppose because we sell stationery and greeting cards and all that they expect us to sell pens as well."

"Has it ever occurred to you to begin selling pens?" Gordon said quietly, an odd tightness coming over his voice.

"Oh, no, sir," Crenshaw replied. "We don't do pens."

It was at that point that Gordon reached into his raincoat pocket, pulled out the Magnum automatic he always carried in case anyone came onto the Giveaway Gordon's Garden of Pontiacs lot looking for trouble, and finished off Crenshaw in three quick shots. He later instructed his attorney to base his defense on the claim that the shooting had been a crime of passion.

MARTIN APPLEGATE, NEWS DEALER 1911–1970

Applegate, a news dealer on Park Lane, was put to death by LeRoy Bean, a millionaire oilman from Ada, Oklahoma, in the normal course of business. Ironically, the killing was a direct result of Bean's making a special effort to behave courteously to the British. When he wasn't making a special effort to be courteous, Bean made a special effort to be uncouth. He prided himself on his reputation as a crude, self-made wheeler-dealer of the type common in the Southwest—although he was, in fact, a native of Chicago of Latvian descent, a graduate of the University of Illinois in musicology, and a baron of oil only through the happenstance of his wife's father having had control over two hundred and forty-seven million barrels of it.

For years, Bean had been particularly rude to the British, to the intense embarrassment of his wife, who always treated the British with the respect due one's revered ancestors, although all the British she met were live people not related to her. Once, during a reception in Tulsa given by the English Descendants of the Sooner Land Rush, Bean remarked to the British consul that he had by coincidence seen "a whole mess of little-bitty foreigners" downtown that afternoon, knowing full well that the only foreigners who had been downtown were the members of the championship Oxford rugby team who were making a special State Department goodwill tour of eastern Oklahoma. In London, whenever Bean ordered a bartender to bring plenty of ice in his drink, he always added that he realized there were only one hundred seventeen ice cubes in the greater London area at one time. In London restaurants, his orders were always something like, "Bring me one of them chicken pies of yours if you got a crane handy."

After a particularly unpleasant scene in London one night, when Bean insulted the Queen's prize corgi dogs in front of members of the British Natural Gas Association ("Why, in Oklahoma if we ever found a critter that ugly we'd put a bounty on it"), Mrs. Bean announced that if Bean did not make a special effort to be courteous to the British, there would be no more trips out of Ada, a threat she was capable of carrying out, since all of the two hundred and forty-seven million barrels of oil were still in her name.

It was Applegate's bad luck that Bean's first transaction on the morning after Mrs. Bean's dictum was to buy a *Herald-Tribune* on Park Lane. Bean had resolved to be more courteous than the British themselves; the thought of having to spend more than a few months a year in Ada, Oklahoma, surrounded by crude, self-made wheeler-dealers, filled him with dread. Walking down Park Lane, Bean had stopped in front of the Dorchester Hotel's doorman and said, "You got a real fine country here. Real

fine." He had decided that at breakfast he would tell the waiter that only the British were intelligent enough to make breakfast sausages mainly out of bread, thus guarding against early-morning heartburn. When he entered Applegate's shop, he said, "A Paris *Herald-Tribune* please, if you don't mind."

"Thank you," Applegate said. He handed Bean the paper and said "Thank you" again.

"Thank *you*," said Bean, who, after all, had been the one receiving the item in question.

"Thank you very much," Applegate said, as Bean handed him a pound note—and then added, before Bean was able to reply, "Thank you."

"Thanks a lot," Bean said.

"Thanks awfully," Applegate said, handing Bean his change.

"Thank *you*. Thank *you* awfully," Bean said, in a louder voice.

"Thank you very much indeed," Applegate said, somewhat puzzled but trying not to offend a customer.

"Thanks a lot fella—hear?" Bean said. He was almost shouting.

"Thank you, sir," Applegate said. He wondered why Bean was not leaving the store.

"Thank ... you ... sir ... awfully," Bean said, very slowly.

A man in the bakery next door testified that the conversation went for approximately ten minutes before Bean pulled out a long-barreled, pearl-handled revolver—a souvenir his grandfather had come upon during a border skirmish with the Estonians in 1902—and fired at Applegate. The man in the bakery also testified that when the police constables opened the doors of the police van so that Bean could climb in, Bean said, "Thanks awfully."

TIMOTHY PENFOLD, SWEET-SHOP PROPRIETOR, 1902–1970

Penfold, a sweetshop proprietor whose hobby was queuing, had one narrow escape from an American on the same day he eventually met his end at the hands of Myrtle Dougherty of Cleveland Heights, Ohio.

The narrow escape occurred in Penfold's sweetshop. It was a quiet Tuesday morning. Penfold was filling the order of a retired housing inspector who regularly sent a variety of candies in a gift box to the keepers working at a home for worn and misused farm animals in Sussex. It was a complicated order, since the retired housing inspector kept careful notes on the preferences of each keeper, and it often took an hour or so to complete. Penfold and the housing inspector had just spent ten minutes discussing the remarkable fondness of the Deputy Chief Keeper for Mackintosh's Quality Street Toffees when an American walked into the store, picked up a sixpence bag of mixed nuts and raisins from the rack, put a sixpence on the counter in front of Penfold, and said, "OK?"

"Won't keep you a moment, sir," Penfold said to the American, getting right down to adding an eighteen-inch column of figures.

"I'm just leaving this for the nuts and raisins," the American said. He had started out of the shop but had stopped to look at Penfold for an answer.

"I won't be long here, sir, thank you very much," Penfold said, starting to check each candy bar in the box against the numbers in the column.

"But it's the right change," the American said.

Penfold looked up from his figures. "There's a queue, sir," he said, sternly.

Penfold turned back to his figures, and the American reached into his pocket for a .45-caliber pistol he had been carrying for just such occasions. At that point, by chance, the American's wife walked in, reminded him that mixed nuts were high in cholesterol, and led him from the store.

Unaware of his narrow escape, Penfold decided to spend that evening queuing about. He often spent his evenings that way, joining first one queue then another. He had a closetful of items that he had purchased without really needing them, souvenirs of the times when he had been enjoying himself so much that he neglected to leave the queue before arriving at the counter and had to buy something or risk being accused by those behind him of having queued frivolously. Once, on Regent Street, he had been rather embarrassed when he joined what he thought was a short queue

toward a shop door but turned out to be a German tourist ducking out of the wind to light a cigarette. But he continued to find queues irresistible, and he often spent an entire evening strolling from bus stops to cinemas to news dealers and back, queuing happily.

There was nothing frivolous about Penfold's presence in the fatal queue. On closing his sweetshop for the evening, he had decided to go to Hammersmith, where there was an Odeon cinema queue he had always found agreeable. He arrived at the bus stop fully intending to take a Number 74 bus to Hammersmith, although he enjoyed thinking that he was also queuing for the Number 31, which used the same stop. As it happened, there was only one person waiting at the bus stop when Penfold arrived—Mrs. Dougherty, who was returning from a beauty parlor that, according to an article on the women's page of the Cleveland *Plain Dealer*, did the hair of some close friends of Tom Jones, the singer. In Cleveland Heights, Mrs. Dougherty was vice president of her Parent-Teacher Association, recording secretary of the Housewives and Mothers Protection Society Gun Club, and a black belt in karate who had once demonstrated her murderous skill by breaking a Whirlpool washer-dryer with one chop of her bare hand. Penfold stood directly behind Mrs. Dougherty, in the proper queue position. Mrs. Dougherty, sensing someone behind her, moved slightly to the left, in better position if she decided to bring her right elbow back into the assaulter's windpipe. Penfold, not wanting to appear to be breaking the queue, dutifully moved directly behind her again. Mrs. Dougherty moved to the right, and again Penfold moved behind her, silently congratulating himself on attentive queuing. Believing her suspicions confirmed, Mrs. Dougherty faked a left elbow to the lower abdomen, spun around to a kneel-and-fire position, and shot Penfold four times with a small derringer she kept in her passport wallet. Before he expired, Penfold was heard to say, "I hope you don't think I was trying to push ahead."

ROBERT COLES

A domain of sorts

The task of transforming a newborn human organism into a human being knowledgeable about his culture is performed through socialization. To socialize the human being in a small, homogeneous society is relatively simple: Cultural patterns of behavior are clear, and almost everyone agrees about the basic values and attitudes of the society. But what about socialization in a society such as ours? Exactly which behavioral patterns, values, and attitudes are we going to transmit to future members of our society? Because we are divided into numerous subcultures, the generalized other that each child learns to take into account as his self emerges will be mainly a subcultural one. Dr. Robert Coles, a Harvard child psychiatrist, offers us a sensitive portrayal of the socialization of children in Appalachia in this excerpt from his recent book, Children of Crisis.

□□□

They live up alongside the hills, in hollow after hollow. They live in eastern Kentucky and eastern Tennessee and in the western part of North Carolina and the western part of Virginia and in just about the whole state of West Virginia. They live close to the land; they farm it and some of them go down into it to extract its coal. Their ancestors, a century or two ago, fought their way westward from the Atlantic seaboard, came up on the mountains, penetrated the valleys, and moved stubbornly up the creeks for room, for privacy, for a view, for a domain of sorts. They are Appalachian

people, mountain people, hill people. They are white yeomen, or miners, or hollow folk, or subsistence farmers.

From the first months of childhood to later years the land and the woods and the hills figure prominently in the lives of mountain children, not to mention their parents. As a result, the tasks and struggles that confront all children take on a particular and characteristic quality among Appalachian children, a quality that has to do with learning about one's roots, one's territory, as a central fact, perhaps the central fact of existence.

In Wolfe County, Kentucky, I became rather friendly with a whole hollow of Workmans and Taylors, all related to one another.[1] The Workmans had followed a stream up a hill well over a century ago, and Kenneth and Laura Workman are there today, in a cabin Deep Hollow, so named because it is one of the steepest hollows around. Kenneth Workman is forty as I write this. He is now a small farmer. He used to dig for coal in the mines down in Harlan County, Kentucky, but he was lucky enough to lose his job in 1954. Many of the older men he worked with also lost their jobs around that time, when the mines were becoming increasingly automated, but they came back to Wolfe County sick, injured, often near death.

"If we're going to be good parents," Kenneth told me, "we've got to teach our kids a lot about Deep Hollow, so they can find their way around and know everything they've got to know. It's their home, the hollow is. People who come here from outside are not likely to figure out that we've got a lot of teaching to do for our kids outside of school, and it's not the kind they'll get in books. My boy Danny has got to master the hollow; that's what my dad used to say to me; all the time he would

---

[1]At the request of the people mentioned in this essay I have changed their names and some place-names.

From *Harper's Magazine*, December 1971. Reprinted by permission of the author.

tell me and tell me and then I'd be in good shape for the rest of my life."

How does Danny get to master the hollow? For one thing, he was born there, and his very survival augurs well for his future mastery. Laura received no medical care while she carried Danny; the boy was delivered by his two aunts, who also live in Deep Hollow. Danny's first encounter with the Appalachian land took place minutes after he was taken, breathing and screaming, from his mother. Laura describes what happened: "Well, as I can recall, my sister Dorothy came over and showed him to me, and then he was making so much noise we knew he was all right. His birthday is July tenth, you see, and it was a real nice day. She brought me a pail of blackberries that she'd picked and she said they were for later. When Danny was born Dorothy took him over and showed him the blackberries and said it won't be long before he'll be eating them, but first he'll have to learn to pick them, and that will be real soon. Then he was still crying, and she asked me if I didn't think he ought to go outside and see his daddy's corn growing up there, good and tall, and the chickens we have, and Spot and Tan, because they're going to be his dogs, just like everyone else's. I said to go ahead, and my sister Anne held me up a little so I could see, and the next thing I knew the baby was out there near Ken's corn, crying as loud as he could.

"Ken held him high over his head and pointed him around like he was one of the guns being aimed. I heard him telling the baby that here was the corn, there was the beets, and there was cucumbers, and here was the lettuce, and there was the best laying chicken we've got. Next thing he told the baby to stop the crying—and he did, he just did. Ken has a way with kids, even as soon as they're born. He told him to shush up, and he did, and then he just took him and put him down over there, near the corn, and the other kids and my sisters all stood and looked. Dorothy was going to pick him up and bring him back to me, but Ken said he was fast asleep and quiet, and let him just lie there and we should all go and leave things be for a while. So they did; and Ken came in and told me I'd done real well, and he was glad to have a red-haired son, at last, what with two girls that have red hair but all the boys with brown hair. He said did I

mind the little fellow lying out there near his daddy's farm getting to know Deep Hollow, and I said no, why should I."

Shortly after each child of hers is born, the boy or girl is set down on the land, and within a few months he is peering out at it, moving on it, turning over on it, clutching at wild mountain flowers or a slingshot (a present from an older brother) or a spoon (a present from an older sister). Next comes crawling; and mountain children do indeed crawl. They take to crawling and turning over and rolling down the grass and weeds. They take to pushing their heads against bushes and picking up stones and rocks. They take to following sounds, moving toward a bird's call or a frog's. I have rarely seen mothers like Laura Workman lift up babies like Danny and try to make them walk by holding them and pulling them along.

"I never hurry a child. The Lord made them the way He did, and when they're going to do something they're going to, and that's what you have to know."

Certainly she does know that; and she also knows that the chances are her children will leave her very early to wander far over the hills —and in so doing stay close to what she considers "home." When her children grow up, however, she expects they will have little interest in going any farther away than they have already been—even as many other American children, kept relatively close to their parents' small front yard or backyard during early childhood, begin to leave home almost with a vengeance when older. At three, Danny had been all over his father's land, and up and down the hollow. He would roam about with his older brother or sister, tagging after them, trying to join in with their work or play. He had learned how to pick crops and throw a line into a stream and catch a fish. He knew his way down the creek and up the hill that leads to the meadow. He knew about spiders and butterflies and nuts and minnows and all sorts of bugs and beetles and lizards and worms and moles and mice—and those crickets making their noise. He went after caterpillars. He collected rocks of all sizes and shapes; they were in fact his toys. He knew which branches of which trees were hard or soft, unbending or wonderfully pliable. He knew how to cool himself off and wash himself off and fill himself up—all with the water of a high stream. At three, he had been learning all that for about a year.

NAMES WRITTEN IN A BIBLE

At the edge of Logan County, West Virginia, by Rocky Creek, lives Billy Potter, age eight. Billy is tall for his age, with blue eyes and black hair. He has a strong face. His forehead is broad, his nose substantial and sharp, his chin long. Billy is large-boned and already broadshouldered. He is thin, much thinner than he was meant to be. His teeth are in fearful condition, giving him pains in the mouth, and he suffers from dizzy spells; but his cheeks are red and he looks like the very picture of health.

"If I had to choose a time of the year I like best," Billy told me one day when we were talking, "then I'd choose the winter. It's hard in the winter, and you're cold and you shiver, even near the fire; but the creek looks the best, and we all have the most laughing and fun then. My daddy says he's in a better mood in winter than any other time, because there's no place to go, and we just get buried in Rocky Creek, and we have the big sled we built and we go hunting, and it's a real job you have, fooling those animals and catching them, what with the snow and a lot of them hiding and some of them only out for a short time. A lot of time there's no school, because you can't get in here and you can't get out. We play checkers and cards and we take turns picking the guitar and we have the radio with all the music we want, except if there's a bad storm out there. Daddy teaches us how to cut wood and make more things than you can believe. Each winter he has a new plan on what I'm to make out of wood with my knife. He says he's my teacher when there's no school.

"For me, this is the best place to be in the whole world. I've not been to other places, I know; but if you have the best place right round you, before your eyes, you don't have to go looking. I hear they come from all over the country to look at the mountains we have, and Daddy says he wouldn't let one of them, with the cameras and all, into the creek, because they just want to stare and stare, and they don't know what to look for. He says they'll look at a hill, and they won't even stop to think what's on it—the different trees and the animals and birds. The first thing he taught us was what to call the different trees and bushes and vines. He takes us walking and he'll see more than anyone else. He knows where the animals live and where they're going and why they want to go over here and there. He's taking my brother Donald around now. Then he comes home and tells us that Donald is learning—or else he's not learning all he should.

"If I left here and went to live in a city, I'd be losing everything—that's what I hear said by my father and my uncle and cousins. We've been here so long, it's as long as when the country was started. My people came here and they followed the creek up to here and they named it Rocky Creek; they were the ones, that's right. In the Bible we have written down the names of our kin that came before us and when they were born and when they died, and my name is there and I'm not going to leave here, because there'd be no mention of me when I get married and no mention of my children, if I left the creek."

THE EDGE OF THE HOLLOW

On the map, Martin County in Kentucky looks a short distance from Logan County, West Virginia, but ordinary maps tell little about high, nearly impassable hills and mountains and valleys that run north to south rather than east to west—and therefore form a barrier to someone moving across rather than up and down the Appalachians. Marie Lewis is a seven-year-old girl who lives in Martin County, not too far from Inez, the county seat. Marie's father is a good deal better off than Billy's. Mr. Lewis has a fulltime job as a bus driver and school custodian. He works for the county's school board, and considers himself extremely fortunate to do so. Jobs are short in the county, and a steady job makes one secure beyond the comprehension of outsiders. George Lewis's salary by national standards is low, very low; in 1969 it placed him among the nation's poor, among those who make less than $3,000 a year. Yet, as he himself put it: "When others see no money at all, and you get your check every week, you're doing pretty good."

Little Marie, as her father calls her, is almost a picture-book child. She has blond, curly hair, blue eyes, a round face with pink cheeks, and a sturdy body, though even at seven she carries herself like a lady—perhaps like the gentle, sensitive schoolteacher she wants to be. She has such a teacher in school, and she idolizes her. And if little Marie someday does become a teacher, she will substantially consolidate her father's rise in position or class or whatever. Her parents realize this. They see few if any jobs available for their sons, but Marie might indeed be able to become a teacher, unless she marries young, has children, and forgets the whole idea.

"I'd like to have a family—a girl and a boy; but not a lot of children like they do up the hollow. We live right at the foot of the hollow, and we see them all going by, and there are too many of them. My daddy says one thing they could do, since they don't have the money, is stop having all those children, one after another. Susan—she sits beside me in school—must have ten brothers and sisters, I think. She says we live in a real fancy house, and how come my daddy gets to make all the money, and I told her he works hard and he's up before all of them in that hollow."

Marie lives in a modest bungalow, but as she said, the house is luxurious compared to some of the cabins up the hollow, which rises and rises behind the Lewises' house. Still, the Lewis family is poor. They are not towns-people, but by their own description they are "people just lucky enough to get out of the hollow." They are *at* but not *in* the hollow. They enjoy electricity and a furnace and running water. They have a television set and a radio and a refrigerator and an electric stove. They don't have much money for furniture, nor do they drive a car. They will be paying off the house they have built for years and years and years, and it is all the property they have and hope to have.

Marie can be a little casual and even humorous as she talks about things up in the hollow, for all the sadness and misery to be found there. She can point out to her worried and pitying listener that schoolmates of hers, from homes as poor as any in America, nevertheless smile and laugh and jostle one another and get fresh and nasty and tease one another and have fights, "good fights," she calls them, some-

times serious and fierce ones, then make up and become helpful and kind and thoughtful—to everyone, which certainly includes her: "I'd like to marry someone from this county. We have the best people in the world here. The boys can do anything. They can climb every hill, I know they can. They can hunt and fish better than people who live in other places. I know from what my father says. If you go to the cities in Ohio and states like that, you don't know what the people are like. They talk different and they think differ-ent. A lot of them don't go to church, and they're mean to you, unless you're in their family; and they don't help you out the way we do here to everyone who comes by, so long as he means well."

Like a good social scientist (not to mention a person with common sense), Marie talks about the social distinctions she observes, from the grossly apparent ones to others that are decidedly subtle: "The history book the teacher reads to us says our country is made up of different kinds of people, and they come from all over the world, but then in a book about Kentucky she read to us, it said we're mostly the same here in the mountains. I don't agree we're all the same here, and neither does my daddy, because if you look around in school and in church and if you go with my daddy on the bus when he picks everyone up, you'll see we're not the same.

"There's a girl Sally who doesn't want to be a teacher or a nurse or anything. She says she doesn't want to come to school, but her mother tells her she should go just long enough to read and write a little, but not too much. There's a girl Betty who is sick, real bad sick she is, and she should go to a doctor in Inez, and Daddy says she belongs in Lexington, where they have a big hospital, but she's never seen a doctor, and the teacher tried twice to have the nurse come over, but each time Betty didn't come to school that day, and the nurse said she couldn't go up the hollow and she didn't know which house it was that Betty lived in, and the teacher didn't know either. Betty told me one day that the doctors get you sicker, and her daddy has her eating herbs and things, and she'd been prayed over a lot, and she'll be getting better soon, she believes. My mother said it's a shame, and besides Betty being sick there's her whole family: they're all sick with one trouble or another, and they don't have money, and Daddy says they're in the worst shape it's possible to be, and the father is always drinkin'-mad and fightin'-mad, my daddy says. Jamie is her kin, I believe, Betty's kin; and he's maybe nine or ten. He's real good with guns. He can shoot sharper than anyone else, everyone says. Jamie says he's got to know how to shoot, and they're always shooting up there, and not only at animals. They're feuding, feuding real bad all the time, and with liquor it gets worse. They go running up the road and they'll take a shot or two at the first house they come to. They don't dare come down to us and do that, because they know the sheriff would come and have them in jail so fast they wouldn't know what happened to them. Daddy says they fight and drink up the liquor they make because they have to fill up the day, and anyone would surely be unhappy if he didn't have his work and there was no money and all the sickness they have up in the hollow. They're always tossing their mess in the creek—a lot of glass and paper and everything. The dogs go swimming, and they'll get scraps of food if there are any, but food is scarce up there, so they don't throw it away.

"Once the teacher called me over, and she said I was being real nice because I shared my cookies with the kids, and my mother packed me extra ones, because I told her I felt bad eating, when others have nothing to eat. I told her they're hungry from up there, and they need better clothes than they have. I give them the cookies, but they're not going to be saying thank you all the time, and I'm glad they don't! You have to keep your chin up, and not bow and scrape, and people don't like to be asking for favors all the time. Sally said her mother told her not to take anything for free and not to go asking favors of people, and she should have her pride. Sally said her mother told her, 'To hell with people feeling sorry for us, because if they try, they'll get shot real fast around here.'

"Sally takes my cookies though. We'll eat my cookies and she'll tell me she's glad we live where we do, because our house is a good beginning for the hollow, and we're lucky Daddy has the job he's got. I know that's right, because if I was Sally, I wouldn't be thinking of going on to the high school, either.

"When they took in their corn, Sally came down with some, because they grow it and we don't. She said she wanted to thank us for the cookies at school, and the corn was just picked and ripe as can be and real sweet, and her mother said they knew we were good to Sally and they wanted to be good to us. Later, when she had left, my daddy said I should never forget that people in Martin County are the best people in the world, and even if they've got almost nothing except what they grow, they don't go begging and stealing and they don't do much borrowing either. They'll take something and let a favor be done, then they'll keep it in their mind, and when the moment is a good one, then they'll go and pay the favor back. He's told me that a few times, Daddy has—not to forget Sally bringing up the corn. I don't. I won't."

ON ACCOUNT OF THE MACHINES

What of the Sallys who by the thousands live up those hollows and creeks, the poorest of the poor, those whose minds and hearts and souls have significantly given way, having suffered beyond any reasonable limit, even where people know how to take hardship in their stride? They are the families and the children whose extreme condition—of life and limb and spirit—has been described by Appalachian people themselves. Sally, for example, can spell out unself-consciously and even casually some of the distinguishing characteristics that set her apart, say, from Herbie, a boy of eight who lives not far away in the same hollow: "Herbie's daddy had a job in the mines, but then he got fired because they were closing down the mines, some of them, and laying off people on account of the machines. They had some money during the time he was working, and my daddy says once you've had money you never can forget it. Herbie says his daddy can't recall the last time he saw a paycheck, but you can see his folks went and got things with the money—the television and the stove and the refrigerator. In our place there's no electricity, none—so we couldn't have television or a refrigerator, even if we had the money to buy them. We don't need electricity. We have the stove. All we need is wood for it, and my daddy goes and finds coal up the hollow and digs out the pieces. The trouble is a lot of the time he's under, real bad under, and then we have to do his chores, and my mother will be crying and then we all start and it's then I wish I was staying down the hollow, maybe with Herbie and his folks—they're the best people you could meet."

When her father goes "real bad under," he has been drinking too much. Her mother tries hard to stop "the old man's habit," as she refers to him and his drinking. After a while, though, she also starts drinking, first slowly but then with a certain desperate acceleration that strikes terror into the minds of her seven children, who run for cover—to the woods and to kinfolk down the hollow.

Sally's parents live as far up the hollow as one can go. From their cabin one can see a truly splendid view of the Appalachians: the hills close by and far; the low-hanging white clouds and the higher gray clouds; the mist or the drizzle or the fog; and, near at hand, everywhere the green of the trees. The cabin is black, tar-paper black, and stands on four cement blocks. It lacks curtains but does indeed possess that old stove, the place where life-giving food is prepared and life-preserving heat is given off. Near the stove there are three beds with mattresses but nothing else. Ten human beings use the mattresses: Sally's grandmother, her parents, and the seven children in the family. The cabin possesses a table but only one chair to go with it, and two other old "sitting chairs," both of which are battered and tattered, with springs in each quite visible.

The children sit and eat outside under the trees, or inside on the floor, or near the house on the ground; or else they walk out in front of the house, in which case they often remain standing or hunch over their food. The children commonly use their hands to eat, or share a limited number of forks (four), spoons (five), and knives (seven) with their parents and grandmother. The children also share clothes: two pairs of shoes, both in serious need of repair, two ragged winter jackets, and three very old pairs of winter gloves. The children, let it be said, also share something else—the hollow: its hills and land, its vast imposing view, its bushes and shrubs and plants and animals and water and silence and noise, its

seclusion and isolation, and also its people —for Sally a whole crowded, complicated sustaining world.

What I have learned from Sally's life (and her words and her) does not require me to say that a good deal of it is unsatisfying—to her, never mind me. She does not need me to express her central longing that her family find a more coherent, valuable kind of existence. Sally and children like her made it very clear to me that on the one hand they very much like certain things about mountain living, and on the other hand they are troubled and confused and even badly hurt (yes, they *know* they are hurt) by the hunger pangs they experience, the sickness that goes untreated, and, perhaps worst of all, the sight of what their suffering does to their parents. Those Appalachian parents certainly do take notice of their children's suffering—partly because they are parents, and also because they are traditionally proud and defiant people. Children notice their parents noticing, and Sally herself can talk about that kind of watching and counterwatching as it goes on among bruised and offended people, unwilling to let go of their sense of dignity and self-respect, and unwilling also to let go of their love for their ancestors, for their homes, their land, their conventions: "There's nothing that gets my daddy going worse than liquor. Once he told my mother he was going to start drinking because he was upset as bad as he could be, because he'd been down the hollow and over to the welfare people and it was the first time he'd gone and it was going to be the last, even if he starved to death. I guess they didn't give him anything. They said they were sorry. They said there's no money for most people, and that's all they can do in the office there.

"Daddy was more upset that he'd gone over to them than that they had refused him; I know that, because he said so all morning. I've never seen him so fightin'-mad, and he said he was, and we all got more and more scared. My mother told us we'd better go out to the woods and play, and she would take care of everything. Then before we left he looked at me and my sister and he raised up his hand, and I got scared he might come over and take it out on us—but no, he didn't do anything. He told me I was good and he was glad I was good, and he said the day would come when he'd be able to bring home clothes for us and I'd look pretty. He said I already do, but if you have a dress, it helps. Then he said I could go outside and my mother said to go, and I went. The next thing I knew he was drinking and he started screaming real bad after a while. I believe a lot of the time he gets himself upset on account of us, and then he'll go and take to the liquor he makes.

"I wouldn't want to live any other place. What do you do if there's no hill you're on—if it's flat like they show you in the books in school? If I could change anything I wanted, I'd tear down that place Daddy and his friends use to make the liquor. I'd just have the hill here, where we live, and the other ones, to go and look at. I'd have us living in a different house, maybe like Marie's. Then we'd all be happier, I know that. Then I think my daddy might stop his drinking and never start again, like he'll promise us each time that he's going to do."

STALEMATE

Mountaineers look upon life as a sort of stalemate, in which there is plenty of good as well as plenty of bad, plenty to hold onto as well as plenty to wish for, and, as a result "an awful lot of plenty" to be high-strung about, unsettled about, feel torn about. Faced with such thoroughly mixed feelings, mountaineers stand fast and try to persist. In the words of Marie's father, they "stick it out, last it out." Stick out and last out what, one wonders? Does he mean the obvious lack of material things and opportunities? That, yes; but more is at stake than some of us on the outside realize. Marie's father says, "As I see it, up there in the hollow it's real bad—yes, with Sally and her people. But there's plenty they just don't want to lose, an awful lot of plenty, I'll tell you. People come in here and they don't know that. I heard on the TV a man saying we're supposed to be suspicious up in the mountains, and we don't trust no one, except ourselves. What a lot of hooey he had in his mouth, saying that. Sure we're not going to like someone if he comes in here and tells us we're a bunch of damn fools, and we should do this and that and everything they want us, and then we'll be all right.

"Hell, this is our country. We made it. We came here and we stayed because we loved it, and no one's going to get us out—except, I guess, if we're going to starve right to death, and then we'll be gone anyway. But I think we're friendlier here than in those cities you see all the time on the TV, where they pay no mind to anyone but themselves. I'm no expert on anything, except driving a bus and making sure those schools stay warm in the winter and as clean as they can, what with all the kids messing things up every day; but you can walk up any hollow or creek in Kentucky and West Virginia and you'll hear people picking on the guitar and listening to the radio and they'll stop and talk with you, and if you want to stay for supper, that's fine. Now, if you do, they're not going to go and spit on themselves and hold out their hand and say, 'Look here mister, give us a few pennies out of your big fat wallet.' No sir, they're going to put out their best for you, and they're going to show you they've got a lot to put out, that's right.

"Sure, we need more, a hell of a lot more, and you must have figured that out by now. But no one's going to get us feeling kindly by coming on first thing with a lot of that lousy pity stuff you hear on the TV—about the poor people of Appalachia! Hell on that! Hell on it! They start with that and the next thing I know I'm ready to tell them to take themselves and their charity and to try it on someone else, because that's not what a decent, God-fearing man wants, no it's not. You can get suspicious, like they say we are. The coal people come in here, and they're tearing up everything they can get their hands on, and maybe they'll give you the money, the wages, but sure as hell they get more out of it than all of us ever will, and then the next thing you know they've gone, and all we have for it is that they've gone, and all we have for it is that they've torn up a whole mountain and what's left of the mountain is falling down on us in a landslide, and we're supposed to get out, fast. If you don't get suspicious over that, then you're not right in your head. Then you know they've been taking our timber away, by the hillful, since way back, and right in front of our eyes that's what's been happening since I guess Abraham Lincoln or someone was President. So, why shouldn't we go and tell our children to watch out when some big-smiling city slicker comes here with a dozen lawyers standing guard over him?

"Sure we're afraid of them all coming here; we can smell the trouble before it gets to the first hill in Kentucky—or over in West Virginia. But if they came to us and wanted to bring in some work here, and it didn't mean tearing up the whole country, and it didn't mean eating up our lungs, then we'd be just like any American—glad to have a job, you bet your life. We'd want to sit here and be ourselves, of course. We wouldn't want to act like some of the people you see on television. We wouldn't want to dress as they do, and talk as they do, no matter how much money we made. We'd want to live as we do. But we'd be working, and that would sure be a welcome change hereabouts."

Many of us on the "outside" have yet to convince a man like Marie's father that we really understand what we claim is obvious to us; for he thinks we would only pity him and his kin, even as we pity the children of sharecroppers and of migrant farmers. Our pity will give very little to anyone, and it enrages the mountaineers—who know very well what kind of justice they require and what justice we in America have so far done and not done.

DISCUSSING THE ARTICLES

1. In Calvin Trillin's fictional piece, "A Nation of Shopkeepers . . . ," what does the nickname "Giveaway" immediately suggest about the American national character?

2. What other stereotype is illustrated when Gordon tries to write to his congressman about matters in a foreign country?

3. What supposed features of the British national character are illustrated when the ticket seller refuses to sell a ticket because the feature had begun fourteen seconds earlier?

4. In the Trillin piece, list all of the supposed national characteristics of both Americans and British. Do you agree that the characteristics of Americans are indeed national? Have you personally observed them in Americans? In many Americans? In a few Americans?

5. Trillin exaggerates his stereotypes for the sake of literary effect. However, most people would agree that there is a modal, or national, personality type. Refer to the national characteristics illustrated in the piece. What elements in American culture produce such personality types? What is your personal opinion, based on experience, of cultural determinism?

6. In Robert Coles' "A Domain of Sorts," would you say the people described make up a subculture? By virtue of what?

7. What becomes the central fact of existence for Appalachian children? How does this differ from children in your subculture?

8. Is conventional formal education, that is, "book learning," emphasized to Appalachian children? What attitude toward education does your subculture hold? Is this why you are in college, or are you in college in spite of the values of your subculture?

9. Compare and contrast the experience of giving birth in Appalachia and in any urban center. Do you think the birth experience in Appalachia may cause the mother to have different feelings toward her child than does the urban mother?

10. What effect on Appalachian children does their freedom to roam when very young have in later years? How does this compare with most other American children, according to the author? In this case, is geography—the physical environment —responsible for personality?

11. Compare and contrast the learning experiences of an Appalachian child and an urban child. Venture guesses as to how these differences affect the children's attitude toward their environment.

12. How do you suppose Appalachian children are affected by the feeling of continuity they obtain from seeing the names and dates of their kin in the family Bible?

13. How does poverty in the hollows of Appalachia differ from poverty in an urban slum? What effect does it seem to have on the children's perception of themselves? Of others?

14. How is poverty in Appalachia similar to poverty in urban slums? What does it do to people?

15. From the conversation of the two girls Marie and Sally, how would you explain the Appalachians' disdain of welfare? What bothered Sally's father more than the refusal of welfare?

16. How do the Appalachians perceive the outside world? What injustices do they feel have been done to them? From what you know of the problem, would you agree with them? How do you explain that they still like their way of life?

TERMS TO REMEMBER

Personality. A complex and dynamic system that includes all of an individual's behavioral and emotional traits, his attitudes, values, beliefs, habits, goals, and so on.

Biological determinism. Theories centering around the belief that human personality and behavior are primarily functions of biology.

Instincts. Genetically transmitted, universal, complex patterns of behavior.

Psychoanalytic theory. A theory of personality developed by Sigmund Freud. It assumes the existence of unconscious, as well as conscious, processes within each individual.

Libido (Freud). The instinctual drive toward pleasure, which is the motivating energy behind human behavior.

Id (Freud). The representative of the libido in the personality, existing on an unconscious level and making up the primitive, irrational part of the personality.

Ego (Freud). A part of the personality functioning on a conscious level. It attempts to force the id to satisfy its instinctual needs in socially acceptable ways.

Superego (Freud). A final element of personality, existing largely on an unconscious level and functioning to impose inhibition and morality on the id. It is the product of culture and society and corresponds to what people call "the conscience."

Defense mechanisms (Freud). Frequently unconscious actions that protect the individual from anxiety and frustration. They hide his real motives and goals from his awareness and, thus, help him avoid suffering a loss of self-esteem.

Psychosexual stages (Freud). The way the individual attempts to gratify the force of the libido at different periods of his physical maturation. The phases are oral, anal, phallic, or Oedipal, latent, and genital.

Trait. Distinctive and recurring characteristics of an individual's appearance or behavior.

Endomorphs, mesomorphs, ectomorphs. Classification of body types in the theory of personality developed by William Sheldon.

Cultural determinism. A theory in which human personality is viewed as being basically the product of the individual's culture.

National character, or modal personality. A basic personality type developed by each society. It reflects the specific culture of that society.

Behaviorism, or environmental determinism. Theories of personality based on the belief that scientific research can concern itself only with overt behavior. Behaviorists believe that behavior is the result of conditioning, which takes place through reinforcement (rewards and punishment). Also called environmental determinism, behaviorism assumes that the newborn human is extremely malleable.

Maturation. A physical process attained by all individuals in all societies, regardless of cultural or personal experiences.

Socialization. The process by which a biological organism becomes a human being, acquires a personality with self and identity, and absorbs the culture of his society.

Symbolic interaction. The uniquely human ability to manipulate symbols that are commonly understood. The chief symbol is language, through which humans create and transmit culture.

Resocialization. A process that includes the erasure of the individual's present self-concept and identity. It generally occurs when the individual is made a member of a total institution, such as the armed services or a prison.

Looking-glass self (Cooley). The process by which an individual's self-image emerges as he perceives the observed attitudes of others.

Mind (Mead). The abstract whole of a person's ideas.

Self (Mead). The individual's self-conception, or self-awareness.

Symbolic interactionism. A theory of personality by George Herbert Mead centering around the interrelationship of mind, self, and society and including the belief that society and the individual give rise to each other through the process of symbolic interaction.

Taking the role of the other (Mead). A process in the emergence of self in which the individual projects himself into the roles of significant others and, thus, learns their attitudes toward him.

Significant others (Mead). The people important to the individual in the first years of his life, from whom he internalizes his first attitudes.

Generalized other (Mead). The role of society as a whole. When the individual has learned to take the role of the generalized other, he has, in effect, learned the attitudes, values, and expectations of society as a whole, or of that portion of it to which he has been exposed.

"I" (Mead). The initial, subjective element of the self, which is acting, natural, uninhibited, spontaneous, and unorganized.

"Me" (Mead). The later, objective, social element of the self, which represents the organized set of attitudes and cultural and societal expectations that have been internalized by the individual.

Neurosis. A feeling of profound anxiety, which the individual often tries to overcome by using defense mechanisms to excess.

Psychosis. A condition in which the individual tries to adjust his environment to fit into his conception of the world. In this attempt, the individual often loses touch with reality and becomes unable to differentiate between societal norms of "right" and "wrong." Psychosis represents a more serious deviation from the norm than neurosis does.

SUGGESTIONS FOR FURTHER READING

Adler, Alfred. *Problems of Neurosis*. New York: Cosmopolitan Books, 1930. An eminent neo-Freudian gives his views of personality formation.

Benedict, Ruth. *Patterns of Culture*. Baltimore, Md.: Penguin Books, 1946. An interesting account of the emergence of modal personality, by a renowned anthropologist.

Blumer, Herbert. "Sociological Implications of the Thought of George Herbert Mead." *American Journal of Sociology* (March, 1966), pp. 525–544. A restatement and clarification of Mead's theories regarding the social self.

Cooley, Charles Horton. *Human Nature and the Social Order*. New York: Schocken Books, 1962. First edition, 1902. The theorist who coined the concept of the "looking-glass self" examines the social nature of the self.

Elkin, Frederick. *The Child and Society*. New York: Random House, 1960. An interpretation of the socialization of children and personality formation according to the precepts of role theory.

Erikson, Erik. *Childhood and Society*, rev. ed. New York: W. W. Norton, 1964. A well-known psychologist speaks on socialization and personality formation.

Eysenck, Hans J. *The Biological Basis of Personality*. Springfield, Ill.: Charles C. Thomas, Publisher, 1967. The biological factor in personality development is skillfully and exhaustively analyzed.

Fromm, Erich. *Escape from Freedom*. New York: Avon, 1965. A classic on personality, among other things, from a philosopher of psychology.

Goffman, Erving. *The Presentation of Self in Everyday Life*. New York: Doubleday Anchor Books, 1959. A view of the self in everyday interaction, and the ways in which the individual consciously or unconsciously strives to present a favorable impression of himself to others.

Hall, Calvin S. *A Primer of Freudian Psychology*. New York: Mentor Books, 1954. Basic Freudian theories presented in a brief, concise, and rather readable style.

Horney, Karen. *The Neurotic Personality of Our Time*. New York: W. W. Norton, 1964. A neo-Freudian looks at personality.

Janis, I. L. et al. *Personality: Dynamics, Development, and Assessment*. New York: Harcourt Brace Jovanovich, 1969. An exhaustive analysis of research on personality.

Jung, Carl G. *Two Essays in Analytical Psychology*. London: Balliere, Tindall, 1926. The collective unconscious analyzed by a neo-Freudian.

Kinch, John W. "A Formalized Theory of the Self-Concept." *American Journal of Sociology* (January, 1963), pp. 481–486. A detailed explanation of the interactionist theory of the self: that a person's self-concept derives from his conception of how others respond to him.

Lundin, R. W. *Personality: A Behavioral Analysis*. New York: Macmillan, 1969. A behaviorist looks at personality.

Manis, Jerome, and Meltzer, Bernard N., eds. *Symbolic Interaction*. Boston: Allyn and Bacon, 1967. A collection of essays interpreting the theory of symbolic interactionism from the viewpoint of social psychology.

Shibutani, Tamotsu. *Society and Personality*. Englewood Cliffs, N.J.: Prentice-Hall, 1961. A view of the evolution of the social self and the relationship of personality and social interaction.

CHAPTER four

We usually define history as the record of the past deeds of humanity. When we examine the record, however, we note that there is hardly any mention of the countless men and women who lived and died during any period. The people we read about were kings and noblemen, popes and cardinals, presidents and prime ministers, idealists and demagogues. They were the people who discovered continents, built nations, and shaped the destinies of the rest of mankind. They wore brilliant headpieces, but their subjects wore a single gray feather. They were buried with costly jewels in elaborate tombs, but their servants' deaths merited no such refinements. They ate with golden utensils, but the masses scavenged for scraps.

In all known societies save the very simplest ones, there has been a division between the few and the many: The few have led and the many have followed; the few have had much and the many have had little; the few have been powerful, and the many have been powerless. What is the basis for such differences among people? Are some individuals born with special talents for leading and for accumulating wealth and power? And are the majority born without such talents? Or are these abilities acquired through a special set of circumstances?

We need not rely on the past for examples of the division between the few and the many. This division has not changed appreciably through the years. If anything, the gaps may have grown wider. For example, in feudal Europe, the king or nobleman ruled his fiefdom with absolute power. He lived in a huge castle instead of a hut, ate meat rather than mush, and fought and hunted rather than tilling the soil. Nevertheless, his life was basically the same as that of the peasants on his estate. Bad crops and famine affected him as well as his subjects. War and disease killed his kin as well as his serfs'. If he washed out of a golden tub and others out of a tin one, the water for both came from the same river.

What is more, in return for his absolute power, the feudal lord performed a definite function for his subjects. He safeguarded them from attacking enemies, provided them with a livelihood, and settled their quarrels. Also, because he was almost the only literate among illiterates, he made sure that the fire of civilization was kept lit.

Today, modern industrial societies are affluent beyond the feudal ruler's wildest dreams. Yet a very large percentage of that affluence still belongs to a very small percentage of the population. Whereas this small, affluent minority are not always the acknowledged rulers, they still have the power to make crucial decisions that affect the lives of the majority. In addition, there are staggering differences in the standard of living of the minority on top and the majority on the bottom. At one extreme is the person who flies from continent to continent, where he owns different mansions, each of which is staffed with numerous servants and filled with valuable antiques and art collections. At the other extreme is the person who lives in one or two rat-infested rooms, in which the only antiques are the plumbing and heating systems, and the only art the obscene scrawls on walls. At one pole are jet-setters, who can travel, anywhere and anytime the whim strikes, in their own or chartered planes. At the other are city-dwellers, who must use uncomfortable, slow, and hopelessly outdated transportation systems to get to work and to perform other necessary activities. At one end of the scale are those people who wear nothing but designer clothing and eat gourmet specialties. At the other are those who shop in bargain basements and buy starchy fillers to substitute for a lack of expensive high protein food.

The minority on top still performs a function for the majority. It provides employment for many, but by no means all, at the bottom. However, work relationships in vast corporations and in government have become so impersonal that the feeling of security, of being taken care of, provided by the feudal ruler is completely lacking. Other protective functions such as defense and welfare, once performed by the feudal ruler, have been taken over, however ineffectively, by the vast, unwieldy bureaucracy of the state.

Obviously, the contrasts we have drawn between feudal and modern societies oversimplify differences and minimize the very real inequality that existed in the feudal period. Today, in modern industrial societies, there is no longer a clear-cut, twofold division between the haves and the have-nots.

A vast number of people occupy the middle ground between the top and the bottom. Nevertheless, the resources of societies are still unequally divided among their members.

SOCIAL STRATIFICATION, OR SOCIAL RANKING

Sociologists call the phenomenon that we have been discussing *social stratification,* or *social ranking.* These terms refer to a structure existing in every society, with the possible exception of very simple ones that have not yet developed division of labor or produced a surplus. This structure is the result of members ranking one another and themselves hierarchically (from low to high) with respect to the amount of goods and services they possess. Members of societies also rank one another according to the prestige they derive from their possessions and according to the extent of power they wield over others in the society.

Sociologists generally examine social stratification as structure, analyzing its varieties and parts. However, stratification expert Gerhard Lenski points out that the structure of stratification cannot be separated from the process that originates it—the distributive process. All divisions of people into social levels represents an attempt to answer a basic question: Who gets what and why?[1] Naturally, this question is answered differently in different societies. The answer depends on the cultural values of a society and the accessibility of societal goals to members.

[1]Gerhard Lenski, *Power and Privilege* (New York: McGraw-Hill, 1966), p. 3.

The most apparent result of social ranking is social inequality, a characteristic of societies past and present. In most simple societies, inequality has been taken for granted, or considered a natural part of life. In complex societies, however, the issue of inequality has provoked serious debate.

In Eastern societies, social inequality has often been considered not only inevitable but appropriate. Hindus, for example, believe that the position to which a person is born is a reflection of his virtue or his lack of virtue. The poor, then, are considered to be underserving, whereas the rich and powerful reap the rewards of goodness they have displayed in a previous life.

Western people have, in general, been a little less accepting of social inequality. The ancient Hebrew prophets questioned whether it was morally ethical for some to have so much and abuse it, and others to have so little and to be the victims of abuse. Thus, questions about the inevitability of social inequality at least existed in the Judeo-Christian ethic.

Many early sociologists viewed social inequality as inevitable. In the nineteenth century, the findings of Charles Darwin influenced not only biology but also social thought. Early sociologists applied to social systems the principle of the survival of the fittest—Darwin's explanation of why some animal species survived and others disappeared. Thus, many people concluded that because the goods that society values are scarce and because almost all the members of society must compete for them, only the strongest, the most intelligent, or the most virtuous will attain them. People who accepted this viewpoint gave little attention to the way goods were obtained—whether strictly through the individual's efforts or through an accident of birth.

Functionalist Theory

Today, most sociologists accept one of two theories of social inequality. In both, social inequality is considered inevitable.

The first theory is, in part, based on a view of human beings that has been held by many people for centuries. According to this view, humans are basically selfish creatures who must be constrained by society and its institutions to live in peace with their neighbors and to cooperate with them for the common good. Such creatures do not cooperate unless they are convinced that cooperation will profit them.

This judgment of humans is part of the *functionalist theory*. The existence of every society depends on the regular performance of specific tasks that are difficult and require special intelligence, talent, and training. According to functionalist theory, if the most intelligent, talented, and best-trained individuals are to perform these tasks to the best of their abilities, a system of rewards must exist. Therefore, the positions most essential to the welfare of society must be the most highly rewarded. Believers in functionalism are afraid that if a street sweeper and a neurosurgeon received the same pay and benefits, no one would bother training for many years to become a neurosurgeon when it is so much easier to wield a broom!

Perhaps of even more importance to functionalist theory is the way in which not human beings but society is viewed. The early sociologist Emile Durkheim emphasized the order and stability of societies. Today's functionalists have built on this viewpoint. Society is considered an organism that constantly tries to attain balance, stability, and order. A system of stratification, even though it promotes social inequality, is considered an aid to the maintenance of a status quo and, therefore, to the desired stability. The absence of a stratification system could lead to conflict among individuals and groups, who want the scarce resources of society. And conflict disrupts the orderly working of society.[2] Unsurprisingly, functionalist theory is sometimes called equilibrium theory.

Critics argue that this theory is not valid by pointing out that societies do not always reward the members who fulfill essential roles. In our society, for instance, although physicians are well rewarded for their vital role, other professionals whose function seems equally vital (teachers, nurses, social workers) are notoriously ill rewarded. In addition, we seem to reward sports and entertainment personalities exceedingly well for the few hours of entertainment they provide us.

Furthermore, the existence of a stratification system prevents many talented people who do not have access to training from developing their talent. Only through extreme good luck do many talented people in various fields eventually rise to the top. The biographies of famous people provide countless examples. Black leaders Malcom X and Eldridge Cleaver were once well on their way to a life of criminal pursuits; chance alone gave them the opportunity to fulfill some of their talent for leadership. Furthermore, millions of unheard-of people live on the edge of survival and are condemned to gray, uninteresting existences, simply because they were born into a social class in which the chances of attaining "the good life" are weak, or almost nonexistent.

TABLE 4.1 SOCIAL ORIGINS OF AMERICA'S RICHEST MEN, 1900-1950

Social Origin	1900	1925	1950
Upper class	39%	56%	68%
Middle class	20	30	20
Lower class	39	12	9
Not classified	2	2	3

SOURCE: Adapted from C. Wright Wills, *The Power Elite* (New York: Oxford University Press, 1956), pp. 104–105. The percentages are derived from biographies of the 275 people who were and are known to historians, biographers, and journalists as the richest people living in the United States—the 90 richest of 1900, the 95 of 1925, and the 90 of 1950. At the top of the 1900 group is John D. Rockefeller; at the top in 1925 is Henry Ford I; at the top in 1950 is H. L. Hunt.

[2]In the United States, the best-known followers of functionalist theory are sociologists Kingsley Davis, Wilbert Moore, and, with variations, Talcott Parsons.

Conflict Theory

According to *conflict theory*, the natural condition of society is constant change and conflict, not order and stability. Creative change and beneficial dissension among individuals and groups are preferable to stability, because they lead to progress and prevent stagnation. In this view, social stratification, and the resulting inequality, though not ideal, are unavoidable. In fact, stratification is the product of the constant struggle for scarce goods that takes place in every society. Stratification exists because those who have acquired a large portion of the goods exercise their power to keep others from attaining them.

The best-known supporter of conflict theory was the social philosopher Karl Marx. He believed that all of history is a record of class struggles caused by the unequal distribution of rewards in societies. According to Marx, the ruling classes exploit the working classes by upholding an unequal system both by force and by instilling societal values and beliefs that encourage people to believe in the righteousness of the system. Marx predicted that continuous class struggles would eventually lead to a classless society. This prediction has, so far, not been fulfilled, even in the societies that attempt to put his theories into practice.

Is Stratification Inevitable?

Regardless of which theory of stratification we find most plausible, we must acknowledge that stratification systems and the consequent social inequality, exist in every human society advanced enough to practice division of labor and to produce a surplus. In addition, some stratification exists even among many animal species. Chickens have a pecking order, and wolves, deer, and other mammals living in what resemble social groups all have hierarchies of leadership. Are we to assume, then, that biology is the basis of inequality? Undeniably, we are not all born with equal size, strength, degree of intelligence, health, and so on. And such factors definitely determine how well we compete for the rewards of society.

Throughout our lives, also, we are susceptible to accidents, some of which may cripple or handicap us and thus diminish our ability to compete. The greatest accident of all is that of being born in a favorable geographic location and into a family that is high on the ladder of stratification. Even though biology and chance play a part, stratification systems are basically social, or man-made. They are part of the overall system into which societies organize themselves for most effective survival.

It is doubtful, moreover, that stratification systems, and social inequality, can ever be totally erased. Even spokesmen for utopian, communistic, and socialistic solutions to social inequality do not envision societies in which every individual possesses exactly the same amount of goods and is entitled to the same number of services as his neighbor. Societies are perhaps unable to take responsibility for the biological differences that influence the individual's social position. However, societies should attempt to lessen the great gap between those who find themselves at the extremes of stratification systems. In modern industrial societies, it is necessary to first lessen economic inequalities, for it is on these inequalities that most others hinge.

All systems of stratification are constructed in the same basic way, regardless of the kind of society in which they appear. And all are based on the possession of scarce goods, whether the goods valued are cash or the number of wives a man can afford. Every stratification system includes the categories of class, status, and power. These categories are sometimes called wealth, prestige, and privilege.

SOCIAL CLASS

Social class—the division of members of society into a number of strata based on income, occupation, education, residence, and other characteristics —has existed for centuries. Long ago, the Greek philosopher Aristotle wrote that Greek society was divided into three layers. During the feudal era, European society was divided into three distinct estates, or classes: the nobility, the church, and the peasants. Some two hundred years ago, Adam Smith, the popularizer of laissez-faire economics, maintained that civilized society is naturally divided into those who live by rent, those who live by wages, and those who live by profit.[3] Finally, Karl Marx not only accepted the concept of social class but made it the crux of his theory. According to Marx, class struggle was the dynamic force of history.

Yet what precisely is a social class? Can any of us determine with absolute certainty whether social classes exist in our society? If so, can we without hesitation identify ourselves as members of a specific social class? Assuming that we *can* establish the existence of social classes, how many are there? And what are the standards for membership in each class?

Classes in the United States

The most precise answer that we can give to questions of social class in the United States is that we are conscious of the existence and the consequences of social classes. In this country, we supposedly govern ourselves according to the democratic principle of equality. This principle is the basis of the myth that we are a classless society. In short, many believe that because all men are created equal, they are equal in all ways—that they even have equal opportunities to acquire wealth, privilege, and power. But the tremendous gaps that exist among people are made obvious by differences in life styles. Such differences show that the belief in classlessness is indeed a myth.

At the same time, because of the nature of our society, classes are too indefinite to permit a scientifically exact counting and description. The degree of difference between social classes, as well as degrees of prestige and power, is sometimes hardly noticeable. What is more, our society is spread across a vast geographic area, and our population is extremely heterogeneous. These factors encourage strong local stratification systems and make the task of interpreting data on a national basis very difficult. The richest hog farmer in Porkersville, East Carolina, is no doubt considered a member of the upper class by Porkerville residents. But on a national basis, he would be competing with tycoons in finance and industry and would undoubtedly be classified on a lower level.

[3] Adam Smith, *The Wealth of Nations* (London: Dent Everyman Edition, 1910), p. 230.

On a national level, then, we can only observe and agree that because some people have similar occupations, incomes, educations, and life styles, they set themselves apart from the rest of the population. In time, they are set off enough to form a social stratum that is unified enough to be recognized as a social class. Sociologist Gerhard Lenski supplies an all-inclusive definition of social class as "an aggregation of persons in a society who stand in a similar position with respect to some form of power, privilege, or prestige."[4]

The concept of social class includes not only similarity of ranking but also the way in which people operate at dissimilar levels in the everyday experiences of life: how and what they eat, how they play, date, marry, bring up their children, and so on. The way in which each social stratum does such things is the result of similarities in educational experiences, occupation, and residence—in short, of life styles.[5]

Methods of Determining Social Class

Social scientists have used a number of approaches in their attempts to describe and order social classes with some degree of accuracy. In *Middletown*, a classic study of stratification, Robert and Helen Lynd divided the population of a representative Middle-American town into two classes: the business class and the working class.[6] Another classic, the *Yankee City Series*, examined the stratification system of a New England seaside town. Classifications were made according to a six-class division: upper-upper, lower-upper; upper-middle,

[4]Gerhard Lenski, *Power and Privilege* (New York: McGraw-Hill, 1966), pp. 74-75.

[5]Harold M. Hodges, Jr. and W. Clayton Lane, *Social Stratification* (Cambridge, Mass.: Schenkman, 1964), p. 13.

[6]Robert Lynd and Helen Lynd, *Middletown in Transition* (New York: Harcourt, Brace & World, 1937).

lower-middle; upper-lower, lower-lower. These divisions are still the most frequently used ones in the literature dealing with stratification.[7] However, still
other researchers use the classifications of white-collar, blue-collar, and professional middle class.

Sociologists disagree not only about the number of classes but also about
the standards that determine who belongs in which class. It is important to
remember, then, that the categories used by researchers are arbitrary, or artificial. They do not occur naturally in society but are simply a device researchers
use to simplify their work. A researcher may decide that an individual whose
salary has increased by $1,000 per year belongs in a different income category
than he would have before the increase. But there is no law, either of nature
or of society, that supports such a classification. In preindustrial societies, on
the other hand, such natural divisions may exist. In feudal Europe, the social
distance between the nobility and the serfs was so great that the existence
of these two categories could be considered natural.[8]

In general, researchers determine social class by using one of the following
approaches:

1. *Life styles.* People are questioned about their life styles—whom they
interact with, what types of material objects they possess, what types of recrea-

[7]W. L. Warner and Paul Lunt, *The Social Life of a Modern Community* (New Haven, Conn.:
Yale University Press, 1941).

[8]Leonard Broom and Philip Selznick, *Sociology* (New York: Harper & Row, 1968) p. 154.

tional activities they engage in, what organizations they belong to, what speech mannerisms they have, and so on.[9]

2. *Reputational approach.*   People are asked to act as judges in ranking others in their community. This approach sometimes presents problems because it is difficult for a judge to know everyone in his community. Furthermore, a judge's biases may influence the way he ranks a person.

3. *Subjective approach.*   People are asked to rank themselves. This approach has been found unreliable chiefly because the average person often has gross misconceptions both about the stratification system of his society and about his place in it. Many people cling to a belief in classlessness. Others see only a clear-cut division between the rich and the poor. Still others conceive of classes in strictly Marxian terms; to them, society is divided into those who own the means of production and those who labor for them.

4. *Objective approach.*   In this approach, researchers use indicators such as income, education, occupation, and position of authority without relying on the feelings, evaluations, and perceptions either of the individuals who are being examined or of a panel of judges. In other words, the researchers, as impartial and objective scientists, make categories based on income, education, occupation, and so on, and place each person into the appropriate category. Although objective methods permit significantly more exact measurements than do the subjective and reputational approaches, nonetheless they, too, fail to describe reality in all cases. For instance, a researcher following this approach would put into the same category a retired postal worker living on a pension of $6,000 a year and a cub reporter working for the first time on a big city newspaper. Yet $6,000 is the highest income the postal worker will receive during the remainder of his life, whereas it is the lowest amount the reporter will receive during what he hopes will be a prosperous career.

5. *Occupational prestige approach.*   People are asked about which occupations and sources of income are the most prestigious. This approach is sometimes considered part of the reputational approach. However, it depends on a much larger—usually on a national—sample. The true reputational approach is most effectively used in a small community, where people know each other well. The occupational prestige approach has proved to be the best index of social class in the United States because of its practicality. Occupation determines the amount of money that is earned, and the amount of money possessed determines, in many instances, the amount of power wielded and the prestige held. But money alone does not determine social class. Some occupations are rated very high even though the pay for them is relatively low. For instance, in a study compiled by the National Opinion Research Center, the occupation rated highest in prestige by the majority of respondents was that of Supreme Court judge.[10] This occupation provides its holder with some power but not

[9]Harold M. Hodges, Jr. and W. Clayton Lane, *Social Stratification*, pp. 79-81.

[10]Robert W. Hodge, Paul M. Seigal, and Peter H. Rossi, "Occupational Prestige in the United States, 1925-1963," *The American Journal of Sociology* (November, 1964), pp. 290-292.

much income, compared to the incomes of industrial executives, for instance. However, the occupation has high prestige because the number of judges serving at one time is small.

Peninsula People: A Regional Study of Social Class Differences

Using a combination of the above approaches, sociologist Harold M. Hodges, Jr. conducted a study of the attitudes, behavior, and life styles of people living in the metropolitan area of San Francisco, California, in the early 1960s. By his own admission, Hodges's findings cannot be considered binding on a national level. Still, many of the social divisions characteristic of this particular area at this time are, to a certain extent, representative of divisions among the population at large.

Hodges defines social class as not merely a statistical category:

> *Each class level is more nearly a subculture, and the members of a given class, although unknown to one another, are linked because they share similar life experiences, occupational roles, style of life, educational backgrounds, formal affiliations, consumption behavior, leisure-time preferences, and choices of mass media. They tend to think and act alike because they share common "universes of discourse."*[11]

The lower-lower class.   This stratum includes 15 to 20 percent of the population in the sample. People belonging to it are unskilled blue-collar workers who have frequent periods of unemployment. They tend to be school dropouts with minimal education. They marry and have children at an early age but have stormy family lives. They live in slum areas and are heavily in debt, because all their household belongings are bought on time. They are aware of the middle-class goals that the mass media and other institutions publicize and support, but they are also aware that such goals are hopelessly out of their reach. Despair, anger, and apathy are the products of this double awareness.

The attitude of members of the lower-lower class is pessimistic and fatalistic. In other words, people in this class admit that they have no control over their circumstances. They tend to blame others for their own shortcomings and for the world's problems. They see solutions to complex problems in simplistic terms. They are authoritarian, and they believe that wives should stay at home and that children should be extremely obedient and respectful. Their recreation consists of reading "girlie" and movie magazines, watching television, and going to bars. They are suspicious of strangers and think that other people will try to take advantage of them. For the most part, they belong either to the Roman Catholic church or to the sects of Protestantism that accept the literal truthfulness of everything in the Bible. They are—and they know they are—looked down upon by the rest of their community.

The upper-lower class.   Approximately one-third of the population in the sample is placed in this category. The members of the upper-lower class are semiskilled or skilled blue-collar workers who have higher incomes and steadier jobs than do people in the lower-lower class. They have either finished

[11]Harold M. Hodges, Jr. and W. Clayton Lane, *Social Stratification*, p. 30.

or have almost finished high school. Their outlook on life is much less fatalistic and much more optimistic than that of people on the level beneath them. They think of themselves as hard working and speak harshly of the lazy "no-accounts" in the lower-lower class. They are rather authoritarian and quite aggressive. They are sports fans and avid outdoorsmen, especially hunters and fishers. They like to think of themselves as strong and silent types, popularized by movie heroes Clark Gable and John Wayne. They are aware of prestige and are concerned with raising theirs. Typically, they try to move into lower-middle class neighborhoods. In this, they have been helped by trade unions, to which they belong in large numbers. They tend to vote a Democratic ticket and support liberal legislation, as long as it concerns economic matters, that is, unemployment compensation or minimum wage laws.

The lower-middle class. Another one-third of the sample belongs in this classification. Members of the lower-middle class tend to be salesmen, clerks, foremen, or owners of small businesses. They represent "the typical American," or "the common man," referred to in the mass media and in political speeches. They also represent the common denominator to which the mass media address themselves through large circulation magazines like *Life* and *Reader's Digest*, through the most popular TV shows, and through movies that are extremely successful at the box office.

Typically, members of this class are high school graduates whose income is around $10,000. They tend to live in suburban tract homes. Their values are Middle-American, typical of those of people living in small towns: Their morality is puritanical; they believe strongly in the Protestant Ethic (work brings success); and their religion is based on a literal reading of the Bible. They tend to be conservative both politically and economically.

The viewpoint of these lower-middle class Americans is presented in the article "The 'Forgotten American' Revisited," which follows this chapter.[12] According to the author, members of this social class, long forgotten by the problems-oriented media and by academics, have lately attracted notice and have been found to be alienated and dissatisfied. Middle-Americans complain that they work at two and three jobs and still can't make ends meet; that their children have no parks or swimming pools but that no one cares; and that their young can't see any future at all for themselves, but only the gray present. Their realization that they have been neglected seems even more bitter because they had finally acquired all the virtues necessary for success in our society: the work-success ethic, an old-fashioned morality, patriotism, and religiousness.

The upper-middle class. Some 10 to 15 percent of the people in the sample belong to this class. They are professionals, semiprofessionals, independent businessmen, or corporate employees who have attended college at least a year or two beyond the A.B. degree. They are the pacesetters of American society—the first to accept new styles in clothing, house furnishings, residence, and so on. Such adjectives as flexible, democratic, tolerant, and nondogmatic seem to describe them quite well.

---

[12]Peter Schrag, "The 'Forgotten American' Revisited" *World* (July 4, 1972), pp. 53-57.

They are child-centered and have a democratic approach to child discipline. They are less puritanical and more optimistic about human nature than are people lower than they on the social ladder. They are sociable, upwardly mobile, and competitive for themselves and for their children, whom they prepare early for an academic career. They are avid joiners of professional organizations and are civic minded and faithful voters. Although they tend to belong to the Presbyterian church, they consider religion's function to be primarily a social one. They have the lowest rate of broken marriages, are patrons of the arts, read avidly—especially critically acclaimed books—spend little time watching television, and much time listening to music. Because they are geographically mobile, most of them are newcomers to town. Members of this social class possess the social position to which many Americans aspire.

Between the upper-middle and the next class, there is another stratum. Hodges, however, feels that the people in this stratum—a small percentage of the total number of the sample—belong to the upper-middle, from which they are differentiated chiefly because they have more money. Members of this in-between stratum tend to be international celebrities or jet-setters, movie stars, and the newly rich who display their possessions. They want the prestige their social superiors have but must generally wait several generations to attain it.

The upper-upper class.   Only 1 to 2 percent make up this stratum. People belonging to this class have everything: wealth, power, prestige, and the right family background. These are the people whose names appear in the Social Register and who can trace their descent almost as far back as the *Mayflower*. They do not display their wealth in obvious ways but prefer to wear tweedy clothes and drive cars that do not attract notice. However, they do entertain lavishly and often. They have attended private preparatory schools and have graduated from Ivy League universities (Harvard and Yale) or from Stanford.

Members of the upper-upper class are tradition-oriented, ancestor-worshipping, and more authoritarian than are members of the upper-middle class. They tend to follow in their father's footsteps, becoming bankers, stockbrokers, physicians, and architects. They display an unusual blend of strait-laced and eccentric, open and reserved character traits.

We must emphasize again that Hodges admitted that his study of the stratification system in the Peninsula region may be ill defined, overlapping, and in constant flux. Nevertheless, this and other studies do indicate that deeply entrenched values, attitudes, and behavior seem to follow class lines.[13]

STATUS

Status is another category of social stratification. It is a way of ranking people according to the prestige evoked by the roles they perform in society. Previously, status was defined as the position of the individual in relation to other individuals, or as the position of the individual within the social

[13]Harold M. Hodges and W. Clayton Lane, "Peninsula People: Social Stratification in a Metropolitan Complex," in *Social Stratification*, Appendix, pp. 5–35.

system. As it applies to stratification, status is a ranked position—high, middle, or low—and the rank is determined by the role attached to the status. For instance, because the role of physician, particularly that of a specialist in a difficult field, is valued in our society, that position has a high status.

The desire for obtaining high status is built into the individual as part of his socialization. Each of us has many statuses in society: We are sons, fathers, husbands, dentists, Scout leaders, and so on. The combination, or totality, of all of our known statuses makes up our *social status*.

Determining Status

Most people become quite adept at obtaining information and interpreting clues to determine the status of someone they have just met. In the United States today, people determine status by first learning the nature of the individual's occupation, including his area of specialization. Occupation is a good indication of their new acquaintance's income. Then they note how he dresses, how he speaks, what kind of car he drives, where he lives, what clubs he belongs to, what church he is a member of, what school he attended, what schools his children attend, and so on. Before long, a fairly clear picture of the individual's social status emerges.

In assigning a particular status to an individual, the members of society who are ranking him must be aware of what determines high, middle, or low status. The standards by which status is assigned have been publicized by the mass media. Nevertheless, they vary from community to community and certainly from society to society and from era to era. Thus, a penniless nobleman has much less status in the United States, where we value money and achievement, than he has in Great Britain, where aristocracy is still highly regarded. By the same token, in medieval Europe, the person who was thought to be especially religious—who remained celibate and abstained from other worldly pleasures—possessed high status among the members of his society. He was also usually rewarded with a high position in the church.

In our society, the social status of a family derives from that of the male breadwinner. His status is, in turn, determined chiefly by his occupation. A child acquires his status from his family and keeps it until he is an adult. In most instances, a woman also obtains her status from her husband. But this is beginning to change, as more and more women choose careers of their own outside the home.

Today, in the United States, we value high intelligence, efficiency, and productivity above all, and we reward people who have such characteristics with highly prized positions. But such positions are often not awarded on the basis of merit alone. Many intelligent, efficient, and productive people are kept out of rewarding positions by people who derive their status from membership in particular racial, ethnic, religious, and regional groups.

The variables that determine status are occupation and source of income, color, education, sex, age, religion, and ethnic origin. A composite, or a model, of a high status individual would, then, present this picture: The high status individual is a white male in his late thirties who was educated at Harvard and is a corporation lawyer. He is a member of the Episcopalian church, is active in state politics, and can trace his ancestry back to a distinguished English earl who settled in the American colonies.

Status Inconsistency

We might deduce that variables directly opposed to those associated with high status would determine low status. Increasingly, however, in studying industrial societies, sociologists have become aware of *status inconsistency*. This is a phenomenon in which several of the variables traditionally associated with high or low status are lacking, yet the individual enjoys high or low status ranking. For instance, a Puerto Rican immigrant does not have the color, income, education, religion, and ethnic origin usually associated with high status. If he becomes a famous and wealthy baseball player, he is status inconsistent. The same may be said for the descendant of rich industrialists who loses his entire fortune, and his status, through excessive gambling.

Status inconsistency also occurs when an individual has a position that ranks high in status, but that provides him with a comparatively low income. Then, he cannot afford to engage in the life styles of other members of his status group. A *status group*, by the way, consists of all individuals who are ranked similarly and who tend to associate with each other, developing common life styles.

Status inconsistency is frequently found among black professionals, whose claim to high status is thwarted by skin color. In such situations, the individual tends to be judged by his *master status*—the status that a majority of societal members consider the most important of several alternatives.[14]

The Importance of Status

Status is very important to most individuals. Sociologist Gerhard Lenski goes so far as to state that the concern for status "influences almost every kind of decision from the choice of a car to the choice of a spouse. Fear of the loss of status, or honor, is one of the few motives that can make men lay down their lives on the field of battle."[15] He adds that because the desire for status becomes insatiable, many decisions of daily life, particularly the important ones, are heavily colored by elements of status striving.

The extent to which people strive for status and the unexpected areas in which status striving occurs are illustrated in our article "The Christmas Card Syndrome" by anthropologist Sheila K. Johnson.[16] The author concludes that status greatly affects the sending of Christmas cards. In fact, Christmas card sending is an excellent indicator of social status and of aspirations for the acquisition of higher status.

POWER

In all probability, the most important category of stratification is power. *Power* is defined as the ability of one individual or segment of the population to control the actions of another individual or segment of the population, with or without the latter's consent. Power is present in all social systems, from the most simple to the most complex.

Power is multifaceted and elusive. Thus, it is frequently difficult to make definitive statements about its nature, source, and location. Power, as it applies to stratification, can be divided into personal power and social power. *Personal power* is the freedom of an individual to direct his own life in any way he chooses, without much societal interference. In our society, great personal freedom is frequently tied to possession of wealth: If a person is rich enough, he is free to do almost anything he wants to do and can obtain "anything money can buy."

Social power is the ability to make decisions that affect entire communities or even the whole society. Social power may be exercised legitimately, or with the consent of the other members of society. In this case, it is called *authority*. Different levels of authority are represented by parents, teachers, and the government.

Power may also be illegitimate, or be exercised without the approval of society. Organized crime is a case in point. The way organized crime exercises

---

[14]Everett Hughes, "Dilemmas and Contradictions of Status," *American Journal of Sociology*, Vol. 50 (1945), pp. 353-359.

[15]Gerhard Lenski, *Power and Privilege*, pp. 37, 38.

[16]Sheila K. Johnson, "The Christmas Card Syndrome," *The New York Times Magazine* (December 5, 1971), pp. 38-163.

power was vividly portrayed in a fictionalized account of underworld operations, Mario Puzo's *The Godfather*. Those who read the book or saw the movie understand how the underworld group coerces an individual into acting as it wishes. Members of the underworld simply "make him an offer he can't refuse." The offer, of course, involves placing the barrel of a gun dangerously near the person being threatened.

The Power of Power

Although we tend to think of power as a political phenomenon, it affects all areas of human life. Most observers agree that the manner in which a society's goods and services are distributed is chiefly dependent on who has power. Sociologist Gerhard Lenski writes, " ... power will determine the distribution of nearly all of the surplus possessed by a society."[17]

Power is also deeply interwoven with the other dimensions of stratification, class and status. The individual who has power can control decision making so that decisions are favorable to him. In this way, he can obtain wealth. Wealth puts him in an upper social class, which, of course, gives him a high status. In traditional nonindustrial societies, religion and tradition have supported the idea that the rich are powerful and are entitled to rule, whereas the poor are powerless and are in need of being ruled.

In modern industrial societies, the naturalness of such a system has long been questioned. What has happened to power in these societies is that it has been spread among many people, rather than being concentrated in the hands of a very few individuals. Because of universal suffrage, political power has been diffused; decision making is no longer in the hands of one or a few people. But there are well-known means of directing voters' behavior. Furthermore, local power groups such as the urban political machines or family businesses that used to dominate small towns have, in general, disappeared because of increasingly centralized decision making. Centralization, in turn, is a result of "big government," "big industry," and "big labor," phenomena which are discussed in later chapters.

The Location and Use of Power

The exercise of power on a national level has been viewed in various ways. The late sociologist C. Wright Mills suggested that decisions having a crucial impact on national and international affairs were being made by no more than three hundred corporate, military, and political leaders.[18]

On the other hand, David Riesman believes that a number of interest groups compromise on major decisions, attaining among themselves a balance of power. The power each group has is the ability to veto decisions that go entirely against its interests. To a lesser extent, each group also has the ability to initiate some decisions.[19]

Economist John Kenneth Galbraith thinks in terms of "countervailing" powers. According to Galbraith, big labor, big government, and big business are

[17]Gerhard Lenski, *Power and Privilege*, p. 44.

[18]C. Wright Mills, *The Power Elite* (New York: Oxford University Press, 1956), Chapter 12.

[19]David Riesman, Nathan Glazer, and Reuel Denney, *The Lonely Crowd* (New Haven, Conn.: Yale University Press, 1961), pp. 245-255.

in a constant tug-of-war; the power of each is somewhat offset by the power of the others.[20] Talcott Parsons, a follower of functionalist stratification theory, believes that power in our type of economy is not fixed but circulates like money, changing hands frequently.[21]

Regardless of the way social scientists conceptualize power, the average member of society feels that his fate is controlled by a small number of individuals in positions of authority. This has always been so, but must it always continue? Not according to Silviu Brucan who, in *The Dissolution of Power*, claims that man can live without power and that society can exist without it. Brucan views political power as a dominating force that has arisen out of inequalities among classes and nations. He predicts that this kind of power will be replaced by a power based on the common interest of society's members. Brucan's prediction is founded on his belief that equality and distribution of the rewards of society are not simply ideals but are very real requirements in a modern technological society. The participation of all members of society in decision making and in the acquisition of rewards, then, will not forever be impeded by the present power structure.

Unfortunately, Brucan's prediction of an eventual world community based on the power of unity seems too optimistic, or at least premature. In fact, such a world order would require that conflicts of interest among classes, races, nationalities, and other social groups be eliminated.[22]

SYSTEMS OF STRATIFICATION

To simplify analysis, we study stratification as an interconnected system. A *stratification system* is the overlapping manner in which societal members are ranked into classes, status groups, and hierarchies of power. In analyses of stratification systems, the following elements are generally examined: (1) The number and size of the social classes in a society. (2) The degree of social mobility among social classes. *Social mobility* refers to an individual's ability to change his class membership by moving up or down the ladder of social stratification. (3) The differences in life styles among social classes. (4) The conditions leading to class divisions. (5) The distribution of power among classes and status groups.

By considering these elements, especially social mobility and life styles, we can distinguish among different models of stratification systems. There are three models of stratification systems: the open, or class, system; the closed, or caste, system; and the estate system. We must remember that these systems are models. None of them have actually existed in any society. The models represent two extremes and a middle on an ideal continuum. Most societies belong somewhere along this continuum.

The Closed Society, or Caste System

Whether a society has an open or closed stratification system depends on the way its members obtain wealth, prestige, and privilege (also called class,

[20]John Kenneth Galbraith, *American Capitalism* (Boston: Houghton Mifflin, 1956).

[21]Seymour Martin Lipset and Reinhard Bendix, *Social Mobility in Industrial Society* (Berkeley, Calif.: University of California Press, 1959), p. 261.

[22]Silviu Brucan, *The Dissolution of Power* (New York: Alfred A. Knopf, 1971).

status, and power). In *closed societies*, class, status, and power are determined strictly on the basis of family inheritance, rather than on personal effort. In such societies, the individual is born into a specific social stratum, called a caste. Because the social system is extremely rigid, the individual has no opportunity to move out of his caste.

Classical India is a well-known example of a closed society. The caste system that flourished in India for hundreds of years was distinguished by several features. Members of society were divided into definite strata, called castes, and arranged in order from high to low. The castes represented areas of service to society and were ranked according to their importance to it. Some ranking, however, was the result of struggles for power or of conquest by other groups. Religion and tradition forbade members of one caste to intermarry or in any way interact with members of another caste. Each caste was restricted in occupation: Priests could not become political leaders, and vice versa. The status of each individual in a caste was ascribed. In other words, he inherited his social position and was unable to change it. Even if an individual accumulated a great deal of wealth and wisdom, he could not enter a higher caste. The caste system was justified by the religion and the traditional mores of the society.

The Indian castes consisted of priests, warriors, merchants, workers, and peasants. In addition, there were countless other castes and subcastes, united by common professions or kinship. Below all castes were untouchables, who were born without a caste, and outcastes, who had lost their traditional caste membership because of some infraction of the rules.

The caste system permitted no mobility between castes. It designated particular jobs as unclean and required that they be performed by members of the lowliest castes or by people belonging to no caste at all. It even provided elaborate rituals for high caste members who by chance came into contact with lower caste members and untouchables, who were thought to be impure.

Today, India is a democracy and is slowly undergoing industrialization. Industrialization will eventually doom the caste system, because traditions will break down as more and more people live in cities, work in factories, and are given the opportunity to obtain an education. However, even though the caste system has been abolished, people living in rural areas are still influenced by it. In a study of this system published in 1963, an Indian author maintained that the caste system is "still a strong and tenacious force."[23]

To someone reared in a society imbued with democratic principles, if not practices, the Indian caste system must seem incredibly stifling and antilibertarian. In fact, it provides the Indian citizen with some satisfactions that members of Western societies lack entirely. The Indian can almost always see that some castes are below his; provided with underdogs against whom he can legally discriminate, he can increase his status in his own eyes. What is more, permanent membership in kinship and religious groups—the individual knows that he cannot leave them—provides a great deal of security. Finally, people who are not constantly competing for a high social standing do not encounter frustrations and thus experience peace of mind.

---

[23]Subhash Chandra Mehta, "Persistence of the Caste System," *Atlas* (November, 1963), pp. 268-273.

The Estate System

A variation of the caste, or closed, system, though less rigid than it, is the *estate system*. This was the economic and social system of feudal Europe, and it existed, in different forms, in many nations of the East.

As in the caste system, in the estate system, societal positions were divided according to their functions. However, rather than being ranked from low to high in order of importance, they were all considered, in theory at least, to be of equal importance, according to the dictum of the day, "Some fight, some work, some pray."

The three main estates were the nobility, the church, and the peasants. In addition, within each estate, there was a stratified hierarchy of positions. Thus, among the nobility, the hierarchy ranged from the king and his family, down to lesser nobles, and, finally, to local administrative officials. Among the military, whose leaders were recruited from the ranks of the nobility, the hierarchy reached from the commanding staff, down to the officer corps, and to common enlisted men. Among the churchmen, the hierarchy was based on a similar arrangement, with the pope at the top, and beneath him, cardinals, archbishops and bishops, and finally, parish priests. The peasants were divided into villeins, who were semifree, emancipated tenant farmers, and serfs, who were not.

Support for the system came from religion and tradition, as in the caste system. However, the estate system permitted quite a bit more mobility among social strata than did the caste system. As a matter of fact, the second and later born children of the nobility had to enter one of the other estates, because according to law, the firstborn son inherited his family's entire estate.

Because of the vow of celibacy, the estate made up of churchmen had to be periodically replenished from outside the church. Additional churchmen came from both higher and lower estates, although the sons of noblemen and military men tended to become cardinals and bishops, whereas the children of peasants tended to become parish priests and monks. Nevertheless, it was not unusual for an ambitious parish priest to rise within the church hierarchy, and for a simple foot soldier to achieve a position of leadership.

The remnants of this system are still visible in some modern societies, in which there are landed gentry and inherited titles of nobility. Such a system is also the essence of stratification on the vast ranch empires of South America, called *latifundia*, and is easily recognizable as the system existing on American plantations a century ago.[24]

The Open Society, or Class System

On the other extreme of the ideal continuum on which we have placed stratification systems, we find the *open society*, or class system. In theory, such a society should offer each member equal access to material resources, equal access to power, and equal access to prestige. In reality, of course, such ideal open societies do not exist. The closest examples would perhaps be the Israeli kibbutzim or similar utopian communities. These, however, are communities, not societies. On a societal level, modern industrial societies similar to the United States most nearly approximate the model of an open society. Such

[24]Alvin L. Bertrand, *Basic Sociology* (New York: Appleton-Century-Crofts, 1967), pp. 168-169.

open societies have several characteristics in common: (1) Classes do exist, but they are not institutionalized in the way that castes and estates are. (2) Because class lines are unclear, the members of society do not display excessive class consciousness. Nonetheless, inequality stemming from class divisions is apparent. (3) Predominantly, status is achieved. However, there is a great deal of evidence that status tends to be ascribed, rather than achieved, in the lowest and the highest social classes. (4) Social mobility is possible and occurs frequently.

In an open, or a class, system, members of society are not ranked according to their functional specialization; doctors, for instance do not make up a social class, as the nobility did in the feudal era. Instead, people are ranked according to the power and status that derive from the rewards of their positions in society. In other words, doctors, lawyers, or industrialists do not form a social class because of what they are. But wealthy doctors, lawyers, and industrialists, who have status and power because of their important positions, do form a social class. Their occupation does not determine their social class. It is merely an indication of and a channel for the attainment of wealth, power, and prestige, according to which they are socially ranked.

Open stratification systems work best in industrial societies that have market economies. Such societies offer more opportunities for social mobility than do societies in which the market is controlled by the government. In controlled economies, people may not have the opportunity to choose their jobs and to increase their wealth.

Although social mobility is possible and is even encouraged in open systems, it does not extend equally well throughout such systems. Limitations of a racial, religious, ethnic, and regional nature restrict some people's mobility. However, the rigid hold of one's family and caste exists to a much lesser extent in an open than it does in a closed society, and the individual is permitted much more leeway of social movement.

SOCIAL MOBILITY

We have seen that one of the principal differences between open and closed societies is that there is social mobility in open societies, and none or very little in closed societies. In defining social mobility, we said that the term refers to an individual's ability to change his social class membership by moving up or down the ladder of his stratification system.

Sociologists, however, usually distinguish between *vertical mobility*, which occurs in an upward or downward direction, and *horizontal mobility*, which occurs when there is a change of status without a consequent change of class. To illustrate, the secondary school teacher who is made principal is upwardly mobile. The department chairman who is demoted to teacher is downwardly mobile. And the school superintendent who becomes an executive of an insurance company at no greater salary and with no greater or lesser prestige than he had as a superintendent is horizontally mobile.

The Upwardly Mobile Individual

Not all individuals take advantage of the opportunities for upward mobility. According to studies in the field, those who are upwardly mobile display the following traits: (1) They are urban residents; (2) they are only children, or one of two children; (3) they are influenced by ambitious mothers; (4) they acquire more education than their parents did; (5) they marry later than others of their generation and usually above their status; and (6) they wait to establish a family, limiting its size to no more than two children.

It is easy to deduce why such traits are associated with upward mobility. Most industries and businesses are located in urban centers. Thus, urban residence provides an individual with many more chances to obtain a good job than does rural residence. An only child, or one of two children, has more opportunities for higher education than do children who come from large families. Not only is it financially easier for parents to send one or two children to school but it is also possible to give a great deal of time and attention to a small number of children.

Ambitious mothers are able to influence their children to become upwardly mobile because mothers are chiefly responsible for socialization in our society. People who acquire a better education than their parents did take the first step toward a job that is better than their parents'. Consequently, upward mobility is furthered. Marrying relatively late in life makes it possible for an individual to delay the assumption of responsibilities. He can spend time in school, obtaining the education that may lead to a good job. Because they are well educated and have good jobs, upwardly mobile individuals are able to marry people from higher social classes than their own. Finally, by waiting to establish a family, such individuals make sure that they are able to care for their offspring well. By limiting family size to no more than two, they repeat the cycle, which leads to upward mobility for their children.

In sociological terms, individuals like those we have just described display *intergenerational mobility*. In other words, they belong to a higher social class than did their parents. They also display *intragenerational mobility*, in that they do better in their careers, and consequently belong to a higher social class, than do other people of the same generation.[25]

Social Mobility in the United States

It is widely believed that upward mobility is the pattern in the United States and other industrial nations. Advanced technology has freed workers from many unskilled manual jobs, forcing them to train for more highly skilled, better paying jobs. Thus, it has been necessary to extend education to include the formerly uneducated masses.

Perhaps, however, the assumption that upward mobility is a trend is open to question. It may well be true that the upward mobility of professionals and technical workers, managers and executives, and clerical and service workers has become so great that these people will someday form the basis of the upper middle and upper classes.[26] But uneducated and unskilled workers have less opportunity to become upwardly mobile now than they had in the past.

A recent study of mobility provides some evidence of a trend toward downward mobility. Researchers used the transition from a manual to a nonmanual

[25]Seymour Martin Lipset and Reinhard Bendix, *Social Mobility in Industrial Society*, pp. 73–74.
[26]Peter and Brigitte Berger, "The Blueing of America," *The New Republic* (April 3, 1971).

job as an indicator of upward mobility. They found that 28.8 percent of the sons of manual workers became nonmanual workers, whereas 29.7 percent of the sons of nonmanual workers became manual workers.[27] Of course this percentage difference is small, and in terms of money, manual jobs are sometimes better rewarded than are nonmanual ones.

The highest degree of mobility seems to occur within, rather than between, categories of jobs such as blue-collar and white-collar. In short, an assembly-line worker can more easily become a foreman than he can become a junior executive. The points of breakthrough from manual to nonmanual jobs lie in clerical and sales positions and in small businesses. However, special talents, if allowed to flourish, are often the key to spectacular upward mobility. Consider the case of boxing champion Joe Frazier, who made the ascent from penniless sharecropper to millionaire.

Social mobility seems to be insignificant at the extremes of the stratification system. At the very top and at the very bottom of the system, mobility is virtually replaced by a caste system. At the very top, upward mobility is nonsensical because there is nowhere else to go, and downward mobility becomes improbable because huge accumulations of wealth have a tendency to increase rather than decrease. At the very bottom, people have very little chance to learn the skills or obtain the education that would help them improve their position. Thus, horizontal mobility seems to be the norm both at the heights and at the depths of the stratification system.

An Evaluation of Social Mobility

We tend to assume that social mobility is a positive rather than a negative value and that an open society is preferable to a closed one. But the situation is not absolutely clear-cut. We cannot flatly state that social mobility is "good" and that lack of mobility is "bad." A closed society, in which there is a small degree of social mobility, shelters the individual from the frustrations of unsuccessful competition. It does not encourage expectations that cannot be fulfilled. Furthermore, it protects him from the strain of moving to unfamiliar surroundings, of both a geographical and a social nature. The mobile individual must constantly adapt to socially unfamiliar situations—a new class, new norms, new values. But a member of a closed society spends his life in an environment that is familiar to him. In other words, an open society, with its high degree of mobility, does not guarantee happiness. The belief in competition and achievement takes a heavy toll in suicides, neuroses and psychoses, broken homes, alienated youth, and physical illness.

On the other hand, a closed society, in which there is little social mobility, is very likely to stagnate and decline. Heredity does not guarantee that the son of a capable and wise father will be equally capable and wise. A society that does not give talented people from the lower strata an opportunity to advance into positions of leadership will not fare well for long. What is more, such a society becomes marked by hopelessness and despair, for many of its members live without even a glimmer of hope for a better tomorrow.

What are we to conclude, then? Which system is preferable? Would you

[27]S. M. Miller, "Comparative Social Mobility," in Cynthia Heller, ed., *Structural Social Inequality* (New York: Macmillan, 1969), p. 329.

prefer to take the chance of being born into a given social stratum? Or would you prefer to be born into an ideal society—one that is *completely* open? In such a society, any citizen could rise to any height through sheer merit. Then those who would not achieve great heights—and there would always be some—would have only themselves, and their inadequacies, to blame. Does this kind of society seem desirable to you? There is no perfect answer to these questions, of course. But it is worthwhile to remember that a completely open society, in which achievement is based solely on merit, would not be a Garden of Eden.

LIFE CHANCES

Before concluding this chapter, we should mention the concept of life chances, a concept first used by the renowned sociologist Max Weber. *Life chances* refers to the opportunity of each individual to fulfill or fail to fulfill his potential in society. An individual's life chances include his opportunity to survive during the delicate years of infancy and to reach his full potential in physical appearance and health. They include his opportunity to obtain an education equal to his desire and talents, to be exposed to all the things that the culture has to offer, and to live in circumstances that prevent him from becoming a criminal. Life chances also include the individual's inability to fulfill all these potentials.

An individual's life chances are determined by his position within the stratification system. The higher that position is, the more positive his life chances are; the lower his position, the more negative his life chances. What is more, one life chance tends to determine another. Thus, a favorable location on the stratification ladder almost guarantees the fulfillment of most other life chances. A low location almost guarantees that life chances will not be fulfilled, and that they will be repeatedly denied even to future generations.

Life chances exist in and influence all spheres of human life. They are especially apparent in the stratification system, because they are linked to class. If we compare the life chances of an individual born into an upper-upper class family with the life chances of an individual born into a lower-lower class family, the differences become strikingly apparent. Statistics indicate that 27 percent of the total national income is received by the richest 10 percent of the population, whereas only 1 percent of the total national income is received by the poorest 10 percent of the population.[28] Obviously, then, the richest 10 percent can afford to fulfill twenty-seven times as many life chances as the poorest 10 percent.

In addition to differential life chances between rich and poor, there are differences in life chances between whites and other racial groups. A white male with seventeen years or more of education, can expect to earn 53 percent more income than is earned by a nonwhite male with the same amount of education.[29] Life expectancy, mortality rates of mothers and babies, incidence of heart disease, and malnutrition are all related to color and class. In addition, members of the lower class are, according to statistics, more frequently the

[28]Gabriel Kolko, *Wealth and Power in America* (New York: Praeger, 1962), p. 34.
[29]Herman P. Miller, *Rich Man, Poor Man* (New York: Crowell, 1964).

**TABLE 4.2   PERCENTAGE OF NATIONAL PERSONAL INCOME
(AFTER FEDERAL INCOME TAXES) RECEIVED BY THE POPULATION
DIVIDED INTO TENTHS**

	Tenth	Percentage of Income Received
Highest		
	1	27
	2	16
	3	13
	4	11
	5	10
	6	8
	7	6
	8	5
	9	3
Lowest	10	1

SOURCE: Gabriel Kolko, *Wealth and Power in America*, New York: Praeger, 1962, p. 34.

victims of accidents and criminal acts and are punished more severely by the law when caught breaking it than are members of higher classes. Lower class members also join fewer organizations and have fewer friends than do people in higher social classes.

Thus, unequal distribution of income is not simply an economic matter. It results in inequalities that spread into all areas of life. The primary inequality of income and the other inequalities that spring from it are extremely difficult for an individual to overcome, notwithstanding our society's reputation as "the land of opportunity." The worst aspect of the problem is that a vicious

**TABLE 4.3   RELATIONSHIP OF EDUCATION TO WHITE
AND NON-WHITE EARNINGS**

Expected Lifetime Earnings

School Years Completed	White	Non-white	Non-white as Percentage of White
Less than 8	$157,000	$ 95,000	61
8	191,000	123,000	64
9 to 11	221,000	132,000	60
12	253,000	151,000	60
13 to 15	301,000	162,000	54
16	395,000	185,000	47
17 or more	466,000	246,000	53

SOURCE: Adapted from tabular material in Herman P. Miller *Rich Man, Poor Man*. Copyright © 1964 by Thomas Y. Crowell, Inc., publishers.

circle exists. The individual who, through sheer accident of birth, begins his life in a lower-class family is socialized into accepting a particular set of values that do not help him become upwardly mobile. Living in an environment hostile to him, he develops a type of personality that does not aid him either. Thus, his life chances become further impaired. It takes a truly extraordinary person to break such bonds.

SUMMARY

Stratification is a phenomenon present in all societies that have developed division of labor and have produced a surplus. Stratification is the process by which members of society rank themselves and one another in hierarchies (from low to high) with respect to the amount of desirable goods they possess.

The existence of stratification has led to the centuries-old problem of social inequality. In societies that have closed stratification systems, such inequalities are institutionalized and rigid. An individual born into a particular economic and social stratum, or caste, remains in this stratum until he dies. Most modern industrial societies have open, or class, stratification systems. In open stratification systems, social mobility is possible, although some members of the population do not have the opportunity to fulfill their potential.

The three categories of stratification—status, class, and power—are closely interrelated. In the United States, occupation or source of income almost always determines status. In turn, status is related to class membership. Finally, the degree of power held by any one individual depends, to a great extent, on his status and class. Other variables that determine a person's position in the stratification system of the United States are color, sex, age, religion, region, and ethnic origin.

An individual's life chances—his opportunity to become a complete human being and reap the satisfactions that his society has to offer—are greatly diminished if the individual belongs to a low social class or to a nonwhite group. Although American society has been sufficiently open to permit considerable upward mobility, attained primarily through education, it has remained obstinately closed to the lower strata of society. Members of lower classes are further hampered by being socialized to hold values that do not help them become upwardly mobile. In addition, they develop a type of personality that discourages mobility. Spending their lives in a hostile environment, they lack the life chances that many other people have.

Stratification and social inequality may always be a part of human societies. However, modern industrial societies have the affluence and the knowledge, as well as the moral obligation, to narrow the gap between those at the top and those at the bottom of the stratification system. They can at least challenge the homespun wisdom of the saying "The poor will always be with us."

PETER SCHRAG

THE "FORGOTTEN AMERICAN" REVISITED

Sociologists tell us that the lower-middle class individual is "the typical American," "the common man," to whom the mass media address themselves. For a long time, we assumed that he was satisfied watching sports on television, singing in the church choir on Sunday, going to his lodge meetings, and bowling with the boys. Suddenly, the incident of the hardhats in New York and the growing popularity of George Wallace revealed the deep resentment that had built up in "the forgotten American." Furthermore, his situation and outlook are not likely to improve, according to Peter Schrag's insightful article, an excerpt from his soon-to-be published The End of the American Future.

□□□

In the fall of 1968, thanks perhaps to George C. Wallace, the American worker re-emerged from a state of sociological limbo that had lasted nearly a generation and took his place with all those other honorable figures of American alienation: He became the forgotten American, the blue-collar worker, the silent majority. "They call my people the white lower-middle class these days," wrote Pete Hamill in 1969. "It is an ugly, ice-cold phrase, the result, I suppose, of the missionary zeal of those sociologists who still think you can place human beings on charts.... Sometimes these brutes are referred to as 'the ethnics' or 'the blue-collar types.' But the bureaucratic phrase is white lower-middle class. Nobody calls it the working class anymore."

By now, of course, that rediscovery seems like ancient history. The books, the articles, the

By Peter Schrag from *World Magazine*, July 4, 1972.

foundation grants, and the political rhetoric have poured forth in torrents; in a few years, indeed, the white working class may even overtake the blacks as the most cliché-laden group in American society. In our embarrassment for the original oversight—there was a time (remember?) when we endlessly spoke of ourselves as a nation divided exclusively between slums and suburbs—we went to the other extreme. We pictured the American worker in colors so vivified with the patronizing tints of anger or apology that he remained almost as invisible as he had been in all those years when he was blissfully forgotten. What all the speculations about him amounted to, far from a new elevation to importance, was a great demotion. The independent yeoman of Andrew Jackson's age, the common man of the New Deal, the onetime "bone and sinew of the country" re-emerged as Archie Bunker, the boobish protagonist of *All in the Family*. The once and future hero of the great American democracy had become its leading chump.

We began to hear of guys sitting around in bars complaining that they worked like mules and couldn't make ends meet, expressing their mounting resentment toward welfare and hippies and students, and observing bitterly that black kids weren't the only ones who didn't have a place to play or pools to swim in. A whole social landscape came into view —gray, limited, out of style: bowling alleys and union halls, row houses and bus stations at 5 in the morning, dog tracks and roller derbies and greasy spoons. Between Harlem and Scarsdale, betwen Roxbury and Wellesley, we were reminded, there still stretched all those places where the trains didn't stop and the mind never tarried: Astoria, Bay Ridge, Cicero, Daly City, Flatbush, Glen Park, and all the rest.

Here were the hustlers, people working two jobs or even three, driving cabs in the evening, working on the side as painters or mechanics, maintaining phony Social Security numbers, taking their pay in cash or in merchandise or free meals. "I don't think anybody has a single job anymore," a Teamsters official told me back in 1969. "All the cops are moonlighting, and the teachers and the truck drivers. A million guys moonlighting, holding a little back, hiding part of it so they don't get nailed by the IRS or kicked out of the housing projects that they live in. . . . Every one of them is cheating. They're underground people—*Untermenschen.* We have no systematic data on any of this, have no idea about the attitudes of the American worker, the white worker. We've been so busy studying the blacks. And yet the white worker is the source of most of the reaction in this country."

We told ourselves that we were beginning to understand something of the workingman's resentments, his sense of having been betrayed: here was someone who felt he was doing all the right things—working hard, paying taxes, keeping his kids out of trouble, keeping up his dues—and who had found that the nice, fashionable people whom he had once taken as his model held him in contempt. They made fun of his style and his old-fashioned morality. They spoke of him as a beery slob whose greatest pleasures came in the homosexual camaraderie of the Legion post and the bowling league. And meanwhile they allowed *their* kids to break the law, smoke pot, dodge the draft, and burn down the college campus. No wonder, we said, that this man was alienated. He was doing the work while the welfare chiselers were getting the sympathy. *You better pay attention to the son of a bitch (that Teamster official had said) before he burns the country down.* Wallace and Agnew were paying attention.

But this newfound sympathy—what did it really explain? We didn't, after all, really even know whom we were talking about. Was it blue-collar workers? People earning between $5,000 and $12,000 a year? Hardhats? At one end of the phenomenon were people merged with the ranks of the poor, people qualifying for food stamps, low-cost housing and Medicare, and at the other were those who disappeared into the middle class—suburbanites,

heads of two-car families, property-tax payers, holders of mortgages. Perhaps the best definition we have is that proposed by a couple of sociologists who labeled the lower-middle class as those living somewhere above the officially defined poverty level and somewhere below that class of people who take it for granted that their children will and must go to college. But even that isn't fully satisfactory. Our definition needs to be cultural, spiritual if you will, as well as sociological, for what we discovered was a whole class of people —some eighty million of them—who had outlived the mythology that legitimized (and sometimes glorified) their existence. The heroic age of American production had come to an end. We no longer admired the smoking factory chimney, had even come to question the almighty GNP, and retained only a nostalgic recollection of the days when the greatest of civilized achievements—when salvation itself—was something called Work and Production. "Let the detractors of America, the doubters of the American spirit take note," said Richard Nixon in his Labor Day address in 1971. "America's competitive spirit, the work ethic of this people is alive and well. . . . . " Perhaps. But if Nixon was right, how could one explain the thousands of auto workers who that very year had chosen early retirement, how could one explain the industrial sabotage or the high and still rising rate of absenteeism on Mondays and Fridays—at some auto assembly plants it was close to 15 per cent before and after weekends—and the related inside advice not to buy Detroit automobiles that came off the assembly line on days immediately preceding or following holidays? Or the wildcat strikes and the parties that the steelworkers in Gary and Pittsburgh held that August night in 1971 when the big layoffs were announced? On the one hand, people were moonlighting to make ends meet; on the other, they were walking off the job, telling off the foreman, taking every moment of vacation to which they were entitled plus a good many to which they were not.

A few months before Nixon's speech an auto worker at Chrysler who had been harassed by his foreman went home, got a gun, returned to the plant and shot the foreman and two other men dead. His lawyers argued that the stress of the assembly line had produced a state of temporary insanity, that the man had flipped under the pressure of work. The jury acquitted him. Every day workers were lining up at the gates of a thousand plants, like kids waiting to be let out of school, waiting for the whistle to blow, waiting for the day when their pensions would be sufficient to provide. Work had become something you suffered, not something that made you a man.

It is, to be sure, unlikely that American workers ever regarded themselves as heroic figures. American labor's triumphant moments, when they existed at all, came on the picket line and not in the plant, and what was won on that picket line was often lost in the contract. There was little about the mill or the assembly line that reinforced heroic illusions; the work was too dirty, too dull, too demeaning. But there surely was a time when the surrounding culture took work for granted, when the common faith assumed some direct relationship between work and self-respect, between work and success. And although the work itself might not be heroic, the factory was still often regarded as a heroic place, a symbol of energy, a magnificence of brute strength. "The great bulk of these metal workers," wrote Bernard Karsh in 1941 in a study of an Auto Workers local, "have a high regard for their company and their union." Another writer, revisiting the same union thirty years later, concluded that while there have been no recent polls about worker attitudes toward the union, "the widespread grumbling and heckling hardly suggest 'high regard.'" At one time, he said, the workers blamed their own lack of education and training for their condition, but "nowhere among the young white or black workers in Local 6 is this attitude discernible today: Blame is now put squarely on the company, and often on the union." In a society with an industrial rather than a post-industrial mentality, blue-collar work was legitimate without further argument, but in a consumer society even twenty million industrial workers —or a hundred million—constitute a minority, a class of outsiders.

To try to understand such things is inevitably to take oneself through a set of geographical and historical situations that cross the nation, from the abandoned textile mills of Lowell and Lawrence and Haverhill to union offices in Bethlehem and Gary to airplane assembly plants in Seattle and Santa Monica; from a mythology of working-class aspirations to a demonology of reaction and fear; from the certainty of work as salvation to the equally certain desire for immortality in the sunshine developments of the Southwest. Clearly, the old Charlie Chaplin-*Modern Times* imagery of assembly-line drudgery and of workers as struggling drones being gobbled up by machines no longer applies. For example, in the so-called continuous-flow industries (plastics, petroleum, chemicals, where the process is highly automated—and the work force relatively small) there exists a high degree of worker autonomy. The employees are there to check dials, to keep things from going wrong, and are not tied to the predetermined speed of an assembly line or subject to the filth and hazards of say, the steel industry's coke ovens. Yet, the assembly lines and the coke ovens and the common labor pool continue to exist, with the result, as David M. Gordon suggested in a recent issue of *Dissent*, that there is a sort of "dual market," based on subtle but mounting distinctions between "secondary workers" —people in jobs with no expectation of advancement, high turnover, little security, and low pay—and "primary workers" who enjoy some expectation of mobility (though often not much), job security, union protection, and stable wages.

But if *Modern Times* and Karl Marx no longer describe the conditions of work and the worker's life, neither do the facile American generalizations that have replaced them. The "fact" that the nation's work force is now primarily "white collar" or that America has become a "service economy" is pure statistical obfuscation. Even if those "facts" were correct, they would tend to make blue-collar workers—twenty-eight million of them—into a sort of historical anomaly, communicating in effect the notion that because they now constitute a minority they are no longer of much concern. But the statistics tell us even less than this, for those "white-collar" workers include the girls in the typing pool, the office boys, the messengers, the bank tellers, and the insurance company clerks, just as "service workers" include, among others, firemen, garbage collectors, waiters, janitors, and some 400,000 women in dead-end $80-a-week telephone company jobs. The "fact" that American workers are better off than ever before is equally doubtful: Between 1965 and 1970 the real wages of the American worker—after taxes and inflation—probably declined. The worker is supposed to be affluent—to be poor in America is to admit to being black; to be working *and* poor was, until recently, supposed to be nearly impossible. But affluent he is not.

And in the work force, too, one is confronted with the question of generations. There are plants where, as a worker tells you, "the whole night shift is smoking dope—not in the john or the cafeteria, but right on the line, guys stoned from the minute they report for work until the minute they leave." There are mills where the young workers spend more time hanging around the labor shack goofing off than they do on the job, and factories where the executives are, on the one hand, "praying for a good depression that could shape these kids up" and, on the other, realizing that such a depression "will kill us too." A growing percentage of the work force is composed of younger men—in some plants the average age is under thirty—who, by general agreement, "aren't going to take the crap their fathers took," and who will walk off the job with little provocation. At the same time, you can find in the schools in working-class neighborhoods youngsters who might be called children of despair—the sons and daughters of steel-workers or auto workers who, despite the rhetoric of working-class mobility, expect nothing more than a replay of the lives of their parents. You can find unions where there is a constant struggle between the demands for security of the older, depression-conditioned members and the pressure for more wages—cash, not benefits—from the young. The country contains whole regions where the young cannot visualize any future at all, where the gray present continues indefinitely, world without end. "The value system of patriotism, personal responsibility, self-help, hard work, deference of gratification," wrote the sociologists William Simon and John Gagnon, "all still co-exist with values of political cynicism, distrust of strangers, male dominance, demands of obedience from children, and moral and personal inflexibility. In the midst of a rapidly developing and changing society, the working class remains a province not of geography but of history. Its sense of personal accomplish-

ment and success, having shared in the affluence after the Second World War, it still sees as precarious and hard won. The rising expectations of what it perceives as its inferiors by virtue of race or late-coming to the society are threats to its self-earned and visible new gains.... The very intact families and social relationships that continue to operate successfully are one of the elements that make the working class so invulnerable to change.... Its very capacity to survive isolates a large section of the society within these provincial value systems." A province of history.

In Lowell and Lawrence and Enfield, the watchmen sit in front of vacant lofts or in little gatehouses like museum guards, talking—if they are old enough—of days when these brick piles were jammed with looms and shoe machines, when thousands of people worked two or three shifts; it was not good work, and parents often warned their children that anything, even clerking in a department store, was better than going into the mill. But there is also the memory of something else, a remembrance of strength, something monumental, a sense of place and integrity. "Things are better now," says the man who guards the nearly vacant remains of the Appleton Mills in Lowell. He sits at the edge of one of the old canals; a few feet away is the silt-jammed intake of a millrace where the water spilled through to drive the looms and spindles and carding machines that filled the place. "Things are better now," he says again, looking at the darkening road across the canal. "I've got a car and a TV. I didn't have that forty years ago, when I was a steam fitter at Merrimack. But ... " He stops for a moment to watch the automatic street lights come on and marvels at this new form of magic, this electric-eye automation that throws blue shadows on this ancient, unused monument; then he allows that it would be nice to have the rambling structure alive again, recalls that 5,000 people once used to work here and that the little machine shops and electronics companies now scattered through the buildings employ no more than 200.

One can find places like this all over the East and the Midwest, decaying factory lofts and engine shops, multi-story buildings along murky canals ("Lawrence Manufacturing Co.," says the sign in Lowell, "is not responsible for the condition of the canal"), buildings no longer suitable to a technology that demands space to spread out, victims of cheap Southern labor and foreign competitors, places where factory girls from the farms and small towns worked for a couple of dollars a day and where the bosses maintained chaperoned dormitories to see to their morals (though rarely to their health); yet places that, until one or two generations ago, also represented the strength of ages, a future that—despite recessions and layoffs and poverty—was not subject to doubt, a set of relationships not open to question.

This is not something to be sentimental about, but it is essential to some comprehension of the current ambivalence about the meaning of work and about the growing sense that even those once strong enough to exploit, to live in those sumptuous homes, to construct canals and mills (and, later, power plants and assembly lines), that even such people were not strong enough. The old textile towns of New England are now suffering their second recession or perhaps their third. "The whole area," said a poverty worker in Lowell, "has gone down the rotten Merrimack again." World War II saved them once, and then the burgeoning postwar electronics industry around Route 128 saved them again. Now the new laboratories and the assembly plants for electronic components are in trouble themselves; the machine tool industry, the core of Connecticut's industrial economy (and once, as someone said, "the heart of the arsenal of democracy") is weak, the old typewriter factories, Royal and Underwood, have moved their operations to Europe, the portable radios are all manufactured in Japan, the shoes in Italy, the watch and clock mechanisms in Switzerland, and the SST, which might have helped support the big jet-engine manufacturers around Hartford, is not being produced at all. Unemployment in Connecticut rose to something over 10 per cent in 1971; in New Britain it reached 12 per cent and in Bristol it exceeded 24. Moreover, the statistics themselves are subject to doubt because they do not include those who have given up looking for work, the welfare cases, or the "retired." "Unemployment," in fact, sometimes seems a wholly inadequate index as compared with other visible indices of recession: houses for sale, families doubling up, foreclosures, and all the rest.

In any case, it is not the fluctuating unemployment figures that make the future appear bleak. Unemployment exceeded 5 per cent in every year between 1960 and 1965, the era of the Great Society and the New Frontier, when the country was supposed to be full of optimism. Taken now, in the Seventies, to herald a failure of the system, unemployment statistics seem to concretize a more subtle sense of decline, to give statistical substance to the line of junk cars outside the surplus food distribution centers—where the men, too proud to enter, send the wife and kids inside to pick up the month's supply of powdered milk and flour, the beans and butter. They seem to reinforce the physical presence of the accumulating junk around the houses in the inner developments and that of the old men, forced into an early "retirement"—often without pensions —who stand on the streets of small industrial cities, places where the old plant or the mill, now closed, gave life its only focus. What you come away with in these towns is a sense of historic stultification, of fixed limits, an almost European sense of class despair. Increasingly, the industrial cities of the Northeast and elsewhere become invisible places inhabited by invisible people, places that the rest of the world flies over or drives around: Thompsonville and New Britain, Lowell and Manchester, Easthampton and Holyhoke, Chicopee and Altoona, Easton and Bethlehem (not to mention Gary or Newark or Oakland), places where people might be angry or militant, but where they were equally likely to be despondent, to have been so conditioned by two generations of recession and uncertainty as to have no fight left.

In such a condition, doubt becomes endemic: doubt not only of personal possibilities but of the system that was to carry one along. To hold a job in the expectation of growth and mobility is one thing; to maintain the same job for the mere purpose of survival is something very different. A few years ago Robert C. Wood, then Under Secretary of Housing and Urban Development, spoke of the American worker as "a white employed male . . . earning between $5,000 and $10,000. He works regularly, steadily, dependably, wearing a blue collar or white collar. Yet the frontiers of his career expectations have been fixed ever since he reached the age of thirty-five,

when he found that he had too many obligations, too much family, and too few skills to
match opportunities with aspirations.''
Perhaps it was always this way, perhaps things
always closed down too quickly; yet surely
there was a time when—even after personal
mobility and achievement were no longer possible—there still existed the possibility of fellow traveling, of getting a piece of the growing
pie, of sharing not only in the common prosperity of the future but also in the reflected
glory of America the triumphant. Now neither
was certain; increasingly (especially among
young workers) the historic version of the
future made little sense. High-morale jobs
were still around: the ironworkers and the
bridge builders in high steel who can generate
among themselves the intense camaraderie of
a football team or a bomber crew, men who
share risks and who depend on each other,
physically and psychologically, to make those
risks bearable; truck drivers or cabbies for
whom the job becomes a mental as well as a
physical engagement, who pride themselves
on their savvy—the way you get around the
load and hour limits of the Interstate Commerce Commission or around the cops, the
places where you can make a quick buck and
the places to avoid, the hustles and the traps.
Here, too, one can get caught by exessive
generalization. Not all blue-collar jobs are
dreary; not all white-collar jobs (God knows)
are glamorous.

And yet the enclaves of excitement, the
glamor jobs, may simply highlight those areas
where little is possible. For a steelworker in
Gary or Pittsburgh or Bethlehem or an
assembly-line worker in Detroit or Flint, the
choice is between a dead-end job and no job
at all. In Lordstown, Ohio, the young workers
at the Chevrolet assembly plant are demanding
a major voice in determining how the plant
is run, resisting speedups on the line, first with
sabotage and then with a strike, and talking
openly about the limited possibilities of the
job.

There is no single set of responses, no consistency in how people talk about their lives;
too much depends on the man, on his age and

background, and on the place where he lives
and works. Here, too, we lack a language, for
we now seem to have in this country a permanent, quasi-proletarian class without a proletarian ideology. Certainly there is still talk
about a better life for the kids, some lip service
to mobility, but the talk is hesitant and forced,
like an incantation. ''The older people who are
here now,'' said a steelworker in Gary, ''came
at a fortunate time, around the time of the war
when things were booming, when everything
was good. You can't do that anymore. These
mills aren't growing; they're letting people off.
Twelve thousand were laid off by U.S. Steel
in the last year, and most of those people will
never go back. Everywhere you go these guys
will tell you that the country's in trouble, that
it's all gone. At the same time they don't want
to hear the bad news: What they want is
baseball in the morning, football in the afternoon, and basketball at night.''

People celebrate layoffs (with full benefits
in the steel industry, a man figures he does
as well while he's laid off as when he's working
a four-day week) but vaguely, inarticulately,
they also fear the end: What if the mills
automate, as surely they must, and the jobs
never come back?'' A man is a damn fool to
go into the mines,'' said a coal worker to a
newspaper reporter in Virginia. ''Sure, I'm a
fool, but I don't expect my son to be. Breathe
that coal dust and then hear Tony Boyle [the
president of the United Mine Workers] up in
Washington say it ain't gonna hurt you. No,
buddy, a miner's nothing but a slave.'' It is
the same in steel, on the automobile assembly
lines, in textiles. You hate the job, but you also
fear that it will disappear and nothing will
replace it, feel the old guilt and anxiety when
the layoffs go into their eighth week or their
tenth, hang around the bars and talk about
another hunting trip or a day at the races or
about how you cleaned your wife's rug, hope
for a new defense contract or a general increase
in government spending (which inevitably
means defense) but understand also that all
defense work is unstable, that the flag itself
is vulnerable.

SHEILA K. JOHNSON

tHe chRistMAs cArd syNdRoMe

Most human beings are intensely concerned with status. Sociologist Gerhard Lenski claims that this concern not only influences their choice of a car and of a spouse but can also be responsible for their laying down their lives on the battlefield (better a dead hero than a live coward). But who would have thought that a traditional holiday ritual like Christmas card sending has class and status implications? Yet precisely such implications have been uncovered by anthropologist Sheila K. Johnson in the amusing article that follows.

□□□

By the end of this month, Postal Department willing, 50 million American families will have sent one another approximately 2.5 billion Christmas cards, according to estimates made by the National Association of Greeting Card Publishers. That works out to 50 cards per family, although, of course, Christmas-card sending is not that evenly distributed throughout the population. Some people send fewer than a dozen, or none at all, whereas President Nixon mails out about 37,000 a year, dutifully hand-addressed by a volunteer corps of Republican women.

Who sends Christmas cards to whom, and why, is a question that first began to fascinate me several years ago, as I was pawing through a stack of cards that my husband and I had

From the *New York Times Magazine*, December 5, 1971. © 1971 by The New York Times Company. Reprinted by permission.

received and were about to throw away. Here were all the expectable entries from people to whom we had also sent cards: Distant relatives with whom we communicated once a year, good friends who were abroad or who had moved to another part of the country, and my husband's colleagues—both local and far afield. But here too were a number of unexpected entries from people to whom we had not sent cards: Graduate students—both foreign and domestic—who obviously expected my husband at some future point in time to sign their theses, immigration papers or employment applications; newspapermen and politicians for whom my husband had done a favor in the recent past; publishers; insurance agents; a Hong Kong tailor, the local liquor store; the hairdresser; our veterinarian. What did these people have in common with one another, I wondered, except the fact that they were obviously trying to cultivate us, or be "remembered" by us—a sentiment which we had felt no need to reciprocate. At the same time, we ourselves had sent a number of cards to people likely to be influential in our lives but who had not sent us cards.

It was at this point that it occurred to me that Christmas-card sending might be an excellent indicator of social status and mobility aspirations. In other words, the total number of cards a person sends and receives and the percentages of these cards that he sends "upward" or receives from "below," as well as the percentage of "reciprocals," ought to tell us something about his social class, whether he is upwardly mobile or relatively stationary, and whether people are upwardly mobile with regard to him.

Unfortunately, data to test this hypothesis proved to be exceedingly hard to come by. Just as Americans like to think of themselves as a classless society, so people like to think of themselves as sending out Christmas cards for the most noble of motives. Nonetheless, on the basis of information gleaned from a few unsuspecting relatives and cooperative friends, some interesting trends emerge. Several professional couples in their late 30's and early 40's who were upwardly mobile and who also knew a number of people upwardly mobile with regard to them, found that their Christmas cards could be grouped into equal thirds (one-third sent and not received, one-third sent and received, and one-third received but not sent).

This is clearly the pattern for ambitious young professionals, and the writers of the recent movie "Diary of a Mad Housewife" missed this point when they showed the husband counting the Christmas cards he and his wife had received and then remarking to her, "One-hundred-and-fifty-three. That's fine. Three more weeks to go until Christmas and we've already reached the half-way mark. . . . We sent out 300." The husband might be understandably anxious about getting as many cards as possible from the V.I.P.'s to whom he had sent cards, but given his penchant for social climbing he would never (as he did in the film) instruct his wife to note carefully who had sent them cards, so that people who had not could be crossed off their list.

It is only among people at the very top of the social heap that one can expect to find a large number of reciprocal cards combined with a large number of cards received from people trying to curry favor, and very few or no cards sent upward. One would imagine, for example, that President Nixon receives a great many Christmas cards that he can ignore with impunity, but that almost none of the 37,000-odd recipients of the President's card fail to respond. The message would be unmistakable. To whom might the President send a card only to have the gesture spurned? George Meany? Chiang Kai-shek? Wars have been started over less.

Perhaps a more typical Christmas-card profile of a high-status but relatively stationary individual is provided by a diplomat of my acquaintance. No longer very upwardly mobile because there are few posts higher than the one he now holds, he found that only 4 per cent of his cards had been sent upward, while 62 per cent were reciprocal, and 34 per cent came from people trying to cultivate him. At the opposite extreme, a young and ambitious graduate student reported that about 70 per cent of his cards were reciprocal, with 30 per cent sent upward and none received from people who were trying to curry favor with him. This last is clearly the pattern for those with their foot on the bottom rung of the status ladder. With retirement, on the other hand, several people reported that almost all of their Christmas-card sending and receiving became reciprocal, with no cards sent upward (unless, perhaps, unintentionally to friends recently deceased) and none received from people who still looked up to them.

If we look at the sheer numbers rather than percentages of Christmas cards sent and received, these too tell a sociological story. Christmas-card sending is more typical of white-collar and professional people than of either blue-collar or lower-class families. It is a safe bet that almost no blue-collar families send out more than 50 cards, whereas the average for lower-middle-class, white-collar families seems to be between 50 and 100. For professional people it can range from 100 to 300 (typical of professors, government bureaucrats and lawyers—*viz.* the couple in "Diary of a Mad Housewife") to 300 to 500 (typical of bankers, minor "media people" and middle-range business executives). However, for businessmen who head large concerns, well-known show-business personalities and politicians with state or national constituencies, the numbers of Christmas cards sent can range into the thousands. One California politician of my acquaintance (who also happens to be Jewish) sent out 2,400 Christmas cards in 1970—a "light" year, by his own assessment, since in his own election years he sends out as many as 5,000.

The class impact on Christmas-card sending is not difficult to explain. Sociologists have demonstrated that middle-class individuals tend to be much more geographically mobile than members of the working class. Typically, a middle-class professional will grow up in one part of the country, go to college somewhere else, and take a job in still a third area. He may move several times more during the course of his career, and retire in yet another part of the country. In the course of these moves, he will make close friends whom he may not see for years, meet people who may prove useful to him in the future, and loosen his ties with relatives. These are the ideal conditions for the exchange of Christmas cards: a loose and scattered network of friends and relations with whom one "wants to keep in touch," and the need, in one's occupation, to cultivate the right sort of people—be they clients, department heads or political allies.

Blue-collar, or working-class, individuals are much more likely to settle and marry in the area where they were raised and went to high school. Because of this, sociologists have found that working-class individuals depend upon tightly knit family networks and upon neighbors for their friendships. Clearly, there is not much point in sending Christmas cards to relatives whom one is likely to see during the holidays or to neighbors whom one sees nearly every day.

Working-class individuals also do not send Christmas cards to workmates—imagine sending a card to every man on the Ford production line, or to a temporarily assembled construction crew—nor are they likely to send cards upward, as a socially mobile white-collar worker might, since blue-collar advancement proceeds through union-defined grades, and a Christmas card to the front office is not likely to do the trick. Only if a blue-collar worker is upwardly mobile to the extent of trying to leave his stratum and become a white-collar worker, may he take to sending Christmas cards to people who can help him.

Social class has a more powerful impact on Christmas-card sending than ethnic or religious ties. Jews as a group do not eschew sending Christmas cards. True, many working-class Jews do not send Christmas cards, but for reasons which may have more to do with the fact that they are working-class than that they are Jewish. Most middle-class Jews do send Christmas cards, even when they avoid all other aspects of the holiday, such as Christmas trees and Christmas presents. If religious affiliation has any impact at all on Christmas-card sending, it is on the type of card chosen.

Middle-class Jewish businessmen tend to choose completely abstract designs featuring the words "PEACE," "JOY" or "GREETINGS" (but not "NOEL"). Jewish professional families, particularly those—such as politicians—whose religion is well-known and an asset, may choose cards that feature the religious symbols of the world's major religions (including, of course, Moslemism as well as Judaism), or UNICEF cards. Jewish academicians are particularly fond of UNICEF cards or of cards supporting some other cause that they espouse (Another Mother for Peace, CORE, the World Without War Council, but not, generally speaking, the American Friends Service Committee).

Other religious and ethnic groups in the society follow the same pattern. Working-class Catholics are no more likely to send Christmas cards than working-class Jews or Protestants, but middle-class Catholics (or upper-class Catholics such as the Kennedys), who send Christmas cards because of their social status, are more likely to select cards with a religious motif. Blacks and Mexican-Americans send few Christmas cards, but this is not a result of their ethnicity but of the fact that so many belong to the lower or working class. Middle-class blacks and Mexican-Americans are just as likely to send Christmas cards as their white counterparts, and until recently they would have chosen the same types of cards. However, with the emphasis on racial pride, there is now a growing demand for cards that reflect their senders' ethnicity. In 1969 a small man-and-wife-operated Christmas-card firm called Creative Soul, Inc., began to design some cards using not only the black-pride theme but also featuring other minority groups, chiefly Asian-Americans and American Indians. In 1970, Creative Soul sold approximately half a million cards.

The owner of Creative Soul, Hugh Dalton (his wife, Yvette, designs the cards), is quick to acknowledge that his cards sell best in the large, sophisticated cities and, particularly, in mixed neighborhoods, where one is likely to find middle-class blacks. Neither share-croppers nor ghetto dwellers are likely to send one another Christmas cards, regardless of the message. Dalton also notes with interest that the success of his own line of cards has prompted larger firms to design cards aimed at the black middle class. There are, as yet, few blatant soul cards, but Hallmark has at least one card on the market featuring an unmistakably dusky-faced Santa Claus. Surprisingly enough, considering that many black Americans are devout Protestants and most Mexican-Americans are devout Catholics, I could find no commercially designed card featuring a black or brown Madonna and child. However, in previous years CORE has produced cards featuring a black mother and child, in an obvious reference to the Madonna-and-child theme, and this year one of UNICEF's cards depicts a Nigerian mother with a child strapped to her back.

Ethnicity and religious ties are by no means the only influences on the type of Christmas cards that people choose. Whereas people buy a birthday card, or a get-well card, with a particular recipient in mind, Christmas cards are bought boxed or ordered in large numbers, and they are selected, either consciously or subconsciously, to reflect the sender's lifestyle. For example, businessmen who want to make a solid, sober impression on their clients usually select large (expensive), heavily embossed cards featuring abstract bells, Christmas trees or holly wreaths. They tend to avoid religious scenes and sentiments for fear of offending any of their atheist or Jewish acquaintances. Academicians, on the other hand, often choose religious designs (usually in the form of museum cards depicting the Annunciation, the three Magi, or the Madonna and child) to stress their purist, noncommercial, nonhokey appreciation of Christmas. In academic circles it is also common for the most powerful professors to send the smallest cards, a deliberate and snobbish inversion of the business ethic, where the size and heft of a Christmas card are usually directly proportional to the importance of the sender.

One indication of the variety of personal and social functions that Christmas cards fulfill is the great proliferation of cards expressing political sentiments. Hallmark's market researchers argue that there has always been a tendency toward such cards in this country: For example, during World War II, cards with Santas carrying flags were very popular. However, this year (as was also true last year), PEACE is the major theme, and it is more often PEACE with strong political rather than Biblical overtones. There is an absolute flood of cards depicting white doves, and there is also a fair number of commercially produced cards featuring the Committee for Nuclear Disarmament's peace symbol. With-it political sentiments have become so popular that even Hallmark—the majority of whose cards still lean toward Santa Clauses, snow scenes and cute little angels with their halos askew—has introduced a new line of "Christmas Now" cards. One of these, for example, features a cheerful, freckle-faced hippie (a second cousin to the little angels of the past) waving a flower and giving the peace sign. Another "Christmas Now" card displays Santa riding his sleigh while wearing a gas mask. The message: "Silent night, holy night, All is calm and visibility is poor!"

Unquestionably the greatest single beneficiary of the desire to express oneself as being for peace on a Christmas card has been UNICEF, although even its staff did not guess that one of their 1970 cards, depicting a Picassoish dove and angel interwined, would be a run-away best-seller. (Last year one Berkeley professor's collection of cards received included 20 UNICEF cards, six of them featuring the dove-angel design.)

UNICEF last year sold approximately 26 million Christmas cards in the United States, or about 1 per cent of the total number of cards that were sent, going by the estimates of the National Association of Greeting Card Publishers. However, if one looks at the cards received by an average professor's family, one finds that between 11 per cent and 16 per cent are UNICEF cards, and another 6 per cent may be cards supporting other liberal causes: Another Mother for Peace, CORE, the American Friends Service Committee, Project HOPE, and so forth. UNICEF cards have the added advantage of depicting scenes in different countries, often drawn by artists of those countries, so that liberal academicians and State Department people can not only advertise their political sentiments but also their area of specialization.

The prevalence of liberal political sentiments expressed on the Christmas cards sent by professors led me to wonder whether there was such a thing as the conservative Christmas card. Sure enough, there is a small Orange County, Calif., firm, called Granger Graphics, that produces a line of cards sold exclusively through John Birch Society outlets. One of their 1970 cards depicts an American eagle, the Declaration of Independence and a Bible; another features George Washington and the quotation "Almighty God, we make our earnest prayer, that Thou wilt keep the United States in Thy holy protection."

Some Birch Society members are also in the habit of enclosing small printed notes with their Christmas cards saying, "Please do not send me a UNICEF card." UNICEF probably does not need to feel seriously threatened by this movement, however, since in 1970 John Birch Society members bought only about 100,000 Granger Graphics cards. At the same time, many John Birch Society members simply send out regular commercially designed cards, particularly those featuring religious motifs. One pleasant, elderly woman whom I interviewed on this subject said that her chief objection to UNICEF cards was not so much a question of politics as the fact that many of the cards were the work of non-Christians (i.e., atheistic Communists). I did not have the heart to tell her that this year's UNICEF collection includes reproductions of five religious paintings from the Vatican museums and library, made especially available to UNICEF by the Holy See.

If one does not choose to parade one's political opinions on a Christmas card, what other avenues of self-expression and status-enhancement are available? One possibility is the museum card, favored by many academicians and other upper-middle-class urbanites who want to adhere to the mass custom of sending Christmas cards without abandoning their claims to good taste and élitism. As with UNICEF cards, many professors also advertise their area of specialization via a museum card: English professors favor Dickens illustrations or reproductions of illuminated manuscripts, Japan and China specialists tend to choose sumi ink drawings, and historians favor art reproductions drawn from "their" period and country.

Although many museums sell some Christmas cards featuring art works in their collections, the biggest purveyor of museum cards, the Metropolitan Museum of Art, has a clientele ranging well beyond local visitors or museum boosters. The type of buyer the Metropolitan hopes to (and does) attract is testified to by the national magazines in which it advertises its cards: Harper's, Atlantic Monthly, The New Yorker, Book World, and The New York Times Magazine. Although the museum refuses to divulge its annual sales figures, these are probably in the vicinity of one or two million Christmas cards a year. The Metropolitan's engagement calendar alone, used by many New York business concerns in lieu of a Christmas card, last year sold a quarter of a million copies.

Given the extensive advertising done by the museum for its Christmas cards, profits are probably not enormous, and the museum sees its sale of Christmas cards as more of an educational than a profit-making enterprise. Topics for cards are chosen by a committee which includes curators from all departments of the museum, and the final selections are based partly on a desire to display items from the museum's collection that are not often seen, and partly on the ability to reproduce them as accurately as possible. These "art for art's sake" considerations, as well as the unquestionably high quality of cards, make them extremely popular with members of the intelligentsia. It is not accidental, for example, that whereas the Metropolitan's sales of Christmas cards represent only a fraction of those sold by UNICEF (and hence a fraction of 1 per cent of the total number of cards sold every year), among several professional families surveyed, museum cards constituted between 4 per cent and 8 per cent of the total number of cards received.

For people not anxious to advertise either their political opinions or their good taste, there remains the option of advertising themselves. I am thinking, of course, of the multitude of cards consisting of photos of people's children, pets and houses, as well as that most dubious of Christmas blessings: the mimeographed family letter. According to Eastman Kodak, 5 per cent of all Christmas cards sent out last year consisted of personal photographs. Most of these photographs were of very young children, it being a little difficult, these days, to get teen-agers to pose for snapshots. In my private survey of two card collections I found that 8 per cent of Professor A's cards were photographic, compared with only 3 per cent of Professor B's cards—a disparity to be explained almost entirely by the fact that Professor A is in his late 30's and has many friends with young children, whereas Professor B is in his late 40's and has friends with teen-age children.

Photographic cards are not, of course, the exclusive preserve of families with young children. Families temporarily living or traveling abroad often advertise that fact via a photographic card of themselves posed in front of some easily identifiable monument. And families for whom the image of togetherness is an important business asset tend to pose themselves en masse.

This is particularly true of politicians. One acquaintance of ours who is both a lawyer and a political figure last year sent us a photographic Christmas card of himself, his wife and four children that looked suspiciously like a piece of campaign literature. Photographs of single individuals also seem to serve advertising purposes of either a professional or a personal nature. Although Eastman Kodak denies any knowledge of such cards, I have some photographic if unprintable evidence that topless dancers, call girls and homosexuals often send nude Christmas greetings to customers or friends.

The tendency for photographic Christmas cards to constitute advertisements for oneself is even more evident in those that depict houses. The houses that are typically enshrined on Christmas cards are "status houses"—that is, houses which denote a change (usually an improvement) in the social status of the occupant. One friend, who had long been pining to buy a farm and who finally inherited some money with which to buy one, sent us a card of a meadow full of wild flowers and bounded by a rustic fence with his name on it. Of course the biggest status house of them all—the White House—almost invariably appears on the President's Christmas card.

One argument sometimes offered by people who send photographs of themselves, their houses or their children is that such Christmas cards are at least "personal"—they avoid the mass-produced, stereotyped, printed card. People who buy museum cards also find this an attraction, and people who buy cards supporting good causes often reason that while such cards may be mass-produced, at least they are noncommercial. This widespread yearning

to reindividualize Christmas-card sending has led many people to design and manufacture their own cards. Often such handmade cards are partly the outcome of attempts to keep preschool children occupied in the week before Christmas, and the results are little more than clumsily folded and pasted bits of colored paper. But sometimes an artistically inclined wife produces genuinely handsome, homemade woodblock or linoleum prints; and in some families, where artistic talent seems to run high, a family competition is held to choose the annual Christmas card design. In one professional family of my acquaintance such a yearly competition has been won for the last two years by the 15-year-old son, who is a talented cartoonist. His 1970 card featured a hip-looking Santa Claus wearing shades and driving a sleigh that bears a sign reading "No Riders. Notice: Driver Carrys [sic] No Money."

It is difficult to estimate the number of handcrafted Christmas cards currently produced in the United States, but among my sample of professional families they constituted 7 per cent to 8 per cent of the total number of cards received. Clearly, such a trend —if it is at all indicative of other groups in the society—is a potential threat to the large greeting-card manufacturers. At least one of them, Hallmark Cards, is trying to adapt to the desire for more "personal" cards by inaugurating a line of cards that allows the purchaser to write out a message in his own hand and have it reproduced. Among the celebrities who have already selected cards and created such personalized messages are Peggy Fleming, Tim Conway and David Susskind. I am sure all of David Susskind's friends and acquaintances will be thrilled to receive his austere gold card with the hand-written photo-reproduced message, "Joyce and I wish you health, happiness and peace in the New Year."

The idea that it is somehow more personal to have Hallmark print cards containing a hand-written message also lies behind the mimeographed Christmas letter. In actuality, however, mimeographed letters strike many of their recipients as the most impersonal of all. Part of the problem lies with the tone of such letters, which often sound as if they were written for (and by) mental defectives. This is a result of their not being addressed to any particular individual; nor are they apparently written *by* any particular individual, since they invariably adopt the third-person voice.

The mimeographed letter has one comforting aspect: It reminds one that bad taste is not limited to any particular social class or group of people. Whereas the tendency to send sappy, sentimental cards—what I call the Hallmark, or schleppiness, factor—increases as one goes down the social scale, the tendency to send mimeographed Christmas letters rises as one goes up the social and educational scale. Among highly sophisticated, verbal Ph.D.'s, the number of Christmas letters received (almost invariably from other Ph.D.'s) is an alarming 8 per cent to 11 per cent.

Although usually written in a tone of forced cheeriness, the actual content of Christmas letters is often far from cheerful. "Well, this has been an eventful year for us," one such letter begins. "After finishing the school year in June, we closed up our house in Cambridge and left for Delhi, where we had planned to spend our sabbatical year. Unfortunately, in October Dick came down with a serious case of hepatitis, complicated by a recurrence of his old malaria, and Sally developed amoebic dysentery. So we decided to cut short our stay and returned directly to Massachusetts General Hospital, where we were lucky to be able to obtain adjoining beds in a private room. . . ."

Another Christmas letter recounts in the most sanguine terms how son John has decided to beat the draft by going to Canada ("where his lovely fiancée, Julie, plans to join him in time for the holidays") and how daughter Sara is really finding herself now that she has managed to get on the methadone program at Half-Way House. However, the choicest Christmas letter to have come my way recently is a poem (slightly altered, to protect the guilty):

> *This Christmas letter brings you cheer*
> *For both the season and new year.*
> *Alas, the Rays who send you this*
> *Have called an end to wedded bliss.*
> *Next year Don will be in Detroit*
> *While Jane and children in Beloit*
> *Live with her parents for a bit,*
> *Until the kids get used to it.*
> *Jane hopes to find a job again*
> *To limber up her sluggish brain.*
> *And Don has taken up the lute,*
> *(His hippie girlfriend plays the flute.)*
> *But though apart, we jointly pray*
> *That peace and love may come your*
> *way.*
>
> *(To which one can only add:*
> *And at this poem do not laugh too hard*
> *Unless you've never sent a Christmas*
> *card!)*

DISCUSSING THE ARTICLES

1. In "The 'Forgotten American' Revisited" by Peter Schrag, in what other terms is the lower-middle class spoken of? Do the terms have different connotations for you? Which term do you prefer?

2. What happened to the image of the lower-middle class member? Can you say why?

3. Are there any similarities between Peter Schrag's description of the "forgotten American" and Hodges's description of the lower-middle class that was given in the text? In general, what has been happening to the provincial virtues of which "the common man" has been so proud?

4. Is the author of the article sure about how to classify the "forgotten American"? How did the two sociologists mentioned by the author classify him? List some of the problems involved in categorizing people into social classes, or strata. Can you think of a system of classification that is superior to those employed by sociologists?

5. Explain what the author means by a social class that "had outlived the mythology that legitimized (and sometimes glorified) their [members'] existence."

6. According to the author, was work ever related to self-respect and success in our culture, or was it always the attainment of wealth that was related to these characteristics?

7. What is wrong with the generalizations that America has become a service economy and that the work force is now primarily a white-collar force? Would a white-collar occupation automatically promote the lower-middle class individual into a higher social class? What would?

8. Do the younger generation of lower-middle class Americans resemble their fathers? What seem to be their values? Are their values similar to which class in Hodges's study?

9. How does the author differentiate between jobs? Of which social class is the first job description representative; that is, members of which social class might expect to have such a job? The second description?

10. What new characterization does Peter Schrag give of the lower-middle class in America? What does this class lack? Speculate about what is going to happen to his social class. On what will its future depend?

11. In "The Christmas Card Syndrome," how does Sheila K. Johnson, the author, link Christmas card sending with social class, status, and social mobility?

12. What is the pattern of card sending among ambitious young professionals?

13. Among which social class does one find a large number of reciprocal cards, a large number received, and very few sent?

14. Where does the graduate student fit in the stratification system? Can you prove it by the number of cards he sends, reciprocates, and receives? In contrast to what social class does he stand? Can that be proven by the number of cards sent, reciprocated, and received?

15. Where do the people with only reciprocated cards fit in the stratification system?

16. Which dimension of stratification do the percentages of cards sent out and received represent? Which dimension of stratification do the numbers of cards sent and received represent?

17. In which social classes are the most Christmas cards sent? Why?

18. To whom do middle-class people send Christmas cards? To whom do lower-class people send them? Why don't lower-class people send cards upward, to those in a higher stratum?

19. Which has more impact on Christmas card sending: religion, ethnicity, or social class?

20. Who tends to send UNICEF cards? Religious motif cards?

21. What do the cards say about the senders' life styles? Who sends big cards? Small cards? How is this related to the senders' status?

22. What other dimensions of stratification do different types of Christmas cards suggest?

TERMS TO REMEMBER

Social stratification, or ranking. A process existing in all but the most simple societies, whereby members rank one another and themselves hierarchically (from low to high) with respect to the amount of desirable goods and services they possess.

Functionalist theory. A theory of stratification in which social inequality is viewed as inevitable because society must use rewards to make sure that essential tasks will be performed by the most talented and most highly trained individuals. Functionalists maintain that the natural condition of society is order and stability.

Conflict theory. A theory of stratification according to which the natural condition of society is constant change and conflict. Stratification systems, and attendant social inequality, are considered evidence of such conflict.

Social class. A category of stratification. An aggregate of persons in a society who stand in a similar position with respect to some form of power, privilege, or prestige.

Social status. A category of stratification. The individual's ranked position within the social system, the rank being determined by the role the individual performs.

Status inconsistency. A phenomenon in which some of the variables associated with a particular status are missing, yet the individual is still ranked according to that status.

Status group. All the individuals who are ranked similarly and who tend to associate with one another, developing similar life styles.

Master status. The status considered the most important of several alternative statuses by a majority of society's members.

Power. A category of stratification. The ability of one individual or segment of the population to control the actions of another individual or segment of the population, with or without the latter's consent.

Personal power. The freedom of the individual to direct his life in any direction he chooses, without much societal interference.

Social power. The ability to make decisions that affect entire communities or even the whole society.

Authority. Social power exercised with the consent of the members of society. Different levels of authority are represented by parents, teachers, and the government.

Stratification system. The overlapping manner in which societal members are ranked according to classes, status groups, and hierarchies of power.

Social mobility. An individual's ability to change his social class membership by moving up or down the ladder of the stratification system.

Closed, or caste, stratification system. A system in which class, status, and power are ascribed; mobility is highly restricted; and the social system is rigid. Classical India is an example of a closed society.

Estate system. The prevailing economic and social system of feudal Europe, consisting of three estates of functional importance to society. The estates were hierarchically arranged and permitted a limited amount of social mobility.

Open stratification system. A stratification system that retains social classes but permits equal access to resources, power, and prestige, to be attained through achievement. Most modern industrial societies are examples of such a system.

Vertical social mobility. Mobility that occurs in an upward or downward direction in the stratification system.

Horizontal social mobility. Mobility that occurs when there is a change of status without a consequent change of class.

Intergenerational mobility. Mobility that occurs when an individual attains a higher social class than his parents had.

Intragenerational mobility. Mobility that occurs when an individual attains a higher social class than do other members of his generation.

Life chances. The opportunity of each individual to fulfill or fail to fulfill his potential as a human being in society.

SUGGESTIONS FOR FURTHER READING

Bendix, Reinhard, and Lipset, Seymour Martin, eds., *Class, Status, and Power*. New York: Glencoe Free Press, 1966. A collection of essays, this book has become a classic in the field of social stratification.

Bottomore, T. B. *Classes in Modern Society*. New York: Pantheon Books, 1966. The systems of stratification of several modern societies analyzed by an authority in the field.

Budd, Edward C. *Inequality and Poverty*. New York: W. W. Norton, 1967. A series of essays in which economists attack the issues of inequality and poverty.

Coleman, Richard P., and Neugarten, Bernice L. *Social Status in the City*. San Francisco: Jossey-Bass Publishers, 1971. The social class structure of Kansas City, Missouri analyzed in a clear and readable style.

Hamilton, Richard F. "The Marginal Middle Class: A Reconsideration." *American Sociological Review*, Vol. 31 (April, 1966), pp. 192-199. The class and status of white-collar employees examined realistically.

Hodges, Harold M., Jr. *Social Stratification: Class In America*. Cambridge, Mass.: Schenkman, 1964. An exhaustive look at the phenomenon of stratification, with particular emphasis on the life styles of the various classes in America.

Hollingshead, A. B. *Elmtown's Youth*. New York: John Wiley, 1949. A classic in the field of social stratification, this book examines the influence of social class on the young people of a Midwestern community.

Kolko, Gabriel. *Wealth and Power in America*. New York: Praeger, 1962. A critic of American economic and political structure—with its inequalities in the distribution of wealth, power, and privilege—presents a convincing, though incriminating, case.

Lenski, Gerhard. *Power and Privilege: A Theory of Social Stratification*. New York: McGraw-Hill, 1966. Power as the basic manipulative force of social life underlies this theory of a renowned sociologist.

Lipset, Seymour Martin, and Bendix, Reinhard. *Social Mobility in Industrial Society*. Berkeley, Calif.: University of California Press, 1966. A comparative approach, the results of which refute the notion that industrial societies are as open as they seem to be.

Miller, S. M., and Roby, Pamela A. *The Future of Inequality*. New York: Basic Books, 1970. The authors maintain that the notion of poverty is outdated and that the lowest 20 percent of the population must be raised out of their fixed level of living and status.

Mills, C. Wright. *The Power Elite*. New York: Oxford University Press, 1959. A polemical book by a well-known conflict theorist, asserting that power in the United States is the property of an interlocking directorate of top corporate, military, and governmental leaders.

Packard, Vance. *The Status Seekers*. New York: McKay, 1959. America's favorite pastime, keeping up with the Joneses, explored with tongue in cheek.

Shostak, Arthur B., and Gomberg, William. *New Perspectives on Poverty*. Englewood Cliffs, N. J.: Prentice-Hall, 1965. A collection of essays on the theme of the culture of poverty.

Warner, W. Lloyd. *Social Class in America*. New York: Harper & Row, 1960. A classic use of the reputational approach in exploring social class.

Warner, W. Lloyd. *Yankee City*, abridged edition. New Haven, Conn.: Yale University Press, 1963. An interesting and readable analysis of the social system of a New England community seen as a microcosm of the larger American society.

Winter, J. Alan, ed. *The Poor: A Culture of Poverty or a Poverty of Culture?* Grand Rapids, Mich.: William B. Eerdmans, 1971. A series of essays in which the culture of poverty is viewed in a new light.

◨ chapter five

If space travel ever became a concrete reality, and if, in our interplanetary adventures, we chanced upon a species similar to humans, we would, no doubt, be very curious to learn how they organized their lives. We would be especially interested in finding out whether they had succeeded in eliminating conflict on their planet (providing they were ever faced with it). We would also want to know what the chief causes of their conflict had been. We on earth are very far from having resolved conflict. Conflict, which basically centers on group relations, has been a part of every society recorded in history.

To continue our imaginary example, suppose that we found that our extra-planetary friends had skins of red, purple, and sunflower yellow. If on this basis, they organized themselves in a hierarchy of superior beings (purple, a royal color), average beings (yellow, a sunny color), and inferior beings (red, a violent color), we would surely ridicule their irrational classifications. Yet if we reverse our story and suppose that visitors from a distant planet were observing us, what tales would they bring back to their homeland? Wouldn't they report similar divisions based on color? And wouldn't such divisions, when observed from afar, appear ridiculous?

From up close, unfortunately, they seem less ridiculous than serious. It seems that in their need to cling to groups, humans develop such an intense loyalty for some of their groups that they cannot tolerate groups formed by others. Lack of tolerance appears to become sharper the greater are the differences in skin color, language, religious beliefs, and customs.

Group conflict is intimately related to social inequality, and like it, is often based on racial and ethnic considerations. Such group conflict makes up a good portion of world history. In fact, all of history may be considered a massive, continuous struggle in which one human group has been pitted against another.

The twentieth century has seen more than its share of group conflict, and there doesn't seem to be an end in sight. The so-called civilized nations are founded on the principle that personal dignity is every individual's birthright. But that principle has been constantly ignored and denied, whether in Nazi Germany twenty years ago, in South Africa, Ireland and Bangladesh, Southeast Asia and the United States today. Racial and ethnic conflicts carry us further and further away from the ideal of the universality of mankind. Instead, they bring to the surface whatever differences exist among peoples and among nations and set these differences up as a permanent wall that separates humans from one another.

Sociologists approach racial and ethnic conflicts from different directions. Some sociologists study such conflicts as a product of the system of ideas that is racism and trace the development of racism throughout history. Others view racial and ethnic conflicts as phenomena related to personality; they examine the character structure of particular types of personalities and the channels and agencies through which intolerant attitudes are acquired and spread. Finally, a third group of sociologists is interested in the social structure in which such conflicts occur—in the factors in a society that are responsible for conflicts. All three approaches offer us helpful glimpses into the problems of racial and ethnic minorities in our society and in the world.

MINORITIES

The word *minority* was first applied to groups within a society that had come under the control of an outside power as a result of land shuffling during the creation of nation-states. For example, when the Austro-Hungarian Empire was broken up into a number of independent units, or nation-states, many German-speaking citizens suddenly found themselves living in Poland. The German-speaking people, differing from the rest of the Poles in language, customs, and often religion, were a minority group in that nation.

Later, the word minority was applied to any substantial number of culturally, racially, or ethnically alike people who immigrated, voluntarily or involuntarily, into a society differing in some or most of these features. Finally, its meaning was altered once more, and minority referred to large groups of native-born people who had come under the control of another group.

Today, however a minority group is any group in society that remains at the bottom of the stratification system and is subjected to discriminatory practices by the wider society because of differences in culture, race, religion, or sex. Specifically, minority groups "are categories of people that possess imperfect access to positions of equal power and to the corollary categories of prestige and privilege in the society."[1] Such imperfect access is ensured by the power possessed by the dominant group—a power that the subordinate group lacks.

In many instances—in the United States, for example—power was obtained by the first group of immigrants, who subdued the native population and gained control of the economy and government. Having control of these key institutions, the original settlers established an elitist system, in which they gave important positions to members of their own ethnic group. Later groups of immigrants received less desirable positions and consequently suffered in wealth, status, and power.

In such a situation, some conflict is unavoidable, for the dominant group guards its privileged status and thwarts attempts by subordinate groups to take some of it away. Subordinate groups, in turn, eventually decide that their inferior status is unsatisfactory and demand a "piece of the action." Conflict, nonetheless, is not always apparent. In stable, primarily agricultural societies, conflict tends to remain beneath the surface. The dominant group is able to control the subordinate groups by convincing them that it is responsible for them in a fatherly way. In other words, members of the dominant group look upon themselves as kindly masters who take care of their less fortunate "children." In dynamic urban, industrial societies, such conflict is much harder to contain. All groups are made to desire scarce goods, and the competition for them brings conflict out into the open. The present racial situation in the United States is an illustration of open, though not yet armed, conflict.

Kinds of Minorities

Minorities are formed when two or more groups occupy the same territory. This situation can arise from political subdivisions following wars, as was mentioned earlier. It can also arise because people migrate to improve their lives or are forcibly removed from their native lands to other territories for economic reasons—so they can be used to enrich others.

The United States has minorities that were formed on each of these bases. The Indians had their land seized by the conquering Europeans. Ethnic minorities immigrated because of political and religious freedom and/or because they wanted to improve their standard of living. And black people were brought here and made slaves for economic reasons.

Minority groups differ from the dominant group and from one another primarily with respect to race and culture. *Racial minorities* differ biologically; their skin color, hair texture, head shape, and eye color or slant sets them apart from others. Blacks, Indians, and Orientals are the predominant racial minorities in the United States.

Ethnic minorities differ culturally. Their language, customs, religion, food

[1]Norman R. Yetman and C. Hoy Steele, eds., *Majority and Minority* (Boston: Allyn and Bacon, 1971), p. 4.

habits, child-rearing practices, and values and beliefs are different from those
of the dominant group. Immigrants, the largest numbers of whom came in
the nineteenth and early twentieth centuries, make up ethnic minorities. Their
status has varied according to the extent to which their appearance and customs
differed from those of the dominant group. Immigrants from the British Isles
and Northern Europe resembled members of the dominant group in appearance
and had cultures similar to its culture. Thus, they were easily accepted and
attained high status. Immigrants from Eastern and Southern Europe—Russians,
Poles, Italians, Greeks, and Jews—have not been as readily accepted, nor have
recent immigrants from Puerto Rico and Mexico. One significant way in which

ethnic groups may culturally differ from the dominant group is in religion. For some ethnic minorities, religion has been the primary factor in determining low status. This has been true of Jews, Roman Catholics, and the followers of Eastern or extremely unusual religions.

Goals of Minorities

Not all minorities have the same goals when they enter a new social and cultural setting. Some want to keep their own cultural heritage, including religion and language, while coexisting in peace and harmony with the dominant group and with any other minorities in the society. Such minorities are called *pluralistic*. Switzerland is an example of a pluralistic society—one in which various minority groups, each of which keeps its own culture, live together in peace. Pluralism is also sometimes expressed as the goal of the United States.

Other minorities prefer to absorb completely the culture of the dominant group, hoping, in this manner, to gain the high status of the majority. Such minorities are termed *assimilationist*. Assimilation was the goal of many European immigrants to the United States. In recent years, assimilation has lost its appeal for members of many minorities, particularly for blacks.

Some groups want cultural and/or political independence from the majority. They desire, in many instances, self-determination. These minorities are *secessionist*. Nations such as Israel and Bangladesh were created out of the demands of secessionist minorities, whereas French Canadians have been thwarted in a similar attempt.

Finally, still other minorities claim as their goal not merely equality with the dominant group but a reversal of status with it. They want to become the dominant group. These are *militant* minorities, found in a number of African nations that recently gained their independence—Algeria, Ghana, and Libya, for example.[2] Such groups, usually numerically superior to begin with, remain minorities only during their struggle to become the dominant group. They abandon militancy and minority group status once their goal is attained.

Common Features of Minorities

Whatever their differences in appearance, culture, or goals, all minority groups have some features in common: (1) They are usually subordinate groups within complex societies; (2) they have specific physical and/or cultural traits that the majority group considers undesirable; (3) they are aware that they differ from the dominant group and tend to stick together because they are different; (4) for the first few generations, and sometimes much longer, members of minorities tend to intermarry; (5) descent determines membership in a minority group, and such membership is sometimes retained despite the disappearance of obvious physical or racial distinctions.[3]

Even though their general situation is the same, the various minorities in our society are quite different from one another. Thus, they have not banded

[2]This typology of minorities appears in Louis Wirth, "The Problem of Minority Groups," in Ralph Linton, ed., *The Science of Man in the World Crisis* (New York: Columbia University Press, 1945), pp. 347–372.

[3]Charles Wagley and Marvin Harris, *Minorities in the New World* (New York: Columbia University Press, 1958), p.10.

together to create alliances and pressure groups that would strengthen their position in society. On the contrary, many ethnic and racial minorities harbor deep feelings of resentment against one another, as well as against the dominant majority. Separation, rather than cooperation, has been their method of existence, and self-interest their concern.

Why Are Minorities a Problem?

All facets of man's life in groups are of interest to sociologists. This is particularly true of minority groups, whose members, being perceived as different by the majority and perceiving themselves as different from it, have been traditionally given a special kind of treatment. Specifically, they have been victims of prejudice, discrimination, and unequal opportunities in the economic system. Thus, their life chances in all areas of life have been affected.

It is not sufficient to determine the number of minorities in existence in a particular society and list their difficulties. In seeking solutions, we must concern ourselves with the majority as well, for this group controls the economic and political mechanisms of the society and most of its mechanisms for change. Sociologist Robert Bierstedt makes this point when he declares,

> It is the majority which confers upon folk-ways, mores, customs, and laws the status of norms and gives them coercive power. It is the majority which guarantees the stability of a society. It is the majority which ... penalizes deviation—except [deviation] in ways in which the majority sanctions and approves. And it is the inertia of majorities, finally, which retards the processes of social change.[4]

In other words, the problems of minorities do not stem from their inadequacies or deviations from the standards of society, as is often suggested by the majority. Instead, problems stem from the inadequacies of outmoded or repressive social institutions. This view is not readily accepted by the majority. The majority prefers to blame features that many minorities display—high crime rates, school dropout rates, unstable marriages and broken homes, and the inability to rise socially—on the lack of intelligence, laziness, and shiftlessness of the minority group members.[5] Thus, the solutions majorities use to overcome problems arising from the existence of minority groups are often misdirected and are sometimes horribly cruel.

In different societies, the dominant group uses different methods of dealing with minorities. Some majorities welcome assimilation, and others force it under penalty of expulsion. Most preach pluralism, but only a few attain it. Some get rid of an undesirable minority by wholesale population transfers. Others exploit minorities economically, keeping them in a state of ignorance and submission.

If all other methods fail and conflict seems unsolvable, recourse is sometimes made to genocide—the killing off of all members of the unwanted group. As horrible as such a so-called solution sounds, it is employed often enough. The murder of six million people by Nazi Germany and the massacre of millions in East Pakistan are only the most recent examples of this solution.[6]

[4]Robert Bierstedt, "The Sociology of Majorities," *American Sociological Review*, XIII (December, 1948), p. 709.

[5]Norman R. Yetman and C. Hoy Steele, eds., *Majority and Minority* (Boston: Allyn and Bacon, 1971), pp. 7-9.

[6]The so-called solutions employed by majorities appear in Louis Wirth, "The Problem of Minority Groups," in Ralph Linton, ed., *The Science of Man in the World Crisis*, pp. 347–372.

RACE

The largest minority group in the United States is a racial minority. Racial minorities, partly because of their visibility, have traditionally evoked the strongest reactions from the dominant group. For these reasons, the concept of race and the system of beliefs it spawns are worth careful analysis.

The word race is subject to as much misinterpretation as any word in our language. Originally, race was a concept that scientists used to describe specific biological differences occurring in the human species. But race soon became part of the layman's vocabulary, acquiring meanings it was never meant to have. It is common to hear people speak of a Latin, Jewish, or Irish race, when, in reality, Latin refers to a language group, Jewish to a religion, and Irish to a nationality.

The word race is misused because the concept is misunderstood. People have observed the *cultural* differences among groups and have interpreted them as being *biological*, which would make them hereditary and unchanging. Some people believe that the way an individual thinks, feels, and behaves is determined by his appearance. In some societies, this belief has become so ingrained that even though no biological differences are apparent, people perceive them as existing and as being important.

Such attitudes are unfortunate because, in reality, "... all men share innumerably more physical traits in common than they differ on. In comparison to what they share, genetic differences among human groups are almost negligible. Genetic variations within groups, psychological and behavioral predispositions in particular, are far larger than variations between groups."[7]

[7]C. H. Anderson, *Toward a New Sociology* (Homewood, Ill.: Dorsey, 1971), p. 262.

What Is Race?

The term race is coming into disfavor even among scientists because of the confusion and misconceptions it has created. Nevertheless, most scientists would agree on the following statements regarding race.

All of mankind is descended from the same common stock, the species *homo sapiens*. This species may be classified into a number of populations, which are also called races. The classifications are made on the basis of differences in the frequency with which certain genes occur among the populations. Genes, because they transmit hereditary traits, determine what physical traits will be concentrated in the population.

The broad classifications into which populations are divided are Mongoloid, Negroid, and Caucasoid. However, these three classifications are artificial and do not correspond to definite distinctions among humans. Because of frequent intermixture, differences in physical traits can be measured only in relative terms. For instance, if we say that a group can be distinguished because of skin color, we must be aware that skin color is a trait that runs through the entire species and is measured on a continuum from almost colorless to very dark. And if we tried to show every degree of skin color on the continuum, the divisions would reach astronomical numbers.[8] In short, we are all aware that some black people have very light skin and that some white people have very dark skin. Thus, we run into problems when we try to set up the boundaries at which "black" and "white" begin and end.

In addition, and more important, racial classifications do not correspond to national, religious, linguistic, cultural, and geographic groups although geographic isolation in the past may have been responsible for different gene pools. Nor do any social traits or behavior of these population groups have a connection with inherited racial traits. Finally, there is no scientific proof to support the existence of differences in personality, temperament, character, or intelligence among the racial population groups.[9]

Race and Intelligence

The statement that race is not linked to personality and intelligence has frequently been challenged, especially the part concerning differences in intelligence. Psychologists A. R. Jensen of Berkeley and Richard Herrnstein of Harvard have created a furor in intellectual circles with their recent reports. Doing separate research they have reached the following conclusions: (1) According to I.Q. tests, whites prove more intelligent than blacks; (2) I.Q. is hereditary and is not much affected by environment; and (3) because wealth and power in the United States are closely associated with high I.Q., blacks are almost doomed to poverty.[10]

Such conclusions may be criticized, first, on the basis that the research depends on I.Q. tests, which are an inadequate tool for measuring intelligence.

---

[8]Melvin M. Tumin, *Comparative Perspectives on Race Relations* (Boston: Little, Brown, 1969), p. 5.

[9]Oscar Handlin, *Race and Nationality in American Life* (Garden City, N.Y.: Doubleday, 1957), p. 152.

[10]John P. Frank and Gretchen Kagan, "The False Standards of I.Q. Tests," *The Progressive* (February, 1972), pp. 29–32.

Intelligence is a mysterious characteristic, one that it is extremely difficult to isolate from an individual's cultural experience. It does not seem fair to judge a person's intelligence by tests that clearly require a kind of knowledge best provided by membership in an above-average socioeconomic group.

Second, researchers who have tried to determine the extent to which intelligence is inherited have reached contrasting conclusions. The statement, then, that intelligence is primarily hereditary is open to doubt. Finally, there is still a great deal that science does not know about heredity and the human brain.

We must, therefore, be satisfied with approximate theories. There are only a few conclusions that we can safely accept at this time: (1) Intelligence seems to be associated, to some extent, with heredity, or to be genetically linked; (2) the importance of genetic factors in relation to environmental factors—culture, social class, family attitudes—is still not known; and (3) statements that variations in I.Q. among social or racial groups are largely genetic in nature have not been supported by data.[11]

RACISM

Another word that is used imprecisely today is racism. Perhaps used even more vaguely is the adjective racist. Consequently, these concepts too are in need of some clarification. Racism is often interpreted as meaning "hatred toward members of other racial groups." In sociological terms, *racism* is a belief that racial groups display both physical and behavioral differences, and that both physical traits and behavior are inherited. Related to this belief is the idea that the physical and especially the behavioral traits of some racial groups are inferior or undesirable. Thus, prejudice is justified, and unequal treatment of some racial groups—segregation, discrimination, and hostility—becomes excusable.[12]

Racism is not new and was not invented by white supremacists. It probably began when our early human ancestors, moving from place to place, met other groups of humans who not only looked odd to them but whose behavior was different from theirs. Lacking any knowledge of culture-building processes, one group assumed that the other group's odd appearance and behavior were inherited traits belonging specifically to that group. Because of the universality of ethnocentrism—a belief in the superiority of one's own group—each group assumed that it was better than the other.

As old as racism may be, however, most societies, though definitely ethnocentric, are not racist. In the West, racism did not begin to assume the proportions of a full-fledged ideology, or system of beliefs, until the middle of the nineteenth century. At that time, justifications for racism began to be built on misconceptions of new scientific knowledge.

Charles Darwin's theory of evolution, with its concepts of the survival of the fittest and hereditary determinism, was applied to human groups. Darwinian theory was interpreted as meaning that the Anglo-Saxon and Nordic "races" were the fittest peoples—the most highly evolved and civilized. The

[11]Richard J. Light, "Intelligence and Genes," *The Humanist* (January/February, 1972), pp. 12–13.
[12]Paul B. Horton and Gerald L. Leslie, *The Sociology of Social Problems* (New York: Appleton-Century-Crofts, 1970), p. 354.

development of self-rule and representative government were cited as partial proof of their superiority. The genetic laws discovered by the Austrian monk Gregor J. Mendel were interpreted as meaning that the "purity" of the race must be maintained, so humans would not revert to a more primitive form. At the same time, the belief that cultural differences were hereditary persisted.

The Social, Economic, and Political Climate in Which Racism Flourished

The growth of racism was no doubt hastened by social and economic movements that were reaching a climax in the nineteenth century. In the United States, the abolition of slavery required that a new status be found for the freed slaves. On this question, American society was sharply divided. The former abolitionists, who had worked to free the slaves, now asked that former slaves be given full equality and a chance to become totally assimilated. But those who harbored deep feelings about the inborn inferiority of blacks wanted almost complete separation of the races. By the end of the nineteenth century, the latter view had become predominant not only in the South, where it had originated, but also in the North.

The doctrine of racism put the brunt of the responsibility for the unequal treatment of blacks on God, because He had created inferior and superior races. Racism soon spread to include Chinese immigrants. The large numbers of Chinese on the West Coast were disliked and feared because they were willing to work for small wages. In the end, all Orientals and even the European immigrants who were coming in droves from Eastern and Southern Europe encountered the wrath of the racists. The racists' fear that the immigrants were polluting the Anglo-Saxon "race" and bringing in Communistic (and in their view, devilish) ideas, led to legislation limiting immigration into the United States.

On a world level, racism became a rationalization for nations that were busily engaged in imperialism, enriching themselves at the expense of other peoples. Colonialism and other forms of imperialism were explained away by the belief in the "white man's burden." According to this belief, whites had an obligation to hold the reins of political and economic power, so the progress of the world would not be blocked. The implication was, of course, that inferior races were unable to govern themselves.

Racism Today

Ideas die slowly, and racism seems to be taking a particularly long time to die. Nonetheless, research indicates that racism as an ideology has declined markedly among Americans in recent years. As of the late 1950s, 80 percent of the whites in the United States have rejected the idea of black inferiority. However, whites have substituted a new belief for their former belief in inferior traits transmitted through heredity. Many whites now feel that blacks are free to better themselves if only they had the ambition to exert the effort. Such a belief, though not racist according to the former definition of the word, is racist in the sense that there is a refusal to place the blame where it belongs.[13] The blame is placed on blacks who are, in effect, still inferior because they have not bettered themselves. What is ignored is that blacks have not bettered

[13] Norman R. Yetman and C. Hoy Steele, eds., *Majority and Minority*, p. 361.

themselves because racism has seeped so deeply into our institutions that the cards have been stacked against them.

To a racial minority such as blacks, racism is viewed primarily as the action—as opposed to the ideology, or beliefs—of the dominant group in exerting its power to maintain a system of white domination. Therefore, blacks deny that they are guilty of "racism in reverse" when they express hostile sentiments against whites, because they do not have the power to impose their views on the white majority. As sociologists Norman Yetman and C. Hoy Steele note, "Racism in its most inclusive sense must refer ... to actions on the part of a racial majority that have discriminatory effects—i.e., that effectively prevent members of a racial minority from securing access to prestige, power, and privilege."[14] Nonetheless, racism in reverse does exist, at least in the view of the working-class whites of Newark, New Jersey. In this city, the coming to power of a black mayor and of a black political hierarchy have created conditions of prejudice and discrimination directed toward what is now a white minority. The reaction of the whites in Newark to their new situation is explored in David K. Shipler's article "The White Niggers of Newark."[15]

Although it may not be technical racism, there is no denying that hatred against the dominant group exists among blacks. It is natural, of course, that it does. Healthy response to oppression is open rebellion. When open rebellion is impossible because the odds are too unfavorable, the hostility goes underground, and the response becomes one of superficial passive submission.

Underground hostility takes several forms. It can become sabotage masquerading as irresponsibility, as in the case of the worker who does not show up the morning after payday. It can become violence turned inward, on oneself, as in the case of alcoholics and drug addicts. Or it can become violence turned on others of one's own group, as indicated by the high crime rates of ghetto areas.

When hostility comes out from underground, it can become excessive. Then, everything that has to do with the dominant group is automatically bad. Perhaps this is the way back to healthy protest. Or perhaps the opening of real channels of communication, through which complaints may be presented with the guarantee that positive action will be taken, will put an end to all forms of hostility. And perhaps when this happens, we will achieve a true pluralism in which different groups will compete for power and privilege without having to harbor antihumanitarian sentiments. That such sentiments are being strongly expressed is shown by a poem by the popular black poetess Nikki Giovanni. In her poem, Nikki Giovanni urges blacks to learn to kill, to stab a Jew and cut off a blonde head.[16]

ETHNICITY

Because of the inexactness of the word race in distinguishing groups of people, the relatively new term ethnicity is gaining increasing popularity.

[14]Ibid., p. 362

[15]David K. Shipler, "The White Niggers of Newark," *Harper's*, (August 1972), pp. 77–83.

[16]Nikki Giovanni, *Black Feeling, Black Talk, Black Judgement* (New York: William Morrow and Company) pp. 19–20.

Ethnicity refers to a group's distinctiveness on the basis of social factors, rather than biological ones. In other words, the members of an ethnic group share common cultural traits, such as language, religion, values, beliefs, food habits, tribe membership, and so on.

On the basis of such commonly held traits, in heterogeneous nations, they have developed a subculture within the larger society. This subculture is recognized as being distinctive both by the members of the ethnic group and by society at large. The feeling of peoplehood, or oneness, shared by members of an ethnic group is rooted in a common national origin or historical tradition. It is maintained by a strong "we" as against "they" feeling, of in-group loyalty against out-group encroachment. And it implies a belief in a common destiny.

For most of human history, the feeling of oneness on which ethnic groups depend was based on membership in a common tribal unit. When nation-states emerged, they became the focus of ethnicity, although the feeling of oneness was sometimes additionally supported by a common religion. Membership in a nation-state remains the basis of ethnicity in small, homogeneous countries. In large, heterogeneous countries, the basis of ethnicity is varied and overlapping. Race, religion, or national origin may determine ethnicity. Historically, in such large nation-states, the dominant group considers itself the true ethnic group and attempts, consciously or unconsciously, to assimilate all other ethnic groups.[17]

A by-product of the feeling of oneness shared by members of ethnic groups is the presence within them of varying degrees of ethnocentrism. In a way, ethnocentrism is the price a member of an ethnic group pays for the emotional satisfactions—an identity and a way of life—such membership affords him. We say "the price he pays" because carried to extremes, ethnocentrism becomes the basis of racism, prejudice, and discrimination, the unholy trinity plaguing minority groups in many societies. It is important to remember that ethnocentrism is found in all groups. If anyone thinks that ethnocentrism is only a part of so-called civilized societies, anthropologists will remind him that among primitive tribes, the name members very often give themselves is "the people." This implies that others outside their tribe are not "people."[18]

PREJUDICE

Conflicts do not inevitably erupt simply because ethnic and racial groups live in the same society. In many places around the world, ethnic and racial groups live together in comparative harmony. And even in racially and ethnically homogeneous societies, conflicts of a political, social, or economic—rather than an ethnic—nature arise and sometimes result in violence.

As a matter of fact, some social scientists suggest that ethnic and racial groups have acted to prevent conflicts of a political and economic nature from erupting into violence.[19] However, when groups within a society emphasize

[17]C. H. Anderson, *Toward a New Sociology*, pp. 232–233.

[18]Ruth Benedict, *Patterns of Culture* (Cambridge, Mass.: Houghton Mifflin, 1959), p. 7. First edition, 1934.

[19]C. H. Anderson, *Toward a New Sociology*, p. 234.

racial and ethnic differences above all other differences, the result is a racist philosophy, accompanied by prejudice and discrimination.

Prejudice comes from a Latin word meaning "to judge before," or prejudge. Prejudgment is making up your mind about someone before you examine the evidence. Prejudgments are based on stereotypes and hearsay. Prejudice is not only making a judgment before you have the facts but also refusing to change your mind even when confronted with unassailable evidence.

Some amount of prejudgment is necessary in everyday life. When moving to a new town, we have to take other people's word about the best neighborhood or the best store to shop in. It is when we refuse to correct our prejudgment even though the facts have proven it wrong that we become prejudiced. And prejudice is dangerous. Especially dangerous are prejudices toward ethnic and racial groups in our society.

Characteristics of Prejudice

Social scientists, having long probed at the roots of racial prejudice, have reached some pertinent conclusions about it. Prejudice, which is encouraged by insecurity, social isolation, frustration, and the need to rationalize personal failure, displays some specific characteristics.

First, prejudice is learned behavior. Only when children observe their elders' prejudices do they begin to imitate adults and develop prejudices.

Second, prejudice seems to be, to a large extent, unconscious. People who harbor prejudicial feelings are not aware of them, but those who have almost no prejudicial feelings are deeply aware of the few they have. Part of the explanation for this is that prejudiced people accept their prejudices as facts.

Third, prejudice does not originate through contact with the group against which it is directed. An individual need only be exposed to the prejudices of those around him to become infected himself. As you already know, prejudice has no connection to reality. If you have been taught that the Chinese are shifty, you will see them as shifty whether they are or not. If a Chinese acts in a way that seems to prove he is not shifty, you will interpret this action as further proof of Chinese shiftiness. It is this ability of prejudiced people to interpret all facts in the light of their prejudices that enables some of them to hold opposing prejudices. For instance, many people who are prejudiced against Jews are convinced that Jews are rich and interested only in money. But the same people will often blithely declare that Jews are Communists and radical subversives, working against capitalism.

Fourth, prejudice is generally directed toward groups, not toward single individuals. This is probably true because many people have interpersonal relations with members of racial or ethnic groups that are pleasant and do not bear out the prejudiced stereotypypes. But prejudice is irrational; it remains unchanged in spite of such positive personal relationships.

Finally, prejudice persists because it is emotionally satisfying to the individual. Some people may experience guilt feelings about their prejudices. But prejudice is ego-satisfying. It gives the individual a feeling of superiority and a chance to blame his failures on someone else. It also provides him with an opportunity to vent his tensions. For most people, the satisfactions derived from prejudice more than make up for an occasional pang of guilt.[20]

[20]Paul B. Horton and Gerald L. Leslie, *The Sociology of Social Problems*, pp. 356–359.

Who Is Prejudiced, and Why?

Researchers have found that some individuals and some groups in our society are more prone than others to hold racial and ethnic prejudices. Several theories have been constructed in attempts to explain why this is so and to distinguish among different kinds of prejudice.

In one theory, a distinction is made between culture-conditioned prejudice and character-conditioned prejudice.[21] In culture-conditioned prejudice, an individual, in displaying prejudices, is merely reflecting the norms of his community. This kind of prejudice is found mainly among middle-aged and old unskilled laborers and farmers, religious fundamentalists, inhabitants of small towns, and the least educated, poorest members of the lower class. The prejudices of these people may stem, to a large degree, from fear of competition on the job market. Upper class people may be less prejudiced because their social positions are secure enough not to be threatened by members of minorities.

In character-conditioned prejudice, the source of prejudice is within the personality of the prejudiced person. In his now-classic study *The Authoritarian Personality*, T. W. Adorno found a high correlation between the development of prejudice and a type of personality that he called authoritarian. Some of the features of an authoritarian personality include submission to authority, admiration of power and toughness, conventionality, condescension toward inferiors, insensitivity to relationships with others, and a deep-rooted and partly subconscious sense of insecurity. In such a person, prejudice is merely part of a total outlook on life in which situations and problems are perceived in terms of absolutes—good or bad, right or wrong—and in which people are either heroes or villains.

Other theories of prejudice formation place the blame for one group's prejudices against another group on the psychological mechanism of scapegoating. Scapegoating has its roots in ancient times. The Bible describes a ceremony in which people relieved their own minds of guilt by symbolically heaping their sins on the head of a sacrificial goat. In more recent times, people obtain the same relief by blaming a conveniently close group for an unpleasant event or situation. Using this technique, Hitler was able to blame the Jews for the loss of World War I and for the disastrous financial condition of Germany. And by using this technique, many people in our own society blame blacks or Puerto Ricans for whatever unpleasantness they themselves are experiencing or think they are experiencing.

Still other theories are based on the assumption that prejudice is, in a way, symbolic—that we see in other groups specific traits that on the surface we hate or fear but that we really envy and would like to imitate.[22]

We must keep in mind that none of these theories claim to supply all the answers to questions concerning the causes of prejudice. Nonetheless, it is probable that each theory explains some facet of prejudice.

DISCRIMINATION

Whereas prejudice refers to an attitude or a feeling, *discrimination* refers to the actions taken as a result of prejudicial feelings. For example, the belief

[21]Gordon Allport, *The Nature of Prejudice* (Reading, Mass.: Addison-Wesley, 1954), p. 282.
[22]Paul B. Horton and Gerald L. Leslie, *The Sociology of Social Problems*, pp. 359–367.

that all Spanish-speaking peoples are sex perverts is a prejudice, but the formation of a committee to prevent them from moving into a neighborhood is discrimination.

The Relationship Between Prejudice and Discrimination

Prejudice and discrimination usually go hand-in-hand. But they can also occur independently of each other. For instance, you may retain your belief that all Spanish-speaking people are sex perverts. If, in spite of this belief, you let them move into your neighborhood without interference, you are displaying prejudice without discrimination. On the other hand, you may think your neighbors are ridiculous for believing such slanderous things about Spanish-speaking people. Because you don't want to make enemies of your neighbors, however, you sign a petition to keep the Spanish-speaking group out of your neighborhood. Now you are displaying discrimination without prejudice.

In general, prejudice and discrimination are mutually reinforcing. In other words, if there are strong prejudices against a minority group in a society, these prejudices will be acted upon and will result in discrimination. The denial of the vote to blacks and women, the refusal to permit blacks to attend some schools and worship in some churches, and the refusal to permit members of particular racial and ethnic groups to live in some neighborhoods and hold some jobs are all examples of prejudice-inspired discrimination. Today, most forms of discrimination have been legally abolished. But because there are means of avoiding full compliance to the law and because these means are widely used, discrimination still flourishes among us. Some of the forms discrimination takes will be described later in this chapter in our discussion of individual minority groups.

Kinds of Discrimination

Discrimination, not prejudice or a racist ideology alone, is the principal method used by the powerful majority to protect its privileged status, ensuring that minorities have unequal status. There are three kinds of discrimination, each of which seldom appears alone.

Individual discrimination refers to discriminatory behavior that is prompted by the personal prejudice of a majority group member. The basis of individual discrimination is, then, often character-conditioned prejudice. If a white landlord refuses to rent an apartment to a Puerto Rican couple who can afford the rent simply because he thoroughly dislikes Puerto Ricans, he is displaying individual discrimination. According to statistics, instances of such discrimination are on the decline in America.

Institutionalized discrimination refers to discriminatory behavior prompted not particularly by personal prejudice but by the knowledge that such prejudice exists on a societal level. An individual who fails to discriminate, then, may endanger his own interests. The white landlord who has nothing against Puerto Ricans but who is consciously or unconsciously afraid that his tenants will move out if he rents to a Puerto Rican couple is displaying institutionalized discrimination.

Structural discrimination refers to the system of inequalities at work within

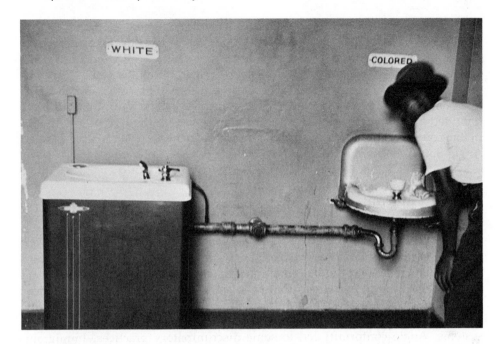

a society, separate from the prejudices and attitudes of majority group members. Because of structural discrimination in our society, most Puerto Rican couples do not have the qualifications necessary for obtaining a good job. Therefore, Puerto Rican couples do not usually have the money to rent an apartment in a nice, quiet, middle-class neighborhood. Structural discrimination denies minority group members the opportunity to become qualified in ways the majority group considers essential to the attainment of a high standard of living.

Of the three kinds of discrimination, institutional and structural discrimination are the most common. Therefore, even if all white landlords suddenly lost their prejudices and no longer practiced discrimination, their apartments would not immediately be filled with minority group tenants.[23]

Lest we think that these forms of discrimination are exclusively American, one of our articles amply demonstrates that we have no monopoly on them. Judith P. Miller, in her article, "Israel's Black Panthers," describes the plight of dark-skinned, Eastern-oriented, Oriental Jews who are trying to live with their light-skinned, Western-oriented neighbors in Israel. The article points to striking similarities among individual, institutional, and structural discrimination in the United States and Israel.[24]

CONCEPTUAL MODELS OF MINORITY ASSIMILATION

In the nineteenth century, especially, people believed that the Statue of Liberty symbolized the United States, a merciful and welcoming land in which

[23]Norman R. Yetman and C. Hoy Steele, eds., *Majority and Minority*, pp. 362–364.
[24]Judith P. Miller, "Israel's Black Panthers," *The Progressive* (March, 1972), pp. 36–40.

the persecuted of the world could find a haven and a new identity. And for many, the United States *has* been a sanctuary and a land of opportunity. But numerous black ghettos, Chinatowns, little Italys, Jewish neighborhoods, and other ethnic enclaves testify that it has not been so for all.

Three major ideologies or conceptual models of minorities and minority assimilation have been accepted at different times in the United States. Each provided guidelines for the way minority groups were thought of and treated in this country. An examination of these ideologies helps to show how a largely Anglo-Saxon, white, Protestant nation has absorbed—or failed to absorb—over forty-one million immigrants from various parts of the world.

Anglo-Conformity

The ideology that has historically had the greatest following in the United States originated in this country. It is called *Anglo-conformity*. The basic principles of Anglo-conformity were that the institutions, language, and cultural patterns of England should be maintained. This attitude stemmed from the belief of the Founding Fathers that even though their new nation had been born of a struggle with England, basic English institutions were sound and might be endangered by immigrants accustomed to less libertarian political systems. Anglo-conformity led to some discriminatory practices. Immigrants from countries that had close cultural ties with England were given preference over other people immigrating to the United States. Generally, though, all immigrants who agreed to embrace Anglo-Saxon customs and language were accepted.

The tangible effects of Anglo-conformity were many attempts at Americanization of the immigrant. In this effort, federal, state, and local agencies together put pressure on the immigrant to learn English, abandon his customs, and ultimately become a naturalized citizen. The final victory of Anglo-conformity was the passage of laws establishing quotas for immigration—laws that discriminated sharply against immigrants from Eastern and Southern European countries because they were "least like us."

The Melting Pot

The *melting pot* ideology developed during the nineteenth century, when Americans began to think that many immigrants could make important contributions to the new nation. The idea then took root that rather than clinging to strictly English institutional and cultural forms, the United States could fuse, both biologically and culturally, all the various stocks within it. The result of such a fusion would be "the New American." This viewpoint received a dramatic expression in a play that was popular at the turn of the century. Written by a young Jewish immigrant, Israel Zangwill, the play was entitled *The Melting Pot*. In it, the hero composes *the* American symphony, in which he expresses his belief that the ideal of the brotherhood of man will finally be realized in this country.

The melting pot ideology and Anglo-conformity were both widely accepted during the first half of the twentieth century. Then, the melting pot view became modified by the findings of a sociologist who studied patterns of intermarriage. She found that British-Americans, Germans, and Scandinavians tended to intermarry with one another, thus creating a Protestant "pool"; Irish, Poles, and Italians also intermarried, creating a Catholic "pool"; and Jews married other Jews, creating a Jewish "pool." In other words, although intermarriage was occurring among people of different nationalities, it tended to be restricted by religion. Out of the melting pot ideology, then, came the triple melting pot theory.[25] The latter paved the way for the ideology of cultural pluralism.

Cultural Pluralism

As the United States became industrialized, it became an urban society. Factories, and thus jobs, were located in cities. Newly arrived immigrants, most of whom had little money, arrived at ports and remained in the cities to work in factories. Urban slums appeared and grew in size and numbers. The worsening conditions of the slums prompted many idealistic members of the middle class to engage in what today is called social work. Social workers, who had personal, first-hand experience with recent immigrants, saw that there was a lack of communication between generations in immigrant families. The children of "dagos," "sheenies," "hunkies," and so on, became filled with self-hate, and the result was family disorganization, juvenile delinquency, and general psychological damage.

Social workers called attention to immigrant problems and argued that it was essential for immigrants to retain their culture. At the same time, America's intellectuals were trying to guide the nation toward liberalism, internationalism, and tolerance. Out of this combination of events, cultural pluralism emerged. *Cultural pluralism* stressed that it was desirable for each ethnic group to retain its cultural distinctiveness, rather than to be assimilated into the dominant American culture. One of its chief spokesmen even suggested that the highest achievement of democracy would be to permit the people of the nation to exist in a federation, or commonwealth, of national cultures.[26]

We hardly need point out that the ideal of cultural pluralism is very far from having been attained. Historical events heightened suspicions against some minority groups, making the goal of cultural pluralism even less attainable.

Despite all this, however, the European immigrant—whether he gave up his native heritage to become an Anglo-conformist, whether he gave up some of it and retained some of it in the melting pot, or whether he still lives in an ethnic enclave that he leaves only to go to work—has, to a great extent, entered the mainstream of American society. His children have college educations, have joined a higher socioeconomic class than his, and have penetrated all levels of the economy and government. We need look at only the Kennedy family (Irish-Catholic), Henry Kissinger (German-Jew), Edmund Muskie (Polish), Spiro Agnew (Greek), and Joseph Alioto (Italian) to recognize that ethnic representation in the power structure of the nation is no figment of the imagination.

The fate of other minorities has been less satisfactory and is yet undeter-

---

[25]Ruby Jo Reeves Kennedy, "Single or Triple Melting Pot? Intermarriage Trends in New Haven, 1870–1940," *American Journal of Sociology*, Vol. 49 (January, 1944), pp. 331–339.

[26]Norman R. Yetman and C Hoy Steele, eds., *Majority and Minority*, pp. 264–278.

mined. These minorities are made up of people who differ greatly from other Americans in appearance. Or they are made up of people who arrived late in the country and lack the skills for functioning in an urban, industrial society. We turn now to these "visible" minorities and their situation today.

BLACK AMERICANS

Making up 11 percent of the population of the United States, black Americans (or Afro-Americans as some prefer to be called) are this nation's largest minority group. Black immigration was not, of course, voluntary, but a result of slavery.

Slavery

The social and economic institution of slavery existed intermittently in many societies over the centuries. In Europe, however, slavery was not deeply ingrained in societies until the discovery of the New World. Then the colonizing fever gripped the most powerful European nations. Both South and North America were colonized chiefly by slave labor, because immigration from Europe proceeded slowly at first.

Although attempts were made to enslave Indians, especially in South America, Indians were susceptible to European diseases and fought against being enslaved either by fleeing into the jungles or simply dying on their masters' plantations. Therefore, black slaves were used. Slaves were either bought from African slavemasters or captured outright on the "slave," "ivory," and "gold" coasts of what today are the nations of Nigeria, Ghana, Togo, and Dahomey. At first, Africans were indentured servants, as were many European immigrants. Indentured servants were committed to work for a specific number of years and could then buy back their freedom. But toward the end of the seventeenth century, slavery was legally institutionalized in the American colonies. Slaves were simply sold to the highest bidder, regardless of whether family members were separated from one another.

Slavery was distasteful to some of the Founding Fathers, who spoke strongly against it and were in favor of ending it. But the Southern states threatened to walk out of the Constitutional Convention and refused to join any kind of federal union in which slavery might be abolished. The Founding Fathers' desire to create a unified nation conquered their distaste for slavery.

The South's determination to retain slavery was based on economics. Improvements in the British textile industry had led to a tremendous increase in the demand for cotton, and cotton was the chief crop of the plantation system that had become deeply rooted in the American South. The cheap labor provided by African slaves made it possible for the vast plantations to function profitably. Such was the power of plantation owners, and of the ship merchants who also profited from the slave trade, that although such trade was outlawed under President Jefferson, it continued to flourish for quite some time to come.

Slavery was legally abolished when the Fourteenth Amendment was passed after the Civil War. But abolition of slavery did not give blacks equality. The South began to pass the so-called Jim Crow legislation, which soon had the people of the region segregated into a two-caste society.[27] This "separate but equal" legislation existed until 1954, and the "separate" portion, though no longer supported by law, continues to be applied, to a large extent, even today.

The Legacy of Slavery

The legacy of slavery has not been easy to overcome. The manner in which the slave responded to his condition—either with rebellion and defiance or with outward passivity—has carried over into the black subculture today. Some blacks are militant separatists, and others, though not passive, are willing to work through the system to attain equality.

These different attitudes became apparent at the beginning of the twentieth century with the emergence of the black leaders Booker T. Washington and W. E. B. Du Bois. Washington, an ex-slave who founded the Tuskegee Institute, counseled blacks to educate themselves and obtain training in marketable skills before aspiring to complete equality. Du Bois, however, argued that all people

[27]Peter I. Rose, *The Subject Is Race* (New York: Oxford University Press, 1968), p. 21.

of African descent should unite and struggle for freedom and political equality right there and then.

Although Du Bois's ideas were too radical for the times, he did spur both blacks and liberal whites into the civil rights struggle, which picked up momentum with the creation of such organizations as the NAACP, CORE, The Urban League, Southern Christian Leadership Conference, and SNCC. Until the mid-1960s, the goal of these organizations and of most blacks was assimilation—or at least inclusion on an equal basis—into the cultural, economic, political, and social life of America. By that time, however, many blacks were becoming disillusioned with what they perceived as the incredible slowness and meagerness of the gains attained through peaceful means. In increasing numbers, young blacks, especially, have vouched to continue the struggle on different terms. These terms include antagonism toward governmental policies and agencies; independence rather than integration as a goal; lower- and middle-class black involvement in the struggle, without white help; and direct action, including self-defense and violence if necessary for the attainment of goals.[28]

Independence, black involvement, self-help, and direct action form the basis of the doctrine of black power. So far, black power has remained more of a motto than a doctrine, and different black leaders have interpreted it in different ways. In general, though, it has been a movement toward the creation of black unity and self-respect through self-help enterprises that would rebuild slums and operate businesses and apartments at fair prices.

The idea behind black power is that the Irish, Poles, Italians, and Jews—and, of course, the white Anglo-Saxon Protestants before them—were able to exert pressure on the government and the economy in favor of their own group. Thus, a strong and well-organized block of black voters can do the same for the black masses. As for the movement away from integration and white coalitions that is obvious in the black power movement, it stems from the strong conviction of some black leaders that the long history of white intervention in black affairs must be ended if self-determination is to become a reality.

The Different Minority

Many members of ethnic groups, somewhat jealous of the attention being received by blacks today, ask, "Why all the fuss? We had the same problems, but we worked hard and pulled ourselves up by our bootstraps." Such people fail to consider several factors that make it clear that blacks are very much different from other ethnic groups.

First, the black has had to contend with the matter of visibility to a much greater extent than have members of any other group. The second or third generation Jew, Pole, or Italian, with education and with perhaps a slight change of name, was no longer noticeable as a minority member but seemed to belong to the majority. Such invisibility has been out of the question for the black.

In addition, all other ethnic groups—including Orientals, who are also visible—were not cut off from their cultures upon their arrival here but continued

---

[28]Jerome H. Skolnick, *The Politics of Protest* (New York: Ballantine, 1969), pp. 129–130.

to be influenced by them. But slavery destroyed the blacks' cultural ties with Africa. Many were brought to this country as individuals and did not even have the ties of family to fall back on.

Living in an alien culture but not a part of it, blacks could hardly fail to accept that culture's negative attitude toward themselves. As black sociologist Kenneth Clark writes:

> Since every human being depends upon his cumulative experiences with others for clues as to how he should view and value himself, children who are consistently rejected understandably begin to question and doubt whether they, their family, and their group really deserve no more respect from the larger society than they receive. These doubts become the seeds of a pernicious self-and-group-hatred and the Negro's complex, debilitating prejudice against himself.[29]

How self-prejudice comes about is made clear by the theories of socialization we examined in Chapter 3. According to Cooley's looking-glass concept, the individual sees himself reflected in others. The type of personality he develops is based on his perceptions of what other people think of him. If significant others—parents, adult relatives—have a low regard for themselves, they will relay their self-image to the child in the process of socialization. Thus, a vicious cycle has been established.

Clark also says that black self-hatred expresses itself in black adults' lack of motivation and fear of competing with whites for jobs. It expresses itself in a feeling of helplessness in political and civic affairs, as is shown by lack of black participation in voting and in community affairs. Finally, it is expressed in family instability created by irresponsibility that arises from lack of hope. Proof of such family instability among blacks is found in the large number of fatherless homes, in which the female has either been abandoned by the husband or has never been married at all. Fatherless homes were frequent during slavery, and in more recent times have resulted from the black male's inability to be an adequate wage earner and provider, and have led to the creation of a virtual matriarchy—a mother-dominated household—with a consequent distortion of the male role.

Many of the other problems that plague the black minority, particularly the large segment still forced to live in central city ghettos, are traceable to the effects of slavery and to the continued repression of the quest for a representative voice in the power structure. Drug addiction, criminality, suicide, homicide, emotional illness, and juvenile delinquency may all be partly explained as escapist responses to intolerable circumstances.

Whether the movements preaching complete separation of the races will lead to a positive solution or whether a pluralistic approach will hasten full equality is a question no one can answer with any degree of certainty. What is certain is that the black minority will no longer tolerate its inferior position. On the other hand, the white majority—especially those whites who have little else but their color to value—will not easily give up its superior position. The two segments of society—black minority and white majority—seem to be currently suspended in an impasse, and solutions could lie in any direction.

We may well hope that whatever the solution, racial hatred will not continue to predominate throughout our entire society. If it should, it would make

---

[29]Kenneth B. Clark, *Dark Ghetto* (New York: Harper & Row, 1965), as reprinted in *Change* (Delmar, Calif.: CRM Books, 1972), pp. 105–106.

a mockery of Martin Luther King's noble dream: "I have a dream that one day on the red hills of Georgia the sons of former slaves and the sons of former slave-owners will be able to sit down together at the table of brotherhood . . ."

JEWS

The second largest minority group in the United States is made up of six million Jews. American Jews suffered from prejudice and discrimination in the past, and to some extent still do. But as a group, they have attained a rather high social status. Although many political offices and some professions—not to mention some neighborhoods and country clubs—remain closed to the Jewish minority, its status may be thought of as largely self-willed. Jews desire no further assimilation but prefer to maintain their own cultural and religious separateness.

The Jews' rise in the stratification system was assisted by some aspects of their heritage. First, having been forbidden to own or cultivate land in the European countries from which they came, Jewish immigrants already had urban skills and were used to an urban way of life when they arrived in the United States. Second, they shared the dominant group's values regarding hard work, success, competition, and education. Third, Jews had a well-developed cultural tradition that they cherished and passed on to their children. Finally, a family group that was tightly knit and therefore cooperative and stable, a strong feeling of community shared with other Jews both here and abroad, and a physical appearance not much different from that of the majority group have all also helped Jews enter the mainstream of society.

SPANISH-SPEAKING MINORITIES

Mexican-Americans, or Chicanos

Five million strong, Mexican-Americans make up the third largest minority in the United States. This minority group is not a unified community, nor does it possess a common culture. Rather, the group is fragmented, because members came to this country at different times and from different places. Some Mexican-Americans settled in rural areas, and others in urban centers. The only thing members really share is the Spanish language and Spanish surnames as well as the Catholic religion.

Most Mexican-Americans, or Chicanos as they prefer to be called, live in Arizona, California, Colorado, New Mexico, and Texas. Most are native-born Americans—descendants of the original *Hispanos* who occupied the Southwest before the colonization of the East Coast. Others arrived here in large migrations at the turn of the century. In spite of this, the Chicanos are one of the few ethnic groups for which there has been no increase in socioeconomic status between one generation and the next.[30] They have consistently remained in the ranks of unskilled and semiskilled blue-collar workers, and are at one of the lowest economic level of the nonwhite minorities.

[30]Celia Heller, *Mexican-American Youth* (New York: Random House, 1966), p. 5.

There are several reasons for the inferior economic and social status of Chicanos. First, they are continually competing with cheap labor, because there is a steady influx of lower-class Mexican immigrants without a corresponding departure of native Chicanos into higher social classes. Second, the nearness of Mexico permits frequent trips back to the native land. Close contact with Mexico and the inefficiency of American school systems have resulted in most

Chicanos' retaining Spanish as their principal language. This may be helpful in maintaining native culture, but it does little to enhance Chicanos' opportunity to get good jobs in the United States. Third, Chicanos are usually born into large families, and this makes upward mobility difficult. Fourth, the Chicano lacks visible models of achievement. In other words, his significant others are not helpful in socializing him to be upwardly mobile. Fifth, the Chicano's group loyalty, which is very strong, prevents him from departing too far from the norms of the group.[31] This is another instance in which excessive ethnocentrism is a disadvantage. Finally Chicano subcultural norms include such features as close ties to the land, a relatively slow sense of time, little stress on formal education, and a social structure founded on personal relationships.[32] It is easy to see that such norms are not helpful to upward mobility in an urban, industrial society.

After World War II, more and more Chicanos began to live in cities. This trend continues today. The Chicano, then, has exchanged his former status of underprivileged rural worker for that of unskilled, semiskilled, or blue-collar urban industrial worker. His new status causes him to share the problems common to all members of the lower-lower class. In addition, his educational achievements have been almost as slow in cities as in rural areas. Urban life has also resulted in the breakdown of traditional Mexican family values, which, in turn, has caused a high rate of juvenile delinquency. These problems are further complicated by discrimination in housing, which forces many Chicanos to remain in urban *barrios*, or slums.

Chicanos have now decided to strive for upward mobility and the attainment of the rewards that this society has to offer. But one very real source of anxiety for Chicanos is whether they want to become assimilated, adopt a pluralist existence, or cling to biculturalism, as well as bilingualism.[33]

Puerto Ricans

Most of the 1.8 million Puerto Ricans live in the cities of the eastern seaboard, particularly New York, and in the large cities of the Midwest. The Puerto Ricans, as do their Chicano counterparts, have one of the lowest standards of living in the country, higher only than that of the American Indians. Other features shared with Chicanos include the Spanish language, the Roman Catholic religion, the high rate of large families, the low educational achievement due principally to the retention of Spanish, and a lack of skilled occupations. All these factors contribute to low social mobility. In addition, many Puerto Ricans encounter racial prejudice and discrimination because their skin color varies from light to very dark.

Puerto Rican problems are complicated because of a lack of commitment to American institutions. Puerto Ricans come here primarily for economic reasons, and many return to their native land as soon as they can. As a result, they have very little political power and thus cannot put pressure on the government to obtain benefits for themselves. (There are, however, indications that

---

[31]Fernando Penalosa, "The Changing Mexican-American in Southern California," in Norman R. Yetman and C. Hoy Steele, *Majority and Minority*, p. 323.

[32]Ibid., p. 325.

[33]Ibid., p. 331.

the young generation is increasingly moving toward political activism, and this should be an asset to the group.) Finally, Puerto Ricans are the latest group of immigrants to arrive in the United States, and traditionally, the latest arrivals have ended up at the bottom of the social scale.

Cubans

In marked contrast to other Spanish-speaking groups, Cuban immigrants who came here in the wake of Fidel Castro's takeover of the country have fared very well. A recent report indicates that the 350,000 Cubans living in the Miami area have attained a fairly high standard of living, with a yearly income averaging $8,000 per family. In addition, more than half of the Cubans in Miami own their homes; one out of every three retail businesses in the city is owned by a Cuban; and Cubans control 30 percent of all new construction in Dade County. Cubans seem to have been accepted socially and are now enlarging their efforts in politics.

One reason for such spectacular success against linguistic, religious, and cultural odds is that most of the Cuban immigrants were members of the middle and upper classes in their society. They came here not out of need but because their superior status in their own country was challenged by Castro. Instead of being unskilled blue-collar workers and rural laborers, then, they are professionals, businessmen, and craftsmen. As such, they have the same goals as the American majority.[34]

AMERICAN INDIANS

No minority is more deserving of understanding than are American Indians. Economically, Indians are truly the forgotten Americans, for they live in poverty and squalor unparalleled by other minorities. The only true natives of America, they have been stripped of their land, and killed by the white man's diseases and by his guns. Because their culture has been almost totally destroyed, they sometimes lead a barren life—on land that no one else wants.

As a minority, the Indians have long been invisible to most other Americans, because after their land was taken, they were moved to the rural areas of the Southwest, where most of them live today. Small groups of Indians do, however, survive in rural sections of some urban states. Of the total number of Indians, some 500,000 live on or near reservations, and 200,000 have moved to cities and towns.

When Indians have been noticed, the majority has displayed indecisive and contradictory attitudes toward them. At various stages of American history, the dominant group has wanted to exterminate the Indians, to assimilate, or Americanize, them, to segregate them, to protect them, and so on. The ravages created by these shifting policies have left a deep imprint on many Indians. Only now, with the growing activism of young Indians, does anyone recognize the Indians' right to decide their own destiny.

Even today, however, the attitude of the Bureau of Indian Affairs, which regulates the lives of reservation Indians, hardly encourages independent and

[34]"Making It In Miami, Cuban-Style," *Life* (December 10, 1971), pp. 37–41.

mature action. Charles H. Anderson reports that on the Pine Ridge Reservation of South Dakota, the ratio of civil service bureaucrats to Indians is about one to one. What is more, if the budget for Pine Ridge were divided among the Indian families, they would have an average yearly income of $8,040, enough to give them a comfortable standard of living, instead of the $1,910 that they actually earn.[35]

Indian problems have been further complicated by their own fierce tribalism. Indians think of themselves first and foremost as Navahos or Cherokees and only second as Indians. Thus, they have never had a unified culture to sustain them; nor have they ever been able to exert political pressure as a united interest group. Even their present difficulties differ from tribe to tribe, so that it is difficult to generalize about them.

In addition, Indians have never been receptive to the European culture the settlers brought to the New World. Therefore, they have resisted numerous attempts at assimilation. At the same time, their various tribal cultures have not fit into our urban industrial society. Thus, Indians have been doomed to a marginal existence.

Most Indians have had to adopt the outward appearances of the dominant

[35]C. H. Anderson, *Toward a New Sociology*, p. 254.

group's way of life. Many Indians farm and raise cattle, and others work in industrial jobs. This is deceptive, however:

> But modern studies of Indian communities show that adoption of the externals of American life is not neatly correlated with accompanying changes in basic Indian attitudes, mind, and personality. Studies ... reveal the same inner Indian feelings about the world and man's place in nature, the same non-competitive attitudes, the same disinterest in the American drive for progress and change.[36]

Belonging to a subculture grossly out of step with the society that surrounds them, many Indians have lost a sense of purpose, a will to live. A young Indian girl living on the Pine Ridge Indian Reservation comments in a recent interview: "Nobody ever asks a child here 'What do you want to be when you grow up?' because there's nothing to grow up to be."[37]

As in the other American minority groups, change also seems to be in the offing for Indians. The change involves primarily the young generation which seems determined to become educated, as increased college attendance shows. Change does not mean that the Indian will choose to become assimilated and pursue the goals of the majority. It does mean, however, that whatever choice he makes, it will be made rationally, and it will be his.

SUMMARY

Although conflict seems to be an integral part of group life, it becomes especially vicious when it takes place because the members of different groups do not have the same outward appearance or cultural traits. Outward appearance and cultural traits distinguish minority groups from the dominant group. The dominant group perceives minorities as inferior and makes them occupy a powerless, subordinate socioeconomic position, despite the fact that they may in actual numbers make up a majority. This is why prejudice, discrimination, and institutions designed to economically exploit minorities have existed in all societies.

Racial minorities have been the victims of the ideology of racism, as well as of prejudice and discrimination. Racism is based on a faulty conception of race. The cultural traits of a group are thought to be inherited. Actually, scientists use the word race to make very broad distinctions among the physical traits of humans, who are all descended from the same stock and are all members of the same species. Minor physical differences are a consequence of the frequency with which some genes appear in some groups classified as races. Aside from physical appearance, no substantial differences have been found to exist among races.

In contrast to race, ethnicity refers to a group's distinctiveness on the basis of social factors such as language, religion, values, beliefs, food habits, and so on. Ethnic groups are subcultures within the larger society. Such groups

---

[36]Alexander Lesser, "Education and the Future of Tribalism in the United States: The Case of the American Indian," in Norman R. Yetman and C. Hoy Steele, eds., *Majority and Minority*, p. 336.

[37]Sally Batz, "Growing Up Is Difficult on Pine Ridge Reservation," *The Cleveland Plain Dealer* (February 2, 1972).

are maintained through a feeling of oneness due to a common national origin or history; through a strong in-group, "we" feeling; and through the belief in a shared destiny. Ethnocentrism—belief in the superiority of one's group—is a part of ethnic group loyalty. But ethnocentrism carried to excess may be the basis of racism, prejudice, and discrimination.

Prejudice is holding stereotyped, unproven beliefs about a minority goup or individual. Discrimination is acting on such beliefs by denying members of a minority group equal access to the sources of wealth, power, and privilege. Of the different kinds of discrimination in existence, the institutional and structural are the most dangerous and yet the most difficult to eliminate.

In the United States, the dominant group has tried various methods of dealing with its minorities. Theories of Anglo-conformity and of the melting pot have failed, and the theory of cultural pluralism has taken their place as an ideal. In a truly pluralistic society, various racial and ethnic minorities would each retain its culture but would coexist with the majority, and all would enjoy equal access to the rewards of society. Before cultural pluralism can become a reality, the stratification system will have to undergo basic rearranging. Then, minorities will no longer be powerless in the political and economic areas of the processes of social change, which are discussed in the next chapter.

DAVID K. SHIPLER

THE WHITE NIGGERS of NEWARK

We are used to hearing of prejudice and dis-
crimination originating from the white population
in the direction of blacks. But what happens in
a situation where the tables are turned? What hap-
pens in a city in which 54 percent of the popula-
tion is black and 13 percent Puerto Ricans, so that
the whites are a distinct minority? Have the les-
sons of prejudice and discrimination been learned
so well that prejudice and discrimination exist,
only in reverse form? Or does the new majority
turn a new leaf and follow a more humane system?
David Shipler, a reporter specializing in urban
affairs for the New York Times, *reports on condi-*
tions in Newark, New Jersey.

□□□

On the other side of the city, far from the
rotting row houses of the black ghetto with its
dropouts and junkies, safe in the sanctuary of
the neat, white, working-class neighborhood,
there is a grimy poolroom that is lit too
brightly. The white kids with long, matted hair
squint as they drift in from the night, forming
knots around the two ratty little pool tables,
their shrill laughter spilling out from under the
scalding fluorescent lights onto darkened
Bloomfield Avenue. Dropouts. A few junkies.
Most are in dungarees, some in Levi jackets,
as if it were a uniform. Only two girls are in
the crowd, both expertly shooting pool, chew-
ing gum seriously, tough girls in tight sweat-
ers. On the sidewalk, kids flick glowing
cigarette butts into the gutter as they lean
against the poolroom's two huge storefront

windows where the faded red letters from
another time can still be seen spelling, "J &
J Confectionery."

Most come here after spending their days
looking fruitlessly for work and groping aim-
lessly for a way out of their own kind of ghetto.
The twenty-two-year-old with the trimmed
beard and the pleading, liquid eyes, who calls
himself "J.B." and says he shoots heroin a
couple of times a week, but gets turned away
by methadone programs that are looking for
harder addicts, especially blacks. The self-
confident eighteen-year-old, Gerard Furrule,
who works his way easily around a pool table,
quit school in ninth grade, worked in a print
shop for a dollar an hour, and now gets $1.90
in the mail room of a big company. In this
candy store turned poolroom, he is considered
a success. He is going to classes in the evening,
trying to get his high-school diploma. College?
"Only niggers go to college," one of his bud-
dies says morosely. Gerard smiles.

These kids are part of a dwindling white
minority in Newark, New Jersey, where blacks
are 54 per cent and Puerto Ricans 13 per cent
of the 382,000 people and where, after long
decades of powerlessness, blacks have taken
political control. The result has been a new set
of angry lines between whites and blacks,
drawn as never before in an American city.
Black power has been converted into reality
with such headiness, and the outside white
establishment has applauded the turnabout so
vigorously, that many whites in Newark have
been left with a corrosive sense of invisibility.
Colleges that send recruiters to Newark do so
in search of blacks, not working-class whites.
Federal programs designed to help youngsters

get jobs, keep them off drugs, provide them with recreation, and improve their schooling are aimed at blacks, staffed by blacks, and located in black neighborhoods. They do not reach the white kids who hang out at the J & J Confectionery.

But simple neglect fails to explain completely the difficulties of Newark's poor and working-class whites, just as it never fully summed up the black experience in America. The whites, especially the Italians, are deeply distrusted by many blacks who have attained power, including the city's first black mayor, Kenneth A Gibson, who sees himself still struggling against the organized crime, corruption, and white racism that gripped the city government under his predecessor, Hugh J. Addonizio. Just before the 1970 election, Addonizio was indicted on sixty-four counts of extortion and conspiracy, along with several city councilmen, former public works directors, and reputed Mafia figures. The indictment, which led to a ten-year federal prison sentence for Addonizio and contributed to his defeat by Gibson, also contaminated all the city's Italians, even those who were disgusted by the corruption, for it reinforced—both to the blacks and to outsiders—a sinister stereotype.

Now, after all the shifts of power, going to Newark is like stepping into a hall of mirrors where familiar images are inverted and twisted into remarkable, confusing shapes that destroy any sense of equilibrium. The familiar American patterns of racism and exploitation dissolve into a mad array of reversals and contradictions.

Gibson is widely regarded by whites as a moderate, undramatic, conscientious man who hasn't the strength to resist the pressure of some militant blacks for the transformation of Newark into what they call "New Ark," a romantic vision of black nationalism and black pride. The major architect of this vision—and of Gibson's election—is the poet and playwright LeRoi Jones, who has adopted the African name of Imamu Baraka. His brilliant pursuit of political power and cultural strength for blacks has frightened many whites, who see in the dashikis of the black councilmen, the clenched-fist salutes of the Board of Education members, and the black-liberation flags in the schools the symbols of a new racism.

The institution most sensitive to this surge of black pride is the Board of Education, always in the past a crucial instrument of white power. Gibson's black appointees have proved more militant than the mayor, and since they constitute the majority of the board, some of them at public meetings sneer and laugh at the white members. Many white citizens say they no longer dare enter the board's hearing room with its dark-stained wood and curved, polished wooden dais. The few whites who do go to monthly hearings are often hooted and ridiculed by the black audiences, and their testimony is ignored by the predominantly black board.

In the spring of 1971, at the height of an emotional teachers' strike, a black physician, Dr. E. Wyman Garrett, rose at a public hearing, pointed to a white board member, John Cervase, and said: "Cervase, we know where you live. We're going to get you. We're really going to get you." Then he allegedly ordered several black men to beat up a white reporter who had written down his threat.

AMATEUR RACISM

We're the niggers now, that's what's happened," said Stephen N. Adubato. "It just is who's on top. The group that's second's gonna catch shit—they're gonna be niggers. This is what this country's really all about." Adubato hunched intently over his desk. "The blacks aren't so sophisticated with their racism. They're just learning what power is about, what America's about. They're more overt, and so are we—we're not sophisticated about our racism as Italians. We're amateurs too." Once a school-teacher, Adubato is emerging as a political leader in Newark's North Ward, the stronghold of the city's remaining working-class Italian-Americans, who make up most of the city's white population. He spent his younger years fighting for the rights of blacks, and he campaigned for Gibson. But as the power of the blacks grew in the city, and as he discovered that nobody was trying to help the Italians, he turned his attention to his own people. He left teaching and won election as Democratic leader in the North Ward.

"Let me give you this analogy," he said. "I see the Italian community in Newark and the black community in Newark face to face, really in a crowd, lined up in a crowd. And the pressure, the momentum, is with the blacks, and they're pushing us backward, and we're not acting like other whites, 'cause we're fighting back, you know, clawing and punching and kicking in the balls and all the rest. But if you reach up and look beyond that line, that black line, you'll see all of the white liberals and do-gooders and the people who really won't meet the problem, pushing, encouraging, you know, and putting on more pressure. It's a nice picture, you can almost see it. D'ya see it?" He laughed.

"And of course we look bad because we're cursin' and swearin', and we say 'nigger' all the time, and the people in the back always said 'Negro' when that was right and now 'black.' They talk the right way, and they're actually assisting. Someone's got to be hurt, that's what I hear, someone's got to be hurt."

Adubato is full of statistics that show the extent of the hurt: a study by the Board of Education, for example, revealing that the percentage of white Newark high-school graduates going to college dropped from 50 per cent in 1969 to 45 per cent in 1970, while the proportion of blacks rose from 49 to 52 per cent.

"There's a great need in the black area for the things that are being done, and they're only scratching the surface," Adubato said. "But take two cases of terminal cancer. The black cancer is more acute, in six months it's terminal; the white cancer is less acute, it would take eighteen months before it's terminal. Now some asshole liberal by looking at that analogy, you know what he says? Well, the whites are three times better off. So what does he do? He goes on the black street exclusively. Nobody attends to the white cancer."

At Barringer High School, white teenagers —who make up about one-fourth of the student body—find themselves engulfed by a whirlwind of blackness: black history, black literature, black culture, black pride, all the components of self-assertion and identity that have been hailed as healthy for a people enslaved and beaten down and brutalized over the centuries. It is not so healthy for the whites. Every morning, "Swahili music" is played over the school's public address system, and some white students find it as offensive and threatening as blacks would find "Dixie." The

day after the Board of Education voted to hang the black, red, and green flag of black liberation in every classroom with a majority of black students (a move ultimately barred by the courts), someone got on the PA system and said, "Brothers be cool, sisters be sweet, and others—well, just others."

Whites stay out of the cafeteria, which is black turf; they don't go to basketball games, since the team is black. And just as blacks used to avoid dances at school in Adubato's day, now whites avoid them, taking the cue from the dance posters in the hallways with pictures of black couples cut out of black magazines. "I never saw a sign in the school of a social event that applied to me," said Stephen Mustacchio, an eighteen-year-old senior. "The same thing with the school chorus: 'Brothers and sisters, if you want to find yourself, join the chorus.' I mean, you know, the white people can't join the chorus if they want to?" One boy ventured into a college recruiter's meeting where it had been announced, as usual, that "a representative will be here today to recruit black and Puerto Rican students," and found talk only of black clubs and black studies, "like I didn't belong there," he said. He didn't apply.

In English class, "you have to read black literature," Steve said. "They never give you any white literature to read. You have to read *Black Voices*, there's a book out called *Black Voices*, then we had to read Malcolm X, then there's another one about a black child. We don't have to read anything about a white person."

Most of the teachers at Barringer are white, but they are fearful of the black students declaring them "insensitive," which Adubato noted means insensitive not to Italians or to whites—just to blacks.

The sense of worthlessness and inferiority that has so long afflicted blacks now seems to threaten these white youngsters, many of whom are struggling to get to college, something their parents could not do. They and their parents see themselves in double jeopardy, a minority in their own city, yet too urban and too Italian to be part of the American mainstream, which they characterize as suburban and WASP.

"When you really feel this is like when you get into college," said Lucille Poet, a bright-

eyed college sophomore whose father is a foreman in a factory. "You can't get a scholarship
because you're not quite poor enough—well,
really, you're not black. And you get into college and they look at you, you come from
Newark, and you're caught in the middle:
you're not rich enough to be really a white person, but you're not poor enough to be a colored
person."

When she finished, a roomful of North
Ward kids let the silence hang for a long
moment.

But the kids fail to see the parallels
between their experience and the complaints
of blacks about predominantly white schools
where no black literature is read and no blacks
appear as characters in American history.
When the similarity was suggested, Lucille's
brother Maurice snapped, "Why should that
affect us?" And Steve Mustacchio explained,
"When I reached high school my whole
attitude changed toward them,'cause I wasn't
really in too much contact with them. I went
to a private white grammar school, I hardly
spoke about them or anything, but when I got
to high school, I had to go to school with them,
I grew to hate them. When I got to school, and
I saw who they were, I came to hate them."

In their candor, the Barringer kids contrast
sharply with another group of white Newark
teenagers, who go to Vailsburg High School,
the last high school in the city in which whites
still constitute the majority, and only 30 per
cent of the students are black. Sitting in a circle
one evening on the floor of a room belonging
to a young divinity student who is trying to
help organize the white community, about a
dozen white Vailsburg students were asked if
they had black friends. "Of course!" they
shouted in an annoyed chorus. Pressed for
specifics, the kids got tense. Only one girl
could name a friend who was black, and her
friend went to another school.

The Vailsburg kids have the luxury of fighting very hard to be, or at least to appear, open-
minded. The same is often true of North Ward
youngsters who have gone to mostly white
private high schools. Everyone in that room
could list clear differences between his own
and his parents' attitudes toward blacks.
Always the parents were bigots or racists.

By contrast, the Barringer teenagers generally agree with their parents' anti-black views,

and Steve Mustacchio even disputes his
mother's liberal attitude that "I work with
them and I get along with them." "She works
in a candy factory with the older type of
people," Steve said. "She don't have to put up
with everything."

Some kids try to resist black pressure, but
others succumb. The Rev. John R. Sharp, a
Presbyterian minister in the mostly white Vailsburg section, describes an effort his church
made to organize a summer basketball team
so white neighborhood youngsters would have
a chance to take part in the downtown recreation programs, which are run mostly for
blacks.

"Our kids would go down and get on the
court and they would freeze, they couldn't
play," Sharp said. "They'd lose their cool, they
would get so uptight playing in an all-black
neighborhood, and the blacks would continue
to take advantage of that and just keep up a
running commentary: 'You better go on back
to white town' and laugh at 'em and call 'em
honkies. And our kids would be on best
behavior—they wouldn't respond. And they
wouldn't go back next time."

Sharp counts himself among the few liberals in Newark. He resembles the young, moderate black leaders of a previous generation,
striving to show the majority that his constituents are human beings who defy easy
stereotypes, who present no threat. He is even
hanging on in the face of open hostility, living
in a mostly black neighborhood and suffering
the telephone calls of some black parents who
tell him, "Keep your honky kids away from
our kids." Sharp explained that the blacks are
worried about the white youngsters eroding
the black identity of their children.

In response to the dominance of the city's
black power structure, especially in the public
schools, Sharp and other white leaders have
tried to do what black leaders in many communities managed years ago—unite the
diverse elements in their neighborhood to
speak with one voice on selected issues. The
result is an umbrella organization known as
the Unified Vailsburg Committee, which contains not only liberals but John Birchers and
Wallace supporters as well. "One of the conservatives said, 'We could probably be more moderate, Reverend, but if we did, they'd walk
over us, and so what we do is go all the way

to the right. We take a position, and we won't move, and we let you guys do all the negotiation.' "

This role as white organizer leads Sharp into some remarkable statements, the kind of statements that were not at all remarkable when black leaders used to make them about their own people. "If they felt they had a voice," Sharp said wistfully of his white constituency. "The great victory is to get the Board of Education to deal with the people and not deal with the stereotype—it's awful hard. Now it's a problem of trying to convince the black majority to be humane and just toward the white minority."

The symmetry of black and white response to power and powerlessness has translated a good many romantic notions into real political questions. "It's the same way as white pride has gotten bad," said Frank DonDiego, who grew up in Newark and now goes to college at Rutgers. "The blacks have gotten their pride, and it started in the beginning really beautiful, but now they've gone into the same white hangups; pride has become a superiority trip."

Adubato's response to the dominance of the blacks is considerably different from Sharp's, but no less pragmatic. He reaches back for his own roots as an Italian, arguing that as a minority ethnic group, Italians should be given the same kind of representation on public bodies, in City Hall, and in federal programs that blacks have won for themselves in cities where they are the minority. He scorns Gibson's two major Italian appointees—one a deputy mayor, one a school board member—as "Uncle Marios" who "think black."

Even though most teachers, policemen, and firemen are still white, the alleged preference of the city's institutions for blacks is an emotional, hate-filled topic of conversation at the Italian social clubs in the North Ward, where men gather in the evenings to watch ball games on television or shoot pool or drink or play cards or eat huge meals they cook themselves in ancient kitchens laden with enormous pots and greasy stoves. The rhetoric swirls back and forth between fact and myth.

"What about Newark Airport? The construction of the new airport? They held up construction for a year already, they stopped all construction on it, being that it's being built in Newark they want 50 per cent of the working force minorities, if they're qualified or not, because they're black or Puerto Rican. That means if I'm a qualified man, a bricklayer, I'm gonna lose a fuckin' job because I'm gonna be replaced by a shine that has no qualifications. But being it's being built in Newark, it's supposedly a majority of fuckin' shines, they want the shines to do the bricklayin', even if they're not qualified." Pete Cannestro, a young truck driver for Sears, shakes his head in disbelief. Then he repeats the complaint that many Italians voice in Newark, that the federal government and private lending institutions give blacks preference when it comes to mortgages or business loans. "They would turn me down and back the shine," Cannestro says. "I know about five people that had experiences like that."

Whether or not such tales are true, they exist with fiery credibility around the card tables in the Italian clubs. These are working men who generally make under $10,000, own $8,000 brick or wooden row houses on dingy streets, cannot get fire insurance because of the 1967 riots in the city's ghettos, pay one of the nation's highest property tax rates (nearly $10 per $100), and submit to what some of them bitterly term a "double tax," the tuition for the parochial schools they feel they owe their children. They are racists, sure, and they like George Wallace and Anthony Imperiale, the beefy white militant and vigilante leader who is now a state assemblyman from the North Ward. But simply to dismiss them as racists and thereby discard their anger and their hurt is to make a sad mistake, one for which they hate the news media and the Establishment in Washington and the suburban executives who crowd downtown Newark during daylight to run the businesses that exclude Italians at least as efficiently as they exclude blacks.

"The liberals are so good at understanding every other group, why don't they want to understand us?" Adubato asks. "Our mothers work in factories—we're the white pigs."

THE URGE TO FLEE

Many whites who have decided to stay in Newark have begun to see themselves as victims not only of the new black power but also of the larger greed and indifference of outside white America. Many understand that they and the blacks are equal victims of the rampant block-busting being attempted in white neighborhoods of their city, where they are barraged by letters and phone calls from real estate agents who spread fear and urge sales at low prices so that the houses can be resold at inflated levels to black families. Signs painted with the word "SOLD" in electric red or orange have been nailed up by real estate agents so that they stick out horizontally from houses, flagging the points of panic on an otherwise peaceful residential block. Some residents of Vailsburg, which has a lovely, more suburban look than the North Ward, have even begun countering with signs declaring, "This House Is NOT For Sale."

The whites who stay expose themselves to the pain of seeing their old neighborhoods, where they and their fathers and grandfathers once lived, ravaged by poverty and decay. They see it every time they drive into downtown Newark, past the old streets, the old corners, past the Boys' Clubs and the YMCAs where they spent hours as children, but where their children cannot go.

Sticking it out in Newark, stopping the trend that saw 100,000 whites leave in the 1960s, is a political strategy in Adubato's terms, essential to his goal of consolidating Italian power in the city. It is also a matter of pride to some, and it stirs sharp debate within families. In one of the shabby brick row houses on a narrow street in the North Ward, a forty-six-year-old man who works the nightshift in a Pabst Blue Ribbon brewery, his wife, and their twenty-two-year-old son talked through the question of leaving. They have lived all their lives in Newark, their parents having arrived there from Italy, but their block has become mostly Puerto Rican, and crime has increased in recent years. The father, a serious, well-read man although he had only two years of high school, was adamant about staying. The mother and the son, a college student who lives at home, wanted to leave. They asked that their names not be used.

"There's no magic in black skin, and some of us are beginning to realize you cannot run," the father said, "because if you run from Wakeman Avenue today, you're going to run from Mt. Prospect Avenue tomorrow, and if it's from Mt. Prospect Avenue tomorrow,

you're gonna run from Llewellyn Park, which is an exclusive suburban residential area, the following day. When do you stop running?" He asked his daughter to get him the Scotch, and he poured some into a shot glass. The bottle in one hand, the glass in the other, he drank and gestured as he talked. His wife, fighting a cold, rubbed her raw nose with a handkerchief.

"I happen to be here all day," she said. "My husband is away at work, so I'm stuck with all the trials that go on, whether they be black or Spanish, so I have the inclination to run. I can cope with the winters, but the summer—it seems as if the warm weather sets everybody off. I don't enjoy the summers here at all. The winters, we close the door, it gets dark early and I'm glad."

"Pride," the son said to his father. "What is the sense of staying in a city, any city, right? Now Newark is just about the worst city in the country. I'm only living in Newark right now because I have to. I'm not running from Newark; I'm running from a bunch of garbage, which is alien to my nature and I don't want to be part of it."

"For you, son, this is okay," his father answered with a tone of finality. "I'm staying in Newark because I simply do not want someone pushing me out. I do not want the idea that I am running away."

Not all young Italians in Newark want to flee. Jim Cundari, for one, a handsome, twenty-seven-year-old lawyer whose family moved from the city a few years ago, found the suburbs barren and came back. "If you go to a shopping center community, you lose that little corner grocery store where you go and get your Italian cheeses and your sausage and bologna, and you lose the warmth and comfort of having the close row houses and the stoops and the kind of social activity. You just lose the closeness with your whole sense of your history and your traditions."

When Newark was authorized by the federal government to expand its Model Cities program to include not just the central ghetto but the entire city, Cundari, with Adubato's help, tried to get a job in the Newark Model Cities agency to represent the Italians. He was refused; the agency remains virtually all black, and Model Cities funds are still not getting into white neighborhoods. Cundari found a post in the office of the city's Business Administrator, but the morning he showed up for work, he was met on the steps of City Hall by an aide to Mayor Gibson and informed that there was no job for him. During the months that followed, he was told repeatedly that the budget couldn't support him. "I was pretty well convinced that the reason I wasn't getting in was because I was Italian and they y didn't want an Italian with a head on his shoulders being in a position of responsibility." Finally, through Gibson's personal intervention, Cundari was hired and put in charge of the city's lobbying efforts in Trenton, the state capital.

Gibson has tried hard to integrate his staff and limit patronage to the less crucial antipoverty-type programs, but an acute apprehension seems to run through his efforts. He complains that white civil servants who cannot be fired subvert his policies by a kind of passive resistance, refusing to do anything they are not directly ordered to do. He has named whites to important posts, such as police director, fire director, and business administrator. But they are not Italians.

Gibson's nervousness is not exactly surprising. The City Council, still mostly Italians, opposes him at every turn. It insisted on retaining as city auditor an accountant who in twenty-four years had never found a problem with Newark's books and who, for the same length of time, had done the auditing for the family of Anthony (Tony Boy) Boiardo, named by law enforcement officials as the Mafia head in Newark. In addition, the most venomous hatred of blacks and of Gibson himself during his campaign came from Italians—the former police director, Dominick Spina, for example, and Anthony Imperiale, who warned of rapists and insurrectionists taking over the city if Gibson became mayor.

When Gibson came into office in July of 1970, he found city government a shambles, mangled to make corruption easy. There was almost no middle management to dilute the power of the top city officials, with the result that there was not much management at all. The city had not a single licensed engineer to check for error or fraud in work done by private firms on millions of dollars' worth of sewer and road projects. Virtually every city contract had been let with a 10 per cent kickback to city officials. Some sewers were built to nowhere, simply ending underground. Corruption heightened the special viciousness about Newark, the rawness in the racism of both whites and blacks. And it damaged the chances for reconciliation.

"There is no real concept of brotherhood in this city," Cundari said. "We all have our own agendas, for the simple reason that we all have such real problems. The consciousness of who you are and what you are is so rampant in the city, as soon as something becomes identified as yours, that's it. There's no one going into an Italian barbershop and trying to challenge whether they'll cut a black man's hair. There's no one trying to implement busing to bring whites and blacks into closer community. It just doesn't work that way. No one wants it. In a city like this, people would be content with separate but equal facilities, and no one would challenge it."

Newark may be the real truth about America, the nation's subconscious finally stripped of its rationalizations and platitudes. The city wallows in the swath of stinking factories that belch filth from the Jersey flats into the shadow of the Statue of Liberty. It has also tarnished the other symbols of America by making hatred look like honesty, by making old dreams laughable.

JUDITH P. MILLER

israel's black panthers

When the terms racism or discrimination are mentioned, chances are that people think of the United States and South Africa as the nations exemplifying such attitudes. But Israel? The homeland of a people finally reunited after centuries of dispersion? Actually, dispersion has had strange effects on the Jewish people: It has divided them culturally, so they are no longer unified. And, in Israel as elsewhere, discrimination follows the pattern of unequal distribution of power, status, and wealth. Judith Miller, a former Middle East correspondent for a New York radio station, has first-hand experience of the situation.

□□□

For years Israel has projected an image of industriousness, purposeful cooperation, and earnest dedication of all Israelis to the task of what is almost their national motto: "building the country." Bound by common dangers and goals—so goes the mythology—the Jews of 101 national origins are fused together and reborn as "Israelis," one people, one race, united by religion, sharing equally in the fruits of their labor and land. This image has prevailed within as well as outside Israel. But recently a small, uneducated group of North African street kids, known as the Israeli Black Panthers, has denounced the image as false, charging that it fosters exploitation of Jews of North African ("Sephardic" or "Oriental") origin.

In response to Black Panther demonstra-

From *The Progressive*, March 1972, Madison, Wisconsin.

tions, the ruling Ashkenazim, Jews of European origin, are hastily instituting reforms of the type familiar to Americans from their own "war on poverty"—"enrichment" programs for college-age youth. Head Start for pre-school children, and the like—to cope with what Israelis call "the Sephardic problem." But far more fundamental questions are inherent in the Black Panthers' demands for such traditional reforms as better housing, jobs, educational opportunities, and admission of former convicts to the army, a gateway to economic opportunity in Israel.

In addition to these demands, the Panthers have raised, often inarticulately and with far less publicity, the question of the suppression of Sephardic culture. They are challenging the Western-oriented Ashkenazi rule of a country which is more than sixty per cent Sephardic and Middle Eastern. They are, in effect, asking whether Israel will continue to be a Beverly Hills or Shaker Heights East, where Americans can cavort in their blue and white "Shalom Israel" caps, feeling perfectly at home with the Western-style economic and governmental machinery and people they encounter, or whether Israel will finally reconcile itself to its geographic and historic position in the Middle East and allow the Levantine culture of the majority of its citizens to determine national government and character.

Most Israelis basically trust their government and are happy with it. They believe that the state of Israel, because it is a "Jewish state," embodies the values and traditions of Judaism —love of justice, wisdom, tolerance, individual freedom, and equality. Therefore, the Panther accusations of massive discrimination have forced Israelis to confront, perhaps for the first time, the very nature of their theoretically democratic, egalitarian state. Ashkenazi Israelis have not yet admitted the challenge to their authority and domination veiled in Black Panther complaints and frustrations.

The Panthers themselves are partially responsible for the failure of Israelis to deal seriously with the more fundamental questions facing the modern technocratic state, for, as was the case with the early black civil rights activists in the United States, many of Israel's Panthers are unaware of the extent of their own oppression and the schizophrenic response to their problems. Their simultaneous desires are to retain their Middle Eastern Jewish traditions and culture and still gain a larger share of economic and social wealth now controlled and distributed by Ashkenazim—principally for the benefit of those who possess or are willing to accept Western values, education, and culture.

Those Panthers who have a measure of political sophistication are reluctant to voice the fundamental question of Israeli identity at this time, for they realize that this tactic would undermine all they hope to win from the existing political system and its rulers. More important, if the Panthers employed such tactics now, it would alienate many of the Sephardim, who, as a rule, want to become more like the Ashkenazim, since they believe in the basic inferiority of their own culture. This sense of inferiority, which borders on self-hate, is reminiscent of black Americans' feelings of personal failure before the advent of the Black Power concept.

The Black Panthers as a group indicate ambivalence toward their "Arabized" ethnic group. They demand, on one hand, all the accoutrements of Ashkenazi "civilized" life, and, on the other, respect for Sephardic traditions—large families, Middle Eastern food, music, and art—not realizing that these traditions are part of what prevents Sephardic Jews from obtaining the economic and social benefits of Ashkenazi life. Because of the ambivalence they feel towards their own ethnic group and the fear that they may in fact be "inferior" to their Westernized brothers, the Sephardim, though an oppressed majority, are the most chauvinistic Israelis, to the point of jingoism, and the most anti-Arab, despite the cultural affinity with Arab neighbors. Most poor Sephardic Jews tend to support Gahal, the leading Israeli right-wing political party.

The underrepresentation of Sephardic Jews in all major aspects of Israeli life is so great that had a "siege" mentality or an actual state of war not existed for so long, a group like the Panthers probably would have emerged years ago. Larger families, less housing, less education, less capital, and less political representation than the Ashkenazim are manifestations of Sephardic inequality. According to *The Jerusalem Post*, ninety-two percent of all large families (those with more than four children) are Sephardic. The average number of children in the Oriental family is 4.3; the mean for the Western family is fewer than three. Government statistics indicate that the average per capita income of Sephardic families is about fifty-four per cent that of the Ashkenazim families. Most of the unskilled jobs not performed by Arabs are held by Sephardic Jews.

Jocharon Peres, an eminent sociologist at Hebrew University, contends that the economic gap between Sephardic and Ashkenazi Jews is increasing. The Sephardim suffer from tremendous overcrowding in settlements which are often situated far from cities and towns. In the political sphere, only one member of the eighteen-member Cabinet, twenty per cent of the Knesset, and three per cent of all top governmental officials are Sephardim. According to government statistics, Sephardic children account for sixty per cent of elementary school enrollment, thirty-five per cent of secondary school enrollment, and only twenty-five per cent of secondary school graduates. In the universities, fewer than twelve per cent of the students are Sephardic.

All of this, Israeli officials defensively claim, has a historic explanation. The oldest members of the Jewish community are the Sephardim who now comprise the membership of the historically elite Sephardic Council, the organization which has represented the Jewish community in Jerusalem for more than 700 years. Paradoxically, however, those generally regarded as the Israeli "pioneers" are the Jews who arrived in the waves of immigration of the early 1900s, and who went on to shape the nation's cultural, social, and political patterns. These Jews came mainly from Russia and Poland, and many had good educations and technical skills. The large Sephardic migrations to Israel had become a state. Most of these immigrants came without skills and education appropriate to a modern, technological state.

This sequence of arrivals, according to government spokesman, explains the current economic and social imbalance. Officials also admit, a bit more uncomfortably, that because the Sephardic Jews lived for so many years in Arab countries and have therefore become "Arabized," the most difficult issue to resolve is cultural differentiation. Most Israelis, however, emphatically deny that the Ashkenazi-Sephardic gap is caused by racism. "No Israeli official," I was told, "would ever be allowed to espouse segregation as they do in your country. We are one race."

Although oppression and separation of the darker skinned, Arab-looking Sephardim have not been a government policy, a kind of unofficial cultural racism does exist. The Western-oriented, technological Israeli society reinforces the feelings of basic inferiority of Sephardic culture held by Ashkenazim and Sephardim alike. Mixed (Ashkenazi and Sephardic) marriages are increasing, but they are still frowned upon by some. Housing reflects the clustering of people by ethnic origin, and the poorest and most overcrowded ethnic neighborhoods are Sephardic. Oriental Jews are sometimes degradingly referred to as "schwartz," Yiddish for black. Since the Panthers, and Oriental Jews in general, look more like Arabs than their Ashkenazi countrymen, they are often stopped at road blocks while European-looking citizens are allowed to pass.

Despite recent exclamations of concern, confessions that neglect did occur in the past, and promises of immediate and meaningful action, the Israeli government has responded only in patchwork fashion to the Black Panthers' demands. Most officials discount the Panthers as a politically motivating force; they claim they are simply responding to a serious problem which has long been overlooked because the state had to focus on more pressing concerns such as national defense.

The army, one of the most important integrative organizations in Israeli society (although it has not one Oriental general), has instituted a program in which some "disadvantaged" youths can forgo the last six months of military service to prepare themselves through a special "pre-academic" course at a university for entrance examinations.

Until this year, secondary school students have had to pay fees to attend, but the government has extended free, compulsory education to the first year of secondary school in an attempt to encourage Sephardic youngsters to stay in school. In addition, the government operates a special program under which Sephardic children need score only seventy per cent of the minimum grade in order to pass. They have also begun to place more emphasis on enrollment of Sephardic children in nursery schools; these, however, are already overcrowded. The government is also attempting to accelerate Sephardic attendance at the universities by providing special scholarships, partially financed by contributions from the United States.

In Jerusalem, the head of the Municipality's Social Welfare Department, Eliezer Jaffe, says that in response to increasing crime rates and growing numbers of prostitutes on the streets (almost all of whom are young Sephardic girls), the Department has greatly increased the number of social workers in disadvantaged areas. He is also working to raise the government poverty line, currently a monthly income of less than $145 for a family of eight, which now encompasses about twenty per cent of the population, most of whom are Sephardic. Within the past year, a renovation fund has been established to provide, on the recommendation of a social worker, loans or grants to families that cannot afford to buy larger flats (most apartments are purchased, not rented, in Israel), but wish to improve or refurbish present accommodations.

Of course, no set of "sweeping reforms" would be complete without a national investigatory committee. Last May, Prime Minister Golda Meir established a twelve-member committee to conduct a "multidimensional" investigation of "Children and Youth in Need." The committee, which is personally chaired by Mrs. Meir, will spend about a year investigating everything from family planning (or the lack of it) to the prisons and correctional institutions which once confined many of the young Panther leaders.

These reforms have basic weaknesses. First, taking the reforms on their own terms, they are seriously inadequate. A quickie pre-university course cannot compensate for what has not been taught in elementary and secondary school. One additional year of free and compulsory education at the secondary level does not effectively meet the dropout problem: Sephardic youngsters drop out not because they cannot afford the fees, since many are on tuition scholarships, but because their families cannot afford to relinquish the income the youngsters could earn if they were working. There is little or no educational reinforcement in the family, and study conditions in cramped flats are almost impossible.

Nor are the problems of prostitution among Sephardic girls or increasing crime rates likely to be solved by employing more social workers, who are often resented in Sephardic neighborhoods. They will not substitute for more realistic welfare subsidies and decent housing.

Improving Sephardic housing conditions, which would be a profound change, involves a direct confrontation with a fundamental national priority: encouraging immigration by guaranteeing new housing for the 2.5 million new immigrants Israel hopes to admit by 1981. This policy of giving the best housing to new immigrants has caused bitterness and frustration among the Sephardim, some of whom have been waiting more than fifteen years to move into better accommodations. A spokesman for Ministry of Housing told me that there is nothing new in this policy; housing has always been provided for new immigrants.

In addition to housing benefits, tax deductions and work opportunities afforded new immigrants serve as a constant irritant to Sephardim, who increasingly feel a part of what the Panthers call "the other Israel."

Mrs. Meir's newly appointed "Committee on Children and Youth in Need" will probably be no more meaningful than its American counterparts. The only value of the committee, an Ashkenazi friend joked, may be that "Golda will have to sit there and listen to the unpleasant truth, whether she wants to hear it or not."

When I asked officials about increased welfare subsidies, free high school education, better medical facilities, job training programs, and the like, I was constantly told that there simply isn't enough money for everything, especially in view of the security situation. Israel spends about fifty per cent of its annual national budget (about twenty-five per cent of annual GNP) on defense.

Even more important than the adequacy of the reforms is the question of their motivation and ideology. These reforms are aimed at helping the poor "disadvantaged" Sephardic Jews take on good Ashkenazi traits and aspirations as rapidly as possible. Most Ashkenazim believe that the heart of the Sephardic problem is that the Sephardim are not like them; the Sephardim are culturally and socially still a part of the underdeveloped, obviously inferior, Arab world. The reforms are created and administered by well-intentioned, paternalistic Ashkenazim who believe that by teaching their Sephardic brethren the virtues of Western civilization and culture—clean houses, birth control, educational (university) tradition, and planning and saving—most of the objective inequalities of Sephardic Jewry will eventually be eliminated. Such attitudes are reminiscent of white American attitudes towards blacks and their culture.

Ashkenazi paternalism is revealed in the almost universal Israeli failure to take the Black Panthers seriously either as individuals or as a political group with great potential. Golda Meir's reaction to her April meeting with the Panthers is indicative of governmental paternalism: "Perhaps they were good boys once, and I hope they will be good in the future. But they are certainly not good boys now."

Similar sentiments are evident in the remarks of Fred Weisgal, an American civil rights lawyer and recently arrived immigrant to Israel, who is working in the Ministry of Justice. He advocates the establishment of a massive "city kibbutz" system to save Sephardic children from the "influence" of their parents.

This emphasis on urban, European middle-class culture, white collar employment, and technologically oriented youth is ironic. The Ashkenazim who rule the country and are now condescending towards the Sephardim are the very immigrants who cast aside their European educations to work with their hands on the land—draining swamps, building highways, and farming the fields.

The Panthers are a loosely structured group. At one demonstration last summer in Jerusalem, more than 3,000 people turned out to support Panther demands for an end to the oppression of Sephardic Jews. Although this number is not impressive by American demonstration standards, it is extremely unusual for Israel, where before the advent of the Panthers demonstrations concerning domestic social issues were virtually unknown. Furthermore, mass public protest and demonstrations have always been considered slightly "subversive" in view of the partial state of war which has existed for so long. In this context, the size of the Panther following is even more impressive.

The Panthers, who speak in simple Hebrew, show political and social sensitivity. Efforts have been made to absorb them into bureaucratic positions, much as the American "war on poverty" attempted to absorb activists in the black movement; thus far, the Panthers have refused political co-optation and personal reward. They continue to work independently in Sephardic neighborhoods, organizing and winning support for their demands. The "bad boys" show traditional Israeli talent for public relations, illustrated in the very selection of their name and through provocative political slogans: WE ARE A SECURITY PROBLEM TOO. HERE IS THE OTHER ISRAELi ALL HONOR TO THE PROSTITUTES. ONE PER CENT IN THE GOVERNMENT, NINETY-SIX PER CENT IN JAIL. They are planning a trip to the United States to "let American Jews know what happens to the dollars they contribute."

In many ways the Panthers resemble black American civil rights leaders of the early 1960s, and they have an undeniably good issue. Many of the Panther leaders combine charisma and dedication. One of the founders of the Black Panthers is Sa'ahdia Marciano, a slender, dark-skinned Moroccan Jew, who speaks with maturity and political sophistication beyond his twenty-one years. Cohavey Shemesh, another leader, chose not to go on the much coveted trip to the United States, because, as he put it, "Someone has to stay to run the shop and teach young Panthers."

Many Sephardim, including some

Panthers, see greater political representation as a solution to their problems. One of the elder statesmen of the Sephardic community, Eli Eliacher, chairman oi the Sephardic Council of Jerusalem, believes that reform of the electoral process—which now decisively favors Ashkenazi control—is necessary to give Sephardic Jews a greater voice in formulating government policy. At present, there are no territorial constituencies in the Knesset, since all members are elected at large by the nation from lists presented by the political parties.

Although Eliacher believes that reform of the system is necessary, he feels it is most unlikely, since it would necessitate a complete shake-up of the existing political structure. The parties are controlled by the Ashkenazim; all pledge before elections to help Sephardic Jews but are unwilling to nominate Sephardic candidates on their national slates. When former Prime Minister Ben-Gurion endorsed a reorganization of the political system to allow for territorial constituencies, his party broke with him primarily over this issue. If Ben-Gurion's prestige was not sufficient to force serious consideration of this approach, there seems to be little promise that the political parties will consent to a decline in their influence by giving up control over candidates.

Thus far, the Panther group has insisted that it is not a "political" organization. While Panthers mock Israeli leaders at demonstrations, they have not publicly endorsed other candidates, nor have they answered questions concerning broader political issues. But within the Panther organization, a few members whose political awareness is highly developed will discuss these issues privately. One Panther said to me, "Do you know what would happen to everything we have fought for if they [the Ashkenazim] could tell Sephardim that we were pro-Arab, or just another political lobby? We have no choice but to continue saying, for the time being, 'no comment' to questions concerning formal domestic politics or Palestinians and Arabs." However, he went on to say that there might come a time when this policy would change. "Every Arab country has its Ashkenazim," he told me. "I am waiting for the coming of the Arab Black Panthers."

Most Ashkenazim, including those in power, are more than willing to admit that something must be done, but few believe that allowing the Sephardic majority power commensurate with its numbers would strengthen the Israeli state. An Israel of and within the Middle East, whose predominant culture would be Sephardic, is anathema to those Israelis who immigrated with their Western culture and values, intending to transform the promised land in their own image. The survival of Israel, they claim, is dependent on maintaining not only military, but economic, technological, and scientific superiority over their Arab neighbors. Therefore, a Western-oriented state, led by those who are comfortable with Western science and technology, is essential.

Eliacher claims that the denial of power and influence to Sephardic communities is the Ashkenazi strategy for safeguarding the control and leadership they now exercise; Jews from Yemen are just as intelligent as those from New York, he argues, and just as capable of leading the Israeli state. But Ashkenazi Israelis point condescendingly to the Arab failure to compete with Israeli scientific and economic achievements and, although it is hardly ever openly stated, imply that Jews raised in such a "backward" environment could not possibly be as capable as those raised in the West.

It is difficult to foresee the evolution of the Black Panthers or the effect they will have on Israeli society in the long run. The Ashkenazi government might be able to buy the Sephardim off with token political representation and reforms, if Sephardic Jews continue to believe in the inferiority of their own culture and aspire to the Ashkenazi "good life." Or Israel may decide to take meaningful and necessarily expensive action in order to hasten Sephardic re-education—that is, to hasten Sephardic assimilation within Ashkenazi society. However, this would necessitate spending less money on military and defense and far more on housing and education. Unless the Panthers convince the Ashkenazim that discontented Sephardim really could be a security problem, a massive program aimed at the transformation of Sephardic Jews into Ashkenazim is not likely.

A third possibility depends to a large extent on the development of the Panthers, or the emergence of a similar ethnically oriented protest group within Israel. If they continue to awaken Sephardim to the fundamental injustices in their society, if they manage to teach young Sephardic Jews pride in their traditions and culture, if they themselves begin to believe that their culture is not incompatible with the progress and defense of Israel, and if they find some political way of manifesting these beliefs, the very nature of the Israeli state could in time be altered.

DISCUSSING THE ARTICLES

1. In David K. Shipler's article, "The White Niggers of Newark," whose roles are turned around?

2. What is unusual about Newark? Has such a situation ever been experienced before?

3. What is the relationship of Black Power to the situation in Newark? Has the concept of Black Power been put to good use? Have the lessons been learned well by blacks?

4. How does the white minority perceive the attitude of the federal government toward themselves? Toward blacks?

5. What type of discrimination does this represent?

7. How do the black militants conceive of the transformation of Newark into New Ark?

8. How have the outward symbols of black militancy been perceived by whites? Is such an attitude justified?

9. How does Stephen Adubato characterize this nation and its racial problem? How is the effect most strongly felt?

10. Is the fact that it is the working-class whites who feel the pinch of the new discrimination in agreement with the contention in the text? Why would discrimination affect those in the lower socio-economic levels?

11. Is reading black literature where the majority is black any different than reading white literature where the majority is white? Does either have any justification, or is there a better alternative?

12. Can what is healthy for one cultural group be made healthy for another? According to the concept of cultural pluralism, how should this be resolved?

13. What is happening to the white youngsters of Newark? Is this a new experience for them? What could be the ultimate outcome of these experiences?

14. Is Newark an optimistic experience? Does it bode well for the future of racial relations in America?

15. In Judith Miller's "Israel's Black Panthers," the Israelis are characterized as "one people, one race, united by religion, sharing equally in the fruits of their labor and land." In view of the way race is defined in your text, are the Israelis one race? How can they be characterized more correctly? Judging from the content of the article, are they even one ethnic group?

16. Which is the dominant group in Israel? Why do you suppose they are dominant? Are they an actual majority?

17. Which is the minority group in Israel? Are they a numerical minority? Which factors make them a minority?

18. According to the article, what is the goal of this minority? What is the sociological term for such a goal?

19. The author states that the Sephardim believe in the basic inferiority of their own culture. Can you make comparisons between the Israeli minority and minorities in our own society? Which minorities here have a similar image of their culture? Is this image changing? What would you say is the current mood of minority groups concerning their cultures?

20. What are the irreconcilable conflicts within the Sephardic group? How are their goals ambivalent? How has this ambivalence affected their attitudes toward their culturally similar Arab enemies? Toward their own nation?

21. What is the paradox of the Israeli "pioneers"? How does this differ from our own situation?

22. What kinds of cultural racism exist in Israel? What kind of discrimination follows from them? What is its connection with the system of stratification?

23. What analogies can you draw from the increasing crime rates and prostitution among the Sephardim? What aspects of socialization are involved?

24. What solutions to Israel's problems would you suggest? Should solutions benefit the society as a whole, or redress the grievances of the minority group?

TERMS TO REMEMBER

Minority groups. Any group in society that is relegated to the bottom of the stratification system on the basis of culture, race, religion, or sex. A category of people that possess imperfect access to positions of equal power and to the corollary categories of prestige and privilege in the society.

Racial minority. A group that differs biologically from the dominant group in such features as skin color, hair texture, eye color or slant, and head shape and dimensions.

Ethnic minority. A group that differs culturally from the dominant group, that is, whose members speak a different language, have different customs, religion, food habits, child-rearing practices, values, and beliefs.

Pluralistic minority. A group that wants to maintain its cultural, religious and sometimes linguistic heritage but still coexist in peace and harmony with the dominant group and with other minorities.

Assimilationist minority. A group that wants to become assimilated into the dominant group, and so share in its privileged status.

Secessionist minority. A group that wants cultural and political independence from the majority.

Militant minority. A group that claims as its goal a reversal of status with the dominant group. It wants to become the dominant group.

Races. The number of populations into which the species *homo sapiens* is divided. Classification into races is made on the basis of differences in the frequency with which some genes occur among the population. The three broad classifications into which populations are divided are Mongoloid, Negroid, and Caucasoid. These classifications do not coincide with national, religious, linguistic, cultural, and geographic groups.

Racism. The belief that racial groups display not only physical but also behavioral differences, and that both are inherited. Related to this belief is the idea that such physical and particularly behavioral differences are inferior or undesirable.

Ethnicity. A group's distinctiveness on the basis of social, rather than biological, factors. Members of ethnic groups have in common cultural traits such as language, religion, values, beliefs, food habits, tribe membership, and so on.

Ethnocentrism. Belief in the superiority of one's own group.

Prejudice. Prejudgment of an individual or group based not on fact or evidence but on stereotype and hearsay, and inability to change this judgment even when confronted with evidence.

Discrimination. Actions taken as a result of prejudicial feelings.

Individual discrimination. Negative behavior prompted by the personal prejudice of a member of the majority group.

Institutionalized discrimination. Negative behavior prompted not by personal prejudice but by the knowledge that such prejudice exists on a societal level. The individual (or group) discriminating against a minority indvidual (or group) is adhering to the norms of his society. He fears negative sanctions against himself if he fails to discriminate.

Structural discrimination. The system of inequalities at work within society. It prevents minorities from having equal access to sources of power, status, and privilege.

Anglo-conformity. A theory of minority absorption holding that the institutions, language, and cultural patterns of England should be maintained.

Melting pot theory. A theory of minority absorption holding that it is possible and desirable to fuse biologically and culturally all the various racial and ethnic groups in society.

Cultural pluralism. A theory stressing the importance and the desirability of maintaining the cultural distinctiveness of each ethnic and racial minority.

SUGGESTIONS FOR FURTHER READING

Bahr, Howard M., Chadwick, Bruce A., and Day, Robert C. *Native Americans Today: Sociological Perspectives.* New York: Harper & Row, 1972. A collection of essays analyzing the various aspects of prejudice and discrimination against the American Indian, and his condition in relation to other minorities.

Brink, William, and Harris, Louis. *Black and White.* New York: Simon and Schuster, 1969. In-depth interviews and opinion polls enrich this combined effort of a *Newsweek* editor and a national opinion pollster about the actual condition of race relations in the United States.

Browne, Robert S. "The Case for Two Americas: One Black, One White," *New York Times Magazine* (August 11, 1968), pp. 12 ff. A case for black separatism effectively and concisely stated.

Clark, Kenneth. *Dark Ghetto.* New York: Harper & Row, 1965. A black sociologist probes several facets of lower-class black culture.

Cleaver, Eldridge. *Soul on Ice.* New York: Dell, 1968. A testimonial, written in Folsom State Prison by the Black Panther Minister of Information, describing the social forces that molded his life and that continue to mold the lives of his black brothers.

Frazier, E. Franklin. *The Negro in the United States.* Rev. ed. New York: Macmillan, 1957. A history of the structure of the black community from colonial times to the middle of this century.

Geschwender, James A. *The Black Revolt.* Englewood Cliffs, N. J.: Prentice-Hall, 1971. An excellent collection of essays examining such contemporary problems as civil rights, ghetto uprisings, and separatism.

Glazer, Nathan, and Moynihan, Daniel. *Beyond the Melting Pot.* Cambridge, Mass.: M.I.T. Press, 1963. A well-documented and readable account of minorities becoming acculturated in New York.

Grier, William H., and Cobbs, Price M. *Black Rage.* New York: Bantam Books, 1968. A vocal and passionate expression of the attitude of black Americans.

Malcolm X. *The Autobiography of Malcolm X.* New York: Grove Press, 1965. The shaping of one of the most dynamic black leaders in recent years, told in his own words.

Meier, August, and Rudwick, Elliott, eds. *Black Protest in the Sixties.* Chicago: Quadrangle Books, 1970. A collection of essays detailing the history of the black protest movement.

Metcalf, George R. *Black Profiles.* New York: McGraw-Hill, 1971. Biographies of black personalities who shaped much of recent black history.

Pettigrew, Thomas F. *Racially Separate or Together?* New York: McGraw-Hill, 1971. Various aspects of the issue of racial integration or separateness analyzed by a distinguished sociologist.

Rose, Peter I. *They and We: Racial and Ethnic Relations in the United States.* New York: Random House, 1964. Minority group relations, especially the social processes of conflict and accommodation as they affect ethnic groups in America.

Rose, Peter I. *The Subject is Race.* New York: Oxford University Press, 1968. Traditional ideologies of race and the teaching of race relations.

Tumin, Melvin M., ed. *Comparative Perspectives on Race Relations.* Boston: Little, Brown, 1969. Intergroup relations in a number of nations.

Van den Berghe, Pierre, ed. *Intergroup Relations: Sociological Perspectives.* New York: Basic Books, 1972. An exhaustive collection of essays on all aspects of intergroup relations.

Van den Berghe, Pierre. *Race and Racism.* New York: Wiley, 1967. A well-written and interesting analysis of the subject matter on an international level.

Yetman, Norman R., and Steele, C. Hoy, eds. *Majority and Minority.* Boston: Allyn and Bacon, 1971. A collection of essays probing into the problems of ethnic and racial groups, their relations, and the discrimination they encounter on individual, institutional, and structural levels.

◎ · chapter six

society and culture in flux

If there is any degree of predictability in human life, that predictability concerns the constancy of change. As if imitating nature, which changes with the time of day, with the seasons of the year, and with the region of the planet, human societies and the cultures they evolve change from day to day, from year to year, and from generation to generation.

Such change has always taken place. But in the past, it was slow and limited to a particular society. Today, change occurs at an unbelievably rapid pace. Not only is the pace fast, but because of mass communication, change in one society is immediately broadcast around the world.

Although change is an obvious part of reality, its opposite—stability, or permanence—is every bit as apparent. For instance, in its two-thousand year history, the family as an institution of Western civilization has undergone several transformations. Yet even today, regardless of all the talk of its obsolescence, it still exists. The same comments may be made about many other institutions, folkways, values, and beliefs.

How do we reconcile change and stability—that things change, yet remain the same, and that some things change and others remain the same? What causes change? Do the frequency and rapidity of change have any effect on people? If so, is the effect positive or negative? The first question is the concern of philosophers. But through observation, partial answers, at least, may be found to the other questions. Therefore, they are in the realm of sociological inquiry.

Of course, we do not have to rely on sociologists to learn that there is evidence of change all around us. As students in your late teens or early twenties, you must be aware that you did not always wear bell-bottoms, that your hair was not always long and straight or worn in an Afro, and that you did not always listen to hard or folk rock. Surely you realize that your older brother never dreamed of burning his draft card and that your older sister would have thought it insane to go without a bra, march for Women's Liberation, or live on a commune. And these are only some of the most visible changes of the past few years.

What of the changes that your parents and grandparents must have experienced? The world they lived in when they were young is not the same world you live in. How, then, could their values be the same as yours? They feel as ill at ease with what is new as you do with what is old.

You can see that although change may be welcomed by some, in most it will create tension. It's not that people think change itself is bad. Most readily equate change with progress and refer to the wonderful inventions and discoveries that have improved human life so greatly. But the human is also a creature of habit; he grows comfortable with old objects and old ideas. When you ask him to constantly readjust to new things and new ideas, he becomes restless and thoroughly uncomfortable. The manner in which he reacts to the discomfort brought about by change and by the direction change takes is the subject matter of this chapter.

SOME EXPLANATIONS OF SOCIAL
AND CULTURAL CHANGE

Questions about what causes change in society and culture have intrigued thinking people throughout the ages. In particular, people have asked these questions: Is whatever determines change universal? Or do specific conditions within a society lead to specific kinds of change? Does change affect every society in the same manner? Or do the effects vary from society to society, and if so, why? People also have raised questions about what types of change prevail in societies: whether change is directed toward definite goals or whether it is haphazard; whether it is constant or occurs in spurts; whether it is inter-related or separate; whether it happens rapidly or slowly. Finally, they have asked whether societies are held together by elements promoting stability or by the dynamism of change.

Sociology has not been able to provide definite answers to all these questions. But sociologists have constructed theories that represent attempts to determine the causes of sociocultural change. If we can discover what causes change, we can control it. If we can find out what brought about the downfall of great civilizations in the past, perhaps we can keep our own societies from disintegrating in the future. This is why many sociologists believe that the study of sociocultural change is the acid test of sociological inquiry.[1]

Cyclical Theories

A number of theories of sociocultural change center on the fact that often societies show significant progress up to a point but then begin to stagnate, and finally decline. One such theory was constructed by the historian-philosopher Oswald Spengler (1880–1936). Spengler claimed that societies follow a life cycle similar to that of living organisms: They are born, they grow to maturity, then they reach old age and die. A society experiences its highest degree of achievement in its maturity. It begins to decline in its old age, and finally disintegrates in death. In his best-known work, *The Decline of the West* (1926), Spengler, using many illustrations, tried to demonstrate that Western civilization was in its old age and was beginning to decline. Although events have not borne him out, Spengler's theory continues to generate a great deal of interest.

Like Spengler, British historian Arnold Toynbee (1889–   ) believes that the history of societies tends to run in cycles. But Toynbee believes that cycles do not necessarily lead to complete decline. On the contrary, history tends to repeat itself over and over, and in every society, the same types of challenges reoccur. If a society responds well to these challenges, it survives and reaches the next stage of its development. If it does not, it disintegrates. About Western civilization, Toynbee is much more optimistic than Spengler. He thinks that it has responded to most of its challenges rather well.

Sociologist Pitirim Sorokin (1889–1968) viewed the rise and fall of societies in terms of three recurring cultural systems. The sensate cultural system stresses physical and sensual needs. The ideational cultural system stresses the needs

---

[1]Robert Bierstedt, *The Social Order* (New York: McGraw–Hill, 1970), p. 509.

of the mind and spirit. The idealistic cultural system, which is a mixture of the other two, exists only in the intervals between them. Using examples drawn from twenty-five hundred years of history, Sorokin illustrates the differences among the various ages. He thinks our age is sensate and contrasts it with Medieval Europe which was ideational in its emphasis on religion and the otherworldly. Although this theory is fascinating, it does not really explain the cause of the action-reaction cycle described by Sorokin, nor does it provide for alternatives to the three cultural systems.

Classic Functionalist Theory

Functionalist theory has already been discussed in relation to stratification, one of the topics in Chapter 4. Functionalists compare society to a living organism. Each part of a living organism functions solely for the organism's survival. To functionalists, all human activity contributes to the continuity of the social system.

Functionalists make an important distinction between changes in the units of society and changes in the form of the social structure. Changes in the units of society are brought about by such daily events as birth, death, and various rituals. Rather than disturbing the social structure, these changes contribute to its survival. They can and do take place when society is in a state of relative stability. On the other hand, internal upheavals, such as revolutions, and external impacts, such as wars, cause changes in the social structure.[2] These changes lead to instability.[3]

Classic functionalists are criticized because they tend to consider social change dysfunctional, or abnormal. They maintain that stability should be the goal of society. Therefore, functionalist research concentrates on the static elements of society, when, in reality, social systems are dynamic, or in constant movement. However, some of the most logical ideas of functionalism have become part of another theory, called structural functionalism.

Structural Functionalist Theory

The theory of sociocultural evolution was widely accepted in the nineteenth century, before classic functionalist theory became prominent. Having undergone specific changes, sociocultural evolution has reinstated itself in the good graces of sociologists. Sociocultural evolution was originally based on the Darwinian theory that biological development proceeds in an evolutionary manner, from simple to complex forms. During the course of this development, only the strongest and fittest survive, and the weaker and less than perfect fall by the wayside. In like manner, societies and their cultures were thought to evolve from so-called primitive to complex forms. The societies and cultures that were considered the most complex were those of Western peoples.

The underlying optimism of evolutionary theory—that societies progress in an upward spiral toward perfection—has long been shattered by events pointing to the contrary. Today, neo-evolutionists have rejected the idea that

---

[2]A. R. Radcliffe-Brown, *A Natural Science of Society* (New York: Free Press, 1957), p. 87. Also, Wilbert E. Moore, *Social Change* (Englewood Cliffs, N.J.: Prentice-Hall, 1963).
[3]Robert A. Nisbet, *The Social Bond* (New York: Alfred A. Knopf, 1970), p. 310.

progress leads to human happiness. But they have retained the idea that progress, as movement forward, does occur.

Neo-evolutionists have joined forces with modern functionalists to produce the *structural-functionalist* theory, which is widely accepted by sociologists. Structural functionalists believe that each society displays some major trends, but the trends are not the same in every society. Even when some of the same trends exist in different societies, they do not develop in identical ways.

One trend common to all societies is mastery of the physical environment. The explanation for the universality of this trend is the cumulative nature of culture, which enables people to learn from past experience. Another trend that is apparent in all societies is the tendency toward specialization, or social differentiation. Specialization arises from the discovery that society can increase efficiency if specific tasks are performed by individuals and groups especially trained for this purpose. A final universal trend is that of functional interdependence. In other words, individuals, groups, organizations, and other units of the social structure become increasingly interdependent in the performance of their tasks.

In brief, neo-evolutionists, or structural functionalists, agree that change occurs in the direction from less to more complex societal forms. But they do not accept the idea that change is always for the better, that all societies undergo the same kinds of change, that change is inevitable, or that it cannot be reversed.

Cultural Lag Theory

The theory of cultural lag emerged in the 1920s. The originator of the theory of cultural lag, William F. Ogburn, argues that it is characteristic of material culture to accumulate. Nonmaterial culture, on the other hand, does not accumulate. In other words, the primitive man who sharpened a piece of wood into an object capable of piercing used the same principle in sharpening stone, which he found to be harder and thus more effective as a weapon or tool. Later, he used the same principle in sharpening bronze and iron, which he found even more useful. Ideas, religious values, beliefs and customs, however, do not build cumulatively but tend to replace one another. This leads to *cultural lag*, an imbalance between material and nonmaterial culture. Cultural lag creates tension in the structure of society which eventually cracks in spots. The cracks are the social problems with which societies are burdened.[4]

Cultural lag does occur in the process of change. But as a total theory of change, it is inadequate. Changes in material culture do not always precede changes in nonmaterial culture. In fact, very few elements of material culture appear unless the need for them is first expressed in nonmaterial culture. Of what possible use would an IBM data processing machine be to a member of a nonliterate society in the Brazilian jungle? Furthermore, in some of the newly emerging nations, a reversed cultural lag is occurring. These nations, in trying to make up for a previous lack of education, have trained more people than they can yet use. Their economies are simply not developed enough for them to need a significant number of such people.[5]

---

[4]William Fielding Ogburn, *Social Change: With Respect to Culture and Original Nature* (New York: B. W. Huebsch, 1922). Revised edition, Viking, 1955.

[5]Neil J. Smelser, *Sociology* (New York: Wiley, 1967), p. 704.

Diffusion Theory

Followers of *diffusion theory* challenged classical evolution theory by demonstrating that there existed many similarities among cultures. These similarities had not arisen independently, but were the result of cultural borrowing, or diffusion, which, in some cases, spanned great geographic distances.

Diffusion theory was somewhat discredited when researchers found that similar cultural elements existed in cultures prior to the time the cultures could have had any contact. In addition, early cultural diffusionists neglected to ask some pertinent questions: why some cultural elements became diffused whereas others did not; how cultural changes affected the society that borrowed elements; and whether changes caused in the society that borrowed caused, in turn, other changes.

Although diffusion theory does not completely account for sociocultural change, there is no doubt that some changes do occur because of diffusion. The rapidity of transportation and the effectiveness of the mass media have spread some of the cultural elements peculiar to one society to the most remote corners of the world. American cowboys are seen on TV screens in places as far away as North Africa. Automobiles cross the sands of the Sahara. And Colonel Sanders' Fried Chicken stands dot the landscape of the polar regions.

Conclusions on the Causes of Sociocultural Change

The large number of theories—and we have only touched upon a few of the most significant—indicates that no one explanation for sociocultural change is completely satisfactory. Thus, the question of what causes such change must for now remain unanswered. All we know is that universal principles of sociocultural change do not seem to exist. As there is variety among human beings, so there is variety in social structures and in the principles guiding social and cultural change within them.[6]

Changes can come from outside society, by the process of diffusion. Or they can come from within, by the introduction of new technology and by the stresses and tensions resulting from everyday interaction. But perhaps we should be aware that, in the words of Robert Bierstedt,

> *Ultimately . . . all social change occurs because of the actions of men and women. Culture is not self-innovating, ideas are not self-creating, and technology is not self-inventing. Somehow, somewhere, in a society, a man breaks however slightly from tradition. He does something in a different way. He finds a shortcut. He has a new idea, or makes a new discovery. When that happens, whether he is a 'great man' or not, he has disturbed the stream of culture and, like a stone tossed into the waters, his ripples may go on forever. The new idea may affect, after a while, all the compartments of culture and all the sectors of society.[7]*

PROCESSES OF CULTURAL CHANGE

Even though we can only guess at the causes of sociocultural change, we have a fair idea of how the changes occur. But first we must distinguish

[6]C. Wright Mills, *The Sociological Imagination* (New York: Oxford University Press, 1959), p. 150.

[7]Robert Bierstedt, *The Social Order*, p. 521.

between social and cultural change. Society, you will recall, is a patterned system of interaction among individuals and groups. Culture is what results from this interaction. *Social change* means change in the patterns of social interaction. When such patterns change, a substantial number of society's members assume new statuses and play new roles. The abolition of slavery was a social change, for it gave former slaves the status of free men. In this position, they fulfilled different roles from the ones they had before they were freed.

Cultural change refers to changes in values and beliefs. Values and beliefs change because of scientific discoveries, technological inventions, new achievements in the arts, and shifts in religious doctrine. The invention of the automobile, which ended the era of the horse and buggy, was a cultural change.

Of course, society and culture are but two facets of the same structure. Therefore, changes in society naturally bring about changes in culture, and vice versa. But although the effects of social and cultural change often overlap, the processes of change are different. On a cultural level, change occurs through discovery, invention, and diffusion. On a social level, change occurs through planning, reform, or revolution. Also, society and culture are both subject to sociocultural drifts.

Discovery

A *discovery* is new knowledge of an already existing fact or relationship. North America existed long before European explorers ever set foot on it. Similarly, principles of physics, chemistry, and mathematics existed before humans did, but it took centuries for people to perceive and even partially understand them. Blood circulation, microscopic life, and the organization of the solar system are additional examples of discoveries.

Discovery only plays a part in bringing about change. Before change can occur, a society must be ready to make use of a discovery and must have technological inventions to support it. For instance, the principle of the steam engine was known some two thousand years ago. The principle was not put into practice because society did not see any use for a steam engine and because parts that would make it workable did not yet exist. Similarly, Leonardo da Vinci was making detailed plans for flying machines in the early sixteenth century. But only in this century did materials essential to the proper functioning of airplanes become available. Only recently, too, did people need means of rapid transportation.

Invention

An *invention* is built on existing knowledge. Cultural ideas or objects already in existence are combined in a new way to produce something more important than the sum of their parts. The boat and the steam engine existed separately in a culture. Brought together, they produced the steamboat—a new, more effective mode of transportation. A four-wheeled carriage plus a steam engine produced a train. When the internal combustion engine came into existence, it was combined with the four-wheeled carriage to produce an automobile.

Invention may occur in nonmaterial culture, as well as in material culture.

For instance, the United States Constitution was a social invention—the product of Western European philosophy and the experiences of the colonists in the New World.[8] Health insurance and traffic laws are other examples of social inventions, in which old ideas were combined in new ways.

Diffusion

Diffusion is the spread of cultural traits from one society to another, and from one group within society to another. Although diffusion as a theory does not totally explain sociocultural change, diffusion is an important factor in the *process* of cultural change. Spaghetti and other pasta and tomato dishes were brought to America by Italian immigrants, but soon the entire population was eating them. Jazz began as the musical expression of New Orleans blacks, but it is now the property of the world. Whether by the conscious effort of missionaries and Peace Corps members or by accident, even minimal contact between cultures produces diffusion. In fact, anthropologists maintain that most of the content of a complex culture is the product of diffusion.

Diffusion is always reciprocal. When two cultures come into contact, each gives something to the other, although the exchange is not always even. In general, more is borrowed by the simpler culture than is borrowed by the more complex culture. Similarly, within the same society, low-status groups try to imitate the life styles of high-status groups.

Not all cultural traits are passively accepted in the process of diffusion. The borrowing culture always displays selectivity. Japan readily accepted Western technology but not the West's system of values. Americans borrowed the idea of representative government from England but gave it a different form.

Borrowing cultures not only select but also modify the traits they borrow. The Indians smoked their pipes as part of a ritual. When they adopted tobacco, Europeans changed the form in which it was smoked—cigarettes, cigars—and altered its function from ceremonial to sociable.

PROCESSES OF SOCIAL CHANGE AND SOCIOCULTURAL DRIFT

Social change, as we have said, occurs through planning, reform, or revolution. The processes of planning and reform are best left to the chapter dealing with political institutions, Chapter 9. Revolution is a social movement that is described later in this chapter, under the topic of collective behavior.

Sociocultural drift refers to the *unplanned* changes that occur in a society. These types of changes appear in all areas of human life. They result from an informally reached agreement among members of society that a particular change is beneficial. Some social scientists believe that unplanned changes are the most effective, because they are not forced on anyone.[9]

We cannot speak of sociocultural change without mentioning the three major factors that have caused change throughout the entire world: population,

[8]Francis E. Merrill, *Society and Culture* (Englewood Cliffs, N. J.: Prentice-Hall, 1969), p. 336.
[9]Norman F. Washburne, *Interpreting Social Change in America* (New York: Doubleday, 1954), p. 21.

industrialization, and urbanization. Population, industrialization, and urbanization are deeply intertwined, and have followed the rapid development of technology. All three have produced problems because the rapidity with which they have occurred has not given humans the time to adjust, physically and psychologically, to their changed condition.

POPULATION

The biblical command to be fruitful and multiply was given when the human species was small in numbers and at the mercy of the forces of nature. With an inadequate food supply, no knowledge of disease control, and no refuge from the ravages of ice and sun, humans did not live very long, and a great many did not even survive past infancy. Life expectancy was extremely low—an estimated 18 years during the Bronze Age, for example.

The total world population of the hunting and gathering societies in existence eight to ten thousand years ago was only 20 million. By 1000 B.C., when many societies had reached the agricultural stage, population had increased to 100 million. But so slowly did population growth occur, that by A.D. 1000, the total world population was only 300 million.

In the middle of the seventeenth century, however, population began to increase in a steady upward curve. Improvements in agriculture, technology, medicine, and sanitation were raising the general standard of living and radically lowering the death rate. At the same time, the birth rate remained unaffected. The low death rate and steady birth rate created an imbalance—more people were being born than were dying. But an increase in population could easily be accommodated in the relatively empty world of the seventeenth century.

Today, this imbalance continues, but it is no longer tolerable. The present rate of world population growth is some 2 percent a year. By the year 2000, then, the current world population of 3.7 billion people will almost double, and will keep on doubling approximately every thirty-seven years.

What effects will overpopulation have on the world? In the industrial nations, overcrowding, or lack of space and privacy, will become a huge problem as additional houses, highways, transportation systems, and sewage systems are continually built to accommodate the onslaught. Air and water pollution and inadequate police and fire protection—already serious problems—will become even more acute.

In the underdeveloped, or developing, nations, the prospect is much more stark: The people will face starvation. Even today, in some areas of the world, an estimated ten thousand people die of starvation or malnutrition each day. Furthermore, the population growth of the underdeveloped nations is now twice that of the industrial nations. By 1980 it will increase to almost three times that of the industrial nations.

Demography and the Malthusian Prophecy

Demography is the study of growth or decrease in population, of its distribution throughout the world, and of its composition. According to demographic research, during the past two hundred years, Europe and the North American continent were the most populated areas of the world. The last few decades of this century, however, have seen a significant increase in the populations of Africa, South Asia and Latin America.

By 1980, South Asia will have 41.7 percent of world population; Africa will have 17 percent; and Latin America will have 14 percent. At the same time, population growth will not be decreasing in the industrial nations. Their rate of growth will simply slow down.

As startling as the population figures are, they are not the first warning we have had of overpopulation. As early as 1798, Thomas Robert Malthus published an essay in which he claimed that under favorable circumstances populations would grow by geometric progression—by 2, 4, 8, 16, and so on. The food supply, on the other hand, would increase in arithmetic progression— 1, 2, 3, 4, 5, and so on. Thus, the food supply would eventually become exhausted. At that time, the death rate would have to increase to reestablish a balance. Although he was quite pessimistic about the possibility of reversing this trend, Malthus suggested the use of preventive checks to control fertility. The checks he favored were late marriage and enforced celibacy.

Although great advances in technology, agriculture, and methods of birth control have made the Malthusian prophecy wrong as it concerns industrial nations, the prophecy still has relevance for developing nations. In the nations of the Third World, agricultural productivity lags far behind population growth, and the yield per acre of foods necessary for survival has actually decreased.

The Demographic Transition Model

Trying to find some solutions for the future from the lessons of the past, demographers have pieced together a conceptual model from the uneven patterns of population growth. According to the demographic transition model, society passes through three basic stages of evolution. In the first stage, birth rates and death rates are both high, leading to a balance achieved through cycles of growth and decline. In the second stage, death rates decline but birth rates remain high, leading to unchecked population growth. In the third stage, there is evidence of a decline of birth rates, leading to a stabilization of population. The model allows for shifts in population growth following unusual events, such as wars and depressions.

According to the model, tropical Africa, tropical South America, and the eastern and middle sections of Asia are currently in the first stage. Parts of North Africa, the temperate part of South America, India, Communist China, and several other Third World nations experiencing unusually high population growth are in the second stage. The United States, Australia, New Zealand, Japan, Canada, the United Kingdom, and northern and western Europe, all of which have a low death rate and a relatively low or declining birth rate, are in the third stage.

Overpopulation in Developing Nations

Unfortunately, there are no guarantees that the third stage of the demographic transition model will ever be reached by the developing nations that have so far made very little progress in industrializing. And without industrialization, food production cannot keep up with population growth.

Besides industrialization, the only solution to overpopulation is birth control. This, unfortunately, does not seem to be an alternative that will be rapidly accepted in the Third World. In a clear example of cultural lag, the societies of the developing nations require birth control for their very survival, but in their cultures it is unacceptable. Children have traditionally been a source of pride and proof of a man's masculinity and a woman's femininity. Furthermore, they have contributed to the family's survival by working on the farm or performing other chores, and they have provided a form of insurance for the parents' old age. What is more, many ethnic groups fear a reduction in numbers, and many religions expressly forbid any tampering with nature.

Underdeveloped nations face a clear-cut choice, then. They must curb population growth because they simply don't have the technology to accommodate such great numbers of people. Population growth can be curbed by only two methods: birth control or an increase in the death rate over the birth rate (caused most likely by starvation). Some demographers are optimistic enough to believe that faced with such alternatives, the human species will be intelligent enough to promote its own survival through demographic regulation, or vigorous methods of birth control.[10] Others, however, fear that apathy and ignorance will eventually cause us all to perish.

Optimistic signs have appeared in at least one nation of the Third World. Birth control has been successfully adopted in Communist China. The acceptance of birth control against great traditional and ideological odds is explained in our article "Neither Marx nor Malthus."[11] The authors, population experts Paul R. Ehrlich and John P. Holdren, describe the special circumstances of China. China has between 750 and 850 million people—and thus is vastly overcrowded—but it is in the grip of Marxist ideology. According to Marxism, population control is unnecessary in a truly just society. It is simply a device invented by capitalists, who want to control the poor so they can continue to exploit them. After several events brought China to the brink of famine and disaster, its policies concerning population control have drastically changed.

Overpopulation in Industrial Nations

Constructed partly on the basis of hindsight, the demographic transition model seems to be an optimistic and accurate interpretation of the history of the industrial nations. In urban nations, which have higher standards of living and higher literacy rates than do developing nations, the birth rate tends to decline or at least remain stable. This happens because conditions in cities do not lend themselves to large families. First, housing is scarce. Second, because industrial jobs are closed to children, a large family is not profitable. Finally, it is expensive to educate and provide health protection for children.

Regardless of the dictates of religion and culture, then, urban families tend to voluntarily curb their fertility. For example, Ireland, France, and Italy are all Roman Catholic nations, and Roman Catholics oppose birth control. Yet the birth rate in these nations is among the lowest in the world and is actually

---

[10]Donald Bogue, *Principles of Demography* (New York: Wiley, 1969), p. 51.
[11]Paul R. Ehrlich and John P. Holdren, "Neither Marx nor Malthus," *Saturday Review* (November 6, 1971), p. 88.

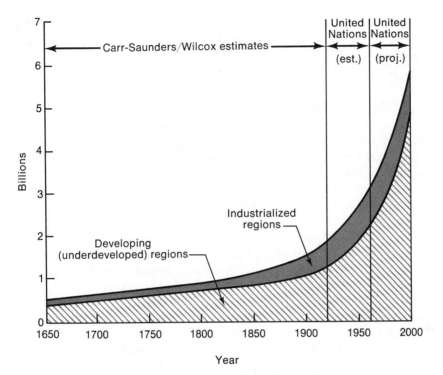

SOURCE: From Bogue, *Principles of Demography* (John Wiley & Sons).

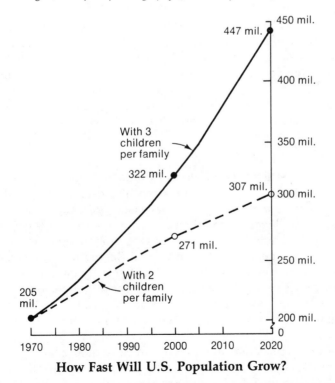

How Fast Will U.S. Population Grow?

SOURCE: Reprinted from *U.S. News & World Report*. Copyright (1972) U.S. News & World Report.

declining in Ireland and France. Sociocultural drift has, then, accomplished what extensive governmental planning and reform in other nations have not been able to do.

INDUSTRIALIZATION AND URBANIZATION

Industrial nations obviously have a privileged position. In each case, this privileged position can be traced back to the occurrence of parallel events: a change in the economy from agrarian, or agricultural, to industrial and a shift in population distribution from rural to urban.

The economic change began with the Industrial Revolution, which first became apparent in England in the middle of the eighteenth century. At this time, England was a rich and powerful commercial nation, which sold its goods around the world. The desire for large profits prodded many people to search for ways to produce goods rapidly and inexpensively. The search produced such inventions as the steam engine, the spinning jenny, and the mechanical loom.

These machines led to the institution of the factory system. Factories were concentrated in cities. And it was there that country people began to move in search of jobs. Some were former tenant farmers who lost their livelihood because of the Enclosure laws, which took away lands they had tilled for centuries for their feudal lords. Others came to cities because science and technology had improved agricultural methods, and less manpower was needed than before. New iron and steel plows, reapers, threshers, harvesters, and finally tractors and combines did much of the work once done by humans. Crop rotation, chemical fertilizers, irrigation, and insect and disease control all increased yields per acre, without requiring much human labor.

The new commercial agriculture, while displacing people from the land, was creating a demand for agricultural machinery. Clearly, the next step was urbanization—the migration of people from rural to urban centers.

Urbanization

Cities were not strictly the products of industrialization. They had existed centuries before the word industrialization had been coined and many had grown large, rich, and powerful. In the past, cities had usually been built in fertile areas, and depended on the surrounding farms for their food supply. In fact, they often reverted to the status of farms following wars and invasions.

The urban trend begun by the Industrial Revolution, however, was of a different nature. It brought together an astonishingly large number of people who had nowhere else to go to earn a living. Because the people were concentrated in a relatively small area, interaction between different groups—rich and poor, educated and illiterate, native and foreign-born—became unavoidable.

People of different backgrounds living in close quarters naturally gave rise to a different life style and to new forms of social organization. In general, life in cities strengthened the importance of economic and political institutions. Religious and primary group ties, on the other hand, lost some of their meaning for the individual. Class structure became more flexible, because fortunes were made, not merely inherited, and social mobility became a fact of life.

Urbanization and Urbanism

Urbanization is the population trend in which cities and their suburbs grow at the expense of rural areas. Urbanization takes place in industrial nations because industry attracts labor to cities and labor attracts businesses. The urbanization trend, which is still going on, will soon lead to a situation in which a large majority of a nation's citizens will be concentrated in cities of 100,000 or more.

Urbanization, however, does not account for all city growth. Because of an increased birth rate, a decreased death rate, or immigration from abroad, cities may grow without a parallel decrease in rural population. Or they may grow because of overall population growth in both rural and urban areas. This is what is happening in developing nations. There, urban growth has not occurred at the expense of rural areas but because both cities and rural areas are increasing in population.[12]

In contrast to urbanization, which is an ongoing process, *urbanism* is a condition, a set of attitudes, a quality, or a way of life distinct from the rural. In other words, the traditional rural values of predominantly agricultural societies are being replaced by urban values on a societal level. Mass communication is causing urbanism to become a characteristic of industrial nations.

[12]Charles H. Anderson, *Toward a New Sociology* (Homewood, Ill.: 1971), p. 341.

Because of television, radio, newspapers and magazines, small towns and big cities are beginning to look and think alike. In Third World nations, however, the opposite appears to be true. Urban dwellers are retaining their previous rural values, or at least are not replacing them with urban ones.

Traditional Rural Values

What are the traditional rural values that urbanism is destroying? They center mainly on life in the open spaces instead of in the cramped quarters of the city and on the closeness and security of living in a large, extended family. Rural values involve the intimacy experienced through personal acquaintance with all of one's neighbors and through friendships developed and maintained because of attendance at the same school, the same church, and the same clubs.

Rural values develop some excellent traits in people, if one is to believe the citizens of Springdale, a town of one thousand people in upstate New York and the subject of a classic study by sociologists Arthur Vidich and Joseph Bensman.[13] According to the study, Springdalers think of themselves as honest, trustworthy, neighborly, helpful, sober, clean-living, and all around good folk!

The researchers saw a slightly different picture. They found a corrupt governing body, elected by a political machine that chose candidates who were willing to keep taxes low and their voices down. What is more, the researchers discovered that the Springdalers depended greatly on the technology and culture of the city. In fact, even their idealized view of themselves as virtuous rural people was chiefly derived from the mass media.

The Urban Transition

A tradition dating back to the biblical prophets holds the city and its people in low esteem. Moralists consider cities dens of iniquity, in which all kinds of exotic sins flourish. Artists and poets decry their physical ugliness, their tall buildings that block out the sun, their general lack of space, and their oppressive look. In all honesty, these critics are not altogether wrong.

Because cities grew so rapidly, very little planning had gone into their development. Thus, much building has been haphazard and ugly. And because of the large concentration of people in cities, buildings have to be close together and tall. It would be difficult, then, to make cities look open, although planning done by people concerned for the physical environment and for appearance could do much to improve them.

As for urban morals, they are of necessity varied. In his transition from rural to urban dweller, the urban resident has had to make adjustments that have had profound effects on his personality and on social organization. First, he has had to limit his family to a nucleus: father, mother, and children. Gone are the grandparents, aunts, and uncles who lent both physical and psychological support and who also made sure that he did not stray from the traditional path. Gone too are the friends and neighbors he knew and talked to every day. In their stead are strangers busy with their own concerns, who do not want to get involved outside of an occasional "Hello." In other words, the urban dweller has experienced the transition from primary groups and a Gemeinschaft (folk, traditional) society to secondary groups and a Gesellschaft (associational) society, a transition we discussed in Chapter 2.

What effect has this transition had on the urban population? Above all, the release from the ties of the primary group has led to increased freedom of action. Freedom of action under circumstances of anonymity—when hardly anyone knows you or cares—may very likely result in behavior that is frowned upon by society. In addition, freedom from the norms imposed by primary groups may also lead to a feeling of normlessness, in which the individual

---

[13]Arthur J. Vidich and Joseph Bensman, *Small Town in Mass Society* (Princeton, N. J.: Princeton University Press, 1958).

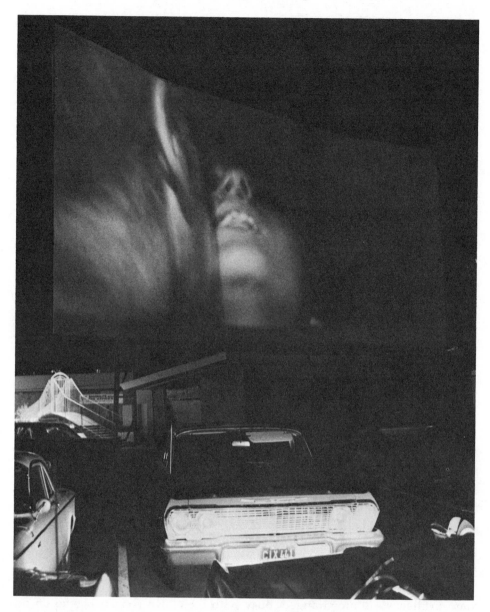

no longer feels that he knows what is right or wrong. Finally, it may bring about a feeling of not belonging to any definite group, of not having anyone who cares.

In some people, such feelings may trigger the onset of mental illness. In others, they may result in delinquent or criminal behavior. Still others may become part of the statistics of our high divorce rate, of drug-induced escapism, and so on. Many express such feelings by assuming a callous, indifferent, dehumanized mask, which they present to the world in self-defense.

The practical result of the decrease in informal controls by the primary group is an increase in formal controls. Without such formal controls, there would be little order. Thus, laws are passed, police departments are formed to enforce them, and more and more activities of the urban resident are controlled by codes and regulations. The urban resident pays dearly for his freedom from primary group interference in general bureaucratization and impersonality of life styles.

Urban Life Styles

The many groups and their subcultures coexisting in large cities have naturally produced different life styles. Urban sociologist Herbert Gans has distinguished five urban life styles.

The first is that of the cosmopolites. The latter are a highly educated, professional group, with a very high income. They choose to live in the city because of its cultural facilities, to which they are drawn, because of their profession, or because of their education. The second life style is that of single, or childless groups. Single people choose to live in the city because there are various social activities and opportunities for meeting people. Single city dwellers tend to be upwardly mobile, and move to the suburbs when they marry or have children. Another life style is that of so-called ethnic villagers. These are immigrants who choose to live as they did in their homeland. Their only contact with outsiders occurs at work. Their interest is limited to their neighborhood, in which they live according to a more or less rural tradition. Still another life style is that of the deprived, who are poor, nonwhite, and live in fatherless households. The deprived live in the city not out of choice but because rents are cheaper, jobs are easier to find, and welfare payments are higher than they are in other areas. The fifth, and last, life style is that of the trapped. This group is made up of elderly pensioners who cannot afford to move out of the city and have to cling to their old neighborhood.[14]

The city is often used as a prime example of the way social disorganization expresses itself in a number of social problems. However, that such a large variety of people, with such different life styles, live so closely together seems to deny this. Modern urban sociologists tend to agree that there is much more social organization in the city than we believe. If that is true, we can be much more optimistic about finding solutions for the city's problems.

The Ecology of the City

Cities are not simply a haphazard collection of residential, commercial, and industrial buildings. Buildings and people are distributed according to patterns within a geographic area. These patterns are related to and dependent on one another. The study of distributive patterns and their interdependence is called *urban ecology*, or sometimes human ecology.

Urban ecologists have found that in each city some *natural areas* come into existence spontaneously. These areas attract people of similar backgrounds, attitudes, and behavior. The people in them depend on one another, but do not actually interrelate with one another to a great extent. A central business district, a rooming house district, and a dormitory district surrounding a university are all examples of natural areas.

---

[14]Herbert J. Gans, "Urbanism and Suburbanism as Ways of Life: A Reevaluation of Definitions," in Arnold M. Rose, ed., *Human Behavior and Social Processes* (Boston: Houghton Mifflin, 1962), Chapter 6.

Cities also consist of *neighborhoods*. These do not arise spontaneously but, in most cases, result from planning. The residents of neighborhoods interrelate more closely with one another than do people in natural areas.

Natural areas and neighborhoods are constantly changing because of the ecological processes at work within them. One such process is *concentration*, or the gathering together of people in a specific area. Concentration is measured in terms of population density, or the number of people per square mile. Another ecological process is *dispersion*, the way in which people are scattered in different areas. Still another is *centralization*, or the tendency for business, industry, and financial and educational facilities to cluster in the central section of the city. *Decentralization*, on the other hand, is a relocation of the above facilities in outlying areas when the central district becomes too congested. *Segregation* is the tendency for different areas of the city to specialize in specific activities or serve as the home of specific kinds of people. The Chinatowns of many cities are examples of segregation. Another example is Greenwich Village in New York City. *Invasion* is the ecological process by which a new group or institution takes over a formerly segregated area. For example, business and industry sometimes take over residential areas, or one racial group takes over a neighborhood previously inhabited by another racial group. When invasion succeeds, the process is called *succession*.

These processes produce rather consistent patterns, at least in American cities. Such patterns have been described by several urban development theories, the best known of which are the *concentric zone* theory, the *sector* theory, and the *multiple nuclei* theory. All three theories have several elements in common. According to all these theories, each city has a central business district; several transition zones housing slum dwellers and industry; zones housing semiskilled, skilled, and clerical workers; and suburban developments on the fringes or outside of the city proper.

Suburbanization and Metropolitanization

American cities are currently undergoing a period of profound crisis. The crisis is related to the trend toward suburbanization and metropolitanization, both movements out and away from the city. According to the 1970 census figures, more than three-fourths of the national population growth occurred in metropolitan, or urban, areas. But the growth was most significant in the *suburbs*—small communities on the outskirts of the central city and somewhat dependent on it. In fact, residents of suburbs now outnumber residents of the central city.

The movement to the suburbs has occurred for several reasons. First, cities expanded so rapidly that industry and business began to take over residential areas. Thus, many people were forced to move further out. Second, a general increase in the standard of living permitted people to build houses that were bigger and more comfortable than those in the city. And there was not much dirt or noise in the suburbs. Finally, improved methods of transportation, especially the automobile, made it possible for people to travel some distance to their jobs.

At first, the suburban movement was limited to the middle and upper classes. But the working classes have increasingly become part of the trend.

Today, suburbs are stratified according to social class and income. There are upper-middle and upper-class suburbs in which almost every head of a household is a college-educated professional. There are suburbs in which residents are chiefly lower-middle class people engaged in service occupations and sales. And there are suburbs containing the inexpensive tract homes of predominantly working-class residents.

For a long time, suburbs were entirely dependent on the city for shopping and for commercial, cultural, and recreational activities. Later, city and suburbs became interdependent, with the suburbs providing the labor force. Increasingly, however, the suburbs are becoming independent from the city. The huge shopping centers of suburbia have been followed by business, industry, and professionals. Thus, both jobs and facilities are now available to the suburban resident.

Suburbs have, of course, mushroomed at the expense of the central city. When people, commerce, and industry moved away, the city lost an important tax base. Without incoming tax money, the city cannot provide important facilities, and even more people, commerce, and industry move out. Thus, the central city is left with a run-down transportation system, outmoded physical facilities, inadequate police protection, and poor schools. Those who have the means can use their own cars, send their children to private schools, and live in guarded apartment houses. Or they too can move to the suburbs. But those without the means must remain in the city and cope as best they can.

The Metropolitan Area and the Megalopolis

Some suburbs have grown so large that they are now called towns and cities. These small cities, regular suburbs, and the central city around which they are clustered make up the ecological city, or the *metropolitan area*. The United States Bureau of the Census is using metropolitan areas as the basis for measuring units of population. The Standard Metropolitan Statistical Area (SMSA) consists of one or more counties containing at least one city of over 50,000 or two cities totaling that number. As of 1965, there were 219 such SMSA's in the United States, embracing about two-thirds of the population.

The large number of metropolitan areas is leading to a new phenomenon in the United States. This phenomenon is "urban sprawl," or the *megalopolis*, in which one metropolitan area follows another without interruption. One such complex is the Great Lakes chain, which begins north in Buffalo and continues solidly to Milwaukee and further west. By the year 2000, an estimated 40 million people will be housed in this complex alone. The Boston-Washington complex is predicted to contain around 80 million people.

Megalopolis proceeds undisturbed despite the damage it does to central cities. Furthermore, it creates problems in local government. Each municipality, county, township, city, or village within the metropolitan area, in fact, maintains its own government. This creates a bureaucratic maze in which agencies and officials of neighboring governments are often at odds with one another. The result is a waste of money and other even more valuable resources.

Urban specialists have long favored some form of metropolitan government. Some attempts to establish such a form of government have been made, but in a nation of individualists, the notion is not popular. Now, however, a federal study has concluded that urbanization in the United States is proceeding so rapidly that even metropolitan governments are no longer efficient. However, broad regional governments may relieve a situation that is presently bordering on chaos. The study proposes that metropolitan complexes such as Boston to Washington and Chicago to Pittsburgh be joined into one metropolitan belt that would touch nineteen states.[15]

CAUSES AND MECHANISMS OF COLLECTIVE BEHAVIOR

Sociologist Robin Williams, in commenting on present urban trends, said, "The rapid, sprawling, uncoordinated growth of these giant conurbations— megalopolises, with their burgeoning outer rings and their crowded, blighted inner cities, creates dislocations, social tensions, and conflicts of great magnitude and difficulty."[16] Under conditions of dislocation, social tension, and conflict, individuals tend to lose their bearings and become confused. Rapid social change produces not only the cultural lag of Ogburn's theory but also the condition that Alvin Toffler called "future shock" in his book by that name.[17]

Future shock is brought about by an imperfect adaptation between the individual and culture because of the speed of change. It shows itself in a disruption of the normal decision-making processes. Toffler observes that there are limits to the amount of change to which the human organism can adapt and "... by endlessly accelerating change without first determining these limits, we may submit masses of men to demands they simply cannot tolerate."[18] We may add that although humans cannot tolerate these demands, they nonetheless respond to them. They respond by behaving in a manner that is unstructured, relatively unpredictable, largely spontaneous, disorganized, and unsupported by existing norms and societal conventions. In short, they are subject to collective behavior.

Under *collective behavior*, sociologists include the kind of short-lived behavior that shows itself in crowds, mobs, riots, rumors, fashions, fads, crazes, and mass hysteria. They also include the more structured and longer-lived behavior that is shown in public opinion and social movements. Collective behavior, though partially a product of social change, is a vehicle for further social change. The purpose of revolutions is to change the political order. The purpose of social movements is to reform various institutions. And riots and demonstrations chip away at the solidity of social organization within society.

Collective behavior has long interested sociologists. Having determined how society is organized through the analysis of social organization, they are faced with completely disorganized, dynamic events in collective behavior. What is more, these events cannot be analyzed at one's leisure. A researcher caught in a riot with his tape recorder or note pad would not fare too well!

---

[15]Jack Rosenthal, "Regional Rule Called Vital as Urbanization Spreads," *The New York Times* (February 6, 1972).

[16]Robin M. William, Jr., *American Society: A Sociological Interpretation*, 3d ed. (New York: Alfred A. Knopf, 1970), p. 114.

[17]Alvin Toffler, *Future Shock* (New York: Random House, 1970).

[18]Ibid., p. 290.

To understand collective behavior, then, sociologists turn to its causes and mechanisms rather than strictly to its external form.

Causes of Collective Behavior

We have already indicated that rapid social change is one source of collective behavior. But collective behavior can be caused by additional factors. One such factor is a conflict of values and norms. The Vietnam war has presented this kind of conflict for many Americans, who are torn between what they feel is an immoral action and loyalty to their country. The indecision caused by not knowing which value to uphold makes them easy prey to collective behavior.

Another factor may be a sudden crisis. People at a rock concert cannot follow traditional norms of behavior—filing out in orderly fashion—when a bomb is thrown in their midst. Faced with temporary normlessness, members of the audience may well respond with panic. On the other hand, if people faced the crisis often enough—as soldiers face crises in combat—they would soon establish new norms to deal with it.

Relaxation of social controls is another possible cause of collective behavior. A group in transition, such as people who have moved from rural to urban areas, frequently becomes free of the controls exerted by close kinship ties. If, in addition, formal controls, such as laws and police, are thought to be inadequate, people may take the law into their own hands. They may, for example, become part of lynching mobs and vigilante groups.

Finally, another cause of collective behavior may be conflict stemming from the heterogeneousness of society. In a society characterized by class, racial, ethnic, regional, political, and economic differences, many people must necessarily be dissatisfied. If they are or perceive themselves as being deprived, they are likely to use forms of collective behavior to remove their dissatisfaction.

Mechanisms of Collective Behavior

Three theories have been constructed to explain how collective behavior originates and spreads. These are the contagion, convergence, and emergent norm theories. Not one of these theories presumes to explain totally the mechanisms of collective behavior. But all three contribute some insights into its origins and processes.

The contagion theory. In the *contagion theory*, collective behavior is viewed as a process. In this process, moods, attitudes, and behavior are rapidly communicated to a collectivity—an aggregation of persons who do not interact on a regular basis. These moods, attitudes, and behavior are uncritically accepted by the collectivity by a further process called *circular reaction*, or *emotional contagion*. For example, someone in a crowd yells, "I see the devil!" Another says, "I see him too!" This reassures the first person, who proclaims his vision even louder. Soon, everyone in the crowd is yelling, "I see the devil!" The same process occurs when an emotion such as anger is displayed.

Other factors involved in contagion are suggestion, imitation, identification, anonymity, and loss of individuality. In *suggestion and imitation*, clues for behavior are readily accepted from others and are then imitated. In *identification*, each person feels a common bond with every other person and with the leader of the event. *Anonymity* and *loss of individuality* make individuals susceptible to a breakdown of inhibitions.

The convergence theory.   Whereas the contagion theory emphasizes the temporary effect of the group on the individual, the *convergence theory* stresses that collective behavior merely brings out into the open feelings already present in the individual members of the collectivity. In short, the collective situation simply brings together people with similar tendencies. When such people are together, they are likely to engage in some form of collective behavior if outsiders are present, individuals not committed to the dominant mores of the society are present, or a target becomes available and no other outlet for frustrations is present.

The emergent norm theory.   In the *emergent norm theory*, collective behavior is viewed as behavior that is governed by norms. According to this theory, norms do emerge in collective situations, although they may be different from the norms that exist in regular group situations. These new norms often indicate that those governing regular group behavior are no longer valid.[19]

CROWDS

A *crowd* is an aggregate of people gathered in the same place at the same time. The crowd may be casual: a line of people waiting to buy subway tickets or a number of people stopped at a red light. Or the crowd may be organized: people attending a football game or a rock concert.

At any rate, the aggregate of people does not become a crowd until it responds to a common stimulus. Even the casual crowd may evolve into a panic crowd, a mob, or even a rioting crowd if the stimulus demands it—if someone yells "Fire!" or "They're shooting at us!" But the organized crowd is much more receptive to mob behavior than is the casual crowd, because people have come together in anticipation of some emotional experience.

Crowds are divided into *expressive* crowds, which are gathered for the purpose of expressing feelings. Religious revival meetings are an example of expressive crowds. Crowds may also be *acting*, in which case they are gathered for the purpose of acting out feelings, generally of a hostile nature. Mobs, riots, and some protests are acting crowds.

People in crowds behave as they do because crowds are temporary, everyone feels anonymous, and there is a relative absence of norms, formal controls, and specific leaders. Under such circumstances, the individual member of a crowd gives up his individuality in exchange for a group feeling. He can, then, perform antisocial acts and shift his guilt feelings about violating norms onto the group: "I didn't do it. The crowd did it."

We have already said that any aggregate may become an acting crowd when stimuli are introduced. Thus, an audience may become a *panic crowd* if a bomb

---

[19]Ralph H. Turner, "Collective Behavior," in Robert E. L. Faris, ed., *Handbook of Modern Sociology* (Chicago: Rand McNally 1964), pp. 382–392.

is exploded in its midst and everyone attempts to flee at the same time. Or it may become a *mob* if people are aroused to a high emotional pitch, and if an available target is suddenly found as a scapegoat for a long-harbored discontent. And the mob may become a *riot* if the discontent is centered around problems of race, religion, ethnicity, and deprivation.

In the 1960s, riots were a frequent occurrence in the United States. Rioting has been thought of as aggressive, violent, destructive, irrational, and ultimately useless mob action. Individuals engaging in rioting were thought to be reacting in frustration against perceived injustices—poverty, repression, discrimination—to which they saw no end.

However, some sociologists are now beginning to look at rioting in a different light. First, they claim that the behavior of the authorities is no less aggressive, violent, destructive, and irrational than that of the rioters. Therefore, value judgments that distinguish between normal and deviant behavior are not valid. Furthermore, the violence of rioting is not useless because it does lead to action and change. As proof, these sociologists maintain that all political revolutions have begun as riots.[20]

RUMORS

In many instances, rumors are the beginning of riots, panics, or mobs. A *rumor* is an unsupported report of an event or a projected event. The report is not backed up by facts but continues to spread by word of mouth or through the mass media. It finds fertile soil in situations of stress in which accurate information is not readily available. In accepting a rumor, people tend to hear what they want to hear. Thus, a rumor may help them rationalize their participation in some form of collective behavior, or it may help to clarify a confused situation.

FASHIONS, FADS, AND CRAZES

Fashions, fads, and crazes differ from the kinds of collective behavior already discussed in that they are not quite as temporary or as action-directed. *Fashions* refer to manners in dress, architecture, or house decor. They tend to reflect the interests, values, and motives of a given society or group within it. *Fads* and *crazes* are minor fashions that are much more irrational and shorter lived than fashions. Crazes have an even more obsessive character than fads. The famous flagpole sitting and goldfish swallowing contests of an earlier era were crazes.

Mass hysteria is similar to fads and crazes in that it is compulsive and irrational. It may exist among a large number of people, such as the screaming fans of a popular singer or group. Or it may express itself in scattered instances—when, for example, a particularly colorful criminal act is followed by a rash of similar incidents.

[20]Jerome H. Skolnick, *The Politics of Protest* (New York: Ballantine, 1969), pp. 335–359. Also, H. D. Graham and T. R. Gurr, eds., *The History of Violence in America* (New York: Bantam, 1969), pp. 4–45.

Although fashions, fads, and crazes begin as a departure from tradition—a bit of nonconformity in a conforming society—they soon establish a new tradition from which new fashions, fads, and crazes will try to depart. Thus, the bearded, long-haired college student who at first represented a radical departure from his Joe College counterpart of the 1950s has been imitated to such an extent that he will have to shave to baldness if he wants to stand out today!

PUBLIC OPINION

A different type of collective behavior involves publics and public opinion. Persons who are geographically dispersed make up a *public* because they happen to share a common interest, because they express that interest, and because others are aware of such an interest. University students, voters, the readers of *Life* magazine, moviegoers, and countless other similar categories of people make up publics.[21]

The composition of a public changes quickly. Although all those watching a TV program at 7:30 on Saturday night are a public, half an hour later they will probably be doing something entirely different and will no longer be a public. We see, then, that a public is an unstructured collectivity in which some members lose interest in the event that made them a public and others replace them. In technological societies, countless numbers of publics exist, many of which are at odds with one another.

Publics are especially important because of the attitudes or judgments they display regarding various societal issues. The attitudes and judgments that publics hold are called *public opinion*. Public opinion has meaning only in a mass society, for only in such societies are the government, business, and industry interested in what the public thinks. Furthermore, public opinion is a creature of the mass media. The mass media attempt to make the public think what government, business, and industry want it to think!

Public opinion is influenced by propaganda and censorship. Both of these devices are manipulative. Manufacturers who want to sell their products, candidates who want to be elected to office, and administrations that want to remain in office all make use of propaganda. *Propaganda* is a deliberate attempt to persuade the individual to accept uncritically a particular belief or to make a certain choice.

A little bit of propaganda creeps into most institutions. Education, religion, and politics—and, of course, advertising and public relations—all make use of propaganda to some extent. However, the effectiveness of propaganda is greatest in totalitarian nations because the government alone has access to it. In democratic nations, its effectiveness is decreased by competing propaganda, by access to various sources of news, and by a sophisticated and well-educated public, which is capable of distinguishing between propaganda and reality.

Censorship is a type of manipulative device that is used to limit the information available to the public. Totalitarian nations also make much more use of censorship than do democratic nations. Yet even in our society, the courts

---

[21]Leonard Broom and Philip Selznick, *Sociology* (New York: Harper & Row, 1968), p. 238.

tell us what we may read or see; the government chooses not to tell us about its mistakes; the mass media reveal some information but suppress other information; and business and industry do the same.

SOCIAL MOVEMENTS

Social movements are collective efforts either to change the sociocultural order or to resist such change.[22] As such, they represent the individual's personal involvement and intervention in directing, redirecting, furthering, or stopping change.

Social movements are rooted in the same kind of discontent that gives rise to many of the short-lived forms of collective behavior. However, members of social movements are interested in long-range solutions. Because of this, they have an ideology that supports their actions. Members of social movements, though separated by continents, are united by a common commitment, by dedication to a cause, and by the idealistic belief in the righteousness of their cause.

Although some social movements are almost entirely unorganized, most are pursued in voluntary groups, or associations. These are secondary groups

[22]Lewis M. Killian, "Social Movements," in Robert E. L. Faris, *Handbook of Modern Sociology,* p. 430.

organized for the attainment of a definite goal. Both social movements and voluntary groups are characteristic of urban industrial societies which are experiencing rapid social change.

The Purpose of Social Movements

Social movements are sometimes called "institutions in the making" because their ultimate aim is to effect change to the extent that it becomes institutionalized. And they often succeed in this. Political parties, international ideologies (socialism, for instance), women's suffrage, and even nations have come into existence as a result of social movements.

Social movements try to accomplish institutionalization by quite unconventional means: mass demonstrations, picketing, organized rallies and disturbances, and the spread of slogans and symbols. Needless to say, not all social movements are successful. Some die from lack of interest and loss of members. Others, however, alter their goals to fit new interests, and are eventually institutionalized in this manner.

The Fertile Soil of Social Movements

We have already mentioned that rapid social change, such as industrialization, tends to produce disorganization in a society. This is because formerly accepted norms and values are being questioned. When norms and values are unstable, people are subject to feelings of anomie and alienation. *Anomie* is normlessness, or not knowing which behavioral guidelines to follow. *Alienation* is feeling that one is separate from society—powerless, normless, and isolated.

In a society in which a high degree of anomie and alienation are present, the soil is fertile for social movements. Social movements, in fact, have a special appeal to people who are restless and confused and who need something to which they can anchor their lives.[23]

Social movements may also emerge when there is general dissatisfaction with the status quo. One source of dissatisfaction is *relative deprivation*. Many people are not deprived in comparison with the deprived of other societies, but they perceive themselves as deprived. In other words, the desert-dwelling Bedouin whose only possessions are a tent, a couple of pans, and the clothes on his back is more deprived than is even an urban slum dweller in our society. But if the Bedouin accepts the values of his social system and his position in it, he does not feel deprived. Not until he begins to question these values and compare his lot to that of others in his society, as the slum dweller has done, does he feel deprived.

Another aspect of general dissatisfaction with the status quo is the failure of rising expectations. *Rising expectations* occur in a society when the standard of living begins to rise. If it then suffers a reversal or does not continue to rise at the same rate, people's expectations are frustrated. They fear that they will lose the advantages they have gained or will not get what others in their

[23]Robert K. Merton, *Social Theory and Social Structure* (New York: The Free Press, 1957), pp 164–169. Also, Dwight G. Dean, "Alienation: Its Meaning and Measurement," *American Sociological Review* (1961), pp. 753–758.

society already have. The masses of the Third World and the underprivileged of our own society are victims of feelings of relative deprivation and the failure of rising expectations.

Closely related to these sources of discontent is the perception of social injustice. The person who feels relatively deprived may also begin to feel that it is unjust for a small elite to live in splendor while he and others like him live in poverty. A passionately perceived image of social injustice, the failure of rising expectations, and a feeling of relative deprivation on the part of the dark-skinned people of the world inspired the revolutionary writings of Frantz Fanon. He was not directly involved in originating any social movement. But he is considered an originator by many members of the social movements that he inspired. Horace Sutton's article "Fanon" examines the personality and writings of this patron saint of the New Left.[24]

The perception of social injustice, however, is not limited to the under-privileged classes. A wealthy person who suddenly finds himself relieved of his fortune may also feel that an injustice has been done him! In any case, the significant factor is not the actual presence or absence of social injustice. It is people's perception that they are victims of social injustice that makes them apt to respond to social movements.

Other Factors Nourishing Social Movements

People subject to status inconsistency are easy prey to social movements. Status inconsistency, you recall from our discussion in Chapter 4, occurs when not all of a person's statuses are ranked on an equal level. For example, in our society, a black doctor tends to be ranked as a black first and then as a doctor. The status of black is considered before the status of doctor. Thus, the black doctor's potential for acquiring the high status of doctor is diminished. Naturally, he feels discontent.

Another factor that encourages people to join social movements is geographic mobility. Geographic mobility, a characteristic of urban industrial societies, promotes feelings of rootlessness. It partly explains why all kinds of social movements flourish in California, a state to which large numbers of people continually migrate.

Social mobility also makes people receptive to social movements. This is especially true of people who belong to a downwardly mobile class or who fear becoming downwardly mobile.[25] But upward mobility also has effects, because it tends to unsettle people.

Social movements also seem to attract people who have weak or nonexistent family ties. The cliché that when you have a mortgage to pay off you can't afford to be involved with hotheads seems to be true. In fact, most members of radical social movements either had no families or had broken all family ties. Campus radicals, too, seem to have been reared in homes in which their parents denied them emotional reassurance and guidance. In short, when family ties are strong, a person feels no need to join social movements. This is

[24]Horace Sutton, "Fanon," *Saturday Review* (July 17, 1971), pp. 16ff.

[25]James A. Geschwender, "Explorations in the Theory of Social Movements," *Social Forces* (December, 1968), Vol. 47, pp. 127–135.

one reason why most revolutionary movements discourage family life and family authority.[26]

Isolated marginal people feel the need to belong to some thing or some group. Isolated people set themselves apart from the rest of society, either voluntarily or because of their occupations. Marginal people are not quite accepted and integrated into society or relevant groups in it.[27]

Now that we have discussed several conditions in which social movements prosper, we should mention that these conditions are not causes of social movements. Their existence merely predisposes people to join such movements. In many of these conditions, moreover, cause and effect are somewhat confused. For instance, geographic mobility causes rootlessness in people. People who feel rootless do not readily accept the norms of the community in which they temporarily live. Therefore, they are more inclined to join social movements than are old-time residents of the community. But which came first, the rootlessness or the mobility? It is, of course, possible that mobility is merely a reaction to an already existing rootlessness. The same may be said for lack of family ties as a factor that predisposes people to join social movements. Are family ties already severed, so that the individual feels a need to belong somewhere, even if it is only to a social movement? Or do ties become severed as a result of the time and effort the social movement takes away from the family?

Some Kinds of Social Movements

There are many kinds of social movements. In some, like *migratory* movements, discontent is eliminated when members leave one geographic location for another. The waves of immigrants who came to this country were members of such movements.

In others, such as *expressive* movements, members' reactions to their environment is changed, because the environment itself cannot be changed. Many religious movements, including that of the young Jesus Freaks, are expressive movements.

Still others are *utopian* in nature. In these movements, an attempt is made to establish new societies with new standards and values. The rash of communes formed by young people in the late 1960s were products of utopian movements.

Finally, in *resistance* movements, people attempt to stem the tide of change because they fear change is proceeding too rapidly. Many organizations of the right and the radical right are resistance movements.

Reform Movements

In the past several centuries, the two social movements that have had the most influence on societies and their governments have been the revolutionary and the reform movements. *Reform movements* represent an attempt to change some feature of an existing social order without changing the entire order.

[26]Herbert Hendin, "A Psychoanalyst Looks at Student Revolutionaries," *New York Times Magazine* (January 17, 1971), pp. 16 ff.

[27]William Kornhauser, *The Politics of Mass Society* (New York: Free Press of Glencoe, 1959), Chapter 12.

Such movements are most successful in democratic societies. In such societies, there is relative freedom to criticize institutions, and there are channels through which reforms can be put into effect.

Our own society offers many examples of reform movements. The most prominent examples are the civil rights movement, which has splintered into revolutionary and moderate factions; the movement for equality and liberation of women; and the movement for removing the social stigma attaching to homosexuality.

It is sometimes difficult to distinguish between a reform and a revolutionary movement, because many generalized movements produce a wide range of action-oriented groups. For example, the Women's Liberation movement includes such organizations as the National Organization of Women (NOW), the aims of which are conservatively reformist, as well as such groups as Radical Women, Women's Liberation Front, and Women's International Terrorist Conspiracy from Hell (WITCH), which surely sounds revolutionary!

Donald McDonald, the author of our article "The Liberation of Women," sheds some light on Women's Liberation. He attempts to separate fact from fancy in this often maligned and frequently confusing social movement. The object of the movement, he maintains, is to discover the nature of woman and to free women so they may fulfill themselves. This, of course, is not as simple as it sounds. It involves not only the removal of legal, occupational, and educational barriers, but also freedom from a sexually directed, rather than a humanly directed, socialization.[28]

Revolutionary Movements

The distinguishing feature of revolutionary movements is that their members do not merely seek to correct some aspect of the present social order. They consider the social order so inadequate, corrupt, unjust, and beyond salvation, that they seek its complete removal and substitution with an entirely new order. In effecting such absolute change, revolutionary movements must often resort to violence.

Revolutionary movements are of two types. In *nationalistic revolutionary movements*, a predominantly foreign government is overthrown and replaced with a native one. *Class revolutionary movements* substitute one ruling class for another in the same society. The American revolution was nationalistic, whereas the French, Russian, Chinese, and Cuban were all class revolutions.

Revolutionary movements should not be confused with revolts, or *coups d'etat*. In revolts, individual members of the ruling class are replaced with other individuals, but the structure of the major social institutions remains the same.

Factors encouraging revolutionary movements. Basically, the same factors predispose people to join revolutionary situations that predispose them to become members of other social movements. Conditions may, however, be extreme or may be perceived as being extreme. This is one reason why revolutionary movements are more characteristic of totalitarian societies than they are of democratic ones. In democracies, public opinion and reform movements exert pressure, which generally leads to the changes desired by the people. In totalitarian regimes, public opinion is ignored, and social movements are not tolerated. The only way people can make changes, then, is by overthrowing the government.

The most important condition for revolution, then, is the widespread reali-

[28]Donald McDonald, "The Liberation of Women," *The Center Magazine* (May-June 1972), pp. 25–42.

zation that the current system of government has failed and that it is necessary to bring about change at any cost. This condition is called a *crisis of legitimacy*. When a crisis of legitimacy takes place, often the government has been ineffective and has not tried to eliminate discontent by making changes.[29]

Revolution is also aided by a breakdown of discipline and efficiency in the ruling body. Some members of this body, especially the intellectuals, become disillusioned and may even join the revolutionary movement. Others, sensing the coming doom, pursue their private pleasures, giving little thought to the task of governing. Therefore, in many cases, very little violence is actually needed to wrest the government from the hands of the rulers. It is already crumbling on its own.

Stages and achievements of revolutions. The actual outbreak of revolution may be sparked by war with another country or by acute economic failures. Members of revolutionary movements may use promises of economic improvements as incentives and combine such aims with the ideology of the movement. During this period, a charismatic leader who is able to unite different factions of revolutionaries often appears. Victory frequently depends on the side the military and the police take. If they take the side of the revolutionaries, victory is almost always assured.

Following a revolution, the new leaders attempt to put together a new government. There is a period of struggle between moderates and radical extremists, during which more violence is apt to occur than occurred during the revolutionary period itself. Finally, a compromise is reached, in which a redefinition of ideology, scope, and function of government takes place. This usually results in some form of document being produced—a constitution—that is supplemented by additional laws and institutions. Thus, the formerly revolutionary becomes the normal, and new radical ideas begin to emerge.

The results of revolutions are seldom as drastic as they promise to be. Customs and institutions are difficult to uproot, and at best only a compromise change takes place. In many instances, in fact, it is precisely the unpleasant features of a society that survive the revolution. At the same time, the history of the modern world would be much different if the French, American, Russian, and Chinese revolutions had not occurred.[30]

SUMMARY

The causes of social and cultural change have interested philosophers and social scientists for a long time. Explanations of change have ranged from theories of evolution, to functionalist theories, cyclical theories, cultural lag, and diffusion theories. No one theory is completely explanatory, but all provide some insights into the causes of change.

The mechanisms of sociocultural change are somewhat easier to determine

---

[29]Seymour Martin Lipset, *Political Man* (Garden City, N. Y.: Doubleday, 1963), pp. 64–79.

[30]The preceding section has drawn on the writings of the following: Crane Brinton, *The Anatomy of Revolution* (New York: Vintage, 1959); Chalmers Johnson, *Revolutionary Change* (Boston: Little, Brown, 1966); James C. Davies, "Toward a Theory of Revolution," *American Sociological Review* (February, 1962).

than are the causes. The principal processes of cultural change are discovery, invention, and diffusion. Change in the structure of society occurs through planning, reform, revolution, and sociocultural drift.

In recent centuries, the major changes that have occurred in the world are population expansion, urbanization, and industrialization. Popslation began to grow in the middle of the seventeenth century. Population growth has now assumed alarming proportions, especially in the developing countries, which are still nonindustrial and can least afford such growth.

Industrialization and urbanization are twin events that followed two important historical changes: a change in economy from farming to industry and a shift in population from rural to urban. The two changes are interrelated: Advances in agriculture forced people to move to cities where they could find jobs in factories. The factory system resulted from advances in manufacturing.

Urbanization is a shift in population in which cities grow at the expense of rural areas. This shift continues into the present, and soon most of us will live in cities with a population of 100,000 or more. Urbanization has, in turn, led to the decline of the inner cities, the spread of suburbs, and the formation of metropolitan areas which become megalopolises.

The rapid social change that has resulted from industrialization has had significant effects on people. Traditional values have broken down, and people often participate in collective behavior. Collective behavior—which is a product of change and leads to further change—is unstructured behavior in which old norms are not considered valid, and new norms emerge.

Collective behavior expresses itself in crowds, which may vary from peaceful audiences to violent mobs and riots; in rumors, fashions, fads, and crazes; in publics and public opinion; and, finally, in the large number of social movements that exist today. Members of social movements may attempt to reform existing features of a social order. Or they may take part in a revolution, in which case they want to completely change the social order.

Total change never takes place in any society. Human beings, the societies they build, and the cultures they develop remain a curious blend of the old and the new. The old is clung to; yet people are receptive to the new. Thus, we must agree both with those who proclaim that there is nothing new under the sun and with those who recognize that new things happen every day.

PAUL R. EHRLICH AND
JOHN P. HOLDREN

NEiTHER MARX NOR MAlTHUS

For many centuries, the dictum "Be fruitful and multiply" was obediently heeded throughout the world—perhaps nowhere as zealously as in China, a nation in which it was important to have children who would care for one in old age and make sure one's memory was respected. It took a long and bloody revolution and then compromise with the nation's new ideology to convince most Chinese that their progress as a nation depended, to a great degree, on population control. How this problem was approached and how it is presently being pursued in China is concisely told by population experts Paul R. Ehrlich and John P. Holdren.

□□□

Mainland China, with between 750 and 850 million people, is the most populous nation on earth. This fact alone makes its attitude toward population limitation a matter of great practical importance. But because China is also a non-white, non-Western, militantly socialist nation, its official posture on population has ideological implications as well. Of special interest in this connection is the claim, advanced by Marx a century ago and parroted by many Western radicals today, that population limitation would be unnecessary in a just society. Indeed, the still fashionable view on the far left is that "the population problem"

From *Saturday Review* November 6, 1971.
Copyright 1971 Saturday Review, Inc.

is merely a fabrication devised by rich, white capitalists bent on continued exploitation of the world's poor. Expanding knowledge of events in Chairman Mao's China contradicts this view. After a few false starts, the Chinese have embarked on a program of population limitation unmatched by that of any other nation.

Considerable information on China's population policies was available even before the recent thaw in U.S.–Chinese relations, much of it through American journalist Edgar Snow. Snow has enjoyed remarkable access to the Chinese leadership and has traveled extensively throughout the country. A selection of prethaw documents on population limitation in China, including two pieces by Snow, one by a former press official in the People's Republic of China, and some translations from Chinese medical journals, was recently published by the Population Crisis Committee (a non-profit, Washington-based organization that disseminates information on population problems). These materials, together with the reports of newsmen and physicians who have been permitted to tour China in the past few months, provide a reasonably complete and consistent picture of China's population programs.

Family planning services (the provision of contraceptive information and supplies to those who want them) have been available in China for many years, hindered only by limitations of production, distribution, and peasant education. Such services, in themselves, merely enable individuals to avoid unwanted children. In addition, however, population control measures (those designed to influence the number of children people actually want) have been pushed vigorously in China, if somewhat intermittently.

The first important population control campaign began in 1956. It consisted of centrally organized propaganda efforts, including films, posters, and public meetings, coupled with increased availability of contraceptives. This campaign encountered many obstacles: illiteracy in the countryside, the prevalence of old values in the group then in the peak reproductive years, and optimism that the Great Leap Forward would make concern with population unnecessary. The campaign was terminated in mid-1958, although family planning services remained available.

The failure of the Great Leap and the associated 1959–62 famine were followed by a renewed and more vigorous population control effort. This time, social coercion was applied to secure conformity with the official norm, which called for late marriage, a three-year interval between marriage and the first birth, similar intervals between all births thereafter, and small completed families. One propaganda slogan was "Two children is just right, three is too many, and four is a mistake." In some localities, economic sanctions were taken against workers who married early or had more than two children; these ranged from denial of ration cards to dismissal from government jobs. Abortion was made widely available and male sterilization was encouraged for those with two or three children. A vast array of party activists was dispersed around the country to carry on birth control propaganda. As a whole, however, the campaign was more successful in the cities, where surveillance was better and offenders had more to lose than in the countryside.

The propaganda and sanctions associated with the second population control campaign were interrupted by the Cultural Revolution in 1966, although contraceptives, sterilization, and abortions continued to be available without restriction. Since 1968—a year of record population growth in China—the government has reasserted itself in actively pushing population control. Many features of the 1962–66 campaign have been restored, and several additional factors make it seem likely that, this time, the momentum of the campaign will be sustained.

First, an apparently very sophisticated contraceptive pill is being manufactured and distributed (free) on an unprecedented scale, and a once-a-month pill is in use in some regions. Second, abortion is now being widely performed by the relatively quick and painless vacuum method, and at the request of the mother alone. Third, decent medical care, contraceptive services, and effective birth control propaganda have now been extended throughout China at the village level, by means of the "barefoot doctors." These paramedical workers are mostly peasants. They receive six months' training by doctors from the cities, who have fanned out across the countryside in a major reorientation of Chinese medicine toward the rural poor. Finally (and perhaps most important), Chinese women have achieved virtual equality with men. They are expected to be full participants in their society—in politics, in acquiring education, in taking jobs—and in this context, large families are a burden to be avoided.

In continuing to support population limitation with an intensity unknown elsewhere, the Chinese sometimes take pains to deny any overtones of "Malthusian" doctrine, and much of their propaganda emphasizes the benefits of small families on the individual level. Nevertheless, in other propaganda and in interviews with journalist Snow, the Chinese leaders have revealed their conviction that progress for China as a nation depends in no small part on the success of population control. Their discomfiture in deserting Marx on this point notwithstanding, the Chinese have set a vital example in recognizing and acting upon the fact that certain principles of biology and arithmetic transcend ideology.

fANON

The cry of "Revolution!" has been heard around the world in recent decades from leaders of dark-skinned peoples. Such leaders are responding to conditions born out of centuries of white oppression and exploitation—a perception of social inequality, feelings of relative deprivation, and a failure of rising expectations. No one has expressed this cry as poignantly and passionately as Frantz Fanon, a black psychiatrist from Martinique, and his words have not fallen on deaf ears: Hardly any black- or brown-skinned person, in America or abroad, has not read or at least heard of this fiery man. Horace Sutton describes the experiences in Fanon's life that prompted his ideas and attitudes for change and the way Fanon's writings have affected today's world revolutionaries.

□□□

The lights in the movie theater dim and the curtain rises. The screen comes to life and there is a scene of arid North Africa. Over this scrabbly background, a quotation appears:

The bourgeois phase in the history of the underdeveloped countries is a completely useless phase. When this caste has vanished . . . it will be seen . . . that everything must be started from scratch. . . .

It is taken from Frantz Fanon.

When Joe Frazier fights Muhammad Ali in the ring, a newspaper runs a series of articles on Ali. It begins with this prelude:

From *Saturday Review*, July 17, 1971. Copyright 1971 Saturday Review, Inc.

I feel in myself a soul as immense as the world, my chest to expand without limit. I am a master and I am advised to adopt the humility of the cripple.

The lines come not from Ali but from Fanon.

In Nigeria, a Frantz Fanon Research Center is opened at Enugu, dedicated to the "mental emancipation of the black man all over the world from neocolonial mentality."

A square in Algeria is named for Fanon.

The former Algerian ambassador to the United States gives a course on him at the University of Massachusetts.

The books Fanon wrote begin to edge toward an awesome three-quarters-of-a-million sale in American editions alone.

A movie treatment of his life has been written. The producers have spoken of seeking Sidney Poitier for the leading role.

Two books about him have appeared this year, and at least two others are pending.

Who is this man so widely quoted, so passionately read, whose name is so frequently invoked, yet who remains so widely unknown?

What is the strange, almost mystic pull exerted by this black man of Martinique dead ten years ago at the age of thirty-six who is being nominated for sainthood in the revolutionary halls of the Third World?

Fanon's career seemed to rise slowly even as a rocket appears to hover momentarily over the launch pad. But then, rocket-like, he roared into the universe leaving a fiery trail. That great forceful thrust died abruptly, but the stars, as from a spent skyrocket, may come floating down for years, for Fanon was and is an effective, articulate voice of the oppressed, of the black man who suffers the dominance of white "superiority," of the native locked in mortal contest with the settler, the colonizer, the oppressor. Fanon's voice is black and intellectual, but it is one with which all the brothers can identify, in Nigeria, in Harlem, in Jamaica, in Angola, and especially in Algeria, whose cause he passionately espoused and whose freedom he helped to win. From Algiers in the heart of Fanonland, Eldridge Cleaver invokes his canons. From his West African sanctuary in Guinea (where his address is c/o President Sékou Touré), Stokely Carmichael drinks deep at the wellspring of Fanon's basic tenets. Holed up in their headquarters in the Bronx, the Black Panthers say that Fanon is required reading for all brothers. He has given them insights, they say, far beyond Marx and Lenin. Marx dealt with economic structures, Lenin with the machinery to bring the economic and military together. But neither came to grips with racism, because, as Panther Minister Zayd Shakur puts it, "They were dealing with European phenomena and they were concerned with whites. Fanon took it to another level. He set down the dialectical contradictions that most oppressed black people are confronted with in a colonized situation."

Nearly all strata of American black society have found their prophet in Fanon. "Many of us were pushing the whole idea of black values and the traumas one suffers from the oppressor and how we try to imitate the oppressor," CORE's Roy Innis recalls now, "but Fanon came along and codified it and gave it authority." In Algiers, far from Harlem, Cleaver remembers the early days. "The feelings and thoughts and passions that were racking us were incoherent and not connected until we read Fanon. Then many things fell together for us harmonizing our attitudes and making it possible for us to organize into a political organization."

To read Fanon now is to find the source of many of the bold moves of the black Left, among them violence itself, the call for reparations for offenses to oppressed peoples, and the summons to effect the rebirth of a native culture and with it a singular identity.

While Fanon was addressing himself to colonized peoples—his experience had been chiefly in Martinique and Algeria—he was heard by all the Third World: by militant blacks in America who consider themselves part of a colonized society; by newly independent nations whose economic lifeline continues to be dominated by white Western capital; and by peoples of color still living in colonial-ruled societies.

To all these, Fanon preached the necessity of violence to bring about abrupt change whether it be "national liberation or national renaissance or the restoration of a nationhood to the people." He played artfully and even eloquently on the obvious truisms of social inequity. *Here* was the "settlers' town," with its brightly lit streets, asphalt sidewalks, garbage cans to "swallow the leavings"—and its white people. *There* was the town that belonged to the colonized people, "whether it be a native town, a Negro village, a medina, or a reservation." It is a crowded town, a hungry town, "starved of bread, of meat, of shoes, of coal, of light . . . a crouching village, a town on its knees, a town wallowing in the mire. . . ."

Colonialism, in Fanon's view, created a Manichaean world, a world of dualism in which there is no distinction between the physical and the ethical. It is a world divided into compartments, and apartheid is a form of compartmentalization. The native learns to stay within his assigned compartment, but to Fanon, the psychiatrist, the penned-in colonial rollicks in dreams of muscular prowess, of running and climbing absurd heights, of bursting with laughter, of spanning a river in a stride. Eventually, this aggressiveness in his subconscious takes a conscious physical form. "This is the period," Fanon wrote in 1961, "when the niggers beat each other up." Watts, Detroit, and Newark were years away.

For the black militant in America, it is a simple matter to substitute the word "establishment," which Fanon used in the Algerian context, for "settler," and the word "black" for "native." Thus, when Fanon writes, "The settler pits brute force against weight of numbers. . . . His preoccupation with security makes him remind the native out loud that there he alone is master," the American militant nods in knowing agreement and thinks about law and order in the United States.

Not only is the native delimited physically with the help of the army and the police, but, says Fanon, he is also painted as evil. The settler depicts the native society as one without values, the native as a person insensitive to ethics, "corrosive, destroying, and disfiguring," indeed "the absolute evil." While Western values are affirmed, the native is disdained in bestiary terms: "the stink of the native quarter," his "reptilian motions," "the breeding swarms."

"During the period of decolonization, the colonized masses," says Fanon, "must vomit up these values, insult them, mock them." But since colonialism is "violence in its natural state," it will yield only when confronted with greater violence. Fanon doubts that this violence will be born of the native elite and the native intelligentsia. "On the specific question of violence," he writes, "the elite are ambiguous. They are violent in their words and reformist in their attitudes." Equally, he suspects the native intellectual who "clothes his aggressiveness in a barely veiled desire to assimilate himself to the colonial world." Thus, it is left to the peasants, for they have nothing to lose and everything to gain, and it is they, among the exploited, who first discovered that only violence pays.

But even after the violence is over and the colonialist powers have run down their flags and withdrawn their forces, the score, by Fanon's count, is far from settled. In the undeveloped world, the capitalists, considering their record of deportations, massacres, forced labor, and slavery, behaved little better than war criminals. And as Germany was required to indemnify those nations it had plundered, then the newly emerging nations also deserve reparations. "The wealth of the imperialist countries," he says, "is our wealth, too." In the Fanon interpretation, Europe is literally the creation of the Third World, because it was the raw materials, the wealth, the slave labor, and the exploited labor of the Third World that enriched the Old World. "When we hear the head of a European state declare with hand on heart that we must come to the aid of the poor undeveloped nations, we don't tremble with gratitude; we say, 'It's just a reparation which will be paid to us.'"

If the Third World is abandoned, then it must create an autarky of its own. But it was Fanon's earnest hope that the Cold War be ended and with it the plans for nuclearizing the world. Rather, large-scale investments and technical aid must be funneled to undeveloped countries. "The fundamental struggle of our time is not the struggle between socialistic regime and capitalism," he says. The fundamental struggle is to "rehabilitate mankind and make man victorious everywhere, once and for all."

Thus Fanon, the prophet of violence, is also the harbinger of hope. He would redress the grievances and employ violent means to do it, but in the end he is not a nihilist. His call for reconstruction, for a re-acculturation of a liberated people, for a new and liberated life, is clear and unmistakable. "If there is any single source that would rise to the status of being sacred writ for all of the New Left, it is Fanon," says Ross Baker, Rutgers's specialist in black and white attitudes of the New Left. "It is the one source that everyone agrees is a seminal revolutionary work. It's become quasi-biblical. It bridges all kinds of otherwise unbridgeable gaps. In many ways, it is tactfully vague. It doesn't prescribe any course of action any group can hold to."

In truth there is something mystical about it, and Fanon's early death has done nothing to detract from that peculiar magic that, similarly, enveloped the demise of other celebrated youth—Patrice Lumumba, Jimmy Dean, Rupert Brooke, to take a few disparate types across a half century of history. About his life, which began in Martinique and ended in Washington, allegedly with a CIA agent at his bedside, there is just enough Michael Caine mystery to add the proper curlicues of romance and intrigue. Even after he died, the dispatch of his body back to North Africa was surrounded with such international huggermugger that ambassadors were infuriated, chancelleries were outraged, and tremors shook diplomatic halls in Washington, Tunis, Algiers, and the Quai d'Orsay.

Fanon's life and times seem to have been spun out of all the marketable elements of international fascination: psychiatry, violence, sex, war, spies, France, and the Arab intrigues of the Casbah. And yet his emergence as a prophet, if not a saint, seems as much a circumstance of fate as that of Marx, the impoverished German Jew who lived in a garret in London and became the father of international communism.

Fort-de-France, on the French Caribbean isle of Martinique, where Fanon was born in 1925, gleams with the luminescence of a Mediterranean city. Unlike Pointe-a-Pitre in neighboring Guadeloupe or Port-au-Prince in nearby Haiti, there is little that is African about it. With its narrow sunny streets, its little bars and shops, and its own setting by the sea, it is rather like a displaced fragment of Menton or Nice.

Fanon's father, a minor customs official, was both a free thinker and a freemason, factors that, in Catholic Martinique, endowed Frantz with a rich sense of independence and a particular appetite for liberty. Of the three young boys who ran together in the years between twelve and fifteen, Jean Valere is now a juvenile judge at Basse-Terre in Guadeloupe, and Dr. Ernest Wan Ajouhu, a physician, is the newly elected mayor of François, a small banana plantation town half an hour's drive from Fort-de-France.

Fanon's middle-class parents produced four sons and four daughters. Frantz's family expected little more of him than gentlemanly comportment. He showed no political motivations when he went to secondary school, but he was a fighter and he readily joined with Wan Ajouhu and Valere as they aligned themselves with older gangs eager to brawl with rival young Martinicans. They fought those who were in a higher social order, never lower. Valere was interested in music and girls, but Fanon was fascinated by philosophical subjects. His friends nicknamed him "Bergson," after Henri Bergson, the Irish-Jewish philosopher who became a naturalized Frenchman and went on to win the 1927 Nobel Prize in literature.

When France fell in 1940, Fanon was barely fifteen years old; it was, as Fanon was later to view it in psychiatric terms, like "the death of the father." Until 1943, Martinique was occupied by Vichy forces, some 10,000 sailors and soldiers whose leaders were collaborating with the Germans, who held France. Blockaded on a Caribbean island, the Vichy forces took over the bars and the girls, brought their families from France, and installed them in requisitioned houses. While the local populace scrimped for food, the military seemed always to be well provisioned. Fanon was later to say that the Vichy occupiers had acted like "true racists," but Martinicans today are inclined to dismiss this allegation. The resentment arose not from racism but from the association of the new Vichy forces with the Germans.

In 1943, the blockade was lifted, and de Gaulle spoke in London of the treason of the soldiers who had surrendered their swords before they had drawn them. The West Indians were assured that *their* France had not lost the war, but that the Vichy traitors had sold it out. Even before the blockade was lifted, Fanon had slipped away in the dark of night to a neighboring British island and ultimately joined the Free French forces fighting in North Africa and in Europe. It was while in the French army that Fanon was to perceive the first real traits of disparity between white and colonial troops and the broad caste lines between the French settlers of North Africa and the Arab natives.

The liberation of Martinique, to which he returned briefly after the war, was to Fanon the birth of the proletariat. In the first election, two of the three delegates Martinique sent to Paris were Communists. One of these was the poet and teacher Aimé Césaire, in whose behalf Fanon had campaigned. It was Césaire (who is mayor of Fort-de-France and still a delegate to Paris, though no longer on the Communist ticket) who first proposed the revolutionary concept that it is fine and good to be a Negro, a version of negritude also advanced by Léopold Senghor, President of Senegal. "Two centuries of white truth proved this man wrong," Fanon was later to write. "He must be mad, for it was unthinkable that he could be right."

His political consciousness stirring now, but not fully awake, Fanon left for France, determined to become a dentist. Bored to distraction after three weeks, he left for Lyons and ultimately went into medicine. When Wan Ajouhu was to see him in France, Fanon was changed. "He spoke now of will and force. He emphasized that it was necessary for us, as colored people, to do more than others. I thought I was talking to Nietzsche."

While continuing his studies, Fanon wrote *Peau Noire, Masques Blancs*, which appeared in 1952. Of all his four books, it deals most aptly with problems translatable to the American scene; yet it was his second book to be published here, appearing in the Grove Press translation in 1967 under the title *Black Skin, White Masks*. The emotional outpourings, the gift for phrasemaking, the spellbinding use of words and imagery that was so pungently to mark *Wretched of the Earth* nine years later were already here. So was Fanon's outrage. His thesis pursued the concept that the Negro camouflages his blackness by adopting the mask of whiteness. Fanon wrote that for the Antillean, especially the Martinican, the process seemed relatively simple: The West Indian was black, but the Negro was in Africa. The Antillean was French. France had given him Rousseau and Voltaire and all the little island functionaries down to the policeman on the corner. The closer one got to France, the more easily one could adopt the white mask. One way to wish one's way into whiteness was to make love to a white woman. "By loving me she proves that I am worthy of white love," Fanon wrote in *Black Skin, White Masks*. "I am loved like a white man. I am a white man. I marry the culture, white beauty, white whiteness. When my restless hands caress those white breasts, they grasp white civilization and dignity and make them mine."

All this Fanon found hypocritical and wrong. In his wishful view he found the West Indian, after the elections of 1945, to be looking not to white Europe, but, having discovered himself to be a black man as well as a Negro, to have turned at last toward Africa as his true motherland. This transference of ancestral allegiance is not as visible among Martinicans today as it is among those black people of other West Indian islands. Yet it was surely true of Fanon, embittered by the inequities he had seen in the French army and enduring the social posture of a black man making it in a European university, albeit in one of the most difficult of all faculties. Completing his training as a psychiatrist in 1953, he sought a post in Senegal, but his appeal to President Senghor, who had known him in Paris, went unanswered. A post as *chef de service* in Blida, just outside Algiers, opened. Fanon applied and was accepted. Still, as Peter Geismar points out so explicitly in his book *Fanon*, he was indoctrinated with negritude, and he wished to get away from Western racism, but when he arrived in Algiers, he was as yet no revolutionary. This supposition is contested by Cherif Guellal, the former Algerian ambassador to the United States, who still lives in Washington and gives courses on Fanon's writings at the University of Massachusetts. The French Communist party was dominant and militant.

France's troubles were in Indochina, in Madagascar, where the uprising had resulted in huge massacres. Tunisia and Morocco were stirring, and the situation in West Africa was highly volatile. Guellal suggests that such a politically charged person as Fanon could not have done other than to head for Africa. It was, after all, the beginning of the African revolution.

For two years at Blida, Fanon lived a double life, a psychiatrist by day—even treating French police who suffered shock from the tortures they had inflicted—and working for the revolution at night. Arrest, interrogation, and torture of Fanon's staff of doctors and nurses began; ultimately, Fanon's work in behalf of the FLN, the Algerian National Liberation Front, became known to French police.

A letter of resignation to the Resident Minister and a bitter, poetic, emotional "Open Letter to a Frenchman," excoriating the French attitudes toward Arabs, did little to improve the security of Fanon's position. Early in 1957 he was formally expelled from Algeria. To linger longer was to ask for imprisonment, torture, or murder. Guellal, then a young FLN revolutionary, barely twenty; received Fanon in Tunis. "Politically the man was loaded," says Guellal now.

Steaming with zeal, with political concepts and revolutionary stratagems, he strained at the bonds of the strict disciplines imposed upon him by the FLN. In Tunis he began to write for *El Moudjahid*, published by the press services of the FLN. His articles, always unsigned, flailed at the colonial system and the war and torture it produced. The racism that he had discovered in *Black Skin, White Masks* in 1952 and that then he considered perhaps "accidental" had, by 1957, revealed itself to him as "part of the pattern of the exploitation of one group by another." He enraged not merely the French Right but also the French Left, who sought only to reproach those responsible for the frightful excesses of colonialism. To Fanon, this was hypocrisy. There was but one solution and that was "total liberation of the national territory." The Algerian revolution was only a phase in the liberation of Africa.

Sent on missions south of the Sahara, he met Lumumba, Mboya, and Félix Moumié of Cameroon. Of the three, Lumumba and Mboya were assassinated. In a bizarre incident, Moumié, a doctrinaire Leftist and a medical doctor, was allegedly poisoned by a Swiss journalist in the employ of the French Secret Service. Diagnosing his own illness as thalium poisoning slipped to him in a glass of Pernod, Moumié died in two weeks.

Fanon was no less a target. While he was driving on the Moroccan-Algerian border, his jeep was demolished. There are many theories: a car accident, a mine explosion, a bomb planted by Leftists within the revolution, or an assassination attempt by the Red Hand, a vigilante band organized by Rightist settlers in Algeria who had killed the FLN agent in Germany and who had tried twice to shoot a German arms dealer. When Fanon went to Rome to recuperate from the accident, he noticed that a Rome newspaper carried an announcement of his arrival, giving the number of his room at the hospital. Fanon had his room changed, and that night two masked assassins sprayed his originally assigned quarters with a fusillade of bullets.

Assigned in 1960 as ambassador from the provisional Algerian government to Ghana, Fanon toured sub-Saharan Africa. Politically he pushed for Pan-Africanism, but his mission also was to recruit volunteers for a new front against the French, a black army that would attack the French positions in Algeria from the south. Flying from Liberia to Guinea, he grew suspicious and decided to cross the border by jeep. Under his pseudonym of Dr. Omar, Fanon was still on the passenger list when, the next day, the French plane was diverted on its Monrovia-Conakry run, making an unscheduled stop at Abidjan, where the Ivory Coast regime of President Houphouët-Boigny, a former minister-councilor of the French government, was on intimate terms with Paris.

Fanon's dreams of Africa were grand. "What I should like: great lines, great navigation channels through the desert. Subdue the desert, deny it, assemble Africa, create the continent." It was to come to nothing, for somewhere on the mission in the south he developed symptoms of what later was diagnosed as leukemia. The FLN sent him to the Soviet Union for the Myleran treatment, but he was as unimpressed by the Russians' care as he was by their psychiatric methods, which he also examined while there. The Russians

objectively suggested that he try the National Institutes of Health in Washington as the most advanced center for the treatment of his disease. The idea at first was unthinkable to Fanon, and, feeling revived, he met Sartre and de Beauvoir in Rome. He had been working on the manuscript for *The Wretched of the Earth*, and Sartre had agreed to write the preface. To de Beauvoir, he seemed furtive and nervous, "sitting down, getting up, changing his money, collecting his luggage, all with abrupt gestures, agitated facial movements, suspiciously flickering eyes." He talked to Sartre for almost an entire weekend, then left to take a rheumatism treatment at Abano, in northern Italy. When he came back ten days later, he was charming, intelligent, witty. "When I shook his feverish hand in farewell," de Beauvior was to recall in *Force of Circumstances*, "I seemed to be touching the very passion that was consuming him. He communicated this fire to others; when one was with him, life seemed to be a tragic adventure, often horrible, but of infinite worth."

He finished *Wretched of the Earth* and collapsed. The FLN arranged for him to go to the United States for treatment at the National Institutes of Health on October 3, 1961. He was met in Washington by an unlikely companion for a Third World revolutionist: C. Oliver Iselin III, Harvard '51, polo player, avid fox hunter, scion of a social family. Barely thirty, Iselin was with the State Department's Bureau of North African Affairs. Fanon was assigned to his charge, and Iselin saw the family to their quarters in the DuPont Plaza Hotel. Eight days later Fanon was admitted to the National Institutes of Health, where he was to die in December. Iselin accompanied the body back to Tunis and then joined members of the FLN, who, as military escort, buried the remains across the border in a part of rebel-held Algeria.

Seven-and-a-half years later, in February of 1969, Joseph Alsop wrote a column purporting that Frantz Fanon—"the chief black hero of the New Left, as Che Guevara is the chief white hero"—had "almost literally died in the arms of the CIA." His unnamed American companion who had visited him daily at the hotel and the hospital had been in fact a CIA case officer. After Fanon died, so Alsop wrote, the case officer, accompanying the body to its burial place, had been photographed with the FLN leaders, which prompted a fiery French protest to the U.S. Embassy. The American Ambassador, Newbold Walmsley, at least according to Alsop, sent the case officer on the next plane back to "the murky depths of his agency."

While working on his book about Fanon, Peter Geismar spotted the Alsop story and hurried to Washington to examine the evidence. Geismar, who himself was to die of cancer at thirty-one a few weeks after his book went to press, was apparently impressed that Alsop's evidence was solid, for he included the tale as fact in his book. Even more incongruously, Alsop, archdeacon of the Old Right, and Geismar, young herald of the New Left, teamed together to write a story line for a film about Fanon, which Universal Studios wanted for Sidney Poitier. Alsop, who continues to chortle about the irony of Fanon's demise "in the arms of the CIA," says of his venture with Geismar, "It came to naught, but we each made a packet."

Iselin, who is a cousin of Alsop's wife, is back in Washington with the Bureau of African Affairs, after having served in Morocco, Tunisia, Algeria, and the Ivory Coast. He claims no association with the agency, even though he is listed in *Who's Who in the CIA*, a volume produced in East Germany. "So is President Johnson, so is Dean Rusk, so is almost anyone who served overseas," he says. Beyond agreeing that Fanon was charming and brilliant, and that the months from October 1961 to Fanon's death in December of the same year were among the most fascinating of his career, he declines to discuss the case. He is writing his own book, he says, and would like to hold "what little information I have."

Retired in Washington, former Ambassador Walmsley can remember no arrangements about Fanon clearing through him. "The first I knew about it was when this fellow showed up for the funeral on the border. I remember my agitation about not having been informed, and I might have asked him to leave in a hurry." Whether these are the smoke rings of a loyal career officer or a true depiction of the events is arguable. About French outrage, there would seem to be little doubt, for Paris was convinced that America was dabbling in the future of Algerian oil. While it seems improbable that in dispatching Iselin to Algeria Washington would have permitted an obscure junior official to jeopardize U.S. foreign policy, the appearance of this young Virginia aristocrat, whatever his actual affiliation might have been, was an indication that the United States was not reluctant to deal with the FLN. Overtures of material aid had already been tendered by private American oil interests to the Algerian rebels as a goodwill gesture that might reap future benefits were the insurrectionists ultimately victorious.

If official Washington was the first Western regime outside France to recognize the existence and possibly the importance of Fanon and his preachments, the New Left in America had only to wait for the appearance of the English-language translation of *The Wretched of the Earth*, which Grove press first issued in 1965. The effects, as one surveys them now, were impressive. Although Fanon is no handbook for revolution, his ideas and concepts are imbedded in the explosive prose dropped into the text, especially in the long introductory treatise on violence. They were found there by Bobby Seale, who recalls in *Seize the Time* that he had read *Wretched of the Earth* six times and "knew Fanon was right" by the time Seale met Huey Newton. In those pre-Black Panther days, Newton was trying to form some sort of organization but had never read Fanon; so Seale decided he had to sell the theories to Newton, who then was more interested in day-to-day survival than in revolutionary enlightenment. Seale arrived at Newton's with a copy:

> *So I brought Fanon over one day. That brother got to reading Fanon, and, man, let me tell you, when Huey got ahold of Fanon and read Fanon (I had always been running down about how we need this organization, that organization, but never anything concrete), Huey'd be thinking. Hard. We would sit down with* Wretched of the Earth *and talk and go over another section or chapter of Fanon, and Huey would explain it in depth.... Huey was one for implementing things, and I guess this is where the Black Panther Party really started.*

An oft-recalled quotation is the statement made by Dan Watts of *Liberation* magazine to Jimmy Breslin of the Chicago *Sun Times* after the riots in Newark and Detroit. It was wrong to think that all the rioting brothers were old wine-sopped ne'er-do-wells. They were all ready to die for something because they had all read Fanon. "You'd better get this book," Watts told Breslin. "Every brother on a rooftop can quote Fanon."

CORE's Roy Innis disputes that assessment as concocted romanticism. "I was in Harlem during the first riot, and some of the brothers on the roof wouldn't have considered reading Fanon or anybody else. They were concerned with redressing grievances. I have my doubts whether that Fanon-reading crowd was on any roof. I'm sure they weren't on the streets. That's too close to reality.

"It is unfortunate that Fanon is used as romantic escape. You don't have to take any action, all you have to do is walk with a couple of Fanons under your arm. That's your badge of courage. That becomes your gun and your revolt. You can go home to your living room and fight the battle right there. Or go see *The Battle of Algiers*. That's really doin' it. And maybe if you're a little bit psychopathic, then maybe you'll knock off somebody and be on trial in New Haven, or maybe you knock some guys off in Harlem, but then you have to be more than romantic, you have to be a little bit stupid and also a little bit psychopathic."

Besides Panthers, what bothers Innis are the campus revolutionaries, "the young blacks on campus who spout Fanon because it is good escapism. They use it to support all kinds of spurious theories they concoct, failing to recognize that Fanon was talking about the Algerian struggle against the majority when the oppressor was not in his own homeland. He was in the home of the oppressed. They don't know how to use Fanon's early experience in Martinique, where the oppressed were the majority. You can use a lot of his formulations and his insight, but one must keep in mind the difference when applied to America and American color problems."

During the frantic revolutionary episodes at Columbia, Fanon was invoked again and again by the graduate students who were giving ad hoc counter-courses to the formal ones being conducted by the Establishment inside the halls. Radical sociology is now an accepted preachment, and a number of university departments teach it. Says William Wilson, a black associate professor of sociology at the University of Massachusetts, "Fanon's tre-

mendous impact on revolutionary nationalism suggests to a lot of scholars that black studies should somehow deal with the whole philosophy of revolution. Many black militants now feel it is necessary to modify black studies programs to include Third World courses." Colleges from Cornell to San Francisco State have Third World courses.

What does all this mean to America? Speaking from Algiers, that fountainhead of Fanon, Cleaver recently said, "Violence in the United States is inevitable. I think what Fanon will do is make that violence more intelligent and more directed and therefore more specific and probably less than it might have been, because it won't be wasted, it will be controlled violence." But Fanon recognized, too, that violence carried to its ultimate conclusion means worldwide holocaust. For him, revolution was only a means to throw off European oppression and to commence a regeneration, as Guellal says, "to reassert the membership of the colonized man, of the damned of the earth, within the human family."

There is a question whether the people of the Third World are in position akin to that of blacks in America. The searing query, especially among militant blacks, is whether we are two intermingled nations or one. Going by the writings of American blacks of two decades ago and a meager personal knowledge, Fanon seems to see a difference between black-white interaction in America and Europe's colonial posture. Black and white in America may build the foundation for a social regeneration and, as Guellal has pointed out, "to Fanon, revolution meant, in the final analysis, regeneration." It may be important to comprehend that "the pediment of his statue in the pantheon of Third World revolutionaries is pretty firmly anchored," as Professor Ross Baker has so eloquently put it. But it is also important to understand that as a revolutionist and a practitioner of violence, Fanon was not teaching a religion of nihilism. He was a builder and, in his last words, a voice of inspirational constructivism. "Come then, comrades," he wrote at the end of *Wretched of the Earth*. "We must shake off the heavy darkness in which we were plunged. . . . The new day which is already at hand must find us firm, prudent, and resolute." He desperately urged the Third World to find a new pathway. "Leave this

Europe," he implored, "where they are never done talking of Man, yet murder men everywhere they find them, at the corner of one of their own streets, in all the corners of the globe. For centuries, they have stifled almost the whole of humanity in the name of so-called spiritual experience. Look at them swaying between atomic and spiritual disintegration."

To imitate Europe is to spawn another United States of America, which "succeeded so well" in imitating its motherland that it "became a monster in which the taints, the sickness, the inhumanity of Europe have grown to appalling dimensions."

If the Third World wishes to respond to the expectations of the people of Europe, it will prove useless to send them back a reflection of their society and their thought "with which from time to time they (themselves) feel immeasurably sickened." Fanon's final printed words to the world were a supplication, ar exhortation to turn over a new leaf, to work out new concepts. "Humanity is waiting for something from us other than ... an imitation ... an obscene caricature...."

"We must try," he wrote, "to set afoot a new man," and it is those words that come booming back across the ten years of time since he set them down, read the final proofs, and then expired.

THE liberation of WOMEN

In the early 1960s, a social movement that had as its goal the "liberation" of women first appeared. It was greeted by guffaws and male remarks concerning "what these women really needed." Most women, too, were mildly amused by what they thought were the exaggerated ravings of a few masculine and, no doubt, frustrated old spinsters. But for many women, the initial amusement changed to a cynical grimace when they realized that the leaders of the movement were not simply raving but were making points that were, unfortunately, true. That the movement has gained momentum, rather than faded away, indicates that it has tapped a reservoir of real resentment in women—a resentment that will not be appeased until women gain the status of human beings. Donald McDonald, the executive editor of The Center Magazine, *takes an in-depth look at the goals and the gains of Women's Liberation.*

□□□

In the introduction to her book *The Second Sex* written in 1949, Simone de Beauvoir noted that woman traditionally has been defined only with reference to man, not as she is in herself. Man is the "Subject, the Absolute—she is the Other. The category of the *Other* is as primordial as consciousness itself." Woman, a "free and autonomous being like all human crea-

Reprinted with permission from the May issue of *The Center Magazine*, a publication of the Study of Democratic Institutions in Santa Barbara, California.

tures, nevertheless finds herself living in a world where men compel her to assume the status of the Other. They propose to stabilize her as object...."

In 1963, Betty Friedan wrote *The Feminine Mystique* because, "gradually, without seeing it clearly for quite a while, I came to realize that something is very wrong with the way American women are trying to live their lives today.... There [is] a strange discrepancy between the reality of our lives as women and the image to which we [are] trying to conform, the image that I... call the feminine mystique."

And in 1970, Germaine Greer wrote *The Female Eunuch* because "we know what we are, but know not what we may be, or what we might have been."

The object of these women, as the object of women's liberation, is twofold. It is to discover the nature of woman and to free women so that they may fulfill themselves.

No small part of the complexity and difficulty of this task is that these goals—discovery and liberation—are also, in relation to each other, means. In order to discover their nature, women are saying, they must be liberated not only from the legal, occupational, and educational barriers in their lives but also from the false self-concepts they have acquired in one way or another—from sexually, rather than humanly, oriented socialization and acculturation processes; from laws, customs, and traditions locked into and handed down by male-dominated societies; from parents, from the men in their lives, from counsellors reflecting uncritically a patriarchal order of things. In this case, women's liberation is obviously a means to the end of self-discovery and identity.

But, women are saying, it is no less true that in order for a woman to know which self-concepts she should liberate herself from because they are false and which she should retain because they are true, she must already know something about her nature as woman; she must know in good part what she "may be" or "might have been." In this sense, self-knowledge is a means to the achievement of ultimate liberation.

The discovery and liberation task is further complicated by the feverish nature of the political, emotional, and psychosocial climate in which the work must be done. The rage and resentment released by a raised consciousness of injustice are indispensable reformist motivations. But they can also blur perceptions and cloud the judgment.

Too, in an age when the politics of problems is crucial, or—what amounts to the same thing—when the politics, because of long smoldering frustrations, *seems* to be crucial, liberationists will be tempted to suppress or deny facts that are politically inconvenient, and to ignore or dismiss arguments and hypotheses that could add clarity and strength to the movement

In a recent article on women and psychoanalysts in *The New York Times Magazine*, Ann Roiphe wrote: "I, like many other women, am often buffeted about by what I read. I am furious when rhetoric of either the right or the left, while promising me new possibilities, turns its back on reality, leading me down some new thorny path where I'll get snarled again by someone's lie.... The life-styles that we will certainly be developing depend on our knowledge and expectations for ourselves as men and women, and it is extremely important that the dialogues now going on reveal, not conceal, the truth, not freeze it in one or another political posture."

This, then, is an effort to get at the truth of women's liberation, both as a movement in itself and as a reflection of the present condition of women in America and what might be done about it.

I will rely on the writings of both men and women. I agree with John Stuart Mill, who said: "The knowledge men can acquire of women, even as they have been and are, with-out reference to what they might be, is wretchedly imperfect and superficial, and will always be so until women themselves have told us all they have to tell." But to consult only women when writing about women would be to invite some of the same disabilities that would afflict a dominantly male approach to this theme. Men, too, can write accurately about women. And when they do not, the refutation of their errors, as women have discovered, can be instructive.

But indubitably what women have to say is of greatest value. Women can speak for themselves. Even when they disagree, their disagreements are expressed within a shared experience; they disagree in the perception and interpretation of the meaning of their experience, not over the fact of the experience. Any effort to understand the phenomenon of feminism which did not rest decisively on the testimony of women would be suspect—and legitimately so—as inauthentic. Way back in 1964, Erik Erikson acknowledged that "feminist suspicion watches over any man's attempt to help define the uniqueness of womanhood." Yet, he said, "It still seems to be amazingly hard for the vast majority of women to say clearly what they feel most deeply, and to find the right words for what to them is most acute and actual, without saying too much or too little, and without saying it with defiance or apology.... Women are tempted quickly to go back to 'their place' whenever they feel out of place."

Erikson's observation may have been accurate—but it would have been no less accurate to observe that the vast majority of either sex finds it difficult to express clearly what it feels most deeply. In any case, eight years and countless consciousness-raising sessions after Erikson's comment, many women have said clearly what it is they feel and what justifies their feeling.

Of course, there has never been a shortage of articulate women, at least not in the literature of liberation. In her book *A Room of One's Own* Virginia Woolf calls to our attention what Lady Winchilsea, a seventeenth-century poet, had to say:

> Alas! a woman that attempts the pen,
> Such a presumptuous creature is esteemed,
> The fault can by no virtue be redeemed,
> They tell us we mistake our sex and way;

Good breeding, fashion, dancing, dressing,
play,
Are the accomplishments we should desire;
To write, or read, or think, or to enquire,
Would cloud our beauty, and exhaust our
time,
And interrupt the conquests of our prime,
Whilst the dull manage of a servile house
Is held by some our utmost art and use.

Margaret Cavendish of Newcastle, a contemporary of Lady Winchilsea, and, like her, a poet whose promise seems to have been narrowed by rage, cried out that "Women live like Bats or Owls, labour like Beasts, and die like Worms...."

The shrill complaints of a disgruntled few? Perhaps. But I keep remembering Mill's comment that "in history, as in traveling, men usually see only what they already had in their minds." One of the great accomplishments of today's women's liberationists is their gathering up of past writings of feminists and, by combining them with current works, forcing all of us to see that what is happening today may be the leading edge of a long and honorable tradition.

That the tradition has always raised the same questions is a measure of their importance. They constitute what Beauvoir has called "the drama of woman ... the conflict between the fundamental aspirations of every subject (ego)—who always regards the self as the essential—and the compulsions of a situation in which she is the inessential." Beauvoir's questions are both the theme and a variation on the theme of The Woman Question: "How can a human being in woman's situation attain fulfillment? What roads are open to her? Which are blocked? How can independence be recovered in a state of dependency? What circumstances limit woman's liberty and how can they be overcome?"

VITALITY OF THE MOVEMENT

It is perhaps pointless to try to pin down the exact date when the present women's liberation movement began. The National Organization for Women (by no means *the* representative of all of women's liberation, but perhaps the best known, most efficiently organized and comprehensive group) held its first national conference in Washington in 1967. At the time of the great mass demonstration of women on the streets of New York in August, 1970 (marking the fiftieth anniversary of American women's winning the right to vote), a *New York Times* writer said that Friedan probably started the movement in 1963 with *The Feminine Mystique.*

Certainly by the end of the nineteen-sixties what looked like a movement was under way. And today the women's protest has all the characteristics of a movement: the untidiness and initial diffuseness of a movement (many voices, many groups); its own "N.A.A.C.P." (NOW) and its crazies (SCUM, Society for Cutting Up Men); street-theater people and "zap" actions; internal conflicts over goals and strategies; quarrels between personalities; conservative, moderate, and radical divisions; and serious differences as to what constitutes an authentically feminist sexual life-style.

Sheila Tobias, a Wesleyan University administrator, thinks that the movement now faces a most difficult choice. If it rests content with getting, say, an equal-rights amendment to the Constitution it will repeat the experience of the suffrage movement which "disappeared without a trace" after women won the right to vote. On the other hand, if women's liberation confronts what she calls the "psychic issues," it will then risk "alienating the women who have made their life choice of marriage and motherhood."

For the moment, these clouds are no bigger than a woman's hand on the horizon. The movement is moving. It is in its springtime. The evidence of vitality abounds:

The mass media, perhaps skeptical at first, have stayed to probe, investigate, and copiously document.

The equal-rights constitutional amendment, which had been introduced in the House of Representatives each year for twenty-three years and each year had been ritually buried by Emanuel Celler, chairman of the Judiciary Committee, was voted for by the House, 346 to 15, in 1970, and again in 1971, 354 to 23. The Senate has also voted for the amendment which must now be ratified by three-fourths of the state legislatures.

MS., a 128-page national Women's Liberation monthly magazine, has been started and its first issue, running to several hundred thousand copies, immediately became a collector's item. Many local and regional feminist publications have been started.

On one crowded weekend recently in Southern California, Gloria Steinem spoke on the movement to two sold-out, all-women audiences, in San Diego and Los Angeles; she appeared on a Los Angeles television documentary on "Womanhouse"; and she was the object of admiring treatment in a story in the Los Angeles *Times:* "Having finally given her their trust, it is doubtful if American women will permit Gloria Steinem to go off and write stories in her brownstone. 'If I could be one person other than myself, she's the one I'd like to be,' said one young woman."

Benjamin Spock is lecturing and writing on the theme "I Harbored Sexism." And he has rewritten what he acknowledges to be the "most objectionable part" of his latest book *Decent and Indecent* eliminating the gratuitous and oversimplified statements he had made about sex and sex roles: "I had written them three to five years ago, when there was no liberation movement.... I [have] changed my thinking a good deal since."

A growing shelf of feminist literature is appearing from book publishers: new material, reprints, and anthologies of both old and new pieces (from Abigail Adams to Shulamith Firestone).

A small sample, yet enough to suggest that Steinem may have been right when she said, "The woman's movement isn't a Hula-Hoop, it isn't going to be over."

But the movement still encounters two objections that are closely linked, though it seems to be encountering them far less frequently than it did as recently as two years ago. The first is that most American women are satisfied with their lives, therefore the movement does not speak for them. The second is that only neurotic, embittered women who have made a failure of their lives are attracted to the women's liberation movement. (Actually current polls show that most American women now favor efforts to improve their status, whereas a year ago the majority opposed such efforts.)

The liberationists' offhand reply to the first

objection is that if a woman is indeed happy, if she is satisfied with her life, then women's liberation has nothing directly to offer to her, although she might entertain the possibility of whether she has any moral responsibility to help her less fortunate sisters. A more analytical and circumspect response includes these points:

The proportion of those in any "under class" who are imaginative and sensitive enough to conceive of more human alternatives has always been small at the outset of any liberationist movement.

If women have been conditioned from birth to adjust their human potential and aspirations to a socially approved, "feminine" life-style which is narrower than, and considerably beneath, their potential, it is not surprising that many of them will settle for that and call it satisfaction. For many, the adjusting continues into their college years and beyond. Women who are excited in the freshman year by the possibility of entering professional and research fields, by the time they are juniors lower their aspirations to more "practical" fields (teaching, nursing, social work, secretarial-administrative work) which may be far below their abilities.

In any event, if women's liberation indeed lacks a substantial basis for its grievances, if social, economic, political, and cultural conditions do not really inhibit women in any significant way, then the movement will collapse and will deserve to collapse.

The objection that only chronic malcontents are attracted to the women's liberation movement has been the standard objection to all reform and protest movements. The labor-union movement, the civil-rights movement, the youth antiwar movement, even the ecology movement were all charged, at the outset, with being simply the work of a few outside "agitators" and inside "troublemakers."

And if some women in the movement are neurotic, their presence may be evidence not of their inability to adjust to a healthy society but rather of the need for a liberation movement which will remove the dehumanizing, neuroticizing conditions in an unhealthy society. Seymour Halleck, a University of Wisconsin psychiatrist, has criticized his fellow psychiatrists who, reflecting community standards, tend to classify as "abnormal" and "aberrant" those patients who wish to change obviously bad social conditions.

Some of the angriest women in the feminist movement are disillusioned dropouts from the New Left—they discovered that New Left egalitarianism was a male-only commodity which was not for export to the female sex. Nor will many soon forgive or forget Stokeley Carmichael's remark that "the only position for women in SNCC is prone."

The feminist movement had always been strongest when it was linked with other social reform movements. Although there was no comparable feminist movement to ally itself with the youth, antiwar, civil-rights, and New Left movements of the nineteen-sixties, those movements were heavily populated with women. It was inevitable that, in "speaking truth to power" on all these fronts, the women would begin putting liberationist questions to themselves, and that they would do so not only within the framework of a potential women's movement but on a scale bounded only by the dimensions of life itself: Who are we? How free are we? How much equality of opportunity do we have? What must be done?

More than a hundred years ago, John Stuart Mill thought he discerned a deep-running historical and—he seemed to suggest—irreversible, trend in the direction of equality between the sexes. If he discerned rightly, that may help explain the emergence today of a women's movement which will no longer tolerate the postponement of equality. Mill said:

> "Existing moralities . . . are mainly fitted to a relation of command and obedience. Yet command and obedience are but unfortunate necessities of human life: society in equality is its normal state. Already in modern life, and more and more as it progressively improves, command and obedience become exceptional facts in life, equal association its general rule. The morality of the first ages rested on the obligation to submit to power; that of the ages next following, on the right of the weak to the forbearance and protection of the strong. How much longer is one form of society and life to content itself with the morality made for another? We have had the morality of submission, and the morality of chivalry and generosity; the time is now come for the morality of justice."

Let us look at the present condition of women, measure it by the requirements of a "morality of justice," and note the extent to which woman is subject to the "compulsions of a situation in which she is the inessential."

THE PRESENT CONDITION OF WOMEN

Alice Rossi writes in *Women in America* that "for the first time in the history of any known society, motherhood has become a full-time occupation for adult women." She adds that it is a "paradox of our social history" that this has happened in "precisely the era when objectively [motherhood] could, and perhaps should, be a part-time occupation for a short phase of a woman's life span."

Because of her increased longevity and the smaller size of her family, the modern mother needs to devote a much smaller proportion of her total life to the rearing of her children. And because of labor-saving devices in the home and the transfer to factories and food-processing plants of many activities formerly done in the home for both family use and profit (weaving, sewing, spinning, candling, brewing, baking, churning, preserving), the modern mother finds neither her time nor her interests filled by housework. What the twentieth-century middle-class American woman finds instead is the "boredom and solitude of spending ten-hour days alone with babies and young children." Under these circumstances, the woman who either does not prepare herself in college or other training program for an occupation or profession or who withdraws from an occupation or profession for which she has been prepared (in the often frustrated hope of reëntering the world of work when her youngest child has grown up) is unhappy with herself, often becomes uninteresting to her husband, and almost inevitably over-invests herself in the lives of her children, at *their* expense.

"I suspect," Rossi writes, "that the things women do for and with their children have been needlessly elaborated to make motherhood a full-time job. Unfortunately, in this very process the child's struggle for autonomy and independence, for privacy and the right to worry things through for himself are subtly and pervasively reduced by the omnipresent mother."

John Stuart Mill observed that "an active and energetic mind, if denied liberty, will seek for power; refused the command of itself, it will assert its personality by attempting to control others. To allow to any human beings no existence of their own but what depends on others, is giving far too high a premium on bending others to their purposes. Where liberty cannot be hoped for, and power can, power becomes the grand object of human desire; those to whom others will not leave the undisturbed management of their own affairs, will compensate themselves, if they can, by meddling for their own purposes with the affairs of others."

Rossi points out that "in a large proportion of cases, the etiology of mental illness is linked to inadequacy in the mother-child relationship." The mother-son relationship has been studied rather closely (because of the high incidence of psychoneurotic discharges of American military men in World War II which could be traced to the young men's overly dependent relationships to their mothers). But "dependence, immaturity, and ego diffusion have been characteristic of daughters as well as sons ... [and] it is the failure of the mother which perpetuates the cycle from one generation to the next, affecting sons and daughters alike."

Noting the pervasive permeation of psychoanalytic thinking in our society, Rossi says that, although psychoanalysts differ widely among themselves, "when their theories are popularized by social scientists, marriage and family counselors, writers, social critics, pediatricians, and mental-health specialists, there emerges a common and conservative image of the woman's role. It is the traditional image—the woman who finds complete self-fulfillment in her exclusive devotion to marriage and parenthood." The woman who wishes to make a different choice is made to feel guilty, defensive, apologetic, somehow suffering from an emotional disturbance.

"Psychiatric counselors of college students," Rossi writes, "frequently have as their chief task that of helping their young patients to free themselves from the entangling web of dependence upon their parents, primarily their mothers, and encouraging them to form stable independent lives of their own. In other words, if the patient is eighteen years old, the analyst tries to help her free herself from her mother, but if the next patient is twenty-five years old with young children at home, the analyst tells her the children would suffer emotional damage if she left them on a regular basis to hold down a job. The very things which would reduce the excessive dependency of children before it becomes a critical problem are discouraged by the counselor or analyst during the years when the dependence is being formed."

If the condition of middle-class underoccupied, full-time mothers is uniquely non-self-fulfilling and potentially damaging to their relationship with their husbands and children, the fate of the forty-three per cent of mothers working outside the home is no better but for reasons of a socio-economic nature. Professors Urie Bronfrenbrenner of Cornell and Jerome Bruner of Harvard, in a recent public criticism of President Nixon for his vetoing of the Child Development Act of 1971, disclosed that four and a half million mothers with children under six years old (totaling six million) are in the nation's work force; many of them are living in poverty or near-poverty; many are without a husband. Most of them desperately "need some help if normal family life is to be sustained." What they need most is massive federal funding of day-care centers for the millions of preschool children not enrolled in a nursery school.

When one turns to the conditions of employment for women, one finds that the "morality of justice" is ill-served indeed. A sampling of the evidence suggests the dimensions of the inequities:

In 1968, the median salary for full-time, year-around workers was $7,870 for white males; $5,314 for nonwhite males; $4,580 for white women; and $3,487 for nonwhite women. After four years of college, women earn 57.1 per cent as much as men with the same amount of education ($7,396 median annual income for women; $12,960 for men). A woman needs a college degree to earn more than a man with an eighth-grade education.

An official of the U.S. Equal Employment Opportunity Commission has charged that women workers at the Bank of America, the world's largest private bank, are paid less for doing the same jobs as men; that they are discriminated against in hiring, job classifications, training, and promotions.

After President Nixon vetoed the Child

Development Act of 1971 Professors Bronfren-brenner and Bruner said that Mr. Nixon's pre-ferred bill (H.R. 1) which he called "my work-fare legislation," is a "put-them-to-work-bill," not a child development bill, and would meet the needs of only five per cent of the children affected.

A report filed in January, 1972 by the Department of Health, Education and Welfare asserts that women are discriminated against in virtually every aspect of American life. H.E.W. acknowledged that sex discrimination exists in its own department: women are sixty-three per cent of the H.E.W. work force but hold only fourteen per cent of the top jobs.

A sex-discrimination suit brought this year against the University of California at Berkeley by faculty members and graduate students noted that only three per cent of the 1,087 tenured faculty positions at Berkeley are held by women, despite the fact that forty-two per cent of the undergraduates, twenty-six per cent of the graduate students, and nineteen per cent of the non-tenured faculty are women. Women in the U.C. management program of the office of the president earn on an average eight thousand dollars per year less than equally qualified and similarly situated males. Only two per cent of the full professors at Berkeley are women.

Seven per cent of American physicians are women; three per cent of lawyers are women; and one per cent of engineers are women.

Although fifteen per cent of graduate degrees granted by Harvard University in recent years have gone to women, only six of the four hundred and twenty-one tenured members of the Harvard arts and sciences faculty are women.

The wives of some male faculty members get maternity benefits at certain universities; women faculty members at the same univer-sities are denied such benefits.

In 1970, of 8,750 judges sitting, three hundred were women (most of them on county courts). There was one woman in the Senate and there were ten women in the House.

Women next ask us to look at the web of interpersonal relationships in our society, at the attitudes, laws, customs revealed in them. If we do, they tell us, we will find women regarded as object, principally as sexual object,

rather than as a person who happens to be female. Again, the evidence is impressive.

Unfortunately, the term "sex object" has been so often pressed into service as a slogan and as a kind of shorthand cipher standing for a thickly textured reality that it has been emptied of all but its genitalized-pleasure meaning. At its roots, it means that woman is instrumental to man. Their relationship is not the "I-Thou" of two persons equal in worth and dignity, but of subject-object, dominant-subordinate, stronger-weaker, superior-inferior. The relationship is sexist rather than human. And even when a man and woman fall in love, the radical feminists argue, the possibility of an "I-Thou" equality is all but defeated in a sexist culture.

One way to see the dehumanization accom-plished by a sexist view of woman is to reverse the roles, put man into the position in which everything he says and does is evaluated according to his sex. Elsewhere in this report I have inserted just such an enlightening exer-cise by Dorothy L. Sayers.

In a society in which woman is *other*, the dependent *inessential*, it is not surprising that the language we invent reflects and reinforces the point. "Man" stands for the race, as does "mankind." Books addressed to the human situation carry male titles: *Problematic Man; Irrational Man; Mirror for Man; The Abolition of Man; The Future of Man; One-Dimensional Man; Man Alone*. The significance of this usage is obviously not that their users are intentional male chauvinists and that women should go to the barricades over language. It is that the identification of man as absolute and as subject has so permeated our society that even its most critical thinkers adopt as their own the lan-guage of that identification.

Perhaps the best one-volume collection of reports and studies of the contemporary scene is *Woman in Sexist Society* (Basic Books, Inc.), edited by Vivian Gornick and Barbara K. Moran. Its thirty essays, all by women (mostly professors, editors, writers), not only report and analyze, but also convey a sense of what it means for a woman to be born into, live, and die in a society in which at every turn and in countless ways, subtle and unsubtle, she learns that her identity is not, as the philosophers say, substantial, it is accidental; it is contingent, not necessary; it is not woman, it is non-man. In an essentially sexist society, whatever power women can achieve is often accomplished on man's terms: women must trade on their sexual favors, flatter, cling, manipulate, use cunning, torture their bodies to keep them "looking pretty." But such power is neither autonomy nor equality. It is, as one woman's liberationist has said, Uncle-Tomming.

And through television, women in a sexist society are bombarded with endless messages by advertisers who portray woman as a somewhat demented person agonizingly obsessed with looking pretty and smelling good to catch a man, and then similarly obsessed with becoming Superwife whose laundry, dishes, kitchen floor, windows, and toilet bowl are so spotless they will evoke envy from the similarly demented housewife next door and a pat on the back from the master when he comes home at night.

WHY HAS THIS HAPPENED?

The question that must be faced is, Why? Why have men wished to dominate women? Why has this state of affairs persisted so long? We shall see, I think, that we cannot answer these questions without also raising fundamental questions about the nature of woman.

Proximate answers are helpful, but not totally satisfying. Women are paid less than men for the same work because that is a profitable arrangement for an employer. Advertisers have typecast them almost exclusively as matrimonial prospects, brides, and housewives-turned-lifetime-cleaning-women because that moves the merchandise. But these forces do not cause. They exploit, perpetuate, and reinforce what they find in society.

Other explanations—women throughout most of human history have been isolated from each other and have not been able to organize a sustained reform movement; women, lacking economic independence, have had no choice but to accept what they dared not resist; many women had perhaps neither the energy nor the capacity under severe stress conditions to imagine a better alternative—all are important but still proximate, they still leave one speculating at more basic levels.

A deeper explanation lies in something Virginia Woolf has commented on, "the enormous importance to a patriarch who has to conquer, who has to rule, of feeling that great numbers of people, half the human race indeed, are by nature inferior to himself. It must indeed be one of the chief sources of his power.... Women have served all these centuries as looking glasses possessing the magic and delicious power of reflecting the figure of man at twice its natural size. Without that power probably the earth would still be swamp and jungle. The glories of all our wars would be unknown.... Mirrors are essential to all violent and heroic action. That is why Napoleon and Mussolini both insist[ed] so emphatically upon the inferiority of women, for if they were not inferior, they would cease to enlarge."

And Mill asks how many thousands of men there must be in every society who "without being in a legal sense malefactors in any other respect, because in every other quarter their aggressions meet with resistance, indulge the utmost habitual excesses of bodily violence towards the unhappy wife, who alone, at least of grown persons, can neither repel nor escape from their brutality...."

But one must probe more deeply still into what Woolf has called "the dangerous and fascinating subject of the psychology of the other sex." Seymour Halleck believes that an important psychological reason for men "fearing women as an equal" is that "if a man is to enjoy the sex act he must have a sense of security that he is not being called upon to perform, that he is not being judged as to his sexual abilities. As long as women are viewed as second-class citizens, the male need not be too preoccupied with his potency."

Would full equality end up, as some traditionalists maintain, by feminizing men, masculinizing women, and increasing the possibility of homosexuality? Alice Rossi thinks not. "If the view of the sex act presupposes a dominant male actor and a passive female subject," Rossi writes, "then it is indeed the case that full sex equality would probably be the death knell of this traditional sexual relationship. Men and women who participate as equals in their parental and occupational and social roles will complement each other sexually in the same way, as essentially equal partners, and not as an ascendant male and a submissive female. This does not mean, however, that equality in nonsexual roles necessarily de-eroticizes the sexual one. The enlarged base of shared experience can, if anything, heighten the salience of sex qua sex."

Rossi writes that many psychoanalysts defend the traditional sex roles—male dominant, female submissive—but that Abraham Maslow is one of the few psychologists who has actually explored the connections between sex experience and the conception of self among women. In one of his important studies, Maslow found, "contrary to traditional notions of femininity and psychoanalytic theories, that the more 'dominant' the woman, the greater her enjoyment of sexuality, the greater her ability to give herself freely in love" because she was able to be completely herself.

Rossi's definition of sexuality equality: "A socially androgynous conception of the roles of men and women, in which they are equal and similar in such spheres as intellectual, artistic, political, and occupational interests and participation; complementary only in those spheres dictated by physiological differences between the sexes."

But what accounts for the tenacity with which so many psychoanalysts and psychologists resist sexual equality and cling to the traditional definition of sex roles? What accounts for it, in great part, is one man, Sigmund Freud.

According to Freud, woman's nature and her fulfillment are dictated by her body. "Anatomy is destiny," is the title of the by now familiar Freudian scenario. Freud held that when the little girl, comparing her anatomy with that of a boy's, discovers she has no penis, she develops penis-envy, a castration complex, and a resentment of her mother for failing to provide her with that organ. Moreover, before puberty, the clitoris—an inferior substitute penis—is the site of the girl's sexual pleasure. But "with the change from girlhood to feminity, the clitoris must give up to the vagina its sensitivity and, with it, its importance. . . ."

Not only is the vagina the proper locus for woman's sexual pleasure, Freud said, but the act of conception and giving birth is the only way in which she can release her sexual energy and fulfill her "unsatisfied wish" for a penis. This wish "should be converted into a wish

to have a child. . . . The girl's libido slips into place by means—there is really no other way to put it—of the equation 'penis equals child.' "

Thus, as Richard Gilman has pointed out, even motherhood, which we "understandably think of as a uniquely female capacity and accomplishment, is indissolubly linked in Freudian thought with woman's inferiority to man."

From his anatomy-is-destiny theme, Freud drew a number of conclusions, all of them underlining the inferior nature of the woman. Because she has to put aside her "childish masculinity" and "change her leading erotogenic zone," she is more liable to be neurotic. Because she has to curb her aggressiveness and be submissive, she is more liable to be masochistic. (Freud indeed asserts flatly that masochism is "truly feminine.") Because of her "wounded" condition (since, without a penis, she thinks of herself as a "mutilated" man), she is more likely to feel shame. According to Freud, woman's shame should not be confused with the virtue of modesty; it is simply her device for the "concealment of genital deficiency."

Gilman quotes the psychiatrist Robert Jay Lifton, who said: "Every great thinker has at least one blind spot. Freud's was women." But at what cost to women and to their relationship with men ever since!

Simone de Beauvoir casts doubt on the universality of penis-envy in women, but, in any case, she says, "the little girl's covetousness, when it exists, results from a previous evaluation of virility. Freud takes this for granted, when it should be accounted for." In other words, what the little girl covets is not so much the penis but all the privileges that her family and her social world confer upon those who possess one.

Naomi Weisstein casts doubt not only on the penis-envy theory, but on Freud's entire methodology. In her essay, "Psychology Constructs the Female," in *Woman in Sexist Society*, she points out that what Freud thought constituted evidence confirming his theories actually fell short of the most minimal conditions of scientific rigor. "In *The Sexual Enlightenment of Children*, the classic document that is supposed to demonstrate empirically the existence of a castration complex and its connection to a phobia, Freud based his analysis on the reports of the father of the little boy, himself in therapy and a devotee of Freudian theory. I really do not have to comment further on the contamination in this kind of evidence."

Erik Erikson maintains, in *The Woman in America*, that Freud's observations of infantile and later sexuality in the female were accurate and that their "psychic truth can be shown by psychoanalysis," but he adds that the truths obtained under the special circumstances of psychoanalysis (the "venting in free association of hidden resentments and repressed traumata") are only "partial truths within a theory of feminine development, which would assume the early relevance of the productive interior [of the woman] and would thus allow for a shift of theoretical emphasis from the loss of an external organ to a sense of vital inner potential; from a hateful contempt of the mother to a solidarity with her and other women; from a 'passive' renunciation of male activity to the purposeful and competent activity of one endowed with ovaries and a uterus...."

Warning that one cannot "entirely reconstruct the ego's normal functions from an understanding of its dysfunctions" and that all vital conflicts are not necessarily neurotic conflicts, Erikson states what he calls a "post-Freudian position," one that is being increasingly found in the literature of psychosexuality, which some feminist critics tend to ignore in their dismissal of Erikson: "The complexes and conflicts unearthed by psychoanalysis in its first breakthrough to human nature are recognized as existing; they do threaten to dominate the developmental and accidental crises of life. But the freshness and wholeness of experience and the opportunities arising with a resolved crisis can, in an ongoing life, transcend trauma and defense."

The key phrase is "in an ongoing life." If anatomy is crucial, no less crucial is the social, familial, and cultural ambience within which the growing girl learns and is led to understand herself and to value herself positively as a woman, not negatively as a mutilated man. Erikson says that while penis-envy exists, it is aggravated in some cultures. He emphasizes that the "first and basic observations" which have "strongly influenced the psychoanalytic view of womanhood," were made by clini-

cians, an important limiting circumstance. He faults Freud and his followers for their "analytic-atomistic" method of studying the human person, a method which works well with matter but when applied to the human being treats the person as a bundle of "isolated fragments" rather than as the constituent elements of an "organic whole."

Erikson agrees that anatomy is destiny, but only "insofar as it determines the potentials of physiological functioning and its limitations.... Anatomy, history, and personality are our combined destiny....

"Woman, through the ages (at any rate the patriarchal ones), has lent herself to a variety of roles conducive to an exploitation of masochistic potentials: she has let herself be incarcerated and immobilized, enslaved and infantilized, prostituted and exploited, deriving from it at best what in psychopathology we call 'secondary gains' of devious dominance. This fact, however, could be satisfactorily explained only within a new kind of biocultural history which (and this is one of my main points) would first have to overcome the prejudiced opinion that woman must be, or will be, what she is or has been under particular historical conditions."

Despite Erikson's caveats and distinctions, despite his corrections of Freud and his own specific denial of any intention to "doom every woman to perpetual motherhood," he has been criticized by feminists because of his insistence on the uniqueness of woman's "somatic [sensory and sensual] design" which "harbors an 'inner space' destined to bear offspring," whether "actual motherhood" is experienced or not. For Erikson, this seems to be a fact established through clinical observations, supported by play-construction experiments with both boys and girls, and reinforced by his own conviction that "the strength of generations (and by this I mean a basic disposition underlying all varieties of human value systems) depends on the process by which the youths of the two sexes find their respective identities, fuse them in love and marriage, revitalize their respective traditions, and together create and 'bring up' the next generation."

But for feminists, this sounds like the same old arbitrary tracking of women by men who, as Naomi Weisstein says, "are assumed to be experts" but who "reflect, in a surprisingly transparent way, the cultural consensus. They not only assert that a woman is defined by her ability to attract men, but they see no alternative definitions."

According to Weisstein, social context, not biological differences, is the crucial determinant of human behavior. "The evidence is accumulating that what a person does and who he believes himself to be will in general be a function of what people around him expect him to be, and what the over-all situation in which he is acting implies that he is. Compared to the influence of the social context within which a person lives, his or her history and traits, as well as biological makeup, may simply be random variations, noise superimposed on the true signal that can predict behavior. . . .

"Psychology has failed to understand what people are and how they act because psychology has looked for inner traits when it should have been noting social context; and theoreticians of personality have generally been clinicians and psychiatrists, and they have never considered it necessary to offer evidence to support their theories. . . . Psychologists must turn away from the theory of the causal nature of the inner dynamic and look to the social context within which individuals live."

I do not propose to mediate between Weisstein and Erikson. But it should be noted, before moving on, that an either/or reductionist stance would certainly be an inappropriate resolution of the differences between them. Social context on the one hand and anatomy and biocultural history on the other do not cancel each other out as explanations of the nature of woman, how she can understand and fulfill herself, and why historically the male-female relationship has been for so long the source of so much injustice and misery. If Erikson has paid insufficient attention to the character- and identity-forming influence of the woman's social context, the feminists tend to dismiss rather too easily her biological and anatomical differences. Because those differences have been used against women, because they have been cited by men as evidence of women's "inferiority," it is understandable why today's feminists have sharply devalued them. If it would repay Erikson to read the second section of *Woman in Sexist Society* ("Woman Is Made,

Not Born," especially the essays by Weisstein, Nancy Chodorow, and Judith Bardwick and Wlizabeth Douvan), it would repay some of the feminists if they would read, or reread, Erikson.

The anthropologist Lionel Tiger, another *bête noire* of the feminists (one of them refers to him as "a man who calls himself Tiger"), may be leaning far too heavily, as the feminists charge, on the evidence of primate behavior to explain human conduct. But in his article, "Male Dominance? Yes, Alas. A Sexist Plot? No." in *The New York Times Magazine*, Tiger presents evidence of significant biological and genetic differences between men and women that is more difficult to refute.

Tiger cites the study made by David Hamburg, a Stanford psychiatrist, who linked the sex hormone testosterone to aggressive behavior in both primates and humans. At adolescence, testosterone increases in boys at least tenfold, possibly as much as thirty times. "On the other hand, girls' testosterone levels only double, from a lower base to begin with. These levels remain stable throughout the life cycle." The significance of this finding, Tiger writes, is that over millions of years, "there was an advantage to the evolving human species in selecting males with high testosterone levels and females with much lower levels." For about ninety-nine per cent of human history, that is until about five thousand years ago, the majority of males hunted (therefore needed high testosterone levels for the aggressive, dominant qualities required of the hunter) and the majority of females gathered and conserved. Today, although such strict sexual division of occupation is no longer required for the survival of the species, the testosteronal secretions continue; they simply must, according to Tiger, be taken into account in any objective study of human behavior.

Tiger presents a second piece of evidence, a "frequency of smiles" study made by Daniel G. Freedman of the Committee for the Study of Human Development at the University of Chicago. "The underlying proposition is that smiling is an affiliative gesture of deference, a permissive, accommodating expression rather than a commanding or threatening one. . . . Freedman and his associates found that among human infants two days old, females smiled spontaneously at a significantly higher rate than males. This was eyes-closed smiling—in the absence of a social relationship—and suggests the affinity for this particular motor pattern which girls have."

If psychologists can rightly be faulted by feminists for failing to look at social-context facts, Tiger suggests that some feminists can be faulted for failing to look at biological data. "The feminist critique," he argues, "takes for granted what important scientific evidence does not permit us to take for granted: that only explicit cultural control—in fact, conspiracy—lies behind the very great differences in certain male and female social behaviors. . . . Because they ignore biological factors (like many other reformers) , the feminists run the risk of basing their legitimate demand for legal and economic equality on a vulnerable foundation."

The feminist Kate Millett has said in her book, *Sexual Politics*: "Groups who rule by birthright are fast disappearing, yet there remains one ancient and universal scheme for the domination of one birth group by another—the scheme that prevails in the area of sex. . . . [New research] suggests that the possibilities of innate temperamental differences seem more remote than ever. . . . In doing so it gives fairly concrete positive evidence of the overwhelmingly cultural character of gender, i.e., personality structure in terms of sexual category."

Tiger's comment: "On generous scientific grounds, it seems clear to me that the evidence which feminists such as Kate Millett and Ti-Grace Atkinson use to support their case is, on balance, irresponsible in its selection and so narrowly and unfairly interpreted that it will finally do damage to the prospects of women's actual liberation."

Tiger's proposition is that "there are biological bases for sexual differences which have nothing to do with oppressing females but rather with insuring the safety of communities [the male's traditional responsibility] and the healthy growth of children [the female's responsibility]."

But, of course, as both the feminists and Tiger know from the social psychology or, more appositely, from the social pathology of the situation, while men do not need the "biological bases for sexual differences" to justify their oppression of women, those bases,

with a powerful assist from Freud's particular interpretation of the data, furnished added justification for their denial of full sexual equality. Dr. Peter Neubauer, of New York's Child Development Center, has said: "When women have fully achieved social equality it will be easier to talk about biology and its relevance, because in a less sensitive time to speak of difference will not be tantamount to insult."

If we add to all of these explanations the historical role that mythology and religion have played in confirming the "naturalness" of male superiority, they seem to have been more effects than cause, they have reflected rather than inspired the phenomenon. Despite some fancy theologizing which makes Eve just as good as Adam in the natural order and Adam just as sinful as the temptress Eve in the moral order, the common understanding down through the centuries has left no doubt in the minds of believers which of the two was the afterthought of the Creator, and also the weaker and inferior. At the same time, the history of religions—notably the Christian religion—has been a history of increasing proscription of man's oppression of women and increasing elevation of the dignity of woman.

Claude Levi-Strauss, acknowledged master of mythological lore (at sixty-three, after twenty years of study and reflection, he has produced four volumes of "mythologiques"), says simply that a "myth is a story that aims to explain why things are as they are." In a recent interview, Levi-Strauss said: "In all this American mythology, [he was referring to the myths of primitive and aboriginal peoples] woman is considered by men as a profoundly dangerous, if indispensable, being—because her natural mechanism constantly threatens to compromise the good order of the universe. Mythology is concerned that day succeed night regularly, that the sun be not too near the earth, since that would provoke a conflagration, and not too far, because that would mean eternal night and universal decay. Just so, one must not marry one's sister, because that is to marry too close, nor seek a wife too far away, because that would expose one to be killed.

"In exactly the same way, it is absolutely indispensable that women have their periods once a month and give birth at a certain time. If a disorder developed in the feminine organism, the order of the world would find itself perverted, there would be no reason why the sun shouldn't approach the earth or disappear, and so on.

"So the first problem of mythic thought is that women must be domesticated. I'd go so far as to say that even before slavery or class domination existed men built an approach to women that would serve one day to introduce differences among men themselves."

For an unsettling journey into the heart of the mythological reading of the human condition, Norman O. Brown's *Love's Body* is perhaps the best guide. It is a brilliant synthesis in which the literature of myth, religion, and psychoanalysis is sorted out and reassembled to produce a vision of the dark, the irrational, the instinctual, and the unconscious. On one level it is a history of what men have thought and imagined; on another, it yields the possibility that what men have thought and imagined might actually be. *Love's Body* is not a probe of sexual politics or the role of intentionality as an explanation of history. It is simply apocalyptic imagery. Not the least of its value is that it stands outside the present rhetoric of feminism and antifeminism.

ON THE MOVEMENT'S AGENDA

What, then, are the prospects for women discovering, liberating, and fulfilling themselves? And what part can the women's liberation movement as such play to that end?

The National Organization for Women has issued a kind of bill of rights, a list of demands, which includes:

enforcement of a law banning sex discrimination in employment;

maternity leave rights in employment and Social Security benefits;

tax deduction for home and child-care expenses for working parents;

child day-care centers;

equal and unsegregated education;

equal job training opportunities and allowances for women in poverty;

the right of women to control their reproductive lives.

These demands have been criticized by radical feminist Shulamith Firestone as a con-

centration on "the more superficial symptoms of sexism." But if they were met they would open up the options; they would create opportunities for women to combine motherhood and outside work if they desired; enable women to achieve that measure of economic independence which is necessary—though obviously not sufficient—for the attainment of psychological and social autonomy; and they would so change the social and cultural climate that sexism would be put at last profoundly and generally in question.

The Women's Equity Action League (WEAL) and NOW have filed general sex-discrimination complaints against nearly three hundred colleges and universities on the basis of a Presidential Executive Order, dated 1965, but amended in 1968 to include sex among the grounds on which federal contractors (including universities) are forbidden to discriminate in their employment practices. The U.S. Office for Civil Rights is now applying that Presidential order, threatening to withhold funds until the universities can demonstrate that they are not discriminating against women employees.

The Federal Communications Commission is requiring all radio and television stations to prove they are not discriminating against women in their hiring practices.

Last fall, the City of New York notified all its suppliers that failure to adhere to new municipal guidelines to end discrimination by business against women would mean cancellation of contracts, withholding of payments, or disqualification from bidding on work for the city.

Alice Rossi believes that concrete institutional changes in the three areas of child care, residence, and education would advance the cause of sexual equality in a major way. Her analysis of what must be done in each of these areas and relating each to the others in the interest of women, their husbands, their children, and the family could be, for liberation groups, an indispensable practical guide to specific institutional reforms.

A new Women's Political Caucus has been started to give women a voice in the decision-making within political parties. Its slogan: "Make policy, not coffee."

Still on the agenda are some very large issues. They are reflected in the questions the women are raising, about liberation and about the movement.

Juliet Mitchell says that a movement is necessary if women are to overcome their isolation, since they inhabit, as a group, neither "geographic nor social space.... The isolation from which women come and into which they are constantly returned, creates serious obstacles for a political movement."

But Pat Williams, an early leader of the women's liberation movement in England, warns that true liberation "implies that free response is not enslaved under any kind of banner," that "mass movements produce change, not liberation," that the "feeling of belonging, the kicks taken from power and status in the group, or the sense of purpose, usually override the ideas which first stimulated the formation of the group."

Women's liberation, as a movement, has not been able to attract black women in any substantial numbers. Toni Morrison has written that America's black women "seem never to have become the 'true slave' that white women see in their own history.... Out of the profound desolation of her reality [the black woman] may very well have invented herself.... She combined being a responsible person with being a female." According to Morrison, "black women have always considered themselves superior to white women"; this only adds to their resentment when black men marry white women. A notable instance of black women joining with white women occurred in the formation of the national Women's Political Caucus. The black women perhaps saw something real there, Morrison writes, "women talking about human rights rather than sexual rights— something other than a family quarrel [between white women and white men]—and the air is shivery with possibilities."

Of all the items on the women's liberation agenda, perhaps the most sensitive and potentially most significant revolves around what Sheila Tobias has called the "psychic issues," specifically the intimate relationship of men and women. The questions that cluster around these issues are being raised and met more and more openly, though what constitutes satisfying answers is still far from clear.

Does the liberation of women require physical separation from men? Can women experience full sexual and psychic satisfaction without men? Is equality possible in heterosexual love? Is marriage essentially a snare and delu-sion for a woman who wants to achieve her identity and fulfill herself?

Betty Friedan proclaimed in the flush of the women's liberation mass demonstrations in August, 1970 that "this is not a bedroom war." Gloria Steinem has said, "Women's Lib is not trying to destroy the American family." (She points out that the family is already in tatters, witness "divorce statistics plus the way in which old people are farmed out with strangers and young people flee the home."

But there are other voices saying other things. Ti-Grace Atkinson, a movement dropout, says, "If you look at the [marriage] laws, it is legalized rape, causes unpaid labor, curtails a woman's freedom of movement, and requires no assurances of love from a man."

Marlene Dixon in *Ramparts*: "The institution of marriage is the chief vehicle for the perpetuation of the oppression of women; it is through the role of wife that the subjugation of women is maintained."

Judith Brown in *Handbook of Women's Liberation*: "[Marriage] does not provide for emotional and intellectual growth; and it offers no political resources. Were it not for male-legislated discrimination in employment, it would show little economic advantage."

In their essay, "Is Women's Liberation a Lesbian Plot?" (in *Woman in Sexist Society*), Sidney Abbott and Barbara Love say: "But today, more and more, it appears that women are socialized into sex roles as well as career roles; there is nothing to prove that heterosexuality is any more normal than homosexuality.... Heterosexuality happens to be the most popular [variety of sexuality] but not necessarily the most valid." "Equality in emotional-sexual relationships is [a] feminist ideal that makes an investigation of lesbian relationships so important for women's liberation.... Love has only recently been analyzed in terms of power, a type of mass domination of women through personal domination in heterosexual love relationships.... Love between equals provides the most fulfilling relationship. Anything short of equality in a love relationship is destructive."

And Abbott and Love make clear what they think of "feminists who continue to live off their husband's incomes and perform the traditional duties of wife and mother at the expense of their own development." Such women, they say, "are hiding and only paying lip service to their cause, much as lesbians who flirt with men in the office. They are trying to escape discrimination by appearing to perpetuate the system."

If the logic of feminism demands that women give up on the effort to be wife and mother and fully human, as Abbott and Love hold, the logic of women's liberation demands, in their view, not only tolerance of lesbians in the movement but virtual identification with lesbianism: "Although women's liberation has insisted on the right of all women to control their own bodies, the subject has only been discussed in terms of abortion. In liberationist thinking the concept of the right to one's own body does not include freedom of sexual activities or freedom of sexual preference, which would logically seem to be a part of the kind of self-ownership and self-determination at the heart of feminist demands. This is probably because such a viewpoint would seem to come frighteningly close to actually endorsing lesbianism."

It is this kind of rhetoric and analysis—an evangelical lesbianism—that has confused some "straight" feminists who want to work for an end to sexual discrimination in employment and politics but who do not want to be accused of hypocrisy because they refuse to leave their male lovers or husbands. It has evoked from other feminists, straight or lesbian, the angry charge that some radical lesbians are doing to their heterosexual sisters what feminists accuse men of doing to women: bullying and dominating, prescribing the terms and conditions under which they can fulfill themselves.

"The lesbian movement," Abbott and Love claim, "is not only related to women's liberation, it is at the very heart of it." Although from the lesbians' viewpoint such a position is consistent with their ideology (i.e., that heterosexual love is a dead end for women, and that marriage is an irredeemable institution), from the standpoint of the women's liberation movement lesbian inflexibility could be much more than an intramural embarrassment.

The sex research of Virginia E. Johnson and William E. Masters, who reported on the successive and powerful orgasms women could achieve through clitoral stimulation alone, gave some feminists ammunition for their cause. Although it was hardly news to learn from Masters and Johnson that the clitoris is orgasmically instrumental, it is the conclusions other have drawn from their research that have stirred controversy within women's liberation. Not only were vaginal orgasm and the double orgasm (clitoral and vaginal) declared dead, or dismissed as Freudian myths, the vagina was said to play no essential role in the ultimate sexual pleasure of the woman.

But Germaine Greer, among others, has entered a critical note: "Many women who greeted the conclusions of Masters and Johnson with cries of 'I told you so!' and 'I am normal!' will feel that [my] criticism is a betrayal. They have discovered sexual pleasure after being denied it, but the fact that they have only ever experienced gratification from clitoral stimulation is evidence for my case, because it is the index of the desexualization of the whole body, the substitution of genitality for sexuality. The ideal marriage as measured by the electronic equipment in the Reproduction Biology Research Foundation laboratories is enfeebled—dull sex for dull people. The sexual personality is basically antiauthoritarian. If the system wishes to enforce complete suggestibility in its subjects, it will have to tame sex. Masters and Johnson supplied the blueprint for standard, low-agitation, cool-out monogamy. If women are to avoid this last reduction of their humanity, they must hold out not just for orgasm but for ecstasy."

When Ann Roiphe recently informed Helene Deutsch, an early disciple of Freud's, and now eighty-seven years old, that Masters and Johnson "seem to have established beyond any question that there is only the clitoral response in women," Deutsch replied: "Oh, oh, that makes me very angry. There is a difference between animals and human beings. In man, the biological is interwoven with the psychological factors. There can be no measurements that have any meaning unless they include tenderness and love."

Perhaps the best brief description of how the totality of a woman's sexuality is engaged in a heterosexual encounter that is characterized by tenderness and love has been furnished by Simone de Beauvoir in *The Second Sex* in a passage all the more remarkable because one encounters in the succeeding chapter an equally sensitive delineation of lesbian love. A portion from the earlier passage may convey a sense of Beauvoir's sure touch and, at the same time, shed light on a question that continues to vex almost every discussion of this theme, namely, the nature and possibility of sexual equality given the obvious physiological-functional differences of the male and female. Following a description of the subtle ways in which both the man and woman can be made to feel, intentionally or not, as object, rather than subject, and of the other ways—when love replaces calculation and when tenderness takes over from technique—in which both remain subjects, Beauvoir sums up:

"Sex pleasure in woman . . . is a kind of magic spell; it demands complete abandon; if words or movements oppose the magic of caresses, the spell is broken. This is one of the reasons why the woman closes her eyes; physiologically, this is a reflex compensating for the dilation of the pupils; but she lowers her eyelids even in the dark. She would abolish all surroundings, abolish the singularity of the moment, of herself, and of her lover; she would fain be lost in a carnal night as shadowy as the maternal womb. And more especially she longs to do away with the separateness that exists between her and the male; she longs to melt with him into one. As we have seen, she wants to remain subject while she is made object. Being more profoundly beside herself than is man because her whole body is moved by desire and excitement, she retains her subjectivity only through union with her partner; giving and receiving must be combined for both. If the man confines himself to taking without giving or if he bestows pleasure without receiving, the woman feels that she is being maneuvered, used; once she realizes herself as the Other, she becomes the inessential other, and then she is bound to deny her alterity."

" . . . she longs to do away with the separateness that exists between her and the male . . . her whole body is moved by desire and excitement . . . she retains her subjectivity only through union with her partner. . . ." This, and the ecstasy Greer begs her sisters to hold out for, are as far beyond the clitoral-only focus and

definition of sexual joy as can be imagined.

Sexual delight is not synonymous with personal fulfillment. But for the woman who has chosen to share her life with another the absence, or even dwindling, of such delight will count as a serious impairment.

It is not fanciful to suggest that for every woman, no matter what life-style she adopts, women's liberation can create the conditions under which fulfillment is possible because all the paths to self-identity are open. In short, there is a direct connection between the seemingly prosaic goals of equal pay for equal work, decent child-care centers, and maternity leave rights, on the one hand and, on the other, the ultimate satisfaction experienced in the purposeful life of an achieving, loving person who is also a woman.

At the end of her book, *Patriarchal Attitudes*, Eva Figes said that she had talked a lot about economic realities not because she was indifferent to the emotional aspects of human relations but rather because one cannot separate states of mind from outer realities. "Economic independence may not be an absolute guaranty of emotional independence," Figes writes, "but it is certainly a necessary *a priori. . . .* When a marriage founders, a wife is risking not only the loss of a lover and companion but her home and her whole way of life, and subconsciously this makes her cling to a man she might otherwise have rejected or released long ago.

"Love, said Byron, was woman's whole existence, and society has seen to it that it was her whole existence. Modern psychologists note that women are more childlike, more emotional, and show a greater degree of dependence, and the reason is still the same. We are all vulnerable to each other, but women have been made particularly vulnerable emotionally because they are more vulnerable in other ways, and we do not need psychologists to tell us this. We have all of us seen evidence of this in our everyday lives, amongst our friends, in ourselves if we are women, in our women if we are men. Our literature bears witness to it, so do the women's pages of newspapers and the advice columns of women's magazines, so do our mental-health clinics.

"I think the remedy lies in our own hands, and it will be found in social change, not on the analyst's couch. The change is one that men should welcome as much as women because female neurosis and dependence does not make the lives of men any happier either."

What women's liberation is saying is that liberation will make that social change perhaps not inevitable but certainly possible.

That possibility and what it leads to seem to be more promising today than at any previous time in the history of woman's efforts to be herself. The sexual life-style that youth have adopted—androgynous in many important respects, rejecting traditional sex roles and manners, equalizing relations between the sexes—this life-style already is embodying, in however attenuated and unreflective a form, and without any political and social support or enabling legislation, much of what women's liberation has constructed as an ideal. These seem to be not so much parallel streams of social consciousness, but rather two currents of a single stream. If that is true, then the stream may well become a river in our lifetime.

DISCUSSING THE ARTICLES

1. In "Neither Marx Nor Malthus" by Paul R. Ehrlich and John P. Holdren, how is population control related to the fact that China is a nonwhite, non-Western, militantly socialist nation?

2. In what stage does China belong, according to the demographic transition model? At what stage of societal development does it become necessary to curb the birth rate?

3. What hinders population control in China? Is this true of other societies? Of primarily what kind of societies?

4. How would you explain why the population control campaign was more successful in the cities than in the countryside? Does this support what we have said about urban life styles? What does it say about rural values?

5. How is women's attainment of virtual equality with men related to the effectiveness of population control? If the Women's Liberation movement in our society is successful in gaining complete equality for women, will our birth rate go up or down?

6. According to the article "Fanon" by Horace Sutton, among whom is the mystic pull of this black man from Martinique particularly felt? Why?

7. What feelings did Fanon put in writing? Are these feelings preconditions for social movements?

8. The author states that Fanon preached "the necessity of violence to bring about abrupt change." What kind of social movement would such preaching produce?

9. Does Fanon believe that the Third World, the black intelligentsia, or the black elite will support a violent movement? From what the text says about collective behavior, in general, and social movements, in particular, what kind of people, from a stratification point of view, would be likely to participate in such movements?

10. Why are the peasants most likely to participate in violent social movements?

11. Does Fanon preach strictly violence? Is his postrevolutionary reconstruction similar to the postrevolutionary periods actually experienced in past revolutions?

12. Is there anything in Fanon's personal past that might have made him susceptible to social movements? Is it one of the preconditions mentioned in the text?

13. "We must try to set afoot a new man," Fanon said. Do you think this can be done by a social movement? Think of previous revolutions. Have they created a new man? What about the Chinese revolution? Has it created a new society? And is a new society not made up of new men?

14. In Donald McDonald's article "The Liberation of Women," what are some of the things the author says women want to be liberated from?

15. What does the author say are indispensable reformist motivations? Are these among the preconditions of social movements mentioned in the text?

16. The author also maintains that reformist motivations can "blur perceptions and cloud the judgment." Which theory of collective behavior suggests that it may?

17. What are the characteristics of the Women's Liberation movement? Is it a unified movement? Is this typical of social movements?

18. What kind of group can women be considered in light of their conditions of employment? Where do they fit in the system of stratification?

19. In the article, McDonald mentions work by anthropologist Lionel Tiger, who reports that until five thousand years ago males hunted while women gathered and conserved. What changes occurred in societies that made such a division of labor unnecessary? Which of the theories reported in the text do you think shows what was responsible for this change? Or do you agree with a combination of the theories? According to Tiger, what other change should have, but has not yet, taken place?

20. According to Tiger, on what ground do the feminist reformers base their demands? Why does he consider this ground shaky?

21. The author states that if the list of demands issued by NOW were met by society, it would lead to such social and cultural changes that sexism would then be seriously questioned. Speculate on the nature of these social and cultural changes. Would you personally feel comfortable with such changes? Is change or stability more important to the health of society?

22. What is the tangible proof that social change prompted by the feminist movement is taking place? Is such change as effective as if it were prompted by sociocultural drift? Might it eventually become a kind of sociocultural drift?

23. What effects might such sociocultural change have on the institutions of marriage and the family? What is the position of radical feminists regarding these institutions?

24. What are the author's conclusions about the probability of social change occurring, through the liberation movement and through sociocultural drift, in our lifetime?

TERMS TO REMEMBER

Social change. Change in the patterns of social interaction, in which a substantial number of society's members assume new statuses and play new roles.

Cultural change. Change in values and beliefs, which may be brought about by scientific discoveries, technological inventions, new achievements in the arts, or shifts in religious doctrine.

Discovery. A process of cultural change in which knowledge of an already existing fact or relationship is newly perceived.

Invention. A process of cultural change in which old cultural ideas or existing objects are combined in a new way, thus producing something more important than the sum of its parts.

Diffusion. A process of cultural change in which cultural traits are spread from one society to another and from one group within society to another.

Sociocultural drift. The unplanned changes occurring in society.

Demography. The study of the growth or decrease of population, its distribution throughout the world, and its composition.

Demographic transition model. A model of population growth, according to which society passes through three basic stages of evolution: Birth rates and death rates are high; death rates decline while birth rates remain high; and birth rates decline.

Urbanization. A population trend in which cities grow at the expense of rural areas.

Urbanism. A condition, a set of attitudes, a quality, or a way of life distinct from the rural.

Urban ecology. The study of the distributive patterns of buildings and people within a given geographic area, and their interdependence.

Natural areas. Areas within each city that attract people of similar backgrounds, attitudes, and tendencies.

Neighborhoods. Areas within each city that are planned and in which the residents interrelate.

Ecological Processes. The processes that cause constant change in natural areas and neighborhoods. They are concentration, dispersion, centralization, decentralization, segregation, invasion, and succession.

Urban development theories. Concentric zone theory, sector theory, and multiple nuclei theory all attempt to describe urban development according to the patterns produced by the ecological processes.

Suburbs. Small communities on the outskirts of the central city and somewhat dependent on it.

Metropolitan area. Small cities, suburbs, and the city around which they are clustered.

Urban sprawl, or megalopolis. One metropolitan area following another without interruption.

Collective behavior. Short-lived behavior occurring in crowds, mobs, publics, fashions, fads, crazes, and rumors. It also includes the more structured and longer-lived behavior in public opinion and social movements.

Contagion theory. A theory in which collective behavior is viewed as a process in which moods, attitudes, and behavior are rapidly communicated to a collectivity, and uncritically accepted by it by the further process of circular reaction, or emotional contagion. Additional factors involved in contagion are suggestion and imitation, identification and anonymity, and loss of individuality.

Convergence theory. A theory of collective behavior stressing that collective behavior merely brings out into the open feelings already present in the individual members of the collectivity.

Emergent norm theory. A theory of collective behavior in which such behavior is viewed as being governed by norms that emerge in collective situations, although distinct from the norms existing in normal group situations.

Crowd. A kind of collective behavior. A crowd is an aggregate of people gathered in the same place, at the same time, either casually or for a predetermined reason, and responding to a common stimulus. Crowds are divided into expressive and acting. An acting crowd may develop into a panic, mob, or riot.

Fashions. A minor kind of collective behavior concerning manners in dress, architecture, or house decor.

Fads and crazes. Minor fashions, short-lived and irrational.

Rumor. A minor kind of collective behavior. An unsupported report of an event or a projected event.

Mass hysteria. Compulsive and irrational behavior of a temporary or scattered nature.

Public. Persons who are geographically dispersed but who share a common interest, who express that interest, and who know that others are aware of this interest.

Public opinion. The attitudes and judgments of publics.

Propaganda. A deliberate attempt to persuade the individual to uncritically accept a particular belief or to make a certain choice.

Censorship. A device used to limit the information available to the public.

Social movement. A collective attempt either to change the sociocultural order or to resist change.

Anomie. Normlessness, or a condition of not knowing which behavioral guidelines to follow.

Alienation. Feeling oneself separated from society—powerless, normless, and isolated.

Relative deprivation. A source of dissatisfaction with the status quo conducive to the rise of social movements. The individual, though not deprived in comparison to people in other societies, perceives himself as deprived in comparison to others in his society.

Failure of rising expectations. The feeling experienced by members of a society when the standard of living has begun to rise, but has then suffered a reversal, or is not proceeding fast enough.

Migratory movement. A social movement in which discontent is eliminated when members leave one geographic location for another.

Expressive movement. A social movement in which the members' reactions to their environment is changed.

Utopian movement. A social movement in which members try to establish new societies with new standards and values.

Resistance movement. A social movement in which members attempt to stem the tide of change.

Reform movement. A social movement in which members attempt to change some feature of an existing social order without changing the entire order.

Revolutionary movement. A social movement in which members seek the complete removal of the present social order and substitution of it with an entirely new order.

Nationalistic revolutionary movement. A revolutionary movement in which a predominantly foreign government is overthrown and replaced with a native one.

Class revolutionary movements. A revolutionary movement in which one ruling class is replaced with another in the same society.

Crisis of legitimacy. The realization that the current system of government has failed and that it is necessary to bring about change at any cost.

SUGGESTIONS FOR FURTHER READING

Allen, Francis R. *Socio-Cultural Dynamics: An Introduction to Social Change.* New York: Macmillan, 1971. Theories of social and cultural change exhaustively analyzed.

Applebaum, Richard P. *Theories of Social Change.* Chicago: Markham, 1970. A brief sociological analysis of current thought on social change.

Barnett, H. G. *Innovation: The Basis of Cultural Change.* New York: McGraw-Hill, 1953. One of the mechanisms of cultural change explored by an anthropologist.

Barton, Allen. *Communities in Disaster: A Sociological Analysis of Collective Stress Situations.* New York: Doubleday Anchor Books, 1970. How individuals and collectivities respond to natural, man-made, and long-term disasters and stresses.

Cameron, William Bruce. *Modern Social Movements: A Sociological Outline.* New York: Random House, 1966. Many examples illustrate this brief survey of social movements.

Cantril, Hadley. *The Psychology of Social Movements.* New York: John Wiley, 1963. Chapter 4 gives an especially memorable description of two lynchings, as seen through the eyes of the lynchers.

Lang, Kurt and Gladys Engle. *Collective Dynamics.* New York: Crowell, 1961. A basic text, but one with interesting chapters on crowds, rumors, panics, fashions, and other forms of collective behavior.

Lipset, Seymour M., and Wolin, Sheldon S., eds. *The Berkeley Student Revolt.* Garden City, N. Y.: Doubleday Anchor Books, 1965. A modern form of collective behavior examined in a collection of essays by two outstanding sociologists.

Mack, Raymond W. *Transforming America: Patterns of Social Change.* New York: Random House, 1967. Changes at work in our society viewed in a straightforward and easy-to-follow style.

Martindale, Don. *Social Life and Cultural Change.* Princeton, N. J.: Van Nostrand, 1962. Social and cultural change in a historical perspective.

Moore, Wilbert. *Social Change.* Englewood Cliffs, N. J.: Prentice-Hall, 1963. A follower of functionalist theory analyzes the causes and effects of social change.

Redfield, Robert. *The Primitive World and its Transformations.* Ithaca, N. Y.: Cornell University Press, 1953. A study analyzing the effects of modernization on nontechnological societies and cultures.

Smelser, Neil J. *Theory of Collective Behavior.* New York: Free Press, 1963. A contemporary sociologist attempts to develop and apply a theory that can be used to analyze collective behavior.

Turner, Ralph H., and Killian, Lewis M., *Collective Behavior.* Englewood Cliffs, N. J.: Prentice-Hall, 1957. A text in which most issues of collective behavior are exhaustively covered.

Van Leeuwen, Arend Theodor. *Development Through Revolution.* New York: Scribner, 1970. Revolution as the process par excellence of social change.

Wirth, Louis W. "Urbanism as a Way of Life," *American Journal of Sociology,* Vol. 44 (July, 1938), pp. 1-25. A classic work in which the urban personality and life style are defined.

PART TWO

SOCIAL INSTITUTIONS

So far, we have looked at the human being as an individual—a personality—as well as a member of various groups. We have seen that humans live in societies and that as a consequence of their interaction with one another in these societies, they develop an abstraction we call culture. We are aware that values and norms are important parts of the culture that a society evolves. They guide and direct human behavior, making it unnecessary for each person who is born into the society to learn through his own personal experience what to do and how to do it, or what not to do.

We have also seen that humans' group way of life, though necessary and comforting in many respects, results in conflicts. Some of the conflicts center around the unequal distribution of the goods and services produced by each society. Unequal distribution gives rise to the universal problem of social injustice. Other conflicts revolve around the heterogeneousness of most modern industrial societies. Because such societies are made up of many racial and ethnic groups and because individuals are victims of hostilities against strangers, prejudice and discrimination arise.

Furthermore, we have established that society and culture, as well as people, are continually changing. Change does not always occur at an even pace. Sometimes it is rapid, and at other times it is slow. Sometimes only particular groups accept change; at other times parts of a culture change before groups are ready for it. These differences create stresses and strains in social organization.

In the following chapters, we look at the patterns of behavior that our culture has established. The term "patterns of behavior" may make you think of lists of do's and don'ts in the vein of the Ten Commandments. And patterns of behavior are, in part similar to commandments. But primarily, they are the habits, or traditional ways of doing things, that have accumulated around an important human function.

Perhaps you recall from Chapter 2 that sociologists refer to such patterns, or habits, as institutions. As is true with most words, sociologists use this word quite differently from the way other people do. For instance, in everyday conversation, we hear people speak of mental institutions, of penal institutions, and of such buildings as orphanages and schools as institutions. But these aren't institutions in the sociological sense. They are only isolated, physical representations of the abstract concept of institution.

Pivotal Institutions

As we have mentioned previously, some human functions are essential to the survival of the individual and the group. One essential function is control of the process of reproduction. Such control ensures a fresh supply of societal members and provides these new members with a nurturing environment. Other essential functions of society include the provision of a livelihood for each member; the guarantee that members contribute to the group, rather than harm it; and the maintenance of order, at least to the extent that people are prevented from killing one another over every disagreement. Then, there is the function of giving important knowledge to each new generation. And, finally, there are ways of answering questions such as, What is the meaning of life? Where do we go after death? Where do we come from before birth?

All human societies have had to provide these functions, and all have risen to the challenge and met it to the best of their ability, though in different ways. To make sure that reproduction proceeds in an orderly fashion and that infants are well taken care of until they are able to be independent, every society has made some arrangement that we call the family institution. To make sure that every member can support himself, every society has some kind of economic institution. To make sure of even a minimal degree of order, every society has some kind of political institution. To make sure that the young of each generation are taught what is important in their society, every society makes provision for supplying an education through the educational institution. Finally, to explain that which cannot be explained if people rely only on their senses, every society provides for some kind of religious experience through its religious institution.

There, in skeleton form, are the basic, or pivotal, institutions of human societies. Around each institution, there have developed a number of folkways, mores, and laws, which all members of society are expected to follow to ease their lives. These folkways, mores, and laws vary from society to society and determine the form institutions take. Thus, the family institution of your society determines whether you marry one husband or many, one wife or many; whether you live with your in-laws or alone; and whether you are the head of your household or subservient to someone else. In the same way, whether you go to the polls to elect your president or whether you watch several young men walking across burning coals to determine which one will be chief depends upon the political institution of your society. The same is true of all the other functions we have mentioned.

Characteristics of Institutions

Because the members of each generation face the same basic problems, and because they maintain ties with both the past and the future through their parents and their children, the organized habits that we call institutions are durable. At the same time, people are not simply conformists but are also individuals. Societal members both follow institutional patterns and continually create new patterns. Therefore, the form of these enduring institutions is constantly changing.

Besides helping individuals satisfy some of their basic needs, institutions also provide the cement that holds societies together. An aggregate of people in which each individual lived in his own way and did only his "own thing" would soon face utter chaos. Without some means of steady support, mothers would abandon their infants or let them die, for mother love is not an instinct but is taught by the family institution. If there were no organized ways of obtaining a livelihood, competition and conflicts would be so fierce that many people could not survive. The law of the jungle would prevail if there were no institution that maintained order. In other words, institutions enable societies to keep functioning. Institutions are, then, the foundations, or pillars, of society.

Institutions not only underlie the very structure of society, but they are also interdependent. Usually, the child first learns about the value of making a good living, about the necessity for order, about religious principles, and about educational goals in the family setting. The family institution, then, supports the other institutions, and is, in turn, supported by them. Even more directly, the condition of the economy in your society sometimes determines whether you can obtain a good job and establish your own family. At times, the government decides whether you finish college or go into the armed services instead. Your religion may teach that birth control is wrong. If you and others are faithful to the teachings of this institution, the overpopulation that results may affect all other institutions.

Within institutions, too, tension between stability and change occurs. Workable ways of doing things, repeated over and over, tend to become rigid forms. Thus, habits become institutions. Looked at from this point of view, institutions tend to maintain stability and the status quo. But as new ways of doing things appear and are found workable, they challenge stability and impel institutions toward change.

Finally, it is important to remember that institutions are simply abstract concepts of organized habits and standardized ways of doing things. We cannot see institutions. What we can see are families, schools, banks, federal buildings, churches, and yes, jails and mental hospitals. But these would be nothing but empty symbols without one vital ingredient: people. The behavior of individuals gives institutions their form. And institutions give form to individual behavior.

CHAPTER SEVEN

THE SOURCE OF life—THE family

British psychologist R. D. Laing levels harsh accusations at the institution of the family:

> The family's function is to repress Eros; to induce a false consciousness of security; to deny death by avoiding life; to cut off transcendence; to believe in God, not to experience the Void; to create, in short, one-dimensional man; to promote respect, conformity, obedience; to con children out of play; to induce a fear of failure; to promote a respect for work; to promote a respect for "respectability."[1]

Can Laing be talking about the institution that is the origin of all institutions and the origin of the individual? Is he referring to the institution that is praised by church and state, that nurtures society's infants to survival, that prepares its members to assume constructive roles, and that offers a haven from the

[1] R. D. Laing, The Politics of Experience (London: Penguin Books, 1967), Chapter 3, p. 35. Copyright © R. D. Laing, 1967.

bruises of life—that is, to paraphrase Robert Frost, where they have to take you in when you have nowhere else to go? Yes, indeed, Laing is talking about this very institution.

From another camp, we hear regretful reactions to the decline of the family's influence. The disintegration of the family will, the prophets of doom declare, lead to the collapse of society and civilization. Whom are we to believe? Is the family too much with us, or not enough? Are we paying too high a price for the initial care, security, and affection that the family offers? Does the family actually perform essential functions, or is it simply a tool society uses to stamp and mold us as it sees fit?

LIFE WITHOUT THE FAMILY

There are others besides Laing who claim that the family has outgrown

its usefulness. These people note that most of its original functions have been taken over by other institutions. And other institutions could also perform its remaining functions, control of reproduction and the care and socialization of the young. Modern contraceptives can solve the problem of unwanted reproduction. And test-tube babies, produced from only the sperm of a living male and the ovum of a living female, are becoming a reality in laboratories today.

Can you imagine a world without families? The child goes from a test tube into a nursery, where he is taken care of by nice women and men (yes, men, because social change will have transformed traditional sex roles). There are hundreds of other babies in the nursery who are all treated as fairly, as intelligently, and as unemotionally as the caretaker can manage. At the proper age, the child enters school. There, understanding, fascinating teachers teach him only what interests him. When the period of schooling is finisheded, the person is free. No one tells him when to come home, what not to eat, what friends to have, and whom to marry. No one nags him about cleaning up his room, driving too fast, or cutting his hair. Pure bliss, right? Or perhaps not?

This kind of world is not merely the product of a science fiction writer's imagination. Centuries ago, the Greek philosophers suggested experiments in socializing the young outside the family. And in this century, Soviet and Israeli societies have attempted communal child rearing. In the USSR, this policy was rapidly reversed, primarily because of a lack of physical and financial resources but also because it failed to produce the type of individual the government required. The Israeli experiment is more difficult to evaluate. First, the kibbutzim on which the experiments have occurred are small, agricultural communes, differing from the urban industrial society that surrounds them. In addition, children are not entirely removed from their parents; they visit them for at least two hours every day and have contact with them at other times if they desire. But most of the responsibility for socialization and education is assumed first by nurses and later by teachers.

A survey of the literature written about these experiments suggests that there is very little difference between children reared in kibbutzim and those reared in the traditional way.[2] In general, however, communally reared children have much lower rates of emotional disturbance and more positive relations with their parents than do children growing up within families. The reason for this appears to be that the communally reared children think of the entire kibbutz as their family. In fact, they marry entirely outside of the group in which they were reared, explaining that they could never marry one of their own brothers or sisters![3] It seems, then, that in the kibbutzim the family has not actually been dispensed with but has simply been extended.

Another interesting result of these Israeli experiments is that communal rearing has been very successful in preparing individuals to fit into the life of the kibbutz. It has not, however, prepared individuals for life in an urban industrial society. In such a society, kibbutz-reared individuals are maladjusted and cannot develop to their full potential.[4]

[2]Larry D. Barnett, "The Kibbutz as a Child-rearing System: A Review of the Literature," in Jeffrey K. Hadden and Marie L. Borgatta, eds., *Marriage and the Family* (Itasca, Ill.: Peacock, 1969), pp. 405-407.

[3]Melford Spiro, "The Israeli Kibbutz," in Arlene S. and Jerome H. Skolnick, eds., *Family in Transition*, pp. 501-508.

[4]Stanley Diamond, "Collective Child-Rearing: The Kibbutz," *Social Problems*, Vol. 5 (Fall, 1957).

All this simply shows that no human being can isolate himself completely from a primary group, whether he calls it his family or his kibbutz, in order to enjoy total freedom. What is more, humans are contradictory creatures: Although we want to be free, we also want to belong; and although we want to be part of some group, we also want to be individuals. Perhaps some family of the future will give us what we are looking for.

The Changing Family

The mass media continually bombard us with information about the family. Numerous articles appear about the crisis of the family and the decline of the good old family virtues. What, in fact, is taking place? Very simply, the family is just another victim of cultural and societal complexity and the rapid pace of sociocultural change.

In simple societies, the family was able to perform all of the functions necessary for human life. It took care of infants, taught children what they had to know, and told them which spirits to worship. It gathered and grew its food supply, made sure each member did not stray too far from the righteous path, helped find each member an appropriate mate, and buried its members when they died.

Societies, however, did not remain simple. They grew surpluses and began trading. They went to war with one another and acquired more land. To ensure the success of their warfare, they decided that their gods had to be worshipped more thoroughly. Members of the family alone were no longer sufficient to work the land. Slaves attempted to escape and had to be punished. Inventions and discoveries accumulated until no father could single-handedly educate his son. The family was breaking at the seams. It could no longer perform all necessary functions in this complicated life.

Thus, other institutions were created to take some burdens away from the family. This led to changes in the family itself. Today, increasingly advanced technology and profound changes in the structure of society have caused additional changes in the family. What's more, technology and social change promise to affect the family even more drastically in the future. But to understand the forms that the family may take in the future, it is necessary to understand the family in the present.

BASIC PATTERNS OF FAMILY ORGANIZATION

The underlying reason for the establishment of the family institution is the regulation of sex. But why must sex be regulated? After all, hunger is a physical drive similar to sex, and when we are hungry, we simply find something to eat. The sexual act, however, does not end with the release of neuromuscular tensions but has further consequences. These, of course, are the conception and birth of children. During the period of pregnancy and for a few years thereafter, the female is a less adequate food provider than she normally is, because she is busy caring for the infant. Therefore, the male who has had sexual access to her agrees to take on the role of protector and food provider. This, in essence, is the basis of marriage, which is, in turn, the chief element of family life.

Forms of Marriage

Obviously, the forms of marriage are different in different societies. But the purpose of marriage is the same: A man and a woman, or various combinations of men and women, live together in a sexual union to reproduce and to establish a family. Their relationship is defined and sanctioned—that is, permitted and encouraged—by tradition or law. The definition of their relationship includes not only guidelines for behavior in matters of sex but also the particulars of their obligations to their offspring, the way labor is to be divided, and other duties and privileges.

The two broad subdivisions in forms of marriage are monogamy and polygamy. *Monogamy* is the union of one man with one woman. *Polygamy* is plural marriage, which can be subdivided into *polyandry*, the union of one woman with several men; *polygyny*, the union of one man with more than one woman; and *group marriage*, involving several men with several women.

Historically, monogamy has been the most common form of marriage. The reason for this may be that an equal number of males and females reach maturity and are available for mating. Or it may be that more than one wife, like more than one car, is not within the financial reach of the average male. Probably, it also has something to do with the way a society views women. If women are considered good workers whose labor brings economic benefits to the family, there is an advantage in having more than one wife. But if women are considered frail and incapable of the same kind of labor as men, they are an economic burden, and one wife is sufficient. In Western societies, the latter view of women has predominated, and so has the monogamous form of marriage.

Polygyny is the most common form of polygamy. It is practiced today in a number of Muslim nations, primarily in parts of Africa. In most instances, having more than one wife is a status symbol attained only by males in high positions. Thus, polygyny is closely associated with social stratification.

The status of women in a polygynous marriage is not much lower than that of women in a monogamous marriage. Often, the first wife in such a marriage encourages her husband to take another wife. This adds to her own status, eases her work load, and offers her the companionship of an extended primary group. Nonetheless, in this form of marriage, the partners are not, by any stretch of the imagination, equal. What is more, polygyny creates physical inconveniences. Because it produces many children, large houses and a good income are necessary. Therefore, polygyny does not fit into urban industrial societies and will, in all probability, disappear with the spread of industrialization.

Polyandry is an uncommon form of marriage, practiced chiefly in areas where physical existence is difficult and seminomadic. Under such circumstances, more than one husband is required to support a wife and her children. Polyandry is usually fraternal—when a woman marries, she automatically becomes the wife of all her husband's brothers. In societies practicing this form of marriage, there is usually a shortage of females, sometimes caused by the custom of female infanticide.[5] Group marriage, though it exists, has never been practiced consistently in any known society.

---

[5]Claude Levi-Strauss, "The Family," in Arlene S. and Jerome H. Skolnick, eds., *Family in Transition*, p. 55.

Limitations on Marriage

Every society regulates its members' choice of mates by specifying whom they may marry and whom they may not. All societies, for instance, require that marriage occur outside a particular group, whether it be family, clan, tribe, or village. In our own society, people must not marry close blood relatives such as parents, sisters, brothers, and, in some states, first cousins. This procedure is called *exogamy*, or marriage outside the group.

Societies also require that people must marry within their own wider group. In simple societies, members must choose their mates from among their clan, tribe, or village. In our society, people are encouraged to marry within their own race, religion, and social class. This process is called *endogamy*, or marriage within the group.

Another limitation is the universal *incest taboo*—prohibition of sexual relations between mother and son, father and daughter, and sister and brother. This taboo has been broken by particular members of past societies—the ancient Egyptians, the Hawaiians, the pre-Columbian Peruvians—and continues to be broken in every society on occasion. Nonetheless, every known society has had clear prohibitions against incest.

Most anthropologists believe that the incest taboo arose because it is functional. In other words, they believe societies prohibit incest because it wouldn't work well and would damage the family. One disadvantage is obvious: Relationships would be extremely tangled. A father would be a husband to his daughter, a brother-in-law to his son, a son-in-law to his first wife, and so on. Second, incest would lead to conflict-producing rivalries within the family and thereby displace patterns of authority. Third, the family would not receive new adult members who could help it economically, but there would be new children to feed. Finally, marrying outside the family builds dependency between families and ensures that new families will be created.[6]

Some anthropologists believe that the incest taboo may have originated as a means of gaining cooperation between competing hunting bands. The exchange of mates between groups helped to ensure friendly relations and prevented excessive fighting over hunting territory.[7]

Forms of Family

The family may be defined as a social group that has the following features: (1) It originates in marriage; (2) it consists of husband and wife and children born of the union; (3) in some forms of the family, other relatives are included; (4) the people making up the family are joined by legal bonds, as well as by economic and religious bonds and by other duties and privileges; (5) family members are also bound by a network of sexual privileges and prohibitions, as well as by varying degrees of such emotions as love, respect, affection, and so on.[8]

The family is divided into two main forms. One is the *extended*, or *con-*

[6]Ibid., p. 55.

[7]Sheldon L. Washburn and Irven DeVore, "The Social Behavior of Baboons and Early Man," in S. L. Washburn, ed., *Social Life of Early Man* (Chicago: Aldine, 1961), pp. 96-100.

[8]Claude Levi-Strauss, "The Family," in Arlene S. and Jerome H. Skolnick, eds., *Family in Transition*, p. 56.

sanguine, family. *Consanguine* refers to blood relationships. The extended family includes a large or small number of blood relatives together with their marriage partners and children. The extended family is typical of traditional, or agricultural, societies, for in these societies, it is advantageous to cooperate in obtaining a livelihood. Such a family provides individual members with many psychological advantages, too. Child rearing becomes the responsibility of many members, and thus one person is not saddled with the entire task. Because the child can form affectionate relationships with persons other than his parents, the emotional content of the parent-child relationship is eased. Physical neglect or mistreatment within the confines of the extended family is almost unheard of. But individuality does tend to be stifled.

The second form of family is the *nuclear*, also called the *conjugal*, form. A nuclear family consists of the nucleus of the father, the mother, and their children. For the children, such a family is *consanguine* because they are related to their parents by blood ties. For the parents, such a family is one of *procreation*, because their relationship does not depend on blood ties but on having produced children.

The nuclear family is usually the product of urban industrial societies, in which there is significant geographical mobility. This kind of mobility results in relatives being left behind in rural areas while new families are established in urban centers. In an industrial economy, opportunities for social mobility are also greater. An upwardly mobile individual tends to break the ties binding him to an extended family, especially if that family is of a low social class.

Another reason why the nuclear family is typical of industrial societies is that functions originally performed by primary groups have been transferred to secondary groups. Thus, a large family group is not essential. Many functions of the family institution—protection, education, health care, money lending, and so on—have also been taken over by separate institutions. Finally, in an industrial society, achieved status is more important than is ascribed status. Thus what a person does through his own effort is sometimes considered more important than his family's social position.[9]

In the United States, the nuclear family followed industrialization and urbanization. But, there are signs that the nuclear family may become the predominant kind of family in many of the developing nations as well. This is probably happening because the life style of the nuclear family is compatible with the values of industrial societies. Almost all developing nations are trying to industrialize, of course, and the values of industrial societies are spreading throughout the world.

Family Organization

In different societies, families are organized in different ways. Differing patterns have evolved regarding such matters as who holds authority, where the family resides, how transfer of property is accomplished, and what obligations parents and their children have. Families in which authority is vested in the oldest living male are called *patriarchal*. This has been the traditional pattern in both Muslim and Western societies, although in the latter patriarchy

---

[9]William J. Goode, *World Revolution and Family Patterns* (New York: Free Press, 1963).

has been progressively challenged. The characteristic of patriarchal families is that the father holds almost absolute power over wife and children.

Less common are *matriarchal* families, in which the source of authority is the mother. Today, matriarchal families are found among the lowest socioeconomic classes of many societies. These families are without a male head of household because the man has left the family or was unable to provide a living. In very few instances have females had authority in both familial and social structures as a normal pattern of behavior.

Today's American family is neither patriarchal nor matriarchal. Although the mother is frequently accused of dominance in the absence of the father, whose occupation keeps him away from home, in reality, it is the father whose income and profession determine the family's status. The word *egalitarian* is sometimes used to denote the contemporary American family. However, families in which the husband and wife have equal authority seem to be more a future goal than a present fact.

Historically, families have also differed in the way by which they trace descent for the purpose of passing along the family name and determining inheritance. In a *patrilineal* arrangement, family name, inheritance, and other obligations are passed through the male line, or the father's ancestors. In a *matrilineal* arrangement, the opposite is true, and descent is traced through the mother's ancestors. In a *bilateral* arrangement, both the father's and the mother's lines determine descent and inheritance patterns.

The residence of a newly married couple also varies according to family organization. In the *patrilocal* kind of organization, the couple takes up residence with the husband's parents. In the *matrilocal* kind, the couple resides with the wife's parents. The current trend is toward *neolocal* arrangements, in which the married couple lives away from both sets of parents.

UNIVERSAL FAMILY FUNCTIONS

We have already discussed briefly many of the functions of the family institution. However, a short summary of the traditional functions performed by families in all societies should indicate how the modern American family differs from or resembles the universal family institution.

Regulation of Sex

Although the basis for marriage is more economic than sexual, no society leaves the regulation of sex to chance. All societies attempt to channel the sex drive so sexual relations take place between persons who have legitimate access to each other—that is, access sanctioned by society, rather than dependent on chance encounters (or what we call promiscuous behavior). Precisely how this is done varies from society to society. Most societies, for instance, permit premarital experimentation and do not give any importance to female or male virginity. But experimentation is not haphazard. There is always a purpose for it—finding a satisfactory mate, proving fertility, and so on. In short, in many societies, premarital sex is institutionalized and is a societal norm, rather than being considered a deviation, as it has been in our society.

Most societies encourage marriage and give high status to married people. They also make a distinction between marriages—unions sanctioned by the society—and unions entered into by consenting partners without such sanction. By the same token, most societies discourage bachelorhood and spinsterhood. In some, there are no unmarried people, because provisions are made for every societal member to enjoy a fairly full sex life. One such provision is the *levirate*. In societies in which this custom is practiced, the brothers-in-law of a woman who has been widowed take charge of her and her children. When the *sororate* is practiced, a widowed man gains access to his wife's sisters. Occasional sexual hospitality and ceremonial license (sexual relations as part of a ceremony) are also used by some societies to permit their members sexual expression.

Reproduction

The reproduction of the species has been a fundamental function of the family institution. In many societies, an individual does not reach the status of an adult until he produces an offspring. Other societies attach no stigma to children born out of wedlock and provide for their incorporation into the family structure. However, in no society has the reproductive function been performed outside of the family institution.

Reproduction remains a basic function of today's American family, but reproduction takes place in vastly changed circumstances. Urbanization and industrialization have caused changes in society, in the economic system, and in values, which have, in turn, caused the American family to decrease in size. Because of the decline in infant mortality, it is no longer necessary for couples to have many children to make sure that at least a few live to adulthood. Furthermore, because the family has ceased to be the basic economic unit, children are no longer needed to work in the fields and around the house. In fact, in an urban industrial environment, children become liabilities. They must be fed, educated, and cared for—an expensive proposition all around.

Increased education has broadened most Americans' horizons. Parents may decide to concentrate on upward mobility. They may wish to travel or pursue specialized careers. In most cases, they want to give their children as many advantages as they can. The chances of attaining these goals are improved if the number of children is small. People are also aware of the dangers of overpopulation and are curbing their fertility for this reason.

The practical means of limiting family size have depended on the continued improvement and distribution of contraceptive devices. Contraception, or some method of birth control, has been known for thousands of years. But reasons for practicing it did not exist until fairly recently. Contraception, however, is not totally accepted even in our technological society. In general, it has greater acceptance in urban than in rural areas, in the middle and upper classes than in the working and lower classes, and among Protestants and Jews than among Roman Catholics and members of the fundamentalist sects of Protestantism.

From all indications, the trend toward small families will continue. This is encouraging for several reasons. First, because of acute overpopulation and a growing worldwide birth rate, it is important that we curb our own birth

rate. Second, several studies have suggested that small families offer more satisfaction, contentment, and self-fulfillment to all of their members than do large families.[10]

Socialization

Most societies depend on the family to socialize their young, although some have attempted to transfer this function to other agencies, as we saw in our discussion of the USSR and the Israeli kibbutzim. At any rate, in almost all societies, socialization within the family is the most important factor in the formation of personality.

In the examination of socialization in Chapter 3, we emphasized that the child's self-concept is shaped by others around him. Because the self emerges only as a reflection of others, it is essential that these others—the significant others, or the family, and later the generalized other, or the society—reflect

---

[10]E. James Lieberman, "The Case for Small families," *New York Times Magazine* (March 8, 1970), pp. 86-89. Also, F. Ivan Nye, John Carlson, and Gerald Garrett: "Family Size, Interaction, Affect, and Stress," *Journal of Marriage and the Family* (May, 1970), pp. 216-226.

a desirable image. Thus, parents play an especially crucial role in socialization. The chances are good that the child will develop into a fairly complete human being and will fit easily into the roles that society will impose on him if his parents offer a successful model for him to imitate and if they provide him with an ego-bolstering looking glass, so he comes to think of himself as competent, capable, and "good." They must also provide him with enough love if he is to become loving, with enough tolerance and understanding if he is to be tolerant and understanding of others, and with enough discipline if he is to learn the importance of self-discipline.

But the chances are good that the individual will grow up into a human being who, hating himself, hates society if his parents are inadequate. Inadequate parents reflect back to the child an image of inferiority and failure. They give little love and much disinterest and neglect, little tolerance and understanding but many commands that must be obeyed, and little discipline but much harsh punishment.

Although the function of socialization has remained basically within the family, institutionalized education—the schools and the peer group—have taken over a large part of the transmission of knowledge. At the same time, some sociologists maintain that the family has become even more important as an agent for establishing the individual's identification and for readying the child to function in the wider society when he reaches adulthood.[11]

In today's family, socialization is particularly influential in the area of selection of mates for dating and marriage. In Chapter 3, we saw how attitudes concerning race, politics, and class are transmitted in the process of socialization without being consciously taught. Largely as a result of this influence, most people do date and marry within their race, religion, and social class.

The family also influences the offspring's political behavior. In harmonious and satisfying homes, the children identify with their parents' political views.[12] Such parental identification is further reflected by a successful adaptation in marriage. In other words, husbands and wives who were the products of happy, loving homes identify with their parents and become well-adjusted partners in their own marriage. The opposite is unfortunately also true, and products of broken homes are themselves good prospects for divorce.

Whereas the content of socialization has become more limited, its quality has become more complicated. Today's parents are much more aware of personality formation, and most try to follow the experts' latest advice on child rearing. This advice has swung widely from extreme permissiveness to extreme rigidity, but children seem to grow up in spite of it! Some social scientists, among them psychiatrist Bruno Bettelheim, have suggested that the recent crop of campus radicals may be the result of permissive upbringing at the hands of their well-educated, affluent, middle-class parents.

Affection and Companionship

The need for affection and companionship appears to be a fundamental human need. Countless studies indicate that a lack of affection in an individual's background may cause delinquency and criminality, emotional

[11]Talcott Parsons, "The Normal American Family," in Seymour M. Farber, et al., *Man and Civilization* (New York: McGraw Hill, 1965), p. 44.

[12]James C. Davies, "The Family's Role in Political Socialization," *Annals of the American Academy of Political and Social Science* (September, 1965), p. 10.

and mental problems, and even physical illness. In fact, children who are given care in a faultless physical environment but who lack affection often become ill or even die.[13]

Companionship may be found in friendship groups and sometimes even in secondary groups such as voluntary organizations. Affection, however, is almost exclusively found within the family group, at least on a fairly stable basis. Because most people today tend to get together with members of their extended family only for Thanksgiving and Christmas and often have very

---

[13]Rene A. Spitz, "An Inquiry into the Genesis of Psychiatric Conditions in Early Childhood," *The Psychoanalytic Study of the Child*, Vol. I (1945), pp. 53-74. Also, Rene A. Spitz, "Hospitalism: A Follow-Up Report," *The Psychoanalytic Study of the Child*, Vol. II (New York: Columbia University Press, 1944).

little in common with them except perhaps a last name, the entire burden of providing affection lies with the nuclear family.

For many reasons, partners in a marriage are not always able to sustain an affectionate relationship. And when such a relationship is lacking, there is not much left to hold the family together. This, then, is the nuclear family's greatest shortcoming: A loveless relationship between the marriage partners is a traumatic experience for all members of the nuclear family, whether or not it ends in dissolution of the family through divorce. Extended families provided a cushioning effect, by which both conflict and affection could be diffused among several members, rather than being limited to the members of the family nucleus.

Status

The family's function of providing the new member of society with his first statuses has remained practically unchanged. The newly born individual acquires the ascribed statuses of sex, age, and order of birth, and he acquires the social, racial, religious, and economic statuses of his parents. As we said in Chapter 4, in our discussion of systems of stratification, the child begins life by inheriting the social class of his family. This, without a doubt, affects his future. In a society with a fairly open class system, social mobility is possible. But if the child is born into a low social class, his parents and others close to him will inadvertently socialize him in such a way that he will tend to remain in this class.

Among the middle classes of our society, socialization is frequently geared toward upward mobility. In other words, children are encouraged to obtain an education in order to attain a high social status. Today, many young people seem to be rejecting these goals. No one can yet determine how their resistance will affect their place in the stratification system.

Protection

The protective function has traditionally been much more pronounced in extended families than it has in nuclear ones. In an extended family, each member is offered whatever help is necessary against whatever threatens him. By the same token, any act committed against a member or by a member reflects on the entire family. For instance, an extended family feels justified in taking revenge against whoever has wounded or killed one of its members. We are perhaps familiar with Southern European or Latin families in which the brothers of a girl take it upon themselves to force a shotgun wedding on the man who seduced their sister. At the same time, the girl who becomes pregnant out of wedlock disgraces her whole family, not only her parents. In short, in traditional societies with extended families, the family acts as a mutual protection association, because there may be few or no other institutions to take care of people.

In the change from the patriarchal to the somewhat egalitarian family, many of the protective functions that were formerly performed by the head of the household have been taken over by federal, state, and local agencies. A father who cannot adequately provide for his family may now appeal to one of the welfare agencies. And a father who mistreats his family can be punished by a legal agency, and his children made wards of the state.

Other functions such as care of the ill and aged members of the family have also been removed from the family sphere. Because of the increased specialization of medicine, sick care is best accomplished in hospitals. And because of the difficulty of caring for aged relatives in households in which most or all members work or are otherwise occupied, special nursing homes for the elderly have come into existence. Many old people resent being disposed of in this manner when they are no longer able to contribute to the family's welfare. On the other hand, life with such aged individuals in the modern nuclear family may be a trying and conflict-producing experience.

Economy

The family in the traditional nonindustrial society is the fundamental economic unit. It both produces and consumes the goods and services essential to its survival. According to an agreed upon division of labor, different members of the family till the soil, plant and harvest, gather additional food and fuel, build the family's shelter, cook the food, and sew the clothes.

In urban industrial societies, these functions have been assumed by numerous other institutions that make up what we call the economy. In fact, it is in this area that the family has experienced the greatest extent of change. The change from a productive unit to a unit of consumption, though resulting in a vastly improved standard of living, has caused difficulties.

When both male and female members of extended families worked around the home producing the necessities of life, young members could identify with them and eventually duplicate their roles in the family economy. Today, the male's work, and increasingly the female's work, is done in factories and offices, away from home and children. The product of such work is not a harvest, or an animal killed in a hunt, or even a building erected by the family but a monetary reward in the form of a check. Clothes are no longer woven and sewn at home but bought in a department store. With the exception of an occasional cake or loaf of bread made from scratch, most cooking is done from cans, frozen packages, and cellophane-wrapped prepared foods. In short, nothing is produced. The family is a place in which things are consumed. This makes it very difficult for the young who are being socialized within the family to assume proper adult roles. Because preparation for occupational roles no longer occurs within the family, and because these roles are largely invisible, the young person has no immediate role to which he can aspire or after which he can model himself.

Other Functions

Among the other functions that were much more a part of the traditional extended family than they are of the modern nuclear one are recreation, religion, and education. In the past, the family was the principal source of recreation and it was the focal point around which recreation revolved. Even when recreation was pursued elsewhere, it was organized and encouraged by the family. Increasingly, recreation has become a function of commercial establishments such as movie theaters, bowling alleys, bars, golf courses, and so on. Television seems to be opposing this tendency to find recreation outside the family. But television often does not attract young adults, who tend to spend free time with one another. Furthermore, it provides a passive experience which does not lead to communication.

Although the family has always reinforced religion—many of the ethical values that the child is taught are couched in religious terms—most of the teaching of religious principles and ritual have become functions of the religious institution. And with the increasing indifference to religion within society, even such customs as saying grace before meals and evening prayers are maintained by an increasingly small number of families.

In like manner, in our complex society, education is now considered largely a function of the schools. There is simply too much information for any one family to teach. However, attitudes toward education—whether it is considered important, desirable, or insignificant—are very definitely acquired in the family setting and are a function of socialization. (We will have further occasion to speak about the religious and educational institutions in later chapters.)

THE AMERICAN FAMILY

Because our society is made up of various racial and ethnic groups, it is difficult to talk about "the American family." Obviously, life in a lower-class black American family differs immensely from life in a white upper-upper class family. Similarly, the experiences of a member of an urban Jewish middle-class family are far removed from those of a person brought up in a family of rural fundamentalists. Nonetheless, there is an American family, at least in contrast to the Russian family or the Chinese family. In other words, for particular purposes, we must speak in terms of stereotypes. In such terms, the American family resembles families in television commercials: white, middle-class, urban, and Protestant.

This generalized American family acquired its forms from the Puritan immigrants. The Puritans brought with them a monogamous form of marriage, a patriarchal form of family organization, and a Judeo-Christian ideology. In addition, they brought the stark and rigid ideas of the Protestant Reformation. Thus, they regulated sexual behavior not only by custom but by law. In the colony of Massachusetts, for instance, adultery was punished by death. Later, the sentence was reduced to being fined and wearing the letter *A* (the Scarlet Letter) on one's clothing. For a period of time, the state of Connecticut punished adultery, homosexuality, and bestiality with the death penalty.

The existence of such laws illustrates society's belief in the damaging effects of sex outside marriage. This belief may be traced to the long-standing philosophical debate between the values of the flesh and those of the spirit. In this debate, the Christian Church has proclaimed the superiority of the spirit, perhaps in overreaction to the pagan stress on the senses. At any rate, throughout the history of Christianity, people have deviated from the formal sexual norms of society. There are no statistics to show the extent of deviation in colonial times. But in our own times, statistics are plentiful. A glance at the data collected by Dr. Kinsey some twenty years ago shows that 25 percent of the women and 50 percent of the men in Kinsey's sample had experienced extramarital relations before the age of forty.[14]

The Liberalization of Sexual Norms

In the past decade, there has been an extreme liberalization of sexual norms. Although a substantial number of people, even young people, still subscribe to the so-called old-fashioned virtues, alternate norms are also widely practiced. Although some of the mass media would have us believe that premarital sex is becoming the norm for both men and women, this has not been generally supported by the facts. Studies indicate that the proportion of brides and grooms who have had premarital intercourse—approximately 50 percent of the brides and 75 percent of the grooms—has remained fairly constant since the Kinsey studies.[15]

Change has, however, occurred—especially in the formality of the relationship between the two people having intercourse—as shown by a study based on the decade 1958-1968. In 1958, only 10 percent of the girls had intercourse while dating, 15 percent while going steady, and 31 percent while engaged; but in 1968, 23 percent had premarital relations while dating, 28 percent while going steady, and 39 percent while engaged.[16]

An even more recent research project by two Johns Hopkins demographers yields much more radical conclusions and seems to indicate that people are having premarital relations at a younger age than they did in the past. The researchers claim that almost half of all single American girls become nonvirgins before they are twenty. Furthermore, 14 percent of the fifteen-year-olds in the sample (a sample that totaled 4,611 girls living at home or in college dormitories) had experienced sexual relations; 21 percent at age 16; 27 percent at age 17; 37 percent at age 18; and more than 46 percent at age 19.

This study also notes marked racial differences, which the researchers think are the result of social class: The percentage of black girls who have had sexual intercourse at age fifteen is 32, whereas the percentage of white girls is 11; at age nineteen, the percentages are 81 for black girls and 40 for white girls. But the white girls, according to the study, are the more promiscuous and engage in sex more frequently. In fact, 16 percent of the white girls reported having four or more partners, whereas only 11 percent of the black girls had the same number. Additional information gathered by the study is that sex is engaged in rather infrequently (70 percent reported a frequency of twice a month) and that teenagers seem naive and ill informed regarding sex and contraception. As a consequence, 41 percent of the black girls, 10 percent of the white girls, and 26 percent of girls of both races were or had been pregnant.[17]

---

[14]Alfred C. Kinsey, Wardell B. Pomeroy, and Clyde E. Martin, *Sexual Behavior in the Human Male* (Philadelphia: W. B. Saunders, 1948) p. 586. Also Alfred C. Kinsey, et al., *Sexual Behavior in the Human Female* (Philadelphia: W. B. Saunders, 1953), p. 416.

[15]Harold T. Christensen and Christina F. Gregg, "Changing Sex Norms in America and Scandinavia," *Journal of Marriage and the Family* (November, 1970), pp. 616-627. Also, Ira Robinson et al., "Change in Sexual Behavior and Attitudes of College Students," *The Family Coordinator* (April, 1968), pp. 119-123.

[16]Robert R. Bell and Jay B. Chaskes, "Premarital Sexual Experience Among Coeds, 1958 and 1968," *Journal of Marriage and the Family* (February, 1970), pp. 81-84.

[17]"Outmoded Virginity," *Time* (May 22, 1972), pp. 69-70.

Such statistics indicate a significant change in premarital sexual behavior patterns. Furthermore, they point to the increasing gap between the conventional ideals of the adult world and the actual behavior of both adults and young people. It may be, then, that we are not witnessing the advent of a new morality but honesty about the old.

Premarital sexual norms are not the only sexual norms undergoing change. Extramarital sex is also taking a new direction, to judge from the number of "swingers' clubs" springing up in most metropolitan areas. There is no doubt that the trend away from institutionalized sex in marriage and toward nonmarital sex with affection (or even just for fun) will have a significant impact on the American family. But in what direction will change occur?

The American Family: Change or Decay?

We have already seen that the institution of the family has provoked controversy. Some people believe that it stifles individuality; others think that society cannot exist without it. But the family has awakened yet another controversy, centering on interpretations of its present condition and its future. There are those who deplore the high divorce rate, sexual permissiveness, the stress on youth, glamor, and the pleasures of the senses, and the declining birth rate. To some people, these trends seem to be very real threats to the family—the institution that acts as a pillar of society. They view changes in the family as symptoms of decay and fear that the decay will spread to the entire society.[18]

Others have interpreted the changes in family structure as functional—appropriate to today's urban industrial society. In such a society, they claim, the family becomes nuclear because specialized functions are best performed by institutions that are separate from it. On the other hand, because the family is nuclear, it can concentrate on such remaining functions as socialization of children and affectional support. At the same time, it can efficiently pursue the values of the society, particularly upward mobility and personal satisfaction.[19]

Still others, though admitting that the family is in a state of disorganization, believe that this condition is only a prelude to change. They see the scope and functions of the family in a state of transition and redefinition. They feel that the emergent family form is that of a unit based on affectionate companionship. In such a family, the giving and receiving of affection would be the foremost concern of the members, who would live in an egalitarian, democratic fashion.[20]

Finally, some researchers maintain that the nuclear family is not so isolated, after all. They have uncovered evidence that much interaction with relatives does in fact go on. Thus, the extended family pattern has meaning even within urban industrial society.[21]

[18]Carle C. Zimmerman, *Family and Civilization* (New York: Harper & Row, 1947). Also, Pitirim Sorokin, *The Crisis of Our Age* (New York: Dutton, 1941).

[19]Hyman Rodman, "Talcott Parson's View of the Changing American Family," in *Marriage, Family, and Society* (New York: Random House, 1965), pp. 262-283.

[20]Ernest W. Burgess, Harvey J. Locke, and Margaret Thomas, *The Family: From Institution to Companionship* (New York: American Books, 1963).

[21]Herbert Gans, *The Urban Villagers* (Boston: Harvard Medical School, Center of Community Studies, 1959), pp. 45-53.

Where does all this leave us? Whose theory are we to accept? Will the American family withstand the onslaught of change, or will it collapse and drag the whole society down with it? As usual, there are no pat answers. And a great deal depends on individual values. People who value a stable, well-disciplined society, in which there is emphasis on the welfare of the group, must be appalled at the changes taking place in the family. People whose chief goal is personal fulfillment think the family is changing in the right direction.

The article "The Family Is Out of Fashion," by Ann Richardson Roiphe, contains a sensitive portrayal of today's nuclear family. The author admits that this type of family organization has many shortcomings. But she concludes that it will survive, perhaps with alterations, because it contains the only workable alternative for our kind of society.[22]

Besides the changes that the family has undergone so far—from extended to nuclear, from patriarchal to quasi-egalitarian, from a productive unit to a consumption unit, from many functions to few—it is presently undergoing additional changes. These involve division of labor and changing sex roles, courtship and marriage patterns, and the dissolution of the family unit.

Division of Labor and Changing Sex Roles

Division of labor between males and females has traditionally been a by-product of marriage and family organization. The definitions of what is man's work and what is woman's work vary from society to society, but the division itself is visible everywhere. In some societies, sex roles are clearly defined and rigidly enforced, whereas in others, they are generalized and casual.

Women's roles. The definitions of sex roles in different societies are not based on strictly biological differences. Rather, the tasks assigned to women revolve around child care, are of a type that can be performed close to home, and are such that they can withstand frequent interruptions. The tasks assigned to men are generally performed away from home and involve much more adventure and risks. Although such a division of labor may be based on common sense (after all, a woman with a baby at her breast is not in the best position to hunt or fish) the interpretation of sex roles has been a distorted one. Generally, men have believed that their tasks are superior, more important, and more meaningful than are women's tasks. An outgrowth of this belief is the image of the male as a superior human being.

What is more, women have become convinced of the same thing. Thus, the patriarchal family, which offered a perfect background for this type of thinking, produced generation upon generation of women schooled in submissiveness and in the belief that "a woman's place is in the home." Women believed that they were incapable of performing any task beyond those involving the kitchen, the children, and the church—the famous three K's from the German *Küche, Kinder, und Kirche.*

Changes in women's roles. The pattern of female sex roles began to break with the shift of production from the home to the factory. Women, and at first even children, began to flock to the factories because work there was considered less demanding than at home. What is more, the income that women brought in strengthened their position in the family to the point that they were almost on a par with males. But even though their strengthened position led to some legal changes—women's suffrage, for example—women are still very far from having acquired equality with men. Such equality will not be forthcoming

---

[22]Ann Richardson Roiphe, "The Family Is Out of Fashion," *New York Times Magazine* (August 15, 1971), pp. 11-34.

until we develop a new process of socialization in which female children are not taught traditional female roles.[23]

Women are seldom considered in the literature dealing with occupation and work, and if they are, they are viewed only as temporary workers, second jobholders in a male-headed family, or primary jobholders in a disorganized family.[24] In reality, however, one-third of the work force in the United States is made up of women. In 1970, this represented 40 percent of American women, of whom 81 percent were married. The new norm seems to be for women to work for several years prior to marriage, stay at home while children are small, and then return to work until retirement age.

In the first decades of this century, the only women who worked were those whose husbands were unable or unwilling to support them. Today, working women are increasingly from the middle and upper social classes. This trend is probably the result of increased amounts of education. Women have begun to realize that their roles as wives, mothers, and housekeepers do not permit them to develop sufficiently as individuals. This realization has led to the rapid spread and wide acceptance of the Women's Liberation Movement.

Working wives create several problems in a nuclear family. Working wives want a new method of division of labor, one that is not based on the traditional male and female sex roles. In other words, when a working wife returns home at the same time as her husband, she does not want to go in the kitchen, prepare supper, and clean up afterwards, while her husband reads the newspaper and sips his martini.

Then, there is the problem of children. In a nuclear family, there are no relatives to care for them. Some couples have experimented by working in six-month shifts so each parent assumes both roles of provider and housekeeper. Day-care centers, which are strongly recommended by feminists, seem to offer an ideal solution.

Many such problems will not be worked out immediately, and many will have to be solved by individual couples. For instance, when both marriage partners work, what happens when one of them gets a promotion that necessitates moving to another part of the country? The other partner is left with the option of following and having to look for a new job or remaining and having to look for another spouse! How does the couple decide whether to stay or go, if both partners find satisfaction in their careers? Some suggest that drawing up individual marriage contracts would help avoid some of these problems before they arise.

Current Sex Roles

Egalitarianism in sex roles is a definite trend, especially among the young, who even reflect this in their appearance—both sexes wear long hair and blue jeans. However, in the majority of today's families, there is an important separation of sex-linked roles. Society defines, and the infant perceives, the mother's role as expressive—as nurturing, comforting, and holding the family together. The father's role is defined as the instrumental one: It is he who

---

[23]William J. Goode, "Industrialization and Family Structure," in Norman W. Bell and Ezra F. Vogel, eds., *The Family* (New York: Free Press, 1968), p. 119.
[24]R. R. Bell, *Marriage and Family Interaction* (Homewood, Ill.: The Dorsey Press), p. 355.

provides the link to the outside world through his occupation and he who is the provider.[25]

If equality of the sexes is the aim, patterns of socialization must be broken, and the expressive and the instrumental roles will have to be shared equally by both parents. If the aim of socialization continues to be the same—if we want to produce individuals who will fulfill the same roles in the same way—the father should be strong and dominant, even if he is emotionally cold, and the mother should be affectionate. A reversal of these roles—a weak and an ineffective, even though affectionate, father and a strong, dominant mother—has been found to be the pattern of socialization among homosexuals.

In this context, a number of sociologists have pointed out that much of the seeming disorganization of the lower-class black family stems from a situation in which there is a dominant, strong mother and a weak, ineffective father. This situation is often the result of socioeconomic forces: The unskilled black woman is in more demand in the work force than is the unskilled black male. Therefore she, more often than he, is the family's breadwinner. Perceiving himself as inadequate, the male increasingly turns to alcohol, drugs, and other unemployed males for companionship. The children, especially the males, are then left with no adequate models from whom to learn roles and with whom to identify.

This popular theory, first set forth by the black sociologist E. Franklin Frazier, was later substantially repeated in a Department of Labor publication, the chief author of which was Patrick Moynihan. Lately, however, this theory has been challenged and partially rejected by a number of sociologists.

Selecting Marriage Partners

We have mentioned before that families influence their children in the matter of selecting marriage partners. The influence runs in the direction of persuading them to marry mates of the same race, ethnic background, and religion. The reason for the parents' desire that their children marry one of their "own kind" tends to be primarily ethnocentric. But as a matter of fact, marriages that are both endogamous—within one's group—and homogamous—between persons with similar characteristics—are also the most successful in terms of duration and quality of relationship.

Of course, people probably tend to marry their own kind simply because most social interaction goes on within groups that are fairly similar. Thus, the selection of marriage partners is a process of narrowing down possibilities to members of groups that are near, either because of residence or because of occupation, and that are alike in age, race, religion, education, and social class.

Marriage partner selection from among limited groups still exists although there has been a tremendous shift from the selection of mates by older members in the patriarchal family to individual choice of mates in the egalitarian family. However, because of the processes of social stratification in the United States, individuals belonging to more or less the same social classes, religion, and race live in the same neighborhoods, attend the same schools, and interact in the same social circles.

[25]William J. Goode, *The Family* (Englewood Cliffs, N. J.: Prentice-Hall, 1969), p. 71.

Interfaith Marriage

Dating and marriage across religious lines, once infrequent and frowned upon, is on the increase. This is especially true among the higher social classes. According to one study, one out of three Catholic college graduates married out of his faith, as against one out of fifteen Catholics with an eighth-grade education.[26]

Among the three principal religions in the United States, Jews have the lowest rates of out-marriage, somewhere between 5 and 10 percent. However, the rate varies according to the availability of Jewish partners. In situations in which there is a lack of available Jewish partners, the out-marriage rate is highest.[27]

Experts interpret the increase in interfaith marriages in different ways. Some believe that the population in general is becoming more homogeneous and sophisticated. Others think that democratic and romantic notions are beginning to prevail over prejudices. At the same time, we are also reminded that interfaith marriages often end because of irreconcilable conflicts, and that the partners in such marriages exhibit weak family ties, weak religious ties, and tend to be products of unsatisfactory homes.[28]

Interracial Marriage

Race remains the strongest barrier to intermarriage in the United States. Although laws against interracial marriages have been removed, there is still a great deal of opposition to them. This is caused by prejudice, which plays such an important part in our society.

The most common interracial marriages, and those that evoke the sharpest degree of criticism, are black-white unions. As of the mid 1960s, the highest percentages of such unions were reported in Hawaii (16 percent) and in California (2.58 percent).[29] Rates have probably increased somewhat during the last five years, but there is little evidence suggesting that there is a clear trend toward interracial marriage.

Typically, in the interracial marriages that have taken place, the male is an upper-middle class black, and the woman is a lower or lower-middle class white. Thus, the woman trades her superior caste position for a superior class position.[30] Both partners, then, gain in different facets of status. Some research projects have challenged the implication that such marriages represent attempts at upward mobility on the part of both husband and wife. However, researchers have not been able to explain why black husbands outnumber black wives in interracial marriages. But the studies do indicate that the trend is changing and that more and more interracial marriages are occurring between partners who are nearly equal educationally, economically, and culturally.[31]

[26]Ibid., p. 36.

[27]Hyman Rodman, ed., *Marriage, Family, and Society* (New York: Random House, 1965), p. 56.

[28]Jerald S. Heiss, "Premarital Characteristics of the Religiously Intermarried," *American Sociological Review* (February, 1960), pp. 47-55.

[29]David M. Heer, "Negro-White Marriage in the United States," *Journal of Marriage and the Family* (August, 1966), pp. 262-273.

[30]William J. Goode, "Industrialization and Family Structure," in Norman W. Bell and Ezra F. Vogel, eds., *The Family*, p. 37.

[31]Todd H. Pavela, "An Exploratory Study of Negro-White Intermarriage in Indiana," *Marriage and Family Living* (May, 1964), pp. 209-211.

Methods of Mate Selection

We take for granted that individuals choose their marriage partners. However, the findings of a comparative study indicate that only five other societies besides ours permit relatively free choice of mates.[32] In most other societies, the choice is made by parents or older male members of families.

In the past, this was true in the United States too. But with the decline of the patriarchal family, the reason for marriage has become much less economic and much more based on ideas of romantic love. Romantic love as a basis for marriage is in sharp contrast with Oriental societies in which "the stability of the family and the maintenance of the social order always come before the happiness of the individual."[33] What is more, the romantic approach to marriage is not being accepted very readily even in areas that have otherwise been susceptible to Western influences.[34]

[32]William N. Stephens, *The Family in Cross-Cultural Perspective* (New York: Holt, Rinehart and Winston, 1963), p. 198.
[33]David and Vera Mace, *Marriage East and West* (Garden City, N. Y.: Doubleday, 1960), p. 124.
[34]George A. Theodorson, "Romanticism and Motivation to Marry in the United States, Singapore, Burma, and India," *Social Forces* (September, 1965), p. 27.

Some elements of romantic love as it exists today in American society include the following: (1) idealization, or choosing to see only the best in the loved partner; (2) fantasy, or withdrawal into an imaginary world with the loved partner; (3) a high degree of emotionality, or a preference for feeling instead of thinking; (4) exclusiveness, or a belief in a unique relationship with the loved partner; (5) the idea of the soul mate, or the belief that the partners were meant for each other; (6) the idea of love at first sight, or the belief that love is experienced on first seeing the loved partner; (7) the overcoming of obstacles, or the belief that a love that is tested is stronger than one that runs smoothly; and (8) the idea of love conquering all, or the belief that love will find a way of overcoming the most pressing problems of everyday life.[35]

Romantic notions of love are the remnants of a long tradition of thought in Western civilization. They have been publicized and emphasized in the mass media, particularly in popular songs, women's magazines, pulp literature, and soap operas. Although no one is naive enough to believe in all of these notions unquestioningly and to select a marriage partner solely on their strength, nonetheless, they do affect many relationships.

The generation that is now of marriageable age shows some signs of rejecting these romantic notions. Much of the current music lacks the "mushy" quality of earlier popular music and stresses love of all mankind rather than only love between man and woman. In the past, most Americans believed that romantic love was not only necessary for marriage but that marriage was the only satisfactory consequence of such love. But this is no longer universally true.[36] Changing sexual norms have made possible male-female relationships that include sex and cohabitation but not necessarily marriage.

Family Disorganization

Family disorganization is the sociological term for a breakup of the family unit resulting from the failure of one or more members to perform his role adequately.[37] There are six major forms of family disorganization: (1) illegitimacy; (2) annulment, separation, divorce, or desertion; (3) male-female, parent-youth conflicts resulting from changes in the definition of cultural roles; (4) the empty shell family, in which members live together but fail to communicate and give emotional support to one another; (5) external events, such as death, imprisonment, natural catastrophes; (6) internal events, such as mental and emotional illness, chronic physical illness, and so on.[38]

Divorce.   Although some of these forms of disorganization have always existed, family breakup following divorce is becoming common and is viewed as a danger to the future of the family. This last view is based on religious attitudes, whereby marriage is considered a holy union sanctioned by God and therefore not dissolvable by mortals. Also, our romantic notion that marriage is based on everlasting love makes it difficult to accept the failure of marriage.

[35]R. R. Bell, *Marriage and Family Interaction*, pp. 108-111.
[36]Ibid., p. 113.
[37]William J. Goode, "Family Disorganization," in Robert K. Merton and Robert Nisbet, eds., *Contemporary Social Problems* (New York: Harcourt Brace Jovanovich, 1971), p. 468.
[38]Ibid., p. 469.

Any situation in which two individuals, with differing needs and desires and possibly with different values and backgrounds, are forced to live together for long periods of time produces some tension and conflict. But tensions must be prevented from becoming destructive to marriage. In some societies, the expectations of what the partners are to find in marriage are not great. In such societies, members value the kinship network over the husband-wife relationship. Some irritations and conflicts are considered unavoidable, and people are expected to live with them for the good of society.

No society has encouraged divorce, but most have recognized that some sources of conflict between husband and wife are so intolerable that it is impossible for them to continue living together. Consequently, safety valves have been provided. In most cases, divorce laws have favored the male, who has found it easy to enter a new union. Even today, women, in some societies, have no recourse to legal action when they are unhappily married, though this situation is rapidly changing.

Divorce in the United States. The high rates of divorce in urban industrial societies reflect the separation of marriage from religion, the emancipation of women, and the change in values to a new emphasis on individuality and personal happiness. Among Western nations, the United States has the highest divorce rates (one out of every three marriages ends in divorce). The majority of divorces are granted to young people (twenty to thirty-five years old), who have been married a short time and who were married when the wife was a teenager. Some 6 percent of married couples have been married three or more times, indicating that divorce occurs more frequently among couples who remarry.[39] At the same time, the fact that couples do remarry indicates that it is not the institution of marriage that is spurned but the individual partner in the particular marriage who is considered inadequate. Marriage itself is a highly prized status.

Some characteristics of marriage partners make them prone to divorce. According to one sociologist, divorce occurs most often among people in particular situations and with particular backgrounds: (1) They live in urban areas; (2) they married at sixteen to nineteen years of age; (3) they married after a short period of acquaintance and/or a short engagement; (4) they grew up with a poor model of marriage presented by their parents; (5) they are nonchurchgoers or of different faiths; (6) their marriage evoked disapproval from their family and friends; (7) their backgrounds are dissimilar; (8) they define their role obligations differently.[40]

Furthermore, research data indicate that marriage instability is inversely proportional to socioeconomic status. In other words, those at the low end of the stratification system, as measured by income and status of profession, have the highest rate of divorce. The reasons for this are not entirely clear. It is possible, however, that husband and wife are dissatisfied with both the quality of the husband's job and its economic rewards, and that this dissatisfaction leads to severe tension in the marriage. [41]

[39]Divorce Statistics Analysis, United States 1963, Public Health Service Publication No. 1000, Series 21, No. 13, pp. 6-39.
[40]William J. Goode, "Family Disorganization," in Robert K. Merton and Robert Nisbet, eds., *Contemporary Social Problems*, p. 500-501.
[41]William J. Goode, *Women in Divorce* (New York: Free Press, 1965), Chapters 4, 5.

The legal grounds on which divorces are obtained range from cruelty, which has come to mean incompatibility (three-fifths of all divorces), to desertion (17 percent), adultery, drunkenness, and failure to provide a living. The real causes for divorce are difficult to determine because the reasons given by marriage partners are frequently superficial. Often, there is an underlying cause of which they may or may not be aware. Women tend to give such reasons as nonsupport, adultery, gambling, drunkenness, and desertion. Men tend to complain about unsatisfactory sexual relations, or frigidity in their wives. And both tend to use lack of affection as justification for divorce.

Regardless of the reasons for divorce, the innocent victims are children. The number of children of divorced parents is increasing, because children are no longer the deterrent to divorce that they were in the past. Statistics indicate that in the decade from 1953 to 1963, the number of children of divorced parents increased by 77 percent. However, there are still about the same number of one-parent homes; because of the decrease in the death rate, fewer parents die than in the past, and thus the situation has been equalized. Moreover, it is debatable whether it is preferable for children to live in a one-parent home or under conditions of continuing conflict with both parents.

The Generation Gap: Parent-Youth Conflict

Another aspect of family disorganization is the familiar "generation gap," or the lack of communication between parents and their adolescent and young adult children. It is useless to deny the existence of such a gap. Simply because there is usually a difference of at least twenty years between parents and children, their values and experiences are dissimilar. This is particularly true in a society in which sociocultural change occurs so swiftly that the older generation has not lived the same kind of life that the new generation has.

In the current generation, a new phenomenon has occurred. It has been brought about by rapid sociocultural change added to the usual influences of the peer group and the mass media. Beginning in the mid 1960s, young Americans began to act as young people do in times of revolution. They have rejected their parents' values, philosophies, and political attitudes as irrelevant and have demanded that parents give up their positions of authority. Furthermore, some have been organizing themselves into voluntary associations—the SDS, other New Left groups, the Yippies, and more temporary political movements in support of specific candidates in an election year—to better pursue their goals. In this manner, the basic conflict between parents and their children—which is simply the children's attempt to become free of parental authority—has become a conflict between the young and the old in general, or the "generation gap."

Some experts, therefore, believe that the current generation gap is different from any previous parent-child conflict. They believe that it will definitely result in changed national priorities when the young people begin to occupy positions of leadership in the government and the economy.[42] Others minimize the importance of such conflicts and quote research findings indicating that parents and their children are in much closer agreement than is generally

[42]William J. Goode, "Family Disorganization," in Robert K. Merton and Robert Nisbet, eds., *Contemporary Social Problems*, pp. 527–32.

thought.[43] These studies show that rather than a generation gap, there is an education gap. The differences in attitudes seem greater between college-educated youth and noncollege-educated youth than between either group and their parents. This difference in attitudes is also reflected between college-educated youths and their noncollege-educated parents.

All researchers, regardless of their point of view, agree that parent-youth conflicts present little danger to the family as an institution. Sooner or later, in one way or another, parent-youth conflicts diminish or come to an end. In most instances, relationships between parents and their offspring are maintained throughout the parents' lifetime.

Tomorrow's Family

We have indicated that today's American family is still experiencing the aftereffects of changes begun by urbanization and industrialization. The nuclear family, which has replaced the extended family of former years, is under attack both from laymen and from some social scientists who consider it particularly susceptible to disorganization.

Even young people criticize the nuclear family, claiming that it is isolated, and thus inadequate in providing the security and stability needed by individuals, or, on the other hand, that it is restrictive, and thus destructive of personal freedom. Their alternative has frequently been communes. Communes are not new, having cropped up in many previous eras. However, none have survived for more than one generation. It is difficult to estimate whether the contemporary communes will have a longer life. At any rate, they do express a real need that is perceived by the present generation.

Today's communes differ from one another in goals and organization. Some are organized along religious lines; others around vegetarian, hippie, artistic, or political philosophies. Some are run democratically; others are dictatorships. In most communes, survival depends on subsistence farming and welfare assistance. Work tends to be shared, as are sexual partners and sometimes children.

Reports indicate that communes tend to be unstable communities, with many members continually drifting in and out of them. This is especially true of communes in which the members are not committed to any specific cause. One reason for their instability could be the irreconcilable differences between the members' wish to remain completely individualistic and "free" and yet to live in a group. Extreme individualism and group existence are incompatible.

What may we expect of the American family tomorrow? It does not seem likely that the commune movement will bring back the extended family. This kind of family simply does not function well in an urban industrial society. It is likely that the family will retain its emotional and reproductive functions and a great deal of the socialization function, although socialization will no longer be the sole province of the mother.

A fascinating account of family life twenty years from now is presented in the article "North American Marriage: 1990," by Leo Davids. Tracing the current trends to their logical conclusions, the author foresees an almost total

[43]Daniel Seligman, "A Special Kind of Rebellion," *Fortune* (January, 1969), p. 67. Also, Ann F. Brunswick, "A Generation Gap? A Comparison of Some Generational Differences," *Social Problems* (Winter, 1970), pp. 358-371.

end to notions of romantic love. He also predicts that people will be able to choose the type of marriage most suited to their own condition, that the roles of husband and wife will be equalized once and for all, and that reproduction will be subject to community control and undertaken only after intensive training in parenthood.[44]

THE RUSSIAN FAMILY

How distinct is the American family from families in other societies? We would expect it to differ greatly from families in nonindustrial societies. But what about family life in a society that has experienced rapid urbanization and industrialization, although under an economic and political system different from ours? What differences in the family institution does a totalitarian ideology produce? A quick glance at the family of the USSR should provide some answers.

Marxian Beliefs

The earliest policy of the Soviet regime was directed at attacking the evils of the family under the capitalist system, as these were perceived by Karl Marx.[45] These evils consisted of a clear inequality of the sexes; not only was there a double sexual standard but women were actually owned by men for the production of offspring. Because women had to remain chaste and men were permitted sexual freedom, the result was prostitution and the further degradation of women. Women also had to suffer the humiliation of bearing illegitimate children.

To prevent this vicious circle from repeating itself, the Soviet regime proposed to transfer the care, education, and maintenance of the child from the family to society. This transfer, it was thought, would not only produce the new Soviet individual, free from the vices of his capitalistic ancestors, but would also lead to happier marriages. Husbands and wives would no longer have to stay together "for the sake of the children." They would stay together only as long as they were in love and happy. If they became unhappy, the marriage could be easily dissolved. (Note the similarity with marriage in our own society, which is naturally drifting in this direction.)

For this purpose, legislation was enacted. Marriages became a simple matter of registration at a civil registry, and divorce could be obtained when one of the spouses asked for it. In addition, differences between legitimate and out-of-wedlock children were eliminated, and abortions were legalized. As for the children, they were to be cared for in a maternity house; and from the age of two months, by a creche, which was similar to a day and night nursery. This, according to Lenin, was to become the "germ cell" of the new communist society.

This plan never went into full effect largely because the state lacked the personnel and the resources. Available personnel and resources were needed

---

[44]Leo Davids, "North American Marriage: 1990," *The Futurist* (October, 1971).

[45]The following section is based largely on Mark G. Field and David E. Anderson, "The Family and Social Problems," in Allen Kassof, ed., *Prospects for Soviet Society* (New York: Praeger, 1968), pp. 386-417.

for the industrialization of the nation, the goal that had top priority under the new regime. But even in the largely urban centers where the program was tried, it failed to meet expectations. The children reared in the state creches lacked the kind of socialization that results in self-disciplined, controlled, steady, and persevering individuals who are needed in a postrevolutionary society. The government had undermined the influence of the family without substituting other beneficial influences. The child, then, was left to the undesirable models offered by the street peer group.

At this point, a sharp about-face was decreed by the regime. Marriage and divorce were again made serious matters. Divorces were especially difficult and expensive to obtain. Abortion was abolished; socialization of the child within the family was made a matter of importance; and parents were made responsible for the conduct of their children. Illegitimate children were again stigmatized by having to take their mothers' names. Mothers were unable to sue for support or recognition of paternity. Finally, large families received state aid and a decrease in taxes, in addition to other privileges.

Once again, in the post-Stalinist era, there was a relaxation of divorce laws, the legalization of abortion, and the taking of the father's name by illegitimate children. The bulk of a child's socialization, however, has remained the task of the family.

The Ideal Family

How well has the Russian family responded to the challenge of producing ideal Soviet citizens? Judging from the amount of space dedicated to the problem of the family in the Russian press, not too well.

In one study of the Russian family, authors Mark G. Fields and David E. Anderson divide the institution into four analytical models. The first model is called the "ideal family" and represents the official blueprint of what the regime would like future communist citizens to be. It serves as a model to be emulated and is not taken from reality. Its object is to produce an unspoiled and a well-guided individual.

According to the model, the ideal family should be a fairly closely knit group of people. They should live in harmony and cooperation and direct their children toward the attainment of communist morality, including patriotism, proletarian internationalism, socialist humanism, optimism, self-discipline, collectivism, honesty, and a self-critical attitude. Parents should socialize children in such a way that they will not know the meaning of laziness and self-centeredness but will devote their life and talents to society.

The Bountiful-Neglectful Family

The second kind of family model is taken from real life. It is the bountiful-neglectful family. Such a family is a phenomenon of the Soviet upper classes, that is, of members of the power elite and the highest ranks of the intelligentsia, such as nuclear physicists. In these families, parents tend to have worked hard for their high positions and lack time to devote to their children. They try to make up for this neglect by providing their children with all the material things they themselves never had and with many privileges. The children grow up thinking that they are "golden youth" and beyond the reach of the law. Often, goaded by boredom and idleness, they commit unlawful acts, from petty larceny to rape and even murder. In such cases, the parents exert their considerable authority to help their child avoid punishment.

Far from being ideal Soviet citizens, members of this group become parasites, loafers, and often criminals. Their existence is particularly disturbing to Soviet society, because they mock its basic values, stressing the importance of having the "right connections" for getting along. Besides, they represent a leisure class, which is also repulsive to Soviet ideology. Contrary to the model of the ideal family, the bountiful-neglectful family produces individuals who are spoiled and unguided.

The Overprotective Family

The third kind of analytic model is based on families found especially frequently among the middle intelligentsia, that is, white-collar workers, professionals, artists, writers, and musicians. Such persons are traditionally interested in intellectual and artistic pursuits. This makes them different from the class above—in which members tend to be the newly powerful—and from those below—who tend to be minimally educated. The standard of living of members of the middle intelligentsia is much lower than that of the upper classes, but they make up for it as far as their children are concerned by extreme pampering and a highly emotional relationship. The parents' overwhelming "love"—it is often a neurotic compulsion of some sort—creates problems for the child who eventually considers himself superior and therefore distinct from others.

Individuals raised in such families are not acceptable to Soviet society either. They seem unable to be loyal to persons and institutions other than their family and have a difficult time severing their emotional bonds with their family even in adulthood. Because of this, they often do not become involved in the social and economic life of their nation. The overprotective family produces individuals who are spoiled and misguided.

The Undersupportive Family

The fourth type of analytic model of the family is found predominantly among the working and lower socioeconomic classes. It offers the child an unstable home life, peculiarly similar to the home life of the disadvantaged classes in all industrial societies. Typically, both parents work, but the financial situation is always insecure. The living quarters are overcrowded, and the family suffers from a great number of symptoms of disorganization: desertion, separation, promiscuity, alcoholism, brutality, and general conflicts.

Rather than providing the wrong kind of socialization, this type of family provides almost no socialization. Because of a lack of supervision, the child soon takes to the streets. The poor models from whom he learns his social roles contribute to the deviant and delinquent behavior often found among such children. The undersupportive family produces a badly socialized individual who is unspoiled but also unguided.

If this typology describes Soviet families fairly accurately, the ideal model set up by the regime has not been reached in actual practice. This is not surprising. Probably every society aims to create perfect societal members, but all fall somewhat short of this ideal. The analytic models simply indicate that Soviet society has not yet found the right combination of socialization methods to produce the type of individual it desires. The models also indicate that socialization processes differ according to social class, even in a society that wanted to rid itself of social classes. Both of these conditions exist in our society also.

Stages in the Life of a Soviet Citizen

During the first stage of a Soviet citizen's life, from age one to six, he is either entrusted to the care of an elderly relative—a custom frowned upon by the state—or enrolled in state-operated nurseries. The nurseries may be located at the mother's place of work, so she is able to feed her baby at intervals. Or they may be boarding school kindergartens, where children can be enrolled from age four to six and where they remain all week until Saturday afternoon. The state does not legally require any family to place its children in nurseries. However, it is considered desirable to do so, because the child will supposedly receive the correct upbringing for a member of a collectivistic society—an upbringing that the family has not been able to provide, as we have seen.

During the second seven-year stage, the child must attend school. There is a choice of either a regular public school, an extended-day school, or a boarding school. In the extended-day school, children are kept in until the parents return from work. At this time, children also join youth organizations run by the school authorities. These organizations are supposed to supplement the pupil's education and provide an environment in which he can pursue his hobbies. In reality, however, school personnel use them to organize, control, and manage the children. Perhaps because of this, youth organizations are not very successful, and many Soviet children prefer to engage in nonapproved activities, often of a delinquent kind.

Another problem, besides delinquency, frequently crops up in the second seven-year stage of development. This is lack of identification with a male model. Soviet children are primarily exposed to female educators, as are American children. Yet in the larger society, males are expected to play a masculine role. Often, then, boys display excessive belligerence in an attempt to assert their masculinity.

The third stage is the most critical for the Soviet citizen. It signals the end of childhood and the beginning of adulthood. At this stage, the role of the family becomes progressively weaker, and the individual decides upon a career and further schooling, or immediate employment. The greatest amount of dissatisfaction is found among this age group (fourteen to twenty years of age). In bountiful-neglectful families, parents force their children to continue their education, even though they may lack the talent or inclination. The places they occupy at universities are, therefore, denied to students of less privileged backgrounds who may have the desire and the ability to learn but who lack the proper "connections." This situation creates two dissatisfied groups.

Another dissatisfied group consists of those who quit school at this stage, yet are unskilled for jobs in industry. To its considerable embarassment, Soviet society is finding that its planned economy cannot prevent the unemployment, or underemployment, typical of all expanding industrial societies. Unemployment creates a steady number of young idlers, who sooner or later become involved in some illegal activity. The extent of the problem, considered an acute one in the USSR, is revealed by the statistics: 8.9 percent of juvenile crimes are committed by children fourteen and under; 51.4 percent by youths fifteen to sixteen; and 39.7 percent by youths seventeen to nineteen.

The Soviet Family in Comparison With the Family in Other Industrial Societies

Ideology and economy aside, the evolution of the Soviet family has, in general, followed the evolution of the family in other industrial societies. In all such societies, the family becomes small and nuclear as it becomes urbanized. It also gradually stops performing many of its functions, because, technologically, it is no longer fit to perform them. However, no satisfactory substitutes have been found to take over the function of socialization, even though the family often fails grossly in its duty.

Other similarities that the Soviet family shares with Western families is, first, the sexual revolution, or sexual anarchy. As an illustration, the number of abortions performed in one city, Leningrad, was three for every one live birth. In addition, 20 percent of these abortions were performed on unmarried women under twenty-four years of age. According to Russian sociologists, the spread of premarital promiscuity is due to overcrowded housing, alcoholism, and imitation of Western life styles, as well as to reduced control of family and neighbors.[46]

A second similarity is that the extended family of prerevolutionary years, which often included three full generations, has been shrinking in the USSR. However, the Soviet nuclear family often includes two generations, primarily because of lack of housing.

A third similarity lies in the area of disorganization. Soviet families are becoming less authoritarian in their relationships than they were but also more subject to breakup and divorce. The divorce rate varies according to areas. In large urban centers, such as Moscow, the divorce rate is 3.6 per thousand population; in the rural and Asian regions of the country, it is only 0.4 per thousand. On the other hand, urban centers have the lowest birth rates, whereas the rural and Asian regions have the highest.

In predicting the future of the Soviet family, one can point to some family-related areas in which change is likely to occur in this century: prudish sex education, casual courtship and marriage rituals, state restriction of religion, austerity in family budgets, the difficult conditions of working women, overcrowded housing, and the productivity of the family (many families still raise their own crops).

What will almost surely *not* change is the coexistence of family and state, even in the face of problems such coexistence may create. In fact, the state wants to reestablish a strong family structure in order to encourage the healthy

---

[46]Most of the information for the following material was found in Peter Juviler, "Soviet Families," in Paul Hollander, ed., *American and Soviet Society* (Englewood Cliffs, N. J.: Prentice-Hall, 1969), pp. 206-212.

emotional development of offspring. At the same time, the state is aware that such a family structure is not helpful to collectivism and to the building of a communistic society. One American observer maintains that the family is an effective, though slow-working, enemy of totalitarianism and that the resistance to totalitarianism may prove to be the Soviet family's most significant function.[47]

SUMMARY

The family is the most vital of all societal institutions. At one time, its functions included the regulation of sex, the control of reproduction, the socialization of the young, the provision of affection and companionship, the setting of social status, the protection of its members, the production of goods and services necessary for survival, education, maintenance of law and order, religion, and recreation. Today, in urban industrial societies, most of these functions have been greatly reduced, having been taken over by other institutions. The family functions that do remain are control of reproduction, socialization of the young, and provision of affection and companionship.

The family institution has also undergone changes in form because of the transition from a traditional to an urban industrial society: It has become nuclear, more or less egalitarian, and neolocal. Within such a society, the preferred form of marriage is monogamy, which appears to be more functional than the polygyny generally practiced in traditional societies. Marriage partners are not chosen by families as they are in traditional societies. However, even in urban industrial societies, mate selection is not random. It is greatly influenced by endogamy, or marriage within one's group, and homogamy, or marriage to partners with similar characteristics. In most marriages, then, the partners are of the same race, religion, and social class.

Although the nuclear form of family is better adapted to life in an urban industrial society than is the extended family, its isolation from the extended family group and the intensity of the emotions within it make it particularly susceptible to disorganization. Divorce and the "generation gap" are two prominent results of family disorganization.

In predicting the future of the American family, which is typical of families in urban industrial societies, we may say that its functions will remain the socialization of the young and the provision of affection and companionship. However, alternative forms of marriage and family organization have, to some extent, already come into existence and will probably continue to do so. These will result from continuing changes in female sex roles and consequent shifts in division of labor.

A comparison of the family in the USSR and the United States shows many similarities. In its postrevolutionary, rapid transition from a traditional agricultural society to an urban industrial one, the Soviet family has also become nuclear and more or less egalitarian. It is neolocal to a lesser extent than is the American family because of a shortage of housing in the USSR. Rapid

47Kent Geiger, "The Soviet Family," in Paul Hollander, ed., *American and Soviet Society*, pp. 212-216.

social changes have also led to some of the same problems of disorganization: promiscuous premarital sexual relationships, leading to a high rate of illegitimacy; a high divorce rate; and high rates of juvenile delinquency.

Following the revolution, the state tried to weaken the family's influence by taking away its socializing function. State-run nurseries and boarding schools were established. Their purpose was to develop the total Soviet citizen of the future. Partly because of a lack of funds and partly because of poor results, this project was abandoned. Today, the state is again emphasizing the importance of the family in socialization. Soviet leaders realize, however, that healthy individualists, who are produced within the family, are not the most suitable people to live in a collectivist society.

THE family is out of fashion

The institution of the family has been subject to severe and incriminating criticism for some time now. Psychologists accuse it of repression–of producing stunted, conforming, fearful, neurotic, and even psychotic personalities. Women's Liberationists blame it for making prisoners of women, trapping them in roles they became unable or unwilling to relinquish. The young criticize it both for trying to mold them in the pattern of their elders and for not being supportive and affectionate enough. The alternatives offered are several: communes, which provide a return to the extended family; socialization that would lead to completely separate, self-realized individuals; or perhaps even total population control through the pursuit of homosexual love. Among this whirlpool of angry voices, Ann Richardson Roiphe's is heard, as she offers a sensitive and sensible viewpoint of the nuclear family.

□□□

"Blood is thicker than water only in the sense of being the vitalizing stream of a certain social stupidity."
—"The Death of the Family,"
by David Cooper.
In a silent room on West 79th Street in New

New York Times Magazine, August 15, 1971. Reprinted by permission of Brandt & Brandt and the New York Times Company. © 1971/1972 by the New York Times Company.

York City, 10 women rub their large, pregnant bellies while their husbands stare at stop watches, encouragingly giving hand signals. The couples are in training for natural childbirth with Mrs. Elizabeth Bing, who has spread the gospel in this country that male and female should share in the dramatic event of the birth of their child. Fifty to sixty new couples sign up for this course a month. What are they all doing? What are they doing several months later, walking around in their nursing bras, buying mobiles that swing from crib tops and potties with musical boxes and on and on into a future radically different from that of their childless past? Don't they know, this army of young people pushing strollers through the park, that they are behaving in a reactionary way? The nuclear family is not now a thing of fashion.

Weary from long discussions on economic theory and wasted by years of futile peace marches, bored by campaigns for compromise candidates and stunned by pollution and ecology reports, the intellectual community has turned with primal fury against a newly discovered evil: the family. Women's Liberation points out again and again how burdened, minimal and trivial is the life of the woman who tends the family. Books are appearing that attack the nuclear unit as the source of the alienated, bomb-throwing society we have come to know all too well. The call is out for new structures, babies brought up in day-care centers, new communes—or perhaps, as Germaine Greer proposes, let us do away with connected permanent relationships entirely. Let each man, woman and child shift for himself. Like the insects that fly singly throughout the ephemeral summer days.

One night my teen-aged step-daughter tearfully accused her father of being interested in her only if she was accepted into a good college so he could enjoy a little reflected status. My God, I thought, she's talking about the man who burped her, carried her to the zoo, played endless games of Monopoly and Clue, and stood in 100-degree heat to watch her ride dumb beasts in meaningless circles around a dusty ring. She's talking about the man who carried 10 bottles of ketchup all through Europe because she wouldn't eat anything without it. How did she miss the tenderness, despair, passion, pride and fear he feels for her? Of course, I knew the facts. She has to grow away, to tear apart the first love and start again—but how painful the ripping of the sinews, how wretched we all become in the process.

I looked at our new baby. "Da, da," she says with joy, pulling off her father's glasses. He kisses her on the stomach. She laughs, cosmic, total, beautiful pleasure—but where is it going? Is it worth it? Sometimes it seems as if the tensions, the angers we have accumulated against each other will get together and flood out this family, each of us floating apart on a river of nightmares, to drown eventually.

The other day I looked at my 10-year-old. "Fix your hair," I said, "wash your face. You look like an orphan. Why won't you wear any of the dresses that hang neglected, wasted, in the closet?" Then I listened. It wasn't my voice speaking at all. It was my dead mother, out of my own body, screeching from the grave the very words I had so loathed. Within me the ghost of values past was possessing, displacing the present. Family of origin, family of procreation, tied together, despite my heroic efforts to separate them, to create a pure and different life. Patterns of the past, rejected or accepted, have a way of imposing themselves on the present. We all live with the dark designs of our early loves; our hates and our attractions are colored by the intense experi-

ence of family life. We cannot easily be freed. It is true as David Cooper in "The Death of the Family" says, "A thousand ghosts roam within us." They depersonalize, limit and bind us. We are like natives with large disks protruding from distorted lips or like primitive tribes with earlobes stretched to elephantine proportions.

Most people suffer from anxieties, are neurosis-riddled, limited, uncreative, socially normal, but inwardly cut off from feelings of self. That is the usual result of our family system. No one I have ever known has made it through without scars on the psyche that became open wounds on the backs of the next generation and yet I feel as I struggle over the bikes, sled and carriage that block access to our stairway that I and my contemporaries, male and female, are truly engaged in a revolutionary drama. We who live in families are the frontiersmen of a new world. That this was equally true of the generation before, and will apply to the generation after, is not discouraging but from a certain distance merely the stuff of history.

Margaret Mead in writing a text to a photography book on the family, has said that "no society anywhere has ever sanctioned illegitimacy." This means that every society from aborigine to Maoist China has structured some form of family life to raise, socialize, protect the children—to guarantee institutionally the social, sexual needs of the adults. Some of these systems have worked better than others, all of them have demanded a price from the participants—some personal freedoms and instinctual pleasures must be abandoned when human groups are formed and it is these very restrictions that enemies of the family are now calling abominations.

Germaine Greer would have us set no limit on sexual pleasure, submit to no discipline of nursing schedules or possessive needs. She would have us abandon ugly security for free flight. David Cooper and R. D. Laing incriminate the family unit as the originator of all pathology, personal and political. They envision a utopia of people truly separate from one another, each self-realized and alive in his own present. David Cooper suggests that mothers should learn not to pick up babies when they wail in the first year of life, but allow them to experience the desolation and aloneness of their position. If we do this he promises we will create people who are not tied to others, not destroyed by the family romance.

His method seems extreme but the goals are unarguable. We all want better human beings. We want to create a society in which each man can live creatively and experience self-love and love of others. We want fewer divorces, fewer psychotics, no Lee Harvey Oswalds, and finally, in a wonderful new world, no Lyndon Johnsons, no George Wallaces, no bigots, no liars, no destroyers—the Pentagon turned into a botanical garden. But the question is, how do we make better people, how will we perfect, tame, simultaneously harness and free the conflicting forces of aggression and love that are an absolute part of every human child that opens its new eyes on the jaded world of its parents?

I cannot believe that further disconnection of child from parent, an atomization of each human unit into a single orbiting star will achieve anything more than the certain death of the species. It seems self-evident that we are now stuck with one another, parent and child, male and female, and that the changes that must be made need to take into account the necessary balances we have to find in order to assure the separate dignity of each living soul. It is my baby's right to take her first steps away from me and my obligation to follow, not too close but not too far, for the next moment when she needs to be restrained from pulling the boiling soup down on her head.

As my husband and I go about our day, we are trying to form between us the shape of a family that will enable our children better to integrate the pressures on them from without and within, and to make them freer, their ghosts more benign than ours, their limitations less paralyzing. We try not to let our time go dead with security and wooden with known experiences. We attempt to do better than our parents—some days we succeed. Very often we definitely don't.

There are alternatives to the nuclear family. I think about them on bad days, when croup has kept us up all night, I've gotten a call about a child turning into a wild thing at school, and some disappointment has turned up in my own work; all combine in a depression, a fatigue common to the battles of family living. First I romanticize the extended family. Why don't I have a loving aunt to walk the baby, a wise uncle to cover the math homework, a niece to do the shopping and a mother to organize the whole of my day? Why am I so alone in my house without the blood ties, the relatives who would connect me firmly into their tribe and end my recurrent nightmare of standing alone on the edge of a cliff that turns into talcum powder wherever I put my foot?

I imagine myself in a compound in Africa. I see myself as a little girl secure in the bosom of my large family and all the goats they commonly own. I think of myself as a woman pounding grain beside my sisters-in-law. I think of myself as an older woman carrying my daughter's baby in my arms, singing an age-old chant. I compare that image to the image of myself as the unwanted old lady I may live long enough to be, sending expensive presents to distant places, hoping against hope to be invited somewhere for the holidays.

Why not? We could gather five or six cooperative apartments, break through the floors, build interior staircases. The eldest could have the final say in matters of marriage, finance, careers and summer vacations. We could have a large common kitchen, a playroom, bedrooms and office space for the several professionals in my family.

The more specifically I consider this solution, the more I must face certain horrible truths. I would rather live in a swamp of stinging mosquitoes and biting crocodiles than spend a month with my very own blood ties. Because of educational differences, because of major value disagreements, because of the peculiar American experience that allows us to develop, peas from the same pod, into a multitude of fruits and vegetables so different from one another they can no longer cling to the same vine.

We could no longer live together. We speak as many languages as destroyed the Tower of Babel. I have an aunt who wins rumba contests at Grossinger's and another whose daughter was presented at a debutante cotillion. I have a bigoted uncle and children at the United Nations School. I have a religious, orthodox father-in-law and an avant-garde cousin who paints blue lines on mountain ridges. It is no longer possible for us to reintegrate into an extended-family unit without violating the development of personality, of free choice, of education, of varied cultural growth that was so dearly won, so bitterly fought for by several generations of uneasy Americans.

Is our specialness worth the pains we suffer in not belonging to a homogeneous, easy-to-understand, easy-to-connect-with culture? In a unified society there would be fewer private disasters, kids lost in a drug haze, others mouthing Zen prayers in hope of mystic union when we give them only personal responsibility and individual terror. There might not be the internal deadness that the search for security inflicts on seekers after better lawn mowers and swifter crabgrass killers, but there would also not be radicals, poets, painters, surgeons, merchants, technocrats or newspapermen. We would all be herding goats, or nut gathering or hunting fierce beasts. Today we have no choice—we cannot live in extended-family units and move in any direction except backwards, where, despite the comfort offered, most of us are unwilling to go.

But then there is the other much-discussed alternative to the nuclear-family problem and that is the commune. The family then becomes a chosen one, of friends who share cultural, social, political outlook, and the society within the commune can be as homogeneous as that of any Samoan island anchored peaceably in the Pacific. Children could know many relationships and grow up in a microcosmic world in which they could trust themselves and others.

This prospect has always interested me and I have often thought about it, flirting with the possibility of emigrating to Israel, to the hills of California or the farms of Pennsylvania—wherever a congenial group might be. I have in fact never moved a muscle to make this a reality and I have finally had to ask myself why. I think it has to do with the task of personal realtionship. If it is hard for me to manage with honesty, spontaneity and pleasure the limited number of people with whom I am now living—how ever will I be with many others? Diluting love experiences will not necessarily enrich them. If I care for 10 with the passion I now care for one, I will be less to everyone, or so it seems.

I wonder why so many communes break apart. They are forming and reforming, blasting and changing with such rapidity that a scientist I knew, attempting to do research on the communal experience, found that as soon as his sources gave him the location of a commune, the chances were 50 to 1 that commune would already have been a thing of the past. It seems others besides me would and do have difficulty in group living.

We are a greedy murderous, cannibalistic and sexually excitable species. This is clear to anyone who has ever taken care of a 2-year-old over an extended period of time. We were thrown out of the Garden of Eden because of our imperfections. It may be that the same humanity which later led Cain to smash in the head of Abel makes commune living problematic. I am not ready to say it is impossible and I would think that there will be movement toward greater community in the near future. As women tend to go out and work, they will need at least partial dependence on one another; as men move to take over some of the burden of domesticity, they may also turn to closer associations with one another. It may be that voluntary groupings, associations of friends, will emerge as a solution to many of the burdens now crushing the nuclear unit.

This will take time to effect and it will take strong, undestroyed people to pioneer in new relationship styles and make them work. Not our weakest, youngest, drug-addled population, but our finest products of education and personal strength will have to venture into new forms of family living if a real social change is to take place. If we are to create more viable forms of family and political life, we need people who can be loving without being inhibited. People who are sufficiently self-controlled so all their emotions don't run amuck, but not so controlled that they don't function creatively in relation to whatever task is set before them. This may be our children, or our grandchildren, or even many generations still to come. The more we learn about how a child grows, the more our schools improve, the more our homes and schools adopt the principles of empathy and love, the closer we will come to positive change.

The communes of America are now isolated from the political and social mainstream of the culture and this also makes it hard to join them and hard for them to sustain themselves. In Israel the commune is a part of the political system, serving both the defense and cultivation of the country. Its members are nourished by their ideological relationship to the rest of the nation. This tells us that the way any family lives is indeed a politcal event. If in America we cannot employ the commune properly, we can still contribute to the future of our country through the kind of people we are and the kind of children we raise. I am not suggesting family life as the only form of political agitation, only that it is one of the available tools.

The current attacks on the nuclear-family structure must not turn our attention away from the need for better child care, more love, not less, from men and women fully exploring the possibilities of love between themselves. If only the potential of male and female is deemed worthy of concern, we will throw away the real revolution that is in the making: that is, changing society by changing the potential of individual citizens. Each single child now in its stroller, pulling and pushing on the beads that hang before it, sucking at its fingers, mouthing its pacifier, stroking a bit of blanket or ragged toy—each of those babies may grow to be a radically new generation that will make miracles or little steps towards miracles.

It is probably true that revolutions so far have all been corrupted by the tyranny that possesses men when they gain power. It would seem that all the isms of the political spectrum are subject to the same malfunctions of the individuals who live within them. But perhaps a revolution will one day succeed when the children who lead it are less damaged by what has come before.

This is what I am doing, running around to nursery schools, looking at the animals in the zoo, waiting for hours in an Indian Walk shoe store to buy a pair of baby sandals. I have a child afraid of the wind and even a slight breeze sends her rushing for cover. I have another who remains convinced the dark is populated with evil spirits that grind little girls into phosphates, the better to pollute our oceans with. I can't seem to make anyone totally happy or well but the battle is nevertheless joined. I won't do worse than was done before.

The Women's Liberation attack on the nuclear family has made several valid points. Women must have more in their lives than children and homemaking. If they don't, they wait like a lit hand grenade sitting on the dining-room table. In due time, the family is certain to blow up. They have also correctly emphasized freedom of choice for women. Marriage is not to everyone's liking and no modern society, groping for new and better ways, should coerce or ostracize, call sick or anti-social, people whose sexual choices or life styles differ. But the Liberationists' de-emphasis on child care, child development, male and female love, is equally destructive. Women can work, men can share the responsibility for the home, without the family dissolving and without our losing sight of the primary human connections: man, woman and child, each important, not one neglected for the other. These days I feel a cultural pressure not to be absorbed in my child. Am I a Mrs. Portnoy sitting on the head of her little Alex? I am made to feel my curiosity about the growth of my babies is somehow counterrevolutionary. The new tolerance should ultimately respect the lady who wants to make pies as well as the one who majors in higher mathematics.

Now the ecology problem looms. An anthropologist friend of mine pointed out that the antifamily feelings, the rise in active homosexual organizations and the Women's Liberation Front itself are all part of a cultural, collective, unconscious move on the part of the species to save itself from the certain ruin of overpopulation. I have a hard time imagining or visualizing the collective unconscious at work, but then I have a hard time believing in molecules dancing around in the floor beneath my feet. It seems plausible that the turn against the idealization of family life is a form of population control. I also agree there should be room on the earth but I'm still interested in the quality of the life we are preserving. A nation of Jill Johnsons, a universe of gay bars, a world of men and women staring each other down across the barricades, seems bleak. I cannot imagine a decent library without "Babar," "Winnie-the-Pooh," "The Secret Garden," "The Wizard of Oz," etc.

The women in Mrs. Bing's apartment, practicing their breathing techniques, the ladies waiting in pediatricians' offices, the men who ride their babies on the back of their bikes around the park, who buy tickets at the carrousel, who wipe Italian ices from small chins stained like the rainbow in the sky, have confronted and daily do confront the drama of fate, of love, of age, of biology. Tenderness and fury we all know, failure, fear and envy of our friends' greater successes we all have experi-

enced. Our mettle is tested and we are often found wanting. We face our past each day. We are humiliated by our absurd ambitions. We observe our petty and great sins magnified or modified in our children—but, brothers and sisters, nuclear-family people, for better or worse the future is ours.

NORTH AMERICAN MARRIAGE: 1990

Everyone agrees that the family is undergoing tremendous changes. But what can we expect from the family of tommorow? Will our children's children really trace their descent according to test-tube numbers or sperm banks? Or will they continue to complain about the impossibility of living in stifling nuclear families, as we do now? Taking current trends as a point of departure, sociologist Leo Davids presents a realistic picture of the family twenty years from now.

□□□

As a preamble for this attempt to predict the options and regulations defining marriage and family life in North America a generation from now, let us consider some of the powerful long-term trends in this area which can be discerned either at work already, or coming very soon. These provide the causal principles that will be extrapolated here to provide a scientific indication of what the mating and parenthood situation is going to look like in another two decades. The remainder of the paper is essentially a working-out of this prediction exercise so that an account of the new situation is built up, which is the best way we have to predict the nature of marriage in 1990.

"PARENTHOOD IS FUN" MYTH WILL DIE

1. The foundation of almost everything else that is occurring in the sphere of marriage and family life today is a process which will go right ahead in the next decade or two, and will continue to have a vast effect on people's thinking and their behavior. This process is what Max Weber called the *entzauberung*, the

The Futurist, October 1971, pp. 190-194. Reprinted by permission of the World Future Society.

"demystification" or "disenchantment" of human life, which is a hallmark of the modern orientation. Young people, especially, are continually becoming more sophisticated—due to television, modern education, peergroup frankness about all spheres of life, etc.—and they are no longer accepting the myths, the conventional folklore, upon which ordinary social interaction has been based during the past few decades. Thus, for instance, young people are gradually rejecting the myth of "parenthood is fun," realizing that parenthood is a very serious business and one which ought to be undertaken only when people are ready to plunge in and do a good job.

Another grand complex of myths that is gradually being rejected is that of romantic love, under which it is perfectly acceptable to meet a person, form a sudden emotional attachment to that person without any logic or contemplation, and to marry that person on no other basis than the existence of this cathexis. Similarly, the whole institution of "shot-gun weddings," in which an unwanted, unintended pregnancy (usually occurring with a lower class girl) leads to what is called "necessary" marriage, is going to become a quaint piece of history which will be considered with the same glee that modern readers feel when they read about "bundling" in Colonial America. With young men and women who are all fully-informed about reproduction and what can be done to prevent it, such things will occur very rarely; romantic mate-selection, likewise, is going to continue only among the impoverished and marginally-educated segment of society.

Insofar as family life remains almost the only area of modern behavior that has not yet become rational and calculated but is approached with unexamined, time-honored myths, we can expect that this area is "ripe" for fundamental change. When serious, critical examination of all this really gets moving, very great changes will come about in quite a short time.

PROCREATION CAN BE SUBJECT TO COMMUNAL CONTROL

2. The second independent variable leading to the developments that we are discussing is the total control of human fertility which advances in medical technique have made possible. There is no need here to discuss the pill, intra-uterine device (IUD), and the many other ways that are in use already to separate sex from reproduction, and therefore to free relations between men and women from the fear or risk of begetting children who would be a by-product, an unintended side-effect of fulfilling quite other needs. This control of human fertility means that what procreation does occur in the future is going to be by choice, not by accident. Both illegitimacy and venereal disease will be almost extinct, too, in 20 years. It also means that reproduction and child rearing can henceforth be subjected to communal control, will be potentially regulable by society at large. Without contraception, all the rest of these trends and changes would not be occurring at all.

HUSBAND-WIFE EQUALIZATION IS "INEVITABLE"

3. Women's Liberation, I believe, is not a fad or a current mass hysterial but is here to stay. Once the schools had instituted coeducation, male dominance was doomed. Let us rephrase that term for present purposes, calling it Husand-Wife Equalization, as a general name for certain tendencies that have been evident for many years and are continuing today. We all know that marriage has shifted, to borrow a phrase, from institution to companionship. Indeed, through the demystification-sophistication of young women, their employment in full-status work, and because of the control over reproduction that has now become a reality, the equalization (in regard to

decision-making) of wives with their husbands become inevitable. The implications of this are already being voiced, to some extent, in the platforms and proposals of women's rights organizations, and some points will be touched upon herein.

It must be remembered that there will remain in the foreseeable future, a traditionalist minority even in the most advanced and change-prone societies. This segment will expend much effort to maintain patterns of marriage and family living that they feel are right, and which are consistent with the patterns they experienced when they were children. This traditionalist minority will certainly not be gone, or vanished to insignificant numbers, in the short span of one generation; therefore, any predictions we make must take into account not only what the "new wave" pattern is going to be, but also the fact that there will be a considerable number of people who elect to maintain the familiar value system that they were socialized with, and to which they are deeply committed.

LAW WILL ACCEPT ABORTION AND NEW FORMS OF MARRIAGE

4. Another trend which is already at work and which, we may assume, is going to accelerate in the future is that legislatures no longer attempt to shape or create family behavior by statute, but are, and increasingly will be, prepared to adapt the law to actual practice, so that it accepts the general viewpoint that public opinion has consensus on. I think that ever since Prohibition, legislators have been forced to agree that sooner or later legal reform must narrow the gap between law on the books and what is really happening in society. It is likely that this reforming and correlation is going to be speeded up in the next few decades, so that the extent to which there is an uncomfortable and problematic contradiction between the law in force and what people are really doing will be virtually eliminated. Thus, all of the ongoing changes with regard to contraception, abortion, new types of marriage contract, etc., will—it is here assumed—be accepted and in a sense ratified by the Law, as the old-style moralists who can

still be found in our agencies of social control cease to fight a rear-guard action against the new norms that are, whether they like them or not, emerging. All modes of birth control will become medical problems, free of an statutory limitation.

5. An important consequence of widespread social-science knowledge among young people today, which is coupled with a greater use of principles drawn from sociology and anthropology in the process of law reform, will be the recognition that continuity or consistency for each person or married couple is necessary, in regard to the larger questions at least, for a particular marriage system to work well in the long run. If the agreements entered into, whatever their content, involve major inconsistency, if people seem to be changing the fundamental norms between them in midstream or giving much more than they receive, then obviously the community has unwisely allowed these people to enter a situation which must lead to disorganization and conflict sooner or later. This realization from our functionalist understanding of how marriage—or any continuing relationship—operates, will lead to acceptance of the clear necessity for such predictability and fairness in every particular case.

So much for the preamble. What are the consequences? **Two major principles underlying our model of marriage in 1990 emerge from the forces and trends listed above. They are: a) the freedom to personally and explicitly contract the type of marriage one wishes; and b) formal public or communal control over parenthood.**

What is meant by the word "marriage," here? To include the newer forms, we require a looser, broader definition than would suffice in the 1950s. Marriage should therefore be understood to refer to a publicly-registered, lasting commitment to a particular person, which generally includes certain sexual or other rights and obligations between these people (that would not be recognized by their community without such married status).

Free choice of the sort of marriage one wishes does not mean that a man and woman (or two men or two women?) will write their own original contract incorporating any combination of rules and arrangements that they like. The reason that such freedom would be beyond that envisioned in our thinking, as argued above, is that they would be able to invent a contract that has severe internal inconsistencies or flights of self-delusion, and which therefore sets up strains for their relationship from the outset. The sophistication which anthropological functionalism has brought to us will lead society to channel the choice of marriage into a selection from among a number of recognized types, each of which has been carefully thought through so that it is tenable in the long run. Thus, people will select from among various ways of being married, each of which makes sense by itself and will enable them to function on a long-run basis once they have made this choice. Neither monogamy nor indefinite permanence are important in this respect, so they will not be required. However, the agreed-upon choice will be explicit and recorded so there's no question of deception or misunderstanding, as well as to provide statistical information, and official registration of this choice is an element of marriage which will remain a matter of public concern.

PEOPLE UNFIT TO BE PARENTS WILL BE SCREENED OUT

The right of society to control parenthood is something than can be predicted from a number of things we already know. For one thing, the rising incidence of battered and neglected children, and our almost total inability to really cope with the battered child's problem except after the fact, will certainly lead legislators to planning how those people who can be discovered, in advance, to be unfit for parenthood may be screened out and prevented from begetting offspring who will be the wretched target of their parents' emotional inadequacies. **Furthermore, increasing awareness of the early-childhood roots of serious crime and delinquency will also lead to an** attempt to prevent major deviance by seeing to it that early socialization occurs under favorable circumstances. It does not appear that there will be many other really effective ways in which rising crime rates could eventually

be reversed. This, however, will again mean that those who raise children will have to be evaluated for this purpose in some way, so that only those parents who are likely to do a respectable job of early socialization will be licensed to release new members of society into the open community. If such testing and selection is not done, we have no way to protect ourselves from large numbers of young people who have been raised in a way that almost inevitably will have them providing the murderers, rapists and robbers of the next generation. **Since we now begin to have the technology and the knowledge to prevent this, we may confidently expect that parent-licensing is going to come into force soon.**

One other trend, perhaps phrased from the negative side, must also be mentioned here as we try to describe the norms that will probably circumscribe marriage in another generation. This trend is the decline of informal, personal social control over married couples which was formerly exercised by kinsmen and neighbors. It would not make sense to anticipate massive changes in the law and explicit contractual entry into marriage as the normal way to shape married life, if mate selection and the interactions between husband and wife were still under the regulation of custom, vigilantly enforced by aunts, grandfathers or brothers-in-law. It is precisely because the vast mobility of modern living has led, along with other factors, to the isolation of the nuclear family —which is the source of so many problems in the family sphere today—that this new kind of regulation will be called into force and accepted as necessary and proper. The recognition that marriage has left the sphere of *Gemeinschaft* will help to bring about a consensus that the regulation of this area of life will have to be handled like any other kind of socially-important interpersonal behavior in today's *Gesellschaft* civilization.

COURTSHIP MAY BE "DUTCH TREAT"

What will courtship be like in about twenty years? We can assume that courtship will, as it does currently, serve as a testing ground for the kind of marriage that people have in their minds, perhaps even dimly or unconsciously. Thus, insofar as particular young men or women may have begun to feel that the type of marriage they would like is Type A rather than Type B, their courtship would be of the sort that normally leads to Type A, and in a sense tests their readiness to build their relationship along those lines. Only the traditionalist couples will keep up such classic patriarchal customs as the male holding doors, assisting with a coat, or paying for both meals when a couple dines out together. The egalitarians would go "Dutch treat," i.e. each paying for himself, during this spouse research period. Thus, courtship will be of several kinds corresponding to the kinds of marriage that we are about to describe, with the conventional acts and phases in the courtship signalling the present intention of the parties involved to head toward that kind of marriage. Thus, pre-marriage and marriage will exhibit a psycho-social continuity, the early marriage centering on the basic interpersonal stance that is already represented in courtship.

Of course, courtship will serve this testing and assessing function after people have been approximately matched through computer mate-finding methods. Random dating and hopeless courtships will have been largely prevented through the provision of basic categoric information which people can use to screen possible spouses, such as total years of schooling completed, aptitude and IQ scores, major subjects (which are related to intellectual interests in a very direct way), religiosity, leisure and recreation preferences, and similar things.

For remarriage suitors, data on wealth or credit and occupation would also be used, along with some indication of attitudes concerning home life and procreation. Since homogamy (similarity between spouses) is recognized as an important indicator of marital success, such information will be systematically gathered and made available to cut down on the wasteful chance element in mate selection. It is only when people are continuing their search for a spouse within the appropriate "pool," defined in terms of those who are at the right point with regard to these variables, that courtship as a series of informal but direct experiments in relationship-building will come into play.

CELIBACY WILL BE LEGITIMIZED

Explicit choice of the kind of marriage one enters into is, is of course, an effect not only of the emancipation of women, but of men as well. What will some of the major options be? With the insurance functions that were formerly secured by having children (who would provide during one's old age) being completely taken over by the government (assisted by unions, pension funds and the like), there will be little reason to warn those who choose childlessness against this course. With celibacy no bar to sexual satisfaction, society will accept the idea that some segments of the population can obtain whatever intimate satisfactions they require in a series of casual, short-term "affairs" (as we call them today), and will never enter any publicly-registered marriage. With celibacy or spinsterhood fully legitimized, and with no fear of destitution when one has retired from the labor force, there will undoubtedly be a sizeable number of people who decide not to enter into a marriage of any sort on any terms.

TRIAL MARRIAGE FOR THREE OR FIVE YEARS

Another not-unfamiliar option in this regard will be the renewable trial marriage, in which people explicitly contract for a childless union which is to be comprehensively evaluated after three years or five years, at which point either a completely new decision can be reached or the same arrangement can be renewed for another term of three or five years. This would not be, then, a question of divorce; it is simply a matter of a definite arrangement having expired. The contract having been for a limited term, both parties are perfectly free to decide not to renew it when that term is over. This would be a normal, perhaps minor, part of one's "marital career."

A third option, which introduces very few complications, is the permanent childless marriage; the arrangement between the two adults is of indefinite duration, but they have agreed in advance that there will be no offspring, and of course, there is no question but that medical technology will make it possible for them to live up to that part of the arrangement. Some will choose sterilization, others will use contraceptive methods which can be abandoned if one changes his mind and is authorized to procreate.

Compound marriages will also be allowed, whether they be polygamous, polyandrous or group marriages. However, these communes will not be free of the same obligations that any marriage entails, such as formally registering the terms of the agreement among the members; any significant change in the arrangements among members of such a familial commune will have to be recorded in the appropriate public place in the same way as marriages and divorces which involve only one husband and one wife. There will be great freedom with regard to the number of people in the commune, but internal consistency concerning the give-and-take among the members, their privileges and obligations, will be required. The fuctional, pragmatic ethics emerging in today's youth culture will be strictly adhered to, some years hence, not as moral absolutes, not because people have come to the belief that these represent the true right and wrong, but in order to prevent serious conflict.

LESS THAN THIRD OF MARRIAGES WILL PRODUCE CHILDREN

With the majority of young people in society choosing one of the foregoing patterns, the number of marriages in which children are expected will be relatively small; perhaps 25% to 30% of the population will be so serious about having children that they will be prepared to undergo the rigorous training and careful evaluation that will be necessary for them to obtain the requisite licenses. The marriages intended to produce children will usually be classic familistic marriages, in which the general pattern of interaction between husband and wife, as well as the relationship between parent and child, may be fairly similar to the contemporary upper middle-class marriage that we know in 1970. However, three-generation households will probably increase.

I see no reason to believe that all of child rearing will be done in a collective way, as in an Israeli kibbutz or in the communes which have been set up in some Communist countries; infant care may gravitate in the direction of day nurseries, however, while school children will live at home, as now.

WOULD-BE PARENTS WILL HAVE TO PROVE THEIR SUITABILITY

The familial pattern, then, explicitly chosen by some men and women to perpetuate the classic familistic marriage, will be intended to provide a home atmosphere approximately similar to that which can be found in those middle cla s families of today's society that have the best socio-emotional climate. The community will be assured that this home atmosphere is, in fact, most probable, since it has been prepared for, rather than left to an accident of kind fate and to happenstance talents that people bring to parenthood nowadays. All those who desire to become parents, and therefore to exercise a public responsibility in an extremely important and sensitive area of personal functioning, will have to prove that they are indeed the right people to serve as society's agents of socialization. Just as those who wish to adopt a child, nowadays, are subjected to intensive interviewing which aims at discovering the healthiness of the relationship between husband and wife and of the motivation for parenthood, the suitability that the man or woman displays for coping with the stresses of parenthood, as well as the physical and material conditions that the adopted child will be enjoying, the evaluation of mother and father applicants in future will be done by a team of professionals who have to reach the judgment that this particular individual or couple have the background to become professionals themselves: that is, recognized and certified parents.

PARENT-TRAINING WILL BE INTENSE

The course of study for parenthood will include such subjects as: human reproduction and gestation; infant care; developmental physiology and psychology; theories of socialization; and educational psychology. Starting with a foundation of systematic but abstract scientific knowledge, the practical and applied courses in hygienic, nutritional, emotional and perceptual-aesthetic care of children will follow, in the same way training for medicine and other professions. In addition to the subject matter referred to above, prospective parents will be required to achieve some clarity concerning values and philosophy of life, in which they will be guided by humanistic scholars, and will also be required to attain a clear understanding of the mass media, their impact on children, and how to manage mass media consumption as an important part of socialization in the modern urban environment. **One side effect of such parent training may be a sharp drop in the power of the peer group, as parents do more and with greater self-confidence.**

Suitable examinations will be devised, and only those who achieve adequate grades in these areas will be given a parenthood license. Some young men and women are likely to take the parenthood curriculum "just in case"; that is, although they have not yet thought through the type of marriage that they desire or the kind of spouse they are looking for, they may continue their education by entering parenthood studies and obtaining the diploma, should it turn out that they elect a classic, child-rearing marriage later on. **Possibly, fathers will be prohibited from full-time employment outside the home while they have pre-school children, or if their children have extra needs shown by poor conduct or other symptoms of psychic distress.**

One of the more striking areas of change, which can serve as an indicator of how different things will be then from what they are now, is age. Age of marriage now is in the early 20's, and child bearing typically occurs when women are in their middle twenties. Also, husbands today are usually about three to four years older than their wives. In another generation, the age of child bearing will probably be considerably advanced, as people who have decided upon parenthood will either be enjoying themselves during an extended childless period before they undertake the burdens and responsibilities of child rearing, or completing the course of study for certification to undertake the burdens and responsibilities of child rearing, or completing the course of study for certification to undertake parenthood. It is probable that women will bear children when they are in their middle and late thirties, so that they will have enjoyed a decade or a decade and a half of companionate marriage in which there was full opportunity to travel, to read, or just to relax before they have to spend 24 hours a day caring for a small child. As to the age difference between husbands and wives, which is essentially based on the patriarchal tradition that the man is the "senior" in the home, it will probably disappear in the case of all forms of marriage other than the classic familistic one; there, where people have explicitly decided that the kind of marriage they want is the same as their parents had back in the medievaloid 1970s, or the ancient 1960s, the husband will continue to be a few years older than his wife.

This picture of the marriage situation in 1990 leaves open various questions and problems, which should be touched upon briefly in conclusion. One of the difficulties in this scenario is the question of what authority will make the necessary decisions: What sorts of committees will be in charge of devising the various internally-consistent kinds of marriage, working out the parent education courses, and certifying people for parenthood? There are, after all, political implications to controlling marriage and parenthood in this way, and the general public will have to be satisfied that those who exercise authority in this area are, in fact, competent as well as impartial.

Another problem is that of securing complete and valid information: (a) for those who are preparing to locate suitable mates through computer matching, or who are preparing to

make a commitment in some specific form of marriage; and (b) concerning those who apply for the parenthood course and later for the license to practice parenthood. Unless we can be sure that the inputs used for making such judgments contain information which is adequate in quantity and true as well, these new systems will not be able to function without a great deal of deviance, and might easily engender problems which are worse than those which we confront today.

WILL CHILDLESSNESS LEAD TO LESS LONG-RANGE INVESTMENT?

A third issue is that of parenthood having tied people to the community, and given them a commitment to the environment. What will childlessness do to one's motivation for planning/preserving; will it de-motivate all long-range investment? Research on this could start now, comparing parents with the childless.

Finally, we have assumed that marriage is going to continue, in some way. That is based on the belief that people will continue to desire a secure partnership with another person or small group, and that youth will feel it is better to institutionally buttress their sharing of life, in general, by setting up a marriage of some kind. This depends, in fact, on the interpersonal climate in communities, and the extent to which people feel isolation and unmet needs that marriage will solve. When marriage is not desired, then we will have discovered new forms of warm, dependable primary association replacing the old institution which has supplied psychological support to people through the millennia.

DISCUSSING THE ARTICLES

1. Ann Richardson Roiphe's article, "The Family Is Out of Fashion," points to certain sources of criticism of the family. What are these sources? Are they justified in their criticism? To what extent are they justified?

2. When the author nags her ten-year-old daughter to fix herself up, who does she say is speaking through her? What does she mean? What does this indicate about the process of socialization? Is she justified in nagging her daughter? Is it a part

of the daughter's individual freedom to go around looking sloppy? Does it prepare her for her roles in society?

3. According to the author, what is the result of our family system? Do other systems produce similar results? In what respect are we "the frontiersmen of a new world"?

4. What price have all family systems demanded of participants? Is this true of only family systems?

5. From what you know about the process of socialization, speculate about what kind of adults would result if people followed David Cooper's suggestion that babies not be picked up when they cry during their first year of life? Does the author agree with Cooper's thesis?

7. What are the author's feelings toward the extended family? In what ways is it supportive of the individual? What are its shortcomings?

8. What kind of people are necessary if social change is to occur in the family? Are these the kinds of people who are forming communes?

9. What is the author's attitude toward Women's Liberation? Does it seem justified? What is the anthropological explanation of Women's Liberation and the increase of homosexual organizations? Does it seem plausible?

10. From your own experiences in your family setting, would you say that the family is in need of reform? Should it continue in its present form? What would you consider an improvement?

11. In the article "North American Marriage: 1990," from what basis does Leo Davids attempt to predict marriage and family life a generation from now?

12. Which myths will be the first to die in the process of changes in marriage and the family? Why is this area ripe for change?

13. Has the separation of sex from reproduction already taken place? What of the author's statement that both illegitimacy and venereal disease will disappear in twenty years? Does this statement agree with the findings of recent research quoted in the text? Are young people truly sophisticated in matters of sex and contraception?

14. What result will the Women's Liberation movement have on marriage and the family? Will it have been a successful social movement, then?

15. Should an individual be able to contract the type of marriage he wishes to have? Can a society exist if everyone has a different kind of marriage? Is it a matter of defining marriage? Will such marriages still be monogamous?

16. Do you think society has the right to control parenthood? Should anyone, for any reason, be prevented from becoming a parent? Is it a breach of individual freedom to have to be evaluated before becoming a parent?

17. Whose control will decline in another generation? Of what kind of society is this typical?

18. What will be the role of government in another generation? Is this a continuation of a current trend, or will this be a new development? Will more people tend to get married, or fewer?

19. According to the author, will the family, as we know it today, cease to exist?

20. What effect will parent training have on the power of the peer group? Would you add other subjects to the author's list of prerequisites for parent training?

TERMS TO REMEMBER

Institutions. Patterns of behavior, or habits in the form of mores, folkways, and laws that have clustered around particular human functions. Members of society are expected to follow them to simplify their lives.

Monogamy. A form of marriage consisting in the union of one man with one woman.

Polygamy. Plural marriage.

Polyandry. A form of marriage consisting in the union of one woman with several men.

Polygyny. A form of marriage consisting in the union of one man with more than one woman.

Group marriage. A form of marriage involving several men with several women.

Exogamy. Marriage outside the group.

Endogamy. Marriage within the group.

Incest taboo. Prohibition of sexual relations between mother and son, father and daughter, and sister and brother.

Extended family. A form of family common in traditional societies. It includes a number of blood relatives together with their marriage partners and children.

Consanguine. The extended family; the nuclear family as it appears to children who are tied to their parents by blood ties.

Nuclear, or conjugal family. A form of family consisting of father, mother, and their children.

Procreational. The nuclear family as it appears to the parents, who are related not by blood but by virtue of having produced children.

Patriarchal. A family organization in which authority is vested in the oldest living male.

Matriarchal. A family organization in which authority is vested in the mother.

Egalitarian. A future goal of family organization in which authority will be vested equally in the mother and the father.

Patrilineal. An arrangement for tracing descent. Family name, inheritance, and other obligations are passed through the male line, or the father's ancestors.

Matrilineal. Descent traced through the mother's ancestors.

Bilateral. Descent traced through both the father's and the mother's ancestors.

Patrilocal. Family residence determined by husband's parents.

Matrilocal. Family residence determined by wife's parents.

Neolocal. Family residence away from both sets of parents.

Sororate. A custom in which a widowed man gains sexual access to his wife's sisters.

Levirate. A custom in which the brothers-in-law of a widow take charge of her and her children.

Family disorganization. A breakup of the family unit as a result of the failure of one or more members to perform his role adequately.

SUGGESTIONS FOR FURTHER READING

Bell, Robert R. *Marriage and Family Interaction*. Homewood, Ill.: The Dorsey Press, 1971. The latest edition of a text that examines exhaustively, yet in a readable manner, the subject matter of marriage and the family.

Benson, Leonard. *The Family Bond*. New York: Random House, 1971. Another basic text, with a particularly fine last section on the past and future of the family institution.

Geiger, H. Kent. *Comparative Perspectives on Marriage and the Family*. Boston: Little, Brown, 1968. A collection of essays probing particular aspects of marriage and the family at a cross-cultural level.

Gordon, Michael. *The Nuclear Family in Crisis*. New York: Harper & Row, 1972. A collection of essays exploring the communal alternatives to the nuclear family.

Graburn, Nelson. *Readings in Kinship and Social Structure*. New York: Harper & Row, 1971. Another collection of essays emphasizing the kinship systems of various societies from an anthropological point of view.

Kirkendall, Lester A., and Whitehurst, Robert N. *The New Sexual Revolution*. New York: Donald W. Brown, 1971. Sixteen essays probing human sexuality, morality, cultural influences on sex, the marital ideal, and population growth.

Komarovsky, Mirra. *Blue Collar Marriage*. New York: Random House, 1964. A classic examination of lower-class marriage, illustrating the way it differs from marriage in other social classes.

Lemasters, E. E. *Parents in Modern America*. Homewood, Ill.: Dorsey, 1970. The parental role analyzed from a sociological point of view.

Murdock, George P. *Social Structure*. New York: Macmillan, 1949. The family and kinship systems of two hundred fifty societies examined by an anthropologist.

Otto, Herbert A. *The Family In Search of a Future*. New York: Meredith, 1970. A series of essays exploring alternatives to the nuclear family of today. Written by sociologists, psychologists, anthropologists, and other experts in human potential.

Reiss, Ira L. *The Social Context of Sexual Permissiveness*. New York: Holt, Rinehart and Winston, 1967. A fairly recent analysis of premarital sexual behavior, showing great changes in numerical incidence.

Roszak, Betty and Theodore. *Masculine-Feminine: Readings in Sexual Mythology and the Liberation of Women*. New York: Harper & Row, 1970. A collection of readings on the feminist movement.

Scanzoni, John. *Sexual Bargaining*. Englewood Cliffs, N. J.: Prentice-Hall, 1972. A readable paperback in which the author contends that modern marriage is neither collapsing nor passé.

Schulz, David A. *The Changing Family*. Englewood Cliffs, N. J.: Prentice-Hall, 1972. A comprehensive new text addressing itself to questions of the function and future of the family.

Skolnick, Arlene S. and Jerome H., eds. *Family in Transition*. Boston: Little, Brown, 1971. An excellent collection of essays on all aspects of the family.

Wiseman, Jacqueline P. *People As Partners*. San Francisco: Canfield Press, 1971. An anthology of selections viewing marriage and the family from the point of view of individual relationships.

cHAPTER EiGHT ◉

We are not accustomed to thinking about economic principles in terms of poetry. Yet perhaps it takes a poet to reduce complicated forms to their bare essentials. For instance, this is how the poet Kahlil Gibran saw the institution of the economy:

> And a merchant said, Speak to us of Buying and Selling. And he answered and said: To you the earth yields her fruit, and you shall not want if you but know how to fill your hands. It is in exchanging the gifts of the earth that you shall find abundance and be satisfied. Yet unless the exchange be in love and kindly justice, it will but lead some to greed and others to hunger.[1]

In this stanza, the poet has expressed the function of the economic institution: to show people how to fill their hands with the gifts of the earth so they

[1]Kahlil Gibran, *The Prophet* (New York: Alfred A. Knopf, 1951).

may survive. What is more, its purpose is also to aid people's organization and enable them to exchange goods and services, so all may enjoy them.

If, today, "the economy" suggests giant corporations, free enterprise, competition, stocks and bonds, inflation, and so on, it is only because we live in an exceedingly complex society. Our chief mode of subsistence, however, was not always industrial production of a highly technological order.

WHAT IS THE ECONOMY?

The functioning of a society's economy is usually analyzed by economists. But because the economy is an abstraction that stands for certain relationships occurring among people and groups and because the economy revolves around specific societal concerns, it is of interest to sociologists too. Of particular concern to sociologists is the structure of the economy, including details of division of labor and occupational specialization, the property system, structural changes (such as that from agriculture to industry, for instance), the structure of the factory, and industrial relations.

The *economy*, or the *economic order*, is essentially the human relationships that exist in society as a result of the necessity to produce, distribute, and consume goods and services.[2] Examples of such relationships in modern society are, to mention only a few, buyer and seller, employer and employee, and government agencies and the industries they regulate. In the term economic order, "order" should not indicate that the economy is controlled in any unified or orderly manner. It simply points to the existence of a structure of relationships that revolve around a common activity.

The Political and Economic Orders

People also engage in relationships centering around the need to make authoritative decisions for society. These relationships, called the political order, will be examined in the next chapter. Examples of relationships in the political order are those between ruler and subject, voter and candidate, and government agencies and the industries they regulate.

The economic and political orders not only affect each other and frequently overlap but are sometimes one and the same. In most traditional societies and in communist nations, the economic order is part of the political order, because political authority makes economic decisions for the society. In most modern industrial societies, the two orders are interrelated, the political order regulating and supplementing the actions of the economic order. In historical perspective, the political and economic orders have been interdependent, to some degree, in all societies. In the recent past, however, differences of opinion regarding the functions each order should perform and the degree of interrelationship between them have crystallized into separate ideologies. These ideologies—communism, socialism, fascism, and capitalism—have divided people and nations.

The ideological divisions that arise from different ways of implementing

---

[2]In the following section, we have relied on information from Nathaniel Stone Preston, *Politics, Economics, and Power* (New York: Macmillan, 1967), pp. 2–10.

decisions would make little sense if the purpose of the economic institution were solely to ensure survival. But that purpose now includes a much broader objective: the attainment of the good life, as that concept is interpreted by the various societies of the world. Some goals of the good life include a wealth of material objects, the freedom of individual self-expression, a striving toward the development of ethical behavior, and freedom from oppression, foreign or internal. Each society decides for itself what priority to give these goals and how to interpret their meaning. And it pursues the attainment of the goals largely through the interplay of relationships between the economic and the political orders.

A final point is actually a reminder from our discussion of stratification in Chapter 4: In a modern industrial society, economic and political power

are often interchangeable. In other words, a person who has a powerful position in the political order—the president of the United States, for instance—can make decisions that affect and sometimes determine the course of the economy. At the same time, managers of giant corporations, who are responsible for decisions concerning what will be produced, how much of it will be produced, and at what price it will be sold, have economic power that affects the political order. So do labor leaders, who can call strikes that paralyze industries and sometimes sections of the country.

A GLANCE AT THE PAST

Although it has been criticized in recent years, in general we accept capitalism as our kind of economy. Some of us may dislike certain of its features and would like it to take a more egalitarian direction, but most agree that capitalism is a fairly workable system.

How did we develop the system called capitalism and the kind of production called industry? Out of all the possible alternatives, why did we develop these? Are there no simpler means of producing, distributing, and consuming the resources of a society? We have said that many factors account for the creation of a culture in a society. And the economic institution is a very important part of each society's culture. We cannot probe into every factor that contributed to the emergence of capitalism, but we can briefly examine the history of capitalism —from feudal Europe to the development of the institution in the United States.

The roots of capitalism lie far back in the past, when societies first engaged in plant cultivation and animal domestication and thus were able to survive in almost any physical environment. This was social change of a revolutionary nature, for it produced an unusual luxury—leisure. In their newly found leisure time, people could think of complex tools and utensils to make and complex rituals with which to enrich their experience. As we saw in Chapter 2, in the agrarian society, there was also, for the first time, a surplus of goods. Surpluses led to even more significant social changes. First, a stratificiation system came into existence. The specifics of this system varied from society to society, but in all societies, there were a ruling class that had access to the surplus and the masses that did the actual labor of production. Second, division of labor occurred. No longer was every member occupied in the labor of production. Finally, a kind of middle class—clergy, servants, soldiers, craftsmen, and merchants —came into being. It mediated between the two other classes and helped the ruling class dispose of the surplus.

Changes in social organization—primarily a trend toward the development of secondary relationships—accompanied the evolution of societies. Kinship ties, no longer sufficient to provide social control, were supplemented by formal ties. Formal ties between rulers and subjects became the basis of the political institution; formal ties between the members of society and the craftsmen and merchants who produced and sold some of the goods of society became the basis of the expanding economic institution. Other communal and ideological ties led to the establishment of other institutions.[3]

[3]Gerhard Lenski, *Human Societies* (New York: McGraw-Hill, 1970), pp. 304–307.

By the time societies had evolved into the agricultural stage, people had already realized the importance of organizing both for efficiency and survival. Such organization was based either on custom and tradition or on the command of an authoritarian ruler. Under the first type of organization, the knowledge of the tasks necessary for survival was handed down from generation to generation. Under the second, the ruler made sure the tasks were done under threat of punishment. The third alternative for economic survival did not emerge until the Industrial Revolution and the Protestant Reformation combined to give birth to the market system, later to be called capitalism. In this type of economic organization, the survival of society is ensured because each individual, lured by the possibility of profit, performs the necessary tasks without the prodding of either tradition or authority.

Feudal Europe: Its Ideology and Socioeconomic System

If you recall our discussion of feudalism in Chapter 4, you will not be surprised to learn that the words most often used to describe the medieval period of European history are "static," "traditional," "orderly," and "spiritual." The predominant socioeconomic system, feudalism, was manorial in nature. In other words, government rested in the hands of a feudal baron who was both the owner of the manor and the ruler of those who inhabited it—villeins, serfs, and peasants. Above the feudal baron, rule extended pyramidically all the way to the king, whereas both above and below the baron there existed a system of mutual obligations.

Rulers and subjects alike accepted the theological rule of the Roman Catholic church. In its ideology, scholasticism, all facets of human life were explained in terms of the Catholic religion, and the ultimate purpose of human life was the salvation of the soul. In this view, the ideal society was one in which order and the common welfare were more significant than was the welfare of the individual.

In medieval society, statuses and roles were rigidly ascribed and could be altered only to a small degree. Work, therefore, was not a means of accumulating wealth or improving one's status. Instead, work was an end in itself, decreed by God as punishment for original sin. Because it was impossible to change one's status, it was useless to make a profit. As a matter of fact, profit met with great disapproval and was condemned as sinful. Merchants and craftsmen were paid for their labor but only well enough so they could remain in the same social position.

The Emergence of a Money Economy

Although the medieval subsistence economy was indifferent to productivity, economic growth still occurred. The sheer expansion of population required more goods and services. And the more people there were, the more they produced. Eventually, the strict isolation that had been maintained by individual manors gave way to exchange among communities. This led to specialization, in which each area produced specific goods and traded them for products from neighboring areas. Ultimately, barter, or trading, was eliminated as a medium of exchange, and money took its place.

A money economy and increased trade led to the development of a new social class made up of merchants, craftsmen, and money lenders. These people became concentrated in cities, which were centers of trade. Because *burg* meant "city," the people were called burghers, and their social class the bourgeoisie.

Mercantilism and the Industrial Revolution

The Industrial Revolution, of which the factory system was an important part, was preceded and accompanied by revolutionary changes in ideology and economic motives. The Industrial Revolution was essentially sociocultural change from subsistence agriculture to production as the basis of the economy. The profit motive, which, as we have seen, was nonexistent in the self-sufficient subsistence economies of feudal Europe, began to take on significance. The voyages of discovery and exploration, by whetting people's appetite for the exotic wares of distant lands, created new markets. In addition, the amount of silver and gold entering Europe was greatly increased by the colonization of the New World, where the precious metals were being mined. Wealth began to be defined in terms of money rather than land.

The face of Europe was changing in yet another respect. The numerous duchies and principalities of the medieval era were being replaced by nation-states. Natural rulers, who were usually absolute monarchs, believed that the goals of a national economy should be a strong, unified, wealthy nation. To reach such goals, it was necessary for a nation to increase its store of gold and silver through trade and colonization.

The new economic policy of accumulating gold and silver and establishing foreign trade monopolies was eventually called *mercantilism*. In many respects it was a shortsighted policy, but it aided commerce, spurred on domestic manufacturing, and encouraged people to develop inventions that would open up new markets and increase international trade. In fact, the willingness of new industries to adopt shortcuts for speeding production was largely caused by mercantilist policies and the New World colonies' supply of raw materials that had to be refined.

The Factory System and Industrialism

The increasing mechanization of infant industries led inevitably to the factory system. Machines were becoming too bulky and too numerous to be used in the homes of individual craftsmen. In addition, the increasingly complex machines became so expensive that they could be bought only by entrepreneurs —individuals in charge of business enterprises. Finally, the invention of the steam-powered loom made it possible to build textile mills in places that were not near running streams in the countryside. The next step was to place all stages of production under one roof in the commercial centers of nations, cities.

Technological advances, particularly the perfection of the steam engine, ensured industrialism of being the chief mode of production for centuries. As a result of the steam engine, the output of coal and iron was increased, transportation was revolutionized, and the production of all goods was speeded up. Obviously, the most industrialized nations also became the most powerful and the richest nations. And the factory system became the key to it all.

THE PHILOSOPHY OF CAPITALISM

Commerce, spurred on and constantly rekindled through the productivity of industrialism, finally brought in the economic order called the market system. This system was so far removed from the feudal economy that it wrought revolutionary changes in the entire social order. The changes were bitterly opposed, and many generations passed before this economic system could be conceptualized in its proper perspective.

First, the mercantilist idea that gold and silver were the basis of wealth had to be rejected in favor of the idea that wealth was based on production. Other factors also had to be digested. Although land, labor, and capital had existed throughout history in the form of soil, peasants, and tools, they now had to be considered the chief agents of production. Each had to be abstracted, dehumanized, and treated as an object to be bought and sold in the market. Land was something to be sold for a profit or bought for the purpose of deriving a profit from the buildings constructed on it. Labor was to be sold in exchange for wages to the highest bidder. And capital was the machinery and tools on which production, and hence profit, depended. How dramatic these changes were is colorfully summarized by Robert Heilbroner:

> Just to commercialize the land—to convert the hierarchy of social relationships into so many vacant lots and advantageous sites—required nothing less than the uprooting of an entrenched feudal way of life. To make "workers" out of the sheltered serfs and apprentices—no matter how exploitative the cloak of paternalism may have been— required the creation of a frightened disoriented class called the proletariat. To make capitalists out of guild masters meant that the laws of the jungle had to be taught to the timid denizens of the barnyard.[4]

Adam Smith and Laissez-Faire

Once the idea of a market system took hold, a philosophy was needed to define it and rationalize it. This task was undertaken by Adam Smith, a Scottish professor of moral philosophy, in his work *The Wealth of Nations*, published in 1776.

Smith agreed with mercantilists that wealth, or abundance, should be the aim of an economy. But he departed from them radically by arguing that wealth should benefit the entire population of a nation. According to Smith, the way to attain wealth was through increased production, which would lead to increased goods that the whole society could then consume. For production to occur most efficiently, the political order could not interfere in economic matters. The principle of noninterference became known as the doctrine of *laissez-faire*, which can be translated roughly into "leave it alone." In Smith's opinion, government should be involved only in military protection, the administering of laws, and the provision of services that the private sector is unwilling or unable to provide, but that are necessary for the orderly conduct of society.

[4]Robert L. Heilbroner, *The Worldly Philosophers*, rev. ed. (New York: Simon and Schuster, 1961), p. 17.

The Self-Regulating Market

Adam Smith believed that the self-regulating market was part of the natural law underlying all economic activity. In his view, the workings of the market were quite simple: In pursuing greed and self-interest, people are working toward the good of society. Smith argued that self-interest is the individual's basic psychological drive. Because they are victims of this drive, people compete withone another, each producing a multitude of goods and services from which consumers may choose.

The demand for goods and services—which goods and services consumers want and have the money to buy—determines the goods and services that are produced and at what price they are sold. For instance, suppose that consumers demand straw hats because they are the latest fashion. The manufacturer of straw hats does very well and has to keep producing more straw hats to satisfy demand. By doing so, he expands his business and continues to increase his profits. A manufacturer of felt hats, which are not in demand, is not doing well. Therefore, he does not produce more of these hats. By not producing and by not selling, he loses money, has to lay off his workers, and eventually has to switch to another form of production or go out of business. Thus, the market works freely, without regulation, according to supply and demand. And consumers determine what shall be produced.

Price is determined in the same manner. If there is a great demand for a good or service but a low supply, the manufacturer charges a high price. If there is a low demand and a great supply, he charges a low price. Thus, the market regulates itself in this way too, and price is based merely on the relationship between supply and demand. Furthermore, if a manufacturer becomes too greedy and raises his prices higher than his competitors' prices, he loses his customers to his competitors. Prices are, then, automatically kept at a level at which consumers consider them fair.

Competition also regulates the incomes of both entrepreneurs and laborers. If profits become high in a one industrial or business sector, many businessmen move into the same field, and profits have to be divided among many people. If profits become too low, entrepreneurs abandon the industry, leaving additional profits for those who remain. In short, what makes the market function without regulation is the pursuit of self-interest, tempered by competition. To Adam Smith, the "invisible hand" of the market was more effective than the hand of government, or a ruler.

KARL MARX'S VIEW OF THE ORIGIN OF CAPITALISM

The origin of capitalism has been of interest to scholars throughout the years. Specifically, many have wondered by what mechanism of social and cultural change the static society of medieval Europe was turned into the dynamic society of the industrial era. Did an idea shape the facts, or did the facts create the idea?

Of the many people who have theorized about the emergence of capitalism, the two most outstanding are Karl Marx and Max Weber. Karl Marx's views on capitalism appeared in 1867, in a chapter of his work *Capital*. These views were later called the philosophy of *dialectic materialism.* According to this philosophy, change within society occurs by a dialectical process—a thesis (old ideas) is challenged by an antithesis (new ideas), resulting in a synthesis (new order). Because the basis of each society is production and exchange, what is produced and how it is produced, exchanged, and distributed determine the society's class system. Thus, roles in the economic system dictate roles in the status system, leading to differences in the wielding of power. Changes in the mode of production and exchange cause changes in the entire social order. Thus, the economic institutions of society determine the course of history.

To prove his theory of dialectical materialism, Marx traced the history of capitalism in England. He viewed the rise of capitalism in that nation as a direct result of the crumbling feudal system, particularly as a result of the Enclosure Acts. Through these acts, the feudal lords and, later, the landowners closed off for their own private use land that had formerly been held in common or open to use by the peasants of the manor. The landowners' actions were prompted by their desire for money with which they could buy, at first, arms and mercenary soldiers and, later, other foreign and domestic luxuries. In short, the lords of the manor and other minor landholders, who previously had been satisfied with subsistence agriculture on their lands, now wanted to put their lands to work and obtain a profit from them.

But the peasants who formerly worked and lived on the land suddenly found themselves landless and homeless. Many fled to the cities, where they made a living by begging and stealing. The most fortunate among them became craftsmen and merchants. Eventually, craftsmen began to sell their labor for wages. Out of this group developed the social class of the proletariat, or the wielders of machinery necessary for capitalistic production. The merchants, who, at first, catered to the feudal lords' insatiable desire for luxuries, eventually became the entrepreneurs of budding industrialism and formed, together with the successful craftsmen, the social class of the bourgeoisie. This class provided the fertile soil in which capitalism was to prosper.

Marx did not believe, then, that an idea or a belief caused a change in the economic system and, eventually, changes in the social system. It was simply the self-interest of the ruling classes—in England, the landowners' desire for liquid assets—that created an ideology. This ideology, masked as religion, was subsequently imposed on the entire society and was the cause of the destruction of feudalism and the ushering in of capitalism. Such a fate was now in store for capitalism itself, which was being challenged, and eventually would be destroyed, by the self-interest of the proletariat.

MAX WEBER'S VIEW OF THE ORIGIN OF CAPITALISM

Weber's theories on the emergence of capitalism appeared in 1904 in *The Protestant Ethic and the Spirit of Capitalism.* Weber's primary interest was not capitalism. He set out to trace the influences of religious ideas on the behavior of individuals. In the process, he challenged Marx's contention that human personality and values are molded by the interest of social class. In short, he refused to accept the theory that economic institutions alone determined the course of history.

Capitalism's Tie to Protestantism

Weber thought it was significant that Protestantism and capitalism emerged at approximately the same time. In attempting to prove a connection between these events, Weber used the comparative method to examine material and ideological factors as they affected societies. He asked himself why capitalism arose in the societies of the West rather than in those of the East—for instance, in India or in China. He noted that India and China had experienced vast increases in population and were rich in silver and gold.

Weber concluded, however, that material factors were not sufficient for capitalism to emerge. Ideological factors must have been at work and must, furthermore, have had economic consequences. To illustrate, Weber showed that the static religious and caste systems in India, which prohibited changes in occupation, contributed to the long life of craft guilds—occupational associations opposed to technological change. Thus, an economic situation was the direct consequence of religious ideas.

Comparisons between the East and the West strengthened Weber's belief that the dual emergence of capitalism and Protestantism —he actually proved that Protestantism preceded capitalism—was not merely an accident of history. He pointed out that the *official* teachings of religion are not necessarily those that influence people's behavior. It is people's reaction to these teachings or the needs religion fulfills for them that are important. Thus, in the Middle Ages, Catholicism provided the common people with an escape mechanism in the form of forgiveness of sins upon confession. Repentance and confession gave the individual a chance to go to heaven, regardless of his position in this life. This escape mechanism made it easier for people to accept their lot in life and consider their position as part of the total scheme of things, or as part of natural law. Thus, there was acceptance of traditional standards and of the status quo. Weber's point was well made; the attitude that all worldly endeavor was vanity was indeed encouraged by the religious ideas of scholasticism.

Luther and Calvin

The Protestant Reformation, based on the ideas of Martin Luther and, later, of Calvin, changed religious teachings. Endeavor was no longer simply vanity. Instead, all men had a calling to serve God, and the service was best accomplished through work. Calvin further expanded this notion, arguing that work is a useful and dignified way to decrease anxiety concerning salvation. The anxiety he spoke of results from the Calvinist doctrine of predestination, according to which each person is part of a preestablished plan and from birth is destined for eternity either to burn in hell or live in the sight of God. There is little the individual can do to change his fate, but he can see signs of what that fate will be. Those who through hard work and diligence accumulate wealth and are successful on earth are, in all probability, the lucky ones destined for heaven.

With such a doctrine, it is easy to see why people worked hard to accumulate wealth! Such ideas particularly appealed to members of the emerging bourgeoisie in England and Holland, who were later called Puritans. They had already been pursuing wealth and treasured such virtues as hard work, saving, thrift, denial of sensual pleasures, and so on. And they were delighted to learn that such activities were pleasing to God as well as being satisfying to themselves.

The Puritan Ideology and Capitalism

Much of the behavior considered virtuous by Calvin—working hard, investing wisely, stilling the demands of the senses, being independent, suffering little interference, being steadfast in purpose—is also essential if an economic system of the scope of capitalism is to function properly. Therefore, Weber concluded that capitalism did not arise automatically or randomly after feudalism collapsed or as a result of the self-interest of any social class. Rather, capitalism arose because Calvinist ideology had affected the behavior of individuals. Unknowingly, Calvinists had shaped social change into a capitalistic mold. That is why the Catholic and Lutheran countries of Europe—which remained tradition-bound and in which people continued to believe in salvation solely through faith instead of through faith in addition to personal effort in the service of God—experienced capitalism only much later.[5]

Whether social change begins with an ideology, as Weber contended, or whether it is caused by the selfishness of the powerful, as Marx declared, is a question that has not been completely answered. Surely, much of history has been shaped by the powerful, and conceivably, many of them were motivated by greed. On the other hand, no social structure survives for long without a supportive ideology that rationalizes it and makes it acceptable to the people. As to which appears first, the ideology or the institution, we might as well ask, Which came first, the chicken or the egg?

AMERICAN CAPITALISM

The Puritans who settled in New England brought with them the Calvinist ideals of the Protestant Reformation. They further refined these ideals to the point that work and virtue came to be considered one and the same thing. Many colonial men of letters emphasized that work brings advantages to people on earth as well as being pleasing to God. This theme is nowhere better illustrated than in the works of Benjamin Franklin, who achieved fame and wealth through hard work and who gave advice to his contemporaries: "Time is money;" money generates more money; industry and frugality are the ways to wealth; "a penny saved is a penny earned;" and so on.

In the change from a feudal to a market economy, new ideas had also begun to spread throughout nations. These ideas affected the system of stratification and gave force to the French and American revolutions. Ideas such as the basic equality of each human being and individual freedom fired people's imaginations and produced such slogans as "Liberty, Equality, Fraternity" and "Give me liberty or give me death!"

Here again, as with the rise of capitalism, ideas originating in separate

---

[5]N. Birnbaum, "Conflicting Interpretations of the Rise of Capitalism: Marx and Weber," *The British Journal of Sociology*, Vol. 4 (June, 1953), pp. 125–141. The idea that Catholic theology encouraged the development of capitalism to the same extent that Protestant theology did was set forth by A. Fanfaniin *Catholicism, Protestantism, and Capitalism* (London: Sheed and Ward, 1935).

fields came together to create a new situation. Ideas of human equality were in perfect accord with a market economy. The rewards of the new economic system were attained through competition. Competition works best in a society in which status is achieved, rather than ascribed, and in which accomplishment, rather than heredity, is valued.

The Growth of Capitalism in the Nineteenth Century

The Horatio Alger novels not only captured the spirit of American society in the nineteenth century but they perpetuated the myth that hard work and self-discipline would lead any man of virtue, regardless of how poor he was, to his well-deserved reward of material wealth and high status. In reality, most of the famous entrepreneurs of this era of rugged individualism, the Rockefellers, Carnegies, and Morgans, came from upper-middle class backgrounds. They made use of a booming economy to attain their vast wealth and high status.[6]

The type of capitalism practiced in the nineteenth century was called *family capitalism* because most huge business enterprises were controlled by members of one family. This form of capitalism differed considerably from the corporate bureaucracy we know today. It was a capitalism based on the principles of a strictly laissez-faire, or free-enterprise, economy, and competition was absolutely ruthless. How tough competition was is suggested by the name "robber barons," given to the tycoons of the era.

The huge family enterprises tended to be in mining, manufacturing, and transportation. Capitalism centering on these fields is called *industrial capitalism*. However, these enterprises eventually grew too complex for family leadership. Capitalism then entered a new phase: finance capitalism.

Finance Capitalism

At the turn of the century, family capitalism had been so successful that it had created gigantic industrial complexes. In other words, competition had worked so well that it had destroyed competition. Although the government tried to step in and check the growth of monopolies through legislation—The Sherman and Clayton Anti-Trust Acts, the Federal Reserve Act, the Federal Trade Commission Act—the monsters seemed to grow new limbs as soon as the old ones were chopped off. Conglomerates and other semilegal devices were used to maintain the vast enterprises.

The complicated enterprises did not lend themselves to leadership by one or a family of owners, and many found themselves in situations of crisis, despite their size and wealth. At this point, bankers, who controlled the money and credit market, stepped in and reorganized the industrial sector. Their interference signaled the beginning of finance capitalism.[7]

The most important result of finance capitalism is the *corporation*. It is an enterprise organized for large-scale production and includes an all-encompassing bureaucracy. The corporation emerges when the owners of an enterprise offer a number of shares of stock for sale on the market. This is

---

[6]Daniel Bell, *The End of Ideology*, Collier edition (New York: Free Press, 1961), p. 41.
[7]Ibid., p. 42.

generally done to amass rapidly a large amount of capital which may be needed for expanding the enterprise. Those who buy the shares—the shareholders, or stockholders—become coowners of the enterprise. Actually, they may become more powerful than the original owners if they own a majority of the shares. In the eyes of the law, the corporation is separate from its owners, an entity of its own, and it endures regardless of what happens to individual shareholders.

The responsibility for operating the corporation no longer belongs to the former owners. In their stead, executive managers, hired by a centralized board of directors, assume this burden. The board of directors is, in turn, elected at the annual stockholders' meeting, with each share of stock counting for one vote.

Features of Finance Capitalism

Finance capitalism exhibits these characteristics: (1) Industry is dominated by investment banks and insurance companies; (2) tremendous amounts of capital are formed, much more than any single company could accumulate; (3) managers, instead of owners, run the enterprise; (4) the holding company appears.

Under finance capitalism, banks and insurance companies frequently control corporations because they have the money at their disposal to buy up large numbers of shares. Thus, industry has become controlled by a few financial enterprises. The government has made attempts to break up financial giants, but as with all such attempts against monopolies, it has not been entirely successful.

Because finance capitalism enables corporations to amass huge amounts of capital in a short period of time, they can take advantage of situations favorable to profit making. Also, corporations receive numerous tax benefits and are protected by the Limited Liability Clause. According to this clause, the individual stockholder is not financially responsible for a corporation's debts. If a corporation goes bankrupt, then the individual stockholder loses only the shares he owns. In private ownership, the owner can lose all of his property to his creditors.

The separation of ownership from management means that the real owners of the corporation—the stockholders—are absentee owners. Technically, this separation is supposed to enhance efficiency and fairness, because the hired managers are not as interested in profits as real owners would be. In reality, a great deal of power and control lies with the board of directors, the members of which are frequently elected by a small number of shareholders who have large portions of stock in the corporation. In effect, then, this powerful minority owns the corporation, because it controls it.

Finally, finance capitalism is responsible for the *holding company*. This enterprise does not produce anything but still makes profits. Holding companies make profits from the stock that the company owns in producing corporations and from management fees that it charges such producing organizations. The holding company is the ultimate triumph of finance over industrial capitalism.[8]

___

[8]Edward McNall Burns, *Western Civilizations*, Vol. I (New York: W. W. Norton, 1963), pp. 677–686.

CORPORATE POWER

The corporation has so pervaded our economic system that many see in its continued quest for ever greater concentration of power a real threat to our political system. Because of the tendency to merge, today two hundred of the top manufacturing corporations control about two-thirds of all assets held by other corporations that engage primarily in manufacturing. Furthermore, "About half of U.S. manufacturing sales are made by industries in which the four largest firms produce thirty percent or more of the total output, and more than ten percent of all sales involve industries in which the four largest firms are responsible for more than seventy percent of production."[9] Such high industrial concentration, called *oligopoly*, has for some time caused heated debates among economists and the public alike.

Those who defend the centralization of economic power argue that the complexity of today's technology requires highly sophisticated machinery and specialized personnel to run it. In addition, huge outlays of capital are necessary to pursue experimentation. Large amounts of capital are available only to giant corporations, which can afford pilot research, costly sales campaigns, and are able to absorb eventual financial failures.

These arguments are increasingly countered by criticism pointing out that most experimentation and initial production of new articles occurs in small firms that are later bought out by the giants. A late executive of General Electric admitted that small companies discovered and initially produced such articles as electric ranges, refrigerators, washers, dryers, irons, and many more. The giant corporations, including General Electric, have a record of moving in, buying out, and absorbing small concerns.[10]

Such maneuvers, of course, deal deadly blows to competition, making a farce of the classical economic theory that the market will work freely through competition. In 1963, the revenues of General Motors were fifty times those of the state of Nevada and only slightly less than one-fifth of those of the federal government. Clearly, corporations of this dimension do not have to conform to demand: They can both control demand and fix prices.[11]

The power of corporations is increasingly being compared with the power of the government. In fact, some suggest that government is often a tool of the corporation. Consumer rights advocate Ralph Nader states, "Much of what passes as governmental power is derivative of corporate power whose advocacy or sufferance defines much of the direction and deployment of government activity."[12] Even as conservative an observer as President Dwight D. Eisenhower, on his retirement, warned the American public against the powerful influences of the military-industrial complex. In a recent incident, ITT allegedly donated $400,000 to the Republican party (by offering to pay for the GOP Convention) in return for which the Justice Department dropped an antitrust case against the corporation. If this did, in fact, occur, it gives ample proof of the influence corporations have over the government. This same corporation—a huge conglomerate with approximately $6.7 billion in assets—ap-

---

[9]Daniel B. Suits, *Principles of Economics* (New York: Harper & Row, 1970), p. 358.
[10]Morton Mintz and Jerry S. Cohen, *America, Inc.* (New York: Dial Press, 1971), pp. 66.
[11]John Kenneth Galbraith, *The New Industrial State* (New York: Houghton Mifflin, 1967).
[12]Morton Mintz and Jerry S. Cohen, *America, Inc.*, p. 11.

parently regards politics as an investment opportunity. At one time, ITT executives made contributions to both parties in an effort to "butter up both sides so we'll be in a good position whoever wins," in the words of one of their former vice-presidents.[13]

The Consumer

Corporate power resembles government power in another way: Corporations are powerful enough to dispense with the consumer's money and life. However, when the cost of living goes up, people tend to blame either labor or taxes, without realizing that corporate profits are usually at fault. In the period 1960–1966, when consumer prices rose by 12.1 percent, corporate profits after taxes had risen 88 percent, and unit labor costs had gone up only 2.1 percent.

In addition, by refusing to install safety features—for instance, an impact-absorbing steering assembly, patented in the 1920s, which would prevent the crushing to death of the driver during a collision—corporations such as General Motors have been contributing to the high rate of deaths in automobiles.[14] Of course, if we are to believe University of Chicago economist Milton Friedman,

> The social responsibility of business is to increase its profits.... [If businessmen declare that] business has a 'social conscience' and takes seriously its responsibilities for providing employment, eliminating discrimination, avoiding pollution and whatever else may be the catchwords of the contemporary crop of reformers,... [they are in fact] preaching pure and unadulterated socialism.[15]

Such an attitude is all too often taken by the corporations, to the consumer's disadvantage.

The corporate irresponsibility of the people making decisions about what will be produced is vividly described in Colman McCarthy's article "The Faulty School Buses."[16] In the name of profit, corporate managers cut the thickness of metal, eliminate parts, use cheap grades of material, and fast assembly-line methods. Ultimately, many such decisions have tragic consequences, but the men making the decisions are so far removed from the consequences that their consciences apparently can remain untouched. In "The Faulty School Buses," the trials of a school bus owner whose conscience would not let him forget the possible consequences, and his head-on collision with General Motors, are reported by one of the editors of the *Washington Post*.

Because of corporations' power and command of the mass media through advertising, the consumer is at a distinct disadvantage. If an advertising campaign can convince you that Ultrabright toothpaste will give you sex appeal, it can convince you of anything, including that increased high profits for corporations are benefiting the consumer.

[13]TRB from Washington, "Gobble, Gobble," *The New Republic* (March 18, 1972), p. 4.

[14]Morton Mintz and Jerry S. Cohen, *America, Inc.*, p. 24.

[15]Milton Friedman, "The Social Responsibility of Business Is to Increase Its Profits," *The New York Times Magazine* (September 13, 1970), p. 32.

[16]Colman McCarthy, "The Faulty School Buses," *Saturday Review* (March 11, 1972), pp. 50–56.

What is so discouraging is that the private citizen has little opportunity to protect himself from the encroachment of corporate power. Private organizations, such as Consumers Research and Consumers Union, though helpful in consumer education, are reaching only a small percentage of consumers. The government, through its agency the Food and Drug Administration, has been cracking down on obvious corporate misdeeds. Legislation such as the Truth in Lending Act is also intended to protect the consumer. However, billions of dollars continue to be spent by consumers on products and services sold under false pretenses: meat and poultry containing high percentages of water and fat; patent medicines and aids to beauty that do nothing, or next to nothing, and are frequently harmful; fraudulent home improvements; and the accident-injury industry which provides insurance, medical, legal, and repair services at the cost of $12 billion a year to the consumer, an expense that could be largely avoided if cars were being safely and sensibly designed.[17]

Some members of the young generation, who are returning to organic foods and utilitarian clothing, give indications of wanting to break free from the hold of corporatism. But concern on the part of the entire consuming public, as well as a change in values, is needed if corporations are to respond positively to the real needs of the people.

The Spread of Multinational Corporatism

The danger of economic power being concentrated in the hands of a few people, whether they are in the public or private sector, has long been recognized. People with different political and philosophic attitudes admit that in such a situation the risk of tyranny or a police state is great. Even if tyranny does not result, the concentration of economic power means that citizens lose power to direct their fate and contribute to their welfare. Yet the concentration of economic power among a few giant corporations is not limited to our society. With the new phenomenon called multinational corporatism, there is production at an international level. In other words, corporations no longer simply export goods to foreign countries; they produce them in the the foreign countries. For example, PepsiCo operates 512 plants in 114 countries outside the United States.

Because of the growth potential of such multinational corporations, they might soon present a very real threat to the host countries. A single giant multinational corporation could conceivably become the largest economic entity in the world, larger than most individual nation-states.

As of now, almost 100 percent of Canada's automotive industry, 64 percent of its oil industry, and 54 percent of all manufacturing are owned by foreigners, most of whom are Americans. Knowing the connection between economic power and political power, we can see what effects multinational corporatism will have on the host nations.

Many people in these nations suspect that the United States is merely using the corporations to control their economies. They also believe that corporations are, in effect, undermining their nations' ability to pursue the best course of economic development for their people. Clearly, the further spread of multi-

[17]Ralph Nader, "A Citizen's Guide to the American Economy," *The New York Review of Books* (September 2, 1971), pp. 14–18.

national corporations without legislative controls of some kind could prove disastrous to international relations. An expert in the subject concluded that to counteract the imbalance between the multinational corporations and the national states the corporations must be made accountable to a body that has multinational powers and takes into consideration multinational interests.[18]

THE INDUSTRIAL HIERARCHY: MANAGEMENT

Industry has evolved into a system composed of a complex machine technology and an executive and administrative bureaucracy, which includes the white-collar labor force and the blue-collar labor force, made up of those who actually run the machinery of production. At the top of this hierachy are the managers of America's corporations.

We have already suggested that some confusion, or perhaps naiveté is shown by the public in regard to the power of corporations and the role of corporate management. The corporations themselves like to give the impression that they are owned by "the people," that the mangers are actually public servants, that the profit motive has all but disappeared, and that the corporation is a trustee of society, a socially responsible entity wielding only as much power as do the government and labor unions.[19]

The reality of corporate power is quite different. In the Western world, industry primarily serves capitalistic economies in which the drive for profits is of overriding concern. The profit motive, then, is of great importance and strongly influences both the corporations and their executives. Even though the selling of stocks has made ownership diffuse and corporate management has been transferred to experts, the managers' success is still measured by the amount of profit they create for the organization employing them. Thus, managers are hired to make profits.

The experts who are officers of the boards of directors of corporations and are collectively called the management, virtually run the entire organization. An observer remarks that in spite of governmental regulation and the image of corporate democracy, the corporation presents a picture of omnipotent management and impotent shareholdership.[20] To mask the impotence of shareholders, the corporations attempt to give them an illusion of power. At the annual stockholders' meetings, impressive-looking reports are handed out. Plants are toured and products inspected, and officers speak of "your" company and listen carefully to the suggestions made from the floor. At these meetings, however, no important stockholders are present and no important decisions are made. Economist John Kenneth Galbraith notes that annual meetings of large American corporations are an elaborate exercise in popular illusion.[21]

Precisely who are these aristocrats of the twentieth century, the corporation executives? Are they the "men in the gray flannel suits" of fiction, who sacrifice their private lives and happiness for their mistress, the corporation? Are they

[18]Raymond Vernon, *Sovereignty at Bay* (New York: Basic Books, 1971), p. 284.

[19]Gabriel Kolko, *Wealth and Power in America* (New York: Praeger, 1961), pp. 55-56.

[20]Bayless Manning, as quoted in Melvin Aron Eisenberg, "The Legal Roles of Shareholders and Management in Modern Corporate Decision-Making," *California Law Review* (January, 1969), pp. 23-24.

[21]John Kenneth Galbraith, *The New Industrial State*.

frustrated conquerors, who satisfy their lust for power in corporate maneuverings? Or are they average Joes simply trying to make a living the best way they can?

Functions of the Executive

Specific functions of the corporation executive are difficult to pinpoint because his role is generally varied and diffuse. However, each executive's primary responsibility is decision making at a policy level. Presumably, his decisions are then carried out by the various departments of the organization. His second function is that of coordinator and troubleshooter. In this function, he must make sure that things are done ttto specifications and on time. In other words, the ultimate responsibility for the operation and organization of the plant is his. Finally, the executive must be concerned with maintaining favorable relations between his organization and outside forces—consumers, bankers, union leaders, and so forth.[22]

Strain in the Executive Role

The functions that the executive must perform create strains. First, he must make decisions quickly, often without having all of the information at his disposal. And he is under intense pressure—these decisions must be the right ones. Second, he must display impersonality in his relations with others, to whom he may have to issue unpleasant orders and whom he may even have to dismiss.[23] Obviously, then, the role strains that we described in Chapter 1 are particularly pertinent to corporate executives.

The reactions to such strains vary, depending on the individual executive. In general, however, executives tend to indulge in scapegoating against external forces, generally the government, labor unions, and competitors. The executive also creates a self-image based on the idea of the "man of action," the aggressive decision-maker. Such a man supposedly makes the right decisions either through intuition or because of superior common sense, which is more accurate than is the knowledge of experts. Executives also tend to develop psychosomatic diseases, such as ulcers, and are subject to nervous breakdowns and heart failure. Finally, executives attempt to control the environment by influencing public opinion, prompting political action, and manipulating competition. They usually do this through legal, though sometimes unethical, channels. However, executives have also been found guilty of "white-collar crime," which includes such offenses as evading taxes, ignoring safe working conditions, knowingly producing defective materials, and making obviously false advertising claims.[24]

The Personality Type of Executives

A composite image of the personality of an executive shows definite characteristics. The executive has broken emotional ties that he thinks interfere with his career. He has a strong sense of self-discipline, can keep emotionally cool,

[22]Chester I. Barnard, *The Functions of the Executive* (Cambridge, Mass.: Harvard University Press, 1958).

[23]Neil J. Smelser, *The Sociology of Economic Life* (Englewood Cliffs, N. J.: Prentice-Hall, 1963), p. 75

[24]Edwin H. Sutherland, *White Collar Crime* (New York: Dryden Press, 1949).

and submits easily to authority. He is unusually ambitious and able to forgo immediate goals for future benefits. He has an element of ruthlessness, because he must be successful at all costs—failure represents the ultimate tragedy. Finally, he is a man who lacks affective empathy, that is, he does not know how people respond emotionally. This may be a defense mechanism developed in response to role strain. Because his role demands that he run his organization as efficiently as possible, it is inevitable that the executive will, from time to time, have to deal harshly with individuals in the organization. He can best perform this chore if he lacks empathy, at least from the point of view of the corporation. Above all, he has a great need for power and for managing, and he approaches management with limitless confidence in his ability to make the right decisions.[25]

A final point about managers and chief executives is that they are overwhelmingly drawn from the upper social classes. This was true at an earlier stage of industrialism, in which rugged individualism supposedly prevailed, and it is true today. The reason for this is simple: Executives are chosen by other executives. It is natural for the chooser to prefer someone who displays similarities in background, beliefs, educational attainment, and so on. And people who display similar life styles belong to the same social class, as we saw in our discussion of stratification in Chapter 4.

THE INDUSTRIAL HIERARCHY: MIDDLE MANAGEMENT

Sandwiched between the lofty position of corporation executive and the masses of blue-collar industrial workers, there is a large segment of the industrial bureaucracy collectively called middle management. This segment includes executive vice-presidents, specialists, office workers, and foremen. Some members of middle management, such as foremen, belong to the *line* divisions of the organization—the divisions responsible for the actual production of goods. Others, such as vice-presidents, belong to the *staff* divisions—those divisions that are supportive of or helpful to line.

The Vice-President

In each organization, there are usually several vice-presidents. Their function is to implement and help carry out decisions from the top. Vice-presidents are generally not involved in the decision-making process per se. Rather, they do whatever the executive hasn't the time or the inclination to do and whatever is outside the realm of other employees' functions. In short, a vice-president is a jack-of-all-trades. Among vice-presidents, then, rivalries are especially acute, and there is competition for executive approval and, ultimately, the executive position. The result is that fear and distrust become the hallmarks of corporate relationships, and much of the information upward is filtered to make it agreeable to the chief executive.[26]

It is easy to see how competition among vice-presidents and the filtering

[25]J. Sterling Livingston, "Myth of the Well-Educated Manager," *Harvard Business Review* (January, 1971).

[26]Delbert G. Miller and William H. Form, *Industrial Society* (New York: Harper & Row, 1964), p. 189.

of information to top management can harm the consumer. To show his efficiency and management ability, a vice-president may order cheap materials to be used in the manufacture of a product. By saving money and increasing the profits of his organization, he will look good to his superiors, but his decision could prove tragic to the consumer, as our article on faulty school buses demonstrates.

Specialists

A specialist is a middle-management employee who is a professional trained in a rather narrow field of specialization. His authority comes from his exclusive knowledge of a particular subject. The role of specialists is especially significant in technological fields, but specialists are becoming increasingly important in advertising, public relations, market analysis, and so on.

Specialists exist because of the complexity of modern technology. Technology has made it necessary to train people in limited fields of specialization, so they deal with only one aspect of the production process. The research programs that many corporations have initiated to enhance their corporate image also require specialists. As a result, specialists—scientists and technicians, in particular— are the fastest growing segment of industry.

Office Workers

In the bureaucracy of the corporation, the position of office workers is quite a bit below that of specialists. As a group, office workers are difficult to place either in the staff or line segment of corporate organization. In reality, the role of the office worker is similar to that of the assembly-line worker, especially recently, because a large amount of office work has become automated or

mechanized. However, the workers themselves prefer to make the distinction between white-collar and blue-collar jobs.

Although they lack the authority and the salary of other middle-management employees, white-collar workers enjoy the status that comes from mingling with executives. That office workers identify with executives has been advantageous to management. In fact, management has had at its disposal an efficient labor force that has been particularly resistant to unionization. Recent studies, however, seem to indicate that this identification is coming to an end.[27]

Foremen

The foreman in the industrial plant, very often a man in the middle, has a role that is ambiguous and difficult to classify. Theoretically, he is part of management and of the line segment of organization. In practice, however, his functions have been taken over by specialists, and he is left with the task of implementing decisions that have already been made. His power to hire and fire employees has also been taken over by management.

Because of the unionization of blue-collar workers, grievances are now processed through a shop steward. Thus, the foreman's relations with workers have become weaker than they were in the past. His remaining functions are limited to maintaining discipline and carrying out instructions from above. His role is, therefore, one in which his identification is split between management, workers, and other foremen.[28]

Conflicts Between Staff and Line

We have mentioned that relationships, particularly at vice-presidential levels, are often of a conflicting nature. Frequent conflict within large industrial organizations also occurs between line and staff managers. According to one sociological study, this conflict has generational and stratificational overtones.[29] Line officers tend to be older, noncollege-educated, former blue-collar workers who have worked their way up. Staff officers, on the contrary, tend to be younger than line officers are, college-educated, and hired to fill managerial positions. Resenting the staff officers' easy ascent, line managers often refer to them as "college punks." They tend to ignore or sabotage any suggestions that come from the staff officers. In turn, the staff officers blame the line managers' lack of cooperation on their ignorance and the stubborness that supposedly comes from old age. Whatever the causes, these strained relationships make for unpleasantness for both segments.

THE INDUSTRIAL HIERARCHY: BLUE-COLLAR WORKERS

One of the far-reaching effects of industrial production and of capitalism was the establishment of a labor force unlike any known before. It brought

[27]Charles Wright Tucker, Jr., "Occupation and Work Self-Identification," *Sociological Quarterly* (Autumn, 1967), pp. 537–542.

[28]Robert David Leiter, *The Foreman in Industrial Relations* (New York: Columbia University Press, 1948), pp. 32–41.

[29]Melville Dalton, "Conflicts Between Staff and Line Managerial Officers," *American Sociological Review*, Vol. 15, (June, 1950), pp. 342–351.

into existence the proletariat, a working class that labored in exchange for wages. As befits a market economy, wages were determined according to the law of supply and demand. If there were many workers willing and able to perform a task, wages were low. If there were few, wages were high.

The transformation of the working man into a member of the urban industrial proletariat took place over a long period of time, and it left deep scars. In the economies of the feudal era, the worker was made to feel protected and secure. He might be penniless and live in the same conditions as his master's animals did, but he didn't have to worry about a roof over his head or about his next meal.

The factory system brought a sharp change in working conditions. First, the worker was made responsible for his own transportation to and from work. Second, the place of work was often a dark, humid, smelly building, into which he was herded with hundreds of other workers. Once there, he was told exactly what to do—usually an insignificant task that he repeated numerous times—and how much he was expected to finish within a period of time. He was told when to come to work and when to go home. Even though some of the work was not difficult, it was tedious, one long hour following another for an average day of twelve to fourteen hours. Accidents and injuries frequently occurred because buildings almost totally lacked hygienic, safe facilities. The final indignity was that wages were so pitifully low that the entire family, children included, had to work.

Owners no longer felt any moral obligation toward their workers. With increasing bureaucratization, workers became mere names on a ledger and could be fired without a second thought if it seemed convenient. The urban industrial worker, then, felt unprotected and alone in an unfriendly environment in which he was considered the country bumpkin. He was exploited by having to work for low wages, live in substandard housing, and eat substandard food. He totally lacked any type of health protection or access to medical

care, even for industrial accidents, which occurred with great frequency. What is more, his very job depended on the mercy of his boss or on a business cycle.

Naturally, the worker didn't display loyalty to an owner he seldom even saw. No longer responsible for producing an article but merely for performing a task that he often could not relate to the finished product, the worker took no pride in what he was doing. This was the beginning of the impersonality and anonymity of industrial relations. That problems of impersonality still exist is demonstrated by a recent strike in a General Motors plant in Ohio. Our article "Luddites in Lordstown," by Barbara Garson, probes into a situation that workers find unbearable. The split-second timing required for the performance of their trivial operation, which leaves them no time to scratch their noses; the juvenile discipline according to which they must raise their hands to be permitted to go to the restroom; and the Armylike atmosphere in which they must obey the direct order of a foreman, regardless of how unfair it is, are all things that in the eyes of the workers cancel out the high wages and good benefits they receive.[30]

ORGANIZED LABOR

In the last decades of the nineteenth century, an increasing number of workers began to realize that the only way to put an end to the horror in which they were living was to organize. Individually, they could do nothing; together, they represented a force to be reckoned with. As industry consolidated into larger and larger enterprises, efforts at unionization increased. Additional factors spurred workers on: growing mechanization, which was displacing skilled artisans; the rapid spread of anonymity resulting from the large size of plants; the lack of loyalty to a management that was by now entirely separate from ownership; and the general depersonalization of working conditions.

Labor organizers, however, had several problems to surmount before effective unionization could take place. First, American workers were anything but homogeneous, representing as they did different ethnic, religious, and cultural backgrounds. Thus, they were often at odds or suspicious of one another. Second, American workers were not conscious of themselves as a working class. Instead, they believed in the "rags to riches" mythology as much as other Americans did. Often, they considered their factory job as a temporary step on the way to wealth and power, and so did not see any reason to organize a group they would soon leave. Finally, the federal government, the state governments, and the American public, in general, were not sympathetic to labor and its efforts at improving working conditions. The heroes of the time were the captains of industry and business who had become powerful tycoons, according to the mythology of the period, through hard work and perseverance. If workers wanted to improve their lot, they could follow *their* example!

The AFL-CIO

In spite of numerous obstacles, American workers did organize several national labor unions. In 1881, the American Federation of Labor was founded,

[30]Barbara Garson, "Luddites in Lordstown," *Harper's* (June, 1972), pp. 68–73.

and soon grew to include a large membership. Later, the Committee for Industrial Organization, or CIO, was formed. After seventeen years of independent existence, the two organizations joined forces in 1955 as the AFL-CIO.

The AFL-CIO is structured on a federal model. This means that below the federal level, unions are organized at national, local, or regional levels. Local industrial and regional craft unions are chartered by their national union, which permits them to exercise only those powers that were initially approved. A large number of national unions are affiliated with the AFL-CIO, but they have given up little actual power. In reality, then, the national union has much power within the federal structure.

Union Goals and Functions

Contrary to labor movements in other countries, in which attempts were made to produce radical changes in the economic, political, and social systems of society, organized labor in America had no such plans. Its goals have been, and continue to be, the attainment of economic and social opportunities for its members. Labor, then, is primarily interested in obtaining favorable working conditions, fair wages, and advantageous fringe benefits. This bread-and-butter philosophy has kept labor from becoming embroiled in ideological controversies and helps explain the basic conservatism of the American worker.

The most important function performed by the union for its members is collective bargaining, which includes daily grievance procedures, negotiations, arbitration, and mediation. Collective bargaining, a process that has become

TABLE 8.1   AMERICA'S LARGEST LABOR UNIONS

	1960 membership	Present membership	Change
Teamsters	1,484,400	2,020,000	Up 36%
Auto Workers	1,136,100	1,350,000	Up 19%
Steelworkers	1,152,000	1,200,000	Up 4%
Brotherhood of Electrical Workers....................	771,000	977,295	Up 27%
Machinists	898,100	900,000	Up 0.2%
Carpenters	800,000	808,000	Up 1%
Laborers	442,500	650,000	Up 47%
Retail Clerks	342,000	650,000	Up 90%
Meat Cutters*	436,000	550,000	Up 26%
State, County, Municipal Employees	210,000	525,000	Up 150%
Communications Workers	259,900	500,000	Up 92½
Service Employes	272,000	480,000	Up 76%
Hotel, Restaurant Employes	443,000	450,000	Up 2%
Ladies' Garment Workers	446,600	442,300	Down 1%
Operating Engineers	291,000	400,000	Up 37%

*Meat Cutters figures include those for former Packinghouse Workers Union, now merged.

SOURCE 1960 figures, U. S. Department of Labor; 1971 figures, union sources as reported to USN & WR.

an accepted institution in our society, has helped eliminate the bitterness and violence that characterized earlier relations between labor and management.

The Union Today: Big Labor

As has happened to the corporation and to the government, organized labor has grown so large and unwieldy that it has suffered the effects of bureaucratization. Because large size leads to power, and power to abuse, the government has had to intervene in the affairs of labor, as it has had to do in those of business and industry.

As a result of its large size, too, the power and authority once belonging to the rank and file have been transferred to a hierachy of leaders. To some extent, however, the lack of democratic procedures is unavoidable, partly because the membership has become apathetic and partly because in a complex society even union leadership must be specialized. Increasingly, then, union leaders resemble the corporate and government "organization men," whose specialty is the running of the organization, not the recruitment of members or the development of new ideas.

Another criticism of organized labor is that it has failed not only to champion social causes but even to integrate its own ranks. The reason for this is, in large part, the fear of white workers that they will lose their jobs to blacks. At any rate, racial discrimination in unions may further weaken the labor movement, already considered stagnant by some people. In fact, although such fields as heavy industry, transportation, public utilities, and construction are still heavily unionized, union membership has declined and union growth has slowed down.

There are several explanations of why the labor movements have lost ground. First, labor movements experience the greatest growth during periods of severe economic depression and war. When the economic security of workers is not seriously threatened, they tend to ignore the labor movement. Second, American workers have acquired middle-class goals, and many believe that they have attained a middle-class standard of living. Consequently, workers have lost their identification with labor. Finally, union leadership is changing. Not only have leaders become "organization men" but, today, few dedicated young men are willing to take up the cause of labor. Promising young people of the working class tend to be upwardly mobile and to look for careers in business and industry. And the middle-class intellectuals who felt ideologically sympathetic to labor in the past have abandoned it in disgust with its strictly materialistic goals.

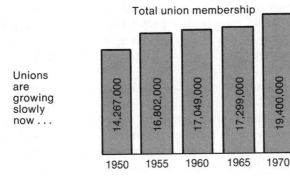

Total union membership

Unions are growing slowly now . . .

14,267,000 — 1950
16,802,000 — 1955
17,049,000 — 1960
17,299,000 — 1965
19,400,000 — 1970

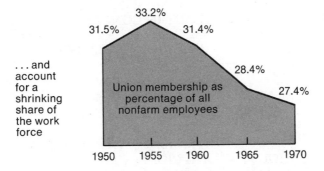

. . . and account for a shrinking share of the work force

Union membership as percentage of all nonfarm employees

31.5% — 1950
33.2% — 1955
31.4% — 1960
28.4% — 1965
27.4% — 1970

Source: U.S. Dept. of Labor

Problems Facing Labor: Automation

For some time now, the labor force of industrialized societies has feared automation. *Automation* is a process by which machines that were previously controlled and run by humans become controlled and run by other machines. In the short run, automation leads to a decrease in the number of workers that are needed to produce the same number of goods and services. The worker, then, is faced with unemployment.

Economists, however, maintain that, in the long run, automation creates more jobs than it eliminates. Each technological change that simplifies some process of production by creating an improved machine requires that parts be produced for the new machine and that people be available to maintain it. Thus, jobs are not actually taken away from workers: They simply must be redistributed. Unfortunately, displacement caused by automation generally hits the blue-collar, semiskilled, and oldest workers first and hardest. And this group is the most difficult to retrain and redistribute.

Another Problem: Alienation

A long-standing problem of the industrial worker is the feeling of alienation he experiences in relation to his work. Karl Marx was one of the first to describe workers' feelings in terms of alienation. Marx applied this word to the sentiment produced by the changed relationship between owner and worker brought about by the factory system, and sharpened by the antagonism between the new social classes, the proletariat and the bourgeoisie. In this new relationship, workers felt utterly powerless and insecure. Their importance was further diminished by increasing specialization, which meant a lessened need for skill and training.

Even though the working conditions of industrial workers have been much improved since Kark Marx's time, the boredom and meaninglessness of their jobs have remained the same. The result has been low productivity and a high rate of absenteeism in industry. Management has tried to solve these problems, for they represent a loss of profit. The concern has become so great that new fields—human relations and industrial psychology—have arisen as a result of the many experiments on the subject.[31]

[31]The classic study in this field is the experiment by Harvard professor Elton Mayo, *Human Problems of an Industrial Civilization* (New York: The Viking Press, 1966). First published in 1943.

TABLE 8.2   LABOR'S CLOUT IN CONGRESS IS BREAKING

	IN 1961-62	IN 1971
SENATE	Tests won by AFL-CIO: 10 Tests lost: 1	Tests won: 5 Tests lost: 7
HOUSE	Tests won by AFL-CIO: 9 Tests lost: 2	Tests won: 7 Tests lost: 5

SOURCE: Reprinted from *U.S. News & World Report.* Copyright (1972) U.S. News & World Report, Inc.

THE RISE OF BUREAUCRACY

In discussing industry and labor, we have noted that both display one startling similarity: a bureaucratic type of organization. This type of organization is part of every industrial society, and the more complex the society, the more bureaucratization there is. Moreover, bureaucratization is not limited to the economic institution. It embraces all institutions except for the family.

A *bureaucracy* is a type of formal organization that all large-scale enterprises have. In its ideal form, a bureaucratic organization includes, first, a clear-cut division of labor. Power and authority are hierarchically divided among a number of individuals, each of whom knows exactly the limits of his decision-making power. The clear-cut division of labor clarifies the responsibilities of each person in the chain of command. Second, labor is divided into such routine tasks that individuals performing the tasks can be easily replaced. Third, in a bureaucracy, people employ rational means, rather than emotional ones, to solve problems. Fourth, rules are applied in an impersonal manner and are considered unbreakable by members of the organization.[32]

Bureaucratic organization exists simply because it is functional for large enterprises. Max Weber, who analyzed bureaucratic forms of organization, maintained that their superiority was the same as a machine's superiority to a human being in efficiently and rapidly producing an object. Besides being the fastest, most efficient, clearest, and frictionless method of organization, bureaucracy is also functional because it is dehumanized. In short, it eliminates from human interrelations such emotions as love, hate, anger, envy, and so on. Thus, it is efficient, predictable, impersonal, rational, objective, and routinized.[33]

The very characteristics that make bureaucracy seem valuable to an organization also breed destructive side effects. In trying to follow rules by the book, the individual often loses sight of the objectives of the organization, becoming fixed in a self-perpetuating, useless routine. Excessive specialization, or the pigeonholing of tasks, also leads a person to develop blind spots with respect to any subject that is not within his sphere of competence. Therefore, bureaucratic organization makes for narrow-minded, petty individuals, who cannot function in unusual situations and who have dificulty thinking creatively.

People who level the most serious criticisms at the bureaucratized society accuse it of always placing the good of the abstract system ahead of personal human needs. Human goals are limited to selling oneself successfully on the market. To obtain the good job with a high income so people will admire you, you become what others want you to be. You learn to feign the right emotions at the proper times. You smile or you frown according to the clues you pick up from others. Similarly, you dress in particular ways, buy a home in the right neighborhood, and send your children to the proper schools.[34] In short, the bureaucratic society is a kind of "taking the role of the other"

---

[32]Thomas Ford Hoult, *Dictionary of Modern Sociology* (Totowa, N. J.: Littlefield-Adams, 1969), p. 48.

[33]Hans Gerth and C. W. Mills, *From Max Weber* (New York: Oxford University Press, 1946), p. 214.

[34]William H. Whyte, *The Organization Man* (New York: Simon and Schuster, 1956). Also, Joseph Bensman and Bernard Rosenberg, *Mass, Class, and Bureaucracy* (Englewood Cliffs, N. J.: Prentice-Hall, 1963).

gone wild, in which genuine human feelings are scarce, and phoniness and manipulation prevail.

We can see a reaction against the bureaucratization of society among the young people who are part of the counterculture and among the increasing number of young people who, though part of the "straight" society, wish to see changes made. In fact, some people claim that the present bureaucratic structure has reached the point of no return—that it is no longer functional. These observers predict that a new type of bureaucracy, dependent on automation and computers, will soon evolve and that decision making will become decentralized while attention will be given to creative thinking.[35]

THE AMERICAN ECONOMY TODAY

The American economy today, though a direct descendant of laissez-faire, or free market, theories is best described as a mixed market economy. Although production is still largely dependent on consumer demand, the government intervenes in the economy by being a large investor in it and by regulating and stabilizing it. We have already seen that the economic system is never entirely divorced from the political system. But an especially close association developed between the two after the Great Depression of 1929, when followers of the British economist John Maynard Keynes tried to reestablish capitalism as a viable economic system.

The Keynesian Solution to Economic Cycles

A weakness of capitalism became apparent when experts were unable to explain why economic growth did not proceed in a regular fashion but followed ups and downs of prosperity, falling prices, and unemployment. The experts finally decided that if increased amounts of money and credit were made available to business and industry when prices were falling, business would be lured into expanding, and the economy would once again be on an upswing. But although money and credit were provided during the depression, business did not expand. What did expand were the bread lines, a source of food for a quarter of the unemployed labor force.

The depression, coming at a time when wealth for everyone was anticipated as being just around the corner, was devastating to the nation. National income declined from $80 to $40 billion in the decade from 1927 to 1937. Wages fell abruptly for those lucky enough to have a job, and a general panic, following the closing of banks, led to welfare rolls strained to their utmost.

In the midst of this chaos, people turned to a work by a brilliant English economist who had accumulated a large fortune. The economist was Keynes, and his book had the formidable title of *The General Theory of Employment, Interest, and Money*. In it, Keynes stated that economic cycles are unavoidable because of the amount of guesswork in a market economy. However, preventive measures could be taken to avoid an economic slump from becoming a world disaster. Such measures should involve intervention in the economy

[35]Robert Townsend, *Up the Organization!* (New York: Alfred A. Knopf, 1970).

by the government, which should "buy and sell, invest and save, tax and make payments to the public in such a way as to counteract the forces that lead to 'boom and bust.'"[36]

Economic Stabilizers

Some of the measures designed to stabilize the economy that were put into effect in the 1930s were welfare programs such as Social Security, Workmen's Compensation, and Unemployment Compensation. Each of these programs was, in part, aimed at putting money into the hands of those most likely to spend it for consumer goods. These and other efforts helped to relieve some of the distress during the depression but the economy did not fully recover until the nation's industrial machinery was set into motion for World War II.

The legislative act that was clear evidence of the government's determination to be responsible for the welfare of the people was the Employment Act of 1946. According to this act, the goal of the economy is to attain and maintain the full employment of its citizens. The act also established the president's Council of Economic Advisers, a body that takes some of the guesswork out of business decisions by issuing reports on the state of the economy. Finally, the act defined the nature of the fiscal and monetary policies that act as the chief stabilizers in guiding the direction of the economy.

Fiscal policies. Fiscal policy is determined by the elected leaders of the nation, the president and Congress. Chiefly, it involves government spending and taxation. An increase in government spending speeds up production, whereas a reduction in government spending checks the rate of production. If tax rates are increased, consumer purchasing power is reduced, which has the effect of slowing production. If tax rates are reduced, however, demand grows, and production is eventually stimulated.

The fiscal policy is more effective in theory than it is in practice. First, those who implement it must act rapidly. And second, it is difficult both to cut back on programs begun during a period of government spending and to increase taxes after a period of low taxation.

Monetary policy. The Federal Reserve Board performs the activities required by the monetary policy, a measure designed to prevent unemployment and serious inflation. The Federal Reserve Board controls bank reserves and lending power. To stem the tide of unemployment, the board can (1) lower discount rates to increase the lending power of banks, (2) acquire securities to increase bank reserves, and (3) reduce the assets on reserve in Federal Reserve banks, thus releasing more money into circulation.

Through these devices, money becomes available to busineses for investment at lower rates of interest. Businesses also can more easily obtain mortgages, which, in turn, stimulates home buying and the building industry. Finally, consumers obtain better terms for installment buying. When inflation, rather than depression, is the problem, the board follows an opposite course.

[36]Nathaniel Stone Preston, *Politics, Economics, and Power,* p. 65.

Fiscal and monetary policies are designed to bring society close to the goal of ever-increasing abundance. They do this by providing everyone with sufficient money and the desire to spend it. To maintain and increase abundance, government has become the largest buyer, employer, landowner, borrower, and investor in the economy. It counters and corrects swings in the market by spending when others do not spend and saving when others do not save.[37] That ever-increasing abundance has not been the unmixed blessing people hoped it would be and that the economy has urgent need of a new goal are themes often repeated among modern economists.

The Affluent Society and the Other America

A few final comments critical of the American economy come from economist John Kenneth Galbraith and social observer and critic Michael Harrington.

[37]Ibid., p. 71.

BETTER TIMES COMING FOR AMERICANS

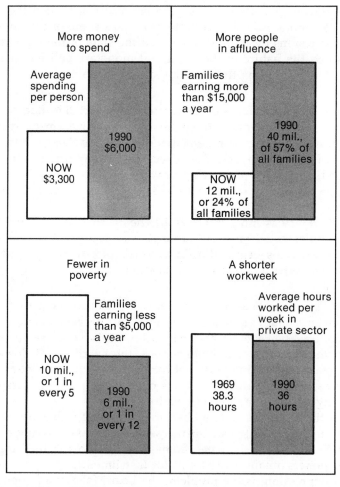

Source: Reprinted from *U.S. News & World Report.* Copyright (1972) U.S. News & World Report, Inc.

Galbraith points out that, in the past, the economy was one of scarcity—there were never enough goods produced to satisfy the needs of society. But now the situation has been reversed. In our present economy of plenty, physical needs have long been satisfied. Yet more and more is constantly being produced, for the sake of "growth." To sell the extreme surplus, a whole new industry—advertising—has come into being. Its sole purpose is to create artificial needs, because real needs have already been satisfied.

Growth for the sake of growth, according to Galbraith, has created a social imbalance in which private demands take precedence over public needs. As a result of this imbalance, in some income brackets, every family has at least two, and sometimes more, cars. But the private demand for cars has far outstripped the public need for highways on which to drive them. Therefore, we must stop worrying about *how much* to produce and start worrying about *what* and *for whom* to produce it.[38]

A more serious shortcoming of our economy is that it does not work equally well for all Americans. In *The Other America*, Michael Harrington reports that a full 20 to 25 percent of Americans do not share in the affluence of the wider society.[39] The problems facing this quarter of our population are complex and cannot be solved by simplistic methods. But a way for the economy to solve them must be found, if the economy is to be truly functional and if capitalism is to survive.

SUMMARY

The economic institution came into being because people organized for survival. In preindustrial societies, organization was sometimes based on custom and tradition. For instance, in feudal Europe the knowledge necessary for performing the tasks essential to survival was handed down from generation to generation, from father to son. In other cases, organization was based on the command of a central, authoritarian ruler who made sure that tasks were performed. This pattern was followed in the early stages of mercantilism, as it had been followed for centuries in the societies of the ancient world.

A third alternative pattern of organization emerged with the development of a market economy. In this type of economy, each individual, lured by the possibility of personal gain, performs the tasks necessary for survival without the intervention of either tradition or authority. The theories explaining and rationalizing the market economy came together in the ideology of capitalism.

Before capitalism could be accepted as a viable economic solution, there had to be a number of changes, both material and ideological. First, profit, which in feudal times was considered sinful, had to seem desirable. Second, statuses and roles, which in feudal society were ascribed by tradition, had to become achieved—subject to change through achievement and the accumulation of profits. Third, there had to be a demand for more and better goods and services. And fourth, the elements for a new mode of production had to be present.

Such changes occurred in Western Europe. They were brought about partly by a growth of commerce, by products imported from the New World, and

[38]John Kenneth Galbraith, *The Affluent Society* (Boston: Houghton Mifflin, 1958).
[39]Michael Harrington, *The Other America* (Baltimore: Penguin Books, 1964).

by new agents of production—land, labor, and capital. Additional changes were the result of Protestantism, which encouraged hard work for profit, and the creation of two new social classes, the proletariat and the bourgeoisie.

The mode of production of capitalist economies is industrialism. Industrial organization consists of a complex machine technology and a bureaucratic corporate structure, including executives, middle management, and a blue-collar labor force. In our society, corporations have grown so large that they wield great power on both a national and an international level. Their power has robbed the consumer of his ability to choose how much will be produced, what will be produced, and at what price it will be sold.

Among the earliest victims of industrialism were workers. Today, industrial workers are effectively unionized and even suffer some of the same ills of bureaucratic organization that corporations do. Unionization has not, however, as yet solved the two major problems workers face today: the fear of automation and alienation in relation to their work.

Today, the American economy is no longer a market system but is mixed. The government intervenes in the economy because "pure" capitalism failed to keep the economy in balance. Besides being a heavy investor and employer, the government attempts to regulate the economy through several stabilizers, among which are the fiscal and monetary policies.

Although the American economy has been functional for a majority of our population, it has not worked for all. Increasingly, critics are suggesting that our economic priorities should be reexamined. A reordering of priorities can take place only if pressures are brought to bear on the political institution, the subject of our next chapter.

THE faulty school buses

Our social critics remind us often enough of the dangers inherent in the power of the corporations. But although we may be temporarily appalled by the high profits, the incredible salaries, and the large share of the market that the giant corporations claim (against all the tenets of the capitalistic market economy and its reliance on competition), we soon forget and once again trade in our car for this year's model. There is a limit, however, that the public should not permit the giant corporations to pass: The limit is set at human life becoming the victim of corporate greed. The following passage, excerpted from a book illustrating many forms of corporate greed, shows what happens when planned obsolescence is equated with progress, and that idea is sold to the public.

□□□

In the board rooms of General Motors, the world's mightiest corporation, decisions are routinely made that affect the lives of Americans in ways that the actions of Congressmen in Washington seldom do. By the hard measure of dollars, little doubt exists about the comparative importance of Detroit and Washington. In a recent peak year, 1969, the board chairman of General Motors was paid $655,000, or fifteen times the salary of a United States Senator and more than three times what Americans pay their President. General Motors has $24-billion in gross annual sales (1969 figures), a sum larger than the budget of any

Saturday Review, March 11, 1972. Originally appeared in Doubleday & Company's *In The Name of Profit.*

of the fifty states or that of every nation except the United States and the Soviet Union. According to GM's records, its cumulative profit from 1947 to 1969 was $22-billion.

One reason for the corporation's Gargantuan size—it has 55 per cent of the American automobile market—is that its customers keep coming back to buy its products, especially its cars, trucks, and buses available at some 13,000 GM dealerships. Many customers return because they have been conditioned to crave the chrome, horsepower, and gizmos that GM puts into its vehicles. Others are the trapped victims of a corporate philosophy candidly described in April 1970 by former board chairman James M. Roche, forty-two years with GM: "Planned obsolescence, in my opinion, is another word for progress."

It is unlikely that any GM executive ever sends out memos to his staff saying things like, "Make the exhaust systems out of cheaper metal this year," or, "Order a lower-grade iron for the engine mounts." Yet in many cases he might as well, for underlings in the auto industry are quick to divine the intentions of their superiors. In February 1969, GM was obliged to notify 5.4 million owners to bring in their GM vehicles for correction of possible safety defects. Some 2.5 million of these were recalled to be checked for exhaust-system leaks. According to the Center for Auto Safety, the leaks were acknowledged by GM to have caused four deaths. The most recent GM recall, in January, set a national record: 6.6 million Chevrolets for possible engine mount failure. The Department of Transportation said it knew of 500 reports of such failures. The Public Interest Research Group, a Ralph Nader organization in Washington, reported at least six deaths and a dozen persons seriously injured in resulting crashes.

Down the line of corporate responsibility, someone had those thoughts about cheapening the exhausts and mounts, someone seconded those thoughts, and someone else carried them out. Death and injury resulted, and surely GM regrets it. Yet many millions of dollars of the $22-billion profit resulted also, and it is not likely that GM has regrets about that.

Consider the front bumper of the 1966 school bus, if a model in Washington, D.C., is representative. It is one-quarter-inch thick. On the 1969 model, it is one-eighth-inch thick. Thus in three years the bumper's thickness was cut in half. Considering the thousands of buses manufactured with the thinner and cheaper bumper, the savings must have been considerable. But so was and is the risk of injury and death to the thousands of school children who might be better protected with the thicker bumper.

Incredibly, as if more juice could still be squeezed from these lemons, the bumpers on these vehicles were the object of further GM cheapening. Behind the front bumper of the earlier model is a piece of steel extending from the frame in each direction about one foot, reinforcing the bumper. From the 1969 model, however, this piece of reinforcing steel is gone. And anyone who wonders why the 1969 bus rides so roughly need only measure the leaf springs that support the body. Compared to those on earlier models, the springs are seven inches shorter.

If GM cheapens parts that a layman can detect, what may it have done to parts hidden under the hood and within the chassis? General Motors, and its brother corporations such as Ford, Chrysler, American Motors, and foreign motor companies, assure prospective buyers that they can get into their products and go tearing off at high speeds. Yet between 1966 and 1970, some thirteen million vehicles, or 38 per cent of all vehicles manufactured, were recalled for possible defects. With 55,000 persons killed by automobiles in 1971 and nearly five million injured, it is reasonable to believe that not all the carnage was caused by drunk or wild driving. Much was doubtlessly caused

by defective cars, and many of those defects resulted from decisions to cut costs.

One citizen who has experienced the cheapness of a GM product is John Donovan. Unlike most owners, who have only themselves or their families to account for when they drive, Donovan has responsibility for some 250 school children, the elementary and high school students he transports to and from six private schools in the vicinity of Washington, D.C. Ever since the famous Huntsville, Alabama, crash in May 1968, when the brakes of a GM school bus failed, killing one child, Donovan has watched his vehicles closely, servicing them frequently and driving carefully. At the time of the Huntsville tragedy, he owned two GM buses, and he didn't want any injuries or deaths due to faulty equipment or anything else.

A short, broad-chested man of thirty-six, born in Oklahoma, a former Marine Corps drill sergeant, brusque in speech, John Donovan first went to Washington as a student at Georgetown University. He stayed on, married, and wound up teaching at a private school—Ascension Academy in Alexandria, Virginia. Students there describe him as a friendly, approachable man with a skill for fairness and discipline. The graduating seniors twice voted him Ascension's most popular teacher.

Donovan began in the bus business in 1963 when a neighbor in the northwest section of Washington asked him if, for a fee, he would take his child to and from Ascension every day. Donovan agreed and took out the proper commercial-carrier insurance. He soon had other requests for the same service. By the 1968–69 school year, Donovan's business had grown; he spent $5,000 to purchase a 1966 GM sixty-passenger bus and a 1959 Chevrolet thirty-seven-passenger model.

In the spring of 1969, the chance to expand still further came along, so that with more school buses he could transport 260 children. The average yearly fare was $200. Many of the children in Donovan's buses were the sons and daughters of Senators, Ambassadors, judges, prominent lawyers, doctors, and other important and powerful Washingtonians. Encouraged by his wife and with confidence in his capacity for hard work, Donovan decided to buy three new 1969 GMC-V-6 school buses. Each cost $8,146.80. The body of this model was made by an independent company; everything else—basically, the transmission, the wheels, the engine, the electrical system, the gas tank—came from General Motors Truck and Coach Division, Pontiac, Michigan.

Early in September 1969, Donovan went to High Point, North Carolina, to pick up his three new buses. Accompanying him were two drivers, as well as a GM dealer from Laurel, Maryland, from whom Donovan had what he called at the time "a little trouble." One bus required sixteen quarts of oil for the 3000-mile trip. On the second bus, things went fine until the accelerator spring snapped. This meant that the driver had to put the transmission into neutral, find a place to pull over, get out, lift the hood, and, with the engine still roaring, try to adjust the throttle spring with a pair of pliers. The third bus worked well until dusk, when the driver tried to switch on the headlights. They didn't work.

All of this irritated Donovan, but he understood that kinks are part of a new product and no cause for alarm. Except for rattling transmissions, Donovan's buses functioned normally for three days. He and his wife were proud of the buses. They had risked most of their savings on them and believed that no finer company existed than General Motors. Donovan named the buses after his wife, Virginia, and their daughters, Regina, who was three, and Colleen, just six months old.

In mid-September, as required by law, Donovan took the vehicles to be inspected before using them to carry children. One bus passed, two did not. One rejection was caused by a faulty brake-hose suspension. GM, Donovan believed, either had not installed the right part or had not installed any part. Thus, the brake hose, which is essential for stopping and which should be suspended several inches away from the wheel, was rubbing the wheel drag line on turns. Amazed that a slip like this could occur, Donovan was nevertheless grateful that the inspectors had caught it. "Thank God," he said to his wife. "Otherwise, the rubbing eventually would have broken the hose, and the brakes could have failed."

The second bus did not pass inspection because the exhaust-pipe hanger was faulty. It allowed the long exhaust pipe to dangle, thereby increasing the chances of its snapping. If it broke, carbon monoxide would seep out beneath the passenger compartment. "I thought the inspectors would be astonished, as I was," said Donovan, "that two brand-new General Motors buses, serviced by a GMC dealer, would fail to pass inspection. But they weren't surprised at all. They just said, 'Go get them fixed and come try again.'"

His amazement and annoyance slowly turned to dismay, for Donovan was serious about his responsibility for the lives of the children who rode his buses. Besides the Huntsville tragedy, Donovan knew of other failures of GM buses. Only the year before, eighteen children from the Accotink Academy in Springfield, Virginia, were riding in a new GM bus on Highway 236 in Annandale. The brakes failed. Somehow the driver managed to steer clear of traffic and coast the bus to a stop without an accident. The brakes were subsequently fixed three times by GM. The next year, another Accotink bus, a 1969 GM, was being driven along a highway in Fairfax County, Virginia, when the brakes failed completely. The driver steered into a pasture, and the bus lurched to a stop. *Those were new GM buses*, Donovan thought to himself, *and these three buses I just bought are new GMs, too*. His mind easily pictured one of his buses, full of children, crashing into a tree or into an oncoming car or truck. He became even more determined to do all he could to keep his three new buses in the best condition possible.

That commitment was made early in Donovan's ordeal, even though he had no way of knowing exactly what it would cost him—in loss of money, time, and peace. Between September 6 and December 6, 1969, according to Donovan's diary, he spent more than 225 hours either repairing the buses himself or hauling them to Central Motors, a GM dealership in Alexandria, Virginia. This averaged out to more than two hours daily, seven days a week. Additionally, he had to pay three of his drivers to do an extra ninety hours of repair work and hauling. A pattern emerged. When the buses finished the afternoon run about 4:30 or 5 p.m. and came to the parking lot in Washington, Donovan would ask what, if anything, had broken or malfunctioned that day. The drivers would tell him, for example, that the clutch had burned out for the second time, or that the left rear tire had leaked air for a second day, or that the bolts were falling out of the motor mounts the way they had last week, or that the wheels were wobbling, or that a gas tank was leaking, or that the power steering had failed.

The waking nightmare would now begin. Donovan would get into the broken bus and head for Central in Alexandria. Donovan's wife and two daughters would follow in the family car, so they could take him home when the bus was dropped off. It was a half-hour trip each way from Donovan's apartment in northwest Washington to Central Motors. After telling the mechanics what needed repairing, Donovan and family would return home. The girls would be fed and put to bed. He and his wife, staring at each other numbly, would have supper and wait for a call from Central—which stayed open until 2 a.m. The Donovans would wake the girls—no sitters were available at that hour—dress them, get in the car, and head for Alexandria. Donovan would pick up the repaired bus and drive it to the lot in Washington, his wife and children tailing. Donovan's records show that they made this trip approximately twenty-five times in the first three months of ownership. When two buses malfunctioned on the same day, two round trips were needed. Sometimes, since he needed to be up at 5:45 in the morning to call the drivers for the morning run, Donovan slept only three hours. During this period, both he and his wife lost weight, and friends found them unusually snappish. Donovan and his wife went out to dinner only twice in three months, and to a movie not at all.

The repairs made at Central Motors were seldom covered by the warranty. Trying to plug the dike through which money was beginning to flood, Donovan traveled to Laurel to talk with the dealer from whom he had bought the buses. "The dealer," said Donovan, "told me my buses were obviously special cases, that these problems certainly weren't universal." Nothing could be done, said the dealer, except to notify the factory representative. Donovan called the GM public relations office in Washington and was told the man who would help him was John Nickell, the truck-and-coach field representative for that area.

Between the breakdowns of his buses, Donovan tried locating Nickell. He called several garages that were, according to the local office, on Nickell's list of places to stop. The response was always the same: Nickell either had just left or was expected at any minute. Donovan never found his man this way. Finally, in a stakeout, he went one morning to the dealer's garage in Laurel, where, the owner had said, Nickell was scheduled to appear that afternoon.

He did. Donovan, momentarily elated at talking to a live GM face, detailed the problems, from the burned-out clutches to the leaky gas tanks. According to Donovan, Nickell's reaction at this meeting, and at several to follow, was astonishment—no other operators in his area were having these troubles; therefore, aside from warranty work, GM could not be held responsible. "It must be my drivers, Nickell told me," said Donovan.

Up against a wall and wanting his conscience to be clear if any of the buses ever crashed and perhaps killed someone, Donovan wrote a letter to the parents of the children he served. "In order to facilitate safe transportation for your children with a minimum of maintenance expense," said the letter, "I purchased three new 1969 GM buses in September of 1969. It verges on the impossible to run the routes safely and on time. The reason is that these three new GM buses continue to break down. The vehicles have been fixed, refixed, and re-refixed. These malfunctions are not minor. They are major mechanical failures that often involve the safety of your children." He listed the problems and concluded: "If this pattern continues, we will have to discontinue the service."

A copy of this letter happened to come my way. I called Donovan and asked if I could examine his records and look at his buses. After several meetings in his apartment, I concluded that his complaints were valid. In any event, his anguish was real. He and his wife had put their savings into the buses, and now they appeared lost. One evening after school, Donovan asked me to take a drive with him in one of his lemons. "I'm only going to get it up to twenty miles an hour," he said, "and then I'll put on the brakes." When he applied the brakes, the bus halted with an abruptness that threw me forward. "We were only going twenty," said Donovan, opening the door and going around back. On the road were two black skid marks. The two rear wheels had locked when Donovan put on the brakes. "Can you imagine what happens," he asked, "when a bus is going fifty or sixty and the driver has to stop suddenly?"

After again looking through Donovan's material, I approached General Motors to get their side of the story and give them a chance to be heard. I tried contacting John Nickell. I left my name at his office several times, but my calls were never returned. I visited Central Motors one morning—"He'll be there all day," said a secretary in his office—but like Donovan before me, I did not find Nickell that day or any other day. Workers at Central said that Richard Lockwood, the service manager, co-ordinated with Nickell and that he perhaps could help me.

I approached Lockwood. He preferred not talking about Donovan's problems. "General Motors has official spokesmen for questions from the public. You ought to ask them." When pressed for an explanation of why so many parts on Donovan's buses kept breaking or malfunctioning, Lockwood said, "Some of Donovan's problems are real, some are fanciful." Asked for an example of Donovan's fancy, Lockwood recalled a visit to him by Donovan when he asserted the clutch on one bus needed fixing. "We drove it around for a road test," said Lockwood, "and there was nothing wrong with it." When informed of Lockwood's statement, Donovan agreed; the mechanic did drive it around. "So I took the bus home, with no repairs made. Maybe Lockwood was right that time. But two days later the clutch burned out."

At 6:45 on the evening of December 9, Donovan phoned me at home. "Guess what," he said with elation, the first happy note I had heard from him since our initial meeting. "GM finally knows I exist. Three of their men are coming over to see me in an hour. They said they want to talk things over with me about the buses. That's all they said." Donovan asked me if I could come over and sit in on the meeting; it might be interesting. I said that I'd be there in twenty minutes.

When I arrived, the Donovans were on the last bites of a meal of meat loaf, canned peas, apple sauce, bread, and milk. Their apartment, a third-floor walkup in a housing project, was in mild disorder, a crib in the middle of the room, a chair holding a drawer filled with

Donovan's records, a filing cabinet in a corner, and a card table covered with invoices, receipts, and other papers. I asked Donovan why he thought GM wanted this meeting. "Hard to tell," he replied. "Maybe they see my complaints are real and they finally want to square it all up. I've heard of things like that happening."

"I haven't," cut in Donovan's wife, Virginia, "especially not from a bunch like this. The bigger they get, the less they care." A short, sandy-haired woman, second-generation Polish, a user of short, bright sentences, Virginia Donovan was perhaps the wearier of the two. Home all day with the girls, she had to phone the parents when a bus broke down and inform them that their children would either not be picked up in the morning or be late in the afternoon. She had typed the letter to the parents as well as earlier letters to GM president Edward N. Cole, President Richard Nixon, Virginia Knauer, the Presidential consumer adviser, the Federal Trade Commission, and the National Highway Safety Bureau. She also had opened and filed the depressing form-letter replies. "It'll be a snow job, John," she said. "Just wait and see. The drifts will be so high, not even a bus could drive through."

Donovan speculated that GM had heard, probably from Richard Lockwood or someone else at Central Motors, that I was looking into the problem. "They hate bad publicity," he said. "Just the thought of a possible story in a major newspaper has flushed them out. It's funny. GM hasn't really been so bad. They've done a faithful job on the work they say is covered by the warranty. The mechanics at Central are superb. I get fast service; they're courteous. The eerie thing is that I can't find anyone who'll take responsibility for what's gone wrong."

At 7:30 the GM men arrived. Donovan, putting the infant in the crib and the three-year-old on a chair, went to the door and opened it. "Hello, Mr. Donovan," said the out-front man. "I'm Webb Madery of General Motors." Round-faced, heavy in the waist, he rubbed his hands briskly and commented on the cold outside. Madery introduced Jerry Fender and John Nickell. Donovan invited them in. The three were cheery, almost bouncy. Donovan introduced them to Virgina.

Madery, with a large smile, said that he was happy finally to meet Mrs. Donovan and that everything her husband had said about her certainly seemed true. The woman did not respond to Madery's pleasantry. She knew her husband had spoken with him on the phone several times, but she also was sure her husband wouldn't have mentioned her. "What a nice little place you have here," said Madery, not letting up. He was unaware that the housewife didn't consider her apartment "nice" at all; she had told me five minutes before that her family would have moved into a house that fall if repairing the three buses had not consumed so much of their money, time, and emotions. Still icy, she took the gentlemen's coats and hung them up.

Of the trio, Madery was the oldest—sixty-two—and, as the Washington zone manager, was highest on GM's ladder. His career in the automobile industry began in 1933. After one year of college at William and Mary, he worked for International Harvester, then Chrysler. In 1958 he accepted an offer from General Motors to become heavy-duty truck manager in the Detroit zone. A year later he moved to Washington.

Fender was a trim, short-haired man of fifty-eight, with the longest GM service of the three, having begun in Oakland, California, as a twenty-four-year-old factory helper. Slowly rising from the bottom, he became shop clerk, parts manager, and so on, eventually moving to Washington as zone service and parts manager.

Nickell, forty-nine and gray-haired, had started with GM in 1940 on the assembly line in the Pontiac truck plant. He also went to school at that time, earning a B.A. in history from the Detroit Institute of Technology. Then he became a parts supervisor and began his climb.

Standing in the uncarpeted living room of the Donovan apartment and not yet down to business, the three GM men continued their cheeriness. They said they had just come from a delightful meal whose main dish was pheasant under glass. "You'd really like pheasant," said Madery to Mrs. Donovan with an over-warm smile, apparently determined to thaw her somehow. The woman could still taste the meat loaf she had just cooked and eaten, so the news about pheasant had a contrary effect upon her.

Moving from the living room into the adjoining part of the L-shaped area, Donovan introduced the three officials to me. I stated clearly that I was a *Washington Post* writer and had begun investigating Donovan's troubles. Still engaged in the busywork of cordiality, the GM men did not seem to notice the significance of having a newsman on hand while they went about the work of customer relations. Only John Nickell, an alert, lively-eyed man, looked twice at me. My name may have been familiar, perhaps from the message slips of my phone calls. Yet, after shaking hands with me at the Donovan apartment, Nickell, lowest of the three in corporate power but closest to Donovan's daily problems, seemed to let the fact of my presence pass. If his superiors weren't concerned, why should he be?

Everyone gathered around a small dining room table, everyone except Mrs. Donovan. She sat on a living room chair within hearing and took out yellow scratch paper, ready to take down in shorthand the important remarks of the conversation. The GM men produced a folder of records covering what they said was the past twelve weeks of Donovan's ownership of the three buses. As the senior official, Madery led off, explaining amiably that the reason for calling the meeting was that "GM wanted to make things right." He said that his corporation had a long record of being concerned about producing safe vehicles, especially those that carry children, and that since Donovan was concerned about safety, GM was most concerned about him. GM, he said, likes to satisfy its customers.

Impatiently Donovan broke in. "I've heard all that talk before," he said. "What I'd like from GM right now is a detailed report of the repairs you've made on my buses and also the modifications you've made on them." Donovan's request, made in a quiet but firm voice, was based on a desire to keep an accurate maintenance record. He explained that "this is the same as wanting information from your surgeon about what he cuts or takes out while operating on your insides. How can you find out unless the surgeon tells you?"

Madery laughed, saying with a final, happy grin that he had undergone operations where the surgeon never told him what he had fooled with. Donovan didn't laugh. On seeing this, Madery nodded to Nickell. "Mr. Donovan should certainly have his records," said Madery. "That's only fair." Nickell said he would get them to Donovan later that week without fail.

As the GM-Donovan case unfolded during the next year, the company never supplied Donovan the records he repeatedly asked for and GM repeatedly promised. In the week immediately after the December 9 meeting in the apartment, Donovan says, he was told by Jerry Fender that high-level officials in Detroit had made a decision not to release the records "at this time in these circumstances." The circumstances were that the first of my series of articles on Donovan and his plight had just appeared in *The Washington Post* and had been circulated by its wire service. Donovan believed GM refused to release the enormous record of repairs and replacements on the grounds that the public—specifically other owners—would learn of it and thus expect similar treatment. Donovan never learned precisely who in GM ordered the embargo. The question came up again at a meeting in January 1970 in Falls Church, Virginia, with Robert Stelter, general sales manager for the GMC Truck and Coach Division, who entered the case when it became a public issue. Donovan says he asked Stelter directly why GM had refused to release the records. Stelter, the superior of Madery, said he himself never understood why. He directed John Nickell, also present at this meeting, to pass along the records. Nickell said he would, but he never has.

At the December 9 apartment gathering, the next topic was an itemized reading by Nickell of the repairs made at GM's expense. The list was long—including leaking oil gaskets, broken motor mounts, flawed gasoline tanks, ruptured rear-wheel seals, uneven brakes, bad tires, wobbly wheels, weak tailpipe hangers. Anyone not knowing the whole story would wonder why Donovan was complaining when GM had done all this work free of charge.

"What about those tailpipe hangers?" asked Donovan. Nickell, shooting a confident glance at his boss as if to say the question was a routine grounder and easily fielded, replied that GM had replaced them on warranty. "I know that," said Donovan, "but the replacements were of the same design as the original ones. So where does that take me?" For my benefit, and looking at me, Nickell explained in layman's terms the nature of a tailpipe han-

ger: a metal, straplike device hung from the frame of the bus and attached to the exhaust pipe to keep it from dragging along the road and breaking.

At this point, the smooth GM presentation showed signs, like Donovan's buses, of falling apart. The customer insisted on getting across his point that replacing a flawed hanger with another flawed hanger, however new, is not really a victory for safety. Visibly annoyed at wrangling over such a small item and apparently sensing a no-win situation, Nickell broke in to admit that "the hangers were just not strong enough. The factory made them too flimsy."

Madery looked sharply at Nickell—either startled or angered at this frank concession. He jumped in to say that studies of the hanger were already under way in Detroit and that a better one was being designed. Donovan said he was happy to hear that. He asked, however, if GM was going to warn other owners of 1969 GM buses around the country that this particular part was made "too flimsy." Madery said the decision would have to be made by higher-ups in Detroit. "I'm sure they'll tell the public," said Donovan sarcastically, "because, as you say, GM cares about its customers and the safety of children." (The flimsy tailpipe hangers have never been recalled.)

All GM cheerfulness had now evaporated. The next topic involved the leaky gasoline tanks on Donovan's buses. Nickell reminded Donovan that three weeks earlier, to show GM's good faith, he had promised to repair the leaky tanks free of charge. That was a gesture of pure largess, Nickell made clear, because GM did not make the tank. Madery looked pleased. Nickell's statement backed up Madery's earlier one of wanting "to make things right."

"I'm not impressed," said Donovan, his anger growing. "After you told me that GM didn't make the gas tank that was leaking, I called up Thomas Body [Thomas Body Company, High Point, North Carolina, the firm that had produced the bodies for Donovan's buses and fitted them onto the GM chassis]. Mr. Thomas personally told me—categorically—that his company does not make the tank, GM does."

Nickell could do nothing but admit error. Coming back fast, however, Madery explained to Donovan that, even though Nickell was wrong about the maker of the tank, it actually didn't matter, because the leak was later found by mechanics not to be in the GM-made tank but in the extension from the tank to the exterior of the bus. "That is a Thomas product," said Madery firmly. He said that GM had nothing to do with it.

Donovan could not argue further, at least not then. The next morning, however, he was on the phone again to John Thomas. I also called Thomas within the week. Thomas said, with no equivocation, that his company did not make the tank-neck extension, that it was a GM product. To be certain, I asked him to check his file and read over the phone Donovan's order page for the bus bodies; it was number 9–12202, and the facts again fitted. A few days after the apartment meeting, Donovan reported to the GM men what he had learned from Thomas. The officials, according to Donovan, "just kind of passed it off, admitting they were in 'error' again but attaching no importance to it. But I attached plenty of importance to it. I was being lied to. Not by the men who had anything to gain from the lies, but because it was corporate policy. Put me down, brush me off, keep me happy—but don't ever tell me the truth or give me new buses."

As the meeting continued, Donovan running through his list of complaints, GM running through their list of solutions, the question came up of whether or not these problems were limited to Donovan's buses. They had to be, said Madery; otherwise, GM would have heard from other owners. "What about Tom Gist and Billy Jubb?" asked Donovan, referring to two owners of 1969 GM school buses in nearby Maryland, with whom he had spoken at length about their mechanical and safety problems. Donovan remarked that both were experiencing difficulties similar to his own and that both said they had seen John Nickell. His memory refreshed, Nickell said that was right, he had seen Gist and Jubb. Their problems, however, were different from Donovan's, said Nickell. Once again Donovan could not refute this with absolute surety. The following day I called Thomas Gist in Sykesville, Maryland, the owner of two '69 GMs. As was so with Donovan's buses, the power steering was bad, riding was rough, the clutches and brakes needed constant adjustment and fixing. I mentioned Donovan's name. Gist recognized it, laughingly saying they were fellow sufferers. Billy Jubb, in Pasadena, Maryland, owned four '69s and called them "the worst I've ever owned." Each had a broken clutch. What he said about clutches echoed John Donovan: "I'm always taking the damned things to the dealer to have them adjusted."

"How does GM explain all these failures of clutches?" Donovan asked Madery. "Driver abuse," replied the GM man, starting on a brief monologue about the many ways drivers ride the clutch, pump it unnecessarily, use it wrongly. Donovan replied, again with anger, that his drivers were not heavy-footed amateurs who loved clutch-riding but were veterans of the road with a least five years' experience in driving trucks and buses. None had ever burned out a clutch on earlier-year buses. Thus, said Donovan, it was unlikely they would have ruined the clutches at the rate they were being ruined on the new buses: Two had already burned out in each of two buses; three had burned out in the third.

The talk went back and forth, Donovan repeating his concern for safe buses because children's lives were involved, Madery cordially reassuring him that GM had made things right with its warranty work and that this was a fluke problem. He had a way of feigning surprise, as if to say wordlessly to Donovan, "You're not actually saying, are you, that GM is not 'the mark of excellence'?" Not once did Madery or his two companions offer sympathy to Donovan or ever admit there might be a safety problem. If a problem was admitted, it was inevitably "not safety-related." On specific points the reply was either, "Here, this is what GM has done, so why are you complaining?" or, "Here, you should have done this, and if you had, this problem would never have happened." Nor did the GM men ever mention that their buses had been the object of recalls two years running and that this year was an extension of patterns of work developed then.

As the hour neared 10 p.m., Donovan was still spirited, but Madery, Fender, and Nickell, the taste of pheasant long gone, were tiring. As they tried to wind things down, the phone rang. Mrs. Donovan answered. "It's for you, John, from Detroit, person-to-person." Donovan took the phone and was greeted by Robert

Stelter, Madery's superior. "He wants to know how things are going with my buses," Donovan remarked to the group. Answering Stelter, Donovan said the buses were just as much broken-down lemons as ever. The two talked for about five minutes, Donovan asking for his records and repeating that he worried about his brakes, clutches, gas tanks, wheels, and everything else that wouldn't stay fixed, no matter GM's diligence in repairing them.

I signaled Donovan that I would like a word with Stelter. Identifying myself and my intentions clearly, I asked Stelter how three new buses could be so flawed. The company, he replied, was doing all it could to make things right. Beyond making things right, I asked politely, would GM make things better and do as Donovan thought it should—replace the buses? The official seemed surprised that Donovan had even thought of such a solution.

After expressing curiosity about what kind of story I might be writing but careful to remain pleasant and assuring, Stelter asked to speak to Madery. As GM Detroit spoke to GM Washington, there was little but "Yes, sir" and "No, sir" from the latter. Madery concluded his conversation by saying he would call Stelter in the morning. The phone hardly back on the receiver, the GM official looked at me in astonishment: "You're a reporter?" I nodded. Nickell nodded too.

Abruptly, the GM men began putting away the materials they had spread out on the table during the evening. The phone call from Detroit, apparently meant as final proof to Donovan that GM really cared, because his troubles had reached the ears of high powers in Detroit, had had the opposite effect. GM had learned that rather than having put down a customer, it had instead fired up a customer, one who had the crust to interest a reporter in his troubles.

Madery rose, as did Nickell and Fender, and recapturing his earlier verve, smiled broadly at Donovan and said that the evening was certainly well spent. Madery even had one last happy word for Mrs. Donovan, throwing her a compliment about "what wonderful boys" the Donovan's two baby girls were. Donovan got the men their coats and saw them to the door.

I remained for a few minutes. Mrs. Donovan said, "Let's get the snow shovels and clear out this place." Her husband saw the evening a little less bitterly. GM now knew, he said, that it could not talk its way out. "They didn't refute a fact I threw at them. That's the test. They would have slapped me down hard if one fact of mine, one record, or one document, was slightly off. But they didn't. Sure, they tried to scare me off, calm me down. What do you expect?"

After telling Donovan I would call him in a few days to check whether anything happened, I said good night.

My story of Donovan's ordeal appeared in the *Post* on December 15 and 22, 1969. On the day of the second installment, General Motors and the White House Office of Consumer Affairs held a joint press conference to announce two investigations of the 1969 buses, one by the government and the other by the company. The press conference statements of GM vice president Martin Caserio were oddly similar to the GM presentation at the Donovan apartment. Caserio said there were no complaints about the buses from other owners. Asked about the 1969 school bus that had suffered brake failure and careened into a pasture, Caserio said he believed the braking equipment on that vehicle was not the same as on Donovan's, adding, "I'm not certain about that yet." Like Madery, Caserio stressed GM's concern for safety. Thus, the faulty exhaust-pipe hanger should not be classified as a safety-related defect, because if it broke the driver could hear the exhaust pipe clattering along the ground and have repairs made before any harm was done to occupants. (But what if it merely cracked?)

Reporters pressed Caserio on Donovan's problems. For the first time the company gave a little, Caserio conceding that some of Donovan's complaints were legitimate. But always added to these admissions was the qualifier, "They are not safety-related." One reporter listed all of Donovan's problems—from brakes to clutches—and said Caserio's claiming these were nonsafety problems was an "incredible observation." The press conference did produce one memorable statement: "GM," said Caserio, "does not duck any responsibility for the finished product that bears our name."

Two months later, on February 19, 1970, a total of 4,269 school buses were officially recalled by General Motors, including John Donovan's three. Also recalled were 21,681 trucks using the same model chassis. "Some of the vehicles," said the announcement, "will require installation of new brake-hose retaining springs. Some will require inspection and possible alignment or replacement of a rear steel brake line. A few will require both services."

At my request, GM sent me a list of forty-four owners around the country who operated more than five buses. When I called them (four people were not GM owners, and one owner couldn't be reached because he had been dead years), I found that a recurring theme was clutch problems. One owner was a GM dealer who had so much trouble with his seven 1969s that in 1970 he bought Fords. Asked if he thought it odd for a GM dealer to buy a competitor's product, he answered, "What should I do—keep on buying buses that I know are nothing but trouble?"

Within the next year, the GM buses were recalled two more times. The second call-in involved the brakes again—possibly faulty brake-fluid reservoirs that caused the braking fluid to leak out. The third recall was for possibly flawed clutches; the clutch linkage was found to be weak—meaning, in lay terms, that the bus could lock in gear and thus be unstoppable.

In a simpler day a consumer with a complaint about, say, shoes, had only to visit the local shoemaker to get justice. "Here," the customer would say, "these shoes are falling apart." The shoemaker, because he was ethical or simply aware that word would spread through the village about his sloppy work, quickly repaired the shoes or replaced them. The exchange was straightforward and there were no evasions. What's more, the shoemaker was *there*, he had a familiar face, he breathed, and the only separation between the consumer and him was his shop counter.

Things have changed. Seeking relief or re-dress from GM with its 750,000 employees is an agony. So it is with any large bureaucracy. The vice presidents at the top are protected from the consumers' complaints at the bottom by the mass of employees between; the latter will catch it first if the brass learns that the consumers are mad. So the vice presidents do not measure the company's success by the consumers' voice, as the shoemaker did, but by sales reports, profit charts, and the smiles of stockholders. If tens of thousands of cars are sold every year, the high-ups conclude that the public must be happy. Otherwise, why are sales up? When profits aren't up, however, or when management thinks profits can be bigger, the decision often made seems to be to cheapen the product. When such a decision ends in death, then the ethical numbness encouraged by the profit system becomes grimly apparent, and the need for remedy becomes urgent.

John Donovan's friends jokingly called him a "giant killer," since he had taken on GM and won. "Won? How can they say that?" he asks. "I never got new replacements from GM for my buses. I never got a cent for my lost time. They never compensated my drivers for the overtime spent in hauling the buses to the garage. They never even apologized to my wife for all those nights she spent trailing me over to Central Motors. What's even more chilling, after three recalls, I have yet to hear from the GM crowd even the slightest hint admitting they may be doing something wrong in the way they build buses. But lives are involved; those are alarm clocks that they're selling.

"That's the true horror of all this—not that they tried to screw one owner like me. It's the corporate callousness. If I were in the business of making school buses—an engineer, a vice president, a local representative like Madery—and someone came along with proof that dangerous defects were in my product, well, I think I'd jump pretty quick to correct them before I had any blood on my hands."

BARBARA GARSON

luddiTiEs iN LordsTOWN

The movement to humanize working condi-
tions in industrial plants is probably as old as
industrialism itself. Much time has passed since
the original Luddites—bands of English workers
who, in the early nineteenth century, went on a
machine-destroying rampage— claimed that
machines were taking away their jobs. But despite
the shorter hours, the absence of children, cleaner
and more hygienic surroundings, higher wages
and fringe benefits, and the alleged strength of
labor in the political and economic sector, workers
today express many of the same concerns as the
nineteenth-century workers. They must perform
rapidly and almost without interruption the same
trivial operation a large number of times per hour
(101 in the case of the Lordstown plant). They
are continually controlled, observed, and disci-
plined in an undignified way. As a result, they
very often act like children, throwing stink bombs
inside cars and generally making mischief. Barbara
Garson, author of the controversial play Macbird,
offers a vivid portrayal of the latest incident in
which man is pitted against machine, or rather
man is pitted against bureaucracy.

□□□

"Is it true," an auto worker asked wistfully,
"that you get to do fifteen different jobs on
a Cadillac?" "I heard," said another, "that with
Volvos you follow one car all the way down
the line."

Such are the yearnings of young auto workers at the Vega plant in Lordstown, Ohio. Their

average age is twenty-four, and they work on
the fastest auto assembly line in the world.
Their jobs are so subdivided that few workers
can feel they are making a car.

The assembly line carries 101 cars past each
worker every hour. Most GM lines run under
sixty. At 101 cars an hour, a worker has thirty-
six seconds to perform his assigned snaps,
knocks, twists, or squirts on each car. The line
was running at this speed in October when
a new management group, General Motors
Assembly Division (GMAD or Gee-Mad), took
over the plant. Within four months they fired
500 to 800 workers. Their jobs were divided
among the remaining workers, adding a few
more snaps, knocks, twists, or squirts to each
man's task. The job had been boring and
unbearable before. When it remained boring
and became a bit more unbearable there was
a 97 per cent vote to strike. More amazing—85
per cent went down to the union hall to vote.[1]

One could give a broad or narrow interpretation of what the Lordstown workers want.
Broadly, they want to reorganize industry so

[1]The union membership voted to settle the
twenty-two-day strike in late March, but the agreement appeared to be somewhat reluctant; less than
half of the members showed up for the vote, and
30 per cent of those voted against the settlement.
The union won a number of concessions, among
them full back pay for anybody who had been disciplined in the past few months for failure to meet
work standards. Meanwhile, however, UAW locals
at three other GM plants around the country
threatened to strike on grounds similar to those
established at Lordstown. In early April GM recalled
130,000 Vegas of the 1972 model because of a possible
fire hazard involving the fuel and exhaust systems.

that each worker plays a significant role in turning out a fine product, without enduring degrading supervision. Narrowly, they want more time in each thirty-six-second cycle to sneeze or to scratch.

John Grix, who handles public relations at Lordstown, and Andy O'Keefe for GMAD in Detroit both assured me that work at Lordstown is no different than at the older assembly plants. The line moves faster, they say, but then the parts are lighter and easier to install. I think this may be true. It is also true of the workers. These young people are not basically different from the older men. But they are faster and lighter. Because they are young they are economically freer to strike and temperamentally quicker to act. But their yearnings are not new. The Vega workers are echoing a rank-and-file demand that has been suppressed by both union and management for the past twenty years: *Humanize Working Conditions*.

Hanging around the parking lot between shifts, I learned immediately that to these young workers, "It's not the money."

"It pays good," said one, "but it's driving me crazy." "I don't want more money," said another. "None of us do."

"I do," said his friend. "So I can quit quicker."

"It's the job," everyone said. But they found it hard to describe the job itself.

"My father worked in auto for thirty-five years," said a clean-cut lad, "and he never talked about the job. What's there to say? A car comes, I weld it. A car comes, I weld it. A car comes, I weld it. One hundred and one times an hour."

I asked a young wife, "What does your husband tell you about his work?"

"He doesn't say what he does. Only if something happened, 'My hair caught on fire,' or, 'Something fell in my face.'"

"There's a lot of variety in the paint shop," said a dapper twenty-two-year-old up from West Virginia. "You clip on the color hose, bleed out the old color, and squirt. Clip, bleed, squirt, think; clip, bleed, squirt, yawn; clip, bleed, squirt, scratch your nose. Only now the GeeMads have taken away the time to scratch your nose."

A long-hair reminisced; "Before the GoMads, when I had a good job like door han-

dles, I could get a couple of cars ahead and have a whole minute to relax."

I asked about diversions. "What do you do to keep from going crazy?"

"Well, certain jobs like the pit you can light up a cigarette without them seeing."

"I go to the wastepaper basket. I wait a certain number of cars, then find a piece of paper to throw away."

"I have fantasies. You know what I keep imagining? I see a car coming down. It's red. So I know it's gonna have a black seat, black dash, black interiors. But I keep thinking what if somebody up there sends down the wrong color interiors—like orange, and me putting in yellow cushions, bright yellow!"

"There's always water fights, paint fights, or laugh, talk, tell jokes. Anything so you don't feel like a machine."

But everyone had the same hope: "You're always waiting for the line to break down."

The Vega plant hires about seven thousand assembly-line workers. They commute to Lordstown from Akron, Youngstown, Cleveland, even as far as Pittsburgh. Actually, there is no Lordstown—just a plant and some trailer camps set among farmhouses. When the workers leave, they disperse throughout southern Ohio. GM presumably hoped that this location would help minimize labor troubles.

I took the guided tour of the plant. It's new, it's clean, it's well lit without windows, and it's noisy. Hanging car bodies move past at the speed of a Coney Island ride slowing down. Most men work alongside the line but some stand in a man-sized pit craning their necks to work on the undersides of the cars.

I stopped to shout at a worker drinking coffee, *"Is there any quiet place to take a break?"* He shouted back, *"Can't hear you, ma'am. Too noisy to chat on a break."* As a plant guard rushed over to separate us I spotted Duane,[2] from Fort Lewis, shooting radios into cars with an air gun. Duane had been in the Army while I was working at a GI coffeehouse. He slipped me a note with his address.

When I left the plant there were leafleteers at the gate distributing *Workers' Power*. Guards with binocular cameras closed in, snapping

[2]Since many workers were afraid of losing their jobs, I have changed names, juggled positions on the line, and given facsimiles for identifying details.

pictures; another guard checked everyone's ID. He copied down the names of leafleteers and workers who took papers. He took my name too.

DUANE'S MILITARY-INDUSTRIAL COMPLEX

That evening I visited Duane. He had rented a two-bedroom bungalow on the outskirts of a town that had no center. He had grown his hair a bit but, in fact, he looked neater and trimmer than when he'd been in the Army.

I told him about the incident at the gate. "Just like the Army," he said. He summarized life since his discharge: "Remember you guys gave me a giant banana split the day I ETSed [got out on schedule]? Well, it's been downhill since then. I came back to Cleveland; stayed with my dad, who was unemployed. Man, was that ever a downer. But I figured things would pick up if I got wheels, so I got a car. But it turned out the car wasn't human and that was a problem. So I figured, 'What I need is a girl.' But it turned out the girl *was* human and that was a problem. So I wound up working at GM to pay off the car and the girl." And he introduced me to his lovely pregnant wife, of whom he seemed much fonder than it sounds.

A couple of Duane's high-school friends, Stan and Eddie, wound up at Lordstown too. Stan at twenty-one was composed and placid, a married man with a child. Eddie at twenty-two was an excitable youth. Duane had invited them over to tell me what it's like working at the plant.

"I'll tell you what it's like," said Duane. "It's like the Army. They even use the same words like *direct order*. Supposedly you have a contract so there's some things they just can't make you do. Except, if the foreman gives you a direct order, you do it, or you're out."

"Out?" I asked.

"Yeah, fired—or else they give you a DLO."

"DLO?"

"Disciplinary layoff. Which means you're out without pay for however long they say. Like maybe it'll be a three-day DLO or a week DLO."

Eddie explained it further: "Like this foreman comes up to me and says, 'Pick up that piece of paper.' Only he says it a little nastier, with a few references to my race, creed, and length of hair. So I says, 'That's not my job.' He says, 'I'm giving you a direct order to pick up that piece of paper.' Finally he takes me up to the office. My committeeman comes over and tells me I could of lost my job because you can't refuse a direct order. You do it, and then you put in a grievance—ha!"

"Calling your committeeman," says Duane. "That's just like the Army too. If your CO [commanding officer] is harassing you, you can file a complaint with the IG [Inspector General]. Only thing is you gotta go up to your CO and say, 'Sir, request permission to see the Inspector General to tell him my commanding officer is a shit.' Same thing here. Before you can get your committeeman, you got to tell the foreman exactly what your grievance is in detail. So meantime he's working out ways to tell the story different."

Here Stan took out an actual DLO form from his wallet. "Last week someone up the line put a stink bomb in a car. I do rear cushions, and the foreman says, 'You get in that car.' We said, 'If you can put your head in that car we'll do the job.' So the foreman says, 'I'm giving you a direct order.' So I hold my breath and do it. My job is every other car so I let the next one pass. He gets on me, and I say, 'It ain't my car. Please, I done your dirty work and the other one wasn't mine.' But he keeps at me, and I wind up with a week off. Now, I got a hot committeeman who really stuck up for me. So you know what? They sent *him* home too. Gave the committeeman a DLO!"

"See, just like the Army," Duane repeats. "No, it's worse 'cause you're welded to the line. You just about need a pass to piss."

"That ain't no joke," says Eddie. "You raise your little hand if you want to go wee-wee. Then wait maybe half an hour till they find a relief man. And they write it down every time too. 'Cause you're supposed to do it on your own time, not theirs. Try it too often, and you'll get a week off."

"I'd rather work in a gas station," said Stan wistfully. "That way you pump gas, then you patch a tire, then you go to the bathroom. You do what needs doing."

"Why don't you work in a gas station?" I asked.

"You know what they pay in a gas station? I got a kid. Besides, I couldn't even get a job in a gas station. Before I got in here I was so hard up I wound up selling vacuum cleaners —$297 door to door. In a month I earned exactly $10 selling one vacuum cleaner to a laid-off steel worker for which I'll never forgive myself."

"No worse than making cars," Eddie said. "Cars are your real trap, not vacuum cleaners. You need the car to keep the job and you need the job to keep the car. And don't think they don't know it. They give you just enough work to keep up the payments. They got it planned exactly, so you can't quit."

"He's a little paranoid," Duane said.

"Look it," says the paranoid reasonably. "They give you fifty, fifty-five hours' work for a couple of weeks. So your typical boob buys a color TV. Then they cut you back to thirty hours. There's not a married man who doesn't have bills. And the company keeps it like that so there's no way out. You're stuck for life."

I asked about future plans.

Eddie was getting out as soon as he saved enough money to travel. He thought he might work for three more months. He'd said three months when he started, and it was nine months already, but "things came up."

Duane figured he'd stay till after his wife had the baby. That way he could use the hospital plan. After that? "Maybe we'll go live on the land. I don't know. I wish someone would hand me a discharge."

Stan was a reasonable man—or a boob, as Eddie might have it. He knew he was going to stay. "If I'm gonna do some dumb job the rest of my life, ', I might as well do one that pays."

Though none of them could afford to quit, they were all eager for a strike. They'd manage somehow. For Stan it was a good investment in his future job. The others just liked the idea of giving GM a kick in the ass from the inside.

THE BLUE-COLLAR COMMUNE

Later in the week I stayed at an auto-workers' commune. Like so many other young people, they were trying to make a one-generational family—a homestead. Life centered, as of old, around the hearth, which was a water pipe bubbling through bourbon. The family Bibles were the Books of the Dead—both Tibetan and Egyptian. Throughout the evening, six to twelve people drifted through the old house waiting for Indian Nut (out working night shift at Lordstown) and his wife Jane (out baby-sitting).

Jane returned at midnight to prepare dinner for her husband. By 2:00 a.m. she complained: "They can keep them two, three, four hours over." Overtime is mandatory for auto workers, but it's not as popular at Lordstown as it is among older workers at other plants.

At two-thirty the Nut burst in, wild-haired, wild-eyed, and sweet-smiled. He had a mildly maniacal look because his glasses were speckled with welding spatter.

"New foreman, a real Gee-mad-man. Sent a guy home for farting in a car. And another one home for yodeling."

"Yodeling?" I asked.

"Yeah, you know." (And he yodeled.)

(It's common in auto plants for men to break the monotony with noise, like the banging of tin cans in jail. Someone will drop something, his partner will yell "Whaa," and then "Whaa" gets transmitted all along the line.)

"I bet there's no shop rule against farting," the Nut conjectured. "You know those porkers have been getting their 101 off the line again, and not that many of them need repairs. It's the hillbillies. Those cats have no stamina. The union calls them to a meeting, says, 'Now don't you sabotage, but don't you run. Don't do more than you can do.' And everybody cheers. But in a few days it's back to where it was. Hillbillies working so fast they ain't got time to scratch their balls. Meantime these porkers are making money even faster than they're making cars."

I ask who he means by the hillbillies. "Hillbillies is the general Ohio term for assholes, except if you happen to be a hillbilly. Then you say Polack. Fact is everybody is a hillbilly out here except me and two other guys. And they must work day shift 'cause I never see them.

"Sabotage?" says the Nut. "Just a way of letting off steam. You can't keep up with the car so you scratch it on the way past. I once saw a hillbilly drop an ignition key down the gas tank. Last week I watched a guy light a glove and lock it in the trunk. We all waited to see how far down the line they'd discover it.... If you miss a car, they call that sabotage. They expect the sixty-second minute. Even a machine has to sneeze. Look how they call us in weekends, hold us extra, send us home early, give us layoffs. You'd think we were machines the way they turn us on and off."

I apologized for getting Indian Nut so steamed up and keeping him awake late. "No," sighed Jane. "It always takes a couple of hours to calm him down. We never get to bed before four."

Later that day, about 1:00 p.m., Indian Nut cooked breakfast for all of us (about ten). One nice thing about a working-class commune: bacon and eggs and potatoes for breakfast—no granola.

It took about an hour and a half to do the day's errands—mostly dope shopping and car repair. Then Indian Nut relaxed for an hour around the hearth.

As we talked some people listened to Firesign Theatre while others played Masterpiece or Monopoly. Everyone sucked at the pipe from time to time.

A college kid came by to borrow records. He was the editor of the defunct local underground paper called *Anonymity*. (It had lived up to its title before folding.)

"I've been trying to get Indian Nut to quit working there," he said.

"Why?" I asked.

"Don't you know? GM makes M-16s."

"Yeah, well, you live with your folks," said one of the Monopolists.

"You can always work some kind of rip-off," replied the ex-editor.

Everyone joined the ensuing philosophical inquiry about where it was moral to work and whom it was moral to rip off.

"Shit," sighed Indian Nut. "It's four-thirty. Someone help Jane with the dishes." Taking a last toke, the Nut split for the plant.

As I proceeded with my unscientific survey, I found that I couldn't predict a man's militancy from his hair length, age, or general freakiness. But you could always guess a man's attitudes by his comments on the car. When someone said, "I wouldn't even buy a Vega, not a '71 or a '72," then he would usually say,

"General Motors—all they care about is money. Not the worker, not the car, just the goddamn money."[3]

A nineteen-year-old told me bitterly: "A black guy worked next to me putting sealer into the cracks. He used to get cut all the time on sharp edges of metal. One day his finger really got stuck and he was bleeding all over the car. So I stopped the line. [There's a button every so many feet.] Sure they rushed him to the hospital, but boy did they get down on me for stopping the line. That line runs no matter what the cost."

The mildest man I met was driving a Vega. He was a long-haired, or at least shaggy-haired, twenty-one-year-old. He thought the Vega was a "pretty little thing." When I asked about his job he said, "It's a very important job. After all, everybody's got to have a car." Yes, he had voted for the strike. "Myself, I'd rather work, but if they're gonna keep laying people off, might as well strike now and get it over with." Anyway, he figured the strike would give him time to practice: he was second guitarist in a band, and if his group could only "get it together," maybe he could quit GM. He had other hopes too. For instance: "The company lets you put in suggestions, and you get money if they use your suggestions." He was a cheerful, good-natured lad, and, as I say, he liked the Vega.

There's a good reason why attitudes toward the car correlate with attitudes toward the company. It's not just "hate them, hate their car." It's also hate your job and hate yourself when you think you're making a hunk of junk, or when you can't feel you've made anything at all. I was reminded of this by a worker's mother.

While her son and his friends talked shop—DLOs, strike, rock bands—I talked to her in the kitchen. Someone in the supermarket where she worked had said, those young kids are just lazy: "One thing, Tony is not lazy. He'll take your car apart and put it together any day. Ever since he's been in high school we haven't had to worry about car trouble. The slightest knock and he takes care of it. And

[3]Ironically, the Vega gets high marks from car buffs. In its May issue, for example, *Car and Driver* magazine reported that its readers had voted the Vega "Best Economy Sedan" (vs Datsun, Volkswagen, etc.) for the second year in a row. [Ed.]

he never will leave it half done. He even cleans up after himself.

"And I'm not lazy either. I love to cook. But supposing they gave me a job just cracking eggs with bowls moving past on a line. Pretty soon I'd get to a point where I'd wish the next egg was rotten just to spoil their whole cake."

At the Pink Elephant Bar I met a man who'd voted against the strike, one of the rare 3 per cent. He was an older man who'd worked in other auto plants. "I seen it before. The international [union] is just giving them enough rope to hang themselves. They don't ever take on speed-up or safety. And they don't ever help with any strike *they* didn't call.

"Meany and his silk shirts! Reuther's daughter hobnobbed with Miss Ford, but at least he didn't wear silk shirts. . . . Woodcock?[4] Who cares what he wears.

"Like I was saying, they see a kicky young local so they go along. They authorize the strike. But it's just giving you enough rope to hang yourself.

"They see you got young inexperienced leadership—I'm not saying our leadership is young and inexperienced but what it is, is—young and inexperienced.

"So they let 'em go ahead. But they don't give 'em no help. They don't give 'em no funds. They don't even let the other locals come out with you. When it comes to humanizing working conditions you might as well be back before there was any unions.

"So the strike drags on, it's lost, or they 'settle' in Detroit. Everybody says, 'There, it didn't pay.' And the next time around the leadership gets unelected. See—they gave 'em enough rope to hang 'emselves."

Other GM plants are having labor troubles, but no coordinated union action has been authorized. It is difficult for an outsider to tell when the UAW International is giving wholehearted help. But with or without the international, workers will continue to agitate for better working conditions.

Local 1112 at Lordstown defined their demands as narrowly as possible. They asked GM to hire more men. They do not, they hasten to explain, want to limit the speed of the line. Gary Bryner, president of the local (an elder

[4]President, UAW.

statesman at twenty-nine), said, "We recognize that it's management's prerogative to run the plant. But all we've got is our labor, so we want to see that our conditions of labor are okay."

Despite this humble goal, local 1112 is undertaking a fight that the international union has backed away from, even suppressed, in the past.

Every three years for the past fifteen, Walter Reuther bargained with auto manufacturers for higher wages and better benefits—off the job. And every three years for the past fifteen, auto workers rejected Reuther's contracts, demanding, in addition, better conditions—on the job.

In 1955 more than 70 per cent of GM workers went on strike when presented with a contract that failed to deal with speed-up or other local grievances. After the 1958 contract an even larger percentage wildcatted. In 1961 the post-contract strike closed all GM plants and many large Ford plants. Running from the rear to the front of the parade, Reuther declared the strike official. However, he failed to negotiate for the demands that caused the wildcat. In 1964 there was a rank-and-file campaign before negotiations began. Near all large plants, bumper stickers appeared on auto workers' cars, saying, *Humanize Working Conditions*.[5]

The underlying assumption in an auto plant is that no worker wants to work. The plant is arranged so that employees can be controlled, checked, and supervised at every point. The efficiency of an assembly line is not only in its speed but in the fact that the workers are easily replaced. This allows the employer to cope with high turnover. But it's a vicious cycle. The job is so unpleasantly subdivided that men are constantly quitting and absenteeism is common. Even an accident is a welcome diversion. Because of the high turnover, management further simplifies the job, and more men quit. But the company has learned to cope with high turnover. So they don't have to worry if men quit or go crazy before they're forty.

The UAW is not a particularly undemocratic union. Still, it is as hard for the majority of

[5]This information was given to me by Stan Weir, a former auto worker. His article "U.S.A.: The Labor Revolts" appears in *American Society Inc*. (Markham Publishing Co., Chicago, 1970).

its members to influence their international as it is for the majority of Americans to end the war in Vietnam. The desire to reduce alienation is hard to express as a union demand, and it's hard to get union leaders to insist upon this demand. Harder still will be the actual struggle to take more control over production away from corporate management. It is a fight that questions the right to private ownership of the means of production.

DISCUSSING THE ARTICLES

1. In Colman McCarthy's article "The Faulty School Buses," how is the relative importance of Detroit and Washington evaluated? On what grounds? Does the difference in salaries of the president of the United States and the president of General Motors support the functional theory of stratification?

2. If General Motors has 55 percent of the automobile market in the United States, can the other automobile manufacturers compete on an equal basis? In what ways can General Motors destroy competition?

3. Why, according to the author, do General Motors's customers come back? What facet of collective behavior is involved?

4. What are some of the consequences of former board chairman Roche's statement equating planned obsolescence with progress? What kinds of needs, in John Kenneth Galbraith's terminology, are being catered to in such a philosophy?

5. Is General Motors morally responsible for the death of the people who perished as a result of defective cars? Why did defects exist? In trying to cut corners by employing cheap and flimsy materials, isn't General Motors following the precepts of sound business logic?

7. What does Donovan's statement that he can't find anyone directly responsible for the malfunctioning of the buses demonstrate about the nature of industrial organization? Of what kind of organization is industrial organization typical?

8. Do any of the personality characteristics of the three GM minor executives resemble those quoted in the text as representative of the executive personality? Might there have been strain in their roles, especially if they were parents whose children rode school buses?

9. In his conversation with a superior in Detroit, the highest ranking GM executive who was conferring with Donovan spoke in what terms? What does this illustrate about a hierarchical chain of command typical of bureaucracy?

10. What does the author say is the problem with seeking satisfaction from GM as opposed to seeking it from the village shoemaker? How would you state this problem in sociological terminology? What is your personal reaction to corporate callousness?

11. In Barbara Garson's article "Luddites in Lordstown," what is the workers' wistful desire? What aspect of industrial organization does it illustrate? What did Marx call it?

12. Why did GM speed up the assembly line and fire several hundred workers? How does this benefit the corporation? How does it affect workers?

13. How do the workers at Lordstown differ from their older counterparts on assembly lines throughout the country? Do they differ basically in their demands? What is at the bottom of their demands?

14. In the workers' description of work on the assembly line, what is the recurring theme? How do the workers try to remain human? Is there potential danger in such a situation?

15. What does the fact that guards photograph and take names of workers who distribute strike pamphlets, as well as of those who take the pamphlets, indicate about the power of the corporation? What do you suppose will happen to those workers? Does it seem to be in line with our Bill of Rights?

16. Many workers compare working at Lordstown to being in the army. What do the army and large organizations, in fact, have in common? Why don't the grievance procedures work, both in the army and in large organizations?

17. How does one of the workers describe the military-industrial complex that traps the little man?

18. In the article, are there any indications that the young workers are not as imbued with the Protestant Ethic as are their older counterparts? How might that affect the industrial mode of production? Should industry continue to produce more and more? Is it filling real needs or artificial ones?

19. How do attitudes toward the car coincide with attitudes toward the company? How does a majority of workers feel toward the Vega? Do they have a feeling of pride when they see the finished product?

20. Are the workers confident in the national union? Do they think its leadership supports them satisfactorily? According to the older worker the author interviewed, what has happened to the top union leaders? What does such a situation do to the relationship between leaders and rank and file members?

21. What kind of sociocultural change must take place in industrial organizations before conditions are improved?

TERMS TO REMEMBER

The economy, or the economic order. Those relationships among humans in society that exist as a result of the necessity to produce, distribute, and consume goods and services.

Dialectic materialism. Karl Marx's philosophy that the course of history is determined by the economic institutions of society.

Family capitalism. A type of capitalism in which huge business enterprises are controlled by members of one family.

Industrial capitalism. A form of capitalism in which business enterprise is concentrated in the fields of mining, manufacturing, and transportation.

Finance capitalism. A form of capitalism in which (1) investment banks and insurance companies dominate industry; (2) large amounts of capital are accumulated; (3) managers run the enterprise; (4) the holding company appears.

Corporation. A product of finance capitalism. A form of enterprise organized for large-scale production that includes an all-encompassing bureaucracy.

Holding company. An enterprise that does not produce anything, but makes its profits from stock it owns in other corporations and from management fees it charges them.

Oligopoly. A high industrial concentration.

Staff. Divisions within the corporation that are supportive of or helpful to divisions in which goods are actually produced.

Line. Divisions within the industrial organization responsible for the actual production of goods.

Vice-president. A member of the middle-management segment of the industrial bureaucracy. The vice-president's function is to implement and help carry out decisions from the executive.

Specialist. A middle-management employee who is a professional trained in a very narrow field of specialization.

Middle management. A segment of the industrial bureaucracy located between the lofty position of corporation executives and the masses of blue-collar industrial workers.

Automation. A process in which machines, rather than humans, control and run other machines.

Bureaucracy. The type of formal organization all large-scale enterprises have. Bureaucracy includes a clear-cut division of labor; a division of work into routine tasks, so employees can be easily replaced; the solving of problems by rational, rather than emotional means; and impersonality in applying rules.

Fiscal policy. An economic stabilizer determined by the president and Congress. It involves government spending and taxation.

Monetary policy. An economic stabilizer wielded by the Federal Reserve Board, which controls bank reserves and lending power.

SUGGESTIONS FOR FURTHER READING

Edwards, Richard C., Reich, Michael, and Weisskopf, Thomas E. *The Capitalist System.* Englewood Cliffs, New Jersey: Prentice-Hall, 1972. The structure, functioning, problems, and alternatives to American capitalism, from a radical viewpoint.

Galbraith, John Kenneth. *The New Industrial State.* Boston: Houghton Mifflin, 1967. The role of the economy in industrial society discussed by one of America's best-known economists.

Heilbroner, Robert L. *The Worldly Philosophers*, rev. ed. New York: Simon and Schuster, 1961. The thinkers who shaped our economic fate in an extremely well-written and interesting account.

Heyne, Paul T. *Private Keepers of the Public Interest.* New York: McGraw-Hill, 1968. Corporate organization's lack of social responsibility is critically evaluated.

Hoselitz, Berthold F., ed. *The Progress of Underdeveloped Areas.* Chicago: University of Chicago Press, 1966. A collection of essays centering around industrialization and economic growth and including methods and effects of industrialization.

Jacobs, Norman. *The Origin of Modern Capitalism and Eastern Asia.* Hong Kong: Hong Kong University Press, 1958. An investigation into why Japan developed industrial capitalism and China did not, based on Weber's position that values mold institutions.

Kerr, Clark, et al. *Industrialism and Industrial Man*. New York: Oxford University Press, 1964. An examination of the cultural conflicts that arise in the wake of industrialization.

Roman, Richard, and Leiman, Melvin. *Views on Capitalism*. Beverly Hills, Calif.: Glencoe Press, 1970. Capitalism as an economic philosophy examined from radical, liberal, and conservative viewpoints.

Shepard, Jon M. *Automation and Alienation*. Cambridge, Mass.: M.I.T. Press, 1970. In this study, both office and factory workers were examined, and the conclusion reached is that alienation is a direct result of specialization.

Sirkin, Gerald. *The Visible Hand: The Fundamentals of Economic Planning*. New York: McGraw-Hill, 1968. An attempt to demonstrate that the visible hand—planning—is more viable than the self-regulating market.

Smelser, Neil J. *Social Change in the Industrial Revolution*. Chicago: University of Chicago Press, 1959. The new division of labor and occupational differentiation in the British cotton industry following the Industrial Revolution.

Smelser, Neil J. *The Sociology of Economic Life*. Englewood Cliffs, N. J.: Prentice-Hall, 1963. The sociologist's concerns in the discipline of economics as well as in the institution of the economy.

Vernon, Raymond. *Sovereignty at Bay*. New York: Basic Books, 1971. The dangers involved in the multinational spread of American enterprises.

CHAPTER NINE

THE political institution

Words such as "government," "the state," "politics," "democracy," and others in a similar vein are part of even children's vocabularies. But although they are used liberally, most people would have difficulty providing a clear definition of them. Such words evoke emotional responses. Government is something you are supposed to obey, except of late, when you demonstrate against it. Democracy goes together with mother and apple pie to mean something strictly American, but, of late, its image too has become slightly tarnished. Politics is a dirty game involving some unsavory people who wish to be elected. The vital importance of the institution of government thus tends to be forgotten in a sea of stereotypes.

Descriptions of the structure and processes of government and the concepts concerning government are properly in the sphere of political science. But because government is first of all a social institution of great importance in human society, sociologists have also been interested in it, directing their efforts toward research in specific areas. The field of political sociology basically involves the analysis of the social organization and cultural values of a society, upon which the political order depends. It also involves the analysis of the social foundations of political behavior—who participates in political processes, why, and which kind of processes they participate in—and the social component of political processes—the kinds of groups that exist and the way they interact as they affect the political order.

The institution of government has become particularly challenging to sociologists in recent years, because attacks on it have increased. In the words of one political thinker,

> We are living in a decade of crisis. [There is] a political crisis, a crisis of public authority.... There is serious doubt about efficacy and justice in the agencies of government, the processes of policy-making, leadership selection, and the implementation of decisions.... Protests and militancy, black and white, are the outward signs of decaying respect for public symbols and destroyed trust in public objects. The emergence of hostilities long suppressed reveals the awesome possibility that the national political system is no longer capable of maintaining the ideal of one nation indivisible. [1]

Are such bleak statements justified? It would seem that they are, judging from a recent poll that measured the faith of Americans in their social and political institutions. This poll repeats one taken five years ago, in 1967. The findings of the two polls are shown in Table 9.1.

What has caused this decrease in faith, this crisis in leadership? What has happened to the political system, once the pride and joy of every American? Is it suffering symptoms of old age? Is the system unable to cope with new forces that have been unleashed in society? Has democracy become bankrupt? Before discussing such fundamental questions, we would be wise to define with some precision the institution of government, the kind of social relationships involved in its processes and the people who participate in them and

[1]Theodore J. Lowi, *The End of Liberalism* (New York: W. W. Norton, 1969), pp. xii-xiv.

TABLE 9.1   FAITH OF AMERICANS IN SOCIAL AND POLITICAL INSTITUTIONS

Americans Who:	Percentage in 1967	Percentage in 1972
Have faith in leadership of corporations	55	27
Have faith in banks and financial institutions	67	37
Have faith in the military	62	27
Have faith in Congress	41	19
Have faith in the executive branch	41	23
Have faith in the scientific community	56	32

Source: Bayard Hooper for Louis Harris and Associates, *Social Education* (March, 1972), as reported in *Intellectual Digest* (May, 1972), p. 49.

to what extent. We should also determine why a group setting inevitably leads to government and political processes and why such processes cannot be divorced from social organization. Finally, we should analyze the values that underlie government, the political systems that values create, and the behavior of members of society in reaction to values and systems.

GOVERNMENT

Opinions about government have varied greatly. Some people have believed that government is, at best, a necessary evil and, at worst, an intolerable one. Others have believed that it is a masterpiece of human wisdom designed to provide for human wants. Regardless of which opinion you tend to support, you must agree that the nature of humans' group life makes government essential. In fact, no known society, no matter how small or simple, has existed without it. Of course, not every group has had a government like ours—a body that collects taxes, sends young men to war, deals with other nations, punishes offenders against its laws, keeps order within our society, and protects us from enemies outside our society. But at some level of organization—family, clan, tribe, or village—a society must agree to accept the authority of some body that directs behavior for the good of the group, or it must disband in chaos.

Government, then, is an institution that arises out of the need for social order. As is true with other institutions, its breeding ground was the family, from which it became separated with the increasing size and complexity of societies. Second to the family, government is probably the most important institution because the remaining institutions depend on government to lend them support. A banker who commits fraud, a father who does not support his children, and a priest who sets fire to his church are all breaking the rules of several institutions. But they must eventually answer for their rule-breaking to an agency of government: a court of law.

Expanding Aristotle's statement that man is essentially a political animal, political scientist Robert MacIver concludes, "Government is an aspect of society."[2] What do these two thinkers, separated by many centuries, mean? Basically, they mean that because it is the nature of humans to live in groups, they must accept a degree of order sufficient to keep the group functioning. Absolute freedom is impossible for humans because it invariably impinges upon the freedom of fellow humans. If you blast your trumpet in the middle of the night, your neighbor is not free to sleep; if he is free to punch you in the mouth to teach you a lesson, you may not be able to blast your trumpet again for a long time, day or night! It is thus necessary that some kind of body have the authority to decree that you can play your trumpet only at specific times and in specific places and that your neighbor cannot use physical violence as punishment. Social order, then, is a by-product of group life. When social order becomes institutionalized—when it becomes sufficiently laden with customs and traditions to set a pattern—it is called government.

[2]Robert M. MacIver, *The Web of Government* (New York: Macmillan, 1947), p. 20.

Social Control: Moral and Political

Social order is imposed on members of a society through the implementation of social control. In Chapter 2 we saw that social control is an outgrowth of social organization. It results from the web of responsibilities that each individual assumes in the different statuses and roles that accrue to him as a member of society. In fulfilling his various roles, the individual is guided by the values, norms, folkways, mores, and laws of his culture. In short, if the individual is well integrated into various groups in society and if he does not deviate greatly from his cultural norms, he is submitting to social control. In this manner, social order is automatically served.

In small, relatively simple societies, social order may be sufficiently maintained through moral control. *Moral control* is within the individual. It is internalized cultural learning acquired through socialization. It makes the individual behave in ways his culture considers right, whether or not anyone is present to force him to behave in this way. In a complex society, social order can be maintained only if moral control is supplemented by political control. *Political control* is exerted by forces outside the individual. In other words, the individual does not behave in a particular way because he thinks it is right. He behaves that way because if he does not, he may be punished, and if he does, he may be rewarded.

Because the members of a society recognize that complete individual freedom is impossible in a group setting, they invest one person or a group of persons with the authority to exercise political control. When and how political control is to be exercised become part of the processes of government.

The Nature of Authority

What does it mean to have or to accept authority? Concerning this question, sociologist Robert Bierstedt makes several interesting points. First, he claims that authority pervades each and every association in society, regardless of how small or temporary it may be. Second, he says that authority is not necessarily conferred because of competence. Third, he points out that authority is attached to statuses, not to individuals. The president of General Motors has the authority to make policy changes in the corporation only as long as he remains president of it. Once he retires or is removed, his authority within the corporation ends. Fourth, Bierstedt maintains that people accept authority because they recognize it as representing the group of which they are a part, and they want their group to be stable and to continue. Finally, he defines authority as institutionalized power, which in some instances rests upon consent, and in other instances upon coercion.[3]

Types of Authority

Max Weber, who was interested in power as a significant factor in the social interaction that takes place in political processes, distinguished among three types of authority.[4] According to Weber, *traditional authority* exists even

[3]Robert Bierstedt, *The Social Order* (New York: McGraw-Hill, 1970), pp. 329–340.

[4]Max Weber, *The Theory of Social and Economic Organization*, trans. by Talcott Parsons (New York: Macmillan, 1964), pp. 328–363.

before government is institutionalized. It derives its acceptance from reverence for the traditions that have been transmitted from generation to generation. The chief reason for obeying the norms of traditional society is that these norms "have always been there." Both the religious authority of the church and the political authority of the government are accepted on this basis. Traditional authority tends to predominate in relatively homogeneous, non-technological societies. In such societies, the members hold similar group identifications, sharing fairly similar values, beliefs, and attitudes.

Rational-legal authority, on the other hand, appears in complex societies that are multigroup. In such societies, members are heterogeneous, belonging to many subcultures. In addition, such societies usually experience rapid social change, resulting in a lack of uniformity in values, attitudes, and beliefs. The United States is an excellent illustration of a society with a rational-legal base of authority. Rational-legal authority is not accepted simply because it has always been there. It is accepted because the members of society are convinced that holders of authority are using rational methods for the benefit of society. For the benefit of society, too, laws are continually being enacted or changed in response to social change.

In both types of societies—those in which authority is traditional and those in which it is rational-legal—*charismatic authority* may appear in the person of an exceptional leader. To their followers, charismatic leaders seem to possess special characteristics that are magnetic, fascinating, and extraordinary. The authority such leaders hold does not rest on tradition, reason, or law. It rests on their outstanding qualities as leaders and as unusual human beings. Much of the authority of Chinese Chairman Mao Tse-tung and Cuban Premier Fidel Castro is based on their charismatic personalities.

Power

It is difficult to separate authority from power, because one can't exist without the other. We have seen that Bierstedt considers authority to be institutionalized power, that is, power around which customary patterns have evolved. But what then is power? In Chapter 4, we defined power as the ability of one person or group to influence the behavior of another person or group in a desired direction. This ability is ultimately based on force or the threat of force. Force effects a change in the actions of an individual or group. The change occurs against the individual or the group's wishes, and no alternative is offered. In short, when an armed robber holds a gun to your back and demands your money, he has power over you because he has only to pull the trigger to kill you. Because you don't want to die, you give him your money, although you would have preferred to keep it. Unfortunately, you were not offered an alternative that was desirable to you. We may conclude, then, that force or the threat of force underlies power. And power is the backbone, or the raw material, of authority.[5]

Legitimacy

Is authority—backed by power, which carries the underlying threat of force—always accepted by members of society? The answer is that only *legitimate authority* is accepted. "Legitimacy," writes Seymour Martin Lipset, "involves the capacity of the system to engender and maintain the belief that the existing political institutions are the most appropriate ones for the society."[6] In other words, before the authority of a government is accepted, that government must convince a substantial number of members of society that the power it holds is justified, or legitimate. Government is generally considered legitimate if its goals and values coincide with the goals and values of a majority of the citizens. At any rate, no government, not even one born out of violence and functioning through force, can survive long without legitimacy.

When a government has legitimacy, its laws are followed and its officials respected by a substantial majority of society, regardless of the members' feelings toward both the laws and the enforcers. If you consider your government legitimate, for instance, even though you think that the law prohibiting the smoking of marijuana is ridiculous, you will refrain from smoking it, at least in public. And even though you may not like your senator, you will probably shake his hand if he offers it and look respectful in his presence. If you and the majority of others in your society deliberately flaunt the law by smoking marijuana and by throwing stones at the senator, you are indicating the presence of a *crisis of legitimacy*. As we mentioned in our chapter on social change, such a situation tends to occur during a period of rapid social change and is particularly severe if major institutions are threatened or if major groups in society have no access to the political system.[7]

---

[5]Robert Bierstedt, *The Social Order*, pp. 347–349.
[6]Seymour Martin Lipset, *Political Man* (Garden City, N. Y.: Doubleday Anchor Books, 1963), p. 64.
[7]Ibid., p. 65.

THE STATE

Whereas government provides social control, the *state* is the formal counterpart of government. The state has become an institution that incorporates the institution of government. Government is the working, active arm of the state, through which the state formulates and enforces its laws. Although the individuals and groups that make up the government—and their laws and procedures—change with time and with administrations, the state goes on.

The basic components of the state are territory, population, government, and sovereignty.[8] Within its territory, through its government, on the basis of its sovereignty, and for the benefit of its population, the state performs certain functions. Its goal is to impose organized political control for the protection of each citizen. It does this by formulating and enforcing laws based on the behavioral norms of the society. If these laws, revolving primarily around the protection of life, limb, and property, are violated, the state, through its governmental agencies, makes sure that the violator is punished. The state can do this because it has a monopoly over the legitimate use of force within its territory.

In addition, the state protects its citizens from enemies outside its territory, for which purpose it maintains a military establishment. Finally, the state plans, regulates, and runs a large number of activities that are designed to further protect and benefit its citizens.

States emerge when the activities involved in the process of government become so numerous and complex that special individuals must be assigned to carry them out. At this time, the customs and traditions revolving around the activities of government also crystallize into a body of laws, the breaking of which results in punishment. A state comes into being, then, when the society, and, with it, the process of government and a body of law, has reached a particular stage of development.

Political philosophers and scientists have long speculated about the precise time and circumstances of the emergence of the state. One of the most interesting theories is that of Morton H. Fried, a political anthropologist. He finds a relationship between the development of a political state and a society's economic evolution. In the first stage of societal evolution, humans live in an *egalitarian society*. In this kind of society, no individual dominates the activities of another because there are as many positions of prestige as there are individuals capable of filling them. (This stage corresponds to the one in other typologies in which a surplus has not yet appeared.)

In the second stage, large groups of humans live in a *rank society*, in which there are fewer positions of prestige than there are individuals capable of filling them. But although positions of prestige are filled by only a few, all continue to have equal access to the basic resources necessary for survival.

In the third and final stage, humans live in a *stratified society*—one in which they are divided into social classes. Stratification occurs because the individuals filling the prestige positions have gained greater access to the resources neces-

---

[8]Sovereignty is the supreme political power vested in the state, which gives it the ultimate authority to administer a government. Sovereignty is recognized both by the citizens of the state and by other states.

sary for survival than have most of the people. Stratification causes a system of inequalities in which the few have more than the many. To maintain such a system, it is necessary to have leaders who can force their followers to obey or accept the system. Because kinship groups are not powerful enough for this coercive social control, the state emerges. Essentially, then, according to Fried, the state emerges to maintain a system of inequalities.[9]

Fried's explanation is of course, only one theory. The emergence of a state cannot be pinpointed to a precise time in history. States emerge gradually, growing and changing in response to the needs of society. At any rate, in most societies today, the state has definitely come into existence.

THE NATION

The same processes that were responsible for institutionalizing social control in the state (with its working institution, the government) have also been responsible for the creation of nations. The continuous growth in size and complexity of societies led people to seek political organization first in clans based on kinship, later in tribes that were collections of clans, and, finally, in city-states. In the fifteenth century, city-states gradually emerged as nation-states. Whereas the state represents a politically organized society that functions through a government, the *nation* is a culture group residing within the territory of the political state. What makes a group of people a nation is the spirit of nationhood.

The factors that help unify a people into a nation are (1) geographic boundaries—separation of an area by mountains, rivers, or the sea; (2) the development of commercial ties throughout this geographic area; (3) a common language, or if there are different linguistic groups, the knowledge of a common language. With the establishment of a central government, these factors become even more significant, and additional factors appear: an attempt to subordinate older loyalties to the new political order and the development of a common literature, a common history, and a sense of a common future. Eventually, the people making up a nation come to have a "we" as against "they" feeling toward those who are not part of the nation. This sense of unity is so strong that, in spite of deep cleavages among the people of the nation, they consider themselves as separate from all others, whom they designate as foreigners.

Of course, the creation of a nation-state does not guarantee that people will feel this spirit of nationhood. Nor does it guarantee that, once attained, the spirit remains intact forever. Events may lead to its erosion and death. Nationalism, which is the ideology behind the nation-state, has played an important part in modern history. It has been essential to the creation of modern societies, for it has destroyed the narrow provincialism of loyalties to family, kin, and community typical of preindustrial societies. At the same time, however, it has created a nation-centered ethnocentrism that may be harmful to international relations. In fact, ethnocentrism, which we try to justify as patriotism, affects our dealings with other nations and builds antagonisms we can ill afford.

[9]Morton H. Fried, *The Evolution of Political Society* (New York: Random House, 1967).

POLITICAL IDEOLOGY

In his excellent book on the subject of government in general, Robert MacIver asserts that it is not force but the myth complex of society that makes governors acceptable to the governed. This myth complex lends government a justification without which no prince or parliament, no tyrant or dictator, could ever rule a people.[10] We have already seen that this was true when we spoke of a government needing legitimate authority. But this does not explain how authority is legitimitized and what makes up the myth complex MacIver mentions.

The underlying fabric of authority is ideology. An *ideology* is a system of values, ideas, beliefs, and attitudes that a society, or groups within it, shares and accepts as fact. Political ideology is such a system of beliefs that explains, interprets, and rationalizes why a particular kind of political order is best for the society. The political order may already exist, or it may merely be planned. Political ideology, in addition, offers a definite strategy for the attainment or maintenance of the preferred political order, including processes, institutional arrangements, and other programs. Therefore, political ideology may be likened to a blueprint for the good society, complete with practical instructions about how to reach it and keep it.

A graphic definition of political ideology is offered by Robert Lane:

> [*Political ideology refers to concepts that*] *deal with the questions, (1) Who will be the rulers? How will the rulers be selected? By what principles will they govern? (2) constitute an argument; that is, they are intended to persuade and to counter opposing views; (3) integrally affect some of the major values of life; (4) embrace a program for the defense or reform or abolition of important social institutions; (5) are, in part, rationalizations of group interests—but not necessarily the interests of all groups espousing them; (6) are normative, ethical, moral in tone and content; (7) are (inevitably) torn from their context in a broader belief system, and share the structural and stylistic properties of that system.*[11]

Those who advance a political ideology expect their followers to become totally committed to it and to act on it. In other words, a political ideology is expected to result in political behavior, its ideas translated into action. Political parties, social movements, interest groups, and, of course, the political system itself are all motivated by ideologies. By examining political ideologies, we can uncover some interesting facts about the people who formulate them and believe in them. We may see, for instance, how the people of a particular society see themselves in relation to their environment; what their goals are; how and why they expect to attain those goals; and what the final consequences of their views and beliefs are.

DEMOCRACY

Democracy has many meanings and has been applied to the political systems of nations that make strange bedfellows. Many communist nations refer

---

[10]Robert MacIver, *The Web of Government*, p. 17.

[11]Robert E. Lane, *Political Ideology: Why the American Common Man Believes What He Does* (New York: Free Press, 1962), pp. 14–15.

to themselves as "People's Democracies," and titles such as "democratic dictatorship," "new democracy," and "democracy with leadership" are common.[12] *Democracy* is an ideology, a philosophy, a theory, and a political system. In each democratic nation, people have borrowed some elements of the ideology and rejected others, adapting democracy to their own particular circumstances. In addition, democracy was not created by one person at a definite period of time. It emerged in ancient Greece, but it did not gain wide acceptance until this century. And even now, it has as many detractors as it has followers.

Assumptions and Principles of Democracy

One of the basic assumptions of democracy is the value of the individual. Whereas in most political systems, the individual is considered only as part of a larger social mass, in democratic political systems, the human being is considered the primary unit of society. From this basic assumption, it follows that in the democratic frame of reference the ultimate purpose of the state is to ensure the self-fulfillment of every individual.

The ideology of democracy is founded on specific beliefs about the nature of humans. In particular, followers of democracy believe that individuals are free, rational, moral, equal, and possess certain rights. Equality does not imply that each individual has the same qualities as every other individual. Equality refers to each person's possession of particular moral and rational faculties, by virtue of which he is entitled to the same freedoms and rights as any other person. Democracy, then, recognizes and respects the uniqueness of each individual.

Democratic ideology is based on the principle of popular sovereignty. Popular sovereignty is the idea that ultimate power resides in the people. The assumption is that a person is not subject to any authority but his own and is capable of directing his behavior. This is a basic article of democratic faith, for if man is free and self-governing, he must be in control of political power.

Another principle of democracy is the belief that each person is entitled to freedom and the opportunity to pursue his goals. As applied in democratic political systems, this principle means that the citizen is guaranteed the right to vote; the assurance that political information is freely accessible; the freedoms of speech, of the press, of religion, of movement, and of assembly; the right to seek public office; the right to criticize public officials and programs; and the freedom from arbitrary persecution.

The principle that the only legitimate basis of rule is the consent of the governed is derived from the notion of popular sovereignty. The governed empower the state to pass and enforce laws to protect them from without and from within society. The state, then, becomes the trustee of powers given to it by the people and has no purpose or authority not assigned to it by them. Thus, the state and its government are instruments created and maintained for the benefit of the people.

[12]Reo M. Christenson, et al., *Ideologies and Modern Politics* (New York: Dodd, Mead, 1971), pp. 178–179.

Democratic Capitalism

In the preceding chapter, we emphasized that political and economic systems are invariably intertwined. Societies that have accepted a democratic ideology tend to have either a capitalistic or a socialistic economic system. These may be considered subideologies, or subdivisions of ideology, because their form and processes depend on the political ideology of the society.

In modern capitalistic societies, most property is held privately, and there are few limitations set on its accumulation.[13] The democratic belief in liberty is reflected in the capitalistic belief that limiting the amount of private property held by any one person would be an infringement on personal liberty.

Modern capitalists, however, recognize that if there were no governmental regulation, a few people would be able to control the entire economy. This in itself would destroy the liberty and equality of opportunity of a great number of people! Thus, capitalists today accept some limitations, so property may be distributed among a number of people. Limitations are set by the government, which as we saw in our discussion of the economic institution, regulates the economy and also supports a vast welfare system.

The relationship between capitalism and democratic ideology is closest in the areas of equality of opportunity and economic freedom. Capitalists argue that capitalism offers the individual more freedom of action than does any other economic system. Anyone who has some capital and is willing to work hard can invest in the system and receive rewards. How a person is to obtain that initial capital, of course, is left unanswered.

Today, equality of opportunity is still very much of a problem in the United States. The welfare system, originally designed to ensure that each person could enter the economic system, has not succeeded. On the contrary, it has excluded those who depend on it from the mainstream of the economic system.

Equality of opportunity may cause democratic capitalism, which has already changed considerably from its original form, to undergo future reinterpretations. In attempting to reach the goal of true equality of opportunity, capitalism has, to some extent, begun to resemble democratic socialism and may resemble it even more closely in the future.

Democratic Socialism

The basic assumption of democratic socialists brings them more closely in tune with democratic ideology than are their capitalist counterparts. Democratic socialists believe that citizen participation in decision making should not be limited to the political sphere but should extend to the economic sphere. Socialists argue that because politics and economics are closely interrelated, the voter should be able to decide his economic future through his control of government, in the same way that he decides his political future. In the socialist view, capitalism permits too much power to be concentrated in private hands—power that cannot be effectively checked and controlled.

Democratic socialism differs from democratic capitalism in several ways:

[13]L. T. Sargent, *Contemporary Political Ideologies*, (Homewood, Ill., Dorsey, 1972), p. 84.

(1) Major national industries are owned by the public; (2) the profit system and the competitive spirit of capitalism are held in low esteem; (3) higher priority is given to public needs than to private wants; (4) national planning is relied on to a greater extent than is the operation of the market; (5) government is trusted to manage the economy; (6) an equal distribution of wealth, allowing for only a small spread between top and bottom, is favored; (7) a comprehensive welfare state gives people security from the cradle to the grave; (8) attempts are made to eliminate special privileges and create true equal opportunity; (9) there is great concern for the working class.[14]

In a nutshell, the basic point of reference in democratic socialism is society—the public as a whole—rather than the single individual as it is in capitalistic ideology. Capitalism is chiefly an ideology of economics that is influenced by the democratic ideology of the political sphere within which it usually operates. Socialism is an all-encompassing ideology, underlying both the political and the economic spheres and offering a program for the welfare of the entire society. The capitalist assumes that equality and freedom of action are essential to the attainment of the good life. The socialist believes that no real equality and freedom of action can exist unless every individual in society is economically secure. This belief, when acted upon, gives rise to the comprehensive welfare state.

Actually, the two subideologies are more alike than different. Labels have made distinctions between them seem greater than they are. Socialism has been identified with communism and many of the other isms that patriotic Americans consider subversive. In reality, the differences seem to be more a matter of degree than of kind.

AUTOCRACY

Autocracy is the ideology most directly opposed to democracy because, according to it, government should be in the hands of one individual or group that holds supreme power over the people. Autocratic government has taken many forms throughout the ages: primitive kingships, despotism, tyranny, and absolutist monarchies of the type that existed in Europe as late as the early twentieth century (Czarist Russia, for instance). Military dictatorships and other forms of temporary, or emergency, rule may also be considered autocratic. The distinguishing feature of autocratic regimes is that the ruler does not have to account to anyone for his actions. He makes all decisions and reaps the consequences of them. Thus, he is not subject to any law but is, in effect, the law.

Having been reared in a democracy, we tend to label autocracy as "bad." However, it has been functional, working for many centuries and for many peoples. In modern times, traditional autocracy has been replaced by ideologies of the right and of the left that we call totalitarian. Totalitarian regimes differ in major ways from the autocracies of the past. They are kinds of autocracies based on modern technology and mass legitimation.[15]

[14]Reo M. Christenson, et al., *Ideologies and Modern Politics*, pp. 256–257.
[15]Carl J. Friedrich and Zbigniew Brzezinski, *Totalitarian Dictatorship and Autocracy* (New York: Praeger, 1966), p. 4.

Totalitarianism

The word *totalitarian* is comparatively new. It came into existence when what were thought to be short-lived dictatorships of the left and the right seemed to have become permanent regimes. Although totalitarian regimes differed from each other initially, and continue to differ today, they all share some common features.

First, their official ideology expresses a revolt against present society and idealistic hopes for a future society of perfect men. The ideology is totalist—it embraces all facets of human life. In effect, it deals with the total individual and attempts his total reform.

Second, totalitarian regimes maintain a single party that functions as the organization through which the ideology is fostered and kept alive. The party is frequently—or at least initially—led by a charismatic leader and is hierarchically arranged into a political elite that is either superior or equal to the governmental bureaucracy.

Third, and finally, in such regimes, there is a secret, government-controlled police. In addition, the ruling elite has absolute control over mass communication, weapons, and the economy.[16]

The destinies of political systems that have evolved from totalitarian ideologies—fascism, national socialism (Nazism), communism Soviet, Chinese, Cuban)—have all been different. World War II put an end to fascism and national socialism, which have reappeared only sporadically in various nations. However, totalitarian solutions to modern problems still hold appeal, as is evident in Mary Simons's interview with the head of the Italian neo-fascist party, which follows this chapter.[17] This appeal has much to do with the snail's pace at which change within a democratic political system occurs. In such a system, many groups must compete and compromise, and often only partial solutions are obtained. It also has much to do with the charismatic party leader, because such leaders are particularly effective in totalitarian political systems.

Communism has continued to prosper and has made inroads among the nations of the Third World. Part of the explanation for this may be that the ideology of communism has not remained static but has continued to evolve. Rulers of totalitarian nations are continually in the process of transforming ideology. Carl Friedrich states that both Mao Tse-tung and the Soviets have elaborated their ideologies and that these "changes illustrate the plasticity of [totalitarian] ideology, and therefore its vitality, rather than its end."[18]

Authoritarianism

There are types of autocracies in existence today that can be best described as authoritarian in their ideology. In these regimes, power is held by either an absolute monarch or dictator or a small elite. However, power is limited to the political sphere, and the ruler makes no attempt to invade other spheres of human life. Such regimes are more or less like the totalitarian model. With

[16]Carl J. Friedrich, Michael Curtis, and Benjamin R. Barber, *Totalitarianism in Perspective: Three Views* (New York: Praeger, 1969), p. 126. Also, A. James Gregor, *Contemporary Radical Ideologies* (New York: Random House, 1968), pp. 20–21.

[17]Mary Simons, "Almirante & The Once & Future Fascism," *Intellectual Digest* (May, 1972), pp. 21–23.

[18]Carl J. Friedrich, et al., *Totalitarianism in Perspective*, p. 138.

time, they may become more totalitarian or less so. Under de Gaulle, France experienced such a period of authoritarianism, and today Spain, Portugal, Greece, South Africa, and many smaller nations are in this category.

This brief examination of the ideologies underlying the political systems of modern societies indicates once again that humans' behavior is dependent on their normative system. In Chapter 2, we saw that norms direct our behavior in all aspects of our lives. Our political behavior is no exception. To a very great extent, it is shaped by the values of the prevailing political ideology of our society. This ideology not only molds the institutions we establish to carry on the political process but also the way we respond to these institutions. Of course, because of our individual and group differences, we do not always interpret the ideology in the same manner. Therefore, both our political institutions and our political behavior do not necessarily always reflect our ideology. How much the actual political system in our society differs from its ideology will be discussed in the remaining sections of this chapter.

IDEOLOGY IN ACTION: DEMOCRACY IN THE UNITED STATES

Democratic ideology does not develop in a vacuum, nor is the political system that emerges from it adaptable to every circumstance. That is why many of the nations that have recently become independent have chosen totalitarian or authoritarian political systems. We who believe in democracy may find their choice inconceivable. But democracy needs a very special soil if it is to flourish.

Preconditions for Democracy

At one time, it was widely believed that democracy could take root only in a small nation. Democracy on a large geographic scale was thought impossible, or at best difficult. However, researchers seeking to determine how closely democratic principles are followed in small-scale local government seem to refute the notion that size is important to democracy.[19] Of course, participatory democracy—in which every individual participates in every decision—depends on small groups.

A national feature that is more significant than size is socioeconomic status. Political sociologist Seymour Martin Lipset, whose views have been supported by the research of other sociologists, found that the wealth, degree of industrialization and urbanization, and the level of education in a society were directly related to the degree of democracy practiced in it.[20] It's not difficult to see why. In a society in which citizens must use all their energy merely to survive and in which there are huge gaps in the distribution of income and much illiteracy, people do not have the time, the inclination, or the knowl-

---

[19]Roscoe C. Martin, *Grass Roots* (University, Ala.: University of Alabama Press, 1957), pp. 56–58.

[20]Seymour Martin Lipset, *Political Man*, p. 50. Also, Robert A. Dahl and Charles E. Lindblom, *Politics, Economics, and Welfare* (New York: Harper & Row, 1953); Daniel Lerner, *The Passing of Traditional Society* (New York: Free Press, 1958).

edge to pursue democratic ideals. Such a society is, in general, susceptible to extremist politics and to rule by a dictator or a small elite.

In urban industrial societies, a rather large middle class tends to develop. This class acts as a damper on conflict, favoring moderate, more or less democratic political procedures. Furthermore, education and financial security tend to be widespread in industrial urban societies. Because of this, the working classes—the people who are generally the most dissatisfied—accept political processes that bring about gradual change.

Although high social, economic, and educational development is, according to Lipset, an almost necessary precondition for democracy, we must not discount the influence of unique historical factors on the political system of a society. "Germany is an example of a nation where growing industrialization, urbanization, wealth, and education favored the establishment of a democratic system, but in which a series of adverse historical events prevented democracy from securing legitimacy and thus weakened its ability to withstand crisis."[21] In India, on the other hand, wealth, industrialization, urbanization, and education were largely lacking. Yet the nation established a fairly stable democratic system. Perhaps, however, the long history of English colonial power in India was responsible for the establishment of a climate receptive to a democratic ideology.

The Distribution of Power in the United States

The United States is a society in which the preconditions for democracy exist. It is rich in natural resources, it is the most urbanized and industrialized nation in the world, and it attempts to educate all of its citizens. If, however, we questioned some Americans about democracy in our society, they would maintain that, as a political system, democracy is a sham and a farce and that fascistic elements grow more evident every day. If we questioned other Americans, they would claim that democracy has degenerated into socialism and that the welfare system supports parasites. What a majority of Americans would agree on, however, is that, contrary to democratic principles, power does not belong to the people.

Pluralism

There are two opposing schools of thought on how power is distributed in our society. One is the school of political pluralism, or broker rule. According to this view, power is diffused among numerous interest groups rather than being concentrated in any single place. Although interest groups continually compete with one another, when it is to their benefit, they unite in coalitions and attempt to reach compromise solutions to the problems of decision making.

A model of political pluralism includes the following assumptions and arguments: First, the basis of politics is the struggle for power, and the parties to this struggle are organized interest groups. Second, the stability of the political system is promoted by the great number and the diversity of these organized interest groups; by the role of politicians as brokers; by overlapping member-

---

[21]Seymour Martin Lipset, *Political Man*, p. 28.

ships in interest groups; and by the possibility of new interest groups being formed. Stability is further ensured by an underlying consensus that acts to restrain group conflicts. Change, as well as stability, is provided for through the emergence of new groups. Although group bargaining is performed by elites—small groups with power to make significant decisions—elites are responsive and accountable to the people through elections.[22]

In other words, those who agree with political scientist Robert A. Dahl that power in our society is distributed according to a pluralistic model believe that neither a majority nor a minority is responsible for governmental decision making. Rather, such decision making results from "steady appeasement of relatively small groups."[23] And the process through which appeasement occurs is continual bargaining.

Of the groups that control decision making through continual negotiations, the most powerful are economic. They represent the interests of business, labor, farming, and related groups. Other interest groups are of a regional and sectional nature (the South, the West, for example) or of an ethnic and religious nature (blacks, Jews, Catholics).

Major interest groups employ the services of lobbyists to influence congressmen into voting for legislation favorable to their employer. This influence seems to reach into the innermost recesses of the political system. No presidential candidate can hope to be successful without the solid support of a number of interest groups, or at least of those interest groups that count. [24]What the candidate needs from interest groups, besides support, is money. Money provides access to the mass media, buys votes, and generally makes or breaks a candidate. The high cost of campaigns and the dependence of candidates on interest groups—unless the candidate is independently very wealthy—is illustrated in our article "The Frog-Hair Problem," by Senator Fred Harris of Oklahoma. The senator announced his candidacy for president in the summer of 1971 but had to withdraw by late fall because of lack of funds. One problem of our political system, then, is that we choose not from among the best candidates but from among the wealthiest or best supported.[25]

"Influence peddling" lends itself to underhanded methods, and lobbying has come under severe criticism in the wake of scandals. In Chapter 8, in our discussion of the giant corporations that dominate our economy, we mentioned that they, and labor as well, exert an unduly heavy influence on government. Their superior economic strength ensures them of a receptive audience. However, small interest groups, lacking funds, are frequently denied access to the channels of governmental power. The unequal influence exerted by different interest groups leads many social thinkers to believe that access to power is open only to elites.

Elitism

Directly opposed to the pluralist view is the elitist view. The late C. Wright Mills was, in this century, a vocal supporter of elitism. Mills believed that

[22]John C. Livingston and Robert G. Thompson, *The Consent of the Governed* (New York: Macmillan, 1971), p. 107.

[23]Robert A. Dahl, *A Preface to Democratic Theory* (Chicago: University of Chicago Press, 1956), p. 146.

[24]John C. Livingston and Robert G. Thompson, *The Consent of the Governed*, p. 104.

[25]Fred R. Harris, "The Frog-Hair Problem," *Harper's* (May, 1972), pp. 12–20.

the most significant decisions, including those concerning war and peace, are made by a handful of men who represent the corporate rich, the military upper echelons, and the political directorate. According to Mills, the consensus that supposedly exists in this nation is, in reality, brought into existence by elites, who manipulate the masses through mass communication. Pluralist competition, then, occurs only when issues are minor. Elitists do not deny the existence of innumerable interest groups, but they question whether their interaction results in a diffusion of power.

Although Mills' views are considered too extreme to accurately reflect reality, elitist theory has lately challenged pluralism, which many find incurably romantic. As it is understood today, the theory of elitism is based on several observations. Primarily, society is considered as being made up of the few who have power (the elite), and of the many who do not (the masses). The ultimate fate of all organizations is to be run by a small minority, or an elite. The elite differs from the masses because, predominantly, it originates in the upper socioeconomic classes. Thus, members of the elite tend to share a common life style and resemble one another. Moreover, their identification as members of the elite is more important to them than their identification as leaders of specific interest groups.

Because of their status, members of the elite control the resources of the society. In addition, they mold and uphold the values of the society in their formulation of public policy. Because one of their values is the stability of society, they do permit some nonelites to attain elite status, but only slowly and after being certain that the newcomers have embraced the elite consensus. This consensus, shared by all members of the elite, centers around the essential values of the social system and around the desirability of preserving it.

Finally, public policy reflects not the demands of the masses but the values of the elites. Changes in public policy eventually occur through the gradual enactment of legislation but not through any radical change. Part of the reason for this is that elites are active, whereas the masses are apathetic. As a consequence, elites are not influenced much by the masses, but the masses are influenced and directed by elites.[26]

We must not think, however, that there is constant conflict between the elites and the masses or that the elites necessarily work against the public interest. Neither should we think of elites as always agreeing and as forming a monolithic power structure that never changes and that has exclusive control of economic resources. Theorists think of elitist features in a relative manner: Elites may be monolithic, or they may be more or less competitive. They may control economic resources, or they may control organization, communication, and information. They may be influenced by the masses, but more likely, they will influence the masses.[27]

Who Has the Power?

Which is the reality of the American situation? Can we determine who has the power? Political scientists Dye and Ziegler suggest that power may fall somewhere between the conceptions of the ruling elite and the plural elite.

[26]Thomas Dye and Harmon Zeigler, *The Irony of Democracy* (Belmont, Calif., Wadsworth, 1970), p. 6.

[27]Ibid., p. 6.

In neither view is the power thought to be in the hands of the people. Both views agree, in fact, that people are too apathetic, ill informed, and self-interested to participate in the kind of system that democratic ideology prescribes. The pluralists however, maintain that those who exercise power are responsive to the people, as uninterested as the people may be. Ultimately, then, instead of government by the people, there is government by elites approved by the people. In short, the pluralists maintain that because people are not interested in political issues, politics is taken over by professionals. But politicians remain accountable to the people because they attain their elite position through people's votes. The people, then, don't make the decisions, but they choose the men who do.[28]

The elitists do not have much faith in the elites' accountability to the people. They, in fact, claim that elites are able to manipulate the masses into a false consensus. Issues, then, that concern the public welfare but are against the interest of the elites are simply not raised. For instance, although socialized medicine might contribute to the welfare of all the people in our society, the issue does not receive any serious attention because Americans supposedly prefer to be attended by private doctors. Of course, Americans have never voted on this issue. It is simply assumed that a consensus exists.

Conflict and Consensus

Whether one tends to interpret the location of political power according to the pluralist or the elitist theory also depends on how one views the interplay of conflict and consensus in society. Obviously, both conflict and consensus

[28]John C. Livingston and Robert G. Thompson, *The Consent of the Governed*, pp. 114–115.

must exist in society. Because politics revolves around the question of who will have power, conflict among individuals and groups is unavoidable in the political process. At the same time, if there were not at least a general consensus on the way conflict is to be mediated—in other words, on the rules of the game—the political system could become chaotic. However, although everyone agrees that both conflict and consensus exist, there is disagreement about which element predominates in American society.

Pluralists tend to belong to a consensus school of thought. You became familiar with functionalist, or equilibrium, theory, as it was applied to social change. Functionalists emphasize the stable elements of a system. Thus, consensus theorists, though not denying that conflict exists, insist that it takes place within a general framework of consensus. Historian Richard Hofstadter, for instance, suggests that all the participants in American political conflicts are still in fundamental agreement with the principles of liberal democratic capitalism, sharing an ideology of free enterprise, self-help, competition, and beneficent greed.[29]

Elitists usually belong to the conflict school of thought, believing that, ultimately, force holds society together. However, force is seldom displayed by the elite. Instead, it is disguised as an ideology supporting the status quo. This ideology, forced on the masses by a manipulative elite, becomes an apparent—though not real—consensus. If this line of reasoning sounds familiar, it is because you have heard it before. Karl Marx was the forerunner of the conflict theorists, in that he maintained that social change is prompted by the self-interest of the ruling class. In discussing the emergence of capitalism, Marx described a consensus that was brought about by a religious ideology, Protestantism.

[29]Richard Hofstadter, *The American Political Tradition* (New York: Vintage Books, 1954), p.vii.

Consensus: Fact or Fiction?

Conflict and consensus views have alternated in popularity depending on the temper of the times. Since the end of World War II, the consensus view has been predominant, just as politicians and educators have favored pluralism as the explanation for the distribution of power. In fact, the stability of the American political system in the face of external and internal conflicts was said to depend on the existence of a widespread consensus.

Of late, however, a number of critics have begun to question the extent of the alleged consensus. Furthermore, they point out that stable or not, the political system has not solved many long-standing conflicts. In addition, critics have challenged the assumption that consensus is necessary if a democratic system is to function. Some maintain that consensus is actually harmful to democracy because it tends to stifle diversity and dissent.[30]

One research study reveals that although a measure of consensus exists when democratic principles are presented in an abstract form, consensus ceases to exist when principles are translated into specific practices.[31] For example, most people agree with the principle that anyone is entitled to buy a house in any neighborhood, so long as he can afford it. But the principle is forgotten when members of a minority group try to move into some neighborhoods. The same study demonstrates that there is wide agreement on the principle of free speech. However, people show great disagreement on the issue of permitting communists or avowed atheists to speak from a public platform.

An even more significant finding emerged from a study undertaken by political scientist Herbert McClosky. He found that what consensus there is on democratic values does not exist among Americans in general, but among political leaders and activists—that is, the political elite.[32]

The authors of the studies on consensus conclude that consensual agreement on the fundamentals of democracy is not necessary for the survival of the democratic political system. Furthermore, those who are outside the democratic consensus disagree in a passive, rather than in an active, way. Their disagreement, then, is based on ignorance and apathy instead of conviction.[33]

Passive disagreement might have been the rule in the past, but recent events indicate that disagreement is being expressed more and more actively. Disagreements on numerous policies and discontent with the slowness with which the government recognizes important concerns as issues have been repeatedly voiced through riots, protests, and demonstrations. Calls for major institutional change, including constitutional reform, are not merely the lone cries of wild-eyed radicals but of respected and conventional personalities. In a recent publication, political theorist Theodore Lowi maintains that the national political system is out of step with the times and that its programs and policies are hopelessly out of touch with the conditions they are supposedly correcting. In effect, he believes that we need a new ideology that addresses itself to

[30]Carl J. Friedrich, *The New Belief in the Common Man* (Boston: Little, Brown, 1942), p. 173.

[31]James W. Prothro and Charles W. Grigg, "Fundamental Principles of Democracy: Bases of Agreement and Disagreement," *Journal of Politics* (May, 1960), pp. 276–294.

[32]Herbert McClosky, "Consensus and Ideology in American Politics," *American Political Science Review* (June, 1964), pp. 361–382.

[33]Ibid., pp. 374–377.

the fundamental issues: "what kind of government, what forms of government, what consequences of government."[34]

The End of Ideology?

The "end of ideology" debate gained popularity in the 1950s during a lull in political conflict. It was developed by such well-known sociopolitical writers as Daniel Bell and Seymour Martin Lipset. The debate centers on the assertion that the fundamental values of American and Western politics no longer produce conflict: They have already been established and are widely accepted. Thus, there is no reason to worry about whether there was consensus over democratic principles. Consensus now has to revolve around specific solutions to the problems that continually arise in society. Because these problems are not ideological, ideology is no longer important or desirable. In fact, a strong ideology leads to extremism and fanaticism, sharpens political passions, and makes people an easy prey to unprincipled leaders, who oversimplify complex problems.

The "end of ideology" view has never been unanimous, and many a debate has raged on the subject.[35] In fact, disagreements about whether our nation is consensual and pluralistic indicate that ideology is still very much with us. But the "end of ideology" view seems particularly ill-conceived now, when the emergence of the New Left and the radical right, to say nothing of the peace movement, the black nationalist movement, and the Women's Liberation movement, seem to point to a rebirth of ideology. In fact, people involved in these movements often complain that the lack of commitment to an ideology—except perhaps the commitment to profit—has caused our political system to stagnate by offering superficial and short-term reforms rather than solutions to basic problems.

EXTREMIST POLITICAL IDEOLOGIES: RIGHT AND LEFT

We have seen that there are individuals who are "deviant," in that they choose not to live by the norms of society. There are also people who are deviant in terms of the political system. These individuals prefer to remain outside the broad—and imperfect—ideological consensus existing within society. But the point of departure for their deviant ideologies is usually found within our political system—they simply stretch political expression to extremes. For instance, extremists of the right stretch the conservative viewpoint to extremes that are contrary to the ideology of our system. Extremists of the left stretch the liberal viewpoint in the same way.

The Radical Right

Radicalism usually occurs when people become polarized over specific issues. However, radicalism—or political intolerance, as Seymour Martin Lip-

---

[34]Theodore J. Lowi, *The End of Liberalism* (New York: W. W. Norton, 1969), p. xi.
[35]Chaim I. Waxman, *The End of Ideology Debate* (New York: Simon and Schuster, 1969).

set calls it—has always been a part of the American political process.[36] The current complaints of the radical right are that there is a breakdown of the moral fiber of the nation; that there is a conspiracy that is controlling the government for the purpose of eventually selling it out to the communists; and that liberal ideas serve the communist cause.[37] Political scientist Robert E. Lane calls the conspiracy theory that runs through radical movements "cabalism." He explains cabalism as the "idea that there is some secular but distant and incomprehensible power in the world controlling the destinies of men."[38] The conspiratorial group that operates behind the scenes in the United States is said to be made up of members of big business families (the Fords, DuPonts, Rockefellers), international bankers, Jews, union bosses, racketeers, or communists.

Political sociologist Daniel Bell, among others, suggests that the politics of the radical right appeal to people who are under stress because of anxieties relating to their status. These anxieties are suffered both by those who are downwardly mobile and those who are upwardly mobile. Status inconsistency appears in periods of rapid social change and technological innovation. In such times, wealth, status, and power tend to fluctuate. Some of the people whose status has previously been secure begin to feel less secure. Others find that although their status has improved in some ways, it remains low in other ways. Thus, they feel frustrated. For instance, a white Protestant who has worked very hard all his life and has reached a secure middle-class standard of living may feel threatened by the ethnic family moving in next door who have prospered because they own a small business. The member of the ethnic family, though proud of his new wealth, feels that he has a lower status than has his Wasp neighbor. Both of them are likely candidates for radical right politics. They may be attracted to a form of superpatriotism, and release their hostilities against targets such as the United Nations and the eastern intellectuals.

Bell concludes that the radical right is really fighting modernity or social change under the guise of slaying the dragon of communism. In reality, what the radical right tries to defend is its fading dominance. This dominance was once exercised through the institutions of small town America, which controlled social change. But it is precisely these institutions that a modernist society is increasingly questioning.[39]

The New Left

The radical youth movement known as the New Left emerged recently. It bears little resemblance to the traditional American left, represented by New Deal reformers, or even to the Old Left, represented by the followers of classical Marxism. In fact, the most radical members of the Old Left have no interest in reshaping American society: They simply express sympathy toward the

[36]Seymour Martin Lipset, "Three Decades of the Radical Right," in Daniel Bell, ed., *The Radical Right* (Garden City, N.Y.: Doubleday Anchor Books, 1964), p. 446.

[37]Daniel Bell, *The Radical Right* (Garden City, N.Y.: Doubleday Anchor Books, 1964), p. 8.

[38]Robert E. Lane, *Political Ideology* (New York: The Free Press, 1962), p. 114.

[39]Daniel Bell, *The Radical Right*, p. 16.

Soviet Union and China. As for members of the liberal middle class, they accept the mechanics of the American system—consensus and coalition politics—but disagree with some of the goals and procedures of the system. In contrast, members of the New Left distrust and are disillusioned by the political system. In fact, they desire change in the very foundations of society.

It is important to recognize that the label New Left is imprecise. It covers a wide range of individuals and groups—some that deny the label, and others that claim but do not warrant it. The New Left includes strains of several other movements in its background. It borrows from existentialist philosophy the principle that although our lives may be meaningless, we create our own meaning through our actions. Our actions, then, should be directed toward the rejection of murder, the insistence on the value of all men, and the establishment of world peace and prosperity. The Beatnik, civil rights, and antiwar movements have all contributed important elements to the New Left movement.[40]

Other generalized goals besides the goal of profound change unite the movement: participatory democracy, equality, liberty, and community. However, hardly any specific goals or tactics give it unity. The generalized goals appeal to a large portion of the population because they are the basic values of the democratic ideology. But the values have basically remained goals. Consequently, although our children are taught that peace, justice, equality, and freedom are elements of our political and social systems, they eventually learn that this is true only in theory. The reality is much different and much less appealing.

[40]Parts of this section are based on Lyman T. Sargent's *New Left Thought: An Introduction* (Homewood, Ill.: Dorsey, 1972), pp. 1–10.

THE POLITICAL BEHAVIOR OF THE AMERICAN VOTER

Sociologists have been particularly interested in the social bases of politics. They are concerned with discovering which social dimensions affect the political behavior of members of society, with what ultimate results in the political system. Some of their findings reveal that the political opinions we hold, and express through our political behavior, are hardly arrived at in a logical, rational manner. For instance, in one study, researchers discovered that people who are insecure and frightened of the future tend to be politically conservative. They find solace in the promise of stability, the praise of old values, and the warnings against experimentation with newfangled ideas.[41]

Political Socialization

Another factor affecting political behavior is political socialization. Socialization differs according to the individual's particular set of circumstances: his social class, race, ethnic group, occupation, sex, age, religion, and geographic region. Political socialization is one aspect of our general socialization; it initiates us into the concepts, knowledge, and opinions of our political system. This process will have indelible results on our own political opinions and behavior.

Political socialization begins in the family and continues in school and throughout our adult lives. Research indicates that a vast majority of children express sympathy for the political choices of their parents.[42] Furthermore, parental party preference is maintained throughout adult life by 69 percent of those who remember their parents' party preference.[43]

Even though the family is important in shaping political preferences, recent studies show that the school is an even more important and effective instrument of political socialization, especially in the development of specific political opinions.[44] Of course, the political opinions taught in schools reflect the dominant values of our society. Schools, then, are expected to turn out loyal, law-abiding citizens. They are eminently successful in this attempt in white, middle-class areas and much less so in what are called disadvantaged areas. In disadvantaged areas, the schools attempt to present a false image: The ideal citizen is more loyal than politically active.[45]

Perhaps there is a connection between attempts to teach political passivity and the low rate of political participation by members of low socioeconomic classes. Statistics on the 1968 presidential campaign indicate that whereas 18 percent of upper-middle class persons engaged in six or more kinds of political campaign activity, only 4 percent of those in the working classes participated

[41]Herbert McClosky, "Conservatism and Personality," *American Political Science Review* (March, 1958), pp. 27–45.

[42]Robert D. Hess and Judith V. Torney, *The Development of Political Attitudes in Children* (Chicago: Aldine, 1967), Chapter 2.

[43]V. O. Key, Jr., *Public Opinion and American Democracy* (New York: Alfred A. Knopf, 1961), p. 301 and Table 12.1, p. 296.

[44]Robert D. Hess and Judith V. Torney, *The Development of Political Attitudes*, p. 101.

[45]Kenneth P. Langston and M. Kent Jennings, "Political Socialization and the High School Civics Curriculum in the United States," *American Political Science Review* (September, 1968), p. 864.

to that degree.[46] This study is only one of the more recent of numerous studies in which the findings were significantly similar.

Class-Conscious Voting

Class consciousness is not an important factor in the United States—in one study, only 60 percent of the respondents admitted that they thought of themselves in class terms, and 5 percent rejected the idea of classes outright. Yet class identification has a recognizable impact on political attitudes.

[46]Marian D. Irish and James W. Prothro, *The Politics of American Democracy* (Englewood Cliffs, N. J.: Prentice-Hall, 1971), p. 174 (Table 5–2).

TABLE 9.2   WHO VOTES FOR EACH PARTY: DIFFERENCES IN VOTER
SUPPORT GIVEN THE DEMOCRATIC AND REPUBLICAN PARTIES
(BY MAJOR SOCIAL GROUPS)

	1948		1956		1960		1964		1968	
	D	R	D	R	D	R	D	R	D	R
Religion										
Protestant	47%	53%	36%	64%	37%	63%	63%	37%	38%	62%
Catholic	66	34	52	48	83	17	79	21	60	40
Jewish	100	0*	74	26	89	11	89	11	93	7
Race										
White	53	47	40	60	47	53	64	36	41	59
Negro	65	35	82	18	72	28	100	0*	97	3
Education										
Grade school	69	31	49	51	55	45	80	20	62	39
High school	54	46	43	57	53	47	69	31	48	52
College	24	76	26	74	36	64	54	40	37	63
Age										
34 and younger	63	37	45	55	52	48	72	28	48	52
35 to 44	61	39	45	55	51	49	68	32	52	48
45 to 54	47	53	42	58	55	45	69	31	43	57
55 to 64	43	57	35	65	44	56	70	30	41	59
65 and over	50	50	36	64	38	62	55	45	45	55
Sex										
Male	57	43	43	57	53	47	65	35	45	55
Female	53	47	40	60	46	54	69	31	47	53
Occupation										
Professional and managerial	19	81	32	68	45	55	58	52	38	62
White collar	50	50	35	65	48	52	65	35	45	55
Skilled and semiskilled workers	77	23	52	48	59	41	77	23	52	48
Unskilled workers	74	26	68	32	59	41	83	17	60	40
Farm operators	64	36	37	63	33	67	64	36	45	55
Union membership										
Non-union families	44	56	36	64	44	56	62	38	56	44
Income										
Lower (less than $5000)	65	35	42	58	47	53	74	26	51	49
Lower middle ($5000-$9999)	69	31	46	54	46	54	71	29	45	55
Middle ($10,000-$14,999)	38	62	26	74	46	54	56	44	52	48
Upper middle ($15,000+)	49	51	42	58	55	45	71	29	32	68
Community Size										
Metropolitan areas	60	40	43	57	58	42	72	28	60	40
Cities (over 50,000)	—	—	52	48	50	50	64	33	55	45
Towns (2,500849,999)	48	52	37	63	40	60	61	39	45	55
Rural (under 2,500)	67	33	39	61	48	52	69	31	37	63

*Fewer than 1 percent of respondents favored the Republican candidate in these instances
†Rounding error.

SOURCE: Survey Research Center, University of Michigan. (Composite from SRC studies.)

A very general observation is that those who think of themselves as middle class tend to be politically conservative, whereas those who think of themselves as working class are politically liberal. However, these labels have several dimensions and convey different meanings to different individuals. Thus, although low-status individuals accept the liberal belief that government should intervene to help the underprivileged, they are not wholly liberal in their attitudes toward social change and in their tolerance for the rights of others. For instance, on the bread-and-butter issue "Should the government make sure that people have more jobs and better wages?" 32 percent of the working-class individuals strongly agreed, but only 13 percent of upper-middle individuals agreed. However, on the issue of open housing, which would allow blacks to move into white neighborhoods, 6 percent of the working class and 10 percent of the upper-middle class strongly agreed.[47]

Class consciousness is more apparent and persistent in voting behavior. Generally, members of the working class vote Democratic, whereas the middle and upper classes tend to vote Republican. However, because there are no sharp differences among classes, and very little difference between Republicans and Democrats, both parties receive votes from all social classes. In addition, recent elections have shown a marked decrease in class-aware voting. The significance of such voting patterns is further reduced by issues of war or foreign relations or by the appearance of charismatic candidates. The relationship between voting and class awareness is most apparent during periods of economic depression and may persist into periods of prosperity.[48]

Regional Voting

Although, at one time, regional differences were considered very important, the mass media have had a leveling effect, and there are now more similarities than differences among regions. Generally, the South, the Far West, southern New England, and the urban centers still vote Democratic, whereas the Midwest and rural areas vote Republican. But the real difference seems to lie in the extent to which nonconformity is tolerated in different sections of the country—to a great extent in the West and to a small extent in the South. In short, then, although regional differences show minimal influence on broad political issues, attitudes on some specifics remain regionally distinctive.[49]

Ethnic and Religious Voting

Class status has a much more profound influence on political opinions and behavior than has religion. On a national level, however, Congregational, Presbyterian, and Episcopalian voters display more conservative attitudes and vote more heavily Republican than do Jewish, Catholic, and Baptist voters, who tend to vote Democratic.

For Jews and Catholics, religion does seem to play a more significant role than does social class. These two religious groups tend to vote Democratic even when they belong to an upper-middle class group. Such voting behavior on the part of Jews may be explained by their long-standing liberal tradition and by the Democratic party's opposition to Nazism abroad and anti-Semitism at home. The voting behavior of Catholics may be explained by their ethnic background. When immigrants from Italy, Poland, Ireland, and other Catholic countries arrived in eastern cities, they were absorbed by the Democratic party machinery. Because party identification is the strongest influence on political behavior, the descendants of these immigrants may simply be expressing old loyalties by voting Democratic.[50]

[47]Ibid., p. 178.
[48]Ibid., p. 181.
[49]Ibid., p. 182.
[50]Angus Campbell and Homer C. Cooper, *Group Differences in Attitudes and Votes: A Study of the 1954 Congressional Elections* (Ann Arbor, Mich.: Survey Research Center, Institute for Social Research, University of Michigan, 1956), p. 36.

Race and national origin have the same effect on voting and political opinion. A group suffering from a low status because of race or national origin will tend to vote on issues and candidates that represent the group's interests. Black Americans show evidence of being interested in gaining local control of their communities. Thus, on a city level, they are organizing behind black candidates. On a national level, they are the most issue-oriented group, tending to vote as a group on issues and candidates.

SUMMARY

The institution of government arises out of man's need for social order. When social control can no longer be adminstered on a family basis because of the size and complexity of a society, some kind of agreement is entered into by members of society and one or a group of their representatives. The customs and traditions that build up around this process become the institution of government.

To be acceptable to members of society, government must have authority. Authority may have a basis in tradition, in reason and the law, or in the charisma of a leader. Authority may be defined as institutionalized power. In turn, power is the ability of one person or group to influence the behavior of another person or group in a desired direction. Ultimately, such an ability is derived from force or the threat of force.

The authority of government must also be legitimate to be accepted. Thus, a substantial number of citizens must believe that the power of government is justified because it reflects their own beliefs and values. Some governments begin in violence and earn legitimation; others begin legitimately but undergo a crisis of legitimacy when they engage in actions contrary to the central beliefs of a society.

The state is the formal, abstract counterpart of government. Its elements are territory, population, government, and sovereignty. The state's chief aim is to impose organized political control over its citizens, and it can do so because it has a monopoly over the legitimate use of force within its territory.

The organization of society into nation-states is a comparatively recent event in history. The creation of a central government to oversee a particular territory in which people had similar characteristics developed in those people a sense of unity. This sense of unity became so strong that, despite great differences, the people of a nation think of themselves as "we" as opposed to "they"—they being all outsiders, or foreigners.

Government ultimately derives legitimate authority not simply through force but because of an ideology. An ideology is a system of beliefs, attitudes, and values that members of a society accept as valid and true. Political ideologies attempt to explain, interpret, and rationalize why one kind of government is best for a society. The ideologies that underlie the most prominent modern political systems are democracy, totalitarianism (fascism and communism), and authoritarianism. Sociologists consider that ideologies are important because they determine, to a great extent, human political behavior.

The political system of the United States is based on the ideology of democracy. However, many democratic principles have not been put into practice.

Among the most important is the principle that power is centered in the people. In our mass society, power has been transferred into the hands of an elite composed of the leaders of various interest groups. According to pluralist theory, the ruling elite is responsive to the will of the people through elections. Pluralists also maintain that competition and rivalry among interest groups keep the leaders from becoming a true ruling elite. Decision making in the United States is a process of negotiation and bargaining among many interest groups. On the other hand, according to elitist theory, the elite pursues its own interests, which may not be in conflict with the interests of the people but nevertheless do not reflect their will.

When issues polarize the citizenry, a proportion of it becomes subject to extremist political expressions. Such political expressions are considered deviant because their principles and procedures contradict the ideology of society. The radical right often attracts people who are experiencing frustrations caused by a change in some dimensions of their status. The radical left, represented by the New Left, is essentially a youth movement, the goals of which are in the tradition of Western civilization. The New Left attracts people disillusioned with the disparity between the ideals and practices of the political and social systems.

The American voter is influenced in his political behavior by psychological and, particularly, social factors. His political opinions and party identification are largely acquired in the process of socialization within the family and school. Social class, religion and ethnicity, and geographical region also influence party identification and voting behavior.

Almirante & the once & future fascism

Fascism was the Italian version of the totalitarian ideology of the right. It offered post-World War I Europe quick solutions to complex problems and propelled it into a second horrible holocaust. Supposedly dead since the end of World War II and the creation of the Italian Republic, neo-fascism is increasingly coming back to life in a nation in which democracy has not taken deep enough roots and in which problems continue to outnumber solutions. The appeal of quick, authoritative solutions—though they are arbitrary—of a charismatic leader, and of a messianic hope for the future seem unabated. The following interview with the leader of Italy's legal neofascist party (MSI) may offer some clues to the fascination this ideology has for many.

□□□

Rome

In the last two years a growing number of Italians have voted for the extremist Right [5 percent in 1970 regional elections, 14 percent in 1971 local elections, mainly in the south]. Some political pundits say their vote is one of disgust with the slow pace of change, the frustration of constant strikes, the rising cost of living and unemployment. Others point

to a man, the Honorable Giorgio Almirante, National Secretary of the Movimento Sociale Italiano (MSI), Italy's legal neofascist party.

Giorgio Almirante did one stint as the party secretary in the late forties. His return to power and to a position as deputy in parliament marks a resurgence of interest in his neofascist party politics. But to be a rightist in Italy, which can also mean being a member of the Liberal or Monarchist parties, is one thing. To come right out and say you are a neofascist and a member of the MSI is another. For although there are many who still remember Mussolini as the man "who made the trains run on time," the vocal majority loathe the neofascists.

But Giorgio Almirante pulls thousands into the piazzas. The Romans love what he says, and they adore the pomp and circumstance of his performance. His speaker's platform is the highest in town, and the music is martial. His voice combines the melody of a priest at high mass and the syrup of a Latin lover.

Almirante's headquarters are in a seedy palazzo. It's shabby, but people are working. The Onorevole has his entourage on the floor above. The waiting room's brown velvet chairs are the essence of the style known as Mussolini modern. His own office has a sky-high ceiling, creamy brocade walls, parquet floor and big, stiff antique furniture. Flags and banners festoon the walls. Giorgio Almirante is the only one who doesn't look lost in the theatrical setting. . . .

Q: How long have you been a member of the Movimento Sociale Italiano?

Almirante: I was one of the founders of the party 25 years ago. I served as secretary from 1947 until 1950 and began again as secretary in 1969.

Q: Was your involvement in the Fascist party an intellectual one or did you just slip into it, as many Italians say they did?

Almirante: I began as a boy. I remember becoming a *balilla* when I was nine. Then I became an *avanguardista* and finally a member of the GUF movement, that is, a university Fascist.

Q: What does fascism mean to you?

Almirante: It means a remarkable part of my life. I remained a Fascist until the very end. I was 31 when Mussolini died. They were important years for me, the years in which a man becomes a man, years of war and of peace. I saw many of my friends killed. I remember that period of fascism with the same affection one feels toward a woman one loves. I'm no saint. I have erred as a man, but from a political standpoint I did nothing wrong. I fully shared the idea of fascism.

Q: But what was that idea, exactly, the idea of fascism?

Almirante: I repeat, it was part of my life. Millions of Italians lived the same experience. I am pained that most of them feel they have to deny it. I am proud of it. But after the war I found myself in a different world, a world I didn't know, the world of democracy. But I was fortunate. In 1948 I was already a government deputy, a representative of the MSI. In parliament I became well acquainted with Italian democracy, and I have learned to value liberty. As a member of the opposition, a member of what many people call neofascism, I have had to defend my own freedom. Our party is the only one that has never had responsibility in government, has never been in the majority. All the others—Liberals, Monarchists, Communists—have been in the majority. But we have always been persecuted, politically and personally. I was persecuted, sentenced to a year of political confinement for giving a speech in Piazza Colonna.

Q: What was that speech about?

Almirante: I gave the speech in 1947. I was all sentiment, and I defended the fighters who struggled to win for fascism. They were people like me who believed in what they had done. The minister of the interior, Onorevole Scelba, feared and hated us because we were gaining popularity. He sent the police, and they threw me off the platform and sentenced me to a year of political confinement. I, who was a Fascist and therefore totalitarian, tyrannical and I don't know what else, had been free under the Fascist regime but was persecuted under the democratic regime for my ideas, not my actions. So I learned, right there, the value of liberty. In these last years I have also recognized the defects of Italian democracy. It is hopelessly inefficient. In parliament they don't speak of real problems, interests and business but of center Left and center Right—things people don't care about or understand. This Italian system does not defend the real interests of the nation. Much of what I learned under Mussolini is valid today.

Q: What is valid today?

Almirante: Love of country, the idea of the state, the need for law, order and discipline. We need cooperativism, collaboration between classes to oppose the Marxist class struggle and capitalist classism.

Q: What do you mean by cooperativism?

Almirante: Let me explain. I am a deputy of the MSI, a part of the party. My party and all the others present to the voters a list of men who are loyal party members. So what we elect is a parliament that represents only parties, not economic interests. We should have representatives elected by the engineers, doctors, professors in addition to those who represent political ideas. Then we would have a parliament marrying politics and techniques with competence and interests.

Q: Where does fascism exist today?

Almirante: Nowhere. There are authoritative regimes in Spain, Greece and Portugal, but it is inexact to call them fascist.

Q: Then what is the difference between totalitarianism and fascism?

Almirante: Fascism under Mussolini was a totalitarian regime without a doubt. The neofascism of the MSI is not totalitarian because I value freedom and intend to defend it for myself and for others.

Q: What are the aims of the MSI?

Almirante: Like all other parties, we want to become the majority and to rule the country. However, our political aim is justified by a programmed end.

Q: If the MSI governed, would there be other parties in the political arena?

Almirante: No one can answer that. Suppose, to be absurd, we got 320 deputies. We would then govern alone. But if we get 50 or 100, we cannot govern alone.

Q: Who needs neofascism today?

Almirante: The program of the MSI is valid in every Western country. It's not so different from what de Gaulle had begun to realize in France. Classes are represented in their parliament, and their social system invites collaboration between employer and worker.

Q: Onorevole, I have lived in Italy for four years, and I have seen the country change precipitously. There is an economic crisis, unemployment and a rise in the cost of living. The crime rate in Rome has risen tremendously. There are strikes almost every day. What does the MSI propose to do about the situation?

Almirante: The economic crisis is very serious, as are all the other conditions you mention. We maintain that all of these conditions have a political cause. Conditions here began to deteriorate exactly 11 years ago, when Italy's political system turned toward the left. The ills we suffer right now are the fault of the Christian Democrats [DC], the center party. They began in 1960 and 1961 to collaborate with the Socialists and then with the Communists. At the same time, they completely closed out the parties on the right.

Q: Why did the DC close off the Right?

Almirante: Because the DC suffers from an old Italian ailment—leftism.

Q: What would the MSI do?

Almirante: Easy. We'd keep the Left out of the government. That would be the beginning of responsible government.

A: Do you find a parallel between the situation that existed in Italy at the time of Mussolini's rise to power and today?

Almirante: Yes, it's very similar. Then too there was the Communist and Socialist attempt to take over. There were strikes and violence in the piazzas. There was widespread discontent. But the economic situation was different. Italy had a balanced budget after World War I.

Q: Do you think there is an Italian national character, and if so, does it need to be ruled by authoritarianism?

Almirante: The Italians have a Mediterranean mentality. They are highly individualistic and undisciplined, so in important moments they need authority and discipline. A system that is too tolerant is a mistake in this country.

Q: What is your position on the much-discussed divorce law?

Almirante: We're against it. The standard of living in Italy is very low. Many men emigrate to find work. They leave their families behind. Being Italians, they need women, and they forget about their wives and their 12 children. With the Italian divorce law all you have to do is to live apart for five years. It's up to the judge to decide how much financial support must be given to the wife. Maybe she gets only $50 a month. Then tragedy strikes. The wife shoots the husband or vice versa. Sometimes the wife ends up as a streetwalker. When the divorce law was passed, we were alone in opposing it. Now there is talk of modifying the law to give guarantees to the children and wives.

Q: What is your position on abortion?

Almirante: The party has no stand, but I maintain that legal abortion could be useful if carefully applied.

Q: And what about birth control?

Almirante: That is indispensable. Mussolini's fascism was mistaken when it said we should produce many children. We are already too many.

Q: What do you think of the Catholic church today, the Christian church as liberalized under Pope John?

Almirante: I think that the Church cannot be liberal, modern or progressive. Either you believe in God or you don't.

Q: This new liberal Church, which says that every man should live under the direction of his own conscience, and the MSI, which says that under a neofascist regime every man lives first for the state and secondly for his own conscience—how could the two exist together?

Almirante: The countries that support the so-called modern Church are the ones that supported Martin Luther 400 years ago. If Luther was right that man can communicate with God without the mediation of an established church—and this is what the modern Catholics say—then the pope should step down because he's not needed. But if the Holy Father remains and the Vatican preserves its spiritual dominion and its wealth, then the Church should not accept these Protestant theses. I think the Church should let us believe in God the way we were taught to.

Q: What would the schools, theaters, newspapers be like under neofascism?

Almirante: They'd be free but clean.

Q: What do you mean by clean?

Almirante: It's enough to open the newspaper to see the dirt. For instance, there are 30 ads today in *Il Tempo* for "social relations." That means prostitution, which by Italian law can be practiced in the open but not in a closed place. These ads are punishable. But no one gets punished. Under neofascism we'd either abolish the law and say, "Ladies and gentlemen, prostitute yourselves," or we'd enforce it. Take the schools. In Rome two teachers were fired because they were of the Right. That wouldn't happen with us.

Q: What about the state theaters?

Almirante: I don't want to establish a preventive censorship because the theaters are supported by those who go, but I think we should produce films and plays that would be healthy and useful to public opinion, above all for youth. If we are not going to have preventive censorship, then we must have education of the people by the state. Perhaps in the theaters we'd just have the classics.

Q: From where do the student strikes emanate? Aren't students dissatisfied with the rote learning they get in Italian schools?

Almirante: No. All the student strikes in this country and everywhere in the world are fomented by the Left. Even in your country. You see university students marching against the Vietnam war. If they were not taught by the Left, they'd be marching to support the soldiers.

A: But in the United States there are many who oppose the war.

Almirante: They oppose the war because they don't want to fight. I admire the Americans who have fought in Vietnam for years. They're in Vietnam not because it's a war of conquest but because their country and their flag orders them to be there. The boy who goes there, risks his life, often dies. He can't even bring home a piece of Vietnamese earth to say

to his woman, "I conquered something." It pains me that the American students don't respect these men, and that they are opposed by a lazy, worthless bunch of drug addicts. It's not a question of a just or unjust war. Many wars are unjust. The Trojan war was unjust, but everyone admires Hector and Achilles.

Q: What is your opinion of Mussolini?

Almirante: I loved him. In the last years, when we fled to the north together, we were very close. He lost because events were bigger than he was. It's ugly to lose.

Q: And what did you think of Hitler?

Almirante: I never liked him.

Q: Do you think that Mussolini made a mistake by going along with Hitler?

Almirante: It was a mistake made by those who threw Mussolini into Hitler's arms. Mussolini hated the Germans, right up to the end. He tried to reach an agreement with Laval and Chamberlain.

Q: Who threw him into Hitler's arms?

Almirante: The English, Americans and French. Laval and Mussolini made an agreement early in 1935 to maintain the Italian-French-English alliance in Europe. In return we were to be given a free hand in Africa. After Laval got back to France, he was overthrown, and France and the others promoted sanctions against Italy.

Q: What was Mussolini's attitude toward the Jews?

Almirante: He had many Jewish friends. The first financiers of the party were Jews. There were Jews in the government.

Q: Are there Jewish members of MSI?

Almirante: Yes. many. We recently won the elections of the Council of the Order of Lawyers of Rome. The second man elected was a Jew.

Q: Where do most of your votes come from, geographically and socially?

Almirante: More from the center south than from the north. Socially from many classes, but chiefly from small businessmen and the proletariat. We do have some noblemen.

Q: If [Premier Emilio] Colombo is unable to form a new government and there are elections this spring, will there be a swing to the right?

Almirante: Without a doubt. We will get lots of votes. If we won, we'd keep the Communists out of the government.

Q: If the government moves to the right, what do you think Nixon's reaction will be?

Almirante: He won't be sorry. Remember that your Rogers said that Americans liked Italian spaghetti but not with Chilean—that is, communist—sauce. Our spaghetti won't have any communist sauce.

Q: Do you think that the Mediterranean is in danger?

Almirante: Listen, the Mediterranean is threatened by communism. When Tito dies, there will be trouble in Yugoslavia. Don't be duped by Italians who talk of free communism or Italian communism. They take their orders from Russia. Believe me, the whole West will be delighted if Italy elects a rightist government.

tHE fROG-HAiR pROblEM

We have long lived with the myth that any red-blooded American boy can grow up to be president. But of late we are hearing from many sources that to become and remain even a candidate for political office, one must have money. This reality is very uncomfortable to live with, especially for people nurtured in the ideology of democracy. According to this ideology, the best-qualified individual, and the one favored by a majority is elected to public office. As it turns out, the one who has the most "frog hair" (money) or the one who is able to get it is the successful candidate. The trials of one politician who is not independently wealthy, and who was not willing to say only what pleased his actual or prospective supporters, are reported in the following autobiographical sketch by Senator Fred R. Harris from Oklahoma.

□□□

The summer I graduated from law school, I was involved in the unsuccessful Oklahoma campaign of Roy J. Turner to unseat the incumbent United States Senator, Robert S. Kerr.

Both Kerr and Turner were oil millionaires. As the impending clash between these colossi of roads (asphalt) grew more apparent and ineluctable, observers rightly foresaw the greenbacking, if not the greening, of Oklahoma in the campaign days ahead.

The sharp ones came out in covies, as they would in any state. Some wanted to be county or town campaign managers for whichever candidate would pay the most. An unprincipled preacher offered to bargain away sup-

Reprinted by permission of Senator Fred R. Harris from *Harper's Magazine*, May 1972.

posed influence with his unsuspecting congregation. An Avon saleswomen was willing to consider—for a price—adding a pitch for a candidate to her usual sales promotion to regular-route customers. And there were the ubiquitous importunings of hundreds of poll haulers and hangers-on. They wanted everything from $25,000 to carry a county to a half pint of whiskey to make the day. From fifty dollars for "gas and expenses" to get to the district church conference, to a thousand dollars to pay back taxes to keep a weekly newspaper publishing.

While most were turned away, a common saying of the time was: "The Kerr-Turner race is better than a cotton crop for Oklahoma and twice as easy to pick."

One young man in the Turner headquarters had as his principal duty running to the Federal Reserve Bank every day as soon as it opened to bring back a thousand or so dollars in cash to be doled out to those who came in declaring that victory in their counties required a little money "to put on a barbecue" or "to hire some women to pick up old folks on Election Day." The great old political wizard who managed the Turner campaign, H. W. "Coach" McNeil, would call the young man into his office each morning and hand him a draft to be cashed at the bank. "My boy," he would say every time with solemn and ritualistic regularity, "we're a little short on frog hair." And just as regularly as the scarce "frog hair" came back from the bank in the form of crisp new bills, it was regularly dispensed by the Coach before the sun went down.

That was 1954; a lot of oil has gone under the bridge since then. Ironically, Turner, as rich as he was, had to pull out of the race for lack of money. Robert Kerr went back to the Senate.

I ran, successfully, myself, for the United States Senate from Oklahoma ten years later. By then the big money was in television, rather than individual payments. But the overall campaign costs had actually increased.

I was able to win without the individual payments of the earlier political era because of a skillfully advised use of free news and paid television. I even won in Muskogee, the home of my principal Democratic opponent, the late Senator J. Howard Edmondson, without having spent a *traditional* dime—a fact that damn near destroyed already-ailing paid politics.

In getting elected to the Senate in 1964, I raised money in three stages: bluff and personal loans; bluff and big first contributions; and bluff and a lot of small contributions.

Most of the money eventually came from a lot of small contributions. And I am told now by friends and others involved that the entire campaign—consisting of an unusually tough Democratic primary and runoff with former governor Raymond Gary and former governor and incumbent Senator Edmondson, as well as an arduous general-election contest with the famous Oklahoma football coach Charles B. "Bud" Wilkinson—probably cost around $750,000.

It seems incredible that I could have spent that much. I remember only the deadlines, the daily crises. "WKY-TV is going to release the television spots they have allotted to you at four o'clock this afternoon unless you can come up with $4,500." "The billboard people have to have $3,200 in the morning or they're going to sell the space to Wilkinson." "We can't get our new bumper stickers from the printers unless we can come up with $2,000 by noon." It was a daily—and sometimes hourly—scramble.

I borrowed the beginning money on my personal note at the Security Bank and Trust Company of Lawton, Oklahoma. Three thousand dollars, later increased to six thousand. And we bluffed a lot. The press and the pros will not take you seriously unless you have the money. It doesn't matter what you're saying or what kind of candidate you are. If you don't have the money, they figure you're not going anywhere. So why bother? My

friends and supporters put out the word that the financial situation was better than we had ever expected. The press wrote me up as a serious contender. And the pros read the press.

Next came the big first money. When it's time to spend money—to buy advertising, to hire staff, to open an office—you either have it or you don't.

A lot of old-time Oklahoma farmers still won't plant potatoes, say, unless the signs—astrological signs and the phase of the moon—are right. In campaigns, not many people will give you money or write in a newspaper that you have a chance unless the signs are right. That means unless you seem to have the money.

I spent a great deal of personal time soliciting big contributors. Some were people who liked me and what I said and hoped I'd win. Most were people who disliked Raymond Gary or Howard Edmondson or Bud Wilkinson and thought I presented the best chance of beating the one they most disliked. A few were afraid I might win and decided to put a little on me for insurance.

We parlayed these contributions into a winning campaign. We puffed them up and trumpeted them about. We waved our checks around and dropped every name that would make a thud. And press people and pros began to write and say, "You know, this young Harris may surprise a lot of people." That's all you need. It is not necessary that the opinion molders write or say that you will be a winner. It *is* necessary that they say you *can* be a winner.

We were able to raise enough initial money to come to the attention of those who should have been the natural constituents of what I was advocating. And, most important, we had special coffee-schools for hundreds of those who volunteered, to convince them that they, themselves, could be opinion molders if they were willing to speak out without fear of ridicule for supporting me, and to give them the skills to do so. Advertising we saw as a means of identifying and reinforcing supporters.

I won the 1964 Senate race by being able to identify and enlist the vigorous support of thousands of volunteers. Then, the last—and main—money, as well as work, came from them. But the crucial financial stage was the successful solicitation of a few first big contributors. It only takes a few, but it was here I fell down in my short-lived Presidential campaign in 1971.

The question is: how do you harvest frog hair without getting warts?

Between July, when I decided to run for President, and November, when I announced I was having to close down because I was broke and $40,000 in the hole, I spent $200,000.

About a third of that amount was raised in relatively small contributions (around $100 each) from a great many friends in Oklahoma. About a third of it came from friends and supporters in Los Angeles, Miami, and elsewhere in the country whom I had come to know when I was chairman of the Democratic National Committee. The most crucial—and initial —third came from the personal contributions and solicitations of Herbert A. Allen, Jr., a brilliant young New York investment banker who had gotten involved in politics during the 1968 Presidential campaign, primarily because of his interest in ending the war in Vietnam.

Most people cannot conceive of how costly campaigns are. In the 1970 Senate campaigns, eleven of the fifteen major candidates in the seven biggest states were, themselves, millionaires. The four who were not millionaires lost.

Nelson Rockefeller spent $10 million getting reelected governor of New York, and John Lindsay spent $3 million in his campaign for reelection as mayor of New York City.

The Presidential campaigns of 1968 *reported* expenditures of $44.2 million.

I ran for president because I believed people want—and are entitled to—fundamental change in their lives and in their society. People feel powerless, and they despair of the political process's being able to change much because there is too great a concentration of political and economic power in too few hands. The two hundred largest corporations in America, for example, now account for 60 per cent of all manufacturing, as compared with only 46 per cent at the end of World War II.

I wanted to see the big monopolies like General Motors broken up into more human-size companies, so that the free enterprise competitive system could be given a chance to work. I wanted to reverse the trend toward more and more concentration of economic

power, which translates into an inordinate concentration of political power.

I wanted to see an end to unfair tax loopholes. I believed that a realization of America's promise and ideals requires these and other fundamental and structural reforms to bring about a more equitable distribution of income and power.

You might imagine that these doctrines of the New Populism went down a little better in union halls, college auditoriums, old folks homes, and minority rallies than they did at fund-raising luncheons at "21."

I tended to get more radical when I spoke to a rich group. And there were always some who were willing to bet a little on a candidate who told the truth about the need to try to make the system work and help America live up to what we always said it was. Often my hosts at fund-raising sessions were disappointed, however, that I wasn't a little less candid about what I planned to do if I were elected President. "You lost so-and-so when you mentioned you were against the investment credit."

One man who had given me a sizable beginning contribution and had promised more quit me after I said in a speech that my daughter wondered why a government that could trace Angela Davis to a motel room couldn't stop the heroin traffic if it wanted to. "When he accused the FBI of being racist, that did it for me," he was reported to have said.

Another of my principal backers (neither of these was Allen) became increasingly alienated by my talk about breaking up the shared monopolies that dominate 35 per cent of American industry and artificially set prices at least 20 per cent too high. "Couldn't he just stick to the dope traffic and safe subjects like that?" he asked my campaign manager.

Worst of all was any talk about the capital-gains provisions of the tax laws that are particularly lucrative for Wall Street brokers. Liberals don't get much money from the oil industry, and it's therefore not too difficult to talk of doing something about the oil-depletion allowance. But liberals get a lot of money from Wall Street. Joseph Duffey, former president of Americans for Democratic Action who ran for United States Senator from Connecticut in 1970, chilled some of his best contributors to the point of freezing their pocketbooks when he included the capital-gains tax in his list of tax reforms needed.

Primogeniture is the rule by which the king's eldest son succeeds to his father's throne. It has sometimes been defended on the ground that while you get a lot of bad kings that way, you save a lot of trouble. Americans, at least in principle, would never agree to that kind of system for determining who will exercise political power.

Nor would we agree in principle to the "one dollar, one vote" political system that the oil-rich reactionary H. L. Hunt once advocated in a self-promoting novel he wrote.

Yet consider that the Mellon family in 1968 gave nearly a quarter of a million dollars to the national Republican party, that Nelson Rockefeller and one sister gave over $100,000, and that the Pew family gave nearly $200,000. One thing these families have in common is that their inherited fortunes have large dependence on oil interests. This, taken together with the fact that members of the National Petroleum Council gave the Nixon campaign more than $200,000 in 1968, may not have been unrelated to President Nixon's later veto of his own task force's recommendation that the protective oil import quota system be scrapped in favor of a less protective tariff system. One man, one vote? The overcharged customers in fuel-hungry New England would probably not say so.

Insurance executive W. Clement Stone of Chicago, who gave the Nixon campaign $500,000 in 1968 and who contributed around $1 million to various GOP candidates in 1970, when asked about the size of these contributions, and those he expects to make in 1972, responded, "If a family has wealth in the neighborhood of $400 million, what's a million in gifts?"

Maybe not much to Mr. Stone. But it's quite a bit to a man who has only one vote. And it's no easier to take when he sees he pays more than his share of taxes—while a lot of rich men like Mr. Stone do not—and yet he can't afford essential things like medical care.

It is not just a matter of whether one agrees or disagrees with the political philosophy of the big contributors. Consider Stewart Rawlings Mott, a thirty-four-year-old bachelor who lives in Manhattan and cultivates an extensive penthouse vegetable and flower garden. He recently said, "I go to sleep at night worrying about the right way to plant radishes."

No threat to democracy in that, you say. But Mr. Mott is a political philanthropist whose second hobby, next to gardening, is giving money to politicians who agree with his views in favor of peace and population control, or who will change their views to suit him. During a ten-week period in 1968, he publicly pledged $50,000 each to the Presidential campaigns of Nelson Rockefeller and Eugene McCarthy. He wound up making political contributions, mostly to McCarthy, totaling $365,000 that year.

My father, a small farmer in southwest Oklahoma, is a better gardener than Mr. Mott. He doesn't go to bed worrying so much about the best way to plant things as he does about whether they'll be worth anything after they come up. Presidential candidates do not, as a rule, line up to ask my father his views on national and international affairs. That may be one reason that so many small farmers like him are being pushed off the land by the rich and corporate farmers who receive huge tax and farm payments subsidies.

Mr. Mott is also a good example of why it is so difficult to get liberal politicians to advocate changes that would do more than just *tinker* with fundamental wrongs or simply *add* a little more to existing New Deal-type programs. Mr. Mott probably believes in the free enterprise system of General Motors, which has more revenue than all but nine countries and which should be broken up into at least five companies under present antitrust laws. For the basis of Mr. Mott's inherited political largess is stock in the General Motors Corporation. His father, Charles Stewart Mott, ninety-six, is the senior director of GM and, together with his wife and children and personal foundation, owns four million shares in GM worth something over $300 million.

President Harry S. Truman came to Oklahoma City during his uphill 1948 reelection campaign. After a personal appearance and a national radio speech, he was told by railroad officials that they would not move his campaign train unless he came up with a sizable cash payment. He was President, and, despite the humiliation, he scraped it together with a lot of urgent late-night telephone calls.

I couldn't get *my* train moving again in 1971—just when the populist constituency was beginning to be stirred. But somehow, with the help of those who share my populist belief in the need to turn this country around before it's too late and return it to the people, I intend to keep raising the issues.

One of the prime issues is the fundamental threat to the democratic process posed by the exorbitant costs of campaigning and reliance on the rich to pay them.

The press could be more helpful. *Washington Post* columnist David Broder wrote on November 16, 1971, after I announced out of the Presidential campaign: "Harris quit because he was flat broke, and the prospects for raising money to back a 'populist' candidate who proposed to talk in blunt terms about the maldistribution of wealth and income and taxes in America were nil."

He wrote that if I had been able to stay in the race, win or not, I might have forced the other Democratic candidates—and even President Nixon—to respond to these issues.

Then Broder suggested the contrast between my fate and that of Senator Henry Jackson of Washington, who, he wrote, "... has no more popular support for the presidency today than did Fred Harris.... What Jackson does have is a record that makes him very popular with a certain few people ... who happen to have money to spend on politics. Whatever happens to Jackson's candidacy, the Democratic nominee will have to respond to those [Jackson's] issues, but not Harris's issues because Jackson, not Harris, is the kind of candidate who can raise the money to run a campaign."

The irony is that the *Washington Post*, itself, contributed to that result. As Tom Bethell has written, too harshly, in the *Boston Phoenix:* "To a considerable degree, I think, the campaign of Senator Fred R. Harris of Oklahoma for the Democratic nomination failed because the *Post* decided not to cover it. Most of the Washington press corps followed suit, and Harris found it impossible to be taken seriously—a fatal liability when you're trying to give people reasons to contribute money to your campaign."

Bethell then quoted a letter he had received, responding to his criticism of the *Post,* from Executive Editor Benjamin Bradlee in which Bradlee stated, "We left Harris out because, in the opinion of our experts, he never was anything but a non-starter..."

It's a circle. The press doesn't take you seriously because you haven't got the money. You don't get the money because the press doesn't take you seriously.

What's a poor candidate to do?

He can raise hell and hope that others get as alarmed about the problems and the implications for democracy as he is.

He can do what he can to get new laws. Federal subsidization of and incentives for small contributions to candidates and parties. Rigid and enforceable limits on campaign expenditures, particularly for broadcast media, and size of contributions. A minimum amount of television time at greatly reduced cost for each party nominee for President, Congressman, and Senator.

Meanwhile, he can help to popularize his views—and pay his debts—by giving lectures and writing books and doing magazine articles.

DISCUSSING THE ARTICLES

1. In Mary Simons' interview with the leader of the Italian neofascist party, "Almirante & the Once & Future Fascism," what is the combination of causes for the growing proportion of votes the extremist right is able to muster?

2. Is it popular in Italy to be a self-confessed neofascist? Is it going against the predominant ideology?

3. What is it about Almirante's appearance and his performance that the public likes? Is this typical of totalitarian ideology?

4. Almirante says he feels toward fascism the same affection one feels for the woman

one loves. What does this say about totalitarian ideology? What sort of absorption does it demand? Can one separate other areas of life from the political area?

5. According to Almirante, what are the irony and the shortcomings of Italian democracy? Does American democracy present similar problems?

6. What kind of interest groups would Almirante include as representatives in the political process? Do you think his idea may work better than does lobbying from the sidelines?

7. Does Almirante distinguish between fascism under Mussolini and the neo-fascism of his own party? Why does he state that a tolerant political system—presumably democracy—is a mistake for Italy? What is his view of a modal personality?

8. What do Almirante's ideas about religion, morals, entertainment, education, and patriotism indicate about his commitment to totalitarianism? In what respect are his opinions reflective of this ideology? What of his characterization of antiwar Americans? Does it fit in with the ideology?

9. According to Senator Fred Harris's article, "The Frog Hair Problem," why do most people offer to support candidates to political office? Is there any mention of this in the ideology of democracy? Would this occur if we had a classless society?

10. When do the press and other politicians take you seriously? Does what you say or what kind of candidate you are matter? Does this situation make for responsible government?

11. For what reasons did most people support Senator Harris in his 1964 Senate race? How do you get the attention of the constituents? Whose contribution was crucial in that campaign?

12. What does the senator mean by the question, "How do you harvest frog hair without getting warts?" Do you think most politicians get warts? What does this indicate about interest groups and broker politics?

13. The author states that in the 1970 Senate campaigns, eleven of the fifteen major candidates were millionaires. Does this support the elitist theorists? Especially because the four who lost were not the millionaires?

14. Why did the senator run for president? With which theory of the location of power does he seem to sympathize? Does he favor socialism?

15. What happens to a candidate who says something that displeases his wealthy supporter, or that goes against his interest?

16. Which seems to be predominating in America, one man one vote, according to the democratic ideology, or one dollar one vote, according to the elitist theory?

17. How does Senator Harris characterize himself and his views? Do many echo his ideas? Why isn't something done about it? Why are some issues that are important to the majority never even raised? In your opinion, has this situation created a crisis of legitimacy?

TERMS TO REMEMBER

Government. An institution arising out of the need for social order; it developed within the family, and it lends support to the other institutions of society.

Moral control. Self-control developed by the individual through the process of socialization.

Political control. Control exerted by forces outside the individual.

Traditional authority. According to Max Weber, authority that is based on reverence for tradition—particular actions are right because they have always been done in that way.

Rational-legal authority. According to Weber, a type of authority accepted by members of society because it is based on rational methods and laws and is exerted for their benefit.

Charismatic authority. According to Weber, a type of authority based on the leadership of a person with charisma. A charismatic leader is thought to possess special gifts of a magnetic, fascinating, and extraordinary nature.

Power. The ability of one person or group to direct the behavior of another person or group in a desired direction, under the ultimate, though not always obvious, threat of force. Power underlies authority.

Legitimate authority. Authority that a substantial portion of members of society consider justifiable. A government is considered legitimate if its goals and values coincide with the goals and values of a majority of the citizens.

Crisis of legitimacy. It occurs when the authority of government is not considered justified.

State. The formal counterpart of government, which develops when the activities involved in the process of government become numerous and complex, necessitating special persons to carry them out, as well as a body of laws to define and maintain certain societal values and mores.

Egalitarian society. A stage in the development of society in which no individual dominates the activities of another because there are as many positions of prestige as there are individuals capable of filling them.

Rank society. The second stage in the development of societies, in which there are fewer positions of prestige than individuals capable of filling them. All, however, have equal access to the resources of society.

Nation. A culture group residing within the territory of a political state.

Stratified society. The third stage in the development of societies, in which society is divided into social classes because the individuals filling the prestige positions have gained greater access to the resources of society than have most people.

Ideology. A system of values, ideas, beliefs, and attitudes that a society, or groups within it, shares and accepts as true.

Democracy. An ideology, a philosophy, theory, and political system assuming the basic value of the individual, his rationality, morality, equality, and possession of certain rights.

Autocracy. An ideology directly opposed to democracy, in that government rests in the hands of one individual or group who hold supreme power over the people.

Totalitarianism. A kind of autocracy, of the left or of the right, characterized by a totalist ideology, a single party, a secret government-controlled police, and a monopoly over mass communications, weapons, and the economy by the ruling elite.

Authoritarianism. A type of autocracy in which power is held by an absolute monarch, a dictator, or small elite. Power, however, is limited to the political sphere.

Pluralism. A theory of the distribution of power in our society, according to which power is diffused among numerous interest groups that continually compete with one another and occasionally unite in coalitions to reach compromise solutions.

Elitism. A theory of the distribution of power, according to which crucial decisions are made by a handful of men representing the corporate rich, the military upper echelons, and the political directorate. Neo-elitists claim that the leaders of all organizations eventually come to consider themselves an elite and that their personal interests become the interests of this elite.

SUGGESTIONS FOR FURTHER READING

Aiken, Michael, and Mott, Paul E. *The Structure of Community Power*. New York: Random House, 1970. A collection of readings based on research into the foundations of social power in a community.

Bell, Daniel, ed. *The Radical Right*. Garden City, N. Y.: Doubleday Anchor Books, 1964. Distinguished sociologists contribute to this exhaustive analysis of ultraconservative groups in our society.

Bendix, Reinhard. *State and Society*. Boston: Little, Brown, 1968. Essays in political sociology from a comparative point of view, with particular emphasis on the impact of modernization on various political systems.

Christenson, Reo M., et al. *Ideologies and Modern Politics*. New York: Dodd, Mead, 1971. An up-to-date, readable, and complete account of current ideologies.

Colfax, J. David, and Roach, Jack L. *Radical Sociology*. New York: Basic Books, 1971. Part III of this book contains essays on our political system viewed through the eyes of radical sociologists.

Dryer, Edward C., and Rosenbaum, Walter A., eds. *Political Opinion and Electoral Behavior*. Belmont, Calif.: Wadsworth, 1967. A series of articles drawn from research on the subject matter in the title.

Etzioni, Amitai. *Demonstration Democracy*. New York: Gordon and Breach Science Publishers, 1971. The role of demonstrations in contemporary political life.

Gillam, Richard, ed. *Power in Postwar America*. Boston: Little, Brown, 1971. The distribution of power among different levels of American society as viewed by a number of distinguished social scientists.

Gregor, A. James. *Contemporary Radical Ideologies: Totalitarian Thought in the Twentieth Century*. New York: Random House, 1968. A readable and concise critique of radical ideologies of the left and of the right.

Hoffer, Eric. *The True Believer*. New York: Harper & Row, 1951. A longshoreman turned intellectual speculates on the reasons for joining radical causes.

Horowitz, Irving Louis. *Foundations of Political Sociology*. New York: Harper & Row, 1972. How the state functions in relation to society.

Kolko, Joyce and Gabriel. *The Limits of Power*. New York: Harper & Row, 1972. U.S. foreign policy during the decade 1945–1954, showing the interaction between Congress and the White House and the pursuit of power on an international basis.

Lane, Robert E. *Political Ideology.* New York: The Free Press, 1962. The impact of ideology on political behavior analyzed through psychological concepts.

Lipset, Seymour Martin. *Political Man: The Social Bases of Politics.* Garden City, N.Y.: Doubleday Anchor Books, 1963. A classic of political sociology, the first part of which deals with the underlying motives for the creation of democracy in modern societies.

Mills, C. Wright. *The Power Elite.* Fair Lawn, N. J.: Oxford University Press, 1956. The original elitist theory of the twentieth century persuasively presented.

Miller, Delbert C. *International Community Power Structures.* Bloomington, Ind.: Indiana University Press, 1970. Community power elites in four world cities, their composition and efficacy.

Nordlinger, Eric A. *Politics and Society.* Englewood Cliffs, N. J.: Prentice-Hall, 1970. A collection of essays in comparative political sociology.

Rose, Arnold M. *The Power Structure: Political Process in American Society.* New York: Oxford University Press, 1967. A sociologist gives a pluralist explanation of power distribution in the United States.

Waxman, Chaim I., ed. *The End of Ideology Debate.* New York: Simon and Schuster, 1968. A series of essays by distinguished social scientists on the subject of whether, having attained the good society, we no longer need ideology.

◨ CHAPTER TEN

THE EDUCATIONAL INSTITUTION

In all probability, the majority of us have some unpleasant memories of school. This is unfortunate, because humans are thinking animals who derive great satisfaction from their ability to understand their environment. And education, as organized by the school, has the key to such understanding. But although it is unfortunate, it is hardly avoidable.

Education, or the formal, institutionalized aspect of socialization, does make demands of us. It demands that at five and six years of age, we give up our freedom to play, run, sing, or roll in the grass to be confined in one room. It demands that we submit, perhaps not for the first time but in definite terms, to discipline. It demands that we pay equal attention to many fields of knowledge, though we may be interested in only a few. Finally, it demands that we accept someone else's judgment about what we should study and know.

Because of these demands, almost every child, even one who finds the scholastic experience enjoyable, shares in the triumph that comes at the end of the school year that is well expressed in the ditty, "No more pencils, no more books, no more teachers' dirty looks." Of course, the exhilaration brought by the sudden freedom from routine soon changes into boredom, and perhaps in secret longings to be back in school.

The function of education has changed tremendously in modern society. Education has assumed the burden of training people not only for professions but for almost all jobs in society. In some respects, it even trains people for living in a complex technological society. Because of this fundamental change in function, not only is a large majority of the population educated—in the sense that most people have attended school for a number of years—but, increasingly, people are spending a significant portion of their lives in educational institutions. Naturally, such fundamental changes in the fabric of the educational institution have caused some problems. In fact, education has been and continues to be criticized on many levels and from many sources. Some criticisms are justified, others demand of education something it cannot give. But none can be ignored, for all involve an institution indispensable to a technological society like ours.

THE EVOLUTION OF THE EDUCATIONAL INSTITUTION

In our discussion of culture in Chapter 2, we noted that humans lack a highly developed instinctual system. We also said that humans have the unique ability to engage in symbolic interaction. These human characteristics necessitate and make possible the development of culture. People everywhere prepare new generations for life in society by transmitting their culture. The vehicle through which a society's culture is transmitted is education—a universal institution in all but the most simple societies. But education was not the same as schooling until comparatively recently, because universal schooling is a product of urban industrial societies.

In traditional folk societies, the transmission of culture occurs within the family. In such societies, cultural transmission consists chiefly in teaching the skills necessary for survival in the society, as well as the knowledge of ritual and perhaps mythology or religion. This type of learning generally climaxes in puberty rites, which mark the beginning of adulthood. The knowledge transmitted in traditional societies is easily absorbed by the child as he goes about the business of living, following his parents and trying to imitate them. Thus, there is no need for any outside agency to take care of culture transmission.

In ancient times and the medieval era, cultural transmission through formal means—that is, whereby a definite person was given the function of teaching others a concrete body of knowledge—was the privilege of a small number of men in each society. Only the rich men of Athens were able to enroll their sons in Plato's Academy or Aristotle's Lyceum. And only those studying for the ministry and a few noblemen's sons studying theology or law were admitted to the monastic schools of the Middle Ages.

For the next several centuries, the situation remained much the same throughout the Western world, including the United States. Everywhere, education was reserved for those of means or of noble birth. Even today, education and socioeconomic status are interrelated, as we shall see in this chapter.

The first steps toward mass literacy, if not mass education, were taken in the sixteenth century. The leaders of the Protestant Reformation thought that everyone should be able to read the Bible. The schools established in Protestant nations taught religion and the three R's. Anything more sophisticated was reserved for the leisure class. In fact, the word "school" is derived from a Greek word meaning "leisure."

In preindustrial societies, education was reserved for a small elite because the productivity of the economy depended on those who worked with their hands. The educated person, who did no manual labor, was considered unproductive. Today, the situation has been reversed. In industrial societies, the uneducated person is considered unproductive. There is such a wealth of information and so many specialized occupations that an apprenticeship is inadequate in all but the least skilled jobs. This brought about another change in the role of education. The vast numbers of skilled technicians and professional experts needed by a technological society must be trained by the educational institution. Thus, the goal of education has shifted from the production of a cultivated individual to the production of an expert. And this is true as much in the society in general as in education itself.[1] In many schools, in fact, the individual who is a specialist in methodology, or knows *how* to teach, is preferred by administrators over the individual who has a broad educational range, and knows *what* to teach.

FUNCTIONS OF EDUCATION

We have already touched on the primary function of education: the transmission of culture, which includes the individual's indoctrination into, or his internalization of, his society's culture. You may remember that this function is performed through the process of socialization. Much socialization occurs on an informal basis, in the family before the child is of school age and, later, in the school and neighborhood. *Education* is the formal aspect of socialization—a specific body of knowledge and skills is deliberately transmitted by a corps of specialists.

Innovation and Preservation

In the change from the traditional to the industrial society, the function of cultural transmission changed from simple preservation of culture to *dissemination and innovation*.[2] Traditional societies are stable; change and innovation occur accidentally and infrequently. However, industrial societies are not only characterized by rapid social change but some of their institutions are specifically designed to promote cultural and social change. For instance, research departments of universities and private corporations exist for the purpose of finding new ideas and new methods in different areas of production. Such innovations in theory and technology eventually result in some cultural and social change.

Of course, the *preservative* function of education does not disappear in

[1]Burton R. Clark, *Educating the Expert Society* (San Francisco: Chandler, 1962), p. 3.
[2]A. H. Halsey, "The Sociology of Education," in Neil J. Smelser, ed., *Sociology* (New York: Wiley, 1967), p. 389.

industrial societies. Schools transmit a people's cultural heritage. In them, the child learns the history of his culture, along with its heroes and villains. He reads literature through which he determines the values, beliefs, and attitudes of society. However, more and more time is spent in the instruction of technical and scientific subjects, so students are prepared for life in a technological society. This tendency is deplored by many educators and intellectuals, who maintain that technological instruction, if carried out at the expense of the humanities, will mold us into arid automatons with computer brains.

Recruitment and Preparation for Social and Occupational Roles

To recruit and prepare people for the specialized roles they will fulfill in society is an educational function that arises with growing industrialization. In traditional societies, in which there is little division of labor and hardly any specialization, everyone receives a common upbringing. In industrial societies, in which there is a very specialized division of labor, it is necessary to select and train people for their future highly diversified occupations. Schools perform this function in a twofold manner. First, they familiarize the student with the countless occupations that the society offers. And, later, they train him for whatever occupation he chooses.

The first function is performed informally, by exposing the student to literature and conversation dealing with occupational roles available in society. Who does not remember having to write a theme about "What you would like to be when you grow up"? The second function is deliberate. Beginning with high school, courses are especially geared so enough students will receive the kind of training that will enable them to enter the job market, or at least will give them a start in that direction. It is the responsibility of the schools to make the right training available in the right proportion to fit the job market.

The majority of industrial societies have open stratification systems in which status is achieved. The school system, then, acts as an agent of selection and of allocation of statuses and roles. In short, the individual's performance in school frequently (perhaps always) determines the length of time he remains in school, his choice of a professional or vocational course of study, his eventual occupation, and his consequent status with its attendant wealth and prestige.

Education also functions to prepare us for positive social roles by exerting social control. Through socialization and education, we develop internal controls, that is, we make part of us the fundamental values of society. And the way in which we internalize societal values determines, to a great degree, the kind of person we become. Education also exerts social control through a selective process by teaching us some things and ignoring others, by preparing us for some occupations and not for others. For instance, not even the most progressive school lists courses on how to steal in its curriculum. The role of thief is not one our society is anxious for us to play! By such subtle means, the educational institution prepares us for the roles it considers supportive of the social order.

All human societies display the processes of person selection and person formation. *Person selection* is the process by which people are chosen to perform the tasks needed by society. *Person formation* is the process by which society ensures that such persons will be constantly available.[3] In our society, the educational institution is chiefly responsible for these processes. And because of this function, education is distinctly supportive of the Establishment: It is a bulwark of society.

Integration and Custody

In a heterogeneous, pluralistic society, the schools function as an integrating mechanism to reinforce our feelings of nationhood. For instance, in our society, a major function of the schools has been to integrate waves of immigrants into the mainstream of society. In today's schools, the purpose of integration has shifted from transforming children of immigrants into full-fledged Americans to turning children from various conflicting and disadvantaged subcultures into individuals with a shared cultural identity and purpose. Because we are instructed in the same language, play the same games and engage in the same sports, and are exposed to the same values, we all eventually speak English, play baseball, learn to compete and to be a good sport, at least to some extent. In short, the schools level our most striking differences to make us fit into the scheme of our social system.

Another function typical of advanced technological societies is the custodial function. In our kind of society, young people must remain outside the job market for a long period of time, simply because the economy has no use for them. There are no jobs for young people because most jobs require a great deal of training; jobs requiring little skill are performed by machines. Consequently, a new situation has been created. A larger and larger proportion of young people are spending the best part of their young adulthood—well into their twenties—in institutions of higher education. In effect, then, schools

[3]Hans Gerth and C. Wright Mills, *Character and Social Structure* (New York: Harcourt Brace, 1953), pp. 165 ff.

are occupying young people that the economy doesn't need. Although not all of them graduate from college with degrees, the time they spend there may have a cooling off effect by deflecting the potential hostility of an unemployed and a relatively idle group.[4]

Thus far, we have been discussing the principal functions of the American educational institution. Naturally, some of these functions are the same in all nations. Other functions, however, differ from society to society. China is one nation in which the educational institution is in great ferment because education is one of the means through which leaders hope to create a new human being. "How the Young Are Taught in Mao's China," by Rhea Menzel Whitehead, offers a comparison of the functions of the Chinese educational institution with those of our society.[5]

Additional Functions

Additional functions of education include the bringing together of young people to form friendships and prospective marriages. For many, education becomes the means to self-discovery, to the satisfaction of intellectual curiosity, to the realization of creative potential, and to a general enrichment of life. Perhaps of even more importance is the increased level of tolerance and the heightened commitment to democratic ideals that seem to result from prolonged education.

The relationship of education to democracy was already pointed out in Chapter 9, in which we noted that a certain level of education is essential if democracy is to emerge. Seymour Martin Lipset, who was responsible for the major study in this area, showed that in stable democratic nations the population is almost entirely literate (96 percent). Latin American democracies, which are unstable, have a much lower level of literacy (74 percent). And the literacy rate in Latin American dictatorships is still more significant—only 46 percent.[6]

Lipset's conclusion is supported by other research. One study showed that college graduates have a more tolerant view of minority groups than do high school graduates. It also showed that the more education a person has, the more involved he is in cultural and political events.[7] The findings of another study indicated that educational attainment was closely associated with tolerance toward nonconformists in social, political, and religious areas and with recognition of nonconformists' freedom to express their views in public.[8] Still another study showed that each year of college increases a person's willingness to grant civil liberties to those who lack them. Thus, almost half the seniors in this study were ranked as highly libertarian, but only one in five freshmen was so ranked.[9]

The evidence, then, points overwhelmingly to the positive influences of

[4]Burton Clark, *The Open Door College* (New York, McGraw-Hill, 1960), pp. 569–576.
[5]Rhea Menzel Whitehead, "How the Young Are Taught in Mao's China," *Saturday Review* (March 4, 1972), pp. 40–45.
[6]Seymour Martin Lipset, *Political Man* (New York: Doubleday Anchor Books, 1963), p. 37.
[7]Burton R. Clark, *Educating the Expert Society* (San Francisco: Chandler, 1962), pp. 27–30.
[8]Samuel S. Stouffer, *Communism, Conformity, and Civil Liberties* (New York: Doubleday, 1955).
[9]Hanan C. Selvin and Warren O. Hagstrom, "Determinants of Support of Civil Liberties," *British Journal of Sociology* (March, 1960), pp. 51–73.

education on such values as egalitarianism, democratic principles, and tolerance of minorities and opposition views. There remain, however, questions concerning whether the effects of education are permanent and whether they influence actual behavior. One study, for example, showed that twenty-five years after college graduation, a predominant number of the alumnae polled held values that reflected their social class rather than a liberalizing college influence.[10] Another study claimed that the college-educated show as much actual prejudice as the less educated but that it is of a different kind. The educated may tend to support legal equality, but they also tend to deny social participation to members of groups against whom they discriminate.[11]

STRATIFICATION: IN AND OUT OF SCHOOL

In discussing the evolution of education, we mentioned that there is a relationship between education and the stratification of society. We should change this statement slightly: Education itself is a stratified system, in which the more successful are at the top and the less successful are at the bottom of the scholastic heap. Furthermore, because educational attainment is directly related to an individual's status in society—the more money an individual has, the more schooling he obtains, and vice versa—the institution of education reinforces the stratification system of the society. The schools in our society hold the keys to the student's future. Statistic after statistic points to the increased lifetime earnings obtained by those with high educational achievement. From the discussion of the operation of the stratification system, we know the effect high earnings have on life chances and the way social mobility affects status. Education may be the way out and up for some, but many are, unfortunately, kept in and down simply because they don't have it or because it has been inadequate to their needs.

Cause and Effect

The school you enter and the education you receive largely depends on the social status of your family. Because of the local nature of school systems, pupils attend schools in their own neighborhoods. Inasmuch as residence is a reflection of the stratification system, a lower-class child attends school in a lower-class neighborhood. Thus, the child is immediately at a disadvantage. (It is precisely this type of situation that a number of urban school systems is attempting to change through the busing of pupils to schools in outlying areas. As of this writing, however, the busing issue has not been resolved.) Geographically, the school is likely to be located in an urban area. It is also probably old and run-down because the people in the neighborhood cannot afford to pay high enough taxes for the school board to make repairs. It undoubtedly has only a minimal amount of teaching aids and perhaps not the best of teachers.

But the child's greatest disadvantage comes from his own background. The

[10]Mervin B. Freedman, "Studies of College Alumni," in Nevitt Sanford, ed., *The American College* (New York: Wiley, 1962), pp. 847–886.

[11]James L. Price, ed., *Social Facts: Introductory Readings* (New York: Macmillan, 1969), pp. 287–290.

life style of the poor does not include many of the objects and activities that stimulate intellectual curiosity. Many lower-class parents, most of whom have had very little formal education themselves, do not encourage a positive attitude toward education in their children. Furthermore, schools and their officials are often viewed with the same hostility as other representatives of the Establishment, like policemen and social workers: They are people to be avoided or outsmarted.

The lower-class child has not been socialized to display the personal qualities by which his largely middle-class teachers judge him. He may not be self-disciplined, clean, polite, diligent, and neat. Such a child often has communication problems, too. His family may be non-English speaking, as with Puerto Rican and Mexican immigrants. Or he may have been exposed to an English dialect used in his subculture which, though it may be direct and expressive, can differ considerably from middle-class English.

These negative factors have several effects on lower-class children, especially on those belonging to minority groups. First, such children begin school less prepared and receptive than their middle-class contemporaries, the gap widening until by the twelfth grade, they are 3.3 years behind in academic performance.[12] Second, a huge number drop out of school without completing the requirements for a high school diploma, even though unemployment figures for people lacking a diploma are twice as high as those for people with it. In effect, if a child belongs to a low socioeconomic class and attends school in a lower-class neighborhood, he is, with few exceptions, doomed to a life of unemployment or underemployment or to illegal means of obtaining a livelihood.

This situation is not something that applies only to today's poor. In a recent publication, historian Colin Greer states that the view of the school as the great equalizer, taking in the ill-fed children of immigrants and turning them out as productive members of the middle class, is a myth. In reality, at the turn of the century, the children of immigrants dropped out of school in as great numbers as today's disadvantaged. But they dropped out earlier, in elementary school, and were able to enter the job market as a cheap labor force, whereas today's dropouts have great difficulty finding jobs as unskilled laborers. In his study of school records dating back to 1890, Greer found that about 40 percent of the pupils failed to finish public school. He concludes that school performance seems consistently to depend on the socioeconomic status of a student's family, and that the school thus acts to screen out the poor.[13]

Quality of Education

Not only is the length of time spent in school severely curtailed for a majority of lower-class children, but the quality of instruction they receive in their schools is also below that received by more fortunate children. In a 1961 study, the author reveals that the amount of money spent on schools and, consequently, their quality, is directly proportional to the income of the families

[12]James S. Coleman, The Coleman Report, as quoted in the *San Francisco Chronicle* (April 9, 1969).
[13]Colin Greer, *The Great School Legend* (New York: Basic Books, 1972).

living in a particular neighborhood.[14] Thus, in the same city gross inequalities can exist between schools that are only a few miles apart. It is a good bet that it is the school in the poor, inner-city neighborhood that is old and lacking in adequate facilities, that is understaffed, that has an outdated curriculum and irrelevant counseling, that has large classes, and that has inadequate methods of measuring and testing student performance.

Schools, in addition, are segregated not only by social class, but by race, because the white middle class has all but abandoned the cities for the suburbs. Some communities are attempting to right the existing segregation—which is by law unconstitutional—through the busing of students from the inner city to the suburbs, and vice versa. But these communities are waging an uphill battle from elements, including those in high governmental positions, opposed to changing that stalwart American institution, the neighborhood school.

Here again, we find ourselves faced with a vicious circle of such proportions that a solution is difficult to find. Because lower-class persons—mostly members of minority groups—tend to inhabit slums and ghettos in the inner city, their children must attend the old schools of their neighborhood. And because the people in those neighborhoods are poor, there is an inadequate tax base, so the schools have inferior facilities and often an ill-prepared and a temporary staff. The results are an inferior education for the child, who becomes either completely turned off and drops out or apathetic. In either case, he does not acquire enough knowledge or skills to prepare him for college or a job.

This situation is particularly tragic in light of the findings of a national survey on educational opportunity (1966). In it, James S. Coleman and his associates state that although differences in facilities and curriculum had little impact on the performance of white pupils, they had considerable impact on black pupils. In other words, whereas white children of a low socioeconomic class performed more or less equally regardless of the quality of their schools, black children performed considerably better when the quality of their schools was improved. In particular, their performance improved when the school contained a majority of middle-class children of both races. Other factors that had a positive effect on performance included well-trained, capable teachers, an increase in the number of whites in classes, and the provision of an integrated environment for children at an early age.[15]

Class Conflicts: Middle-Class Teachers, Lower-Class Students

Another factor that is not helpful to the lower-class child's success in school is his teacher. Here again, we must speak in generalities, for undoubtedly there are many idealistic, self-sacrificing teachers who do their best for their students. Nevertheless, the majority of teachers are recruited from the middle class and are upwardly mobile. Consequently, their values often collide with those of their charges.

We have already noted that language is often a barrier to effective communi-

[14]Patricia Cayo Sexton, *Education and Income: Inequality in the Public Schools* (New York: Viking, 1961).

[15]James S. Coleman, et al., *Equality of Educational Opportunity* (Washington, D.C.: U.S. Government Printing Office, 1966), pp. 9, 12, 22, 23, 29, 32.

cation between teacher and student. It does not help the self-image of a child to be told that the way he speaks is incorrect and incomprehensible—especially when his speech is perfectly comprehensible to his peers and family. On the other hand, if the student is encouraged to maintain his speech, he will be effectively cut off from the best-paying positions on the job market. Ultimately, then, the child is damaged in one way or another.

Perhaps the worst offense that teachers commit is making prejudicial judgments about students. These judgments often result in a self-fulfilling prophecy. In other words, because teachers expect little or nothing from their lower-class students, that is often precisely what they receive. Two researchers proved this point by administering a battery of IQ tests to a number of students in a lower-class neighborhood school. The researchers chose a number of names at random. Then, they told the teachers that these children were "potential spurters"—special children to be watched because they should do well in their schoolwork. Later retesting of the children proved the researchers' point. Although these students' IQs had not been higher than those of the other students tested, two years later, the IQs of the students selected had risen above the others. The researchers concluded that preferential treatment by teachers stimulated the selected students to perform well.[16] In short, the "looking-glass" principle is again at work: The reflection of ourselves that we receive from those around us is the image we return, or the kind of person we become.

Higher Up in the Stratification System

In a two–year study of education in New York State, a striking fact emerged: The white, affluent student whose father is a college graduate has a much better chance of succeeding in the public schools than does the student who is not white and affluent and whose parents are not college graduates. The commission entrusted with this study also found that those most likely to achieve low scores on standardized tests, to drop out of high school, and to fail to attend college were the sons and daughters of urban, poor, minority-group parents. The commission concluded that this close parallel between school success and the student's socioeconomic level indicates that American education has failed in some way.[17]

These findings only support what has been known for a long time: The school experience is both more rewarding and more successful for middle- and upper-class children than it is for lower-class children. We can see why by describing the lower-class child's situation in reverse. First, the middle-class child comes from a background similar to that of his teacher. Thus, he meets most of his teacher's expectations immediately and without conflict. Second, he comes from a home in which at least and often both, parents are college graduates. He is motivated, therefore, to follow in their footsteps. In fact, because his parents may simply assume that he will attend college, they reward and strongly encourage academic excellence. Finally, middle-class values

[16]Robert Rosenthal and Lenore Jacobson, *Pygmalion in the Classroom* (New York: Holt, Rinehart and Winston, 1968).

[17]Gene I. Maeroff, "Home Life Linked to School Success," *New York Times* (January 30, 1972).

include self-discipline, responsibility, postponement of gratification in expectation of future rewards, and a strong belief in achievement.

Furthermore, the middle-class child attends school in affluent neighborhoods, which have a favorable tax base. Thus, he has the advantage of pleasant surroundings, up-to-date instructional aids, and the best-trained, most capable teaching and counseling staff. Clearly, all of these features combine to give affluent students a good chance for success in the classroom.

It is not difficult to see why the children of families from high socioeconomic strata are much more likely to remain in school, attend college, and obtain advanced degrees than are those from low strata. Moreover, a college degree is not only a status symbol in our society but confers increased earning potential. For example, in 1968 the mean annual income of males twenty-five years old and over was slightly under $4,000 for those with an eighth-grade education, slightly over $8,000 for high school graduates, and slightly under $13,000 for college graduates. Income, of course, does not follow ironclad rules: Some high school graduates earn more than college graduates. But if lifetime earnings are considered, the earning potential of college graduates is, in general, considerably higher than that of high school graduates. According to one estimate, the person who has a limited education receives in his lifetime one-fourth the income of the well-educated individual.[18]

CRISIS IN THE CLASSROOM

If you were not already aware of it, the preceding discussion should have demonstrated that all is not well in the American system of education. And although many of the problems are directly or indirectly of an economic nature, this is not the only area of concern.

Whatever the root of the problems, American education has, in recent years, undergone a barrage of criticism. Some critics blame the initiation of universal education—according to law, young people must attend school until they are sixteen years old. These people deplore the relaxation of scholastic standards and feel that education has become intellectually inadequate. And, in fact, it is no secret that large numbers of children can't read and that many college freshmen have only minimal standards of literacy. Other critics of American education maintain that because the schools are unnecessarily authoritarian, they effectively destroy children's creativity, spontaneity, and intellectual curiosity. Still others believe that the schools are too permissive and tolerant and that they should teach only the three R's, all other subjects being unnecessary frills.

One of the most vocal critics of the schools is author Charles Silberman. Commissioned by the Carnegie Foundation, his book *Crisis in the Classroom* was the result of a three-and-a-half-year study of education and educators. In it, Silberman describes American schools as grim, joyless places. The atmosphere is oppressive because of petty rules, it is sterile and aesthetically barren, and it is characterized by a supreme lack of civility and contempt toward students. According to Silberman, schools do not teach children how

[18]H. P. Miller, "Annual and Lifetime Income in Relation to Education, 1939–1959," *American Economic Review* (1960), pp. 962–986.

to learn or prepare them for life. Instead, they prepare children to earn a living. They do not teach the appreciation of beauty or the way to use knowledge. Instead, they concentrate on order and control.

Regimentation and Distrust

Because everything in school happens according to the clock, the teacher becomes, in effect, a timekeeper, making sure that the schedule is followed regardless of what must be interrupted. This regimentation results not only in a great deal of wasted time, but it also requires students to spend most of school time waiting for the next activity to begin. Lesson plans add to regimentation. These are adhered to so rigidly that teachers are expected to follow them regardless of what other interest intrigues the students at the time.

Rigidity is part of a basic confusion of ends and means in which the ends are forgotten in the maze of means. Silberman mentions schools that have built fantastic libraries but that do not permit students to read the books. Students only practice taking books off the shelves and returning them. As another example of confusion, a principal sent a memorandum to teachers stating that they were to keep all books away from students because one student had thrown a book out the window.

The emphasis on order and control is particularly noticeable in administrators, who see themselves in the role of managers of an efficient organization. They force teachers to assume the roles of disciplinarians and timekeepers. Furthermore, discipline is defined in very simplistic terms: the absence of movement and noise. Principals seem to be obsessed with preventing children from talking to one another and from moving about. One principal who visited a school for deaf-mutes expressed his admiration for the silence in the school! Silence is unnatural, and so is sitting in one position for long periods of time, especially for children. But the ban on speaking and movement continues throughout school, even in the upper grades in which students must have passes and special permits to use school facilities.

Silberman claims that petty rules (one principal even limited the number of minutes a student was permitted to spend in the lavatory—no more than three) are necessary because the system operates on mutual distrust. Distrust extends all the way from the school board to the students. By the time it reaches the students, it is of such proportions that they are not trusted with anything. The distrust shown by teachers and administration does not permit the student to develop reliability and motivation. On the contrary, it encourages him to remain chronically dependent and makes him think of himself as worthless and incapable of regulating his own behavior.

The Stifling of Independence

Perhaps Silberman's most severe criticism is that schools discourage students from developing a capacity for learning on their own. School personnel assume that education is provided for the student by the teacher. This attitude destroys the student's intellectual curiosity and his desire and capacity to think for himself. At fault is the teacher-student relationship which, Silberman writes, is one of institutionalized dominance and subordination. The teacher represents the taskmaster, the adult world, and the established social order,

whereas the student is most interested in life among his peers. This conflict, though not always apparent, is always present.

Nowhere is the conflict more obvious than in the school's preoccupation with evaluation, which follows the student throughout his scholastic life. Evaluation per se is necessary and helpful, if used in the proper perspective: as a diagnostic tool that shows both teachers and students the areas in which they are weak. However, evaluation is actually used to rate and categorize students into rigid classifications from which they can seldom escape. Evaluation used in this way can have disastrous effects on a student's self-esteem and may lead to the self-fulfilling prophecy of perpetual failure. Of particular concern is the exaggerated importance given to IQ scores, the validity and reliability of which are far from perfect.

The Teacher

Silberman mentions several causes of the school's destructiveness. Above all, he considers the teacher a victim of the system. He thinks the teacher would act with care and concern if he were treated in a professional, trusting manner. But the teacher is not given respect either as a professional or as a human being. Research shows that teachers are given the shabbiest of environments and that they are held in low regard by the rest of the community, as witnessed by their low salaries and their ranking of thirty-fifth from the top in a study of occupational prestige. Teachers work in an atmosphere of meanness and distrust, punching time cards and being ignored on decisions involving curriculum and textbook selection. They work long hours and perform an astonishing number of clerical and menial tasks. Finally, they receive

very little guidance from their supervisors, but are themselves judged not on how well their students learn but on how quiet and orderly their classes are.

Silberman argues that Americans, in the final analysis, have the types of schools they want. He quotes the findings of a Harris poll: Two-thirds of the parents of high school students think that maintaining discipline is more important than student self-inquiry. An innovative teacher, then, risks not only the displeasure of his own administration but of his students' parents as well. It is a small wonder that many teachers become insensitive and brutalized by the system.

The Student

As for students, they develop different systems for survival. The goal of education becomes for many to get through school with a satisfactory record and minimum discomfort. Thus, learning is no longer the purpose of going to school. Instead, the performance of daily tasks is an end in itself. Survival tactics include finding out which answers a particular teacher wants—the answers need not be correct but must simply be those the teacher thinks are right. Other tactics are acting in a passive manner, cheating to obtain higher scores, suppressing one's feelings, retreating into apathy, and being docile and conforming.

One of a few black students in a predominantly white school has his own survival kit, which is described in our article "The Integration of Harry Benjamin," by Thomas J. Cottle.[19] This student's method of survival is to think about an eventual student-led revolution. Such ideas have appealed to many students recently, but according to Silberman, students are too brainwashed

[19]Thomas J. Cottle, "The Integration of Harry Benjamin," *New York Times Magazine* (April 23, 1972), pf. 14.

into accepting the paternalistic school system to take revolt seriously. Thus, a majority of high school students claim that they want no power, that they would not know what to do with it if they had it, and that schools are authoritarian, abusive, and stultifying because "that's the way things are." In Silberman's view, then, the function of social control has been performed so well by the educational institution that students have been turned into virtual zombies.[20]

THE TRIALS AND TRIBULATIONS
OF AMERICAN EDUCATION

Is the condition of education really as bad as Silberman paints it? To anyone who has been through the primary and secondary schools of this country, many of his accusations ring true. But perhaps American critics should have studied in a European school, as one of the authors has, to know the extent of the pain, ruthless authoritarianism, bureaucracy, and ego-deflation a European student must face!

Before indicting American education as utterly unsuccessful, we should be aware of some of the difficulties it has faced and continues to face today. First, the United States was the first nation in the world to attempt to educate everyone. This attempt was based on democratic ideology, which assumes the existence of an informed and intelligent electorate. Fifty years ago, education was a privilege for the very few, as it is in many nations today. Then, it was aimed at continuing a genteel tradition, not at training people for skills with which they could earn a livelihood.

When both the scope and the aims of education changed—to educate all, not only the few; to educate for an occupation, not only for pleasure—the content of education had to become more specialized in some areas and more diluted in others. According to some critics, the natural lowering of standards, has, however, resulted in a situation in which almost everybody obtains a diploma but almost nobody knows very much! The fundamental conflict of bringing education to every level of society, and to every individual regardless of his intellectual potential, and retaining a high standard of intellectual attainment has not as yet been resolved.

What is more, the institution of education is an integral part of the fabric of society and reflects, to a great degree, its conflicts and problems. We have seen how closely the type of education obtained by an individual is associated with his socioeconomic status. By the same token, the disaffection of members of lower socioeconomic groups with this society is reflected in their behavior in and against schools.

A look at urban schools amply supports this point. A recent survey indicates that truancy in inner city schools is averaging 30 percent and is often as high as 60 percent. Despite attempts at changing curricula and providing compensatory education, parents in ethnic neighborhoods complain bitterly that their children cannot read, and businesses complain that many high school graduates

---

[20]The material for this section is based on Charles E. Silberman, *Crisis in the Classroom* (New York: Random House, 1970).

are, for all practical purposes, illiterates. Obviously, then, not much learning is taking place.

In addition, violence in urban schools is a growing menace. Extortion, robbery, rape, stabbings, and even occasional gunfights force such strict security rules that many schools resemble fortresses. This state of affairs has led the director of the Public Education Association to say, "People say I shouldn't talk about it, for fear it will spread. But it's here and it's real. The myth of universal education is no longer as American as apple pie."[21] If he is right, what is the alternative? We live in a society in which literacy is a key to survival—even crossing a street becomes dangerous if one cannot read the signs. Surely we cannot condemn a whole stratum of society to the fate of illiteracy.

Compulsory universal education, however, can be attacked on several grounds. For a democratic system to be completely functional, an educated electorate is essential. But we could argue that forcing everyone to go to school for twelve years is also undemocratic. We could further argue that freedom *from* participation is as fundamental a right as freedom *of* participation in the democratic process. That is precisely the argument of one subculture; the Amish reject public education for their children beyond the eighth grade because it is contrary to their religious beliefs. Clearly, some alternative system of education will have to be devised. Sooner or later, we must accommodate the Amish and other groups that have societal and cultural goals vastly different from those of middle-class America, as expressed by our public schools.

TRENDS IN EDUCATION

In 1971 the American educational establishment, including full-time students, teachers, and administrators, numbered 63 million people, and students alone accounted for over 60 million. In the school year 1959–1960, the total enrollment in American schools was 46 million students. The increase in a little over ten years has occurred at the level of higher education. Thus, it does not simply reflect the increase in the number of young people but indicates genuinely expanded educational participation.

It is estimated that enrollment in American colleges and universities will reach 10 million by the academic year 1977–1978. As a basis for comparison, note that in 1900, only 4 percent of those between the ages of 18 and 21 were enrolled in such institutions. This figure had risen to 35 percent by the beginning of the 1960s and to almost 50 percent at the end of that decade.

The figures concerning high school enrollment and graduation are even more spectacular. At the turn of the century, some 7 percent of students were graduating from high school. By 1940, this figure had increased to 40 percent, and today it is approximately 80 percent. In addition, today, the median number of school years completed by the American labor force is 12.3—the equivalent, and slightly more, of high school.[22] An increased amount of education for increasing numbers of people can safely be considered a trend of the future, as it has been a trend during this century.

[21]"Doomsday for Urban Schools?" *Newsweek* (April 3, 1972), p. 50.
[22]U. S. Department of Labor, as cited in the *New York Times Almanac* (1970), p. 44.

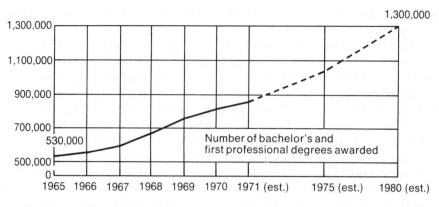

A GROWING PARADE OF DIPLOMA HOLDERS

SOURCE: Reprinted from *U.S. News & World Report*. Copyright (1971) U.S. News & World Report, Inc.

What are some of the changes we can look for in the near future? Can we hope for reforms that will make education meaningful to those who find it irrelevant? Obviously, we cannot return to a simpler time in which little education was needed to survive in society. But can we make large amounts of education palatable? There are indications of change in the institution, but it is difficult to predict their success.

Reforms in Education

At the college level, the numerous junior colleges that have sprouted in recent years are giving many young people a second chance to enter higher education because of their open-door policy. To counteract the rising cost of higher education as well as the crowded conditions in high schools and colleges, there are plans of offering degrees after three years, instead of the traditional four. This can be accomplished either by offering a speeded-up three-year course, by accepting students after their junior year of high school, or by letting high school graduates enter at a sophomore level. The premise that traditional four-year courses can be successfully condensed into three, or even two years, seems to be well supported. A report on twelve- to fourteen-year-old students in rural Norway who were taught only half time showed that more time spent in school made very little difference in terms of mastering basic skills, as measured by achievement tests.[23]

Alternatives to Existing Schools

At the high school level, attempts are being made to do away with the impersonality of urban schools and make them relevant to their student body through alternatives that range from free schools, to community schools, to the school-within-a-school concept, and to mini-schools. All these alternatives attempt to reverse the image of the public school by being child-centered, unstructured, small, individualized, and unoppressive.

The efforts of American educators have been inspired by the success of

[23]Torsten Husen, "Does More Time in School Make a Difference?" *Saturday Review* (April 29, 1972), pp. 32–35.

the British open schools which follow some of the methods outlined by such progressive theorists as Maria Montessori, John Dewey, and Jean Piaget. Although no comprehensive theories have been developed by the British, the teachers following this methodology assume that learning is most effective when it reflects the interests of the learner. They also assume that active learning is better than passive rote learning, that the student must be first convinced that it makes sense to be literate before he can be taught basic skills, and that students should be treated as individuals. The ultimate aim of the methodology is to influence students to become thinking, sensitive, independent human beings.[24] So far, the British schools have been most successful at the lower grades, in which this reform movement began.

American free schools.   The American version of free schools has been somewhat less encouraging than has the British because of the high rate of failure. In a recently published book, *Free Schools*, Jonathan Kozol states that free schools have an average life span of nine months. The author has been deeply involved in the free school movement, both as a teacher and as an organizer, and was particularly active in establishing such schools in urban slum neighborhoods.

The reason Kozol gives for failure is that such schools do not teach the kinds of skills that lower-class children need to acquire. Much of the difficulty lies with the upper-middle-class, idealistic teachers who most frequently teach in these schools. Having been educated in a rigorous, expensive, traditional fashion, the teachers insist on waiting until their students *ask* to be taught reading and other skills. Needless to say, sometimes students never ask. In the meantime, the students in these schools are busy—and supposedly contented—weaving headbands, making pottery, and growing organic food. Such

[24]Joseph Featherstone, "The British and US," *The New Republic* (September 11, 1971), pp. 20–25.

activities infuriate lower-class parents who want their children to acquire those very skills which, though despised by the free school teachers, enable them to be a part of a high socioeconomic class.[25]

Mini-schools.   The mini-school experiment in New York City seemed destined for success until the larger system took over the idea. The first attempt at creating small independent schools was made by the New York Urban Coalition in cooperation with a publishing company and the Board of Education. The mini-school that was set up contained one hundred students who were formally enrolled in a large high school in which 90 percent of the students were either black or Spanish-speaking. According to school system officials, the hundred students chosen were habitual troublemakers and were not functioning well in regular schools.

The mini-schools were modeled after the successful street academies originated by black nationalist leaders in black neighborhoods. They were housed in makeshift quarters, and students had a part in the selection of teachers. Classes were flexible, subjects being covered according to the mood of the students, rather than according to a prepared lesson plan. To counteract reading problems that stemmed from a dislike of books, one teacher let her students read pornography in class. It seems to have worked! Students were permitted to smoke in class and had other privileges unheard of in conventional schools. Unfortunately, what worked so well in small doses became the same old grind once it became part of the large bureaucratic system. And because the mini-schools were an experiment intended to be transferred back to the large high school, they made only a temporary dent in the monolithic school system.[26] Nevertheless, the initial success of these mini-schools may encourage dedicated educators to pursue the goal of small, centralized, community schools, which would eventually make the large system obsolete.

HIGHER EDUCATION: STRUCTURE AND ISSUES

As do all other institutions, education displays characteristics that reflect the changing demands of a modern industrial society. Thus, what is true of the economy and the political structure is true of education also—it is large, bureaucratized, impersonal, and subject to influences of interest groups. Many critics of the institution claim that higher education, in particular, is resembling the other giants of our society—industry, business, labor and government. The resemblance is striking at several points. First, universities and colleges tend to process their students on an assembly-line basis. To a great extent, universities treat students as if they were raw material to be put through the machinery of academe and turned out as finished products.

In addition, the corporate groups that are so influential in the political and economic spheres exert a similar influence on education. In many cases, college and university trustees, presidents, and even professors who have acquired

[25]Jonathan Kozol, *Free Schools* (New York: Houghton Mifflin, 1972).

[26]Diane Divoky, "New York's Mini-Schools: Small Miracles, Big Troubles," *Saturday Review* (December 18, 1971), pp. 60–67.

a reputation are on intimate terms with business, industry, and government leaders.[27] Through generous grants and other special privileges, such leaders may be able to influence academicians to act—or fail to act—in directions favorable to themselves or to the interest group they represent. Such influence may affect both curriculum and academic freedom.

The relationship is not one-sided. In a technological society, institutions of higher learning are essential to the maintenance and development of society, because a great deal of technological research is done within their walls.[28] Moreover, colleges and universities train the specialists needed for the smooth operation of the economy. In any case, interdependence between higher education and the economic and political spheres of society sometimes leads to dubious ethics. When a large corporation, interested in profit, engages the research department of a university to develop an effective weapon, and when this weapon is used by our government against the women and children of a mythical enemy, the contribution of the university must be weighed from the standpoint of morality.

Issues in Academe

Not only is higher education in a precarious position because of some of the company it keeps, but it is divided within itself on several fundamental issues. Chief among them is the argument over the primary goal and function of higher education: Should the main goal be the production of well-rounded, cultivated individuals, attuned to the world of the intellect and aesthetics, or should it be the practical training of individuals for occupations and for life in general? In short, should colleges teach knowledge for knowledge's sake or knowledge that can be used for practical purposes? This dilemma is not new. It is usually brought to the surface in debates between humanists and scientists. Basically, the view one takes depends on one's idea of the meaning of life: According to the scientific viewpoint, material progress is more important than personal self-fulfillment; according to the humanist viewpoint, the opposite is true.[29] Two thousand years ago, Socrates argued in favor of education in the service of the "examined life" rather than in the service of the marketplace. But the pendulum has often swung in the opposite direction. Many philosophers and social thinkers have favored the practical over the strictly rational, among them Jean Jacques Rousseau (1712–1778) and the American John Dewey (1859–1952).

For all practical purposes, the fundamental conflict between the scientific and humanist viewpoints can be translated into the question of whether we, as a society, are obligated to provide class, or elite, education or mass education. Do we maintain high standards and permit only a few to become educated, or do we lower the standards and permit all to become barely informed? Do we train people to become specialists capable of functioning

[27]James Ridgeway, *The Closed Corporation: American Universities in Crisis* (New York: Random House, 1968).

[28]A. H. Halsey, Jean Floud, and C. Arnold Anderson, eds., *Education, Economy, and Society* (New York: Free Press, 1961), p. 456.

[29]George Levine and Owen Thomas, eds, *The Scientist vs. the Humanist* (New York: Norton, 1963).

within only a narrow occupational sphere, or do we offer them education in all fields, taking the chance that they will be unable to function in any one occupational sphere of our technological society? Do we feed them facts, or do we teach them how to think? This dilemma has no either-or solutions, and shouldn't have. With our wealth and resources, we should be able to provide both educational approaches.

Other Thorns in Academe

We have mentioned that a side effect of the large size of the educational institution is bureaucratization. We are all familiar with some of the forms of bureaucratization, both at lower levels and in higher education. One particularly unfortunate result is the reduction of the student's intellectual life to concern with academic credit and the grade system. High school becomes something that the student goes through to obtain the subjects and the grades necessary for college; and college is something that the student goes through to obtain a degree. Even in graduate school, learning is not emphasized: The race for the Ph.D. has often been compared with an obstacle course, made up of outdated requirements that test a student's endurance rather than his ability to reason. Thus, diplomas and degrees lose all meaning. They become little more than licenses for obtaining jobs.

Another aspect of bureaucratization is the hierarchical organization of all those involved in the institution. From Charles Silberman's account, we have seen that in the public schools this system is characterized by coercive authority running from the School Board all the way down to the students. In colleges and universities, the authority is perhaps not as coercive, but it is as systematic, with money and privileges heavy at the top and spiraling downward. This makes for competition among socially mobile faculty members. One evidence of competition is the "publish or perish" syndrome. Because the amount a faculty member publishes is one basis for determining promotions and status—and, hence, rank and tenure—many engage in it at the expense of teaching. The result is large quantities of published material that would have been better left unpublished and a dissatisfied student body taught, to a large degree, by graduate students. We are, of course, making generalizations about the situation: Publishing significant material is valuable, and many dedicated faculty members do their own teaching. But the situation does exist and does cause concern.

Additional consequences of large size and bureaucratization are the increasingly huge classes that make a relationship between instructor and student impossible. Furthermore, the student has no voice in the setting up of curricula, a situation that has prompted many accusations of irrelevancy to be leveled at institutions of higher learning. Dissatisfactions with these aspects of bureaucratization, and many more too numerous to mention, have undoubtedly been responsible for much of the student protest of recent years.

Dissatisfactions have also been responsible for the establishment of experimental colleges, on the model of the free schools of lower education. Whether or not such schools will be practical on a large scale, they deserve encouragement because they seem to fulfill the needs of at least some students.

THE STUDENT SUBCULTURE

Students, who are the beneficiaries of the bulky institution of education, have been the subject of conversation and have captured headlines since the early 1960s. They have been pictured as spoiled ingrates, products of an affluent society who out of boredom turn to political activism and the destruction of the Establishment for which their elders labored so hard. They also have been represented as almost saintly innocents, angellike creatures who are preparing the world for Consciousness III. In Consciousness III, the future earthly paradise predicted by Charles Reich, there will be an end to materialism, injustice, and all kinds of social evils.[30] As may be expected, today's students—and we are speaking of both young people in institutions of higher learning and those in the last years of high school—are neither angels nor devils. As are people everywhere, they are probably a combination of both.

In previous chapters, we have referred to the extensive youth subculture. Each year, it has become more visible, more exclusive, and more isolated from the world of the adults than it was the year before. It has created its own music, morals, clothes, hair styles, and literature (not to mention its own diversions, such as smoking marijuana!) However, when this subculture comes into conflict with the adult world, it has no mechanism for working through the established political system and thus for eventually reaching compromise. Therefore, it must rebel.

According to an English historian, if we want to end the rebellion of the young as well as their subcultural existence, we must reverse the trend of the last four hundred years and make youth once again part of adult life. Before the era of modernity—an era that took some two hundred years to develop—children and adults shared the same life styles, wore the same clothes, played the same games, and had the same morals. Children were almost miniature adults. In the modern era, however, there has been a new outlook on children: They are viewed as innocents who must be protected from the immoral actions and pastimes of adults. Along with a change in outlook, there came the physical separation of children from adults, especially among the upper classes, in which children even lived in their own quarters and only occasionally visited with their parents. Everything, from clothing to literature, from food to games, became distinguished into that which was meant for children and that which was meant for adults.

The underlying reason for this gradual but definite separation was that the social needs of modern societies dictated that a pool of skilled and trained individuals be made available for new professions and commerce. Such a pool was ensured by discipline enforced by regular schooling. However, the constant separation of youth from the adult world, as well as the repression, conformity, discipline, and exclusion that went along with it, had side effects. It propelled young people to create a world of their own, to which they kept attracting ever younger members. Perhaps this world is a repressive and an artificial one, from which the young are straining to be liberated.[31]

---

[30]Charles A. Reich, *The Greening of America* (New York: Random House, 1970).
[31]J. H. Plumb, "The Great Change in Children," *Intellectual Digest* (April, 1972), pp. 82–84.

Preactivist College Subcultures

For some time, college age youth have formed subcultures—perhaps because they resent being excluded from adult society or maybe simply because exclusion causes them to be together in the same place at the same time. Sociologists Burton R. Clark and Martin Trow have classified the subcultural peer groups found on American campuses during the decade of the 1950s and in the early 1960s.[32] As with all typologies, Clark and Trow's is oversimplified, but their classifications are instructive when contrasted with current classifications.

The first subculture is the *collegiate* and is best characterized by the Joe College type. The star athlete, the homecoming queen, and parties and dances symbolize this group. Its values do not include serious studying but simply getting by. Its supporters are usually drawn from the upper and upper-middle social classes, and it tends to be most active on residential campuses. Members of this subculture develop a strong loyalty to their college and for a long time furnished the media with its image of college students.

The *vocational* subculture develops in institutions catering to working- and lower-middle class students, who are interested in education as a means to upward mobility. They are concerned primarily with taking as many hours of courses as possible in the briefest amount of time, hoping that a degree will bring a good job. Because many are married and have families to support, they tend to work from twenty to forty hours a week at an outside job. Sports, fraternities, and scholarship for its own sake are luxuries members of this subculture cannot afford. Members are not very visible on campus and do not interrelate with one another to a significant degree. They view their educational experience in the light of training.

The *academic* subculture consists of students who pattern their behavior and values after the concerns of the faculty. They are interested in the world of ideas and knowledge, are hard-working, and obtain the best grades. They plan for future careers that involve work in graduate school and divide their time in college among the library, the research laboratory, and the seminar. These students come from all social classes, but are most often from upper-middle and upper-class homes, in which the parents are educated.

The fourth subculture among college students is the *nonconformist*. Although nonconformity takes many directions and is labeled in different ways—bohemian, beatnik, radical—aggressive nonconformism is the predominant style. In other words, members of this subculture tend to be critical of the Establishment, hostile to the college administration, and rather detached from the college environment. Their concerns are intellectual, artistic, and political, but in the frame of reference of the adult society. In their search for a distinct identity, nonconformists frequently adopt styles of dress that shock their more conformist peers. Members of this subculture, apparently recruited from all social classes, are concerned with ideas, as is the academic subculture, but they lack the latter's loyalty to and involvement with the college.

The authors of this study noted that the collegiate subculture was on the decline, whereas the vocational one was on the rise. Of course, since that

[32]Burton R. Clark and Martin Trow, "The Organizational Context," in *College Peer Groups: Problems and Prospects for Research* (Chicago: Aldine, 1966), pp. 17–70.

time, it has become apparent that the nonconformist subculture has become predominant. But there is no doubt that all such subcultures exist, to a greater or lesser extent, on all college campuses and that one individual may participate in several subcultures.

The Generation Gap and Generation Units

The decade of the 1960s saw a sharp revival of student commitment to politics for the purpose of social change. The consensus has been that this political reawakening is a result of a generation gap—in other words, that the interests and values of the young are in direct conflict with those of the older generation. According to Seymour Martin Lipset, who has written in depth about youth activism, the generation gap factor is vastly over-emphasized.[33] In fact, there are as many differences within the younger generation as there are between the generations. Lipset suggests that generation gap be replaced by the term *generation units*, which sociologist Karl Mannheim applied to differing views in existence within the same generation or within the same span of time. Although Lipset admits that there are many generation units among the youth of today, he denies the novelty of their views. On the contrary, many features show continuity with the views of past generations.

But though their views are not new, the methods young people choose to express them are action-directed. Orientation toward action, Lipset says, is natural, considering the impulsiveness of youth and their socialization. Impulsiveness directs youth to act on their ideals, to emphasize ends without giving much thought to the means. And their socialization directs them to live up to the ideals of society in absolute terms. Therefore, compromise, which from a mature outlook is considered the only solution to the inevitable conflicts of values and beliefs that arise in society, is viewed by the young as a violation of basic morality. The young are impelled to action wherever they see a gap between ideals and reality. Only when they see their way completely blocked do they react with cynicism and withdrawal.

Lipset believes that there are primarily four generation units among American youth. First, there are the right-oriented youth who support Wallace. They want to maintain traditional society, which they consider threatened by the changes of liberal elements. This group is opposed by another generation unit made up predominantly of black, militant youth. This group wants to change traditional society but only enough to permit blacks to enter the economic system. In other words, this group is basically interested in maintaining wealthy, industrialized America, but with a radically changed stratification system, particularly as it concerns the distribution of power and income. Lipset thinks that this group is ideologically close to the Wallace supporters, even though it is backed by radical left college students who want to change American society drastically and think they can do so through black anger.

The remaining two groups—radicals and renunciators—are composed largely of university students. Although radicals and renunciators are often confused with each other, they are quite distinct. Radicals are closer to Wallace supporters than are renunciators because, although they want to change soci-

[33]The following section draws on Seymour Martin Lipset, "Youth and Politics," in Robert K. Merton and Robert Nisbet, eds., *Contemporary Social Problems* (New York: Harcourt Brace Jovanovich, 1971), Chapter 15, pp. 743–791.

ety, they too are basically concerned with owning it. In other words, they want the system to work for them. The renunciators, on the other hand, are interested in disowning their society. They reject much of what we call modern, especially technology and urbanization. Thus, their views are actually closer to those of classic conservatives than to those of any radical or revolutionary movement. Among protesting students, then, there may be different emphases, and the rejection of the system follows two distinct social tendencies.

The Role of the University in Protest

The university is a center from which radical and renunciatory behavior is initiated and from which it is expressed. Some suggest that scholarship is so closely related to ideals and abstractions and to processes of creation and innovation that antagonism and a rejection of the status quo naturally occurs. In fact, Lipset quotes an American intellectual of the nineteenth century who said that the foremost function of the scholar in politics was to oppose the established and to offer intellectual leadership to radicals. Lipset also points out that political protest was common among the university students of Europe, having played an important role in the social and revolutionary movements of the first part of this century. Even some of the personal renunciatory styles of that time are strangely reminiscent of today: long hair for men and short hair for women, dirty clothes, irregular life styles, the free use of obscene language, and colored glasses!

There are additional reasons why students engage in political protest to a greater extent than do other members of society. Students' roles are marginal in society. They are partly dependent on their family's status and partly in search of their own status. They suffer, therefore, the same problems as do

others whose roles are insecure. Furthermore, education shows students how far their society departs from the ideal. Also, students are freer than other segments of youth, and certainly freer than adults, to act without fear of the consequences of their actions. Finally, students are free in other ways—they are economically free to do what they choose and have both the time and energy to do it.

Student Activism

Although most people treat student unrest as a phenomenon peculiar to this time—something that never happened in the "good old days"—in reality, student dissent has a long history even in America. Lipset quotes Samuel Eliot Morison who, in a study of Harvard University, noted that the typical student of the 1790s was an atheist in religion, a rebel to authority in politics, and an experimentalist in morals. Again, the differences dissenters had with the rest of society were not generational differences but differences within generations. Such dissent, expressed mainly in renunciatory behavior, was stilled in some periods because of, for esample, the Great Depression and the fear of the expansion of communism during the Stalinist era.

The discovery that communism was not the nation-devouring monster it was thought to be and the struggle for civil rights renewed dissent and protest in the United States. Civil rights was an ideal issue to provoke protest because the denial of civil rights represented a major departure from the ideology of democracy. According to Lipset, the tactics of civil disobedience—mass demonstrations, including some violence—were taught to students by white Southern segregationists who refused to obey the Constitution, thereby showing that peaceful democratic methods were not functional.

The student protest movement that arose during the Vietnam war took two main directions. Some groups accepted the rational political mode of expression, either by supporting candidates such as Kennedy and McCarthy, by joining Bolshevist or Maoist factions of leftist organizations, or by embracing racial militancy. Other groups totally renounced rational politics and the Establishment. Their renunciation was expressed in drug use, which reduces a person's contact with reality. The characteristics of this last generation unit are a bias against rationality; cynicism toward social reforms, which they feel cannot be attained and made to work; and rejection of the political process. Some members of this group argue that their renunciatory behavior is a form of political dissent. The political activists, however, maintain it is politically counterproductive. It alienates many potential sympathizers who agree with the issues—peace, civil rights, economic maldistribution—but disagree with some aspects of countercultural life styles.

Finally, it is necessary to point out that activist students are decidedly a minority of the students on American campuses. Opinion polls have consistently shown that young people were less opposed to the Vietnam war than were older people. The majority of college students remained prowar until 1968, though to a lesser extent than their noncollege counterparts. A majority of students also looked favorably on Vietnamization as a means of disengagement. And in the fall of 1969, a poll showed diminishing student interest on the issue of war and a growing passivity and preoccupation with self. After the Cambodian incursion, however, political participation rose to 50 percent, and student attitudes moved to the left on all issues.

Surveys for the years 1968 through 1970, however, show student unrest in perspective. During this time, no more than some 10 percent of college students referred to themselves as radical, alienated, or dissident. And this figure diminished to 7 percent in November, 1970. At the same time, a Harris poll taken in May, 1970 indicated that 15 percent of college students identified their politics as conservative. In short, the image we receive from the mass media, of university students collectively engaged in tearing down the walls of the Establishment, is essentially false. Undoubtedly, there is a nucleus of politically active, radical students, dissatisfied with the status quo and working for change. But the great majority of students appears to be apolitical, reacting only in spurts to what they consider particularly outrageous governmental action.

SUMMARY

The fundamental function of the institution of education is the transmission of culture. In traditional society, this function is performed by the family, but in industrial societies, it has been taken over by the schools. The complexities of a technological society have added functions to the educational institution: innovation, recruitment and preparation for social roles, and integration and custody. The institution also performs other functions: It acts to develop tolerance and acceptance of democratic principles, it brings young people together, and it satisfies intellectual curiosity.

In our society, education is closely associated with social class. The length of time spent in school and the quality of education received depend, to a great extent, on the individual's socioeconomic status. Because school systems are local, children attend schools in their neighborhoods. Consequently, schools in lower-class neighborhoods, which lack an adequate tax base, tend to be old, run-down, lacking in facilities, understaffed, and overcrowded. Lower-class children lack, in addition to adequate schools, the kind of socialization that prepares them for their experiences in school. They are seldom provided with toys and books, their scholastic achievement is not particularly encouraged, and often their manners and language are at odds with the manners and language of their predominantly middle-class teachers. The result of this conflict is that many lower-class students either drop out of school as soon as their age permits it, or they languish in school in apathy, without benefiting from the experience. Such students, once out of school, become the permanently unemployed or underemployed, or they make their livelihood through illegal means.

Children of middle- and upper-class families enter schools in affluent neighborhoods, which have a generous tax base. They tend to come from homes in which their intellectual curiosity was stimulated and in which one or even both parents are college graduates. They are strongly encouraged to excel academically. What's more, their manners, language, and expectations do not conflict with those of their teachers. Consequently, their scholastic experience tends to be rewarding—or at least tolerable. They go on to colleges and universities, after which they obtain jobs that are quite a bit above those of their lower-class contemporaries.

But inequality of education is not the only problem confronting schools. Our schools have increasingly come under attack from various directions. In *Crisis in the Classroom*, Charles Silberman lists some grievances: Schools are grim, joyless places; they stifle children's curiosity, creativity, and individuality; and they are basically repressive institutions, based on a relationship of distrust.

Admittedly, American schools do have problems. A major problem, and one that has not as yet been resolved, is how to educate every individual, regardless of his intellectual potential, and still maintain academic excellence. It must be remembered that the United States is one of the first nations to have attempted universal compulsory education. Previously, education had been the privilege of a few, rather than the right of the many. Trends in education indicate that there will continue to be increased amounts of education for increasing numbers of people. Innovative teaching techniques in the form of free schools and mini-schools offer hope for the educational institution.

Higher education is also confronted with problems. Academic life has become bureaucratized, and professors frequently do not have enough time to devote to teaching. Furthermore, political activism has rocked the academic community. However, research indicates that political activism has been overemphasized. University students, here and abroad, have a long tradition of voicing dissent and calling society to task for its departures from ideology. But the vast majority remain in the mainstream of society.

How the young are taught in Mao's China

In our democratic open society, education has become the foremost mechanism for upward social mobility. Universal education, seen in this light, permits large numbers of people to attain high social status, with all its attendant privileges. Education in the People's Republic of China has an entirely different function. People try to improve themselves not to gain money or personal prestige but to better serve their society. Rhea Menzel Whitehead, who visited China with a delegation from the Committee of Concerned Asia Scholars, reports on educational methods that attempt to fulfill this purpose.

□□□

HONG KONG

Nearly everyone in the People's Republic of China seems to be involved in some form of education or re-education. Mao-thought study groups, literacy classes, part-time study programs for workers and farmers, and cadre schools for the re-education of government office workers supplement the usual schools. Throughout the country one has the feeling of a whole people intent on improving themselves. Their expressed purpose, however, is not monetary gain, higher position, greater

Saturday Review, March 4, 1922. Reprinted by permission of *Saturday Review* and the National Council of the Churches of Christ in the U.S.A.

prestige, or even individual satisfaction, but the following of Mao Tse-tung's concept of serving the people.

It is impossible to understand Chinese education without an awareness of the role of Mao's thought. For him, practice is both the source and the test of all knowledge. At every level of Chinese education heavy emphasis is placed on the application of knowledge on the farm and in the workshop, the laboratory, and the factory. Experienced workers and farmers are called in to give practical lessons to students because education must be intimately connected with life so that it will be related directly to the pressing needs of society.

The continuing struggle between the exploited and the exploiters is also central to Mao's thought. Such "class struggle," says Mao, continues in China even today. And since the educational process takes place within the context of social struggle, there must be constant effort to combat exploitative thinking and action.

Mao believes both that man is the product of his social condition and that he has an almost infinite potential for re-education. As a result, the Chinese are confident that they can create a new man and a new society in which the needs of others come before those of self. They are determined to make education serve the majority of the people, rather than just a privileged few, and are trying to avoid the kind of elitist education they see evolving in the Soviet Union.

By 1966 Mao had concluded that a thoroughgoing revolution was necessary to eliminate the vestiges of elitism and special privilege that remained. That summer the Cultural Revolution exploded. Schools closed. The central Ministry of Education was dismantled. Teachers, administrators, and textbooks came under bitter attack. When the schools reopened more than a year later, they set out to translate into practice Mao's conception of the role education should play. Now, more than four years later, the Chinese freely admit that their educational revolution remains unfinished.

The thrust of the future, however, seems clear. More than ever, schools will reflect the conviction that education can never be neutral. "Abstract education that does not serve the politics of a given class does not exist in the world today," one teacher told me. This is a rephrasing of Mao's belief that within education, as in all of society, there is a constant struggle between the exploited and the exploiters. The Cultural Revolution, the Chinese say, has been a victory for the exploited. In place of academic authorities, workers and peasants, who are assumed to know best what kind of people are needed for socialist revolution and construction, now have overall direction of the schools.

Traveling in China, as I did this past summer, one feels that this "festival of revolutionization," as the Chinese refer to the Cultural Revolution, has brought a renewed vitality and consciousness to Chinese education. Young people are convinced that they are playing a role in the creation of the future of China and the world and appear to be motivated by the concept of service rather than by personal gains. No one is considered worthless; even the deaf-mute and the cripple can make a meaningful contribution to society. The values children are taught are pride in the new China as led by Chairman Mao, selflessness, modesty, a willingness to learn from others, perseverance in the face of difficulties, and determination to struggle against anyone or anything that hinders the creation of a new society.

How then do the Chinese translate this philosophy and spirit into classroom practice?

Any attempt to generalize on the state of education in a country of 800 million must be done with caution. The sprawling urban complexes of Shanghai, Peking, and Wuhan are as different from the isolated villages of the northwest as New York City is from rural Mississippi. But some general changes can be identified. School courses have been shortened; textbooks are being revised. Greater flexibility in meeting local needs is encouraged. Emphasis on manual labor, pushed during the Great Leap Forward in 1958 but rejected during the early Sixties for lowering the quality of education, has returned. And other dimensions of the picture can be filled out from what is happening in individual schools.

Chen Hsien Primary School in Nanking, which I visited one sultry July day, is made up of a group of pleasant one-story classroom buildings surrounding a large courtyard. The din of children playing basketball, Ping-Pong, and a Chinese version of Drop the Hanky could have been that of an American school recess except for the political content to the game's song.

Classes in the school are large; I counted between forty-eight and fifty-six children to a room. While this is due partly to a continuing shortage of teachers and space, the Chinese do not consider a class of forty a problem. Children begin school at age seven for a five-year course, one year less than before the Cultural Revolution. The curriculum for the first three years includes politics, Chinese language, arithmetic, physical and military training, and "revolutionary culture" (music and art). Beginning in the fourth year, students learn English, natural science, agriculture, and industry.

Classroom organization is traditional, but the atmosphere varies considerably from room to room. I groaned inwardly at the classroom style of fourth-graders studying an essay on the revolutionary sculpture *The Rent Collector's Courtyard*, a scene of peasant exploitation. The class followed while the teacher animatedly read a six-page essay, occasionally wiping tears from her eyes. A period of rote reading and recitation followed. We heard well-rehearsed answers to questions about the nature of the oppression the peasants had endured. Students responded promptly and boldly, always standing when recognized. Discipline was impeccable, the students ignoring their visitors' presence completely. A bulletin board at the back of the classroom displayed the students' work—Mao poems they had copied. Other visual effects included a large world map, four political posters, and, as in all classrooms I observed, a small picture of Chairman Mao at the front of the room.

Fortunately, not all classes are so rigid. First-graders, each with an abacus on his desk, worked on two-column addition and subtraction problems. Children took turns demonstrating problem-solving processes on a huge abacus hung on the blackboard. The young teacher patiently explained and corrected when necessary. There was no automatic raising of hands, and youngsters helped each other in a quiet, relaxed manner.

In the past decade Mao has strongly advocated the abandoning of authoritarian teaching methods, and many articles in the Chinese press claim this is under way. Nevertheless, in conversations with the teachers, all insisted that in some subjects rote learning and class recitation were necessary, especially at the elementary level.

In other schools we did see children working in small clusters. Group discussions and evaluation have replaced memorization-type exams, the bane of traditional Chinese education. Class trips to historical shrines and museums are common and aid in developing a sense of China's past. Canton youngsters visit the Peasant Movement Institute, where Mao first started training revolutionaries. In Peking a fifth-grade class spent a whole week investigating life on a long avenue. Older shopkeepers told them stories of the past, when shops sold primarily foreign goods, workers had no rights, and ricksha pullers strained to deliver purchases to the wealthy few. Small class groups investigated different types of shops, houses, working conditions, and areas in need of improvement.

Many teaching techniques considered standard practice in America are regarded by the Chinese as individualistic and antisocial. Choice is collective rather than individual. Instead of exploring with finger paints or hammering abstract creations of scrap metal, Chinese first-graders remove the cork from bottle caps to facilitate their recycling. Others clean the streets, run errands for the elderly, make crystal radio sets and lantern slides, or learn sewing and barbering. The energy of the child

as well as that of the adult is spent for the development of the nation.

Clearly, the most innovative part of Chen Hsien School is its workshops. Beginning at age eleven, children spend a half-day a week producing items actually used in bus production. Girls in flowered skirts hand-file grooves in metal plates for bus steps. Others electroplate, work machine presses, or make oil filters for carburetors. No fixed quotas are set. Such work is meant to instill respect for physical labor, reinforce lessons learned in math and science, and contribute to the school's operating funds.

Workshops are part of schools all over China. Following the principle of self-reliance, the Chinese are proud that shops are set up with minimal expense. Often nearby factories send workmen to the schools to help the students. And most urban primary schools also have garden patches where youngsters learn how to grow vegetables.

Most cities maintain specialized schools, such as the Canton deaf-mute school where I saw acupuncture used along with more traditional forms of treatment, or a Sian arts training school where eleven- and twelve-year-olds enter a program of disciplined dance and musical instruction. New schools are also being established for the education of the mentally handicapped.

Since the Cultural Revolution, decentralization and relaxation of "state standards" have allowed a great deal more local control of schools, both urban and rural. Communist China has always relied heavily on private, run-by-the-people schools to provide supplementary school places. These schools have sometimes come in conflict with official regulations on academic standards, school hours, and age requirements. Many begun during the Great Leap were later closed. More recently, they appear to be flourishing anew as factories, neighborhoods, and rural brigades organize their own schools. Education in China, incidentally, is not free. Almost all students pay a rather insignificant fee of from 3 to 8 yuan per year ($1.20 to $3.20 in U.S. money).

Rural primary education continues to expand rapidly and flexibly. In one Inner Mongolian region, itinerant teachers ride horseback to points where one to five students gather in the homes of herdsmen or in the fields. Spring and autumn holidays allow pupils to care for new lambs and work during the harvest.

Classes focus on animal husbandry, agriculture, first aid, and acupuncture along with basic literacy training and cultural information. Several provinces report that universal primary education has been "basically introduced."

A firm principle of rural development has been self-reliance. But self-reliance alone will not help the countryside overtake the cities. Chinese whom I met seemed aware of the problem and spoke of the need to further equalize resources. Yet the "spirit of the pauper" cannot be considered unhealthy for a developing nation with limited resources. It is inspiring to be shown buildings made from local stone and straw, desks and benches made from bricks and stone, without encountering the familiar Asian attitude of "this must not be as good as you have in America."

Before the Cultural Revolution, the discrepancies in opportunity between city and rural youngsters were even greater at the secondary than at the elementary level. Middle School No. 31 in Peking, formerly a British-run missionary school with a chapel and swimming pool, remained an elite boys' school with strict entrance exams until 1966. Despite attempts to include manual labor in the curriculum, the emphasis remained on academic studies and university preparation. The curriculum, amazingly, varied only in superficial detail from what one might find in academic secondary schools anywhere in the world.

Now it is a coeducational institution accommodating all neighborhood youngsters who complete their primary studies. Students study politics, Chinese language, math, English, physics, chemistry, agriculture, health science, history, geography, and athletics and also prepare performances of revolutionary songs and dances. The curriculum, as in all urban middle schools, has been reduced from six years to five. Students spend one month at a Peking low-voltage electrical appliance factory, another on a farm, besides time in the school-run factory located on the premises. Getting students out of school and into factory and farm work offers the opportunity for a close partnership among students, workers, and peasants. Yet some of the factory's production plans do not integrate well with on-the-spot teaching of more theoretical lessons; therefore, the school's own workshops are important. Students not only repair desks and renovate water boilers but also produce electrical wirings and fluid brake lines for 2,000 heavy-duty trucks annually.

Many urban schools have set up rural branches where students live for periods varying from a month to a year. Students of these schools build houses, dig fish ponds, and sink wells, all the time studying related math and physics. Chinese authorities are hoping to equip urban youngsters with skills and attitudes applicable to life in rural areas, where many of them will eventually settle.

None of China's secondary school graduates now go straight to the university. Upon graduation they spend at least two years at manual labor—in the factory, on the farm, or in the army. Most will remain workers or farmers indefinitely; a few will be selected by their working units for further education. It is hoped that this process will eliminate the "three-door students," those who have gone straight from the door of the home, to the door of the school, to the door of the office, where they become bureaucrats who have little contact with real life or ordinary people.

Rural secondary schools are frequently part of an integrated seven- or nine-year school system (five years elementary, two or four secondary). Although many rural children, especially in the remote districts, still do not go beyond the primary level, current programs of expansion augur well. The students' practical work emphasizes agricultural experimentation and the development of farm mechanization. Meanwhile, spare-time education is still considered necessary for some. In one mountainous Fukien commune of fifty-two villages, for instance, secondary schools hold midday and evening classes for those busy with other chores.

Chairman Mao has said: "The question of educational reform is mainly a question of teachers." Viewed with suspicion as harborers of bourgeois ideas, especially the emphasis on intellectual development, teachers were severely criticized during the Cultural Revolution. Yet very few have actually been removed from their posts. The overwhelming majority are depicted as wanting to transform their outlook and are encouraged to "study well; make progress every day."

In Liu Ling, near the old revolutionary base of Yenan, one teacher talked of how her previous teaching had been motivated by an unconscious assumption that the bright student was superior. She had felt great pride in students' intellectual achievements and led bright pupils to avoid manual labor. Others she subconsciously regarded as inferior. Now her first goal is to cultivate her students' concern for people and the environment.

Chinese authorities admit that the doubling of school enrollment since 1966 has created a situation in which both the numbers and standards of teachers are inadequate. Young people with middle school experience and demobilized servicemen are given a training course of three to twelve months and then are used to augment the teaching force. Workers and peasants themselves are often used as part-time or temporary instructors to give political and practical lessons.

On-the-job training is pursued intensively. To tackle specific problems, mobile teaching groups tour areas setting up seminars on map reading and surveying for secondary math teachers. The staff at one teachers' training college held a twenty-day course for all eighty teachers of one commune to discuss common problems. Correspondence courses are becoming popular. "Tutoring stations" are set up on a city- or countywide basis. Here teachers meet regularly to exchange experiences, gather supplementary aids, and collaborate in the writing of reference materials. In keeping with the Maoist view of knowledge, new methods and materials are not private but are to be as widely disseminated as possible. Some areas have instituted a "teachers' study day," when teachers on a swing basis are given one day a week away from classes to help in a factory or on a farm and to pursue solutions to professional problems.

Part of the Chinese teaching style is to publicize models for emulation. The exemplary teacher is one who consistently battles for the cause of mass education, who modestly accepts criticisms from students, workers, and peasants, and who regularly takes part in productive labor. He develops a close relationship with his students and sets high educational and political goals for himself as well as for them. He treats students with patience and commends rather than scolds. Just because a pupil is considered a problem is no reason to "write him off." Mao Tse-tung's thought encourages thorough investigations into causes and patient help to the person who is trying to change.

Teachers have cooperated with workers and farmers to produce academically and politically sound new textbooks. In retrospect, pre-Cultural Revolution texts appear surprisingly free of political content. Today, politics dominates language lessons (English is in; Russian out). In one school I heard nine-year-olds reciting "I am a Little Red Guard"; in another "Sunflowers [the people] always face the red sun [Chairman Mao]." Arithmetic problems illustrate class exploitation. "Calculate how much rice poor Auntie Hsia was cheated out of when the crafty landlord weighed her rice in an extra heavy jar." History texts concentrate on the Chinese Communist Party and liberation struggles of the world's oppressed. Teachers said the books we saw last summer were "experimental," always under review. The simple paperback form in which materials are produced facilitates revision.

The "old" has not been eliminated with one stroke, however. That which can "serve China" is retained. Graceful girls perform Tibetan folk dances, the music and movement traditional, the words in praise of Chairman Mao. School children trudge through Peking's ornate Imperial Palace, learning to cherish the historic treasure as the product of the labor of the working man. The Sian Red Cultural Troupe sound much like Juilliard students, but the skills these budding musicians learn will be used in revolutionary opera and ballet.

The Chinese are making herculean efforts to erase those aspects of their educational heritage that gave special privilege to the educated, often the sons of the rich and powerful. Throughout China one meets young, confident leaders in factories and communes. No longer do workers and peasants feel inferior to the university-trained. The Chinese people have made great strides toward creating a new, indigenous, collectivized educational system to meet China's needs. They are determined to avoid developing an overeducated elite with no function to perform in society, such as that which Western-style education has created in many developing nations. Although the Chinese describe their far-reaching educational experiment as turning "the whole country into a great school of Mao Tse-tung thought," the problems they are grappling with are universal.

THOMAS J. COTTLE

THE INTEGRATION of HARRY bENJAMIN

A major function of the American educational institution has been to provide access to the upper echelons of the stratification system to groups lacking status and power. Students have probably never been totally satisfied and comfortable with educational processes. But additional suffering is undergone by a student who is black, who is in a numerical minority, and whose background is such that much of what is taught does not make sense. For such a student, survival involves developing some kind of defense mechanism. This sensitive account by Thomas J. Cottle, member of the Education Research Center and the Medical Department of MIT, describes Harry Benjamin's defense mechanism–the sweet dream of successful revolution.

□□□

Boston.

For several years in Boston, a school busing operation has been employed to increase racial integration. A small number of black students from Boston's inner city are transported each school day to rather opulent suburban high schools, some of them as many as 25 miles away. Not all the suburban school systems have accepted the busing program, and hence all-white schools, or schools with less than 1 per cent nonwhite populations, still exist.

Harry Benjamin is a black youth, 16 years old, from Boston's Roxbury district. I rode the school bus with him quite a few days, morn-

New York Times Magazine, April 23, 1972. Reprinted by permission of Sterling Lord Agency. Copyright © 1972 by Thomas J. Cottle.

ings and afternoons, hoping that I might come to know a few of the feelings attached to this recent attempt to integrate schools. What follows is a portion of a conversation I had with this young man after knowing him almost two years. We were together at the suburban school he attended, he being one of 70 black students among some 1,500 white students.

"My problem," Harry Benjamin was saying one morning after English class, "is that I just don't know what the hell I'm supposed to make of all this b——— they're teachin' me. Man, they go throwin' some of this stuff around like it's supposed to mean something."

"What were they discussing in there?" I asked him as we marched down the halls of the large suburban school. "Any books in particular?"

"Yeah. Greek tragedy. Now what do I know or care about Greek tragedy? I ask you that, Man, I don't even know where Greece *is*. And that's another thing. Before they go to speaking about this play or that play, like 'Oedipus Rex,' they show us this map of Greece and then they got one of the Roman Empire. I can't get it in my mind where these places are in the world. I ain't even traveled nowhere. I'd like to maybe, though...," and he started to dream: "I'd like to go to Africa someday."

The halls between 9:14 and 9:20 were filled with students running, walking, whistling, moping their way to second-period class. That feeling of school. Everyone knows it. It has anxiety and reactions to authority and giddiness and depression, all the world and all the feelings of the world tied up with it. When I think of that word, "microcosm," which some inevitably apply to the nature of schools, I have to wonder whether they mean a collection of feelings more than anything else. Surely no one would say society is like this, an easy extension of, and an elaborated form of, school. Harry interrupted my thoughts:

"You know, strange thing about this place, you know, you were askin' me before?"

"Yes?"

"School's kinda like the whole world, only in miniature."

"It *is*?" I questioned him, somewhat surprised.

"Sure. Look. This place is doin' its best to teach us who we are. School stinks a lot of the time but that's the way life is. That's what my father always says to me. 'You gotta learn the hard knocks there,' he says, ''cause you're gonna find out there is no perfect smooth sailing anywhere.' He says that all the time. I don't want to conform, you know, be like all the rest of the kids, but you can't always start out and be different. That ain't the way to be. You gotta learn to take orders and give orders."

"But you make it sound a bit like the Army," I replied.

"Yeah, maybe I do." One could see him thinking about his own words. "But school ought to be a little like that. You gotta do things you don't like."

"Even like Greek tragedy?"

"Yeah. Even that. You surprised to hear me say that?"

"Yeah. I am a little, truthfully."

"Well, don't be. See, here's the thing you can't dig, so I'm gonna make you understand."

"I'm ready." I smiled at him.

"Seriously," he started. "I'm black. Right?"

"Right."

"Everybody knows that, right?"

"Right."

"Don't need to tell anybody, right?"

"Right."

"See," he began to giggle although his teeth were closed tightly, "you're gettin' all the answers right."

"You watch me, man," I blurted out unthinkingly, "I'm gonna get straight A's."

"Well, that'll be good, too. 'Least one of us is passing."

"I'm sorry, Harry. Go on."

"Yeah. Yeah. O.K. See, I gotta learn about what the white kids are learning, otherwise I'm always going to be behind them. I'm going to have to work harder at all of this stuff, no matter what happens. I don't dig it most of the time but I'm going to stick it out. Man, there's no one in this school hates it more than I do when some sonofabitch teacher, white or black . . . That's another thing. Don't make no difference, you know. Some of them black teachers can be just as bad or worse on us black kids.

"Like, you know, I'd take Levy over Henkle anytime. Boy, he's a mean s———, that guy Henkle. He ain't been no friendly cat to me, whereas Levy, he's been a good friend, or you know, straight with me. A regular guy."

We were heading now down the main stairs of the building, caught in a trafficking of bodies and a swirl of language, conversations, pinching, smells of high school. Harry Benjamin was the single black person I could see in this entire swarm of persons. I was checking for this as he spoke his piece, but not he. He just kept poking and shoving his way downward, his words flying out for anyone to hear. It wasn't as though he had rehearsed his sentiments exactly; it was merely that nothing he was saying was meant for me alone to hear.

"O.K. So that's the race part of it. Now, like I was saying, they got horrible cats teaching here. They boss us here, they boss us there; don't even give us a chance to listen to ourselves think and figure out what we are or who we'd like to be. But it ain't no matter. I'm going to take it so I can make it like all the families of these kids have made it. I don't want my children to have to be bused out to no white suburb someday. This s——— gonna have to stop. Damn thing which near drives me crazy is how the white kids all think we're something so special or something. They really think we got something on 'em. They should only know."

The crowd of white students was slamming up against us as our feet hunted first for one step and then the next. We had reached the landing above the ground floor. Suddenly, my anxiety of getting trampled to death—actually, a highly unlikely fate—was supplanted by a more intense anxiety connected with the thought that this tide of adolescents might inadvertently sweep me into some classroom from which I would not be able to escape before making an utter fool of myself. And still, as we began the last descent from the landing, I saw no other black faces in the crowd.

"Part I don't like about this school I guess more than any other is how they keep looking at you and pushin' you. It's like they gotta always control us, keep us under wraps or something." For the first time he looked about at the swarm of noisy students making their way toward the various first-floor classrooms. "Now you dig this scene?"

"Man, I've been jostled around in it seems like days," I said.

"Yeah, it's a sonofabitch, ain't it?"

"Yup," I said. He laughed.

"Well," he went on, "who's going to make trouble in a setup like this with all these people starin' at you all the time. Ain't no place to even move an inch, much less get out of line. Man. You hear what I'm saying? Get out of line. They got me talking their way now."

"Matthew [a friend of ours] says that school pressures him like I pressure him," I responded. "The phrase he used which I like is that I give him no corners to hide in and no windows to jump out of."

"I can dig it. I can dig it." Harry nodded assent and pleasure. "Someday there's gonna be one great revolution. All the kids of this country are going to slug the s——— out of their teachers. O-o-o-e-e-e that's gonna be one beautiful day for us. You know, at one designated time all the clocks in all the schools gonna hit their chimes and very slowly, very slowly mind you, all these cats gonna get outta their little chairs and walk up to the front of the classrooms and s-o-o-W-A-N-G, they're gonna knock their teachers right through the blackboards. I can dig it. I can dig it."

"That means some of the good teachers that you like are going to go under with the bad ones, right?" Always my fears about a revolution come back to me.

"That's it. Sorry about that, man, but that's the way it's gotta be in times of revolution." He was smiling broadly. "S-o-o-W-A-N-G and they'll drop like flies. Got to do something about this overpopulation problem we got here in these halls. You just said it yourself. Too many goddamn people here. So we'll start first with the teachers, then, maybe if everything all goes according to plan, we'll knock out the

administration too. Then we'll really be running the show."

"You know," I started to say timidly, "it almost sounds like you've done a lot of thinking about this already."

"You better believe I have. I think about it every day in class." He laughed. "Every day I'm sitting in this class or that class rackin' my poor mind as to how to get school to be more the way I want it. Now you take math here. I got math coming up, right?"

"You'll think about this vision in math too, eh?"

"Sure. Got to, man. Got to. Can't let the dream die, not now before we've gotten something underway. You'll see. Well, you won't see, but I'll be in there and Oates will be crankin' on 'bout math and I'll turn on my revolutionary dream."

"Your what?" I hadn't heard his words properly.

"My revolutionary dream, man. My revolutionary dream." I had heard his words properly. "I'll be sitting in there figuring out just how we get to organize the entire country and get all the kids involved so that they can take over every school. I mean every school, man. Not just these suburban deals. All of 'em. In every state as well as Alaska and Hawaii. Even the school where you once went."

"Five hundred years ago," I muttered, trying to get him to have a little tolerance for an old man, should a revolution come. He wouldn't have any of it.

"C'mon, man," he came back, looking at me as we neared the math class. Only a few minutes to go before that bell would ring, then there would be silence. "You know what? You got a thing about age. You know that? You ain't so old that you can't remember school and your desires to explode it, or take it over. Or were you one of those nice little well-behaved dudes?"

As he said these words two thoughts struck me, almost as arrows might. First, I remembered a vision I once had of blowing up a chemistry lab when I was a high-school junior. A group of boys had gotten together to laugh over the teacher's absentmindedness and misperceptions of the perfectly obvious. We thought we would take the laboratory door off its hinges and get everybody inside and then put the door back before the teacher came in for class. This procedure would be necessary because the door was always locked. What kept us from doing it, we reasoned, and probably rightly so, was that the teacher would never have noticed that we had gotten in without his opening the door for us. So, later on, we thought of total annihilation. I remember the anxiety I had felt then as we spoke of, well, revolution.

The second thought was how much Harry Benjamin had changed as we had moved from the last seconds of first-period English to the minutes just before second-period mathematics. His resolute way, his willingness to adapt to a trying situation whose payoff in 30 years was as visible now as the kids who milled in the halls, and his conformity, all were being altered. His language too, and his resentment of the rules of the game that ultimately constituted his schooling, had undergone tremendous transformations in these few minutes. The fact was, he even seemed more handsome now than he had five minutes before; and if this were only my imagination, then surely he had grown several inches in this time.

"What you thinkin' about?" he asked me.

"About students and schools," I answered him. "Basically what you were saying."

"Yeah. Well, don't take it all too seriously, man."

"Well, I do, I suppose."

"You don't have to. It's only a dream, my stuff. I ain't about to get into any trouble here. If I did, my father would draw the belt on me. I'd have to run away from here rather than face that."

"Well, that may be true," I said, "but you know, school must be terrible if all you're doin' is sittin' in class thinking about ways to overthrow it."

"School s——!" Harry Benjamin looked at me, straight on. Now, at last I believed him to be as close to what he really was, or would be that one day. "It s——! Ain't no one gonna give you any argument there. Very few kids dig it. Every once in a while something good might happen. Might be in class or outside of class. But man, when you gotta take it this way, day in, day out, you gotta be mighty strong or mighty dumb not to be defeated by it. That's

kind of why I plot to take it over. 'Cause I ain't so strong and I ain't so dumb neither."

"That's about the way I felt when I went to school, Harry, years and beers ago." He smiled when he heard me use his father's expression. "I never thought I was dumb, but I also didn't seem to have the strength to do it the way it was supposed to have been done." He was deeply interested in what I was divulging. But it had taken his wild, melodramatic fantasy to get me to dredge up my meager little left-over feelings about school—the feelings which come back to me like an old girl friend's name the moment I step on school grounds, any school grounds, anywhere.

"You know what, dad?" He was about to enter the mathematics classroom. "This has been a groove. You're one of the few people that has leveled with me about this school jazz." But I haven't, I thought. I haven't leveled with you at all, Harry Benjamin. I'm giving you rehearsed, well-baked bits of my childhood that I don't mind parting with at all to anyone. I got millions more like them. Don't you know that they don't mean a thing? "Yup," he was saying, "You're an honest dude, so I'll give you an honest ticket back. In return, like."

"I'd like to hear it," I said, half expecting to hear something like a parade of the raw bits of my history that I give only rarely, and even then reluctantly—and never, never once gave to any teacher that I can think of.

"My dreams about overthrow are extremist and all that. No one needs to tell me that." He switched his books to his left hand in preparation for opening the door with his right. For the first time he looked about wearily, making certain that no one else would hear him. Then he waited for a girl to go into the room. "Hi, Harry," she said softly, the two words brimming full of feeling.

"Hey, what d'you say, mamma." Then he looked at the mustard-colored linoleum floor and began.

"I'm scared, man. I'm scared s—— in this place. Almost two years now I been coming here and I still get the flies in my stomach every day. Every morning before we leave. Every day. I don't belong here, man. Not just 'cause I'm black and everyone's white. It's just that it's all over my head. They got lots of teachers here tellin' me my talents are fine and I'm, you know, gonna be all right. But they're jivin' me. It's gonna be one helluva cold day in hell 'fore I get to makin' it here like you're supposed to. The thing is, no matter how hard I try it ain't never enough. I work harder than any of 'em and I can't do it. I just can't do it. I just can't do it, and I . . . I . . . I don't know who to talk to 'cause it just ain't easy to tell someone you're failing and you know they're keeping you practically no matter what 'cause you're black or you're poor or your father's an alcoholic or your mother's a whore."

The class bell blared in the hall and everywhere around me I heard doors slam. Quickly the noise diminished. A few stragglers dashed about, along with those who were free this one period. "They're doin' the best they can. So am I. I'm doin' the best I can but it just ain't working' out and *you* can't say a thing or figure out anything to do neither, 'cause you know it's true. Every last word I say."

And just like that he was gone.

DISCUSSING THE ARTICLES

1. In Rhea Menzel Whitehead's article "How the Young Are Taught in Mao's China," does education seem to play a greater or lesser role in China than it does in the United States? How is this evident? What is the reason behind it?

2. Do the Chinese go to school for the same reasons we do? What is the expressed purpose of education? What is ours?

3. Would you characterize Chinese education as authoritarian? Do you think it is directed at the production of a cultivated individual or a specialist? Is practical knowledge or knowledge for its own sake stressed?

4. Do the Chinese believe in abstract, neutral education? Is our education neutral and abstract?

5. What group directs schools in China today? Would this work well in our society?

6. How do Chinese students differ from American students in their attitude toward the institution? How is this evident in their socialization? Is this view at odds with the concern with the individual shown in democratic ideology?

7. Do the Chinese methods of elementary education seem progressive? How is the energy of the child channeled in China? Could it possibly work in our society?

8. Do central or local authorities have control of schools in China?

9. Who decides who goes to college and who remains a manual worker? Does this violate individual freedom? What is the Chinese rationalization for this system? Do you think it is valid? Do you think we should adopt this system?

10. How have teachers' attitudes changed? Would our society benefit if our teachers had this attitude?

11. What criticisms do you have of Chinese educational goals? Are they functional for their society? Are they primarily goals of education or of training? Does China need educated or trained individuals? Will a society that has these objectives eventually suffer from some shortcomings?

12. The hero of Thomas J. Cottle's "The Integration of Harry J. Benjamin" has several strikes against him which prevent him from making a successful adjustment to the educational institution. What are they? Which is the most difficult to overcome?

13.   What in Benjamin's background makes Greek tragedy irrelevant to him? Is Greek tragedy irrelevant to everyone? What relevance might we find in it?

14.   In what respects is school a microcosm? In what respects is it like the army?

15.   Why is Harry Benjamin willing to take it? Does he take it passively? What thoughts does he relish? Do most students entertain such thoughts at one time or another?

16.   What does Harry's revolutionary dream do for him?

17.   Harry's admission of his inadequacy points up what problems in American education? Where do the solutions lie?

TERMS TO REMEMBER

Education. The formal aspect of socialization in which a specific body of knowledge and skills is deliberately transmitted by a corps of specialists.

Transmission of culture. The chief function of education.

Dissemination, innovation and preservation. The functions of education that foment social change at the same time that they conserve the traditional cultural heritage.

Recruitment and preparation for social and occupational roles. The functions of education through which schools both prepare students for occupational roles in terms of actual training and select them for specific roles more or less according to ability.

Person selection. The process by which people are chosen to perform the tasks needed by society.

Person formation. The process by which society ensures that people able to perform necessary tasks are constantly available.

Integration. A function of education in which subcultures are integrated into the mainstream of society and given a shared cultural identity and purpose.

Open schools. The British version of experimental schools—child-centered, unstructured, small, individualized, and unoppressive.

Free schools. The American version of open, or experimental, schools.

Mini-schools. Experimental high schools in New York City.

Scientific view in education. A conception of life in which material progress is viewed as the ultimate good.

Humanist view in education. A conception of life in which personal fulfillment is viewed as the ultimate good.

Generation units. Differing views that exist within the same generation or within the same span of time.

Radicals. In Lipset's typology, students who want to change society and make the system work for them.

Renunciators. In Lipset's typology, students who reject society, especially the modern aspects of technology and urbanization.

Collegiate. In Clark and Trow's typology, the typical Joe College subculture. Members are interested in fun, dates, fraternities, and are loyal to the college.

Vocational. In Clark and Trow's typology, the college subculture made up of working, urban, family men to whom the degree represents upward mobility. They are hard-working but are not interested in intellectual pursuits and are not particularly loyal to the college.

Academic. In Clark and Trow's typology, the college subculture interested in intellectual pursuits, patterning its values and behavior after those of the faculty.

Nonconformist. In Clark and Trow's typology, the college subculture interested in ideas but within the context of the wider, adult society. They have become predominant on campuses today.

SUGGESTIONS FOR FURTHER READING

Becker, Ernest. *Beyond Alienation: A Philosophy of Education For the Crisis of Democracy*. New York: Braziller, 1969. The past and present of education is examined, and an alternative for the future is offered by the author.

Caplow, Theodore, and McGee, Reece. *The Academic Marketplace*. New York: Doubleday Anchor Books, 1965. A view of the institutions of higher learning, detailing the "publish or perish" syndrome and other particulars of making it at the university level.

Clark, Burton. *Educating the Expert Society*. San Francisco: Chandler, 1962. The educational institution as it has responded to the demands of an urban industrial society.

Friedenberg, Edgar. *Coming of Age in America*. New York: Random House Vintage Books, 1965. A personal view of the conflict between adolescents and the secondary school as it attempts to imbue them with mass cultural values.

Jencks, C., and Riesman, David. *The Academic Revolution*. New York: Doubleday, 1968. An examination of trends in American higher education from a historical and sociological perspective.

Koerner, James. *Who Controls American Education?* Boston: Beacon, 1969. The takeover of education by small administrative groups furthering their own interests rather than the students'.

Litcher, S., et al. *The Dropouts*. New York: Free Press, 1968. High school students who become the victims of our educational jungle.

Mannheim, Karl, and Stewart, W. A. C. *An Introduction to the Sociology of Education*. London: Routledge & Kegan Paul, 1962. A renowned sociologist and social philosopher's posthumous writings on education.

McLendon, Jonathon C. *Social Foundations of Education*. New York: Macmillan, 1966. A collection of readings in which various facets of education are viewed from the perspectives of the different behavioral sciences.

Ridgeway, James. *Constraint and Variety in American Education*. Lincoln, Nebr.: University of Nebraska Press, 1958. An examination of the leaders of education and of the forces that repress freedom in colleges and high schools.

Sexton, Patricia Cayo. *The American School: A Sociological Analysis*. Englewood Cliffs, N.J.: Prentice-Hall, 1967. The major issues in American education presented with a wealth of relevant details from research done by the author and others.

◨ CHAPTER ELEVEN

THE RELIGIOUS INSTITUTION

Imagine yourself alive at the dawn of history. You are in an unfriendly environment and are forced to compete for food and territory with all kinds of frightening creatures. To make things more difficult, imagine yourself in this situation without all your cultural baggage to guide you. What would you be thinking? Of course, most of your time would be taken up in action, in a simple grubbing for survival. But during the long nights, as you lay in some unobtrusive spot, gazing up at the mysterious darkness pierced now and then by flickering lights, what would you think? And in a storm, when lightning seared the sky, thunder growled, water poured down, and winds bent and tore up enormous trees, what would you think? Would you feel a part of this scene, that you truly belonged? Would you want to know why you were there, where you came from, and where you were going?

If you can put yourself in the place of this mythical prehistoric person, and if you believe that he asked himself some of these questions, you will have answered the first question concerning religion: Why is religion universal, found in every society ever known? Religion is universal because human beings do not live by bread alone. A full belly and a place to lie down are essential to survival. But no one has ever been satisfied with merely staying alive. People have always wanted to know why—why this instead of that, why they and not someone else. That there should be no purpose to their lives and to their world has always seemed inconceivable to humans. This arrogance—the refusal to believe that they might be a sheer accident of fate whose lives and deaths matter to no one except a small circle of people—has led individuals to conceive of themselves as part of a system that includes them but also transcends them. In this system, or cosmos, there is harmony, justice, and purpose. Central to this system is the promise that in the end everything will turn out all right. Unfortunately, we are given only glimpses of this perfect system. Historically, these glimpses have been obtained through religion.

But people are no longer primitive cave dwellers frightened of natural phenomena. Science has explained what causes winds to blow, stars to flicker, lightning to strike, and thunder to roar. Why, then, is religion still a part of our lives? What's more, why do sociologists, who are committed to the rational methods of science, take an interest in it? Religion is of interest to sociologists because it is a social phenomenon. It is found in every society, and its rituals invariably involve groups of people. Furthermore, religion affects human behavior as surely as human behavior affects religion.

Humans need religion today—more than ever, some say—because it fulfills a vital need. We have become disillusioned with the rationalism of the Age of Enlightenment. We no longer believe that human reason alone is capable of explaining everything, including human motivation. In fact, we are finding

that we are not much closer to uncovering many of the causes of motivation than we were before. We are also discovering that we still need to go beyond the here and now—to transcend time and space. Professor Joseph Campbell, who has done much research in the field of mythology, claims that we need myths and ancient legends to act as vehicles of communication between the conscious and the unconscious. In fact, myths and legends do for society what dreams do for the individual: They link him to an unconscious of which he is unaware in his waking hours.

Professor Campbell maintains that the totality of myths in a society form a mythology that expresses the society's views on life, death, and the universe, in general. (This view is similar to sociologist Emile Durkheim's conception of religion as the worship of society, as we will see later in the chapter.) Thus, differences among cultures are indicated by differences in myths. The myths of Prometheus and Job, for example, are indicative of the cultures of ancient Greece and biblical Palestine. In the Greek myth, Prometheus steals fire from the gods of Olympus and gives it to humans. This symbolization of the high aspirations of the human race, even against the powers of nature, characterizes the Greek conception of humans. In the Judeo-Christian myth, Job is beset by trials and tribulations. Job submits to all these trials, declaring his infinite faith in the goodness and justice of God. This symbolizes the conception of humans in Judaic culture. Humans submit to a power even higher than nature, humbly surrendering to a superior, though benign, force.

The functions that myths perform for humans are very real, and the medium through which they are transmitted is, in our society, generally the church and synagogue. However, the increasing indifference to religion in the West has created a void that some people attempt to fill with psychoanalysis and encounter groups, others with membership in exotic cults, and still others with a return to fundamentalist forms of Christianity. Campbell believes that it is essential for our society to reinvent some myths. If it doesn't, we may suffer the fate of many preindustrial societies which have fallen apart when their myths and taboos were destroyed by contact with industrial civilization.

The communist nations already have a mythology—we called it ideology in another context—in the form of Marxism and Maoism. Both promise an ultimate heaven on earth. Leaders such as Churchill and de Gaulle also used myths to bring out fundamental themes of their national culture—themes that inspired people in trying times. America too had its mythology: the endless frontier where one could always make a fresh start and the American Dream, according to which any poor boy could eventually become president. But no one believes these myths any more. And a grand mythology will never be acceptable to everyone again. Each person must find his own myths, wherever he can, for they are a necessary part of life as long as man has hopes and fears.[1]

RELIGION IN THE SOCIAL SCIENCES

When sociologists first became interested in religion, they tended to think of it as an intellectual error committed by primitive man in an attempt to

[1]Gerald Clarke, "The Need for New Myths," *Time* (January 17, 1972), pp. 50–51.

explain his reality. For example, the French sociologist Auguste Comte (1798–1857) believed that human thought passed through three stages, the first of which was the theological stage of early and so-called primitive societies. Writing in the nineteenth century, Comte said that modern societies were in the second stage, after which religion would be replaced by science. Other sociologists, notably E. B. Tylor and Herbert Spencer, sought to explain religion in terms of a universal concern with the idea of soul. In their view, the idea of soul originated among primitive peoples from a wrong interpretation of dreams and death.[2]

Other social philosophers tended to view religion in the light of rationalism—as a relic of man's ignorance. Karl Marx believed that religion originated from a fear of natural phenomena and that it would disappear eventually. In Marx's theory of economic determinism, religion was viewed as a mask for class interest. Class interest, disguised as religion became the ideology of society (the "opiate of the people") and played an important part in social control. The author of *The Golden Bough*, anthropologist J. G. Frazer, approached the phenomenon from an evolutionary standpoint. He maintained that magic and religion would give way to science as a society matured and rid itself of the mistakes in thought caused by confusion and ignorance.[3] In short, these social thinkers viewed religion essentially as "institutionalized ignorance and superstition."[4]

Durkheim's View: Religion as Social Integration

An alternative view of religion was expressed by Emile Durkheim, the French sociologist. He suggested that *religion* deals with the sacred, which, in all societies, is distinguished from the profane. The *profane*, according to Durkheim, includes both the objects and events of everyday life that are usual, explainable, and repetitive. The *sacred* is separate from everyday experiences. It is unusual, unexplainable, mysterious, in some way powerful, and therefore deserving of reverence and respect.

Durkheim argued that primitive people were aware of a force greater than themselves—a force that they had to obey and on which they were dependent for survival. But they did not know what that force was or where it came from: "Men know well that they are acted upon, but they do not know by whom."[5] Thus, they invented the concept of deities who have supernatural powers and control over humans. And they invented rituals with which they hoped to appease their gods.

Durkheim theorized that primitive people arrived at their concept of the divine by imagining that the divine being possesses the characteristics of society. Society has moral authority over the individual. Society frequently has goals that conflict with the desires of individual societal members. Society requires a degree of obedience and sometimes even sacrifices of its members. And society is more powerful than the single individual, even appearing to

---

[2]E. B. Tylor, *Primitive Culture* (London: Murray, 1973), Ch. 11. Also Herbert Spencer, *Principles of Sociology*, Vol. III (London, 1896).

[3]Sir J. G. Frazer, *The Golden Bough*, abridged edition (New York: Macmillan, 1943).

[4]Gerhard Lenski, *The Religious Factor* (New York: Doubleday Anchor Books, 1963), p. 3.

[5]Emile Durkheim, *The Elementary Forms of Religious Life* (New York: Free Press, 1947), p. 209. First published in 1912.

exist independently of him. (This, of course, is an illusion, because a society cannot exist without single individuals.) At the same time, society helps the individual and gives him more power than he would have alone.

Because the characteristics of society and the divine are similar, Durkheim maintained, religious beliefs and practices are not rooted in ignorance and superstition. Rather, they deal with a very real object: human society. Religion, in Durkheim's view, is the expression of human solidarity, of the individual's awareness of his social system, of the web of relationships occurring within it, and of his dependence on it despite its sometimes dictatorial nature.

According to Durkheim, religious concepts, especially rituals, evolved in situations of collective behavior. (As we saw in Chapter 6, in such situations, individuals often seem to be possessed by a superior force or energy. They lose their individuality and take on a group conscience and emotional unity.) During the rhythmic dances and singing of tribal gatherings, the atmosphere tended to promote collective behavior. Primitive people, feeling very different from their everyday selves, thought that a supernatural cause was responsible. Both the occasion and the supernatural cause, therefore, became sacred to them, and they evolved further symbols, myths, and rituals in an effort to worship their deity.

Durkheim also theorized that a clan's god, or *totem*—an animal or a vegetable representation which was the symbol of a particular clan—represented the clan itself. In worshipping the totem, the members recognized that the power of the clan was superior to their power as individuals. In fact, the laws of the god, or totem, were, in reality, the most important laws of the clan. Religion, then, acts essentially to hold together different elements of a society by establishing an order for doing things and ultimate reasons for doing them. This cementing function of religion is what sociologists call the function of social integration. In Durkheim's words, "Religion is a unified system of beliefs and practices relative to sacred things, that is things set apart and forbidden—beliefs and practices which unite into one single moral community... all those who adhere to them."[6]

Weber's View: Religion as Social Control

The German sociologist Max Weber also became interested in religion. You will remember, from Chapter 8, that Weber refuted Karl Marx's theory of economic determinism by speculating that sometimes religious ideas caused social change. Using a comparative methodology, Weber concluded that the reason for the emergence of Western capitalism seemed to have been the Protestant Reformation. The Reformation, especially in its Calvinist and Puritan expressions, reoriented human thinking: Work became a means of glorifying God, rather than a punishment for sins; magic was eliminated from life and religion; and the rational, the systematic, and the unified became the new ideals. As these originally religious ideas took hold, they influenced all of man's activities, including economic matters. Thus, the driving force behind capitalism was not simply greed (a basic assumption underlying the very different theories of Adam Smith and Karl Marx) but a genuine commitment and dedication to work.

[6]Emile Durkheim, *The Elementary Forms of Religious Life*, p. 47.

Weber theorized that religious ideas contributed to social control in the same way they contributed to capitalism. Protestant ideology, for instance, legitimized, or justified, the power that the wealthy exercised in society. According to the ideology, the powerful attained their position through hard work and frugality, attributes pleasing to God.

Religion has also justified power in other political and economic contexts. Ruling dynasties, for example, have been believed to be of divine origin. Monarchies have reigned by virtue of divine right. And in democracies, it is assumed that the individual is born with God-given natural rights.

According to sociologist Peter Berger, religion's legitimizing function is evident "whenever obedience to the agencies of social control is interpreted as religious duty, and disobedience is interpreted as religious sin."[7] In effect, then, the commandment "Thou shalt not kill," which is assumed to be God's will and the breaking of which is a sin, justifies the power of the social agency—the court—to punish for murder. Religion, in short, strengthens the norms of society, thus exerting social control.

FUNCTIONS OF RELIGION

Some features of the human personality and some conditions of humans' social reality keep the need for religion alive. Science, which was thought capable of displacing religion, has so far proved incapable of doing so. People continue to reach out for something beyond life, and beyond science. Thus, today's social thinkers and scientists follow in the path of Durkheim and Weber. They are interested in the functions religion performs for the individual and society.

Functionalist theory, which we have encountered on previous occasions, provides interesting insights into religion's functions. For instance, according to functionalist theory, the individual in society is subject to two fundamental needs. One is the need to adapt, master, and control his physical environment in order to survive. The other is the need to express his feelings, to respond to objects and to the feelings of others, and finally to enter into relationships with others. Modern psychologists have found that this last need, called the expressive need, is of crucial importance to humans. Religion is functional in human societies because it fulfills these needs, and it does so because it transcends the common experience of human beings in their natural environment.[8] But then the question arises, Why do people need to transcend their everyday experience? To answer this, we must examine a few characteristics of the human condition and of human existence.

Religion: A Response to the Human Condition

The first characteristic of the human condition is that we live in perpetual uncertainty. We do not know how or when our safety and welfare may be

---

[7]Peter L. Berger, "Religious Institutions," in Neil J. Smelser, ed., *Sociology* (New York: Wiley, 1967), p. 341.

[8]The discussion of the functional interpretation of religion is based primarily on Thomas F. O'Dea, *The Sociology of Religion* (Englewood Cliffs, N. J.: Prentice-Hall, 1966), Chapter 1.

jeopardized. Death and catastrophe are always at our elbows. Every time you leave your house in the morning, you cannot be sure that you will ever return to it. You may be the victim of an automobile accident, a shooting incident, or even a falling brick. The human condition, then, is distinguished by its *contingency*. Another characteristic of the human condition is that our ability to control our environment is limited. At some point, our condition becomes one of *powerlessness*. You may have a profound desire to become a surgeon, but if you faint every time you see blood, the chances are good that you will have to settle for another profession. A third characteristic of the human condition is that because most societies still have economies of *scarcity*, we face relative deprivation and thus frustration.

In the functionalist view, religion acts as a mechanism through which people adjust to the inevitable facts of human existence. In other words, contingency, powerlessness and scarcity, frustration and deprivation, not to mention death, suffering, and coercion, largely direct human lives. But the regular norms of society provide no comfort during these experiences and no guide for correct behavior in circumstances that seem neither just nor meaningful. What can you say to a mother whose infant son has just died? "Never mind, you'll have another" seems totally unfeeling in view of our cultural values of treasuring life and deriving satisfaction from heirs. Nothing you can say will make the mother believe that there was a reason for her son's death, unless you refer to a system beyond her everyday experience and yours. In the context of such a system, the child's death could appear meaningful and would therefore be less difficult to bear. In the functionalist view, areas in the social structure that fail to provide adequate explanations and guides for behavior under stressful circumstances are breaking points. At these breaking points in the social structure, people reach out beyond their ordinary experience and, through religion, establish a link with the sacred.

Specific Individual and Societal Functions of Religion

Religion provides a view of the beyond. It is a system that clarifies and makes meaningful human deprivation and suffering. Through ritual, it also offers the means by which a relationship with the beyond can be established and maintained.

On an individual level, religion provides emotional support in the face of human uncertainty. It offers consolation for human physical suffering. It furnishes a channel through which humans can search for ultimate meanings. And it helps people overcome their fears and anxieties, whatever their origin. Psalm 23, "The Lord is my shepherd; I shall not want...," is a beautiful and moving example of this religious function. In short, religion strengthens the individual's morale, keeps his disaffection with his environment to a minimum, and gives him a means of attaining reconciliation when he becomes alienated from the goals and values of his society.

Establishment of Identity. As we have said before, through its ritual of worship, religion offers man access to the beyond. In this transcendental relationship, the individual's doubts about his security (What will happen to me?) and his identity (Who am I?) are reassured. In fact, religion contributes to man's recognition of his identity not only in relation to the universe but also in a more limited sense, within his own society. Membership in a religious organization,

in which people share in the same ritual, helps the individual to define for himself who he is and what he is. This function is particularly important in times of rapid social change, in which problems of identity are critical. Thus, a sociological study of religion in America reveals that an important way in which members of our society establish their identity is by recognizing themselves as Protestants, Catholics, or Jews.[9]

Clarification of the World. Religion clarifies the physical world, making it comprehensible, familiar, and meaningful. In teaching beliefs and values, it offers the individual a point of reference for his society's normative system—for what is considered good and what is considered evil. It also uncovers the mystery of the beyond, the explanations it offers becoming certainties in the mind of the believer.

[9]Will Herberg, *Protestant, Catholic, Jew* (Garden City, N.Y.: Doubleday Anchor Books, 1960).

Support of societal norms and values. Because socialization is never perfect, deviance from societal norms is frequent. Religion supports the norms and values of established society by making them divine laws. Thus, religion is an adjunct of the process of socialization.

Sociologist Peter Berger agrees with Weber that religion's support of the norms and institutions of society legitimizes them. Viewed in this light, religion is guilty of falsification or mystification of essentially human products (values and norms) by covering them with a veil of nonhuman mystery. The institution of marriage, for instance, is a human solution to the human problems of regulating sex and reproduction. But, in order for the institution to be accepted and followed, it is necessary "to explain why the particular arrangement that has developed in a particular society, in whatever sequence of historical accidents, should be faithfully adhered to, even if it is at times annoying or downright painful. One efficient way of solving the problem is to mystify the institution in religious terms."[10] Religion says, in effect, "You must marry according to the established rules because God wills it." The deviant, then, when breaking a norm, faces not only the anger of his fellow humans but can also be punished by a supernatural being whose power is supposedly limitless.

Relief of guilt. Religion also provides a means of relieving the deviant's guilt, as well as a way for him to become reestablished in society as a law-abiding member. Most religious organizations provide some kind of ritual for the forgiveness of sins, whether through the sacrifice of an animal or through confession. This function is important because the existence of a large number of deviants who cannot reenter society and are forced to live outside it present a definite threat to a society.

Legitimation of power. It is easy to see that the supportive function of religion is vital to social control. In addition, the supportive function is extremely helpful to the maintenance of the status quo. To use Peter Berger's example, every society is faced with the necessity of distributing power, for which purpose political institutions emerge. In giving these institutions legitimation, the society has to justify the use of physical violence, which underlies power. Here again, religion mystifies the human institution by giving it extrahuman qualities, so the phrase "The King wills it" soon bears the same weight as "Thus sayeth the Lord."[11]

Subversion of the status quo. Religion may, conversely, subvert rather than support the status quo. The prophetic function of religion causes the beliefs and values of society to be considered inferior to the laws of God. Because of its subversive function, religion often leads to protest movements and to eventual social change. The prophets of biblical times had such an effect on their society, and in modern times, the abolition of slavery and the passage of humanitarian laws for the disadvantaged were due, in part, to the influence of religion.

[10]Peter L. Berger, *The Sacred Canopy* (Garden City, N.Y.: Doubleday, 1967), p. 90.
[11]Ibid., pp. 1–92.

Aid in the critical stages of life. Another function of religion is the help it offers the individual in critical stages of his growth and maturation. From Chapter 3, you may remember that psychologists have established that humans develop through progressive stages. At each stage, the individual is faced with new problems. Religion seems to help him to accept the new roles forced on him. It does this through *rites of passage*, the rituals that have been established around critical times, such as birth, puberty, marriage, and death. Some of the tensions the individual feels as he approaches a new stage of life are lessened by his involvement with the ritual. Thus, funerals soften the blow of a loved one's death, whereas wedding ceremonies, initiations, and puberty rites (bar mitzvah, confirmation) instruct the individual in the role he is about to assume.

Feeling of power. A final function of religion may be the feeling of power that members of a religious group derive from their special relationship with a superior being. For example, the survival of the Jews as a religious and ethnic group, in the face of severe and repeated persecution, was largely a result of their feeling of being a chosen people.

Not all of these functions are performed by religion in all societies, or at all times, or for all people. At some times, one function may be more significant than another. For instance, in societies that lack scientific knowledge, religion's most important function may be that of explaining the physical and supernatural environment.

Many of the needs that religion helps to fulfill may be met by other societal institutions. Meaning may be sought in a nonreligious philosophy. Natural phenomena have been and continue to be explained by science. Social control, the overcoming of anxieties, the search for identity, and the critical function can be and are pursued through other institutions and structures of society. Religion contributes, supports, and supplements the other institutions in attaining the same ends. Those deeply committed to religion may feel that it is the only medium for fulfilling personal needs and upholding morality. Those less committed, or uncommitted, may find morality and transcendence in other sources.

To summarize religious functions, we can say that religion, from an historical perspective, seems to be both a world-maintaining and world-shaking force. At bottom, all religions have reflected humans' intense interest in the meaning of life. They have exemplified humans' efforts to make reality meaningful: "In all its manifestations, religion constitutes an immense projection of human meanings into the empty vastness of the universe—a projection, to be sure, which comes back as an alien reality to haunt its producers."[12]

MAGIC AND RELIGION

Another phenomenon existing in all human societies and one that fulfills some of the same functions as religion is magic. *Magic*, which is a part of

---

[12]Ibid., p. 100.

religion, shares with it a belief in the existence of a reality beyond that experienced by humans and in the possibility that humans may establish a relationship with that supernatural reality. But religion, through its ritual, offers only the *possibility* of such a relationship, whereas magic offers a way of manipulating supernatural forces so they operate in a desired fashion. Whereas a religious person would ask God to give him strength in a time of famine, the believer in magic would ask his deity specifically to send him a good harvest and thus end the famine. Anthropologist Bronislaw Malinowski states that magic always has a definite end, for instance, an incantation said to ensure successful childbirth. Religion is an end in itself, and its ritual celebrates the birth of a child for no other purpose than to rejoice.[13] Of course, if we pray for successful childbirth—and this is a common practice among the religions —we are essentially doing the same thing that a believer in magic does.

In nontechnological societies, magic and religion are two facets of the same institution, both performed in the spirit of mystery and awe, respect and marvel. In technological societies, a distinction is made between the two. At least, most religious organizations do not admit to practicing magic. Yet many people use the formulas of magic in the name of religion. How many of us have, at one time or another, prayed for a wish to come true, for the return of someone we love, or even for a good grade on an exam?

Religion: A System Dealing With the Sacred

In discussing the religious theories of Emile Durkheim, we mentioned that he distinguished between the sacred and the profane, characterizing religion and magic as the systems that deal with the sacred. The sacred is created basically by transforming the profane. The quality of sacredness can be attached to anything: an object, a person, an event, a time of day, a specific location. When something is made sacred, it is perceived as special, different, and distinct from the everyday. It is approached with awe, respect, reverence, fear, and admiration. The sacred has a contradictory impact on humans. It both attracts and fascinates them and frightens and repels them. Or perhaps it fascinates them because it frightens them.

The nature and qualities of the sacred were clarified by the anthropological discovery of the concept of mana among the natives of Polynesia and Melanesia. *Mana* is a supernatural force that can attach to any person, object, or event. It is ethically neutral—it can be either good or bad—but because its power always makes it dangerous, people must use caution in dealing with it. The idea that danger is part of the mysterious power of the sacred is equally evident in Western religions. The Old Testament narrates the story of a biblical figure who accidentally touched the ark of the covenant and was instantly destroyed.[14]

After something profane has been invested with sacredness, those who recognize it as sacred have a committment to it. The commitment is like a moral obligation to believe in, obey, and revere the sacred object. The beginning of such a commitment represents the beginning of religious faith. Durkheim suggested that *totemism* was very probably the first kind of religion and that others evolved from it. In totemism, an animal or a vegetable important

---

[13]Bronislaw Malinowski, *Magic, Science, and Religion* (Glencoe, Ill.: Free Press, 1954), pp. 37–38.
[14]Peter Berger, "Religious Institutions," in Neil J. Smelser, *Sociology*, p. 336.

to the society is worshipped as a god or an ancestor, or both. Sociologists believe that such worship began within the family or clan when some extraordinary event occurred and then spread to the rest of the society, perhaps because the particular family or clan became prosperous. In short, members of society thought that if worship of a particular deity was working well for the successful and powerful family, perhaps it would work equally well for them.

Sometimes a religion originates when the sacredness of an individual, such as Christ or Mohammed, is accepted by his followers. Finally, although it is primarily in religion and magic that sacredness is either created or recognized, other institutions can and do collaborate in this task. The political institution invests some symbols with sacredness: the flag and the constitution, for example. And in our culture, we consider human life and, to a lesser extent, motherhood as sacred.[15]

COMMON FEATURES OF RELIGION

Although religious expressions vary greatly from society to society, in their institutionalized form religions have some elements in common.

Beliefs

All religions possess a set of beliefs spelled out in doctrines, or articles of faith. Christian and Jewish beliefs, for instance, are contained in the Bible, whereas Muslim beliefs are in the Koran. Most probably, beliefs appear after other aspects of religion have become established. Their function is to explain and justify the sacred and the ritual attaching to it. Thus, the Old Testament, containing Judaic beliefs, explains why God is sacred. It also presents God in a form easily understood by people—as possessing human sentiments and passions. Furthermore, it explains how and why ritual should be performed.

Within religions today, the role of religious beliefs has grown stronger than it was, whereas the role of ritual and the worship of sacred objects has become weaker. In addition, beliefs have been refined and altered not only to make them consistent with scientific evidence but to give them relevance to behavior outside the religious sphere.

Ritual

Ritualized behavior follows the creation of sacredness and is an important mechanism for maintaining it. Any kind of behavior may become ritualized: dancing, gathering in a specific spot, drinking from a specific container, or eating a particular food. Once something becomes ritualized, however, the behavior and the objects involved are set apart and considered sacred in their own right. Ritual becomes a very important practice because it is considered to be the correct form of behavior toward the sacred. Therefore, ritual eases some of the dread connected with the sacred. In other words, by behaving in the prescribed way toward the sacred, people think that they are protecting themselves against supernatural wrath.

[15]Leonard Broom and Philip Selznick, *Sociology* (New York: Harper & Row, 1968), p. 303.

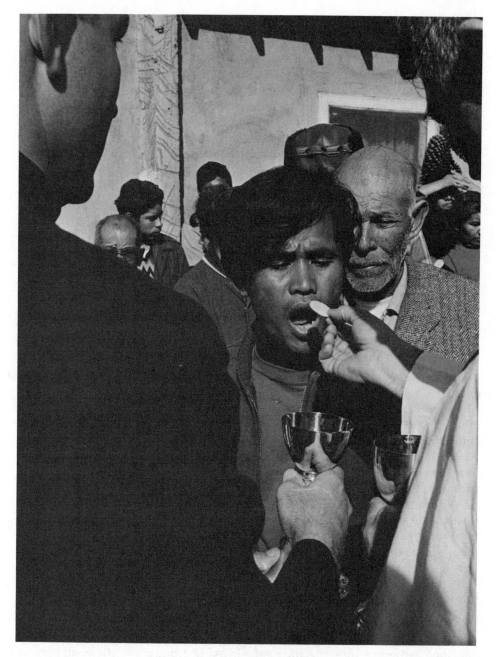

Ritual practices have been incredibly rich and imaginative. They have ranged from the offering up of human sacrifices, a practice engaged in by the Aztecs of Mexico among others, to the consumption of peyote, a hallucinogen, among some North American Indians. Sociologists who have analyzed ritual think that it helps people attain the feeling of self-transcendence (of being beyond and outside oneself), an emotion eagerly sought by those who need a temporary escape from reality. Such an emotion is part of the revivalist ritual associated with the fundamentalist sects of Christianity, which may be one reason why a growing number of young people are turning to similar methods of religious expression.

Today, however, among the major denominations, ritual tends to be restrained: kneeling and praying, celebrating Mass, eating bitter herbs and matzoh for Passover, and so on. However, expressive ritual often coexists with the staid ritual of official religious organizations. For instance, according to a recent report, 90 percent of Brazilians call themselves Roman Catholics. But at least 20 million of them are also followers of spiritism, which embraces everything from witchcraft to extrasensory perception. Among the rituals that accompany the pagan expressions of spiritism is a New Year's Eve celebration on the beach. During this ceremony, offerings—jewelry, perfume, cosmetics —are brought to the sea goddess Iemanja, while some of the faithful receive the blessings of priests from improvised altars, and others dance, chant, and drink to the incessant beat of bongo drums.

In effect, many Brazilians practice two religions simultaneously. They attend both Sunday Mass and Monday evening services in which they invoke their favorite spirits and burn candles to them. Of late, spiritism is attracting not only the impoverished urban masses, who make up its chief followers, but also an educated and wealthy segment of the population. Because spiritism presents a real threat to the Catholic Church, the Catholic clergy is seriously thinking about trying to replace spiritism with something that would fill the people's needs yet remain within the boundaries of Catholicism. This involves reversing a trend in which spirits are invoked more often than are saints.[16]

Observers of our society today view the emergence of new musical expressions, the colorful attire of the young, and their interest in drugs, group encounters, exotic and fundamentalist religions, and magic as a revolt against the lack of ritual in America. Our nation was founded on bleak religious principles, according to which expressions of joy were sinful and worthy of severe punishment. Thus, members of our society have repressed expressions of genuine feelings, substituting for them a kind of artificial fixed smile. Artificial emotion is associated with our present rituals: the Veterans' Day Parade, the political convention, the floats of the Orange Bowl, the funeral at which no one is sad, and the birth at which no one is particularly happy. These rituals do not permit civilized beings to express basic emotions, such as fear, grief, and sexuality. Yet, these emotions clamor for expression.

The current generation is rebelling against this long period of repression and searching for new rituals and for new forms of magic. But the new interest in ritual is dangerous, too, because an excess of passion may be as unsatisfactory as an excess of reason. At any rate, people do not outgrow their need for ritual, magic, and religion so long as they remain aware that they are mortal and insignificant beings in a largely mysterious universe.[17]

Organization

The institutionalization of any societal function requires that it become organized. If religion is to remain effective, people must be recruited to make

[16]"Homage to Iemanja," *Time* (January 10, 1972), pp. 44–45.

[17]Melvin Maddocks, "Rituals: The Revolt Against the Fixed Smile," *Time* (October 12, 1970), pp. 42–43.

sure that there is always a place available for worship, that ritual is conducted in the proper manner, and that followers treat the sacred with the proper respect. In nontechnological societies, institutions are not highly differentiated, so the family or the political institution (as represented by a chieftain) usually performs these functions. Modern societies, however, have developed a hierarchy of personnel that has the specific responsibility of running religious affairs. In Roman Catholicism, for instance, the hierarchy includes priests, bishops, archbishops, cardinals, and the pope, as well as various orders of monks and nuns.

Additional features

All religions also have specific emotions, symbols, and propitiatory behavior. The emotions most commonly associated with religion are humbleness, reverence, and awe, although in some people religion awakens feelings of ecstasy and terror. Symbols, such as the cross of the Christians and the skullcap of the Jews, express the meaning of the sacred. Propitiation is behavior that is thought pleasing to the sacred power, such as church attendance, prayer, confession, and obedience to the injunctions of one's religion.

RELIGION AND SOCIETY

Religion and the social order are deeply intertwined, both reflecting and affecting each other. At first, as we mentioned in passing, there was no distinction between the two. Religion was part of the family, each family having its own gods, spirits of ancestors, or whatever, for whom it practiced a specific ritual. These deities, in turn, were charged with the protection and promotion of the welfare of each specific family. In Greece and Rome, the head of the household was also the high priest, or intermediary between the sacred and the profane, whereas the sacred being was thought to reside within the borders of the family's property. Family membership was reckoned more by who worshipped at the family shrine than it was by blood ties. When a daughter married, she accepted the gods of her husband's family, an act equal to conversion to a new religion today.

For a long time, then, there were many gods, and family units remained tightly knit. Eventually, however, families began to worship gods of nature—symbols of the sun, the sea, and the forest—and worship became shared among a number of families. In addition, whenever one family prospered because of what was thought to be the effectiveness of its gods, other families wanted to adopt that family's worship so they too would have good fortune. Gradually, one set of gods came to be accepted by a whole clan, tribe, and, later, city-state.[18] Religion was then *communal*. In other words, the social and religious identities of the members of society were one and the same. If a member renounced his gods, he was, in effect, renouncing his membership in the social order. In communal religion, religious and worldly roles were also combined. First the head of the household later, the village chief, and finally, the political leader were high priests of religion.

Differentiation of the Institution

We have noted previously that the historic trend in societies has been one in which functions have become increasingly differentiated and specialized. Religion too has followed this trend. It became a separate institution after the functions of dealing with the sacred were taken over by a specialized hierarchy of societal members who made religion their vocation, membership in a particular religion became voluntary, and religious and nonreligious activities became independent from each other.

Because of the growing complexity of societies, authority for dealing with the sacred was given to a special body, the priesthood. This, in turn, led to further differentiation: Priests did not want societal members to interfere in religion and thus threaten their own power and security. By the same token, members of society felt less obligation than they had to listen to religious specialists when they spoke on nonreligious matters. Increasingly, the religious, political, economic, and educational spheres became distinct. Religion's lack of influence on worldly affairs gave the individual increased freedom of choice. He could choose not to participate in religious activities, and later, he could choose from among a number of different religious expressions.

Structural Organization of the Institution

Religious organizations fall into the categories of church, sect and cult.

---

[18]Fustel de Coulanges, *The Ancient City* (Garden City, N.Y.: Doubleday Anchor Books, 1956), p. 125.

Churches. In its sociological definition, the *church* is an association that is thoroughly institutionalized and well integrated into the social and economic orders. It seeks out its members according to residence and family, and participation in it is more or less routine. The highly institutional nature of the church gives it a hierarchically arranged official body of administrators, an official doctrine or ideology intended to meet most of the problems encountered by members, and a traditional ritual. The church is integrated into the social and economic orders because it retains close ties with the family, the school, the state, and the economy, all of which reflect its teachings.

If the church has a monopoly on religious belief, it is called *universal.* For example, the Catholic Church of Medieval Europe was a universal church. When a substantial majority of, but not the entire, population, profess to be members of a church, that church is called an *ecclesia.* In a society that has an ecclesia, the beliefs and values of the secular, or worldly, social system and those of the religious one are closely related. The Anglican Church in England and the Catholic Church in modern Latin America have great influence in nonreligious areas of life.

In a society that accepts a number of religious organizations on an equal basis, the organizations are known as *denominations.* This kind of religious organization is most familiar to Americans and is particularly characteristic of pluralistic societies. Denominations—Episcopalian, Presbyterian, and Methodist, among others in the Protestant Church and Orthodox, Conservative, and Reformist in Judaism— coexist in comfort when there is separation of church and state. They are tolerant of other denominations; their membership is hereditary (although, of course, voluntary); and they do not make great demands on their members for religious commitment but are content with occasional church attendance and financial support.

Sects. A sect differs from a church in several important ways. Frequently, a *sect* is formed by a group that breaks away from either the church or from a denomination of the church. In this sense, it is a revolutionary movement that rebels at the conservatism of the established religious organizations. The sect rejects an official priesthood, preferring to divide religious responsibilities among its lay members. Commitment and participation by the members is thus high and valued. Sects emphasize to a far greater degree than do churches religious emotions and expression and are less concerned with the formal and traditional aspects of religion. Church and sect are, then, frequently in conflict. The sect stresses the need for the purity of religious thought and uncompromising faithfulness to the spirit of religion. The church emphasizes the necessity of maintaining a stable institution and faithfulness to the letter of religion.

Members of sects tend to think they are the elect of God because they have special knowledge and a special relationship with Him. Personal perfection is an acknowledged goal, and a serious infraction of rules or norms may be followed by expulsion. For these reasons, sectarian members tend to be intolerant of both the secular order and other religious groups. In short, members think they have the only answers, and they would rather try to change the world to fit their beliefs than to compromise so their beliefs would fit the world. In time, some sects gain a large enough membership to become institutionalized and develop into denominations. Because this trend is almost unavoidable, some sociologists regard sects as denominations in the making. Most sectarian organizations become transformed by the second or third generation or even last for only one generation.[19] The Anabaptists, Huguenots, Mennonites, Presbyterians, and Baptists, among others, were once sects but all have become denominations since the Reformation.

Although they may be short lived, sects are a vital force in society and are no less alive today than when they began the Protestant Reformation. In fact, whereas membership in denominational organizations is declining, pentecostal and evangelical sects are flourishing. One reason for the popularity of sects is their appeal for members of the lower classes. Lower-class people are attracted to movements offering rationalization for their low status in society and hope for an improved status in an extraworldly system. What religion—especially a sectarian religion—means to the poor is sensitively portrayed by Robert Coles in his article "God and the Rural Poor."[20] The religious zeal of the poor is often misinterpreted by the wealthy and well educated, who consider the highly ritualized and superstition-laden religions of the poor effective mechanisms for compliance to an unjust social order. But Coles maintains that the sincerity of poor people's beliefs gives them spiritual strength, a kind of strength lacking in institutionalized churches.

Cults. The least conventional and institutionalized form of religious organizations—some would deny that it even belongs to that category—is the cult. *Cults* are usually temporary groups of followers clustered around a leader whose teachings differ substantially from the doctrines of the church or denomination, or even from those of the sect. However, persistent cults often develop into sects. A belief in the supernatural or a relationship between man and the sacred are not necessarily part of these organizations. Because membership in cults tends to be drawn from the alienated of society, cults are so small that they do not usually influence the course of society. We will have further occasion to discuss cults when we consider trends in modern society.

RELIGION IN AMERICA

The institution of religion, no less than that of the family, has suffered from the increasing division of institutional functions caused by urbanization and industrialization. Membership in religious organizations has not decreased In fact, statistics indicate the opposite. But the quality of religious feeling has suffered. Religion has become increasingly secular, bureaucratic, and commercial, creating a void that many are forced to fill with substitutes. The substitutes range from psychiatry to satanic cults and from encounter groups to Jesus freaks.

[19]Howard Becker, "Constructive Typology in the Social Sciences," *American Sociological Review* (February, 1940), p. 467. Also, H. Richard Niebuhr, *The Social Sources of Denominationalism* (New York: Holt, Rinehart and Winston, 1929), p. 19.

[20]Robert Coles, "God and the Rural Poor," *Psychology Today* (January, 1972), pp. 33–40.

Characteristics of Religion in America

Religion in the United States had a peculiar character even before industrialization took place—in fact, from the very beginning of the nation. Except at the beginning of the colonial period, the United States has never had a state, or national, religion. Instead, numerous religious expressions have coexisted. The separation of church and state, as well as tolerance for a number of denominations, is a deeply ingrained American tradition. Of course, some religious prejudice and even discrimination are present in our social relationships. But prejudice is probably more closely related to social stratification than to religion.

One effect of the existence of numerous denominations in the United States is that, like worldly organizations, religious organizations must compete for the attention of the buyer, or prospective member. As a result, religious expression in this country is characterized by much more optimism and much less emphasis on self-sacrifice and punishment than it is in other countries. The prospective member is likely to choose a religion that promises him peace of mind and the freedom to enjoy the fruits of his labor than he is to choose a religion that promises him eternal damnation and the need to repress his desire for pleasure. The extent to which religion is sold as a panacea for whatever ails humanity is made apparent in our article "The God-Hucksters of Radio."[21] The Gospel, as preached by the radio preachers, represents an

[21]William C. Martin, "The God-Hucksters of Radio," *Atlantic* (June, 1970), pp. 51–56.

TABLE 11.1   SOCIAL CLASS PROFILES OF AMERICAN RELIGIOUS GROUPS

Denomination	Upper class	Middle class	Lower class
Christian Scientist	24.8	36.5	38.7
Episcopal	24.1	33.7	42.2
Congregational	23.9	42.6	33.5
Presbyterian	21.9	40.0	38.1
Jewish	21.8	32.0	46.2
Reformed	19.1	31.3	49.6
Methodist	12.7	35.6	51.7
Lutheran	10.9	36.1	53.0
Christian	10.0	35.4	54.6
Roman Catholic	8.7	24.7	66.6
Baptist	8.0	24.0	68.0
Mormon	5.1	28.6	66.3
No preference	13.3	26.0	60.7
Atheist, agnostic	33.3	46.7	20.0

SOURCE: N. J. Demerath III, *Social Class in American Protestanism*, Chicago: Rand McNally, 1965, p. 2. Original data derived from National Council of Churches' survey. The precise meaning of "upper," "middle," and "lower" was not designated.

extremely sectarian and marginal religious expression. But it has an audience of tens and hundreds of thousands, as canned and packaged as it is. There is no doubt that whatever is being sold has a market.

Other methods that religion has borrowed from the marketplace include the offering of secondary inducements. Church buildings are now used for recreational purposes—people can play cards, and bingo, discuss books and political issues and candidates, and form interest-related clubs. To keep up with the times, churches concentrate on nonreligious activities that are principally family and child-centered.[22] Even abortion information and drug counseling can be obtained today through church-sponsored agencies.

Finally, there is a new ecumenical movement within American Protestantism. It has been described in business terms—cartelization, or mergers of several denominations for the purpose of cornering the religious market.[23]

[22]Peter L. Berger, "Religious Institutions," in Neil J. Smelser, *Sociology*, pp. 372–375.
[23]Robert K. Merton, Leonard Broom, and Leonard S. Cottrell, eds., *Sociology Today: Problems and Prospects* (New York: Harper & Row, 1959), p. 161.

TABLE 11.2 EDUCATIONAL ATTAINMENT OF HOUSEHOLD HEAD, BY COLOR AND RELIGIOUS AFFILIATION

| | **Education: Highest Grade of School Completed** | | | | | |
| | **Elementary School** | | **High School** | | **College** | |
Religious Preference	**0-6 yrs.**	**7-8 yrs.**	**1-3 yrs.**	**4 yrs.**	**1-3 yrs.**	**4+ yrs.**
White, Total	13.4	24.2	20.5	22.4	10.3	9.1
Protestant total	12.1	24.6	21.0	22.4	10.8	9.1
Baptist	18.8	28.3	22.1	17.7	7.6	5.4
Methodist	9.5	21.0	21.8	26.5	12.2	9.0
Presbyterian	6.4	17.4	23.6	24.7	15.1	12.8
Episcopal	5.0	17.1	8.8	22.5	23.1	23.5
Lutheran	10.5	29.2	21.8	22.5	8.5	7.5
Other Protestant	13.2	26.9	19.0	21.4	9.8	9.8
Roman Catholic	15.1	25.8	20.8	22.5	9.0	6.8
Jewish	12.5	13.4	13.2	28.2	10.8	21.8
No religion	20.5	23.6	19.1	16.3	9.5	11.0
Nonwhite	45.1	21.4	17.5	10.7	3.4	2.1
Baptist	50.4	21.6	16.4	7.8	2.8	1.2
Other	36.2	20.6	18.9	16.4	4.3	3.6

SOURCE: Donald J. Bogue, *The Population of the United States*, New York: Free Press, 1959, based on special tabulation of survey data from National Opinion Research Center.

There are even indications of a coming together of Catholicism and Protestantism. In fact, a joint theological commission reported recently that it had reached substantial agreement on the Eucharist, a doctrine flatly rejected by the Anglican Church after its sixteenth century split from Roman Catholicism. Ecumenicism is, of course a movement designed to minimize religious differences that have been traditionally conflict-producing. But in so doing, ecumenicism cannot avoid contributing to the standardization of religious expression, which ultimately may result in a watered-down, mass-produced, neatly packaged product for consumption.

Religious Membership

Valid statistics concerning membership in religious organizations are difficult to find because the organizations themselves supply the figures, which are neither standardized nor carefully recorded. As of 1968, to the best of our knowledge, 126 million people were reportedly members of 241 religious organizations in the United States. This represents roughly 63 percent of the total population of the nation, a percentage that has increased steadily since the beginning of this century.[24] In general terms, Protestants have the largest membership (70 million), followed by the Catholics (48 million) and Jews (almost 7 million). However, if Protestants are separated into their denominations

[24]Lewis B. Whitman, *Yearbook of American Churches*, 1968.

TABLE 11.3   RELIGIOUS AFFILIATION IN THE UNITED STATES

Roman Catholic	47,873,000
Baptist	23,900,000
Methodist	21,289,000
Lutheran	8,400,000
Jewish	5,725,000
Episcopalian	3,429,000
Presbyterian	3,926,000
United Church of Christ	2,053,000
Mormons	1,892,000
Greek Orthodox	1,770,000
African Methodist Episcopal	1,166,000
Assembly of God	595,000
Seventh-Day Adventist	385,000
Salvation Army	325,000
Jehovah's Witnesses	311,000
Unitarian	283,000
Black Muslims	250,000
Pentecostal Church of God	115,000
Mennonite	84,000

SOURCE: *Yearbook of American Churches*, 1969.

(Baptists, Lutherans, Presbyterians, Anglicans, and so on), they are far outnumbered by Catholics, who have no denominational subdivisions.

Additional statistics regarding religion lend themselves to sociological interpretation. For instance, Jews and Catholics tend to live in urban centers, especially in the Northeast. Baptists and Methodists are concentrated in the South and Midwest. The birth rate is highest among Baptists and Catholics and lowest among Jews and Presbyterians. More men than women report that they have no religious affiliation. Church attendance is highest among professionals, lowest among semiskilled and skilled workers. But the most analyzed relationship by far has been that between religion and stratification.

RELIGION AND DIMENSIONS OF STRATIFICATION

Christ declared that it is easier for a camel to pass through the eye of a needle than for a rich man to enter the kingdom of God. Ironically, however, Christianity has both initiated and helped to maintain systems of stratification. When the Catholic Church became institutionalized and reached the height of its power in Medieval Europe, it continued to emphasize the basic equality of all men in the eyes of God and retained the idea that poverty is a virtue. But Catholicism found no contradiction between these ideas and the stratification system in which many lived in dire misery and a few, including the upper echelon of Catholicism's hierarchy, lived in majestic splendor. Relying on the dictum that "The poor will always be with us" and will obtain their reward in an afterlife, the Catholic Church helped maintain a rigid system of stratification that permitted almost no social mobility.

The Protestant Reformation, controlled primarily by the new merchant middle classes, challenged the established views of Catholicism. We have noted previously that Protestants believe that God looks favorably upon those who accumulate wealth through hard work, a belief that gave added force to the emergence of capitalism. The reverse side of this belief is that those who do not accumulate wealth are obviously not in God's grace. Soon lower-class characteristics became associated with sin: God does not favor the poor because they are lazy, drink too much, and have no self-control and no self-discipline. At the same time, middle-class qualities became established as virtues. Poverty became a condition not to be pitied and remedied but to be reprimanded and censured. Protestantism, then, also helped to maintain a system of stratification. But Protestants did leave the door open to social mobility by encouraging the poor to embrace middle-class virtues and thus rise in the system.

Religious Affiliation and Social Class

In the United States, the relationship between religion and stratification can be seen most clearly in the religious affiliation of different classes. Americans of highest status—members of the several elites—have consistently been Protestant, particularly Episcopalian (Anglican). Those of lowest status have usually been Catholics and members of fundamentalist sects that broke away from denominational Protestantism.

The relationship between church membership and status can be credited both to the effects of the Protestant ethic and to historical circumstances. Historically, immigrants have generally been pushed upward in the stratification system by the subsequent arrival of other immigrants. Because the earliest arrivals here were primarily Protestants, dissenters from the Anglican Church, and the late arrivals were primarily Catholics from Ireland and from southern and central Europe, Protestants automatically formed the upper strata. Moreover, Protestant denominations have been divided along class lines from the very beginning, whereas the Catholic Church has traditionally included all social strata.[25]

Although significant class differences among the members of different denominations continue to exist, caution should be used in interpreting the data. In a very general way, Roman Catholicism has been the faith of the urban industrial masses. Protestantism, on the other hand, draws its members from the business and professional communities. Of the Protestant denominations, the Presbyterian and Episcopalian churches attract the educated elite, whereas the Lutheran, Methodist, and Baptist churches attract the urban middle classes and rural farmers. Small Protestant denominations, such as the Quakers, Congregationalists, Unitarians, and Christian Scientists, tend to attract middle-class and upper-class members on a local basis. Working-class Protestants feel attracted to the colorful rituals of radical sects.[26]

Participation

If measured in terms of church participation rather than church membership, those at both extremes of the stratification system (the upper-upper and the lower-lower classes) engage in very little church activity. Those of high social class may not feel that religion is important enough for them to take time from their numerous other activities. It is also possible that upper-class individuals are uncomfortable with doctrines that preach human equality. The disinterest in church activities on the part of the lower-lower individual is probably related to the general apathy and suspicion he feels against all who do not belong to his own kinship group. You may remember from our discussion of stratification in Chapter 4 that one characteristic of the lower social classes is lack of participation in all types of organization.

Those who participate actively in church affairs are chiefly recruited from the ranks of the upper-lower and the lower-middle classes. Among these strata, church activism and doctrinal belief are most intense. The upper-middle class shows a high degree of participation, but there is reason to believe that their participation is motivated more by the desire for social recognition, or for doing the "right thing," than by moral conviction.[27]

[25]E. Digby Baltzell, "Religion and the Class Structure," in Seymour Martin Lipset and Richard Hofstadter, eds., Sociology and History: Methods (New York: Basic Books, 1968), p. 312.

[26]Ibid., p. 313.

[27]Charles Y. Glock and Rodney Stark, Religion and Society in Tension (Chicago: Rand McNally, 1965).

Income

With respect to income, Jews show a high representation in the upper levels of the stratification system. Sixty-nine percent have incomes of $7,000 and over per year. In second place are Episcopalians, 55 percent of whom are in this income category. Among Baptists only 26 percent are in this income group.

Jews and Protestants are also occupationally more successful and upwardly mobile than are Catholics. In *The Religious Factor*, sociologist Gerhard Lenski provided evidence that white Protestants who had begun life at the same level of the stratification system as had Catholics remained there or rose more frequently than did Catholics. Lenski's explanation for this is the Protestant Ethic, which develops a favorable attitude toward work. In fact, favorable attitudes toward work were found to exist among 52 percent of white Protestants, 48 percent of Jews, and 44 percent of Catholics.[28]

Education

Because of the close relationship among income, status, and education, which we examined in an earlier chapter, clearly, those groups that have the highest income and status also achieve the highest levels of education. Thus, Episcopalians and Jews reach the highest educational levels, whereas Baptists

[28]Gerhard Lenski, *The Religious Factor* (New York: Doubleday Anchor Books, 1963), pp. 84–85.

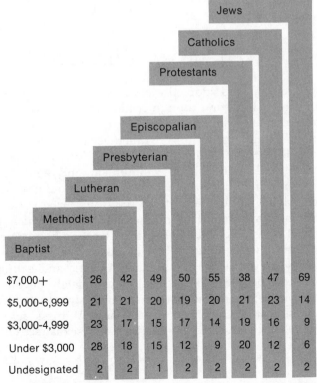

	Baptist	Methodist	Lutheran	Presbyterian	Episcopalian	Protestants	Catholics	Jews
$7,000+	26	42	49	50	55	38	47	69
$5,000-6,999	21	21	20	19	20	21	23	14
$3,000-4,999	23	17	15	17	14	19	16	9
Under $3,000	28	18	15	12	9	20	12	6
Undesignated	2	2	1	2	2	2	2	2
	100%	100%	100%	100%	100%	100%	100%	100%

and Catholics do not. In addition, Gerhard Lenski discovered that the school dropout rate was lowest among Jews (29 percent) and highest among Catholics (52 percent). Lenski theorized that Jews and Protestants may be highly motivated by, once again, the Protestant Ethic and that motivation may be another reason why their income is high. Catholics may be less motivated and may be further handicapped by large families and crowded home conditions.

It is ironic that religion has such close ties to stratification because in almost all religious doctrines humans are declared equals. Although classlessness may have been emphasized in the Judeo-Christian tradition, Judaism and Christianity became institutionalized and thus susceptible to stratification. A system of ranking is a deeply ingrained feature of social orders and is particularly characteristic of systems that are stable and continuous. Thus, because the goal of most religious organizations is to become stable and continuous, they cannot avoid becoming stratified internally. Externally, they also function to maintain the stratification system of the larger social order.

The rigidity that follows institutionalization has been periodically challenged by religious movements emphasizing the spirit rather than the form of religion. The Protestant Reformation was a reaction to the institutionalization of the Catholic Church, and the later splinter groups of Calvinists and Methodists reacted to the institutionalization of the Protestant Church. Thus, in the same way that religion functions both as an integrative and a conflict-producing force in society, it both reinforces the stratification system of society and threatens it on occasion.

CONTEMPORARY TRENDS

We saw how religion has adopted mechanisms of the marketplace to win and keep supporters. But even though it has employed such methods, its influence is progressively waning. At present, religious influence is felt most strongly within the family institution—in other words, on an individual, rather than on a social, level.[29] As a unifying force in society, religion is being displaced by ideologies like nationalism, communism, and democracy.

Thus, a large portion of our cultural beliefs, values, and goals are becoming gradually secularized, or separated from religious, or spiritual, influence. Nowhere is this more apparent than in religious festivals, which have become nothing but social occasions. Undeniably, the Christian holidays of Christmas and Easter and the Jewish holidays of Hanukkah and Passover retain little that is holy. They are occasions for exchanging gifts and eating traditional foods, but, for most people, they are almost completely devoid of spiritual meaning. What is more, the norms that were previously invested with religious sanctions have also lost much of their effectiveness. Witness, for example, the nonchalance with which divorces are obtained and sexual activities pursued.

[29]Peter L. Berger, "Religious Institutions," in Neil J. Smelser, *Sociology*, p. 373.

Finally, religious beliefs are becoming almost universally a matter of personal choice rather than of social necessity.

Bureaucratization

Not only is secularization a distinct trend but the denominations most highly institutionalized have met the fate of most other associations in urban industrial societies. They have become bureaucratized, specialized, and efficient in their administrative functions, particularly in financial matters. Today, denominations have headquarters in downtown skyscrapers and branches in the suburbs. They are, in the words of Harvard professor Harvey Cox, "a perverted form of Christianity, deodorized and afraid of smell."[30] Dehumanized and despiritualized forms of religious expression may help to explain why sectarian religion is flourishing and denominational religion is languishing.

In modern society, then, religious organizations resemble other voluntary associations, offering practical help, and promoting such values as mental health, peace of mind, family togetherness, and even patriotism. Therefore, although religious activity is rather high, the supernatural, or sacred, facet of religious life is definitely declining.

The Ministry

An increasing number of the clergy of all denominations are pursuing careers in addition to the ministry, particularly in such fields as teaching, the law, and social work. This trend indicates that religious organizations are trying to perform functions useful to modern society. But it also indicates that clergymen are working for purely secular causes. In this area, too, the distinction between the sacred and the secular is becoming hazy.

If clergymen are succeeding in their role of social guide, they seem to be failing as spiritual guides. The sermon has been the traditional means for transmitting instruction and leadership to the faithful. However, more and more clergyman are complaining that their sermons seem to be increasingly ineffective and that their messages fall on deaf ears.

Yet a recent survey of Protestant ministers indicated that members do not listen because nothing is being said. Over a third of the ministers surveyed replied that they had never taken any issue to the pulpit. This was true even of issues involving school prayers, racism, drug legislation, sexual behavior, divorce, and pornography, which would seem to be within the sphere of spiritual leadership. In their religious outlook, the ministers were overwhelmingly traditional. They held the most orthodox doctrines of their religion, a factor associated with their poor record of speaking out on political issues. A small minority of modernists were much more vocal on these issues. A whopping 95 percent of them spoke out on the issue of public housing, as

---

[30]"Religion in the Age of Aquarius: A Conversation with Harvey Cox and T. George Harris," *Change: Readings in Society and Human Behavior* (Del Mar, Calif.: CRM Books, 1972), p. 211.

compared with 29 percent of the traditionalists; and 52 percent of the modernists supported the grape strike by farm laborers, compared with only 9 percent of the traditionalists. Even on such an important issues as the Vietnam war, one out of three Protestant ministers were silent.

The reason for neglecting vital issues may be the ministers' conception of the purpose of the sermon. Fifty-nine percent thought that the chief purpose of the sermon was to provide spiritual comfort and to uplift the distressed; 54 percent thought it was to point out the existence of sin; 79 percent thought it was to illustrate the kind of life a Christian should lead; and 73 percent thought it was to apply Christian standards to the behavior and institutions of humans. Obviously, the high percentage that agreed with the last purpose did not apply it in their own ministry, because in their sermons they ignored issues begging for leadership in Christian behavior.

Finally, this survey touched on the function and mission of the church in society. Here, researchers found two conflicting views. The first view is that of otherworldliness. It is represented by evangelism, best illustrated by the Reverend Billy Graham. According to this view, social problems will automatically disappear through individual salvation—in other words, when all people are brought to Christ. According to this view, social problems can best be solved through social and political efforts. In statistical terms, 77 percent of traditionalist ministers agreed with the statement that social ills would take care of themselves if all people were brought close to Christ. Conversely, only 42 percent of the traditionalists, as against 100 percent of the modernists, agreed with the view that it is more important to improve the quality of this life than it is to worry about the next. The authors of the survey concluded that the traditionalist clergy's failure to speak out on social issues can be traced to their conviction that worldly problems are illusory and temporary in comparison with the joys of the next world.

What seems most disconcerting about this survey is that although the modernists are found on college campuses and even in some administrative positions, the traditionalists are in the majority at the parish level. Traditionalists, then, have the most contact with rank-and-file church members. This and other findings of the survey caused the authors to doubt that sweeping reforms will take place in the Protestant Church in the near future.[31]

The Changing Face of the Catholic Church

The Catholic Church, in general, and its clergy, in particular, seem to be undergoing much more revolutionary, or at least more visible, changes than are Protestants. Until a few years ago, Catholics could be easily distinguished from Protestants: Their children attended predominantly parochial schools; they rarely failed to appear at Sunday Mass; they prayed in a distinctive manner, kneeling and saying rosaries; their services were conducted in Latin; and they had a list of sins that only they could commit, such as eating meat on Friday, missing Sunday Mass, or using birth control devices.

[31]Rodney Stark, Bruce D. Foster, Charles Y. Glock, and Harold Quinley, "Sounds of Silence," *Change: Readings in Society and Human Behavior* (Del Mar, Calif.: CRM Books, 1972), pp. 200–204.

Less than a decade later, many of these characteristics of Catholicism are much less obvious. What is taught in parochial schools is often controversial; the injunction against birth control is ignored by a majority of American Catholics; and conflict has replaced consensus among Catholics on such subjects as abortion, aid to parochial schools, and the Vietnam war. In fact, only five years after the late Cardinal Spellman blessed the war as a struggle for civilization, the Berrigan brothers and numerous other priests and nuns were deeply involved in protests against it. In addition, increasing numbers of priests and nuns are leaving their orders to marry or marrying and fighting to remain within the church. Statistically, five priests leave the church (because of death and other reasons) for every two who are ordained into it.

Many older Catholics view the new Catholicism as a different religion, and they do not like it. Furthermore, the church has lost much of its attraction for and power over young members. A Gallup poll reports that more than a third of the respondents no longer attend Sunday Mass; two out of three admit to not having confessed for a two-month period; three-fourths belong to no Catholic organization whatever; only one out of two wants the church to uphold its stand against abortion; and less than 10 percent believe that their children would lose their souls if they left the church.[32] These findings are amazing, for Catholics used to be a united, distinctive religious group.

One interpretation of the changes is that they result from the church's own attempt to Americanize its members. Americanization was considered beneficial for a minority in a predominantly Protestant nation—a minority, moreover, in which members differed ethnically in almost everything but religion. The Irish-Catholics, who resembled the ethnic majority both in looks and culture, were responsible for building the parochial school system. The purpose of parochial schools was twofold: to teach the belief that the Catholic religion was the only true faith and to produce loyal Americans who were even more patriotic than were their Protestant neighbors. The Americanization of Catholics has been completed, particularly since John F. Kennedy became president. However, the reverse side of the process is that in a homogenized America, the church's role diminished. Today, each Catholic tends to face the issues confronting him as an individual, rather than as a member of a monolithic church.

Sociologist Gordon Zahn believes that the upheaval in the Catholic church represents a departure from the Catholic doctrine of the "just war." According to this doctrine, the church asked Catholics to take up arms even against their fellow Catholics on the assumption that the warmaking powers of the national government were just. Catholics felt that it was their patriotic duty to uphold and serve in any war in which their country fought. The majority of Catholics, as well as the majority of the priestly hierarchy, still act according to this doctrine. The doctrine, however, was reversed by the Papal encyclical *Pacem in Terris* (Peace on Earth), which rejected war in the nuclear era as contrary to reason. Nevertheless, in clear defiance of the course prescribed by Vatican II, Catholic traditionalists do not speak out against the Vietnam war or against crimes against humanity such as the Mylai massacre. Because they feel that

---

[32]"Has the Church Lost Its Soul?" *Newsweek* (October 4, 1971), pp. 80–89.

the silence of their coreligionists makes them accomplices in an immoral war, young, morally sensitive Catholics fall away from the church.[33]

The Jesus Movement

Another controversial phenomenon in America is the so-called Jesus movement. Some observers view it as the last gasp before the death of religion, but others regard it as a potential influence on both the church and society. The positive view is based on the movement's emphasis on a personal quest for ultimate meanings. Whatever its eventual fate, the movement seems to be flourishing, judged by the abundance of Jesus rock music, publications, Broadway shows, and other paraphernalia which in America accompany any movement or even any statement thought to be at all saleable. T-shirts, posters, buttons, bumper stickers ("Honk if you love Jesus"), and the rock play *Jesus Christ Superstar* are only the visible by-products of what seems to be the latest outbreak of American sectarianism.

What is unusual about this revivalist movement is its origin. It has sprung from the crash pads, the coffeehouses, and the communes of the counterculture. Its leaders are almost wholly under thirty and are often former drug users, bikers, and political radicals. Jesus freaks seem to be turning to fundamentalist religion because of their disillusion with the condition and goals of modern society and their dissatisfaction with ways they previously used to cope with their disillusion. In statistical terms, the members of the movement have a predominantly middle-class and white-collar background (72 percent indicated this). A majority are high school students, but one-fourth attended college or are attending it now. Sixty-two percent of those over 18 and 44 percent of those under that age admit to drug use before conversion. One-third claim activity in New Left politics, but 76 percent say they have become politically more conservative. Finally, 62 percent confess to having engaged in premarital sex prior to conversion, but fewer than 5 percent continue to do so after conversion.

The movement is anything but organized, embracing many different beliefs and attitudes. In general, the beliefs center on an acceptance of the Bible, a severe moral stance, commitment to the Gospel in daily life, and belief in Jesus Christ as a real presence in daily life, not merely as a historic or symbolic figure. Although the movement does not seem to attract many blacks—who perhaps have more pressing problems to take care of—it does appeal to a number of alienated Jewish youths. One of the leaders of Jews for Jesus explains that these young Jews do not feel that they have defected from their original religion. Rather, they are reaching toward God through Jesus, believing him to be the Messiah foretold in biblical prophecy whom orthodox Judaism refused to accept. Religious scholars are inclined to think that the Jewish converts are victims of an identity crisis, brought about because Jews are no longer held together as a united group either by ghetto walls or by religious persecution.

[33]Gordon Zahn, "The Great Catholic Upheaval," *Saturday Review* (September 11, 1971), pp. 24ff.

The Jesus movement has been criticized not only by the established denominations as reckless and impulsive but also by concerned observers who fear its simplistic approach to life, its emotionalism, and the unflinching certainty of its beliefs. They also fear the Jesus people's disregard for worldly issues. This disregard is illustrated by one Jesus convert who was asked about the issue of race. He answered that he no longer had to think about such things because Jesus would tell him the right thing to do when the occasion arose. Such social blindness has obvious drawbacks in our society, which is in dire need of social reforms, particularly in the area of race.

Some churchmen believe that the Jesus movement will be most effective if it becomes integrated with the institutional churches, in which it may provide a spark of new life. Many groups in the movement are already taking this direction and are becoming increasingly involved in the sectarian movements of the established denominations. This trend may eventually bring about the end of the Jesus movement as countercultural movement and transform it into denominationalism.[34]

Critics and supporters of the movement agree that its popularity, as well as the popularity of other exotic religious groups (such as polytheists, pantheists, and explorers of the occult, black magic, and even satanism), basically results from two unfulfilled needs. The first need is for community participation, for a feeling of oneness with the world and with other human beings. The other need is for personal experience with things and events. Young people are not satisfied to hear others pray or talk about the divine; they want to experience the sacred too. They sought to fulfill these needs through drugs, politics, and liberated sex, but they failed. They hope now to fulfill them, and to reach out for answers to the still unanswered questions of who the human being is and where he belongs in the scheme of things, through a religious expression that is free of the institutionalizing trend of society.

The religious movements of the young may be extreme in their rejection of rationality. And the followers' zeal for personal salvation may cause them to overlook important social problems. But much of organized religion is also unconcerned with these problems. Although most religious leaders insist that they teach their followers moral values, research has shown that religious devoutness is no indication of a sincere concern for the welfare of other human beings. Sociologist Milton Rokeach reports on a survey showing "that the religiously devout are on the average more bigoted, more authoritarian, more dogmatic and more antihumanitarian than the less devout."[35] Rokeach concludes that institutional religions must shift from merely telling people what they must not do to teaching them what good they ought to do. In other words, rather than stressing the Ten Commandments, they should emphasize the Sermon on the Mount.

[34]"The Jesus Movement: Impact on Youth, Church," *U.S. News & World Report* (March 20, 1972), pp. 59–64.

[35]Milton Rokeach, "Faith, Hope, Bigotry," *Change: Readings in Society and Human Behavior*, p. 213.

SUMMARY

When social philosophers first studied religion, they tended to think of religious beliefs as people's faltering explanations of a reality they did not understand. A later view, proposed by Emile Durkheim, was that religion deals with the sacred and that the object of religious beliefs and practices is society itself. Whereas Durkheim's theories of religion stress the function of social integration, Max Weber's stress those of social control.

Modern sociologists view religion from a functional viewpoint. The first function that religion performs for the individual is to relieve his feelings of frustrations which arise because he lives in a situation of contingency, powerlessness, and scarcity. Religion also explains the physical world, making it comprehensible, familiar, and meaningful. It supports and invests the norms and values of society with divine sanctions. Thus, it aids in social control. Religion also provides the deviant with a means of repenting and rejoining society. It helps the individual during the difficult stages of maturation, and it gives him a feeling of power and of being special by virtue of his special relationship with the divinity. On a societal level, religion both maintains the status quo (through social integration and social control) and challenges it on occasion.

All religions have beliefs, rituals, and organization. Before becoming institutionalized, religion was a part of the family. It arose when an unusual event or person was invested with sacredness. Later, ritual and a set of beliefs grew up around the object of sacredness. As one family became particularly successful, other families adopted its divinity and ritual to ensure their own success. In this manner, the worship spread throughout the entire society. With the growing complexity of societies, the authority for dealing with the sacred was given to a special body, the priesthood. This led to further differentiation and specialization of functions and, finally, to the institutionalization of religion.

In structure, religious organizations may be divided into church, sect, and cult. The church is an institutionalized association which is integrated into other institutions. It recruits members according to residence and family and demands only routine participation. The church can be universal, an ecclesia, or denominational. A sect is a revolutionary movement that has broken away from the church or is formed because people find the church inadequate in some way. Although churches and sects are often in conflict, sects tend to become denominations within the church.

Religion in America is denominational. Because of the existence of numerous denominations, the doctrine of the separation of church and state has become firmly established. At the same time, religion has borrowed the methods of the marketplace to recruit and hold members.

Religious and denominational membership are closely related to social stratification. People who have high status are overwhelmingly Protestant, particularly Episcopalian. Many people who have high incomes are Jews and Episcopalians, and so are the highly educated. But the most active participants in religious organizations are members of the lower-middle and upper-lower classes.

Modern trends in religion include secularization and bureaucratization. Religious organizations resemble other kinds of voluntary associations that deal with mental health, family togetherness, and social welfare. A reaction against the growing lack of spirituality, as well as against the lack of leadership on vital social issues, is becoming apparent among the modernists of the clergy, who have been active in the peace and civil rights movements. The emergence of a number of sectarian movements of a pentecostal and evangelical nature and the Jesus movement may be credited to a similar reaction.

god & the rural poor

Many of us well-educated and affluent rationalists tend to sneer at storefront, or rural, churches. We sometimes call their members "holy rollers" because of their emotionalism. But we seldom stop to think what the emotional expression of religious faith means to the followers of fundamentalist sects or what would happen if their zeal were directed at extracting revenge from society for having assigned them to the bottom of the stratification system. Courage to endure, hope for the future, and a rationalization of the present—the only possessions of the dispossessed—are all found in the religion of the poor. Robert Coles offers a sensitive portrayal of people aided by religious faith in this excerpt from his book Children of Crisis.

☐☐☐

Perhaps nothing is more difficult for the outsider to comprehend than the deep and abiding religious faith of black sharecroppers and white tenant farmers, of migrant workers, and of the mountain people of Appalachia.

The social, economic and political condition, not to mention the medical and psychological problems, of the rural poor command wide and sympathetic interest from well-educated people who are truly horrified that America continues to allow some of its people to live in near-peonage. Liberals and progressives try—often enough in a sensitive and fair spirit that shuns condescension—to

comprehend the so-called life-styles of the rural poor. Nor do we merely try to understand; we proudly consider ourselves supporters, well-wishers, champions of the poor and the miserable—America's version of Frantz Fanon's "wretched of the earth."

Limit. The language of tenant farmers, the traveling and living habits of migrants, the music played and sung up in the hollows—all of these we may look upon with discernment and insight and (we hope) not a little compassion. But our forbearance wears thin at the church door. We are likely to think: what hardships they face, in return for a promise that another world will redeem this one's evils! And what energy is week-by-week carried off in a noisy, superstitious tide of prayers and hymns, all meant to make people compliant, slightly dazed, and ridiculously hopeful—in the face of their awful circumstances. Seldom do we react similarly to the dozens of secular ideologies that command compliance, belief and, not uncommonly, real zealotry from well-educated and well-to-do people.

Yet we must come to terms with the faith of "poor, wretched believers," as I once heard a sharecropper woman describe her family, if we are to avoid making people with sincere opinions and passionate beliefs into opiated and deluded victims, or into philosophically duped and neurotically afflicted patients.

God lives for sharecroppers, difficult though that may be for some of their distant friends and allies to accept and believe.

Event. I will try to hint at—maybe this is the way to put it—the animated spirit of the Spirit, as I happened to see and hear and feel that Spirit come alive, become an event.

It *is* an event. Something happens, something takes place. In rural churches one is moved and transported, one is elevated and summoned, one uses arms and the hands and the legs, one bends and straightens out and twists and turns, and yes, finally yes, *arrives*.

The black mother of a Mississippi sharecropper's five children talks about those Sundays:

"It's the only day of the week for me, the only one we count, because then God is there beckoning you, telling you it's all right, just come on over and be with Me, be with Me for a few minutes, yes sir. If you do, if you go to Him, if you be with Him, then, like He says, you'll be all right. When you go back home, you'll be good again."

Passion. Those verbs—*do, go, be*—what are we to make of them, marched out in formation one right after the other, stated so easily and unselfconsciously and knowingly? To that woman, the idea of a Christian church means exactly what she says: *doing, going* and *being*. She says that a time *comes*, a time of truth, a time when one *goes* to be saved, when faith *does* something. There is an orgiastic quality to her kind of worship; no one these days would deny that. The history of theology is full of books in which religious passions are unashamedly, indeed proudly, connected to man's physical and psychological nature, to his lusts and urges and wants and needs.

But we agnostic ascetics or religious puritans aren't used to finding faith "impure"—lusty, driven, sensual, *physical*. For Sally, that woman in Mississippi, church is initially a destination, a place over there that requires the physical effort of attendence —which means hundreds and hundreds of steps taken. The passion behind all those steps, the force of mind and heart that makes them possible, is seen in the effort of traveling down the Appalachian hollows, across the Delta mud, away from migrant labor camps to town, or simply to an open field, this time not so that crops will be harvested, but so that legs can be bent, bodies made to kneel—kneel as on weekdays, but now for a different purpose:

"I kneel all week long with the beans, but on Sunday I kneel to speak with God,

and He makes my knees feel better, much better...all of a sudden I know He's touched me and given me a little of His strength, so I can go on..."

Doubt. How is one to make neurophysiological (not to mention psychological) sense out of all that? Ought I to do a thorough medical examination on her, especially a neurological and psychiatric "evaluation"? I can only take note of her mixed feelings, faith that turns to despair, her high hope that becomes a grim low point. Doesn't she sometimes have her misgivings, her doubts about God and His churches and those ministers who from time to time take so much money from poor migrant workers? Certainly she does:

"You get weak on a lot of days, and your head hurts and your feet, from the top to the bottom. Then you're in trouble, because you start having bad thoughts, one after the other, until you've lost everything, all your belief in God, and you just want to go sit someplace and fill yourself up with all the wine you can find, and steal some if you haven't the money to buy it, and then you're glad when you start going under and you get dizzy and if you go to sleep you hope it lasts and lasts. There have been times, no fooling, when the last thing I could recall was myself saying it would be nice if I slept and slept and never work up... But if you can just remember to catch yourself and be patient with God, and if you know He's coming upon your life, to look it over and do like that, then you won't be killing yourself with the wine and with shouting at everyone when the least little thing goes wrong. That's how I think."

Happen. I can take note of her stubborn, quarrelsome spirit, which returns almost weekly to the struggle. I can also mention the various things that happen to her—I say again, the things that *happen to* her rather than the things that religious faith and attendance at church *do for* her. She actively takes on something when she goes to church. It seems to me, having been with her on those Sundays, that she is taking on all of her life and all of everyone's life, all of *life itself* perhaps, though believe me, I am not one bit sure.

Such worship means prayer and supplication, means the acknowledgment of faith, means the protestation and affirmation of beliefs; but a mind that is worshipping is also at work in other ways. Standards come to mind in those churches. Comparisons are made with what was and what might be. Things fall in place. A sense of sequence emerges. There is the coherence sought and found so helpful, and the reassurance that somewhere one is being noticed and somehow one does matter, after all.

Flush. The self becomes felt, and however hard it may be to prove when and in what form one "feels" that "self," such people know what it is suddenly and for a moment to be agitated and excited, to blush and flush or turn pale, to heave and tremble and warm up, and finally, as a retired Kentucky miner says it, "to get thinking about yourself."

For him, that self inevitably contains the Devil:

> "...God isn't going to let us get completely taken over by the bad in the world, the bad that's in yourself and in others. But like the Bible will tell you, it's a big struggle, and ... you're going to be fighting the struggle all your life, and a lot of the time you'll be near to losing, with the Devil just about to claim you his property, but then you'll be singing a hymn or like that, and you'll turn around and realize you're in danger and get saved in the nick of time, yes sir, right in the nick."

The Devil is there in him, and the Devil must be exorcised. Temptations are to be expected, and they must be challenged, though not with the idea that there is any decisive victory to be had, at least in this life on this earth.

Save. But there is evil out there as well, as this migrant worker has reason to know:

> "You have to have Someone who will save you. A man like me works all the time and crosses all over the country trying to get by ... he's going to need

the Lord ... Once the police picked me up and told me I was drinking too much. I hadn't touched anything like beer or wine, but I was talking to some others and saying we should ask for more money, and I had the picture cards they give you at church, of Jesus Christ on one side and on the other the name of the church and a message from the Bible. They came and grabbed the cards and they thought I was handing out 'Communist stuff,' they said. I didn't know what they were talking about and I still don't, except that you can figure it out: the growers don't want us to become part of a union, and the police work for the growers. The foremen call the police, and they come. And when they're poking you with a gun, it helps if you know that Jesus Christ, the Son of God, was also dragged away and put in jail, or someplace like it, and before He could have known what to do, they were calling Him all the bad names, like they do us, and telling Him either He went along and didn't cause them the trouble, or they'd go and sentence Him—and they did, and they didn't give Him any mercy, none at all."

No, they didn't; nor does this worker get much mercy from those who herd him and his family all over the nation, and pay them sums like 50 or 60 cents an hour for stoop labor. Yet they know the mystery of mercy; they have experienced mercy, the kind that a tired and hurt person receives when he learns that Almighty God Himself was also tired and hurt and repeatedly betrayed. It was merciful of God to appear among them as a humble man, a lonely man, an exile and a wanderer, abused, insulted, mocked, condemned, and eventually tortured and killed. And when one is living an extremely humble life oneself, when one knows from daily experience how arbitrary and mean the high and proper people can be, when one has heard again and again about lynchings or has been pushed and shoved and threatened by the gun-carrying guards of migrant camps—then it does come as rather extraordinary, as almost unbelievable, that God actually saw fit to be so merciful as to choose the kind of life He did.

Sore. These people know the Bible, know some kind of church, know what it means to pray long and hard. They also know in their bones what others talk about and speculate upon: they know and live out "resignation" and "estrangement." They feel a certain soreness of mind and body. They know what it is to feel cursed by the rest of mankind. They know what self-doubt is, and abandonment. They sometimes wonder whether they are not now, right now, in Hell. Heaven is to them a constant vision—even as water is to a thirsty man crossing a desert.

The wife of a sharecropper in Alabama made that last comparison. She reminded me that her life and Christ's are not unlike, which is not a presumptuous or blasphemous thought for her to have, but rather something for all of to wonder about and maybe get nervous over, as perhaps Jesus Christ originally intended:

> *"A lot of the time I'll be thinking that there's no point in going on. Then I'll remind myself that I may feel bad and I may feel sorry for myself, but there's the sky up there and there's the next day coming, and just like there's the next day, there's the next life, and that's when the Judgment Day will be, and we won't be so bad off then, like now. I truly believe so ... Of course, I admit that every once in a while I catch myself getting worried. That's when I'll say to myself that maybe this is Hell, right where we are, right here. And it's not a good thought to have. It's a bad one! But sometimes you can't help yourself. Sometimes you get to thinking."*

There it is, faith and doubt, utter conviction and skepticism, resigned acceptance of God's will and His mysteries, and a gnawing suspicion that maybe justice might never be done, here or "up there" or anywhere.

Ours. Some of the ways these rural churches ease the hellishness of life for their congregations, we can recognize, even support.

Much is made today of the word "community," but in 1962, near Burnsville, North Carolina, I watched a rural mountain community begin to appear and assemble in front of a church and later that day I heard the meaning of the word discussed:

> *"We're a community, and on Sunday you know it most, that's when. You come down from the hills and there she is, our church, that we built with our own hands. We want to see each other, now that the whole week has gone by, and we want to tell the news and have the day of rest and visiting we need—one out of seven. If we didn't go to church, we'd not be neighbors to a lot of people."*

But those churches out in the Appalachian hollows and in the Mississippi Delta and around Florida's Belle Glade and Bean City and Pahokee "do" more than provide for visiting. They provide sanctuary. Poor rural people find in those churches a real chance for escape, for haven, for respite from a tough daily life.

Release. There is also joy that comes with listening to music, with praying, with singing, with saying things—for when things go unspoken too long, moroseness and despair result. A tenant farmer in North Carolina apologetically but earnestly described the way it can get for him:

> *"God forgive me, I sometimes can't say a word and I don't believe in God or anything—only in the mean, mean bossmen; they're always around, and you can depend on them to be watching you."*

But perhaps most of all, such people feel they have somehow obtained sanction. Again and again I have heard from them a virtual cry for approval, for authorization of sorts—and here I feel the awkwardness of language:

> *"I come out of there and I'm taller. I'm feeling bigger. I feel God has taken me to Him. He put His hand on my shoulder, and said, 'Brother John Wilson, the reason that I want you praying to Me is so you won't be looking at yourself and feeling so low' ... My daddy used to tell me when I was a boy that he didn't want my spirit to go and break, and if I prayed to God, He'd keep me strong, and I'd never lose my spirit, no matter how bad they treat you, and*

no matter what words they call you, the bad words—and Lord, you sometimes wonder where they get all those swear words for a colored man, and here I am, working on their land, their own land, and planting for them and harvesting for them ... That's why I'll have my time of praying, and I'll feel like it says in the Bible, a new man—because He's nodded at me and given me His blessing and said, 'Brother John, you're an all-right man, even if you do slip and stumble every once in a while. So you keep right on going, and I'm right up here, looking down on you, and it'll be OK. Bad as it is, you'll come through, yes sir.'"

Balk. The outsider has little difficulty comprehending such needs and the role of rural churches in satisfying them. But the fundamentalist *substance* of the faith that finds expression in those churches balks our rationalist invesitgations. Migrant farm workers, sharecroppers, and the mountaineers of Appalachia have in common not only their closeness to the land but their closeness to God's word. They have a faith that is fundamentalist, that has no desire to reinterpret Scripture in the light of 19th- and 20th-century scientific discoveries. Yet they are not oblivious to the intellectual and political critiques some of us would make of "churchgoing among the rural poor."

In Martin County, Kentucky, where we had heard a minister point out how "transient" and "temporary" all our "worldly ills" are, a one-time coal miner, now injured for life and barely able to live off his small farm, said at suppertime that "temporary" could be a long, long time, it seemed.

I knew the man's laconic, proud, understated ways, and so I was particularly moved to hear him speak—as he sat before a meal of cornbread, pork that was just about all fat, and coffee without milk. I also felt the need to say something myself, so I did. I remarked upon the nice car the reverend drove and observed as quietly as I could that maybe a new car helps one take the long view, helps make life's serious problems seem like nothing, nothing at all. "True, true," he replied, and then hesitated, while I thought he was only agreeing with me:

"I'll wonder a lot about God, and if He meant for us to get near Him by going to church and listening to ministers ... We get them one after the other as they come through. Then they go on to the next church and the next one—their circuit, you know. I don't have anything against them, though. They're no better or worse than the rest of us ... When we were down in the mines ... we'd hear the same thing we hear now—in the church that stands there right beside the mine. The minister would tell us we were so lucky, being poor, because we'd be going to Heaven, while the rich fellow, he'd never go any place but Hell. The way I see it, you don't hold it against the Bible, because it says that. The Bible is trying to tell you the truth, and the truth is that the mine owners are sinners, every one of them, for the way they treat us and sit back and let us get killed in those mines—while they take in the fat profits and send them up to Pittsburgh and New York and wherever the money goes, everwhere but here in Kentucky ... But God can't come down here and run the show; if He could, the world wouldn't be like this.

"I mean to say, God may be on our side, but we're going to have to fight for ourselves; and the reason we pray to Him, that's what I believe, is to get the strength to fight for ourselves...

"My father believed in God. He knew how to read the Bible; that's all he knew to read or ever did read. He could recite passages by heart. He'd do that in one breath, and then he'd tell us that a lot of ministers are holding the hands of the mine owners and getting paid to do nothing much except tell us to be quiet and law-abiding ... My father said that even so we should go to church, and the church belongs to God, and He'll have His bad ministers, like there are bad in every type of person. He was betrayed by one of His disciples, way back there, and it still happens."

Isaiah. He makes his point: there is God and there is the church and there is man. The minister is a mediator between man and

God—through an institution, which is the church. As for the Bible, it is God's word—but heard and written down by men.

He reads the Bible, and in so doing becomes stronger, speaks louder, feels more certain about things. Something happens to him that is physical.

Proud, defiant and independent, he can speak like a prophet, like Isaiah and Jeremiah. He can denounce evil and treacherous people who seem to be everywhere and know in his bones that there is a *point* to denunciation, that Someone is listening, that voices of lamentation and exhortation will be heard by Him, the voice of voices. And such conviction must certainly constitute the very heart of religious faith.

Direct. I am reminded of Kierkegaard's formulations (in *Fear and Trembling* and *Repetition*) because like him this miner in essence demands a *particular* relationship with God, one that in the clutch will gladly dispose of all intermediaries, be they ministers, politicians, secular propagandists, wise neighbors and friends—and yes, overbearing, would-be advocates and helpers. What is more, signs of resignation appear again and again in the miner's words and sentiments—and I say resignation, not depression or despair. He knows what Kierkegaard knew and spent a short lifetime attempting to describe: that the wishes and dreams men have during their brief time on this earth are not the stuff of faith, but rather are obstacles to faith or distractions from it. Yet, again in company with Kierkegaard, the miner understands that he is human, that he is bound to demand and expect the impossible (from himself, from others and from God) but that ultimately whatever goes on between him and Him, as it were, is mysterious and beyond rational calculation or analysis. "Who can ever think he's got God's design figured out but a fool?" I once heard that miner ask. No doubt the tormented Danish theologian would have smiled had he been there to listen.

Abraham. Whether the miner or others like him ever come to the point of Kierkegaard's teleological suspension of the ethical, as in Abraham's willingness to sacrifice his son to God if need be, no man can ever determine. I have often wondered, though, as I talk with miners about to descend into the bowels of the earth, whether in some fashion

many of them haven't in their ordinary, everyday lives made some of the "motions of faith" or "movements of the spirit" that Kierkegaard writes about. Life to those miners (and to so many migrants and sharecroppers) is comically and tragically absurd, yet has to be confronted and not only lived, but in so far as it is possible, understood. If life is absurd, then faith can easily become one more hopeless effort to make sense of the absurd—which is *not* what that miner wishes to do.

Sin. The paradox of faith always has to do with transcendence, with the mind's ability to see what prompts it to faith (one need not be a psychiatrist for that kind of self-awareness; indeed, many psychiatrists sorely lack it) and then go on to renounce precisely that kind of faith—because such faith becomes recognized as an expression of man's sinfulness.

All of this gets complex and unfathomable, which is just the point, because a simple-minded "give-and-take" religiosity (in contrast to religiousness) is exactly what makes the miner and Kierkegaard both shudder. *I am good, so be good to me, dear God*—in a sentence like that, one can summarize the Pharisaical pieties that so many of us manage to embrace at one time or another. If any group of people could perhaps be forgiven such a direction of thought and belief, these people are the ones. Yet, I see little of that kind of religious bargaining among them, perhaps just because they know the concrete experience of hunger and pain and solitariness and abandonment. These people know "existential despair": the assaults of what seems like the entire universe rain upon them and their children all day and in the many waking moments of the night, when the empty stomach intrudes upon the brain's consciousness and those sores and injuries and illnesses conspire to say *no, you cannot possibly escape from the pain and fear and sadness we impose, not even in your sleep or your dreams.* It was Kierkegaard who insisted that men caught up in despair, in "fear and trembling," are not bargain-hungry, churchgoing burghers, and maybe for that reason are nearer to God's Spirit.

Design. The wife of one of the tenant farmers I came to know had her shrill and bombastic times with the language of the Christian religion, but as with the miner, I think she was struggling for something, and out of the hard, tangible, dreary particulars of her life she came up with what she called "a religious philosophy."

> *"You know, don't you, that God has His own purpose, it's a 'design,' like you hear in church, and it's not for us to figure out. But there's one thing I know after all this living—yes sir, after all this living—and that's how foolish you are if you start the day, or the year even, waiting for the good Lord to come into the state of Alabama and straighten everything out and make us all be good to each other. True, later on, we're going to be judged, yes sir, we are, but that's not going to take place in Alabama."*

Tongues. Often I have heard her begin what I suppose can be called "glossolalia" or "speaking in tongues" with that phrase "after all this living." What follows is, of course, largely incomprehensible, if very emotional, earcatching, exhausting, confusing—and at times alarming, at times utterly compelling. But there came a point in most of her "episodes," as I guess I came to think of them, when my mind at last stopped counting, counting this and analyzing that and waiting, always waiting, attentively waiting—for something intelligible, something that can be explained, fathomed, held on to, turned into "material" for formulations. Who can possibly comprehend what is claimed to be His Spirit, the Holy Spirit, coming to its own, dark, cryptic and baffling expression?

Still, she cannot, even when "going off" manage to forget "all this living"; and it is exactly that living that provides for her what I can only call the "substance" of her faith. Put differently, the source of her particular prayers, of her worship, of her emotionally religious allegiance, is her life itself, her life as a black Alabama tenant-farmer's wife.

His. In a nearby county I have come to know (and to go to church with) a white tenant-farmer's family, and heard from the wife of that tenant farmer rather similar religious concerns and convictions. They too are people who live intimately with the land —God's earth, they feel it to be, seized perhaps by greedy owners and manipulators, but ultimately a creation of His.

Amid stretches of "glossolalia" she bitterly and imploringly asks all near to know and never stop knowing Who really owns Alabama's land, Who made it and Who one day will descend from Heaven and take possession of the whole world, let alone the rural South.

As we have learned in this century, the mind is driven by knowledge it both possesses and fears. Driven minds eventually become vocal, because a human being wants to state things, give them the force of utterance—all of which she tries to do, it seems to me, on those long, long, hot, clammy Sundays, when a voice both soft and drawling, yet in a flash high-pitched and sharp and fierce with agitation and earnestness, declares Alabama's rich black loam God's, once God's and eternally God's.

And alas, it is *we* who stand between now and eternity: that is, she, and the landowners to whom she and her husband are tenants, and the politicians and in fact, the whole struggling, sometimes decent, sometimes indifferent, sometimes harsh and unjust world.

Rhythm. Fundamentalist, Pentecostal religion, like all church life, falls back on the rhythm of the worshiper's life. Many migrant families can't attend the same churches week in and week out; migrants go to church less, miss church more, and produce not more skeptics but more people relatively uninterested in religion. "We have to catch our praying on the go," one migrant farmhand told me, and his wife added a few more observations that have to do with their special kind of fate. She said:

> *"Last year we went to a little church in New Jersey ... We had all our children there, the baby included. The Reverend Jackson was there, I can't forget his name, and he told us to be quiet, and he told us how glad we should be that we're in this country, because it's Christian, and not 'godless.' He kept on talking about the other countries, I forget which, being 'godless.' Then my husband went and lost his temper; something happened to his nerves, I do believe. He got up and started shouting, yes sir. He went up to the Reverend Mr. Jackson and told him to shut up and never speak again— not to us, the migrant people. He told him to go on back to his church,*

wherever it is, and leave us alone and don't be standing up there looking like he was so nice to be doing us a favor. Then he did the worst thing he could do: he took the baby, Annie, and he held her right before his face, the minister's, and he screamed and shouted and hollered at him, that minister, like I've never before seen anyone do. I don't remember what he said, the exact words, but he told him that here was our little Annie, and she's never been to the doctor, and the child is sick . . . and we've got no money, not for Annie or the other ones or ourselves.

"Then he lifted Annie up, so she was higher than the reverend, and he said why doesn't he go and pray for Annie and pray that the growers will be punished for what they're doing to us, all the migrant people . . . And then my husband began shouting about God and His neglecting us while He took such good care of the other people all over.

"Then the reverend did answer—and that was his mistake, yes, it was. He said we should be careful and not start blaming God and criticizing Him and complaining to Him and like that, because God wasn't supposed to be taking care of the way the growers behave and how we live, here on this earth. 'God worries about your future'; that's what he said, and I tell you, my husband near exploded. He shouted about 10 times to the reverend, 'Future, future, future.' Then he took Annie and near pushed her in the reverend's face and Annie, she started crying, poor child, and he asked the reverend about Annie's 'future' and asked him what he'd do if he had to live like us, and if he had a 'future' like ours. Then he told the reverend he was like all the rest, making money off us, and he held our Annie as high as he could, right near the cross, and told God He'd better stop having the ministers speaking for Him, and He should come and see us for Himself, and not have the 'preachers'—he kept calling them the 'preachers'—speaking for Him.

"He stopped after he'd finished talking about the 'preachers,' and he came back to us, and there wasn't a sound in

the church, no sir, not one could you hear—until a couple of other men said he was right, my husband was . . . and everyone clapped their hands and I felt real funny. I was a little ashamed and worried, on account of the reverend—he just stood there looking out at us, yes-fl—but I was proud of what had been said and spoken by my own husband. Later on I asked him—it was a few days afterwards, I think—if he still believed what he said, and you know he answered yes, he did; he said he believed in God, but he believed God wanted us to stop moving all over and to settle into one place and live there and get some money each week, like the rest of the people do, enough so we can stay alive and not be hungry. That's what he says he believes, and so do I."

Mix. Unquestionably, not all migrant workers feel so specially, defiantly religious, and so puzzled and perplexed by the ironies that plague man the believer—man the worshiper of a "just God," as He is described by "preachers" like the one denounced just above. Yet I have found among migrants particularly a rather intense mixture of faith and doubt, of prayerful religious devotion and outright scorn of prayer, of loyalty to the church and deliberate, angry avoidance of ministers. Sharecroppers and mountaineers find in the church a place—a place to go and meet neighbors who in fact don't live so near and kin who live a good distance away, especially for people without automobiles. Migrants live abroad in the land and have no such sense of place; indeed, they have an opposite sense, of drifting and wandering.

Hell. What has to be stressed here is that the religious beliefs of a particular people respond closely to a whole range of other beliefs and experiences. The migrant woman whose husband behaved so scandalously believes in God, all right, but she also believes in the unrelenting depravity of the "world." For her the world is no harmless abstraction, nor it it one of a series of ritually descriptive words, such as "the world, the flesh and the Devil." For her and her husband all the terrors of Hell itself are real, living, daily matters—again, matters of the world, this very world. She needs no long poem of Dante's to spell out how diabolical and even grotesque it can eventually be for doomed people; she knows right now what the word infernal means —hellish in the colloquial sense of disgusting and awful and mean and brutish.

Obviously, she and her husband have "mixed feelings" or "ambivalence" toward what they seem to take seriously and embrace wholeheartedly, namely the church, the value of prayer, and above all, the glory of God. Nor are such doubts and moments of defiance absent among Applachian families or tenant farmers, for what binds all these people is *angst*, as some theologians and existentialist philosophers and psychologists put it—in this case an *angst* that is not elusive or metaphysical or associated only with unconscious mental conflicts, but a kind that is thoroughly clear-cut and specific and apparent and very much tied to 'everyday life.' The rural people I have worked with, in some 14 states, simply cannot be overawed by references to the terror ahead after death. For such people the apocalyptic struggle, the ultimate encounter between Good and Bad, between God and the Devil, has an almost prosaic counterpart in the daily struggles they as field hands and farm hands, barely alive and always at the edge of what agricultural economists call "subsistence," constantly wage and often enough lose. (Little Annie died at the age of three; we did get her to a hospital but she was badly malnourished, epileptic, and had a kind of congenital heart defect that ought to have been operated on shortly after she was born.)

In any event, they fight on, the people I have been writing about, and they continue to pray—most often very earnestly indeed. They forthrightly and with not a little desperation ally themselves with Him Who offers them hope, redemption and another, sorely coveted chance. To them, God's suffering requires no complicated explanation, nor do Christ's pain and humiliation, His harassment and exile, His final disgrace at the hands of His persecutors, all of whom were avowedly high-minded, powerful, practical, and full of pieties. Christ's suffering, God's suffering, is Annie's suffering, is her parents' suffering.

Meanwhile, small rural churches continue to receive multitudes. The mystery of God and the world persists. Life for these uprooted and stranded and hidden children of His goes on as well as possible. Muted protests continue in those churches, but minds also become refreshed, relieved, newly at ease in those churches.

Once again we have to take note of the tension between the outside sympathizer (with his own kind of faith) and the recipients of that sympathy. Often enough it is a kind of sympathy that stubbornly and even arrogantly dwells upon exteriors, upon the dreadful surfaces of life, the lack of plumbing and electricity and furniture and money. I can only at this point bring up the words of Annie's father—and he certainly is no apologist for murkiness, self-deception or religious opiates:

"That minister should go and pray for us. He should ask God to give us what we deserve. He should ask God to make him a better minister, so that he'll be able to talk with us and, you know, be more a part of us—know us and not always be giving us those lessons on what we should do and how we should live. He should do some things, too—so he can be better and live better, because it's not just us that have to change our thinking, like he keeps on telling us to do. He says he wants to help us, but he doesn't really want to see the world as we do. Maybe he should do us a favor and hear us for a change, and then go back to his side of the fence and ask himself if the people over there have anything more important to say."

Then I felt close to that minister—and rightly warned.

WILLIAM C. MARTIN

THE GOd-HUCKSTERS OF RAdIO

Sectarian, evangelical movements have always plagued institutionalized churches. The Protestant Reformation was only one of the most successful of such movements. Numerous other movements within Protestantism have arisen since, only to be institutionalized or to become extinct. But the sectarian movements of this century differ from their predecessors in at least one respect: They take advantage of the methods of a technological society to spread their message. So do the "respectable" denominational churches, but their manner is reserved, lacking the flamboyance of a Reverend C. W. Burpo—"spelled B as in Bible." Yet the people reached by sectarian messages—in revival meetings, in storefront, or rural, churches, or over the radio—are the better for it, or feel that they are. Sociologist William C. Martin of Rice University, himself a graduate of Harvard Divinity School, shows a keen understanding of both the pain of such people and of the balm that heals it.

□□□

You have heard them, if only for a few seconds at a time. Perhaps you were driving cross-country late at night, fiddling with the radio dial in search of a signal to replace the one that finally grew too weak as you drew away from Syracuse, or Decatur, or Amarillo. You listened for a moment until you recognized what it was, then you dialed on, hoping to find *Monitor* or *Music Till Dawn*. Perhaps you wondered if, somewhere, people really listen to these programs. The answer is, they do, by the

tens and hundreds of thousands. And they not only listen; they believe and respond. Each day, on local stations that cater to religious broadcasting and on the dozen or so "super-power" stations that can be picked up hundreds of miles away during the cool nighttime hours, an odd-lot assortment of radio evangelists proclaims its version of the gospel to the Great Church of the Airwaves.

Not all who produce religious broadcasts, of course, are acceptable to the scattered multitude for whom "gospel radio" is a major instrument of instruction and inspiration. Denominational programs and Billy Graham are regarded as too Establishment. Billy James Hargis and his Christian Anti-Communist Crusade are too political. Even faith healer Oral Roberts, once a favorite out there in radioland, has become suspect since he founded a university and joined the Methodist Church. For these believers, the true vessels of knowledge, grace, and power are people like Brother Al ("That's AL, Brother Al"); the Reverend Frederick B. Eikerenkoetter II, better known to millions as "Reverend Ike"; C. W. Burpo ("Spelled 'B,' as in Bible..."); Kathryn Kuhlman ("Have... you... been... waiting... for me?"; and the two giants of radio religion, healer A. A. Allen (of Miracle Valley, Arizona) and teacher Garner Ted Armstrong, who can be heard somewhere at this very moment proclaiming The Plain Truth about The World Tomorrow.

The format of programs in this genre rarely makes severe intellectual demands on either pastor or flock. C. W. Burpo (Dr. Burpo accents the last syllable; local announcers invariably stress the first) and Garner Ted Armstrong usually give evidence of having thought about the broadcast ahead to time, though their presentations are largely extemporaneous. Some of the others seem simply to turn on the microphone and shout. Occasionally there is a hint of a sermon. J. Charles Jessup of Gulfport, Mississippi, may cite Herodias' directing her daughter to ask for the head of John the Baptist as illustrating how parents set a bad example for their children, David Terrell may, in support of a point on the doctrine of election, note, that God chose Mary for his own good reasons, and not because she was the only virgin in Palestine—"There was plenty of virgins in the land. Plenty of 'em. Mucho virgins was in the land." Evangelist Bill Beeny of St. Louis, Missouri (Period. Beeny regards the Zip Code as a plot to confuse the nation), may point to the flea's ability to jump 200 times his own length as proof that God exists. Often, however, a program consists of nothing more than a canned introduction, a taped segment from an actual "healing and blessing" service (usually featuring testimonials to the wondrous powers of the evangelist), and a closing pitch for money.

The machinery for broadcasting these programs is a model of efficiency. A look at station XERF in Ciudad Acuña, Coahuila, Mexico, just across the border from Del Rio, Texas, illustrates the point. Freed from FCC regulations that restrict the power of American stations to 50,000 watts, XERF generates 250,000 watts, making it the most powerful station in the world. On a cold night, when high-frequency radio waves travel farthest, it can be heard from Argentina to Canada. Staff needs are minimal; less than a dozen employees handle all duties, from the front office to equipment maintenance. The entire fourteen hours of programming, from 6:00 P.M. to 8:00 A.M., are taped. Each week the evangelists send their tapes to the station, with a check for the air time they will use.

All announcing is done by Paul Kallinger, "Your Good Neighbor along the way." A pleasant, gregarious man, Kallinger has been with XERF since 1949. In the fifties, he performed his duties live. At present he operates a restaurant in Del Rio and tapes leads and commercials in a small studio in his home; he has not been to the station in years. A lone technician switches back and forth between the preachers and Kallingner from dusk till dawn. Kallinger recognizes the improbability of some of the claims made by the ministers and acknowledges that their motives may not be entirely altruistic. Still, he figures that, on balance, they do more good than harm, and he does his best to impress listeners with the fact that "these are faith broadcasts and need your tithes and love offerings if they are to remain on the air with this great message."

Who listens to these evangelists, and why? No single answer will suffice. Some, doubtless, listen to learn. Garner Ted Armstrong discusses current problems and events—narcotics, crime, conflict, space exploration, pollution—and asserts that bibilical prophecy holds the key to understanding both present and future. C. W. Burpo offers a conservative mixture of religion, morals, and politics. Burpo is foursquare in favor of God, Nixon, and constitutional government, and adamantly opposed to sex education, which encourages the study of materials "revealing the basest part of human nature."

Others listen because the preachers promise immediate solutions to real, tangible problems. Although evidence is difficult to obtain, one gets the definite impression, from the crowds that attend the personal appearances of the evangelists, from the content and style of oral and written testimonials, from studies of storefront churches with similar appeals, and from station executives' analyses of their listening population, that the audience is heavily weighted with the poor, the uneducated, and others who for a variety of reasons stand on the margins of society. These are the people most susceptible to illness and infirmity, to crippling debts, and to what the evangelists refer to simply as "troubles." At the same time, they are the people least equipped to deal with these problems effectively. Some men in such circumstances turn to violence or radical political solutions. Others grind and are ground away, in the dim hope of a better future. Still others, like desperate men in many cultures, succumb to the appeal of magical solutions. For this group, what the preachers promise is, if hardly the Christian gospel, at least good news.

The "healers and blessers," who dominate the radio evangelism scene, address themselves to the whole range of human problems: physical, emotional, social, financial, and spiritual. Like their colleagues in the non-miraculous healing arts, some evangelists develop areas of special competence, such as the cure of cancer or paralysis. Brother Al is something of a foot specialist—"God can take corns, bunions, and tired feet, and massage them with his holy love and make them well." A. A. Allen tells of disciples who have received silver fillings in their teeth during his meetings and asks, sensibly enough, "Why not let God be your dentist?" But most are general practitioners. On a single evening's set of programs, hope is extended to those suffering from alcoholism, arthritis, asthma, birth defects, blindness, blood pressure (high and low), bunions, calluses, cancer (breast, eye, lung, skin, stomach, and throat), corns, death, diabetes, dope, eye weakness, gallstones, heart disease, insomnia, kidney trouble, leukemia, mental retardation, mononucleosis, nervous breakdown, nervous itch, nicotine addiction, obesity, pain, paralysis, polio, pregnancy, respiratory problems, rheumatic fever, tuberculosis, tumors (brain, abdominal, and miscellaneous), ulcers, useless limbs, and water in the veins.

The continually fascinating aspect of the healing and blessing ministries is that they do produce results. Some of the reported healings are undoubtedly fraudulent. One station canceled a healer's program after obtaining an affidavit from individuals who admitted posing as cripples and being "healed" by the touch of the pastor's hand. Police officers have occasionally reported seeing familiar vagrants in the healing lines of traveling evangelists, apparently turning newly discovered disorders into wine. But these blatant frauds are probably rare, and a faith healer need not depend on them to sustain his reputation. He can rely much more safely on psychological, sociological, and psychotherapeutic mechanisms at work among his audience.

The testimonials that fill the broadcasts and publications of the healers point to two regularities in a large percentage—not all—of the reported cures. First, the believer had suffered from his condition for some time and had been unable to gain relief from medical or other sources. Long illness or disability can weaken emotional and mental resistance to sources of help that one would not consider in other cir-

cumstances. Second, most of the cures occur at actual healing services, when the deep desire to be made whole is transformed into eager expectation by a frenzied whirl of noise, anxiety, and promise, and the pervasive power of the gathered group of true believers.

In recent years, the miracle-workers have turned their attention to financial as well as physical needs. They promise better jobs, success in business, or, in lieu of these, simple windfalls. A. A. Allen urges listeners to send for his book *Riches and Wealth, the Gift of God.* Reverend Ike fills his publications and broadcasts with stories of financial blessings obtained through his efforts—"This Lady Blessed with New Cadillac," "How God Blessed and Prospered Mrs. Rena Blige" (he revealed to her a secret formula for making hair grow). "Sister Rag Muffin Now Wears Mink to Church," and "Blessed with New Buick in 45 Minutes." Forty-five minutes is not, apparently, unusually fast for Reverend Ike. He regularly assures his listeners, "The moment you get your offering [and] your prayer requests into the mail, start looking up to God for your blessing because it will be on the way."

These men of God realize, of course, that good health and a jackpot prize on the Big Slot Machine in the Sky are not all there is to life. They promise as well to rid the listener of bad habits, quiet his doubts and fears, soothe his broken heart, repair his crumbling marriage, reconcile his fussing kinfolk, and deliver him from witches and demons. No problem is too trivial, too difficult, or past redemption. Brother Al will help women "that wants a ugly mouth cleaned out of their husband." A. A. Allen claims to have rescued men from the electric chair. Glenn Thompson promises "that girl out there 'in trouble' who's trying to keep it from Dad and Mother" that if she will "believe and doubt not, God will perform a miracle."

The radio evangelists do not cast their bread upon the waters, however, without expecting something in return. Though rates vary widely, a fifteen-minute daily program on a local radio station costs, on the average, about $200 per week. On a superpower station like XERF the rate may run as high as $600. The evangelists pay this fee themselves, but they depend upon their radio audience to provide the funds. For this reason, some take advantage of God's Precious Air Time to hawk a bit of sacred merchandise. Much of it is rather ordinary—large-print Bibles, calendars, greeting cards, Bible-verse yo-yos, and ball-point pens with an inspirational message right there on the side. Other items are more unusual. Bill Beeny, who tends to see the darker side of current events, offers $25-contributors a Riot Pack containing a stove, five fuel cans, a rescue gun, a radio, and the marvelous Defender, a weapon that drives an attacker away and covers him with dye, making him an easy target for police. Ten dollars will buy a blue-steel, pearl-handled, tear-gas pistol, plus the informative and inspirational Truth-Pac #4. Or, for the same price, Evangelist Beeny will send his own album of eighteen songs about heaven, together with the Paralyzer, "made by the famous Mace Company." Presumably, it is safer to turn the other cheek if one has first paralyzed one's enemy.

The most common items offered for sale, however, are the evangelist's own books and records. Brother Al's current book is *The Second Touch*: "It's wrote in plain, down-to-earth language, and has big print that will heal any weak eyes that reads it." For a $5 offering C. W. Burpo will send his wonderful recording of "My America," plus a bonus bumper sticker advertising his program, The Bible Institute of the Air—"Be a moving billboard for God and Country." Don and Earl, "two young Christian singers from Fort Worth, Texas," offer for only $3 "plus a extra quarter to pay the postage back out to your house," albums of heart-touching songs and stories that include such old favorites as "Just One Rose Will Do," "A Tramp on the Streets," "Lord, Build Me a Cabin in Heaven," "Streamline to Glory," "Remember Mother's God," "A Soldier's Last Letter," "That Little Pair of Half-worn Shoes," "Just a Closer Walk with Thee" (featuring the gospel whistling of Don), and that great resurrection hymn, "There Ain't No Grave Gonna Keep My Body Down."

In keeping with St. Paul's dictum that "those who proclaim the gospel should get their living by the gospel," the radio ministers do not always offer merchandise in return for contributions. In fact, the books and records and magazines probably function primarily as a link that facilitates the more direct appeals for money almost sure to follow.

Brother Al, sounding like a pathetic Andy Devine, asks the faithful to send "God's Perfect Offering—$7.00. Not $6.00, nor $8.00, but $7.00." An offering even more blessed is $77, God's two perfect numbers, although any multiple of seven is meritorious. "God told me to ask for this. You know I don't talk like this. It's got to be God. God told me he had a lot of bills to pay. Obey God—just put the cash inside the envelope." In addition to cash, Brother Al will also accept checks, money orders, and American Express—surely he means traveler's checks. Seven's perfection stems from its prominence in the Bible: the seven deadly sins, the seven churches of Asia, and so forth. Radio Pastor David Epley also believes God has a perfect number, but he has been reading about the apostles and the tribes of Israel. Quite understandably, he seeks a $12 offering, or the double portion offering of $24.

Brother Glenn Thompson, who also names God as his co-solicitor, claims that most of the world's ills, from crabgrass and garden bugs to Communism and the Bomb, can be traced to man's robbing God. "You've got God's money in your wallet. You old stingy Christian. No wonder we've got all these problems. You want to know how you can pay God what you owe? God is speaking through me. God said, 'Inasmuch as you do it unto one of these, you do it unto me.' God said, 'Give all you have for the gospel's sake.' My address is Brother Glenn, Paragould, Arkansas."

In sharp contrast, Garner Ted Armstrong makes it quite clear that all publications offered on his broadcasts are absolutely free. There is no gimmick. Those who request literature never receive any hint of an appeal for funds unless they specifically ask how they might contribute to the support of the program. Garner Ted's father, Herbert W. Armstrong, began the broadcast in 1937, as a vehicle for spreading a message that features a literalistic interpretation of biblical prophecy. The program has spawned a college with campuses in California, Texas, and London, and a church of more than 300,000 members. Characteristically, the ministers of the local churches, which meet in rented halls and do not advertise, even in the telephone book, will not call on prospective members without a direct invitation. This scrupulous approach has proved quite successful. *The World Tomorrow*, a half-hour program, is heard daily on more than four hundred stations throughout the world, and a television version is carried by sixty stations.

Several evangelists use their radio programs primarily to promote their personal appearance tours throughout the country, and may save the really high-powered huckstering for these occasions. A. A. Allen is both typical and the best example. An Allen Miracle Restoration Revival Service lasts from three to five hours and leaves even the inhibited participant observer quite spent. On a one-night stand in the Houston Music Hall, Allen and the Lord drew close to a thousand souls, in approximately equal portions of blacks, whites, and Mexican-Americans. As the young organist in brown Nehru played gospel rock, hands shot into the air and an occasional tambourine clamored for joy. Then, without announcement, God's Man of Faith and Power came to pulpit center. Allen does not believe in wearing black; that's for funerals. On this night he wore a green suit with shiny green shoes.

For the better part of an hour, he touted his book that is turning the religious world upside down, *Witchcraft, Wizards, and Witches*, and a record, pressed on 100 percent pure vinyl, of his top two soul-winning sermons.

To prepare the audience for the main pitch, Allen went to great lengths to leave the impression that he was one of exceedingly few faithful men of God still on the scene. He lamented the defection from the ministry: "In the last few years, 30 percent of the preachers have stopped preaching; 70 percent fewer men are in training for the ministry. A cool 100 percent less preachers than just a few years ago." He chortled over the fate of rival evangelists who had run afoul of the law or justifiably irate husbands. At another service, he used this spot to describe the peril of opposing his ministry. He told of a student who tried to fool him by posing as a cripple; God struck him dead the same night. A man who believed in Allen's power, but withheld $100 God had told him to give the evangelist, suffered a stroke right after the meeting. And on and on.

When he finished, Brother Don Stewart, Allen's associate in the ministry of fundraising, took the microphone to begin a remarkable hour of unalloyed gullery. At the end of his recitation, approximately 135 people pledged $100 apiece, and others emptied bills and coins into large plastic wastebaskets that were filled and replaced with astonishing regularity. And all the while Brother Don walked

back and forth shouting to the point of pain. "Vow and pay, vow and pay, the scripture does say, vow and pay."

Despite the blatantly instrumental character of much radio religion, it would be a mistake to suppose that its only appeal lies in the promise of health and wealth, though these are powerful incentives. The fact is that if the world seems out of control, what could be more reassuring than to discover the road map of human destiny? This is part of the appeal of Garner Ted Armstrong, who declares to listeners, in a tone that does not encourage doubt, that a blueprint of the future of America, Germany, the British Commonwealth, and the Middle East, foolproof solutions for the problems of child-rearing, pollution, and crime in the streets, plus a definitive answer to the question, "Why Are You Here?" can all be theirs for the cost of a six-cent stamp. On a far less sophisticated level, James Bishop Carr, of Palmdale, California, does the same thing. Brother Carr believes that much of the world's ills can be traced to the use of "Roman time" (the Gregorian calendar) and observances of religious holidays such as Christmas. He has reckoned the day and hour of Christ's second coming, but is uncertain of the year. Each Night of Atonement, he awaits the Eschaton with his followers, the Little Flock of Mount Zion. Between disappointments, he constructs elaborate charts depicting the flow of history from Adam's Garden to Armageddon, complete with battle plans for the latter event. Others deal in prophecy on more of an *ad hoc* basis, but are no less confident of their accuracy. David Terrell, the Endtime Messenger, recently warned that "even today, the sword of the Lord is drawed" and that "coastal cities shall be inhabited by strange creatures from the sea, yea, and there shall be great sorrow in California.... God has never failed. Who shall deny when these things happen that a prophet was in your midst? Believest thou this and you shall be blessed."

To become a disciple of one of these prophet-preachers is, by the evangelistis' own admission, to obtain a guide without peer to lead one over life's uneven pathway. Though few of them possess standard professional credentials, they take pains to assure their scattered flocks that they have divine recognition and approval. Some associate themselves with leading biblical personalities, as when A. A. Allen speaks of the way "God has worked through his great religious leaders, such as Moses and myself," or when C. W. Burpo intones, "God loves you and I love you." Several report appearances by heavenly visitors. According to David Terrell, Jesus came into his room on April 17, about eight-thirty at night and told him there was too much junk going around. "Bring the people unto me." Though some receive angels regularly, they do not regard their visits lightly. "If you don't think that it'll almost tax your nervous system to the breaking point," says the Reverend Billy Walker, Jr., "let an angel come to you." Other evangelists simply promise, as does Brother Al, "I can get through to God for you." In support of such claims, they point to the testimony of satisfied disciples and to their own personal success; the flamboyance in dress affected by some of the men obviously capitalizes on their followers' need for a hero who has himself achieved the success denied them.

In the fiercely competitive struggle for the listeners' attention and money, most of the evangelists have developed a novel twist or gimmick to distinguish them from their fellow clerics. C. W. Burpo does not simply pray; he goes into the "throne room" to talk to God. The door to the throne room can be heard opening and shutting. David Epley's trademark is the use of the gift of "discernment." He not only heals those who come to him, but "discerns" those in his audience who need a special gift of healing, in the manner of a pious Dunninger. A. A. Allen emphasizes witchcraft on most of his current broadcasts, blaming everything from asthma to poverty on hexes and demons. In other years he has talked of holy oil that flowed from the hands of those who were being healed, or crosses of blood that appeared on their foreheads. David Terrell frequently calls upon his gift of "tongues." Terrell breaks into ecstatic speech either at the peak of an emotional passage or at points where he appears to need what is otherwise known as "filler." Certain of his spirited words tend to recur repeatedly. *Rapha*, *nissi*, and *honda bahayah* are three favorites. The first two may be derived from the Hebrew words for healing and victory. Unless the third is a Hebrew term having to do with motorcycles, its meaning is known

only to those with the gift of interpretation. Terrell defends his "speaking in the Spirit" over the radio on the grounds that he is an apostle—"not a grown-up apostle like Peter or Paul; just a little boy apostle that's started out working for Jesus."

Once one has made contact with a radio evangelist, preferably by a letter containing a "love offering," one is usually bombarded with letters and publications telling of what God has recently wrought through his servant, asking for special contributions to meet a variety of emergencies, and urging followers to send for items personally blessed by the evangelist and virtually guaranteed to bring the desired results. One runs across holy oil, prosperity billfolds, and sacred willow twigs, but the perennial favorite of those with talismaniacal urges is the prayer cloth.

Prayer cloths come in several colors and sizes, and are available in muslin, sackcloth, terrycloth, and, for a limited time only, a revival-tent cloth. As an optional extra, they can be anointed with water, oil, or ashes. My own model is a small (2½ × 3½ inches) unanointed rectangle of pinked cloth. The instructions state that it represents the man of God who sent it, and that it can be laid upon those with an ailment, hidden in the house to bring peace and blessings, carried in the purse or pocketbook for financial success, and even taken to court to assure a favorable outcome. One woman told Reverend Ike that she had cut her cloth in two and placed a piece under the separate beds of a quarreling couple. She declared the experiment an unqualified success, to the delight of Reverend Ike—"You did that? You rascal, you! Let's all give God a great big hand!"

These scraps of paper and cloth serve to bind preacher and people together until the glorious day when a faithful listener can attend a live service at the civic auditorium or the coliseum, or under the big tent at the fairgrounds. It is here, in the company of like-minded believers, that a person loses and perhaps finds himself as he joins the shouting, clapping, dancing, hugging, weeping, rejoicing throng. At such a service, a large Negro lady pointed into the air and jiggled pleasantly. Beside her, a sad, pale little woman, in a huge skirt hitched up with a man's belt, hopped tentatively on one foot and looked for a moment as if she might have found something she had been missing. On cue from the song leader, all turned to embrace or shake hands with a neighbor and to assure each other that "Jesus is *all right!*" Old men jumped about like mechanical toys. Two teen-age boys "ran for Jesus." And in the aisles a trim, gray-haired woman in spike heels and a black nylon dress, danced sensuously all over the auditorium. She must have logged a mile and a half, maybe a mile and three quarters, before the night was over. I couldn't help wondering if her husband knew where she was. But I was sure she liked where she was better than where she had been.

If a radio evangelist can stimulate this kind of response, whether he is a charlatan (as some undoubtedly are) or sincerely believes he is a vessel of God (as some undoubtedly do) is secondary. If he can convince his listeners that he can deliver what he promises, the blend of genuine need, desperate belief, reinforcing group—and who knows what else?—can move in mysterious ways its wonders to perform. And, for a long time, that will likely be enough to keep those cards and letters coming in.

DISCUSSING THE ARTICLES

1. In Robert Coles' article "God and the Rural Poor," what is the reaction of well-educated and well-to-do people to the religious expressions of the poor? What are the affluent and educated forgetting?

2. How does Coles explain the faith of the sharecroppers?

3. In sociological terminology, how do you explain the type of behavior that takes place in rural churches? How is it connected to religion?

4. What does religion do for the sharecroppers (in what way is it functional)? How do sociologists classify orgiastic behavior?

5. Is there any evidence in the article that religion has a role in social control? But what does it offer to counter this effect?

6. Do the rural poor of whom Coles writes need a feeling of transcendence? Why? Do they bargain with God for improvement in life on earth? Why are people who are caught up in despair closer to God than are churchgoing burghers?

7. In William C. Martin's article "The God-Hucksters of Radio," why do people listen to the gospel programs on radio? Why aren't they interested in denominational religion? Of what do they become suspicious? What kind of religious expression do they represent?

8. From what facet of our society are the radio preachers' names copied? What methods are employed to sell religion? Can this kind of religion be as genuine as the denominational kind?

9. Are these preachers well educated? What is this typical of? Do they have power over the audience? Could they exert political control?

10. Why do most people listen to the radio preachers? Is this reason peculiar to our time and society?

11. What problems are dealt with by the preachers? Are these problems typical of a particular social class? Could doctors and dentists—who are what most in the audience really need—fulfill the same function as the preachers?

12. Why is faith healing sometimes successful? What kind of behavior is it, in sociological terms?

13. How are our materialistic values reflected in the concerns of the radio preachers and their audience?

14. What are these preachers, all rolled into one? How do they use religion to solicit money? What is the difference between this kind of soliciting and the custom of tithing?

15. What does a preacher like Garner Ted Armstrong offer people for the price of a stamp? How do such preachers demonstrate their special relationship to God?

16. During revival meetings, what special feeling is established among members of the audience? Has this feeling always been associated with the religious experience?

TERMS TO REMEMBER

Religion. A system of beliefs and rituals dealing with the sacred.

Profane. Objects and events of everyday life, which are usual, explainable, and repetitive.

Sacred. An object or a person distinguished from the profane. It is set off from the everyday experiences of people and is unusual, unexplainable, mysterious, powerful, and deserving of reverence and respect.

Totem. A symbolic representation, in the form of an animal or a vegetable, of a clan, tribe, or society.

Contingency. A characteristic of the human condition, whereby people live in perpetual uncertainty.

Powerlessness. Another characteristic of the human condition, whereby people's ability to act is limited.

Scarcity. A third characteristic of the human condition, which results in frustration.

Rites of passage. Rituals established around critical times of growth and maturation: birth, puberty, marriage, and death.

Magic. A belief in the existence of a reality beyond that experienced by humans, in the possibility of establishing a relationship with this supernatural reality, and in the possibility of influencing it to effect change in this world.

Mana. A concept of the natives of Polynesia and Melanesia, according to which there exists a supernatural force that can attach to any person, object, or event.

Totemism. Worship of a totem, or symbol of a clan.

Ritual. Behavior that follows the creation of sacredness and provides a mechanism for maintaining the sacred.

Church. A religious association that is institutionalized, well-integrated into social and economic life, and in which participation is routine.

Universal church. A church that has a monopoly on religious belief.

Ecclesia. A church to which a substantial majority of the population belongs.

Denomination. A subdivision of the church, considered equally as valid as the church.

Sect. A revolutionary movement that breaks away from the church or from one of its denominations. It stresses the spirit, rather than the letter, of religion.

Cult. The least conventional and least institutionalized of the religious organizations. It consists of groups of followers clustered around a leader whose teachings differ substantially from the doctrines of the church or denomination.

SUGGESTIONS FOR FURTHER READING

Berger, Peter L. *A Rumor of Angels: Modern Society and the Rediscovery of the Supernatural.* New York: Doubleday, 1969. The renowned sociologist theorizes that religion is of great importance even in this age of science and rationalism, because many human experiences can be understood only in terms of a belief in the supernatural.

Berger, Peter L. *The Sacred Canopy: Elements of a Sociological Theory of Religion.* New York: Doubleday, 1967. An interesting theory in which religion is viewed as a social product.

Comstock, W. Richard, general ed. *Religion and Man: An Introduction.* New York: Harper & Row, 1971. An overview of religious phenomena as social and historic facts appearing in human cultures.

Cox, Harvey. *The Feast of Fools.* New York: Harper & Row, 1969. The need for festivity, fantasy, and mysticism in human life and in religion.

Goode, William J. *Religion Among the Primitives.* New York: Free Press, 1951. The religions of five so-called primitive societies are analyzed to show the interdependence of religion and other aspects of life.

Glock, Charles Y., and Stark, Rodney. *Religion and Society in Tension.* Chicago: Rand McNally, 1965. Much survey research analyzed to show the strain between today's culture and religious values.

Herberg, Will. *Protestant, Catholic, Jew.* New York: Doubleday Anchor Books, 1960. A comparative historical account of our three major religions, showing that religion is particularly important to Americans as a means of establishing their identity.

Lenski, Gerhard. *The Religious Factor.* New York: Doubleday Anchor Books, 1963. An important sociological work showing the relationship of religious participation and membership to class, politics, and life styles.

Lessa, William A., and Vogt, Evon Z. *Reader in Comparative Religion.* New York: Harper Row, 1972. A comprehensive collection of readings on the general subject of religion from anthropological and sociological perspectives.

Noss, John B. *Man's Religions.* New York: Macmillan, 1967. A text covering religious expressions around the world.

O'Dea, Thomas. *The Sociology of Religion*. Englewood Cliffs, N.J.: Prentice-Hall, 1966. A concise paperback presenting an overview of sociological thought on religion.

Yinger, J. Milton. *Religion, Society, and the Individual*. New York: Macmillan, 1967. A text with readings on all aspects of religion.

Yinger, J. Milton. *Sociology Looks at Religion*. New York: Macmillan, 1963. A readable book in which the author looks at some religious functions, particularly as religion affects social change and group identification.

CONClUSION

A bRAVE NEW WORld?

Oh, wonder!
How many goodly creatures are there here!
How beauteous mankind is! Oh, brave new world,
That has such people in 't!

When one of Shakespeare's characters first spoke these words in *The Tempest*, neither the playwright nor his audience could have imagined, in their wildest dreams, a world like ours. But when Aldous Huxley, in the early 1930s, ironically titled his futuristic novel, *Brave New World*, he could see the shape of things to come. Still, the changes Huxley predicted for the future seemed far off, not likely to come about either in his lifetime or in that of his grandchildren.[1]

Consider, for instance, how Huxley envisaged the world of tomorrow. Soci-

---

[1]Aldous Huxley, *Brave New World Revisited* (New York: Harper & Brothers, 1958), p. 3.

ety was completely organized, functioning with total efficiency and no waste. Stratification consisted of a scientific caste system in which members were bred according to the duties they performed: The highly intelligent were on top, the almost subhuman on the bottom. The society's educational system was based on methodical conditioning of the individual to promote specific behavior. Its masses accepted a condition of servitude because of the daily doses of chemically induced happiness they received. And the right doctrines, which permitted the ruling classes to maintain the status quo, were instilled by nightly sleep-teaching courses.

Huxley's brave new world existed in the seventh century A.F. (After Ford), but the author may have underestimated the rapidity of change. Many of his prophecies seem dangerously near fulfillment in this last third of the twentieth century. For instance, a completely organized and controlled society is the expressed objective of totalitarian governments. And this goal is, to a large degree, being attained in nations like Communist China. In the industrial nations of the Western world, both democratic and authoritarian, the trend is toward substantial, if not total, organization.

Furthermore, *technocracy*—rule by technological specialists—is already an acknowledged fact in the Soviet Union. That supposedly classless society has an upper stratum of university professors, scientists, engineers, and high administrative officials. And in Western nations, if we are to believe the social prophets of today, we are already in the age of the scientific innovator (in contrast with the individual inventor of the industrial age). Scientific innovations affect the entire social system, bringing systemic changes with them. Systemic changes are so complex that already our social and political problems can be understood and coped with only by people who have IQ's of at least 140.[2] Hence, rule by some kind of an intellectual elite appears likely.

Conditioning aimed at producing particular behavior is not foreign to modern people either. The unanimous agreement on goals in China is at least partly attributable to the Little Red Book, which is studied at school, at work, and in leisure hours. In our society, this type of indoctrination has, for years, been the avowed purpose of advertising, particularly in the mass media. Recently, the noted experimental psychologist B. F. Skinner stated in *Beyond Freedom and Dignity* that humans are basically what they are conditioned to be. Proceeding from this assumption, Skinner offers a program of operant conditioning that radically modifies human behavior in order to create a perfect human being. According to him, by using conditioning, we should be able to reconstruct human culture and thus prevent its inevitable collapse. In reality, Skinner says, we are already being conditioned to act in particular ways. Thus, freedom and free will are largely illusions. Why not put behavior control to good use? We could design a culture to fit future requirements, one that incorporates our highest values. Then, we could create an environment in which these values would inevitably become part of human beings. The result would be a perfect society. People would no longer fight wars, riot, pollute, and overpopulate, because they would *want* to achieve the common good rather than their own selfish ends.

Although Huxley's prophecy concerning the servitude of the masses has

[2]Harvey Wheeler, "Technology: Foundation of Cultural Change," *The Center Magazine* (July–August, 1972), p. 50.

not yet been borne out, substantial numbers of people in our society, and in others around the world, are ill fed, ill clothed, ill housed, ill educated, and plain ill. Poverty, hunger, and despair exist because societies still have stratification systems in which power, status, and privilege are the property of those born with particular characteristics. Poverty, hunger, and despair exist because we still permit ethnocentrism, racism, extreme nationalism, and even religion to set individual against individual, group against group, nation against nation. They exist because, without meaning to, we have emphasized quantitative considerations—a preoccupation with the number of things produced—at the expense of qualitative ones.

Finally, the sleep-teaching techniques by which the doctrines of the state were drilled into individuals in Huxley's brave new world are not yet part of our societies. Although the machines and techniques exist, we still believe that, as individuals, we have too much freedom and dignity to use them. But Huxley's fantasy may become reality, in the same way that his other predictions have come true. Scientists tell us that we are now experiencing the passing of the industrial era and that we are about to enter a postindustrial period. The postindustrial era may well be characterized by babies who are conceived in laboratories and nurtured in test tubes, by the purposeful breeding of superior individuals to produce a race of intellectual giants and the breeding of subhumans to perform menial tasks, and by the manipulation of men and women to make them willing participants in the aims of society. It would be interesting to know whether the brave new world that Shakespeare foretold will turn out to be the horror of Huxley's brave new world. In other words, will the nightmares of our wise men come true, or their dreams?

To speculate about the future, we will examine technological society today and the characteristics it has spawned—a bureaucratic form of organization, a mass society, and institutionalization of previously noninstitutional functions. Using the trends apparent in today's society as a starting point, we will speculate about life in the postindustrial era. In addition, we will analyze some countertrends that are also apparent in contemporary society to determine whether they are powerful enough to channel social change in a totally different direction. Finally, we will suggest that what you have learned of sociological concepts may be helpful to you in making individual decisions about the type of sociocultural change that is most desirable.

TECHNOLOGICAL SOCIETY

Many of the changes in the structure and institutions of society occurred during the period of modernization, when a simple technology was replaced by a complex one. The world once consisted of a rather placid aggregate of hunting and later of agricultural societies. During the period of modernization, a number of societies tried to change their mode of production—their economies—through technological knowledge. *Technology* includes all methods, tools, instruments, and devices that help humans to control their environment. The Industrial Revolution heralded the modern technological era in the West. But modernization is not universal in the world today. Many societies are still striving to acquire an advanced technology. They valiantly try to attain this goal because they want to achieve what technologically advanced societies have achieved: a change from a society of scarcity to one of plenty, or abundance.

Technology has performed miracles in freeing human beings from the most demeaning, backbreaking forms of labor. It has enabled us to produce goods in such quantity and of such quality that members of nontechnological societies are astonished. It has given humans additional means of pursuing knowledge. It has created transportation and communication that have shrunk the world so greatly that we can explore every corner of it. It has provided us with such a vast number of comforts that we need not fear most aspects of nature.

But technology has also brought changes that humans neither foresaw nor desired. In many respects, technology has become a Frankenstein monster, which rises up against its human creator. That we have long been aware of technology's dangers is apparent from the popularity of science fiction in literature and movies. A frequent theme in science fiction is the takeover of the world by computers impelled by the desire for power over humans.

Technology For What?

In a basic sense, technology is desirable because it produces maximal human satisfaction with minimal human effort. Thus, the first crude tools of the caveman, later agricultural implements, and four-wheeled, animal-drawn vehicles were as much the products of technology as are our latest space missiles. In the modern era, however, technology has consisted primarily of mechanization and automation. *Mechanization* is the substitution of machines for human muscle. *Automation* is the substitution of machines for the human brain. Mechanization produced great upheavals in societies and displaced many workers from their jobs. But eventually it created additional jobs, so that today we have adequate, though far from total, employment. Automation is a trend that has only begun, and its greatest impact will occur in the future. Many people fear that automation will never create enough jobs to replace those it will do away with. In that case, we will have to find both means of supporting the displaced workers and of providing them with a sense of worth.

The most obvious and important impact of modern technology on humans is the pheonomenal rise in the standard of living. Mechanization and automation permit the rapid production of such a large quantity of goods that their price is low enough for almost everyone to obtain them.

Of course, the standard of living did not rise for all people at the same time. Some social classes achieved high standards of living at the very beginning of the Industrial Revolution, but the industrial workers of the West didn't see the tangible results of the Industrial Revolution until well into the twentieth century. And today, substantial portions of the populations of industrial societies and huge numbers of people in the nations of the Third World have achieved very few of the benefits of advanced technology. These people are involved in the revolution of rising expectations, meaning that they are no longer satisfied with their condition and want a piece of their society's pie.

In previous chapters, we discussed some of the effects of the Industrial Revolution, or modern technology, on population and social organization. The first effect was the spectacular rise in population due to advancements in sanitation and medical knowledge. The second effect was the creation of industrial cities to which workers flocked to obtain jobs in factories. Urban life radically altered living patterns: Families became small and nuclear, friendship circles became restricted, and voluntary associations multiplied, as did the tall concrete buildings that increasingly overshadowed nature.

Impersonal Work Relations

In the factory, the worker was no longer his own man. His life was run by the clock. He had to arrive and depart at definite times. He had to produce a specific amount of work. He usually repeated the same operation without understanding, or feeling pride in, his contribution to the finished product. The increasing dehumanization that resulted from such impersonal relations at work, and the harsh realities of life in an urban environment, are by-products of technology that continue to plague us, for we have been unable to correct them.

Many social critics contend that technology has acquired a more important place in society than the human being. What is more, society has succeeded in socializing most individuals into worshipping the machine and its products. This worship is apparent in such major trends as the secularization of religion and the preeminence of scientific and technological subjects in education. And it is obvious in trivial details, such as the plastic flowers and plants in homes and offices.

The Exploitative Nature of Technology

One by-product of technology of which we have recently become aware is its exploitation of the physical environment. In our zeal to satisfy the demands of technology, we have completely ignored the impact those demands have had on our biophysical surroundings. We have long felt that there are plenty of humans, plenty of water, and plenty of air, so why worry? Well, the humans, the water, and the air, not to mention the fish, the animals, the forests, and the seas, have obviously taken as much abuse as they can stand.

Our awareness that we are on a suicidal course, and thus our current interest in ecology, is due, in part, to the publication, in the early 1960s of Rachel Carson's *Silent Spring*. In her book, Rachel Carson vividly portrayed a world destroyed by chemicals. The author of the book *Earthkeeping*, Gordon Harrison, maintains that our ecological awakening must be followed by radical change. Harrison suggests that change might be brought about by outright revolution that would overthrow systems like capitalism and communism, both of which are equally insensitive to man and nature. Or it might be brought about by a moral and an ethical revolt against the production-consumption society—a change currently being fermented by the counterculture. Finally change might be brought about by radical, though not revolutionary, governmental actions that would challenge the conventional wisdom. All these approaches to change would be far more effective than the mild measures the governments of technological societies are currently employing as remedies.[3]

[3]Gordon Harrison, *Earthkeeping* (New York: Houghton Mifflin, 1971).

No Place To Go: Loss of Individual Freedom

The technological era has also led to a societal interdependence in which each individual depends on another individual, each agency on another agency, and each institution on another institution. This is primarily a matter of economics. Because our economy depends on an equilibrium of production and consumption, a disruption of this equilibrium echoes throughout society. In preindustrial societies, the individual need not depend on the larger economy of the society to such a great extent. For instance, in agricultural societies, almost everyone owns at least a little plot of land that he can depend on for survival in lean times. But in industrial societies, the factory worker and the salaried white-collar worker have no such security. If, in times of economic crisis, they are unemployed, they must depend on some state agency for survival.

This dependence extends to every sector of our lives. We depend on others to build our homes; to gather, package, and often prepare our foods; to sew our clothes; and to make our furniture. We often leave the furnishing of our homes to interior decorators, and the education of our children almost entirely to professional educators. No wonder that standardization and loss of individuality are the norm and that self-sufficiency is impossible. Finally, there is no place for an individual to go where he is not subject to the control of a state or some other body, and where he can live in a totally self-sufficient manner. Thus, the individual is never free of his society and is affected, willy-nilly, by all developments in the international sphere.

Cultural Standardization

Technology has leveled cultural differences around the world. Because of the revolution in communications—rapid transportation, radio, television, the telephone—cultural diffusion has become almost instantaneous. When the same songs are played over the radio in New York City and over a transistor in the Sahara and when the same television programs are seen in both places, it is inevitable that ideas, dress, and architectural styles soon come to resemble one another. Cultural standardization is not necessarily an undesirable product of technology. It seems that we are destined eventually to combine into a world society, and the more we resemble one another, the easier such a process will be. Nonetheless, it is because of our differences, rather than our similarities, that we find one another fascinating.

The Weapons Revolution

The weapons that modern technology has evolved know no boundaries, and the individual cannot successfully isolate himself from them. For many centuries, a favorable geographic location—high mountains, seas, and rivers—was helpful in maintaining a country's security. Today, geography counts for nothing because missiles and bombs may be directed at any target. Moreover, modern technological societies have a dubious distinction—they have the capacity to end human life on this planet. Thus, people throughout the world live with the knowledge that a nuclear holocaust and total destruction could occur at any time. In fact, nuclear war could result not only from irreconcilable differences among the superpowers but from a human or mechanical error. And how easy it would be to make an error, for no target on earth is more than fifteen minutes away from a launching device.[4]

Supposedly, the purpose of possessing nuclear capability is the realization that the possibility of annihilation will deter aggression. However, the constant threat of the complete destruction of life can have peculiar effects on human conduct. One effect may be to incite, rather than deter, aggression. Sometimes, people prefer the certainty of death to the insecurity of living. Another effect is that people simply isolate themselves from the problem and ignore it, which permits military leaders to continue to extoll military priorities and military values.[5]

The Rise of Technocracy

A highly technological society results in centralization of governmental power and technocracy, or domination of most areas of life by a small elite of technological experts. Many projects requiring a sophisticated technology, especially those built on a national scale, can be administered and supervised only by the government. Individuals simply have neither the knowledge nor the resources to carry them out privately.

Furthermore, the more complex technology becomes, the fewer are the individuals who are able to understand it and make intelligent decisions about matters involving it. Thus, technological specialists take on ever-increasing responsibilities and eventually assume enough power to merit the title of technocrats.

Mass Society

In discussing the institutions of our society, we noted that the prevalent trend was toward bureaucratization and the establishment of large formal organizations. In a nation of not only big business, big government, and big labor but also of big church, big school, and big sports, the individual has little power and feels insignificant. In his daily life, he is faced with huge bureaucratic organizations that lack the informality, warmth, friendliness, and feelings of security characteristic of small closely knit groups.

In our society, for instance, a university student attending a branch of one of our multiversities could conceivably find that no instructor, no administrator, and not even another student knows him. He may worship in a church that is part of a large denominational network, and again be known to no one. After he graduates, he might work for a giant corporation in which his name and number are known only to the computer issuing his paycheck. He will pay taxes to a government with which he has contact only through his IRS form (unless he decides not to pay taxes, in which case he will have intimate contact with representatives of a governmental agency!). He might give charity to the United Fund, never knowing whom he has benefited. He might spend his vacation on a prepackaged tour, in which everyone gets a free cocktail and a visit to the local red-light district.

[4]Robert Perrucci and Marc Pilisuk, *The Triple Revolution Emerging* (Boston: Little, Brown, 1971), p. 3.
[5]Ibid., p. 6.

A society in which members are presented with huge, neatly compartmentalized pigeonholes in which to fit their lives is called a *mass society*. A mass society is not simply a society in which large numbers of people live close together. Rather, it is a society characterized by a great deal of anonymity, by a high degree of mobility, by secondary group relationships among people, by increasing specialization of roles and statuses, and by a growing indifference to the traditional values and goals of society.

Our description of the mass society and the lone individual lost in it is, of necessity, generalized and exaggerated. Such a society does not exist in pure form. Even within the most formal organizations that have vast bureaucracies, primary groups develop. In fact, as we noted in our previous discussion of bureaucratic organizations, if the goals of the organization are to be fulfilled, they must correspond fairly closely to the goals of the primary groups within it. Otherwise, loyalty to the primary group overshadows loyalty to the organization, and organizational goals are sabotaged.

Some sociologists have also observed a debureaucratization of formal organizations in cases in which it is advantageous for an organization to promote informal interaction.[6] There is no doubt that "bureaucracy's other face" exists, as sociologist Charles H. Page points out, and that this face's spontaneous features contribute positive functions to bureaucratic organization. And, finally, we must not forget that bureaucratic organization has been called man's greatest social invention because it has made possible modernization and the consequent high standard of living of modern technological societies.

Bureaucratic organization does not necessarily have to be standardized and routinized, impersonal and alienating. Japan, for example, became rapidly and exceedingly industrialized, but jobs are considered extensions of the family. The Japanese employer, today often a huge corporation, takes care of his employees from school graduation to retirement. The workers receive low interest loans, free dormitory housing, gifts marking special occasions for themselves and their children, and after-hours recreational and study facilities. Even marriage can be arranged through a company counselor. The result is a great deal of company loyalty and an almost complete absence of job jumping.[7] But this type of paternalism has dangers, too. It may constitute an invasion of privacy, and it may work against social mobility. Nevertheless, it proves that bureaucratic organizations need not be unmindful of and unconcerned with the needs of the individual. Unfortunately, too often they are.

Effects of Mass Society

What effects does a mass society have on the individual? First, mass society tends to standardize him. He becomes the "average person" toward whom everything in the society—production, consumption, education, politics, religion—is directed. Standardization leads to the development of a cult of mediocrity, in which any behavior very far removed from the norm is discouraged. Political candidates must appeal to the so-called average guy. Politicians, then, must not be too smart or too dumb, not too far to the left or too far

[6]S. N. Eisenstadt, "Bureaucracy, Bureaucratization, and Debureaucratization," *Administrative Science Quarterly*, Vol. 4 (1959), pp. 302–320.

[7]"In Japan: A Job for Life, Free Housing, Even A Bride," *U.S. News & World Report* (July 17, 1972), p. 54.

to the right, not in favor of the rich or in favor of the poor; not too religious but not irreligious either. Not only do the mass media, institutions, and other organizations of society address themselves to the average person, but they actually help to mold such a person.

Thus, in school, we are encouraged to stifle our individual differences in favor of what our teachers consider "a nice personality." Because we have become primarily an employee society and because our employers are big organizations, these organizations force us to fit the pattern they have determined for us, both on the job and off. We know what detailed scrutinies are made of the life and personality of federal employees. We also know how easily school teachers are dismissed for indiscretions in their private lives. In corporations, the rising young executive—as well as his wife and family—is expected to conform to organizational standards or leave the corporation. For example, if the wife of an up-and-coming executive of General Motors suddenly began speaking in favor of militant feminism—particularly if any publicity were involved—her husband's climb to the top would almost certainly be seriously endangered or halted altogether.

During the 1950s and early 1960s, sociologists tended to believe that our mass society inevitably produced organization men, or other-directed personalities. In *The Organization Man*, William H. Whyte pointed to the change in the image of the ideal man in our society. Previously, the individualist, the self-made man, the man of strong ideas and principles was set up as a societal model. Recently, however, the ideal man has been an individual who fits into the organization—in reality, who conforms to the requirements of the organization.

David Riesman presents another effect of mass society in *The Lonely Crowd*.

According to Riesman, in the past, the individual was guided in his behavior by the dictates of his own conscience, but in modern society, he behaves according to the standards of other people, acting as they want him to act. In short, modern people have developed an interior radar that permits them to detect the reactions of others. They then conduct themselves according to those reactions.

Pressures for conformity to an organizational mold result in, among many other things, an attitude of "my organization, right or wrong." Eventually, this attitude embraces all organizations. This may be one reason why many people disapprove of young men who refuse to serve in the armed forces in a war they consider immoral. Even though such critics admit that they too are against the war, they think that the government must be supported because it knows best—"My country, right or wrong."

The Failures of Mass Society

Despite all its shortcomings, mass society is not completely undesirable. If, through mass production, articles are made cheaply enough for everyone to afford them, who is going to argue against mass production? The barefoot Appalachian child who has never owned a pair of shoes doesn't care that his new pair is one of thousands that he will soon encounter on every second pair of feet on the street. Furthermore, the great number of people living in urban centers and the mass organizations that surround them make it possible for urban centers to provide their citizens with the best in specialized schools, with a rich artistic and cultural environment, with countless recreational activities, and with other possibilities for creative growth that no sleepy rural town ever dreamed of offering. Nor is the Gemeinschaft feeling, the primary relationships that we might consider natural in the small rural community, impossible to find in large urban centers. In his book *The Urban Villagers*, sociologist Herbert J. Gans tells how rural Italian peasant life has been made to fit into the urban American pattern and yet retains many of the traditional features of an agricultural society.

Although mass society is not totally unsatisfactory, it has not fulfilled entirely the promise of a good life for everyone. The techniques of mass society have not worked for the benefit of the 20 to 40 million Americans who are classified as being poor, meaning that most of them get only one starch-filled meal a day, are disease-ridden, and are damaged in body, mind, and spirit. When cities envelop humans in ugliness, when the strain of living in them—the overcrowding, the noise, the dirt, the blight—leads to psychological impairment, to high rates of violent crime, to senseless vandalism, and to emotional frigidity, the techniques of mass society have surely failed. When the land, the sky, the sea, and our own bodies are threatened with extinction because of the poisons and pollutants that attack them; when we, as consumers, are made into fools by producers; when our jobs give us little satisfaction, making us feel like merely part of the rat race; when we can find little purpose in life and must seek escape in alcohol, drugs, or the accumulation of material objects, our mass society is not serving us well.

Perhaps the dehumanization representative of the mass society has reached its highest peak in a new business venture thriving in our major cities. The venture is called "Rent-a-Gent" and "Rent-a-Bird." The well-known American ability to make a profit wherever there is a profit to be made has met with a golden opportunity in the lack of primary relationships and in the numbers of lonely people willing to pay for even one evening of warmth and friendliness. For about 55 dollars and all expenses for a six-hour evening, you can now rent a man or woman for companionship, or whatever.[8]

In the past, many have warned against the ultimate results of organization for its own sake, of efficiency for no real purpose, and of formality, rigidity, and dehumanization of life. But the majority, drunk with their sudden wealth, with their cars, radios, televisions, boats, and houses in the suburbs, paid no heed to these voices in the wilderness. The voices are increasing, however. Growing numbers are asking what happened to spontaneity, sincerity, responsibility, individuality, and meaningful relationships among people. They are questioning, in ever louder tones, the desirability of quantity over quality.

REBELS WITH A CAUSE: THE COUNTERCULTURE

Although a reaction against our technological mass society was not foreseen by most social thinkers of the 1950s, such a reaction began in the mid 1960s and has continued at an accelerated pace. The reaction has taken many forms, some of which were mentioned in previous chapters: campus unrest; resistance to military service; refusal to submit to regimented hair styles and clothes; interest in communal life styles; political, especially leftist, activism; a return to fundamentalist religious expressions; and an attempt to go beyond ordinary experience through the use of mind-expanding drugs. Regardless of its form, dissidence seems to be directed against what is perceived to be the drift of postindustrial society and its technetronic future.

Those who dissent are young people, for the most part college and high school students, backed by a number of radical, liberal, or simply sympathetic teachers. The dissidence of youth, based partly on their own feelings of insecurity about their identity and role, is not new. It has been particularly apparent in industrial societies, in which socialization occurs over a long period of time, including time spent in institutions of higher learning, and in which it does not result in a total integration of the individual into society. In recent years, however, perhaps as a partial result of the increasing bureaucratization of society, the conflicts between youth and the older generation, or the established system of society, have become more acute.

These conflicts have led social scientists and the media to refer to today's youth as a subculture, counterculture, youth culture, or youth movement. The widespread use of such terms, unknown a decade ago, indicates that, to some extent, the young have separated themselves from the larger society.

This counterculture, as we will call it, is a visible social phenomenon. As such, it has been written about extensively, the consensus being that it has primarily arisen as a reaction to the current conditions of society and culture. Unfortunately, at this time, no exhaustive sociological research on it exists. Sociologists have studied the phenomenon but have not arrived at any defini-

---

[8]Judy Klemesrud, "If a Rented Gent Makes Passes, Take Two and Go Right to Politics," *New York Times* (June 4, 1972), Travel Section, pp. 1ff.

tive conclusions. Their opinions are widely different. Some believe that the counterculture represents the future of our society, and others consider it merely the latest fad through which the young sow their wild oats. Our own statements regarding the counterculture should be regarded as merely tentative and by no means final. Only the future will tell whether the countercultural movement was the originator of sociocultural change, whether it provided a true alternative life style, and what its sociological significance was. In the meantime, it is a phenomenon that cannot be ignored.

Keniston's View of the Counterculture

Those who have researched student protest movements and the student subculture, in general, agree that it is not a monolithic movement. Kenneth Keniston believes that students can be divided into a subculture of activists and a counterculture of the alienated. The activists are particularly sensitive to the gap between the real and the ideal culture. They are typically from middle- or upper-middle-class homes, have liberal parents, and have been exposed to the inequalities and social problems of society. They generally attend the top academic centers of the nation, and may feel deprived and disillusioned with them because of their high educational aspirations. Many are

graduate students, who are academically superior, though they may be frustrated by the obstacles they encounter in trying to attain higher degrees.

Such personalities, when they have an antiauthoritarian background, are ready for political activism. The institutional setting of a large, impersonal university, in which various subcultural groups may easily assemble under the stimulus of a current event, is sufficient to transform the readiness for activism into real action. Because there are many causes to be protested, there are many opportunities for demonstrations. However, these students will not continue to demonstrate if they see no possibility of obtaining results, if they create a conservative backlash, or if they are frustrated by a long wait from protest to results.[9]

Roszak's View of the Counterculture

Another researcher into the culture of the young does not make such a sharp distinction between activists and the alienated. Theodore Roszak

[9]Kenneth Keniston, *The Young Radicals: Notes on Committed Youth* (New York: Harcourt Brace Jovanovich, 1968), pp. 297–325.

believes that the counterculture developed because of the extreme antagonism and disaffection the young feel for our present culture.[10] They are disillusioned and sickened with political methods, political parties, and political movements. They are revolted by the technocratic totalitarianism of society. They see no purpose in looking for freedom or meaning in a cold, formal, calculating society, which has assigned science the function of manipulating the individual and of devising ever more efficient methods of organization. They will not be satisfied with piecemeal or token renovation; they want nothing short of an "epochal transformation."

Their heroes have been dissimilar, from the now largely discredited Timothy Leary to Herbert Marcuse, a neo-Marxist philosopher; from the poet Allen Ginsberg to the humanist Paul Goodman. They have weaved together in new patterns threads of anarchism, socialism, existentialism, populism, bohemianism, and transcendentalism. Some have dropped out, preferring to turn their backs on a society that is beyond help. Others are engaged in a generalized movement for social change.

Hard-and-fast lines cannot be drawn between activists and counterculturalists, between radicals and escapists, between those who want change and those who would as soon ignore social problems, between those who are seriously committed and the hangers-on. According to the President's Commission on Campus Unrest, the majority of students do not belong to the counterculture except in their appearance and music. Furthermore, there are great differences in the degree to which countercultural ideas are carried out. Nonetheless, such ideas are undeniably having a tremendous impact on society and eventually may provide the alternatives many seek.

Reactions to the Counterculture

Many in our society feel personally threatened by the counterculture and its ideas. But they feel this way because of a basic misunderstanding of its goals. Nowhere, except perhaps in the most radical forms of political activist propaganda, is there any mention of the complete destruction of modern society and culture. A mere 9 percent of young people believe in the use of violence, and that is only as a last resort. Most are repelled by a totalitarian social structure, whether it is totalitarian in the name of Marx or Jesus. When violence against the Establishment is advocated, its nature is more symbolic than real.

THE REVOLUTION: WHEN AND HOW

What chances does the counterculture have of changing our society, of redirecting its course away from an apparently gloomy future? The strong support recently given to conservative and even reactionary political expressions may indicate that the chances are poor. Yet many people predict that a revolution is in store for America. Many of the original flower children have given up, preferring a drug-induced experience to reality. But others persist in predicting a new tomorrow.

---

[10]Theodore Roszak, *The Making of a Counter Culture* (Garden City, N.Y.: Doubleday Anchor Books, 1969). Also, by the same author, "Capsules of Salvation," *The Nation* (April 8, 1968).

Marcuse's View of the Revolution

Herbert Marcuse in his *Counterrevolution and Revolt* upholds the Marxist tradition by contending that capitalism contains within itself the seeds of its own doom. Unlike Marx, however, Marcuse does not think that the revolution will be brought about by the proletariat. In Marcuse's view, new impulses for revolution have arisen because both capitalistic and socialistic societies create needs they cannot satisfy. These societies supply man's basic economic needs. But once these are satisfied, others emerge. People begin to worry about the quality of their lives and about their environment. And modern technological societies that are capitalistic or socialistic are simply not geared to handle such concerns. As a consequence, they are eventually destroyed.

Although Marcuse does not specifically tell how the revolution will come about, he sees the New Left as standing at the forefront of the counterculture. According to Marcuse, the specific aims of the revolution will be a rejection of the performance ethic—by which people are judged by their performance—and the Protestant Ethic; a reassertion of the rights of nature, of the rights of women, of the rights of all the downtrodden; and the re-creation of a new sensibility. The universities of the nation will be the training ground for the cadres of the revolution, and violence may have to be used temporarily to counter the predictable oppression of the Establishment. Marcuse also thinks that the new natural woman—who has remained less brutalized by capitalism than have men because she has been denied access to the system and has thus been insulated from it—will embody the future ideal of peace, joy, and the end of violence. Finally, an important contribution to the revolution will be made by artists because they are the natural enemies of the state and will thus be instrumental in promoting changes in the prevailing consciousness.

Reich's View of the Revolution

A similar, though more idealized view, is taken by Charles A. Reich in *The Greening of America*. This Yale law professor also predicts a revolution, but one that is nonviolent. Rather, the revolution will originate within the individual. Reich argues that this revolution is inevitable because our present system fails to respond to real human needs. In particular, it does not give us an opportunity to experience our own lives. Most experiences, even such intimate ones as love and creativity, are blunted by the demands made on us to perform to our utmost ability in our roles as mothers, housewives, consumers, professionals, workers, or ruling elite. We feel this inability to experience ourselves as human beings, but we tend to blame ourselves or our partners for our incomplete lives. Thus, we lose ourselves in drink, in the accumulation of material objects, in the search for new partners, and so forth. But, according to Reich, the fault lies in our technological, media-directed, militaristic society, which prevents us from achieving a complete experience of our lives.

This society, however, is vulnerable because the Establishment owes its existence not only to its control of wealth and power but also to a widely accepted ideology. The ideology stresses production, consumption, denial of experience, postponement of pleasures, and acceptance of the rules of the game. But these principles are subject to change, and change may be accomplished without violence. The young, by rejecting many portions of this ideology, are making the first dent in it. And the Establishment has no weapons with which to fight the erosion of ideology because it is not being challenged on what it deems important: its control of wealth, power, and privilege. When the sons and daughters of the Establishment become converted to the ideology of the counterculture, as many already have, they will stop worrying about how to preserve their favorable position, giving in to the experience of warmth and community offered by the counterculture.

Reich's book has been thoroughly criticized by both Establishment and non-Establishment critics because he gives the impression that he is writing a scholarly treatise but is, in reality, dealing in optimistic conjecture. In fact, Reich does romanticize today's young generation and the symbols of their culture. But he recognizes the deficiencies of our larger culture that have given rise to the counterculture.

Is Revolution Realistic?

Both Marcuse's and Reich's predictions of how social change will come about are within the realm of possibility. In our type of society, however, change through cultural diffusion seems more likely than change through violent revolution. The system, although repressive of forceful action that challenges it, leaves other channels of operation open. For instance, whereas the Black Panthers were persecuted when their program included armed confrontation, they are now being left alone since they changed their tactics and gave their support to a caucus of black congressmen.

Furthermore, the very system that condemns long hair, rock music, unusual clothing, and the sexual permissiveness of the counterculture packages and sells products symbolic of the counterculture to the entire society. In so doing, the established system makes converts among the wider consuming public, who begin to identify with the ideas of the counterculture, even though they are only following a fad. In time, the conversion may become real. Finally, the Establishment itself is not monolithically anticounterculture. It has its Daniel Ellsbergs and its Ralph Naders, who expose the parts of the system that do not conform to the ideals of democracy. In general, critics within the Establishment use legal means, work within the system, and do not engage in violent confrontation.

WHAT NOW, AMERICA?

And what now, world? We might well ask that question, for America is not the only society suffering the strains of pervasive technology. A recent report, commissioned by the Swedish government after an increase in the number of people committed to mental hospitals, made some rather gloomy conclusions about Swedish society. Sweden is Europe's most industrialized and most affluent nation. It is also a prototype of the technetronic society, in which one of the nation's computerized hospitals award each citizen a number upon birth—a number that he does not relinquish until his death.

In order to maintain its high standard of living, Sweden's technocrats drive their workers into competing ruthlessly to produce at peak rates. The stronger the push toward higher performance, the more workers drop out of the rat race. And the more dropouts there are, the more the economy has to grow—hence the higher the performance expected from the remaining workers—to take care of the dropouts.

This vicious cycle is made even worse by the constant striving for perfection that has become distinctive of Swedish life. After a harrowing day at the factory, one out of four Swedes attends night school in an effort at self-improvement. The results are not only an increase in mental illness but also the highest per capita consumption of alcohol of any nation in the world.

The most chilling conclusion of the study is that the phenomena described are not strictly Swedish. They are apparently occurring in all industrialized societies and are simply more visible in Sweden, a comparatively small, homogeneous, and exceptionally technetronic society.[11]

Of course, we cannot unquestionably accept the conclusions of only one report. Undoubtedly, causes for an increase in mental illness may be sought—and found—in other sources. In addition, we must weigh the negatives and positives of every situation. In Sweden, there are many positives to be considered. Its social and economic systems display great concern for disadvantaged and deviant groups. Many observers think that, from that vantage point, Sweden is the most advanced nation in Europe, if not the world. However, an excessive reliance on technology and the bureaucratization of organizations, in pursuit of increased efficiency, may be causing a standardization of attitudes, as well as other side effects, that are ultimately undesirable.

Trends of Tomorrow

Whether or not our own society will display the excesses of technology that Sweden already shows or whether the counterculture or others will steer it away from such a course is not yet known. But we can foretell the trends of tomorrow from what is taking shape today. The first trend concerns our economy. Because of a growing use of automation, the economy will change from a production to a service economy (that is, more services will be provided for the consumer, rather than more articles produced for his consumption). Even today, it takes only half of our available labor force to produce all of our food and consumer goods. It seems clear, then, that in the future an even smaller portion of the labor force will be needed for this task. The remainder of the population will have to find jobs in service or professional categories.

This change will make a great difference in our society. First, many blue-collar jobs will be eliminated, and many more white-collar, administrative jobs will be created. The massive upward mobility this will bring may eliminate much of the alienation of the blue-collar worker and unsettle the layers of the stratification system. Because automation will replace machine production, scientists and highly trained specialists may attain the status held by the business entrepreneurs and corporate executives of yesterday and today. Because the average person will need a greater amount of education than he does today, much of the labor of teaching and communicating will be taken over by computers and teaching machines. Finally, government, or the public sector of the

[11]Roger Choats, "Harsh, Ruthless Society Unbalances Many Swedes," *The Plain Dealer* (May 29, 1972). Also, Bernard Weinraub, "Sweden Discusses the Impact of Welfare System on Freedom," *The New York Times* (November 12, 1972).

economy, will become predominant over the private sector. Government will also become the largest employer because it will increase the number of agencies that supervise industry, oversee social services, and protect the environment. Thus, government will become even more centralized than it is now and will play a larger part in our lives.

If these trends crystallize, there will be changes in residential and community structure patterns. The center of the city should become the home of the single, the young, and the affluent swinger. The outer fringes of the city will probably house the perpetually poor. The suburbs will be inhabited by family groups and will be divided according to social class and, to a lesser extent, according to age (young families, retired couples, and so on). Thus, our society will become even more heterogeneous because of the creation of additional life styles.

The Peace Before the Storm

Even those who are willing to accept the trends of the future without flinching, those who are not particularly dissatisfied with the quality of their lives, and those who are happy with their things and comforts and cannot understand the goals of the counterculture may be forced to reexamine their goals and values in view of a very real threat to the continuation of our existence. Such a reexamination should yield a change in attitude away from the exploitation of nature by humans and of human by human. So far, exploitation has been the pattern. We have exploited nature, never thinking of what we could put back, only concerned with what we could get out. We have also exploited our fellow humans, with the result that, today, some people worry about whether they experience life sufficiently and others worry whether their empty stomachs will survive another day.

Exploitation, according to a recent study, will ultimately bring disaster unless overpopulation, pollution, and continued economic growth are not brought to a drastic halt.[12] Although this and similar studies have been severely criticized for their use of incomplete data and for computerized methods, they do indicate some realistic possibilities of where the trends of today may bring us tomorrow. The report warns us that our world system is in danger of collapse within a century—a collapse that will bring with it a massive destruction of human life and natural resources. Ecological disaster will inevitably occur if present population trends and economic growth continue unchecked. Economic growth originates when capital is created in such forms as factories, cars, trucks, airplanes, mines, and so on. Capital continues to produce and leads to ever greater wealth and an expanding technology. In turn, wealth and a complex technology create an increase in population because advancements in medicine and hygiene lead to a decrease in death rates.

The larger population, producing and consuming ever more goods, pollutes the environment and exhausts the resources of the planet. And here, continues the research team, the teachings of Malthus are relevant. Whereas people, capital, and pollution grow at geometric rates—or keep doubling—the earth's resources grow only at arithmetic rates—1, 2, 3, 4, . . . — and are finite and

[12]Dennis L. Meadows, et al., "The Limits to Growth," Report of the Club of Rome, M.I.T., as previewed in *Current* (October, 1971), p. 3.

exhaustible. Malthus's error, and perhaps the error of this research team, was to overlook that the resources of the earth may be enhanced by a changing technology. For instance, uranium was not considered a resource until the nuclear age. Many resources may exist for which a technology has simply not yet been developed. But resources are, at some point, finite. Eventually, whether within a century, as this research indicates, or within ten centuries, life-supporting resources will probably be exhausted.

An Ounce of Prevention, But Which Ounce?

The basic question raised by this study is, What can we do to prevent catastrophe? Many, including spokesmen from both the extreme left and the extreme right, have indicated that zero economic growth may be the answer. This proposal, in essence, is based on the halting of not only population growth but also of the growth of economies in the technologically advanced societies of the world.

Naturally, the drastic solution of zero economic growth does not encounter a receptive public in a society as dependent on continued economic growth as is ours. Critics say that opportunity, and hence upward social mobility, would be altogether destroyed in the United States. Many believe that those who have a personal stake in capitalism would not accept such a solution but would resort to violence to maintain their privileged positions.

On an international scale, zero economic growth would have to be accompanied by a redistribution of world income. It does not seem likely that technologically advanced nations would initiate such action voluntarily, because no further economic growth would replenish their empty coffers. And because no organization is strong enough to force them to redistribute income, the condition of developing nations would worsen. Finally, because world population will probably not be checked for many years, population growth without corresponding economic growth could well lead to disaster.

Thus, zero economic growth as a solution to world problems is perhaps too drastic a measure. A workable alternative might be planned, purposeful growth instead of massive, undirected growth. Such growth would make it necessary for us to reexamine our goals as a society and our position relative to the world order.[13] For too long, we have ignored this position. For too long, we have thought of ourselves as individuals, independent of any ecological system. And for too long, as societies, we have thought of ourselves as entirely self-sufficient.

We must begin to think of ourselves as citizens of the world if our search for survival is to be ultimately successful. No nation on earth can exist alone any longer. Nations have long realized that they are economically interdependent. Internationalism in all other areas is not only possible but necessary. Albert Einstein once said that he considered his relationship with the state of which he was a citizen to be no more than a business relationship. We are expecting a great deal when we ask that such an international orientation develop among the ethnocentric citizens of modern nation-states. But develop it must.

[13]Zbigniew Brzezinski, "The Politics of Zero Growth," *Newsweek* (March 27, 1972).

THE SOCIAL WEB

We hope that in the preceding chapters the meaning of this book's title has become clear. The human being as an individual does not exist outside the group. We are not only products of those countless others whose memory we carry in our genes. We are also products of those countless others whose memory we carry in our history and our culture. And we owe to others not only *what* we are but the fact that we *are* at all. To be human, remember, is to be able to employ symbols. Symbols are tools we learn to handle so we can establish rewarding relationships with others who matter to us. Because human beings have always desired such relationships, they have been called social animals, and their nature a social nature.

But the individual within a group and groups of individuals perceive reality in the light of their own unique life experiences. Sometimes, these experiences lead them to seek cooperation, harmony, and community with their fellow humans. At other times, these experiences lead them into conflict. Somehow, we have permitted conflict to distort our feelings of love, empathy, tenderness, self-identity, responsibility—those feelings of personal involvement with others that are necessary to a fulfillment of the self. Somehow, we have permitted the development of institutions that are repressive of some groups, that have legitimized the power of other groups, and that owe their existence to possessive and conflicting interests among groups. The dissatisfaction of many people with life in modern society seems to indicate that we are realizing the error of our ways. What humans have built, they can tear down. And what they have torn down, they can build again. The important point for them to remember is that they cannot do it alone.

SUMMARY

An increasingly complex technology has permitted human mankind to master the environment and thus to transform many societies into societies of plenty. Humans have, however, paid dearly for this transformation. It has led to dangerous overpopulation—there will be 7 billion of us by the end of this century. It has created huge urban centers and megalopolises in which large numbers of people live in overcrowded conditions and are severed from nature and from the security of the extended family and a warm circle of friends. It has depersonalized working conditions, making workers feel less important than the machines they run. It has threatened workers' security through increasing mechanization and automation. It has led to an exploitative attitude toward nature and its resources, according to which we ever extract nature's bounty but return nothing but toxic fumes and trash.

For the individual, technological society has led to a loss of personal freedom and an increasing dependence on other people and institutions. Aspects of different cultures have begun to resemble one another, as distances have shortened and communication among societies has been improved. Weapons are so sophisticated that we cannot defend ourselves against them. We live with the knowledge that an error could erase us forever from the face of the earth.

A complex technology has also led to the increasing organization and bureaucratization of society. Anonymity, mobility, secondary relationships, and specialization of roles and statuses have become the norm. Such a society is called a mass society, and it tends to produce standardized, average people, who are attuned to the demands of the organizations that employ them and to others around them. People living in a mass society are surrounded by creature comforts and objects, but the quality of their life suffers.

Among critics of the dehumanization and continued inequality of the mass society, the strongest voices have belonged to the counterculture. Members of the counterculture, though not in total agreement on goals or organized in a movement, are trying to effect societal change.

Even if we are not dissatisfied with life in a mass society or frightened by the future in a technetronic world, we must reexamine our goals and change our direction because we are faced with real dangers. These dangers include overpopulation, pollution of our natural habitat, exhaustion of natural resources, and total destruction of life through the use of nuclear weapons. Any solutions that seek to overcome these dangers must take an international direction.

TERMS TO REMEMBER

Technocracy. The domination of most areas of life by a small elite of technological experts.

Technology. All the methods, tools, instruments, and devices that help humans to control their environment.

Mechanization. A type of technology in which machines are substituted for human muscle.

Automation. A type of technology in which machines are substituted for the human brain.

Mass society. A bureaucratically organized society characterized by a great deal of anonymity, by a high degree of mobility, by secondary group relationships, by increasing specialization of roles and statuses, and by a growing indifference to the traditional values and goals of society.

SUGGESTIONS FOR FURTHER READING

Aldridge, John. *In the Country of the Young*. New York: Harper & Row, 1970. The author questions the originality and the cultural transformation of the young.

Blau, Peter M. *Bureaucracy in Modern Society*. New York: Random House, 1965. Positive and negative functions and interrelationships between bureaucracy and democracy.

Brzezinski, Zbigniew. *Between Two Ages*. New York: Viking, 1970. An optimistic view of the role of America in the new technetronic era.

Dreitzel, Hans Peter, ed., *Recent Sociology*. New York: Macmillan, 1969. Includes several readings by contemporary sociologists writing on the counterculture.

Ellul, Jacques. *The Technological Society*. New York: Alfred A. Knopf, 1964. The technological revolution seen by a contemporary French philosopher.

Ferkiss, Victor C. *Technological Man: The Myths and the Reality*. New York: Braziller, 1969. A political scientist evaluates technology, concluding that a new type of human being, with a new kind of understanding, must be developed before technology can become valid.

Goodman, Paul. *Growing Up Absurd*. New York: Random House, 1960. The plight of the individual in an organizational society.

Hope, Marjorie. *Youth Against the World*. Boston: Little Brown, 1970. A portrait of those involved in the revolution of rising expectations.

Keniston, Kenneth. *Young Radicals*. New York: Harcourt Brace & World, 1968. A sympathetic, but sociological look, at committed youth.

McLuhan, Marshall. *Understanding Media*. New York: McGraw-Hill, 1966. An enthusiastic commentary on the revolution in communications.

Newfield, Jack. *Prophetic Minority*. New York: New American Library, 1967. An early sociological analysis of the counterculture.

Roszak, Theodore. *The Making of a Counter Culture*. Garden City, N.Y.: Doubleday, 1969. The technocratic society and opposition to it.